Leaving Certificate Biology

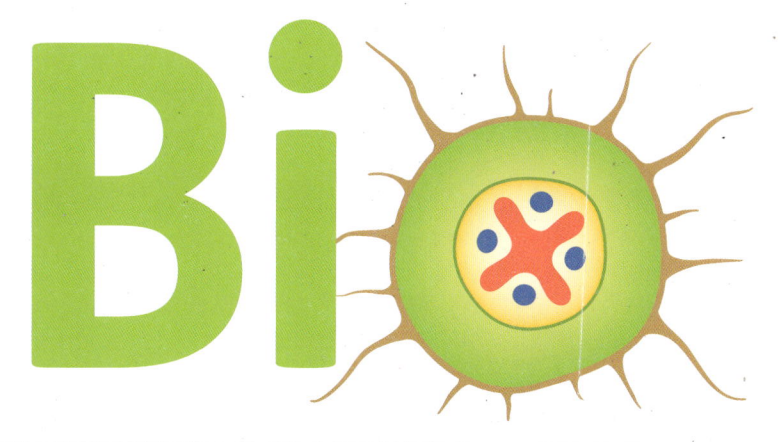

Bio

Ordinary and Higher Levels

educate.ie

John Loughlin

educate.ie

Published by:
Educate.ie

Walsh Educational Books Ltd
Castleisland, Co. Kerry, Ireland

www.educate.ie

Editor:
Ciara McNee

Design, layout and cover design:
Liz White Designs

Printed and bound by:
Walsh Colour Print, Castleisland

Copyright © John Loughlin 2012

First published 2012; reprinted January 2013

Without limiting the rights under copyright, this book is sold subject to the condition that it shall not, by way of trade or otherwise, be lent, resold, hired out, reproduced, stored in or introduced into a retrieval system, or transmitted, in any form or by any means (electronic, mechanical, photocopying, recording or otherwise), or otherwise circulated, without the publisher's prior consent, in any form other than that in which it is published and without a similar condition, including this condition, being imposed on the subsequent publisher.

The author and publisher have made every effort to trace all copyright holders, but if some have been inadvertently overlooked, we would be happy to make the necessary arrangements at the first opportunity.

ISBN: 978-1-908507-43-3

Credits

The author and publisher would like to thank the following for permission to reproduce photographs:

Alamy Images; AQUAFACT International Services Ltd; the Botany Department of Trinity College for the portrait of Henry Dixon (painted by Phoebe Donovan); FSC Cremona, Simms and Ward (2001): Rocky Shore Name Trail; FSC, OP61; Getty Images; Glow Images; iStockphoto; Sciencephoto Library; Thinkstock; Wikicommons for a range of images (Benjah-bmm27 for a ribbon diagram of the structure of haemoglobin; Dezzawong for a photograph of Yakult; Manilus for a photograph of a quadrat used for calculating percentage frequency).

Contents

Introduction v
Practical activities vi

Unit 1 Biology: the study of life

1 The scientific method 2
2 The characteristics of life 10
3 Nutrition 14
4 Ecology 32
5 The study of an ecosystem 56

Unit 2 The Cell

6 Cell structure 84
7 Diversity of cells 94
8 Movement through cell membranes 99
9 Enzymes 103
10 Energy carriers (HL only) 118
11 Photosynthesis 121
12 Respiration 132
13 The cell cycle 144
14 DNA and RNA 155
15 Protein synthesis 166
16 Inheritance and genetic crosses 171
17 Variation and evolution 193
18 Genetic engineering 203

Unit 3 The Organism

19	Diversity of living organisms......212	31	The human circulatory system..316
20	Kingdom Monera......216	32	The human lymphatic system....332
21	Kingdom Fungi......230	33	The human digestive system.....336
22	Kingdom Protista......239	34	The human defence system......351
23	Viruses......242	35	The human breathing system....362
24	Kingdom Plantae......248	36	Human skin (the integumentary system)......370
25	Nutrition in the flowering plant......260	37	The human urinary system......374
26	Response in the flowering plant......269	38	The human endocrine system....383
		39	The human nervous system......392
27	Vegetative propagation......279	40	The human musculoskeletal system......410
28	Sexual reproduction in the flowering plant......284	41	The human reproductive system......423
29	Homeostasis......304		
30	Blood......308		

Glossary......442
Index......450

Introduction

Bio is a comprehensive new textbook for the Leaving Certificate Biology course. It is written for both Ordinary Level and Higher Level students. Material that is for Higher Level students only is clearly marked with a red dotted line.

This colourful and attractive textbook covers all elements of the Biology syllabus, while also bringing the subject to life by including many interesting and current topics in biological research.

This book has been written with the student firmly in mind: simple language has been used throughout to explain even complex topics.

Features

- **Learning objectives** at the start of each chapter indicate what students need to learn. Higher Level only objectives are clearly shown.
- The **wide range of full-colour images and illustrations** will further the student's understanding and stimulate interest in the topics being covered. Many of the images are transmission and scanning electron microscope photographs, which help to explain and give a greater insight into the particular topic being covered. Where relevant, simple illustrations have been used, which students will be better able to **reproduce in the exam.**
- **Syllabus definitions,** which students should learn off by heart, are clearly highlighted in separate boxes and marked with an !. Other important biological terms are also explained. All definitions are also covered in the comprehensive **glossary.**
- **Practical activities** are clearly explained. These sections highlight the method, safety instructions (when applicable), results and conclusions of the activity. Questions at the end of each activity reinforce what the student has learned.
- **End-of-chapter questions** are in the order in which the material is presented in the text. The questions have been designed to stimulate thinking and the language mirrors that of the Leaving Certificate Biology exam. Higher Level only questions are clearly marked.
- **Sample exam questions** are included at the end of chapters, with at least one Ordinary Level and one Higher Level question for almost every chapter.
- The **mind map** at the end of each chapter summarises all topics, key words, terms and definitions covered. Higher Level only material is clearly marked. The mind maps provide an excellent **exam revision tool** for students.
- A comprehensive **index** allows students to easily navigate the text.

In writing this book, I have used my years of experience teaching Biology and correcting the Leaving Certificate Biology exam. I have also drawn on my experience in scientific research and as a joint author of a scientific paper published in 2006 in *Biochemical and Biophysical Research Communications.*

Bio will prepare the student for the Leaving Certificate exam and for further study in Biology at third level. I also hope it gives the student an interest in and love of Biology.

John Loughlin

St Joseph's College, Nun's Island, Galway

April 2012

Practical activities

When carrying out your practical activities, you should fill the details into a hardback laboratory copy. Number each page and leave the first page blank to insert a table of contents. **NEVER** rip any pages out of your lab notebook, even if you make an error in drawing a table, graph or diagram.

You should always record the following when writing up your practical activity:

1 The date or dates on which you carried out your practical activity.
2 The title of the activity.
3 Equipment and chemicals used.
4 A detailed procedure or method followed.
5 All results obtained, even ones that you feel are incorrect, useless or meaningless. Results are a record of what you observed. Do not try to explain results in this section.
6 A concise conclusion. In completing your conclusion, ask yourself what you learned. Give an explanation of your results.
7 An analysis. In this, you should explain your results and conclusions in relation to existing scientific knowledge and describe any ways in which you could improve your experiment.

SAFETY

In carrying out all practical activities, safety must be a major consideration.
- Take extreme care when using glass equipment, blades and scalpels.
- Report all breakages to your teacher and/or laboratory assistant.
- Wear a laboratory coat whenever you are in the lab.
- Wear safety glasses and gloves when necessary.

Important safety symbols

In the course of your practical activities, you will be using many chemicals that are dangerous. There are a number of hazard symbols that you should be aware of. Familiarise yourself with the symbols listed below before conducting any practical activity.

| Corrosive | Irritant | Toxic | Oxidising | Flammable |

List of practical activities

1. Qualitative test for a reducing sugar 17
2. Qualitative test for starch 19
3. Qualitative test for fat 21
4. Qualitative test for protein 24
5. The study of an ecosystem
    - Select and visit one ecosystem 56
    - Broad overview of the selected ecosystem and identify any five fauna and any five flora using simple keys 57
    - Identify a variety of habitats from the selected ecosystem 62
    - Identify and use various ecological apparatus for collecting organisms in the habitat 65
    - Conduct a quantitative study of plants and animals of a sample area of the selected ecosystem 69
    - Investigate three abiotic factors present in the selected ecosystem 73
    - Identify one adaptation of any organism in the selected ecosystem 74
    - Identify the roles the organisms play in energy transfer by constructing food chains, a food web and a pyramid of numbers 75
6. To be familiar with and use the light microscope 87
7. Prepare and examine animal cells (human cheek cells) unstained and stained using the light microscope at 100x and 400x 88
8. Prepare and examine plant cells (onion cells) unstained and stained using the light microscope at 100x and 400x 90
9. To demonstrate osmosis 100
10. To investigate the effect of pH on the rate of action of catalase 106
11. To investigate the effect of temperature on the rate of action of catalase 108
12. To investigate the effect of heat denaturation on the activity of catalase .... 109 *(HL)*
13. To prepare one enzyme immobilisation and examine its application 113
14. To investigate the effect of light intensity OR carbon dioxide concentration on the rate of photosynthesis 127
15. To prepare and show the production of alcohol by yeast 139
16. To isolate DNA from plant tissue 160
17. To investigate the growth of leaf yeast using agar plates and controls 234
18. To prepare and examine microscopically the transverse section of a dicot stem (100x, 400x) 256
19. To investigate the effect of indoleacetic acid (IAA) growth regulator on plant tissue 274
20. To investigate the effect of water, oxygen and temperature on germination 296
21. To use starch agar or skimmed milk plates to show digestive activity during germination 297
22. To dissect, display and identify an ox's or a sheep's heart 326
23. To investigate the effect of exercise on pulse rate 328

OR

24. To investigate the effect of exercise on breathing rate 366

Unit 1
Biology: the study of life

1 The scientific method 2
2 The characteristics of life 10
3 Nutrition 14
4 Ecology 32
5 The study of an ecosystem 56

Chapter 1 The scientific method

Learning objectives After studying this chapter, you should be able to:
- Define *biology* and list three areas of study in biology.
- Describe the process of the scientific method.
- Describe the principles of experimentation.
- Describe the limitations of the scientific method.

Introduction

> **Biology:** the study of life.

Biology is a vast subject area, with many divisions and subdivisions. Some examples of the areas of study† in biology are listed below:

Anatomy	Study of form and function of an organism
Biochemistry	Study of the chemical reactions required for life to exist
Biotechnology	Artificial manipulation of living organisms
Botany	Study of plants
Cell biology	Study of the cell as a complete unit, and the molecular and chemical interactions that occur within a living cell
Ecology	Study of the interactions of living organisms with one another and with their environment
Genetics	Study of genes and heredity
Microbiology	Study of microorganisms such as bacteria (bacteriology), fungi (mycology) and viruses* (virology)
Pharmacology	Study of the effects of drugs on living organisms
Physiology	Study of the functioning of living organisms
Taxonomy	Study of the classification of living organisms
Zoology	Study of animals

NOTE
† For Leaving Certificate Biology, you must know at **least** three of these areas of study.
*It is still being debated as to whether viruses are living or non-living (*see* Chapter 23).

> **Microorganisms** are living things that can be seen only with the aid of a microscope.
>
> **To replicate** means to make a copy of. Viruses replicate and do not reproduce. This is one of the reasons they are considered to be non-living.

The process of the scientific method

Scientists have used the scientific method for many hundreds of years. It involves following a series of procedures as detailed in Fig 1.1 (see page 3).

> **Scientific method:** a process of investigation carried out in order to explain observations made in the natural world.

1 Observation

A scientist makes an observation, usually from previous work he or she has carried out.

> **Observation:** the taking in of information received about the natural world.

For example, a new drug a scientist is working on is observed to slow the growth of breast cancer cells.

2 Hypothesis

> **Hypothesis:** an educated guess or an idea based on an observation.

The new observation leads on to a hypothesis. Using the above example, the scientist reasons that if the drug can slow the growth of breast cancer cells, it might slow the growth, or even kill, other common cancer cells, such as skin cancer cells.

3 Experimentation

Experiment: a test to determine the validity of hypotheses.

Experiments nearly always involve an experiment group and a control group. In this example, the experiment group would be skin cancer cells exposed to the drug. The control group would be to grow the skin cancer cells without the new drug.

4 Collecting and interpreting data

Data: the results of measurements or observations.

Data must be collected at the end of the experiment. In the above case, the data would be the number of skin cancer cells left in each Petri dish at the end of the experiment.

Petri dish: a shallow circular dish used for culturing, or growing, bacteria and other microorganisms.

5 Forming conclusions

Conclusion: an explanation of the results.

In the above example, the conclusion would involve determining whether or not there has been an effect. Has the drug affected the skin cancer cells? Let's say that the new drug in the above example slowed the growth of the skin cancer cells. Our conclusion is therefore: 'The drug slows the growth of skin cancer cells.'

6 Analysing conclusions

Analysing the conclusion involves explaining new knowledge in relation to existing knowledge.

In our example, if there is an effect, is it the same as the effect the drug had on the breast cancer cells? An example of our analysis would be: 'The drug slowed the growth of breast cancer cells more than it slowed the growth of skin cancer cells.'

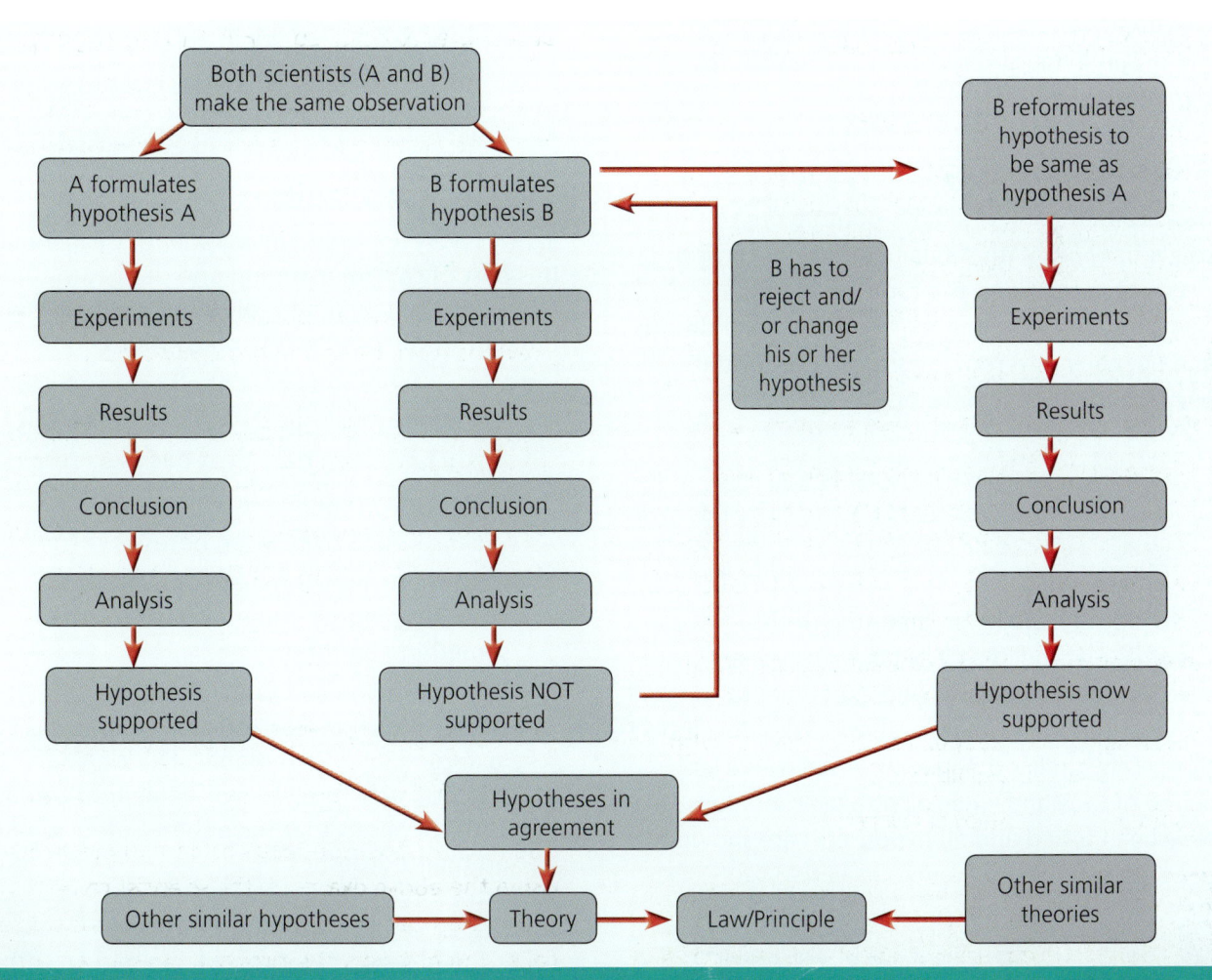

Fig 1.1 Schematic diagram representing the main points of the scientific method

Often at this stage, the scientist will see flaws in their hypothesis and/or the design of their experiment and have to start again.

7 Reporting and publishing results

Reporting and publishing results must always be done in detail and should include all the aspects of the scientific method followed. The scientific community always publish their results in scientific journals.

Scientists are in competition with one another to publish results regularly. They are also in competition to get their results published in prestigious journals such as *Nature* or *Science*. Exciting new scientific discoveries are often reported in popular magazines, newspapers and, if it is a very important discovery, sometimes even on television.

Other scientists, having read the publication, may come up with their own hypothesis. They will then want to test their hypothesis and/or the original hypothesis to see if they get the same results.

8 Development of theory and principle

Eventually, a bank of data is built up on a scientific topic, with similar conclusions having been reached. When the topic has been rigorously tested under many different conditions and by many different laboratories around the world, a theory will develop.

> **Theory:** a comprehensive explanation of an important aspect of nature supported by results gathered over a long period of time.

A law or principle is the final step of the scientific method. It usually takes many years or even decades of research and experimentation to arrive at this stage. Laws and principles develop from many similar theories proposed over a long period of time and when all possible conditions have been tested and all hypotheses are shown to be correct.

> **Law/principle:** a definite, factual explanation of an important aspect of nature.

Principles of experimentation

1 Careful planning and design

It should be obvious, even to a non-scientist, that experiments must be carefully planned. Scientists want to get results that they can rely on. If there are too many unknown factors affecting an experiment, the results may not be what were expected.

Every factor in an experiment must be controlled. For example, if botanists are growing new seedlings in a laboratory, they must control the temperature, air quality and nutrient mixture within previously agreed limits. If they then want to vary something to see what effect it might have on the growth of the seedling, then only that factor (variable) is changed – everything else remains constant.

> **Botanist:** a scientist who studies plants.

> **Variable:** a factor that is changed in the course of an experiment.

2 Safety procedures

Safety is very important in any scientific experiment. It is part of careful planning and design. In the course of your study of biology, you will follow a number of common safety precautions:

- Wear a laboratory coat at all times when in the laboratory.
- If you have long hair, tie it back securely.
- Wear safety goggles when necessary.
- Wear safety gloves when necessary.
- Do not touch your mouth or eyes during an experiment as you may have touched something harmful.
- Familiarise yourself with laboratory safety symbols, such as 'corrosive'; 'irritant'; 'toxic'; 'oxidising' and 'flammable'. During your practical activities you will come into contact with chemicals that have these safety symbols on their bottles.

- Wipe up any spills immediately and inform your teacher and/or the laboratory assistant.
- All breakages must be reported to your teacher and assistant.
- Use the fume cupboard when necessary. This is a ventilation device used to limit exposure to harmful fumes.
- Always wash your hands before leaving the laboratory.

3 Experimental control

As we have learned, there should be only one variable at a time when conducting an experiment. The factor that varies is present in the experiment group. However, we need something to compare this variable with. This is the function of the control.

> **Control:** a factor in an experiment that provides a standard with which the results of the experiment may be compared.

4 Large sample size

Sample size is a very important part of the careful planning and design of experiments. Sample size refers to how many items, chemicals or living organisms are to be included. In general, the larger the sample size, the more accurate the experiment will be. If the sample size is too small, individual differences among the subjects being tested may give inaccurate results.

For example, a research group wants to obtain the mean height of Irish adult males. Taking only 10 adult males will not give as accurate a reading as selecting 1000 adult males. There is a greater possibility of selecting adults of one height range when selecting 10 subjects than when selecting 1000.

Fig 1.2 There is a wide range of heights on the Irish rugby team.

5 Random selection

> **Random selection:** the process of choosing, without method or conscious choice, subjects or items to be scientifically tested.

Using the above example, random selection would involve choosing Irish adult males in no particular order or pattern; that is, in a completely random manner. Once this is done, the males should be representative not only of a wide range of heights, but also a wide range of ages (except under-18), body sizes, fitness levels and occupations.

In this way, the results (mean height in Irish adult males) will be more accurate.

6 Replication

In terms of the scientific method, replication is the repetition of the experiment (using the same conditions) so that variability within the experiment can be determined.

> **Replicate:** a repeat of an experiment.

In our height example, replication of the experiment would involve randomly taking another 1000 Irish adult males, measuring their heights, getting the mean and comparing it to the first result. This result is called a 'replicate' and may be slightly different to the first result. Every experiment should have at least three replicates.

7 Double-blind testing and placebos

> **Double-blind testing:** an experiment where neither the tester nor the patient knows what treatment is being given.
>
> **Placebo:** a substance with no active medication used as a control in an experiment.

Double-blind testing is used to eliminate any conscious or unconscious bias. Experiments can be carried out without double-blind testing, but this introduces the possibility of bias, mostly on the part of the experimenter. For example, if an experimenter (doctor) is administering a trial drug to cancer patients and knows who is getting the active drug and who is getting the placebo, it is likely that they will give the active drug to the sickest patients. The doctor could also unintentionally give clues to the patients who were taking the active drug.

This bias leads to unreliable results. However, double-blind testing can be controversial: many people would believe that is wrong to give very ill patients a placebo.

Limitations of the scientific method

1 Extent of basic knowledge

How much we currently know about the natural world limits the hypotheses we can form.

Consider the question, 'Is there any other life in the universe?' There are two possible hypotheses:

'There is other life somewhere in the universe.'

'There is no other life in the universe.'

It is currently impossible to test these hypotheses experimentally as we are unable to travel to planets many light years away. If it were possible to travel to different solar systems, we could carry out experiments to prove one hypothesis to be correct and the other invalid. Therefore, our scientific knowledge limits what we can discover.

Light year: the distance light travels in one year, almost 10 trillion km.

2 The basis of investigation

The basis of an investigation refers to the reasons for carrying out an experiment in a particular way.

A scientist always wants to carry out an experiment so that it mimics the real-life situation as closely as possible. However, this is not always possible. Lack of equipment, technology, time and money all limit how closely an experiment can mimic a real-life scenario.

For example, 99 per cent of cell research takes place in a Petri dish. Ideally, it should all be carried out in a living organism, as this is where cells are in their natural environment. However, it is neither practical nor possible to conduct all cellular experiments within a living organism.

Scientists must always search for the best alternative way of conducting their experiments. In the above example, the use of Petri dishes for research on cells is the best alternative in the early stages of testing a hypothesis. New potential treatments for many different human diseases are first tested on cells grown in a Petri dish. However, if a treatment works on cells in a Petri dish, this does not mean it can be used in humans. Cells may behave differently in the artificial environment. This is a limitation of the basis of investigation – whereby it is very difficult to replicate real-life conditions in a laboratory environment.

Another example of where the basis of investigation limits the scientific method is in the study of evolution. The fossil record is the main source of evidence of how evolution occurred. Ideally, we would like to reproduce certain aspects of evolution to see how they occurred. However, this is not possible as it would take millions of years for many species. Therefore, our only basis of investigation is studying and searching for new fossils. Fig 1.3 shows the evolution of the human from a common ancestor.

Fig 1.3 The evolution of humans *(Homo sapiens)*.

3 Interpretation of results

One scientist may interpret results differently from another researcher. This can lead to slightly different conclusions.

Sometimes scientists incorrectly interpret the results. For example in 1998, a scientific paper was published which claimed that there was a link between the MMR (measles, mumps and rubella) vaccine and autism. As a result, many parents refused to give their children the vaccine, against doctors' advice. This led to outbreaks of measles and mumps in older children. Some children developed complications and there were a small number of deaths. Further experiments showed that there was no link.

Fig 1.4 The MMR vaccine being administered.

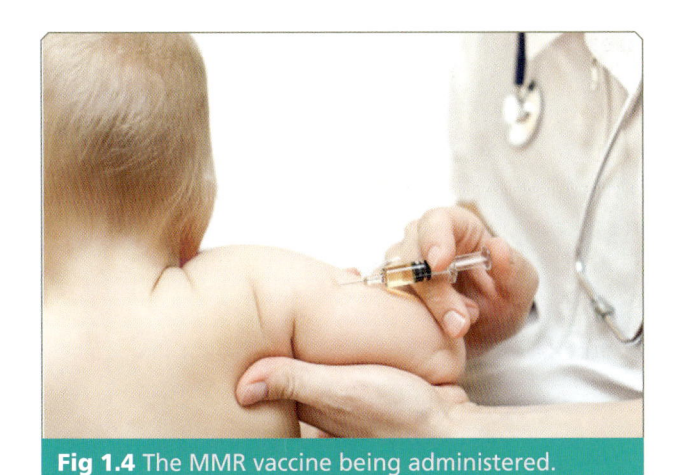

Another example occurred in the 1950s, when thalidomide was prescribed as a treatment for morning sickness in pregnant women. The drug had been tested on animals. However, the drug's effects had not been tested on the animal embryos, nor fully tested on humans. It was later discovered that the drug caused limb deformities in human babies (Fig 1.5) and was quickly withdrawn. It is thought to have affected 20,000 people worldwide.

4 Application to a changing natural world

A discovery today may have a certain effect on us or on the natural world. Over time, this effect may alter as the natural world is in a constant state of change. For example, antibiotics were discovered that killed bacteria. Those same antibiotics have become less and less effective because the bacteria evolved to be able to resist them. This is thought to be partly due to the overuse of antibiotics. Therefore, scientists have had to 'design' new antibiotics.

Another example is the discovery and use of alcohol. Had we discovered alcohol in the modern era, it would most likely have been banned because of its harmful effects. However, humans have drunk alcohol since as far back as the Neolithic period (approximately 10,000 years ago) – and it has become part of our culture.

5 Accidental discovery

In 1928, Scottish scientist Alexander Fleming (Fig 1.7) was researching the influenza virus when he discovered a blue-green mould, called *Penicillium*, growing in a Petri dishes he had left uncovered. Fleming noticed that the mould prevented the growth of bacteria he had placed in the dish. He concluded that the fungus must be producing some factor that prevented the growth of bacteria. Fleming also hypothesised that this factor could be used to fight bacterial infections in humans.

Fleming had the factor purified by chemists to create the first antibiotic, penicillin. Penicillin has saved millions of lives. It is one of the greatest scientific discoveries of all time – and it happened by accident!

Fig 1.6 Growing the fungus *Penicillium* in a Petri dish.

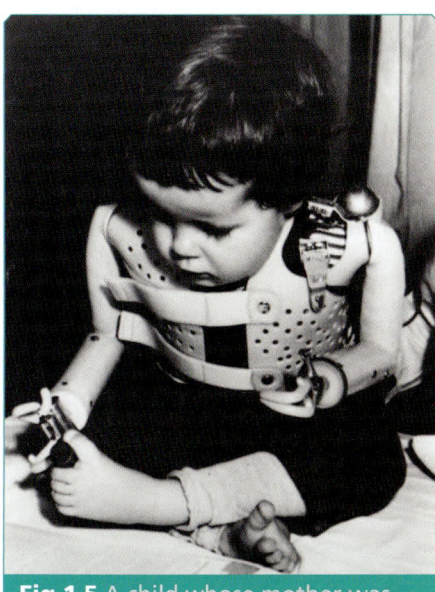

Fig 1.5 A child whose mother was prescribed thalidomide during pregnancy.

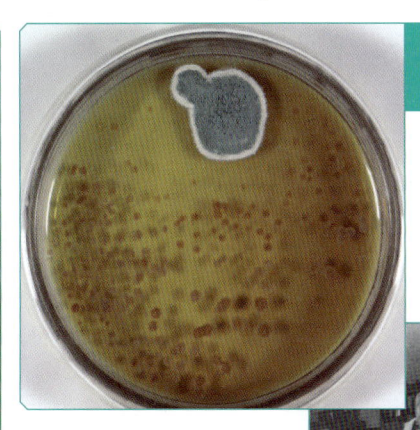

Fig 1.7 Alexander Fleming (1881–1955) discovered penicillin by accident.

Chapter 1 Questions

1. What is *biology*?
2. Name **three** areas of study in biology and give a brief description of each.
3. What is the scientific method?
4. (a) List the first **seven** steps of the scientific method.
   (b) What can scientists formulate after all conditions of a scientific topic have been tested?
5. A new plant has been discovered in the Amazon basin in South America. Local tribespeople have been using its extract as a treatment for fever.
   (a) What is the observation made by the local tribespeople?
   (b) Give a possible hypothesis for this observation.
   (c) Briefly describe how you would investigate whether your hypothesis was correct.
   (d) If the results of your investigation supported your hypothesis, what might you do next?
   (e) What benefit(s) might there be in continuing research on this newly discovered plant?
6. A new fungus has been discovered in the Daintree Rainforest in Queensland, Australia. It had been reported by the Aborigines to prevent infection of wounds and cuts.
   (a) The Aborigines made a hypothesis.
      (i) What is the hypothesis made by the Aborigines?
      (ii) Would it be possible to directly test their hypothesis?
      (iii) What problems might be encountered if a scientist were to directly test the hypothesis made by the Aborigines?
   (b) A scientist's hypothesis might be slightly different but still linked to the Aborigine's hypothesis.
      (i) What might a scientist's hypothesis be considering the hypothesis made by the Aborigines?
      (ii) Explain how you would test the scientist's hypothesis.
   (c) Hypotheses can be correct, incorrect or inconclusive.
      (i) How might you proceed if your hypothesis were correct?
      (ii) How might you proceed if your hypothesis were incorrect or inconclusive?
   (d) The conclusion to your experiment was: 'The fungus is producing a substance that kills bacteria.' Explain the significance of this finding.
   (e) What substance might the fungus be producing that prevents infection?
   (f) What problems are associated with the overuse of this substance?
7. List **three** ways in which a scientist may report or publish their results.
8. Explain, in terms of the scientific method, the following terms:
   (a) *Theory*
   (b) *Law*
9. (a) One of the principles of experimentation is the use of a control. What is a *control*?
   (b) In relation to the control, explain the term *variable*.
10. Give **three** safety precautions that must be followed when in the laboratory or when conducting an experiment.
11. Explain the importance of the following to the scientific method:
    (a) Large sample size.
    (b) Random selection of experimental subjects.
    (c) Conducting replicates of the experiment.
    (d) Double-blind testing.
12. Double-blind testing can be controversial. Discuss.
13. List **two** limitations of the scientific method.

Chapter 1 Sample examination questions

1 (i) The scientific method involves making a hypothesis, carrying out experiments, recording results, and forming conclusions.

Why is it a good idea to repeat an experiment many times?

(ii) Why is a control used when carrying out experiments?

Section B, Question 8 (a) Ordinary Level 2011

HL 2 Answer the following, which relate to the scientific method.

(a) As a result of her observations a scientist may formulate a _____.

She will then progress her investigation by devising a series of _____ and then carefully analysing the resulting _____.

(b) Why is a control especially important in biological investigations?

(c) If a scientist wished to determine the effect of a certain herbicide on weed growth, she would include a control in the investigation. Suggest a suitable control in this case.

(d) The use of replicates is an important aspect of scientific research. What, in this context, are replicates?

(e) Suggest where a scientist may publish the results of her investigations.

Section A, Question 3 Higher Level 2008

Chapter 1 Mind map

The **scientific method** is a process of investigation carried out in order to explain observations made in the natural world.

Biology includes many areas of research, e.g.
1. Anatomy
2. Botany
3. Zoology

Biology is the study of life.

Procedures of the scientific method:
1. Observation: taking in of information received about the natural world
2. Hypothesis: an idea based on an observation
3. Experiment: a test to determine the validity of hypotheses
4. Collecting and interpreting data. (Data: results of an experiment)
5. Conclusion: an explanation of the results
6. Analysing conclusions
7. Reporting and publishing results
8. Development of theory (comprehensive explanation of an important aspect of nature) and principle (a factual explanation of an important aspect of nature)

Principles of experimentation:
1. Careful planning and design
2. Safety procedures
3. Experimental control: factor in an experiment that provides a standard against which the results of an experiment may be compared.
4. Large sample size
5. Random selection
6. Replicate: a repeat of an experiment.
7. Double-blind testing (neither the tester nor patient knows what treatment is given) and placebo (substance with no active medication)

The **limitations of the scientific method** include:
1. Extent of our basic knowledge
2. Basis of investigation
3. Different interpretations of results
4. Application to a changing natural world
5. Accidental discovery

Chapter 2: Characteristics of life

Learning objectives After studying this chapter, you should be able to:
- Describe what is meant by the *diversity of life*.
- Define the word *life*.
- Define the terms *metabolism* and *continuity of life*.
- Name, define and outline each of the characteristics of life.

Introduction

> **Diversity of life** refers to the large variety of living organisms present on Earth.

Life is incredibly diverse. We only begin to appreciate the diversity of living organisms when we study biology or watch a nature programme.

Fig 2.1

A The giant sequoia: the largest tree in the world.

B The blue whale: believed to be the largest animal to have ever lived!

C The frogfish lives in tropical and subtropical seas and oceans.

D The lionfish is a poisonous fish that is found mostly in the Indian and Pacific Oceans.

E The firefly: emits light to attract mates.

F The axolotl: a type of salamander that has an amazing healing ability. It can regrow lost arms and legs!

G The star-nosed mole: a completely blind mammal native to Canada and the USA.

H The starfish stinkhorn: a type of fungus that produces spores in a foul-smelling slime which attracts insects.

I The bobtail squid: a bioluminescent (light-producing) squid from East Timor.

J The aye aye: a primate native to Madagascar.

Organisms have inhabited most places on Earth. There are microscopic organisms (such as bacteria) that cannot be seen by the naked eye and are present almost everywhere! There are huge organisms, such as the blue whale (Fig 2.1B), which can weigh up to 180 tonnes, and the giant sequoia (Fig 2.1A), which can grow to 115 m high! Organisms of all shapes and sizes exist in between these two extremes (some unusual organisms are shown in Fig 2.1C–J).

It is estimated that there are 10 million different species of living organisms on planet Earth. Unfortunately, life is becoming less diverse. Scientists believe that at least 10 species become extinct every year. This is mainly caused by human activities which have destroyed the habitats of many organisms. The disappearance of the dodo is one of the most infamous extinctions of recent times. This flightless bird lived on islands in the Indian Ocean and was hunted to extinction (Fig 2.2).

Fig 2.2 The dodo has been extinct since the mid-seventeenth century.

Even though we all know what life is, it is a very difficult concept to define. Biologists are still trying to devise a complete and concise definition of life. Whole scientific conferences have been taken up discussing this issue! However, life can be broadly defined as follows:

> **Life** describes an organic-based object that possesses the characteristics of metabolism and continuity of life.
>
> **Metabolism** is the sum of all the chemical reactions that occur in an organism.
>
> **Continuity of life** describes how cells arise from cells of the same type and organisms arise from other organisms of the same type.

The five characteristics of living organisms

Metabolism and continuity of life can be subdivided into the five characteristics of living things. In order for an organism to be considered living, and hence have life, it must possess these characteristics:

1. Biological organisation
2. Nutrition
3. Excretion
4. Response
5. Reproduction

You need to learn these characteristics off by heart for your Leaving Certificate Biology exam.

1 Biological organisation

> **Biological organisation** refers to the different levels of complexity in an organism.

All living organisms show biological organisation (also known as the hierarchy of life). This consists of a number of various levels of complexity. Each level represents increased complexity and organisation.

The levels of organisation are:

cell → tissue → organ → organ system → organism → population

2 Nutrition

> **Nutrition** is the way in which living organisms obtain and use food.

All the energy that makes up living organisms on Earth has come from one source – the Sun.

The light energy that comes from the Sun is first captured by plants, algae and some bacteria in the process of photosynthesis and used to make carbohydrates (chemical energy). This chemical energy is then transferred along the food chain and used up in the process of cellular respiration.

There are two main types of nutrition: autotrophic and heterotrophic.

- Autotrophic nutrition is a type of nutrition in which an organism makes its own food, such as photosynthesis in plants.
- Heterotrophic nutrition is a type of nutrition in which an organism must obtain its food from another living organism, such as carnivores killing and eating their prey.

3 Excretion

> **Excretion** is the getting rid of the waste products of metabolism.

Metabolism produces waste products continuously. These must be gotten rid of by the organs of excretion. If they are not excreted, waste products will build up in an organism and reach toxic (poisonous) levels.

All organisms must maintain a constant internal environment (such as mammals maintaining their body temperature at 37 °C), which is called homeostasis (*see* Chapter 29). This is despite possible changes to external environmental conditions. Waste products must also be kept at manageable levels and other molecules at the correct levels in order to survive.

Organs of excretion in animals (lungs, kidneys, and skin) and structures of excretion in plants (stomata, lenticels) are responsible for helping to maintain a constant internal environment for the organism. Less complex organisms (bacteria) get rid of waste by diffusion.

> **Diffusion** is the movement of molecules from areas of high concentration to areas of low concentration.

4 Response

> **Response** is the way in which living organisms react to their environment.

Humans are stimulated by light, sound, touch and so on; plants are stimulated by light, gravity, water and so on. Response in living organisms varies greatly from the extremely quick (electrical nerve impulses) to the very slow (chemicals/hormones causing growth). Response has evolved in organisms as a way of obtaining food and protection from harmful environmental factors.

- Responses in animals to obtain food include catching, killing and eating prey; protection responses include the flight or fight impulse.
- Responses in plants to obtain food include phototropism (growth towards light) and hydrotropism (growth towards water); protection responses include releasing chemicals such as alkaloids (*see* Chapter 26) to protect against herbivores.

5 Reproduction

> **Reproduction** is the way in which new offspring are produced from their parent(s).

There are two methods of reproduction: sexual (involving two parents) and asexual (involving one parent only).

- Sexual reproduction is the more advanced method, as it produces variation amongst members of the same species. It is the preferred method of reproduction for most animals and plants.
- Asexual reproduction is the more primitive method, as it produces identical copies of the organism and produces no variation. Examples of organisms that undergo asexual reproduction are bacteria and members of the protista kingdom (*see* Chapter 22).

Chapter 2 Questions

1. Define the following terms:
   (a) *Life.*
   (b) *Metabolism.*
   (c) *Continuity of life.*
2. Name the **five** characteristics of living things and give a brief description of each.
3. List the **six** levels of biological organisation.
4. Give an example of an organism that demonstrates only the first level of organisation.
5. (a) Where does all of the chemical energy present in living organisms ultimately come from?
   (b) Name the **two** major biochemical processes responsible for transferring energy.
6. (a) What are the **two** types of nutrition and what is the difference between them?
   (b) Give **two** examples of organisms that use each type of nutrition.
7. What is *homeostasis*?
8. (a) Name **three** ways in which animals get rid of waste.
   (b) Name **two** ways in which plants get rid of waste.
   (c) Name **one** way in which single-celled organisms get rid of waste.
9. Give **two** ways in which organisms respond to external factors and give one biological reason for each response.
10. (a) Distinguish between sexual and asexual reproduction.
    (b) Name **one** organism that reproduces asexually and one that reproduces sexually.

Chapter 2 Mind map

Continuity of life describes how cells arise from cells of the same type and living organisms arise only from living organisms of the same type.

Life describes an organic-based object that possesses the characteristics of metabolism and continuity of life.

Metabolism is the sum of all the chemical reactions that occur in an organism.

The five characteristics of living things are:
1. **Biological organisation**
   - Cell
   - Tissue
   - Organ
   - Organ system
   - Organism
   - Population
2. **Nutrition:** way in which organisms obtain and use food.
   - Autotrophic: organism makes its own food.
   - Heterotrophic: organism obtains its food from other organisms.
3. **Excretion:** getting rid of waste products of metabolism.
   - Animal excretory organs: skin, lungs and kidneys.
   - Plant excretory structures: stomata and lenticels.
4. **Response:** way in which organisms respond to their environment.
   - Hormonal/chemical
   - Nervous/electrical
5. **Reproduction:** way in which new offspring are produced from their parent(s).
   - Sexual: reproduction involving two parents.
   - Asexual: reproduction involving only one parent.

Chapter 3 Nutrition

Learning objectives After studying this chapter, you should be able to:
- Describe the function of food and identify the elements present in food.
- Describe the general structures, various types and sources of carbohydrates, lipids, proteins and vitamins.
- Describe tests for starch, lipid, reducing sugar and protein.
- Distinguish between anabolism and catabolism and give examples of each.
- Describe the structural and metabolic roles of carbohydrates, lipids and proteins.
- Describe the metabolic roles of one water-soluble and one fat-soluble vitamin and a deficiency disorder associated with each.
- Describe the requirement and use of two minerals in animals and two in plants.
- Describe the importance of water to living organisms.

Introduction

Nutrition is the way in which living organisms obtain and use food.

As we learned in Chapter 2, some organisms can make their own food (autotrophic organisms) and some need to obtain their food directly from other organisms (heterotrophic organisms). Food is the way in which living organisms obtain their nutrition. Food is made up of six constituents:

- Carbohydrates
- Lipids
- Proteins
- Vitamins
- Minerals
- Water

Humans, and other animals, must take in these nutrients in the correct amounts to maintain health. The food pyramid (Fig 3.1) is designed to give people an indication of the quantities of the various foods they should eat.

The function of food

Food is required by all living organisms because of two major processes: metabolism and continuity of life.

1 Metabolism

Metabolism is the sum of all the chemical reactions in an organism.

In order for chemical reactions to occur, chemical substances are required. These chemicals originate from food, which is the raw material for all the biochemicals (chemicals made in living organisms) that make up an individual organism.

2 Continuity of life

Continuity of life is the way in which living things arise from living things of the same type.

A plentiful supply of food is necessary for the rapid assembly and growth of a new organism.

Fats, oils and sweets
0–3 servings/day

Milk, cheese and yoghurt
2–3 servings/day

Meat, poultry, fish, beans, eggs and nuts
2–3 servings/day

Vegetables
3–5 servings/day

Fruit
3–4 servings/day

Bread, cereal, rice and pasta
6–11 servings/day

Fig 3.1 The food pyramid shows people the quantities of different food types they should eat.

Chemical elements present in food

The food we eat is made up of chemicals. All chemicals are made up of individual elements. There are six common non-metal elements that are present in food in high proportions.

Carbon (C)	Essential elements for the important molecules of an organism, such as all carbohydrates, fats, proteins, vitamins and DNA
Hydrogen (H)	
Oxygen (O)	
Nitrogen (N)	Essential element for all proteins and enzymes
Phosphorus (P)	Essential element for DNA
Sulfur (S)	Essential component for many proteins and enzymes

There are five elements that are very important for such things as bone structure, water retention, nerve impulses and muscle contractions. These are present in our bodies as dissolved salts.

Sodium (Na)	Helps maintain the correct amount of water in an organism
Magnesium (Mg)	Essential for a long list of animal enzymes and an essential component of bones
Chlorine (Cl)	Helps maintain the correct pH of the blood
Potassium (K)	Essential for proper nerve impulses
Calcium (Ca)	Essential component of bone

Finally, there are chemical elements that are only needed by organisms in extremely small amounts. These are called **trace elements.** Humans need many of them, but for the Leaving Certificate Biology course, you need to know the first three only.

Iron (Fe)	Required by haemoglobin
Copper (Cu)	Essential for a long list of animal enzymes
Zinc (Zn)	Essential for a long list of animal enzymes
Iodine (I)	Required to make a hormone called thyroxine
Manganese (Mn)	Essential for a long list of animal enzymes
Molybdenum (Mo)	Used by enzymes involved in protein synthesis
Selenium (Se)	Essential for antioxidant enzymes
Cobalt (Co)	Key constituent of vitamin B_{12} (cobalamin)
Chromium (Cr)	Helps regulate glucose levels

Biomolecules

> **Biomolecules** are organic chemicals produced and found only within living organisms.

The four major types of biomolecules found in food are:

1. Carbohydrates
2. Lipids
3. Proteins
4. Vitamins

Carbohydrates

Carbohydrates are biomolecules, which means they are only present in, and made by, living organisms.

Biomolecular structure of carbohydrates

Carbohydrates are made up of the elements carbon, hydrogen and oxygen in a specific ratio. All carbohydrates have a general formula of $C_x(H_2O)_y$. This means that hydrogen and oxygen are always present in a 2:1 ratio (as in water).

Fig 3.2 Iron (5 g); copper (0.15 g); and zinc (3 g) – the average amounts of three trace elements in the human body.

Carbohydrates are divided into three groups based on their structural size and composition:
1. Monosaccharides
2. Disaccharides
3. Polysaccharides

> The word **saccharide** comes from the Greek word, sákkharon, meaning 'sugar'.

Monosaccharides and disaccharides (sugars)

Monosaccharides and disaccharides are simple carbohydrates (often referred to as sugars) with names always ending in 'ose'. There are three types of monosaccharides and three types of disaccharides.

Monosaccharides	Disaccharides
Glucose (Glc) Sources: fruit juices, sweets and chocolate	Maltose (Glc-Glc) Source: barley
Fructose (Fru) Sources: fruits, fruit juices	Sucrose (Glc-Fru) Sources: table sugar, sugar cane, sugar beet, fruits
Galactose (Gal) Source: dairy products	Lactose (Glc-Gal) Source: milk

NOTE: 'Glc' is short for glucose; 'Fru' is short for fructose; and 'Gal' is short for galactose.

Monosaccharides are the simplest type of carbohydrate, being 'one sugar unit'. They all have the same molecular formula, $C_6H_{12}O_6$, in a hexagonal ring structure (see Fig 3.7), page 18. This means they have six carbon atoms, 12 hydrogen atoms and six oxygen atoms.

Monosaccharides are sweet to taste and soluble in water. Good sources of monosaccharides are fruits such as oranges, apples and pears (Fig 3.3). Good sources of lactose include milk and yoghurt.

Disaccharides consist of two monosaccharides covalently joined together (see Fig 3.7). They are also sweet to taste and soluble in water. They all have the molecular formula $C_{12}H_{22}O_{11}$.

The molecular formula of disaccharides is not exactly twice the formula for monosaccharides. When a disaccharide is formed, it is lacking a H_2O. Every time two monosaccharides join together, a water molecule is left out, in what is called a **condensation reaction.** This is why the general formula for all carbohydrates is $C_x(H_2O)_y$.

Fig 3.3 Fruits and juices of fruits are high in glucose and fructose.

In monosaccharides $x = y$, but in disaccharides $x = y + 1$.

- Maltose is composed of two glucose molecules joined together. It is found in germinating seeds such as barley (Fig 3.4A).
- Sucrose is composed of a glucose molecule and a fructose molecule. Sucrose is more commonly known as table sugar and is obtained from sugar cane (Fig 3.4B) and sugar beet (Fig 3.4C).
- Lactose is composed of a glucose molecule and a galactose molecule. It is obtained from milk.

Fig 3.4 Barley (A), from which malt (containing maltose) is made; sugar cane (B) and sugar beet (C), from which table sugar is made.

Nutrition   Chapter 3

Practical activity: qualitative test for a reducing sugar

A reducing sugar is any sugar that has the ability to reduce (add electrons to) another atom or molecule. To test for a reducing sugar, we use Benedict's reagent (Fig 3.5). Benedict's reagent is blue. When heated in the presence of a reducing sugar, it turns an orange or a brick red colour (Fig 3.6). All three monosaccharides and two disaccharides (maltose and lactose) are reducing sugars.

Method

1. Fill a beaker two-thirds full of water and heat using the Bunsen burner. The water needs to be hot (but not boiling).
2. Label test-tubes A, B, C and D.
3. Dissolve a small amount of glucose powder in 2 ml of water and add to test-tube A (positive control as we know it is a reducing sugar).
4. Add 2 ml of water, using a different dropper, to test-tube B (negative control).
5. Add 2 ml of a fruit juice (for example, apple juice) to test-tube C.
6. In test-tube D, dissolve a small amount of table sugar in 2 ml of water.
7. Add 2 ml of Benedict's reagent to each tube.
8. Place each test-tube in the hot water.
9. Observe what happens to the colour of the Benedict's reagent in each test-tube.
10. Wash all test-tubes out thoroughly at the end of the experiment (otherwise the brick red colour will stain the test-tube).

SAFETY Benedict's solution is an irritant. Be very careful when using it. Wear gloves, a laboratory coat, and safety goggles when handling chemicals.

Fig 3.5 Benedict's reagent. Notice the hazard symbol on the bottle. Care must be taken when using this reagent.

Results

Copy the following table into your experimental laboratory copy and complete the results.

Test-tube	Colour change
A (glucose) – positive control	Blue →
B (water) – negative control	Blue →
C (fruit juice)	Blue →
D (table sugar)	Blue →

Fig 3.6 Test-tubes with sugars of different strengths. The first test-tube is the negative control (no sugar present).

Conclusion

What did we learn from this practical activity?

- Benedict's solution (blue) turns orange or brick red when heated in the presence of a reducing sugar.
- Glucose is a reducing sugar.
- Fruit juices contain reducing sugars.
- Sucrose (table sugar) is not a reducing sugar.

Practical activity questions

1. What is a reducing sugar?
2. Name the five reducing sugars.
3. Which disaccharide is not a reducing sugar?
4. What reagent is used to test for the presence of a reducing sugar?
5. What colour change occurs if a reducing sugar is present?
6. Explain the purpose of a control in this experiment.
7. Give one safety precaution you took during this activity.

Functions of sugars

Sugar	Structural role	Metabolic role
Monosaccharide	None	Energy source
Disaccharide	None	Energy source

Monosaccharides and disaccharides have the same function – providing energy for the organism. All sugars are converted to glucose and then metabolised in respiration to produce energy (see Chapter 11).

Polysaccharides

Polysaccharides are complex carbohydrates made up of long chains of more than ten monosaccharides (usually glucose) covalently joined together. Their general formula is $(C_6H_{10}O_5)_n$.

The table below lists some examples of polysaccharides (see Fig 3.7): starch (amylose), glycogen and cellulose.

As polysaccharides are made up of long chains of monosaccharides, they generally do not dissolve in water.

There are subtle differences at a molecular level among the three polysaccharides. Starch and glycogen are branched, with glycogen being slightly more branched than starch. Cellulose is not branched. Animals cannot digest cellulose because they lack the enzyme needed to break it down. Cellulose therefore acts as fibre in the digestive system, preventing constipation and helping lower blood cholesterol. There is also evidence to suggest that fibre reduces the risk of developing colon cancer later in life.

Good sources of polysaccharides include foods such as vegetables and fruits, wholegrain bread and potatoes.

Polysaccharides	Functions	
	Structural role	Metabolic role
Starch (amylose)	None	Energy store in all plants; energy source for animals
Glycogen	None	Energy store in all animals
Cellulose	Makes up the cell wall of plant cells	Source of fibre in humans; Energy source for herbivores

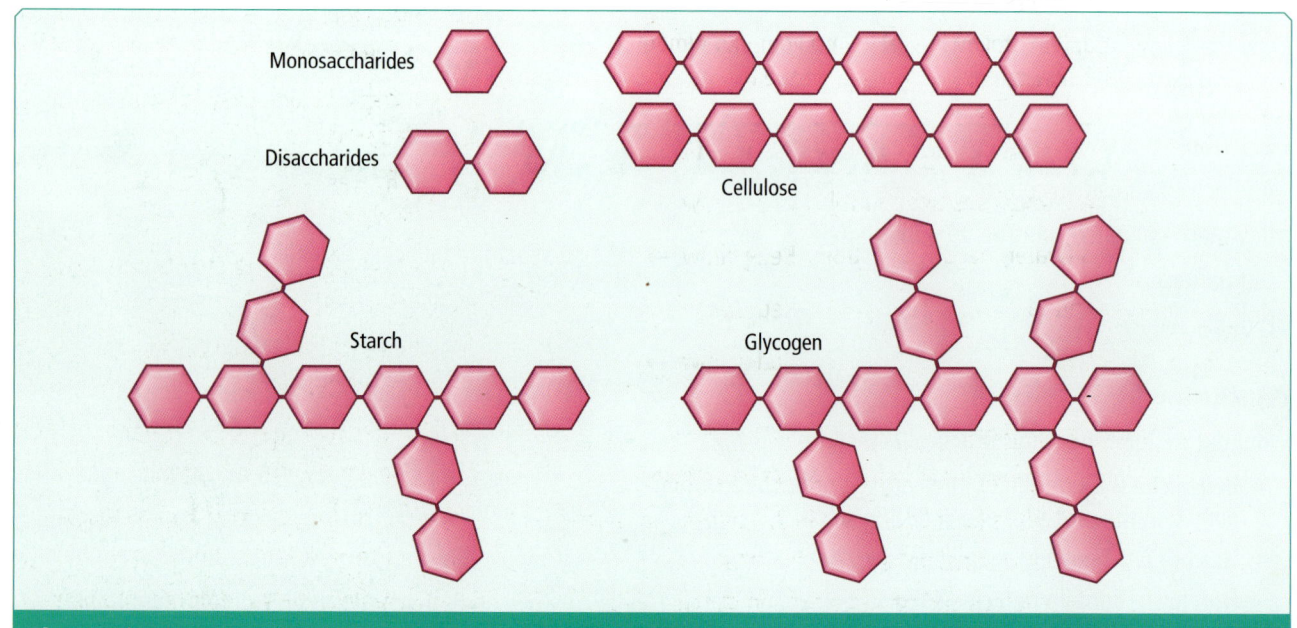

Fig 3.7 The structure of carbohydrates: monosaccharides; disaccharides; glycogen; cellulose; and starch.

Nutrition | Chapter 3

Practical activity: qualitative test for starch

Plants use carbon dioxide and water to make glucose. This glucose is then used in respiration within plant cells. Any excess glucose produced in photosynthesis is converted to sucrose and transferred to other areas of the plant for storage as starch. For example, all vegetables (such as carrots) have organs that are responsible for storing energy. Energy is stored in the form of starch so the vegetable can survive winter, when there is less sunlight to aid photosynthesis.

Iodine can be used to test for starch. Iodine is a red-yellow colour. In the presence of starch it turns blue-black.

SAFETY
Wear gloves and a lab coat when handling iodine.

Method

1. Label two test-tubes A and B.
2. In test-tube A, place a small amount of starch powder and add 2 ml of warm water (positive control).
   Notice that it does not dissolve well – which is why we use warm water.
3. In test-tube B, place 2 ml of water (negative control) using a different dropper.
4. Take a potato and a banana and cut a small portion from each and place each on a piece of tissue paper.
5. Place two drops of iodine into both test-tubes and onto both the piece of potato and the piece of banana.
6. If you wish you may test other food, such as bread, for starch.
7. Observe what happens to the colour of the iodine.
8. Record your results in the table.

Fig 3.8 Iodine is used to test for starch. A blue-black colour indicates a positive result for starch.

Results

Copy the following table into your experimental laboratory copy and complete the results.

Test-tube	Colour change
A (starch) positive control	Red-yellow →
B (water) negative control	Red-yellow →
Potato	Red-yellow →
Banana	Red-yellow →

Conclusion

What did we learn from this practical activity?
- Iodine turns blue-black in the presence of starch.
- Starch does not dissolve in water.
- Potatoes and bananas contain starch.

Practical activity questions

1. What type of carbohydrate is starch?
2. What are the subunits of starch?
3. What is the other name for starch?
4. What is the function of starch in each of the following:
   (a) Plants?
   (b) Animals?
5. Where in a plant would you find starch?
6. Why was warm water used to dissolve the starch?
7. What substance is used to test for starch?
8. What colour change is seen in a positive test for starch?
9. Name two foods that are good sources of starch.
10. Explain the importance of a control in this activity.
11. Give one safety precaution you took during this experiment.

Lipids

Lipid is the general term given to fats and oils. Fats tend to be solid at room temperature, whereas oils are liquid. Good sources of fats are butter and lard.

Good sources of oils are vegetable oil and cod liver oil.

Fig 3.9 Examples of everyday lipids are butter and olive oil.

Biomolecular structure of lipids

Lipids are similar to carbohydrates in that they are made from the same elements: carbon, hydrogen and oxygen. However, in lipids the arrangement of the elements is not in any particular ratio, which means there is no pattern to the frequency of the elements. Also, lipids have very few oxygen atoms present in their molecules. They are composed of mostly carbon and hydrogen.

All lipids contain a glycerol and fatty acids – although the number of fatty acids depends on the type of lipid.

You are required to know two types of lipids for Leaving Certificate Biology: triglycerides and phospholipids.

Triglycerides

> **Triglycerides** are lipids composed of one glycerol molecule and three fatty acids.

The structure of a typical triglyceride is shown in Fig 3.10. Notice that the fatty acids can be all the same or all different, depending on the lipid.

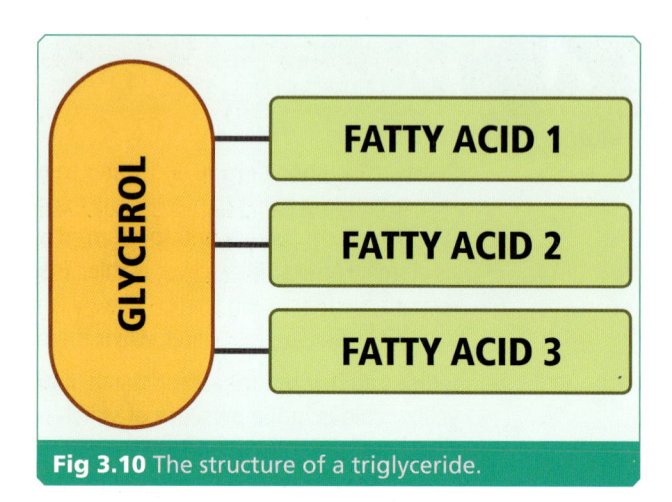

Fig 3.10 The structure of a triglyceride.

Functions of triglycerides

Triglycerides are very important molecules for storing energy. Humans and all other animals store excess energy in the form of triglycerides under the skin (adipose tissue for insulation) and surrounding internal organs (protection). This means that excess energy that is consumed in any form is converted to fat. For example, too much carbohydrate is converted to fat in the liver and sent to various areas of the organism's body for storage. It can then be used when needed, such as during prolonged aerobic exercise.

There is an important reason why animals store excess energy in the form of fat. Fat stores more energy per gram than any other biomolecule. For example, 1 g of sugar holds 4.2 kcal (17 kJ) of energy, whereas fat holds 9.4 kcal (37 kJ) per gram. This makes it far more efficient for animals to store energy in the form of fat. The energy values of protein and alcohol are shown in the table below as a reference.

Biomolecule	Energy per gram
Carbohydrates	4.2 kcal (17 kJ)
Lipids	9.4 kcal (37 kJ)
Proteins	4.2 kcal (17 kJ)
Alcohol	7 kcal (29 kJ)

Phospholipids

> **Phospholipids** are fats that are composed of one glycerol molecule, two fatty acids and one phosphate molecule.

Nutrition   Chapter 3

Practical activity: qualitative test for fat

Fat has unique chemical properties, the most important of which is that it is insoluble in water. Brown paper is used to test for fats and oils. If there is fat present in a sample of food, then the brown paper will absorb the fat molecules and become translucent.

Lipids can also be tested for using Sudan III dye.

Translucent means it allows light through.

NOTE: Do not describe the brown paper as being transparent. Transparent means that light can pass through a substance so that objects on the other side can be clearly seen.

Method
1. Label four pieces of brown paper A, B, C and D.
2. Onto A, place a drop of water (negative control).
3. Onto B, place a drop of oil (positive control).
4. Onto C, place a drop of full fat milk.
5. Onto D, rub a small amount of banana.
6. If you wish, you can add further tests to the experiment, such as butter, peanut butter, margarine, yoghurt and so on.
7. Allow the pieces of brown paper to dry completely by placing them near a radiator or into an incubator for a few minutes.
8. Observe the pieces of brown paper by holding them up to the light.

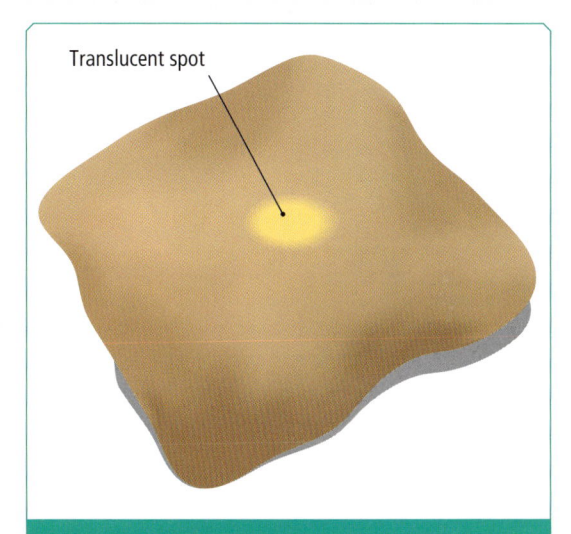

Fig 3.11 A translucent spot present on brown paper.

Results
Copy the following table into your experimental laboratory copy and complete the results.

Substance	Translucent	Not translucent
Water		
Oil		
Full fat milk		
Banana		

Conclusion
What did we learn from this practical activity?
- Brown paper turns translucent when it absorbs fat molecules (Fig 3.11).
- Full fat milk contains fat.
- Banana does not contain fat.

Practical activity questions
1. Why do you think it is important not to use grease-proof paper for this activity?
2. What is the difference between 'translucent' and 'transparent'?
3. Name and draw labelled diagrams of the two types of lipid.
4. Distinguish between the two types of lipid in terms of: (a) Structure (b) Function (c) Location in an adipose tissue cell.
5. Explain why it is important to allow the pieces of brown paper to dry before observing the results.
6. Name three foods rich in lipids.
7. Explain the importance of a control in this activity.

Phospholipids have the same structure as triglycerides except that the third fatty acid is replaced with a phosphate group (P) (Fig 3.12).

Functions of phospholipids

Phospholipids are an essential component of the cell membrane of all cells (*see* Chapter 5). The cell membrane of all cells is made from a double layer of phospholipids controlling what enters and leaves the cell.

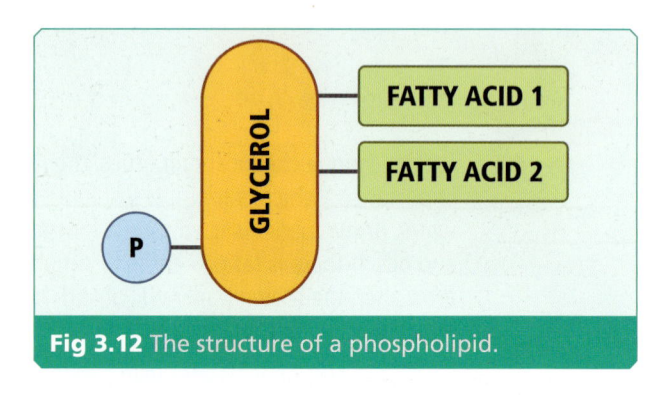

Fig 3.12 The structure of a phospholipid.

Lipid	Structural role	Metabolic role
Triglycerides	Adipose tissue; protection of internal organs, such as the kidneys	Energy source
Phospholipids	Formation of the cell membrane	Transferring chemical signals into the cell

Protein

Proteins are a type of organic biomolecule found in every living organism. They are essential for an organism to function properly. Proteins that do not work properly can result in disease.

Good sources of proteins include fish, chicken and red meat.

Biomolecular structure of proteins

Proteins are composed of at least four elements: carbon, hydrogen, oxygen and nitrogen. Most proteins also contain sulfur and some have phosphorus. These elements combine to form the building blocks of protein, which are called amino acids.

There are 20 common amino acids that make up all the different proteins. There are also a number of rare amino acids. It is the sequence of these common amino acids that determine the type of protein. Amino acids are bonded to one another via peptide bonds. Many hundreds of amino acids – or sometimes even thousands (*see* Fig 3.13) – are required to make up one single protein!

Functions

Proteins can be classified by their shape: **fibrous** or **globular**. This method of classification indicates their structure and function.

- Fibrous proteins are composed of long, straight chains of amino acids with very little folding in their structure. They have structural functions in living organisms.

- Globular proteins are composed of long chains of amino acids with a lot of folding in their structure. They have metabolic functions in living organisms.

Structural functions

Proteins are very important for the structure of all parts of an organism. Examples include:

- Collagen (Fig 3.14) is a fibrous protein responsible for holding tissues and organs together. Collagen is a key component of bone, skin, tendons, ligaments and gums.

- Skeletal muscle is full of the proteins actin and myosin (Fig 3.15), which are responsible for creating movement.

- The protein keratin makes up a large part of our skin, hair and nails (Fig 3.16).

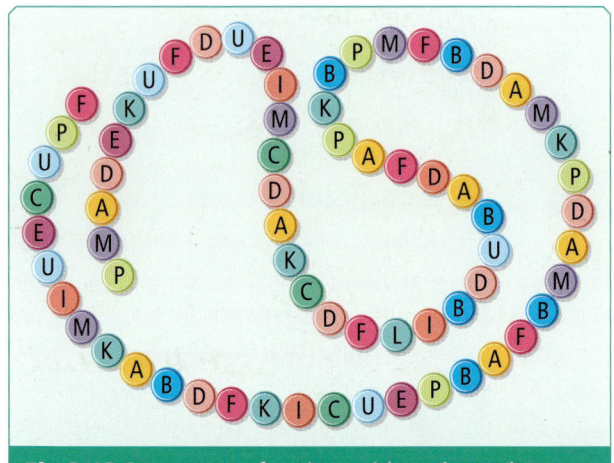

Fig 3.13 Sequences of amino acids make up large proteins.

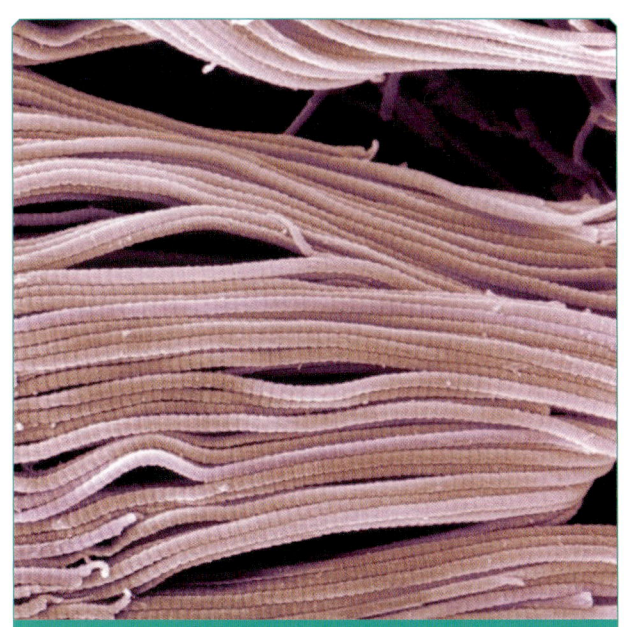

Fig 3.14 A scanning electron micrograph (SEM) of collagen fibres.

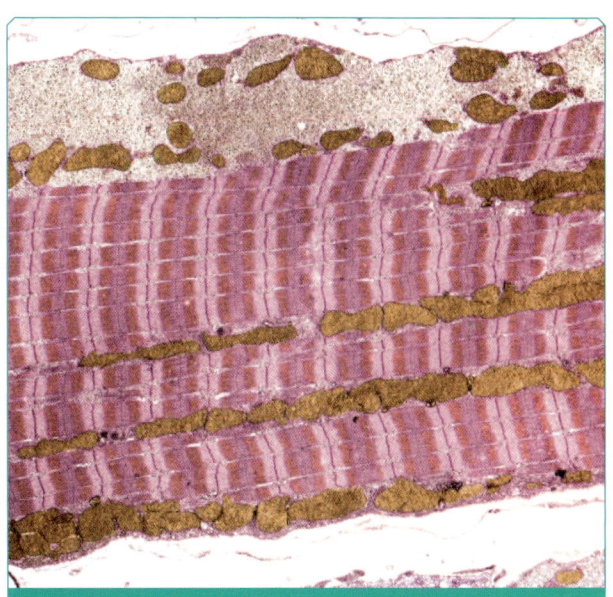

Fig 3.15 A transmission electron micrograph (TEM) of actin and myosin proteins arranged in bands in a muscle tissue.

Metabolic functions

Proteins are involved in all aspects of metabolism. Below is a short list of examples:

- All enzymes are made from protein and speed up biochemical reactions (that is, metabolism). For example, amylase is an enzyme found in saliva that breaks down starch into maltose.
- Many hormones are made from protein (for example, insulin and growth hormone) and regulate metabolism.
- All antibodies are made from protein. Antibodies are produced by white blood cells and help us to fight infections.
- Haemoglobin (Fig 3.17) is a protein present in red blood cells. It carries oxygen around the body.

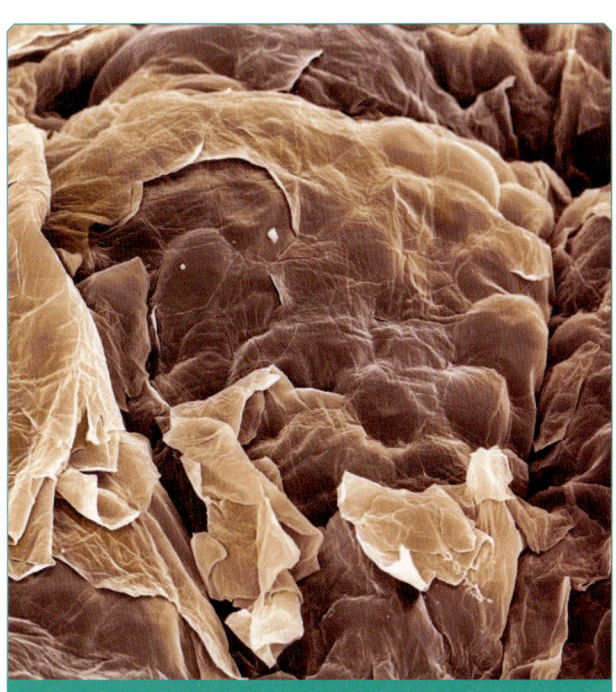

Fig 3.16 A scanning electron micrograph of the surface of human skin. Keratin is a major component of the skin.

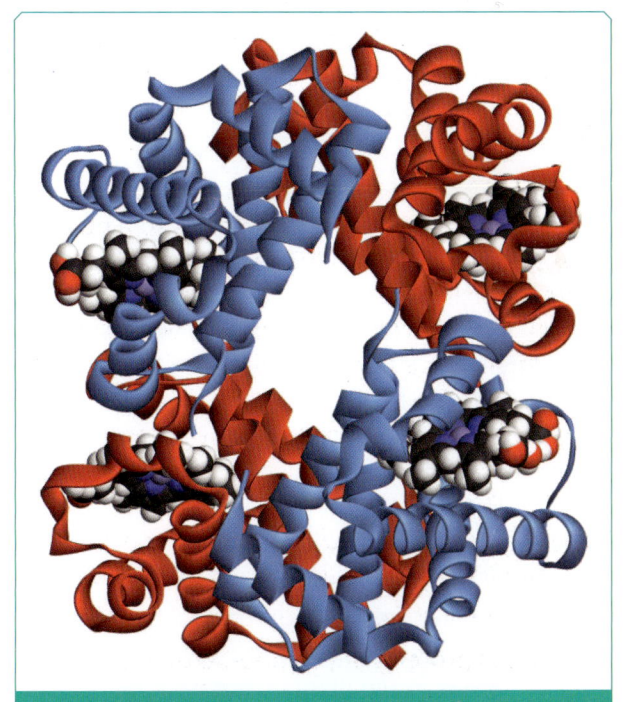

Fig 3.17 A ribbon diagram of the structure of haemoglobin (a globular protein).

Practical activity: qualitative test for protein

Amino acids are the building blocks of proteins and are connected to one another via peptide bonds. It is the presence of this peptide bond that is the basis of this test. Sodium hydroxide and copper sulfate solution are used for this test. A purple colour will indicate the presence of the peptide bond. Alternatively, biuret reagent can be used, which gives the same colour change.

SAFETY
- Sodium hydroxide is a strong corrosive base.
- Copper sulfate is a strong irritant.
- Be careful! Wear gloves, a laboratory coat and safety goggles when handling these chemicals.

Method

NOTE: The chemicals used in this experiment can be dangerous.

1. Label three test-tubes A, B and C.
2. Into test-tube A, place some raw egg white diluted with water, using a dropper, so that the final volume is about 2 ml.
3. Using a different dropper, place 1 ml of milk into test-tube B and dilute to 2 ml using water.
4. Into test-tube C, place 2 ml of water (negative control).
5. Mix each test-tube by swirling it.
6. Place 2 ml of sodium hydroxide solution into each of the three test-tubes using a new dropper.
7. Add a few drops of copper sulfate solution to each test-tube, using a new dropper.
8. Observe any colour changes.

Results

Copy the following table into your experimental laboratory copy and complete the results.

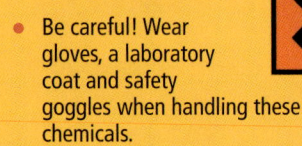

Fig 3.18 Biuret test for protein. A purple colour indicates that protein is present.

Test-tube	Colour change
A (egg white solution)	Blue →
B (diluted milk)	Blue →
C (water)	Blue →

Conclusion

What did we learn from this practical activity?

- Copper sulfate solution and sodium hydroxide are used to test for the presence of proteins.
- Egg white contains protein.
- Milk contains protein.

Practical activity questions

1. What are amino acids?
2. What type of bond binds amino acids together?
3. What two substances are used to test for the presence of proteins?
4. What indicates a positive result for protein?
5. Explain the importance of a control in this experiment.
6. Give two safety precautions you took during this experiment.

Vitamins

A vitamin is an organic molecule needed by organisms in very small amounts because the organisms are unable to make it themselves. Vitamins are made in plants from basic elements they obtain from the soil. Plants require these vitamins just as much as animals do. The vitamins are then passed along the food chain. Some vitamins in humans are not vitamins in other animals. For example, most animals can make vitamin C, but humans and mice cannot! Fig 3.19 shows some examples of disorders caused by vitamin deficiencies.

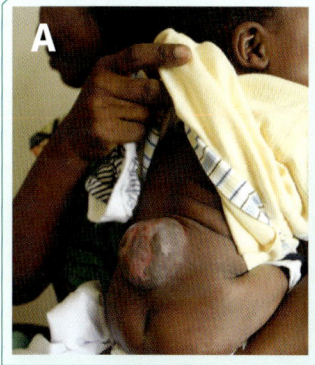

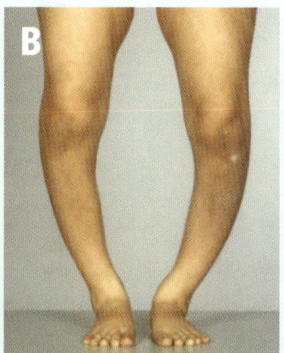

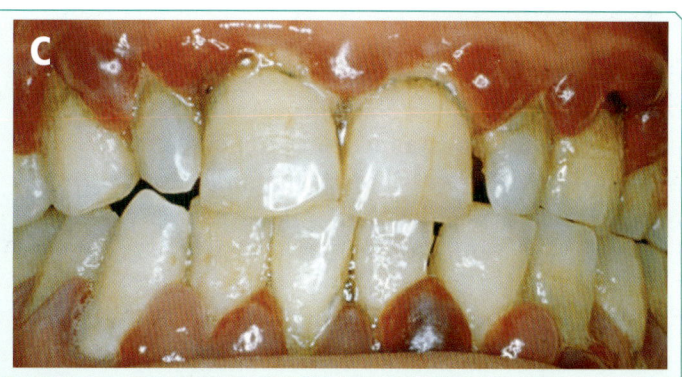

Fig 3.19 Spina bifida (folic acid deficiency) **(A)**; rickets (vitamin D deficiency) **(B)**; scurvy (vitamin C deficiency) **(C)**.

Vitamins are classified by their biological functions and not by their structures. They are grouped into two distinct categories: **fat-soluble** and **water-soluble**. For the Leaving Certificate Biology course, you need to be able to name one fat-soluble vitamin and one water-soluble vitamin and a deficiency disorder associated with each.

- Fat-soluble vitamins are generally found only in food that contains fat; for example, butter, milk, oily fish and red meats.
- Water-soluble vitamins are found in a wide variety of foods.

The table below shows the fat-soluble and water-soluble vitamins along with the deficiency disorder of each.

Fat-soluble vitamins*	Deficiency disorders	Metabolic role†	Sources
Vitamin A (retinol)	Night-blindness	Formation of rhodopsin (pigment in eye)	Cod liver oil, butter, margarine
Vitamin D (calciferol)	Rickets in children; Osteomalacia in adults	Absorption of calcium in digestive system	Sunlight, eggs, milk
Vitamin E (tocopherol)	Poor nerve impulse conduction	Growth in children; Antioxidant in adults (prevent damage to cell membranes)	Eggs, milk, nuts and seeds
Vitamin K (quinone)	Inability to clot blood	Blood clotting	Intestinal bacteria, spinach
Water-soluble vitamins*	**Deficiency disorders**	**Metabolic role†**	**Sources**
Vitamin B_1 (thiamine)	Beriberi (neurological disorder)	Carbohydrate metabolism	Pork, wholemeal bread
Vitamin B_2 (riboflavin)	Swollen mouth	Carbohydrate metabolism	Eggs, meat, milk
Vitamin B_3 (niacin)	Skin lesions (pellagra)	Carbohydrate metabolism	Chicken, beef, tomatoes
Vitamin B_5 (pantothenic acid)	Fatigue and low glucose levels	Carbohydrate metabolism	Wholegrain bread, eggs, meat
Vitamin B_6 (pyridoxine)	Anaemia	Formation of red blood cells	Wholegrain bread, nuts, seeds
Vitamin B_7 (biotin)	Dermatitis and hair loss	Fat metabolism	Nuts, seeds, liver
Vitamin B_9 (folic acid)	Spina bifida in children; Anaemia in adults	Nervous system development; Formation of red blood cells	Spinach, egg yolk, sunflower seeds
Vitamin B_{12} (cobalamin)	Anaemia	Formation of red blood cells	Eggs, milk, fish
Vitamin C (ascorbic acid)	Scurvy	Formation of collagen	Citrus fruits, such as oranges, lemons

NOTE
*For Leaving Certificate Biology, you must learn about one fat-soluble vitamin and one water-soluble vitamin.
†Vitamins have only metabolic roles in organisms. They have no structural role.

Biomolecular structure of vitamins

All vitamins contain carbon, hydrogen and oxygen elements. Some vitamins contain nitrogen and sulfur and one vitamin contains phosphorus and cobalt. Therefore, no two vitamins are alike. They all have their own unique structure and have their own distinct functions in a living organism (*see* table on the previous page). They are essential to the health of the organism despite only being needed in small amounts.

Dietary minerals

Dietary minerals are metallic elements required by living organisms. These minerals are required in small quantities on a daily basis.

> **NOTE** For Leaving Certificate Biology, you must know two dietary minerals required by plants and two required by animals, as well as their respective functions.

There are many minerals required by both kingdoms. The table below shows four minerals for each kingdom.

PLANTS	
Minerals	**Functions**
Calcium	Formation of the middle lamella (cement that holds plant cell walls together)
Magnesium	Formation of chlorophyll (green pigment)
Iron	Formation of a number of enzymes
Copper	Needed for the electron transport chain of photosynthesis and respiration

ANIMALS	
Minerals	**Functions**
Calcium	Formation of bones and teeth
Iron	Formation of haemoglobin (red pigment in red blood cells that carries oxygen)
Magnesium	Formation of bones
Copper	Needed for the electron transport chain of respiration

Water

Water is the most common molecule in living organisms. Depending on the cell, water makes up between 70 per cent and 95 per cent of the cell's mass. Water is required in living organisms for a number of important reasons:

- Water is the medium in which all chemical reactions (metabolism) occur.
- Water is an excellent solvent, meaning many organic molecules can dissolve in it.
- Water can actually take part in chemical reactions. **Hydrolysis reactions** and **condensation reactions** are two very important reactions that water takes part in.
  - Hydrolysis reaction occurs in digestion when water, with the help of specific enzymes, breaks the bonds between the building blocks of carbohydrates, lipids and proteins. Water is used up as each bond is broken. Monomers (single units) of the biomolecules are formed during hydrolysis (Fig 3.20).
  - Condensation reaction: occurs when molecules – such as carbohydrates (for example, glycogen), lipids (for example, triglycerides) and proteins (for example, collagen) – are reassembled within cells. Water is lost after each bond is made. The process is also called polymerisation as polymers of the biomolecules are being made (Fig 3.20).

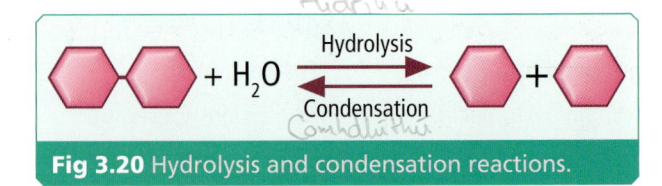

Fig 3.20 Hydrolysis and condensation reactions.

- Water is responsible for transporting substances around cells, into and out of cells and around the bodies of complex organisms.
- Water has a very high specific heat capacity for such a small molecule. Water retains heat very well, making it an ideal solvent for living organisms.

> **Specific heat capacity** is the amount of heat energy water can hold per litre.

Nutrition   Chapter 3

Metabolism: anabolism versus catabolism

As we have already learned, metabolism is the sum of all the chemical reactions in an organism. Metabolism is categorised into **anabolism** and **catabolism**.

> ⚠ **Anabolism** is the building up of large molecules from smaller molecules using energy.

Fig 3.21 An example of the effects of anabolic steroids on the body.

Examples of anabolic reactions

- **Photosynthesis:** where enzymes make glucose from the small molecules water and carbon dioxide using sunlight as an energy source.
- **Protein synthesis:** where enzymes join many amino acids together to make large proteins (anabolic steroids speed up protein synthesis).

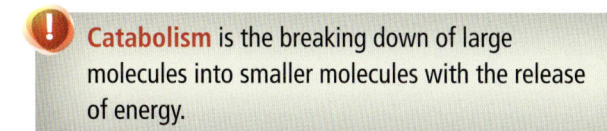

> ⚠ **Catabolism** is the breaking down of large molecules into smaller molecules with the release of energy.

Examples of catabolic reactions

- **Respiration:** where glucose is broken down by enzymes to produce the waste products of water and carbon dioxide, releasing energy in the process.
- **Digestion:** where enzymes break down large molecules into smaller ones, for example, amylase breaking starch (polysaccharide) down into maltose (disaccharide).

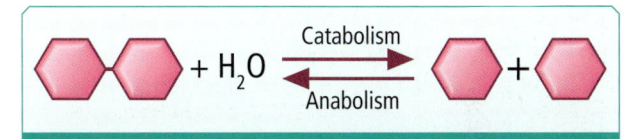

Fig 3.22 Anabolism and catabolism.

Chapter 3 Questions

1. What is *nutrition*?
2. What is the function of food?
3. Where does all the chemical energy in food ultimately come from?
4. There are many elements present in living organisms.
   (a) List the **six** common elements present in living organisms.
   (b) List the **five** elements present in living organisms as dissolved salts.
   (c) There are a number of trace elements needed by living organisms. Explain the meaning of the underlined term.
   (d) Name **three** trace elements.
5. (a) What is a *biomolecule*?
   (b) Which of the **six** constituents of food are considered to be biomolecules?
6. Explain why dietary minerals and water are not considered to be biomolecules.
7. (a) Carbohydrates contain the elements _____, _____ and _____.
   (b) The general formula for all carbohydrates is _____.
   (c) What **two** elements in carbohydrates are in a 2:1 ratio?

8 (a) What is a *monosaccharide*?
   (b) Give the chemical formula for monosaccharides.

9 (a) What is a *condensation reaction*?
   (b) Give an example of a condensation reaction.

10 (a) What is a *disaccharide*?
   (b) Give the chemical formula for disaccharides.

11 Copy the following table into your exercise copy and complete:

Monosaccharides	Function	Source
1.		
2.		
3.		
Disaccharides	**Function**	**Source**
1.		
2.		
3.		
Polysaccharides	**Function**	**Source**
1.		
2.		
3.		

12 (a) What is a *reducing sugar*?
   (b) What reagent is used for testing for the presence of a reducing sugar?
   (c) What colour indicates the presence of a reducing sugar?

13 The urine of a diabetic patient was found to contain glucose.
   (a) What type of biomolecule is glucose?
   (b) What specific test might have been carried out on the urine?
   (c) What was the result (colour change that occurs) of this test?

14 Name the specific disaccharide that is not a reducing sugar.

15 A biomolecule has the chemical formula $(C_6H_{10}O_5)_n$ where 'n' represents the number of repeated units of the biomolecule. What type of biomolecule would have this formula? Describe a chemical test for a member of this group of biomolecules.

16 $C_{55}H_{98}O_6$ is the chemical formula of a biomolecule present in animals.
   (a) What type of biomolecule is this likely to be?
   (b) Of what subunits is this molecule made?
   (c) Give a function of this biomolecule.

17 (a) Lipids are composed of the elements _____, _____ and _____.
   (b) Name the **two** types of lipids.
   (c) Draw and label the basic structure of each type.
   (d) State a biological function for each type.
   (e) Explain why animals store excess energy in the form of fat.
   (f) Describe a test for fat.
   (g) Name **two** foods that are rich in fat.

18 $C_{256}H_{381}N_{65}O_{79}S_6$ is the chemical formula for insulin.
   (a) List the elements present in insulin.
   (b) What type of biomolecule is insulin?

19 (a) The building blocks of proteins are called _____ _____.
   (b) How many different types of these protein building blocks are there?
   (c) Name the elements present in proteins.
   (d) What are the **two** categories of proteins? Give an example of each type.
   (e) Give **two** structural functions and two metabolic functions of proteins in living organisms.
   (f) What are the bonds between the building blocks of protein called?
   (g) Describe how you would test for protein.

20 Name a fat-soluble vitamin, giving its source in the diet, its function and the disorder that results from its deficiency.

21 Name a water-soluble vitamin, giving its source in the diet, its function and the disorder that results from its deficiency.

22 (a) What is meant by *dietary minerals*?
   (b) Name **two** minerals required by plants and **two** required by animals and give the function of each.
   (c) From where do plants obtain minerals?

23 Give **two** reasons why water is needed by living organisms.

24 Distinguish between catabolism and anabolism. Give an example of a catabolic reaction and an anabolic reaction.

Answer the following multiple-choice questions:

25. The elements that make up dissolved salts in living organism are:
    (a) Sodium, magnesium, potassium, chlorine, and calcium
    (b) Chromium, iodine, chlorine, potassium and fluorine
    (c) Iron, oxygen, carbon, zinc, and sodium
    (d) Sodium, fluorine, chlorine, zinc, and copper

26. The trace elements present in all living organisms are:
    (a) Gold, silver, platinum
    (b) Iron, zinc, copper
    (c) Copper, sulfur, cobalt
    (d) Iodine, fluorine, argon

27. The elements that make up most proteins are:
    (a) Carbon, helium, oxygen, fluorine
    (b) Carbon, hydrogen, oxygen, nitrogen
    (c) Calcium, helium, boron, sulfur
    (d) Cadmium, hydrogen, osmium, nitrogen

28. The elements that make up carbohydrate are:
    (a) Carbon, helium and oxygen
    (b) Carbon, nitrogen and oxygen
    (c) Carbon, hydrogen and oxygen
    (d) Calcium, hydrogen and oxygen

29. Carbohydrate is made up of individual units known as:
    (a) Amino acids
    (b) Fatty acids
    (c) Vitamins
    (d) Monosaccharides

30. Glucose, fructose and galactose are examples of:
    (a) Monosaccharides
    (b) Disaccharides
    (c) Oligosaccharides
    (d) Polysaccharides

31. Maltose, sucrose and lactose are examples of:
    (a) Monosaccharides
    (b) Disaccharides
    (c) Oligosaccharides
    (d) Polysaccharides

32. Starch, glycogen and cellulose are examples of:
    (a) Monosaccharides
    (b) Disaccharides
    (c) Oligosaccharides
    (d) Polysaccharides

33. The test used for starch is:
    (a) Iodine
    (b) Bromine
    (c) Fluorine
    (d) Chlorine

34. The test for reducing sugars uses:
    (a) Biuret reagent
    (b) Benedict's solution
    (c) Copper sulfate solution and sulfuric acid
    (d) Iodine

35. The test for protein uses:
    (a) Copper sulfate solution and sodium hydroxide
    (b) Benedict's solution
    (c) Sulfuric acid
    (d) Iodine

36. A deficiency of vitamin A can lead to:
    (a) Scurvy
    (b) Night-blindness
    (c) Beriberi
    (d) Rickets

37. The function of vitamin D in the body is to:
    (a) Maintain healthy bones and teeth
    (b) Help the formation of clotting factors
    (c) Maintain a healthy heart
    (d) Protect the brain

38. Lack of vitamin C in the diet leads to:
    (a) Hearing loss
    (b) Heart enlargement
    (c) Scurvy
    (d) Mental retardation

39. The function of folic acid in the adult human body is:
    (a) Development of red blood cells
    (b) To maintain strong bones and teeth
    (c) To keep eyes healthy
    (d) To prevent skin cancer

40. The function of calcium in the body is to:
    (a) Maintain good eyesight
    (b) Maintain healthy bones and teeth
    (c) Maintain healthy skin
    (d) Prevent diabetes

Unit 1 Biology: the study of life

Chapter 3 Sample examination questions

1. Use your knowledge of nutrition to answer the following questions:
   (i) Carbohydrates always contain the elements carbon, hydrogen and _____.
   (ii) Lipids are made up of fatty acids and _____.
   (iii) Name a fat-soluble vitamin.
   (iv) Name a structural carbohydrate found in plants.
   (v) Name **one** good source of protein in the human diet.

   Section A, Question 1 Ordinary Level 2011

2. Answer any **four** of the following parts:
   (a) Name the chemical elements present in carbohydrates.
   (b) Which **two** of these elements always occur in a 2:1 ratio in carbohydrates?
   (c) Name a structural carbohydrate.
   (d) Give a function of carbohydrates other than a structural one.
   (e) Name a chemical element always present in proteins but not in carbohydrates.

   Section A, Question 1 Ordinary Level 2009

HL 3. Answer **five** of the following:
   (a) In relation to the human diet, what is meant by a trace element?
   (b) Give an example of a trace element.
   (c) State **one** way in which an oil differs from a fat.
   (d) Vitamins may be divided into two groups depending upon their solubility. Name these two groups.
   (e) What is a triglyceride?
   (f) Give an example of a catabolic reaction in a cell.

   Section A, Question 1 Higher Level 2010

4. Answer **five** of the following:
   (a) In carbohydrates, which **two** elements are in the ratio 2:1?
   (b) Cellulose is a polysaccharide. Explain the term *polysaccharide*.
   (c) Name a polysaccharide other than cellulose.
   (d) Where precisely in a plant cell would you expect to find cellulose?
   (e) Name a test or give the chemicals used to demonstrate the presence of a reducing sugar.
   (f) In relation to the test referred to in (e) which of the following is correct?

   1. No heat needed.
   2. Heat but do not boil.
   3. Boil.

   Section A, Question 1 Higher Level 2009

5. Answer **five** of the following:
   (a) Biomolecules of the general formula $C_x(H_2O)_y$ are examples of _____.
   (b) Give **two** functions of water in a living organism.
   (c) Is energy release a feature of anabolic or catabolic reactions?
   (d) How do fats differ from oils at room temperature?
   (e) Name the test or give the chemicals used to detect the presence of protein in a food sample.
   (f) Name a structural polysaccharide.

   Section A, Question 1 Higher Level 2008

Chapter 3 Mind map

Nutrients (from food) are required for metabolism and continuity of life.

Food
- Six constituents of food: carbohydrates, lipids, proteins, vitamins, dietary minerals and water.
- Six common elements present in living organisms: carbon, hydrogen, oxygen, nitrogen, sulfur and phosphorus.
- Six elements present in living organisms as dissolved salts: sodium, magnesium, chlorine, calcium and potassium.
- Three trace elements required only in small amounts: iron, copper and zinc.

Biomolecules: organic chemicals produced by and found within living organisms. Four biomolecules: carbohydrate, lipid, protein and vitamins.

Lipids
- Two types: triglycerides and phospholipids.
- **Triglycerides:** composed of a glycerol and three fatty acids. Responsible for storing energy in adipose tissue.
- **Phospholipids:** composed of a glycerol, two fatty acids and a phosphate. The main constituent of the cell membrane.
- The test for fat is brown paper. A translucent spot indicates presence of fat.

Nutrition is the way in which organisms obtain and use food.

Proteins
- **Amino acids:** the building blocks of proteins. There are 20 common amino acids.
- Proteins are classified based on their structure: fibrous and globular.
- Fibrous proteins (collagen) show very little folding; involved in structural roles: formation of skin, tendons, ligaments and bone.
- Globular proteins show a lot of folding; play metabolic roles such as formation of all enzymes and antibodies.
- The test for protein is the biuret test. Sodium hydroxide added to solution of food to be tested. A few drops of copper sulfate then added; a purple colour indicates the presence of protein.

Vitamins
- Biomolecules required in the diet of an organism when that organism cannot make them.
- Classified as either fat-soluble or water-soluble.
- Vitamins A, D, E and K are fat-soluble.
- Vitamins in the B group and vitamin C are water-soluble.
- Vitamin A required for rhodopsin pigment in the retina and a deficiency leads to night-blindness. Oily fish a good source.
- Vitamin C required for the proper formation of collagen; deficiency leads to scurvy. Citrus fruits a good source.

Minerals
- Metallic elements required by living organisms in small amounts to maintain health.
- Calcium is needed in animals for healthy skeleton and teeth.
- Iron is needed in animals for haemoglobin formation.
- Calcium is needed in plants for the middle lamella of the cell walls.
- Magnesium is needed in plants for formation of the green pigment chlorophyll.

Carbohydrates
- Classified based on structure: monosaccharides, disaccharides and polysaccharides.
- Monosaccharides and disaccharides are sugars with names ending in '-ose'.
- Three monosaccharides are glucose, fructose and galactose. Formula: $C_6H_{12}O_6$.
- Glucose and fructose: fruit juices and fruits. Galactose: milk.
- Three disaccharides are maltose, sucrose and lactose. Formula: $C_{12}H_{22}O_{11}$.
- Maltose from barley, sucrose from table sugar and lactose from milk.
- Reducing sugars are: glucose, fructose, galactose, maltose and lactose. The test for a reducing sugar is to add Benedict's reagent and heat – brick-red colour indicates presence of reducing sugars.
- Three polysaccharides are starch, glycogen and cellulose. All three are composed of many glucose molecules bonded together. Their general formula is $(C_6H_{10}O_5)_n$.
- Starch and glycogen are branched polysaccharides (glycogen more so), whereas cellulose is unbranched.
- Functions: starch is an energy storage polysaccharide in plants; glycogen an energy storage polysaccharide in animals; cellulose a structural polysaccharide responsible for the strength of plant cell walls.
- Iodine is the test for starch. A blue-black colour indicates presence of starch.

Water
Has the chemical formula H_2O and is needed in every living organism for the following reasons:
- The medium in which all biochemical reactions occur.
- Takes part in chemical reactions such as condensation and hydrolysis.
- An excellent absorber of heat.
- An excellent solvent.

Chapter 4 Ecology

Learning objectives After studying this chapter, you should be able to:
- Define a number of terms commonly used in ecology.
- Describe energy flow from the sun to all levels of food chains, food webs and pyramids of numbers.
- Describe the carbon and nitrogen cycles.
- Describe the effects humans have had on ecosystems under the headings of 'pollution', 'conservation' and 'waste management'.
- HL ▶ Describe and give examples of ecological relationships.
- ▶ Describe the factors involved in population dynamics.

Introduction

> **Ecology:** a branch of biology concerned with the study of the interactions of living organisms with each other and with their environment.
>
> **Ecosystem:** a community of organisms that interact with their environment.
>
> **Biosphere:** a region of the Earth where life can exist.

The Earth is one large ecosystem made of many smaller ecosystems. The table below gives examples of ecosystems and their locations.

Ecosystem	Location
Freshwater	River Shannon, Ireland
Grassland	Serengeti, Kenya
Rainforest	Amazon, South America
Desert	Great Sandy Desert, Western Australia

> **Habitat:** a place where an organism lives.

Most organisms live in either terrestrial (land) or aquatic (water) environments. Various factors affect these organisms within their habitat.

Environmental factors

Abiotic factors

> An **abiotic factor** is anything that is non-living and has an effect on living organisms in an ecosystem.

Fig 4.1 The Amazon rainforest in Brazil, a very large and diverse ecosystem.

There are two main types of abiotic factor:

- **Climatic factors:** These are the weather conditions that affect organisms, such as rainfall; wind speed and direction; temperature; humidity; light intensity and day length.

> **Climatic factors** are weather conditions that have an effect on living organisms in an ecosystem.

- **Edaphic factors:** These are anything relating to the soil (pH; temperature; and moisture, mineral and organic matter content) or geology of the land (altitude, aspect, and steepness).

> **Edaphic factors** are anything relating to the soil or geology of land that have an effect on living organisms in an ecosystem.

Biotic factors

> A **biotic factor** is anything that is living and has an effect on other living organisms in an ecosystem.

Biotic factors include availability of food; presence of a predator; interactions between different organisms; presence of pathogenic organisms; competition between organisms; and the presence of humans.

> **Pathogenic:** capable of producing disease.

Energy flow in ecosystems

All of the energy in organisms in an ecosystem has come from our Sun. This light energy is converted into other forms of energy, such as chemical energy (glucose). Plants convert light energy into chemical energy via the anabolic process of photosynthesis (see Chapter 11). This chemical energy is passed along the food chain. Much of the energy is lost as the food chain gets longer.

- When an organism dies, it is decayed by detritus (dead organic matter) feeders, such as bacteria and fungi of decay. This returns the nutrients to the soil. Plants can then recycle the nutrients turning them into chemical energy once again.

- The chemical energy present in plants is then passed on when other organisms feed on the plants (herbivores). Biomolecules are passed from the plants to the herbivores. In this way, feeding forms the pathway upon which energy flow occurs.

- Other organisms eat the herbivores. These are carnivorous organisms. Energy, in the form of chemicals, is passed onto the carnivores. This sequence of organisms, beginning with a plant and ending with a carnivore, is called a grazing food chain.

> A **grazing food chain** shows the sequence of organisms with one species at each trophic (feeding) level.

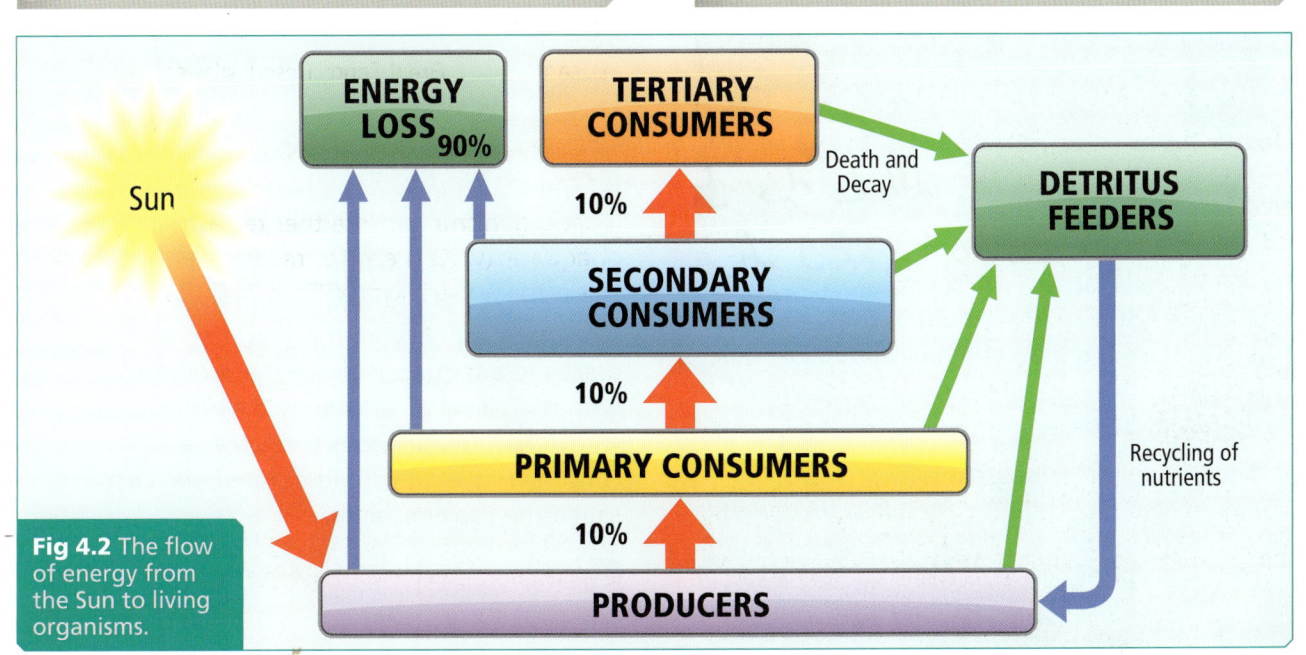

Fig 4.2 The flow of energy from the Sun to living organisms.

Energy is passed along the food chain from one organism to the next. However, as a food chain gets longer, the amount of energy decreases. The living organisms use energy (respiration) while alive and most of the energy is lost in this way. Only around 10 per cent of the energy is passed onto the next member of the food chain. Therefore, food chains are generally limited to a maximum of five organisms.

- The first organism in a food chain occupies the **first trophic level.** The word 'trophic' comes from the Greek word *'trophé'* meaning food. The first trophic level is always occupied by a producer, such as a plant. This is because a plant 'produces' chemical energy from light energy.
- The second organism occupies the **second trophic level.** These organisms are called primary consumers.
- The **third trophic level** is occupied by secondary consumers.
- The **fourth trophic level** is occupied by tertiary consumers and so on.

Fig 4.3 shows a simple food chain along with the various trophic levels.

Producer	Primary consumer	Secondary consumer
First trophic level	Second trophic level	Third trophic level

Fig 4.3 A simple food chain.

Fig 4.3 shows a rabbit, which eats grass. However, rabbits are not the only organisms that eat grass. Similarly, rabbits eat other plant material as well. In addition, foxes also prey on hares, squirrels, birds, rats and mice.

In this way, food chains are interconnected. Interconnected food chains are called food webs.

A **food web** is two or more interconnected food chains.

Fig 4.4 shows an example of a food web.

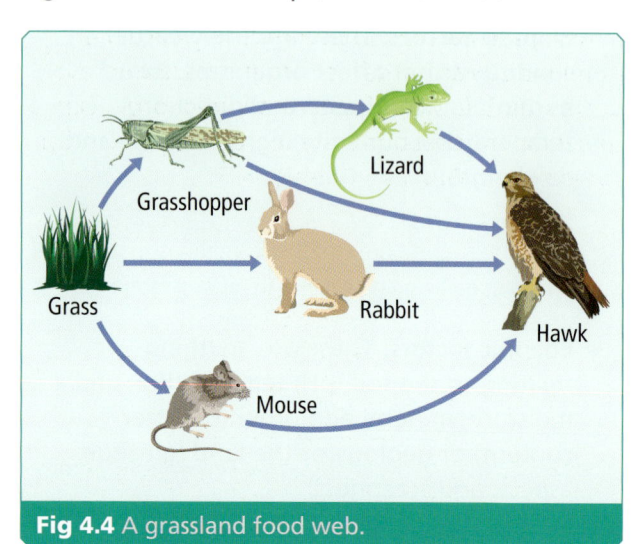

Fig 4.4 A grassland food web.

You may notice that as the food chain gets longer, the number of organisms at each trophic level decreases. As already mentioned, energy is lost at each trophic level, with only 10 per cent being passed onto the next level. You may have also noticed that the size of the organism increases as the food chain gets longer. This is because predators are adapted to kill their prey. One of the most critical adaptations, in most cases, is that they are larger than their prey. There are exceptions to this rule; can you think of any?

Ecological pyramids of numbers

An **ecological pyramid of numbers** shows the numbers of organisms at each trophic level in a food chain.

Pyramids of numbers are constructed by counting the numbers of producers and putting them at the bottom of the pyramid. The numbers of primary, secondary and tertiary consumers are then counted and placed in a sequence above the producers, with each level of the pyramid a different width than the previous level. The last consumer in any pyramid of numbers is often called the top consumer.

NOTE: Ordinary Level Biology students need to study upright pyramids only.

Upright pyramids of numbers

In upright pyramids of numbers (Fig 4.5), the numbers of each organism at every trophic level decreases. The size of each individual organism generally increases as the food chain gets longer, for example, Grass → Rabbit → Fox.

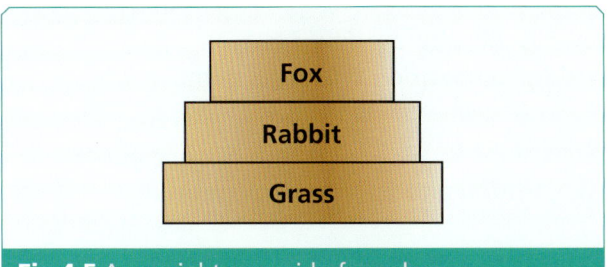

Fig 4.5 An upright pyramid of numbers.

HL NOTE: Higher Level students must also study two other types of pyramids of numbers.

Partially upright pyramids of numbers

Fig 4.6 shows an example of a partially upright pyramid of numbers.

In this pyramid of numbers, there is one hazel tree (the producer) upon which many caterpillars (primary consumers) will feed. A smaller number of blue tits will prey on the caterpillars, and an even smaller number of sparrowhawks (top consumer) prey on the blue tits.

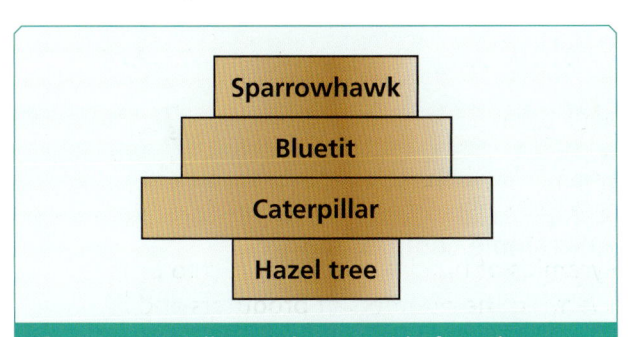

Fig 4.6 A partially upright pyramid of numbers.

Inverted pyramids of numbers

Inverted pyramids of numbers (Fig 4.7) involve a producer that is the largest organism. All organisms that follow are smaller, but more numerous, for example, Beech tree → Caterpillar → Mites

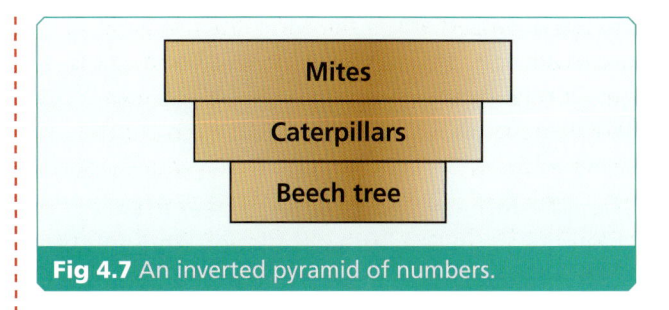

Fig 4.7 An inverted pyramid of numbers.

Limitations of the use of pyramid of numbers

Pyramids of numbers have a limited use in ecology as it is very difficult to draw them to scale.

In addition, pyramids of numbers do not take the size of the organism into account.

It is also difficult to incorporate detritus feeders and decomposers into a pyramid of numbers as they do not feed on living organisms. This means it is often impossible to quantify the number of organisms they feed on.

Niche

> **Niche:** the functional role an organism plays in its habitat.

Every organism has an effect on its habitat and on the ecological relationships within the habitat and the wider ecosystem. For example, if foxes were taken from their habitat, the numbers of hares and rabbits would increase rapidly. This would in turn have an effect on other organisms in the habitat. As a result, vegetation could be overgrazed. Therefore, the niche of a fox is to keep the numbers of rabbits and hares under control.

HL Ecological relationships

Factors controlling numbers of organisms

In the study of the factors controlling numbers of organisms in a habitat or ecosystem, we refer to populations of organisms and communities of organisms.

Populations

> A **population** is a group of organisms living in a habitat that belong to the same species.

Examples include a population of deer in the Phoenix Park in Dublin, a population of dolphins off the west coast of Ireland and a population of lactic acid bacteria in a sample of cow's milk.

Population levels of different species are in a constant state of change, going up and down over a period of years. The balance of nature ensures that the numbers of different types of species in a habitat remains constant over time.

An example of where the balance of nature has been upset is when cane toads were introduced to Australia by Europeans in 1935. The toads were introduced in an attempt to control the numbers of cane beetles that were damaging sugar cane crops. However, the cane toad has no natural predator or parasite in Australia. Therefore, their numbers increased very quickly and invaded many habitats, causing damage and spreading disease.

Communities

> A **community** is a group of organisms living in a habitat that belong to many different species.

The total number of species in any one particular habitat usually remains stable over time. There may be regular fluctuations in the total number. However, barring a natural disaster, the balance of nature ensures the regular fluctuations average out over a long period of time in a habitat.

The factors that help to keep population and community numbers in a habitat steady include competition, predation, parasitism and symbiosis.

Competition

> **Competition** is the struggle between organisms for a resource that is in limited supply.
>
> A **resource** is a stock or supply (such as food) that can be drawn on.

The amount of competition is affected by the amount of resources present. If there are plenty of resources for a population of organisms, then there will be no competition. When the resource becomes scarce, competition will start to occur between members of the same species and between members of different species that use the same resource. This affects the size of a population and a community.

- Numbers of organisms will decrease as competition increases.
- As competition decreases numbers of organisms will increase.

There are two types of competition: **contest competition** and **scramble competition**.

1. Contest competition

> **Contest competition** is the direct fight between two organisms for a resource that is in short supply.

In contest competition, the resource is usually for a mate or territory; an example is the fight between two stags (male deer) for a mate (Fig 4.8).

Fig 4.8 Two stags fighting (contest competition).

2. Scramble competition

> **Scramble competition** is the struggle amongst a number of organisms for a resource in short supply. Each organism gets a small share of the resource.

In scramble competition, the resource does not have to be food. Plants are competing with each other for light, minerals, water and space. This is an example of scramble competition. Fig 4.9 shows another example of scramble competition where a number of vultures descend on a kill, with every vulture obtaining a small amount of the available food.

Fig 4.9 A pack of vultures competing for a portion of the kill made by a large predator (scramble competition).

Fig 4.10 Some plants produce fruits, such as berries and acorns, that are dispersed by animals **(A and B)**. Other plants, like dandelion, disperse their seeds using the wind **(C)**.

Adaptations to reduce competition

Competition limits the size of a population of a species. There is always only a fixed amount of any one resource. However, many species have developed adaptations that give them distinct advantages over other species when it comes to competing for various resources.

- Trees grow tall to gain more light. Any change in a plant species that enables it to grow taller gives it a distinct advantage in competing for light. Other species of plant, such as ferns, have developed the ability to survive in very low light conditions,. In fact, some of these species cannot survive in direct sunlight.

- Plants have developed sophisticated methods of dispersing their seeds so as to avoid competition between parent and offspring. Many plants produce fruits that hold the seeds. Animals are attracted to the fruit, eat it and disperse the seeds over a wide area. Plants such as dandelions have developed mechanisms that involve the seed being carried on the wind (Fig 4.10C).

- Caterpillars and butterflies do not compete with one another as they have different food sources. Caterpillars feed on leaves, whereas the adult butterfly feeds on nectar from flowers.

Predation

> **Predation** is the catching, killing and eating of another organism.

Predators, such as hawks, catch, kill and eat their prey (field mice).

Predation is very useful to humans. We use predation to control numbers of certain unwanted species. It is often used by organic farmers, who do not use pesticides and insecticides.

- Black ladybird beetles are used to control spider mites, which would otherwise damage plants (Fig 4.11).

Fig 4.11 Black ladybird beetles eating spider mites on leaves.

- Ladybirds are used to control aphids and greenflies, which also damage plants.

- A microscopic group of animals called nematodes, which are natural parasites of slugs, are used to prevent crop destruction by slugs.

Adaptations of predators and prey

The predator-prey relationship depends on the adaptations shown by each. If a predator develops an advantage that enables it to catch more of its prey, the numbers of prey will decrease. Eventually, the prey will develop an adaptation that makes it more difficult for the predator to catch them.

Examples of predator adaptations include:

- Polar bears have an excellent sense of smell that enables them to locate their prey from great distances.
- Birds of prey (Fig 4.12) have excellent eyesight so that they can sense movement of small animals from a long distance away.

Fig 4.12 A hawk has excellent eyesight to pick out prey from a long distance away.

- Anteaters have evolved a long tongue and mouth to make it easier to search out and prey on ants and termites that live underground.

Examples of prey adaptations include:

- Stingrays have a well-developed tail (Fig 4.13) with one or more barbed stings, which contain strong venom. These are used not for predation but for self-defence when preyed upon.
- Hedgehogs have a spiny coat of fur and have the ability to roll up into a ball to protect themselves from predators.

Fig 4.13 A stingray has a long tail with barbed stings that it uses to protect itself from predators.

Symbiosis

Symbiosis is the biological relationship in which two species live in close proximity to each other and interact regularly in such a way as to benefit one or both of the organisms.

Symbiosis occurs in every habitat and ecosystem on Earth. There are many different types of symbiosis depending on the type of interaction between the two organisms. The examples listed below are all types of **mutualism** where both organisms benefit.

- Nitrogen-fixing bacteria that live in root nodules (Fig 4.14) of legume plants make nitrates from atmospheric nitrogen gas.

Fig 4.14 Root nodules on a pea plant. The nodules contain symbiotic bacteria.

The plant uses these nitrates to form proteins that it needs for growth and repair. In return, the plant provides the bacteria with a food source and a space to grow.

- There are bacteria in our large intestines ('good bacteria') that produce vitamin K, which we need for proper blood clotting. We do not usually get enough vitamin K from our diet so these symbiotic bacteria are essential to health.
- Many plants rely on underground fungi attached to their roots to absorb enough water and minerals from the soil. In return, the fungus gets nutrient biomolecules, such as glucose, from the plant.

Parasitism

> **Parasitism** is where one organism, called the parasite, lives in or on another organism, called the host, and the host is harmed.

Parasitism is a type of symbiosis. However, the parasite always harms the host.

- Aphids are parasites of plants as they take their nutrients from leaves.
- Athlete's foot is an example of a human parasite. It is a fungal infection of the delicate skin between the toes. It survives there because of the often warm and moist environment.
- Another human parasite is the mosquito, which feeds on blood (Fig 4.15).

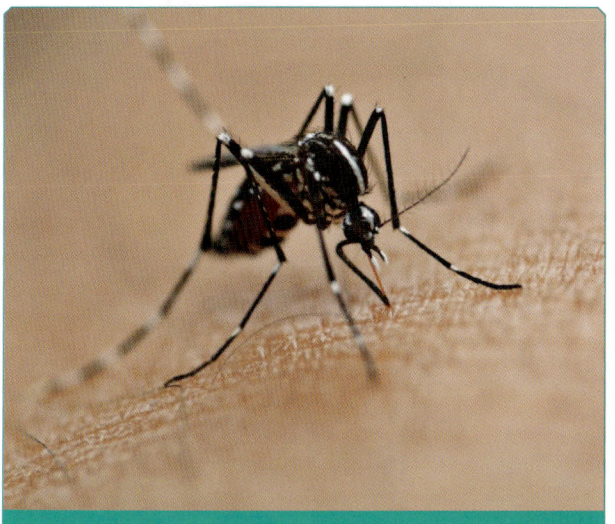

Fig 4.15 A mosquito feeding on the surface of human skin.

Population dynamics

Predator-prey relationships

The relationship between predators and prey depends on various factors such as camouflage, speed of movement, food availability and size of the organism. The numbers of predators and prey usually follow a cycle, whereby when numbers of prey increase, the numbers of predators increase and vice versa.

Camouflage

Many living organisms have excellent camouflage and other methods of hiding. Both predators and prey can demonstrate camouflage.

- Cheetahs, with their spotty, golden fur, blend in well with their environment. They also have the ability to creep up on their prey.
- The grasshopper provides another example of excellent camouflage (Fig 4.16). Its green colour enables the grasshopper to blend in well with the environment. This adaptation minimises the risk of them being preyed upon.

Fig 4.16 A grasshopper is camouflaged on a leaf.

Speed of movement

In many habitats, there are examples of both predator and prey developing the ability to move very fast.

- Cheetahs are the fastest known land animal. They can reach speeds in excess of 80 km per hour! This gives them a better chance of catching their prey. However, when a predator has to move very quickly to catch its prey, it usually means that their prey (gazelles) can also move very quickly. Gazelles have the ability to run fast and are very agile (they can change direction very quickly). This increases their chances of avoiding capture.

- Chameleons have the ability to move their tongues very quickly to catch their prey (Fig 4.17).

Fig 4.17 A chameleon catching an insect with its tongue.

Availability of food

If there is a lack of food in an ecosystem or habitat, the populations may migrate (move) to a new habitat where food is more plentiful. If the population is unable to migrate or is unable to find a new source of food, their numbers may decrease.

Populations of organisms follow availability of food very closely. Fig 4.18 shows a predator-prey relationship where the numbers of prey (the food) have an effect of the numbers of predators. As prey numbers increase so do predator numbers, albeit with a slight delay. Similarly, as prey numbers decrease so do predator numbers.

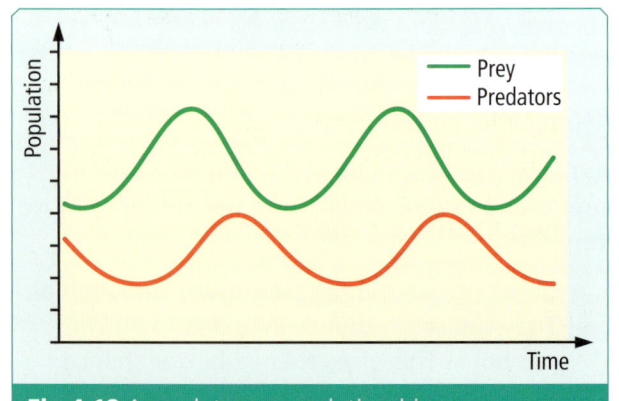

Fig 4.18 A predator-prey relationship.

Size of organism

The size of an organism has an effect on which predator-prey relationships it will be involved in. A small predator that is not preyed on by any other organism is unlikely to prey on an organism that is larger than itself.

- Foxes will prey on smaller animals such as birds, squirrels and hares.
- Ladybirds prey on aphids and greenflies.
- Sharks prey on smaller fish and will not prey on fish larger than themselves.

Human population

The human population is currently 7 billion. There have never been this many humans on Earth before. Factors such as war, famine and disease limited the growth in population. Because of the Industrial Revolution and the major advances in medicine, these factors are no longer as significant.

The Industrial Revolution first occurred in Britain in the eighteenth and nineteenth centuries. There were huge advances in machinery, which made it possible for factories to mass produce goods. During this time, most of the working population moved from agriculture to industry,

Fig 4.20 shows the relatively recent rapid increase in the human population. The past 100 years has seen the highest ever rate of increase in human numbers. However, human population growth has slowed in recent years, especially in well-developed nations. It is predicted that by 2050 the world's population will have reached 9.2 billion. Fig 4.19 shows the effect human populations are having on the land.

Fig 4.19 Ireland and Britain from space : the bright lights indicate dense population centres.

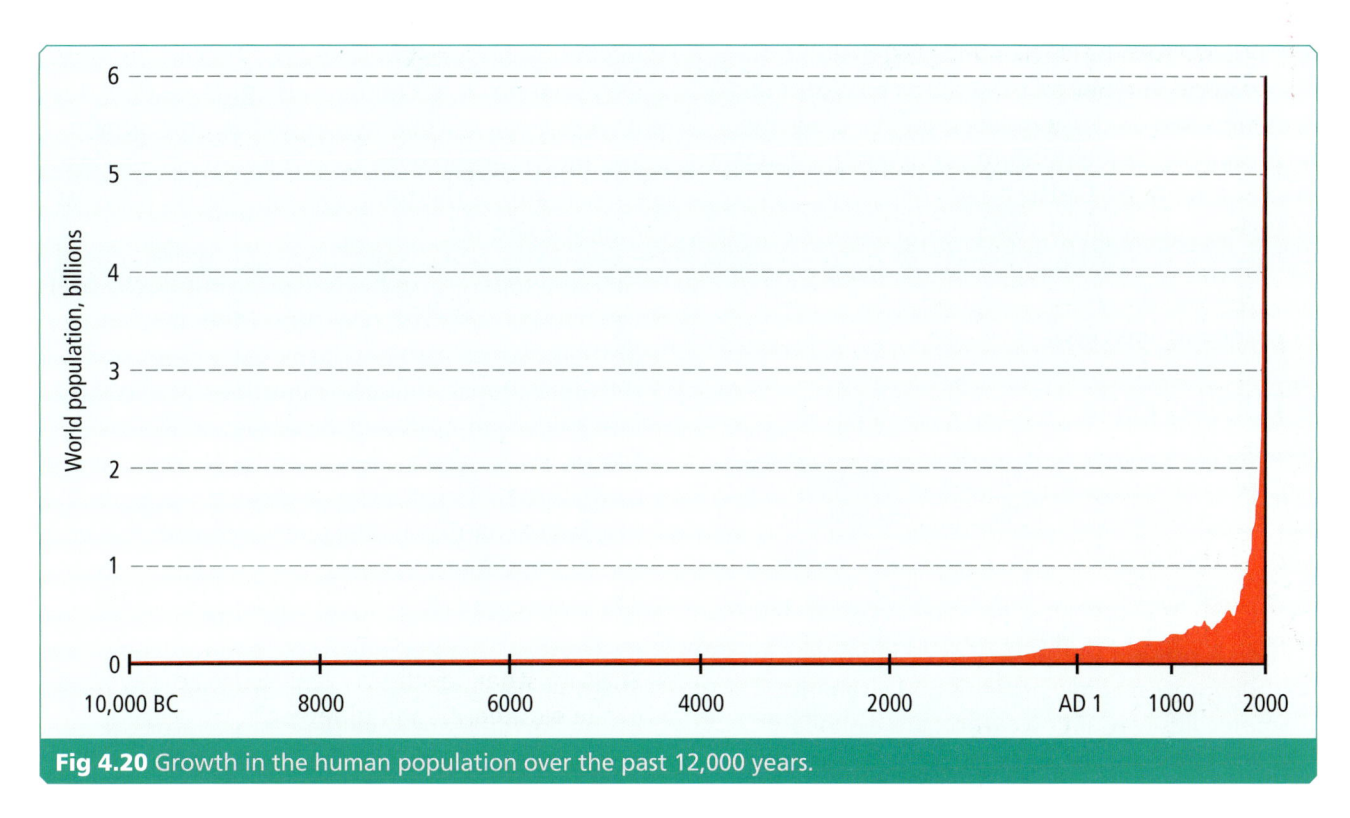

Fig 4.20 Growth in the human population over the past 12,000 years.

The following factors have affected and continue to affect human population to a certain extent:

- **War:** The effect of wars was greater in the past. However, many thousands continue to be killed every year in conflicts around the world.
- **Famine:** Famine is the widespread lack of food. Fortunately, it happens less often in today's modern world. However, despite the emergence of technology over the past century, famines still occur, especially in poor rural areas in less developed countries.

Developing or **less developed countries** are ones which do not have advanced economies and the benefits this brings (improved education, healthcare and so on). Most are located in Africa, Asia and South America.

- **Contraception:** The relatively recent emergence of contraception and its increasing availability has seen average birth rates steadily decline over the last century. However, there are large differences in birth rates around the world. In some developing countries, the birth rate is still very high (up to seven births per woman). Most developed countries have a birth rate of approximately two births per woman. This is enough to maintain the population at its current levels. However, the higher birth rate in developing countries means that the world's population is predicted to reach 9.2 billion by 2050.
- **Disease:** Advances in medicine and vaccine technology have reduced the effect of disease on the human population, especially in developed countries. Despite these medical advances, some diseases continue to have a major effect on human population, especially in developing countries. According to the World Health Organisation, malaria kills almost 800,000 people per year, mostly in Africa, and AIDS kills approximately 2 million people per year worldwide. It is hoped that improved medical supply to developing countries and education programmes can help to reduce these massive death tolls.

Nutrient recycling

Nutrient recycling is the process of exchanging important elements between living organisms and the environment.

Producers are continually taking raw materials from their environment and incorporating them into biomolecules, such as carbohydrates, proteins and lipids. These molecules are passed along the food chain. They exit the food chain during excretion and death and decay, and re-enter the environment. These nutrient cycles continue and are vital to life on Earth.

There are two main nutrient cycles:

1. The carbon cycle
2. The nitrogen cycle

1 Carbon cycle

> The **carbon cycle** is the process through which elemental carbon (in the form of biomolecules) is exchanged between living organisms and their environment.

Carbon is present in the four main biomolecules (carbohydrates, lipids, proteins and vitamins). Biomolecules containing carbon are assimilated into the structures of living organisms. The food we eat has come from other living organisms. Some of those living organisms are producers and some are primary and secondary consumers. When living organisms excrete waste or die, carbon leaves the organism and enters the environment (atmosphere, water and soil).

- Excretion produces carbon dioxide that is released into the atmosphere.
- When organisms die, bacteria and fungi of decay break down the remains.

This returns carbon to the environment in the form of carbon dioxide and also produces humus. Humus is organic material that has been broken down by bacteria and fungi and will decay no more. Compost is an example of humus.

Carbon dioxide in the atmosphere and in the oceans is recycled by producers (plants) in the process of photosynthesis (*see* Chapter 11). This completes the carbon cycle.

Burning fossil fuels, forest fires and emissions from volcanic eruptions are also part of the carbon cycle. Carbon dioxide is the product of burning fossil fuels and forest fires as well as the main gas emitted from volcanoes.

Global warming

The continuing use of fossil fuels as our main energy supply is a significant contributor to carbon dioxide levels in the atmosphere. This is leading to imbalances in the Earth's carbon cycle. Carbon dioxide is a greenhouse gas, meaning that it traps the Sun's energy within the atmosphere. Too much carbon dioxide in the atmosphere leads to increases in the temperature. This is known as global warming.

Global temperatures have been rising slowly over the past century. This has caused the melting of the polar ice caps and large glaciers around the world, releasing large quantities of water into the oceans and causing sea levels to rise. Global warming also increases the temperature of the ocean, which causes the water to expand (thermal expansion). This further contributes to the rise in sea levels, which are rising at a rate of 2–3 mm per year!

Global warming has also caused more severe weather patterns, particularly in tropical regions of the Earth. There have been more large-scale floods and hurricanes in recent decades.

Fig 4.21 shows the main events of the carbon cycle.

2 Nitrogen cycle

> The **nitrogen cycle** is the process through which elemental nitrogen (in the form of biomolecules) is exchanged between living organisms and their environment.

Nitrogen is a major component of biomolecules such as proteins and DNA, as well as of some vitamins. Nitrogen is present in the air, water and soil. Air consists of 78 per cent nitrogen gas (N_2). This atmospheric nitrogen can be converted into nitrites and nitrates by lightning and bacterial action on nitrogen gas (nitrogen fixation). The bacteria that complete this are called nitrogen-fixing bacteria. As we learned earlier in the chapter, nitrogen-fixing bacteria can be found in the root nodules of legumes such as clover and pea plants (Fig 4.14). Clover and other legumes are used regularly by farmers and horticulturists as natural fertilisers for soil. They can be used in crop rotation to ensure a particular field is not depleted of nitrogen.

> **Crop rotation:** growing different types of crops over different seasons or years. It helps to maintain nutrients in the soil.

Fig 4.21 The carbon cycle.

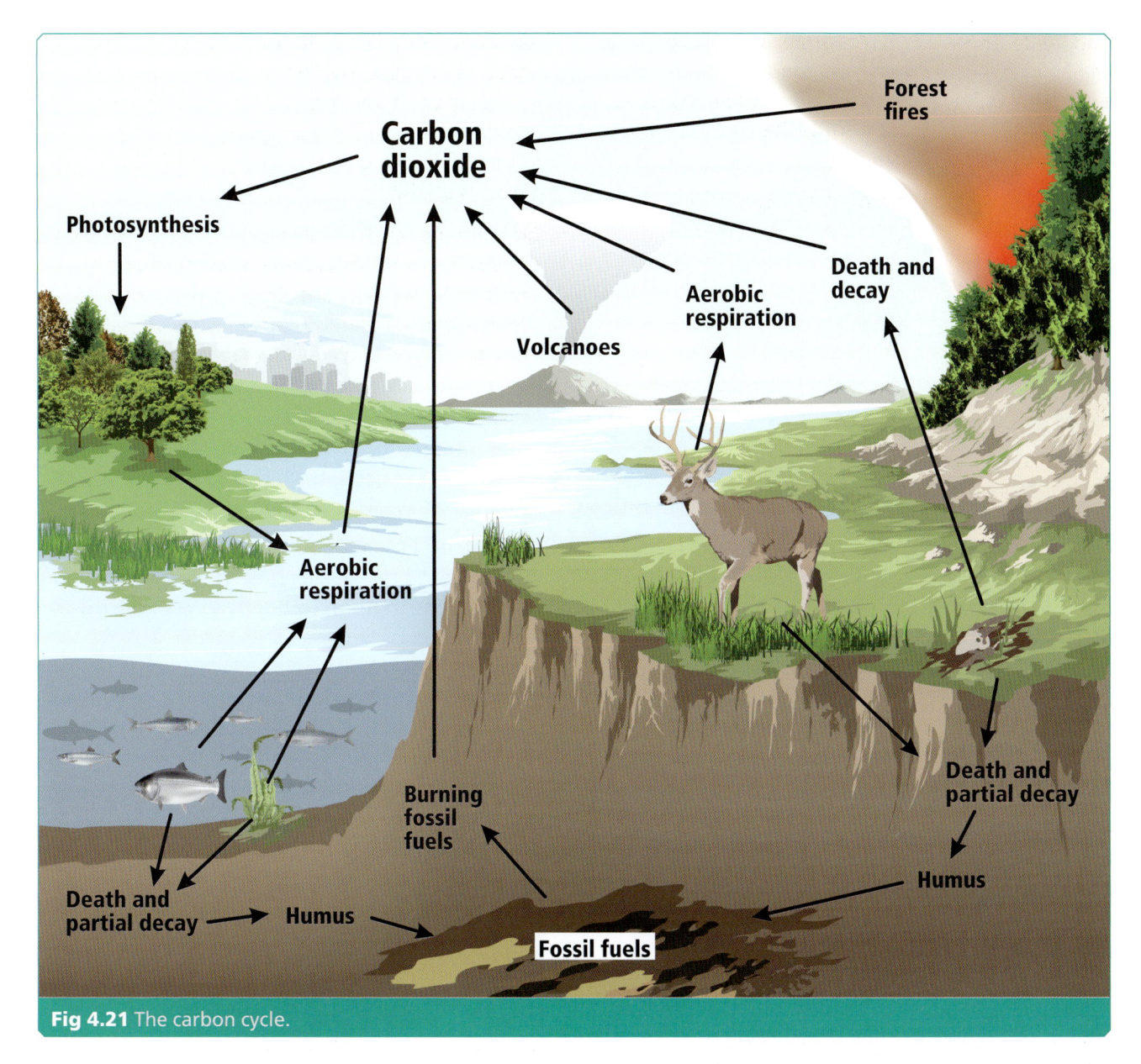

- Nitrates and nitrites produced in the soil or by lightning are used by producers to make plant protein. Herbivores consume these plant proteins and assimilate them into animal protein. In this way, amino acids are passed along the food chain.

- Excretion from living organisms and their eventual death releases nitrogen back into the environment. The remains of dead organisms are decomposed by bacteria and fungi of decay. The proteins and any other nitrogen-containing biomolecules (such as DNA) are converted to ammonia. Ammonia is then converted into nitrites and nitrates by nitrifying bacteria. These processes of decomposition and nitrification occur in the soil and oceans.

- Denitrifying bacteria complete the cycle by converting nitrates and nitrites back into atmospheric nitrogen gas.

- Volcanoes are also significant contributors to the nitrogen cycle as they emit ammonia. This falls to the ground and is converted to nitrates by nitrifying bacteria. It is then assimilated into plant protein.

Fig 4.22 shows the main events of the nitrogen cycle.

Fig 4.22 The nitrogen cycle.

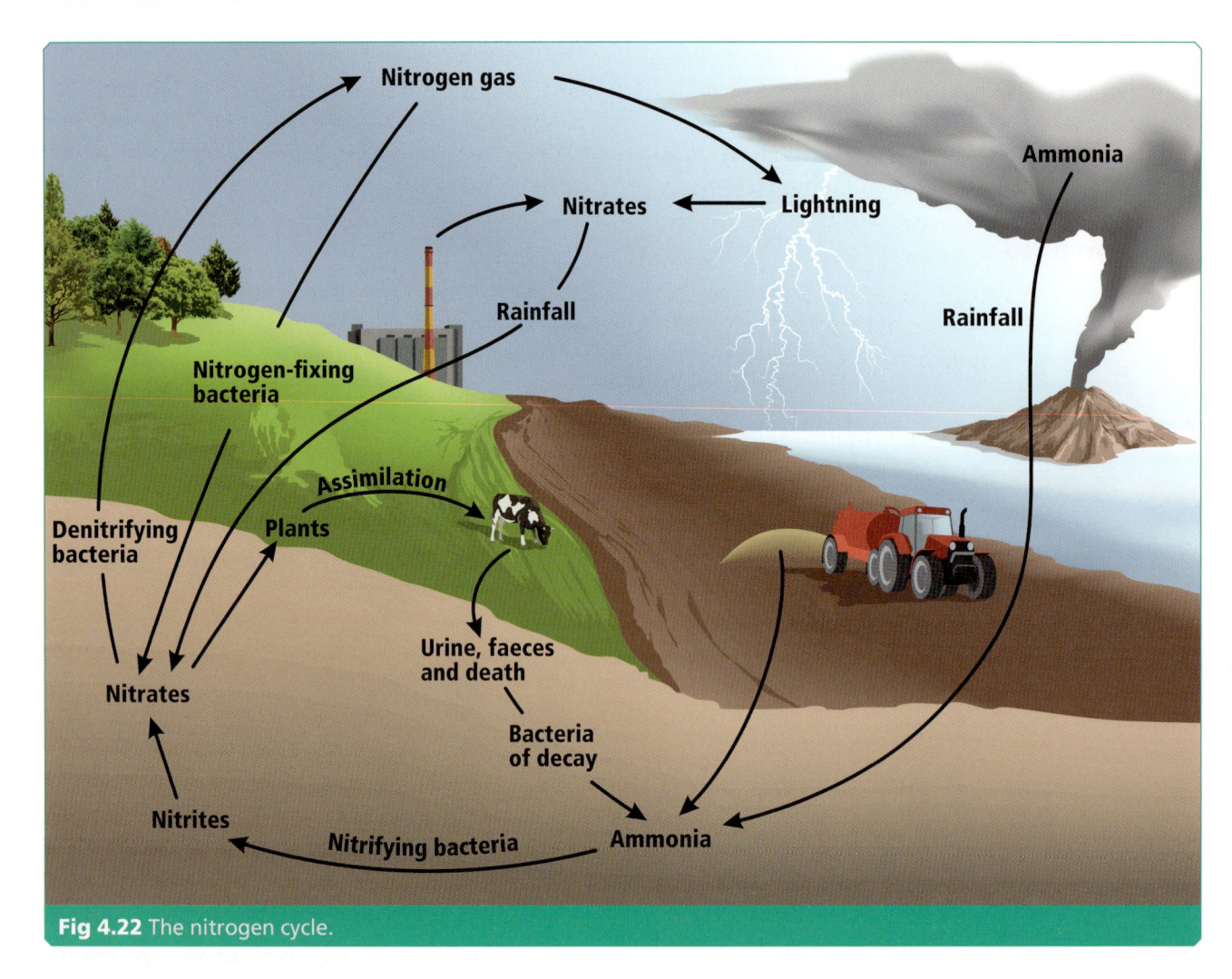

Human impact on ecosystems

Humans have had a huge impact, not just on ecosystems, but on the biosphere as a whole. Human effects on the planet are so vast they can be seen from space! For example, satellite images have been used to document the ice caps melting over a period of years.

Human activities have contributed to rising global temperatures and to reducing the size of the polar ice caps. Any harmful addition to the planet, biosphere or ecosystem is called pollution. Pollution control involves conservation and waste management.

Pollution

> **Pollution** is any harmful addition to the environment.

Affected areas

All areas of the planet have been affected by pollution. Air is continually being contaminated by gases from industry and carbon dioxide from burning of fossil fuels.

Soil has been contaminated by landfill sites, by drilling for oil and also by mining activities.

Fresh water and sea water have been contaminated by sewage and effluent from many different industries. They are also polluted by large oil spills. The most recent significant oil spill was in the Gulf of Mexico in April 2010, where over half a million tonnes of crude oil was released into the water causing an environmental catastrophe.

There are three main categories of pollution: domestic, agricultural and industrial.

> **NOTE:** For Leaving Certificate Biology, you need to study the effects of only one of the three types of pollution.

Domestic pollution

Domestic pollution includes household wastes such as rubbish, liquid wastes (bathroom and kitchen effluent) and hazardous wastes such as used batteries and electrical equipment. Domestic pollution occurs when these wastes are not disposed of properly.

Solid wastes are often dumped at landfill sites, where there is a risk that dangerous chemicals could leach into groundwater.

Waste water from domestic sources usually goes to a water treatment facility where it is cleaned before being released into the environment (see pollution control below).

In many regions around the world, waste water and sewage are still released into rivers, lakes and the sea (Fig 4.23). Sewage contains organic materials and chemicals from detergents, washing powders and disinfectants. Untreated, these chemicals can have serious consequences for the environment.

Eutrophication is the main result of polluted water. Bacteria and algae grow very rapidly because of the nutrient-rich sewage. This uses up all the oxygen in the water, making it inhabitable for fish and other aquatic organisms. A contaminated water supply can also cause disease in humans.

> **Eutrophication:** a process where water receives too many nutrients that stimulate excessive algal growth

Fig 4.23 Sewage being released into open water.

Agricultural pollution

Pesticides and insecticides, which are regularly used in agriculture, can seep into the water supply. These compounds can impact on human and animal health.

Slurry (Fig 4.24) used on farmland as a fertiliser can run off into rivers and lakes if it is not spread at the correct time of year. This contaminates the water supply and can lead to eutrophication. As a result, it is important that farmers spread slurry on fields during dry periods only.

Fig 4.24 Slurry being sprayed onto a field in summer.

Industrial pollution

Industrial pollution involves the release of liquid effluent and gas emissions.

- The food industry releases oils from food processing.
- The steel industry releases waste water containing ammonia and cyanide contaminants.
- The mining industry can release unwanted metals such as zinc and arsenic into the water supply following rainfall.
- Nuclear power stations release small amounts of radioactivity into the sea and oceans.
- Fossil fuel power stations release large amounts of carbon dioxide, along with smaller amounts of carbon monoxide, sulfur dioxide and nitrogen dioxide. These gases contribute to acid rain that can damage plants and buildings.

Unit 1 Biology: the study of life

Fig 4.25 Air pollution: carbon dioxide being released into the atmosphere.

Ecological impact of one human activity

Drilling for oil

Drilling for oil carries a risk of major oil spills. As mentioned already, oil spills have serious consequences for the environment. The oil spill in the Gulf of Mexico in April 2010 (Fig 4.26) resulted in oil being washed ashore along a vast length of coastline. Hundreds of species living in this area were affected. Many birds that feed along the coastline died when the oil contaminated their feathers and entered their digestive systems.

The chemicals used to break up the oil slick can cause the oil to fall to the bottom of the ocean as small dense droplets. This means that this oil spill will continue to have an effect on the organisms that live on the sea floor for many years.

This oil spill has upset the balance of nature, and the Gulf coastline may take a very long time to return to normal.

Pollution control

Pollution control is a way of keeping pollution levels at a minimum. Some methods of pollution control are listed below.

Reduce, reuse, recycle

We can all reduce the amount of waste we produce, particularly by buying products that use less packaging. We can further cut down waste by reusing materials where possible. Finally, when something is of no more use, it can be recycled, especially if it is plastic, paper, glass or metal (Fig 4.27).

Fig 4.26 The Gulf of Mexico oil spill.

Sewage treatment

Sewage is waste water from bathrooms, kitchens, industry and rainwater. Many small towns and individual houses in the countryside do not have access to waste water treatment plants. Instead they dispose of sewage in large septic tanks. Large towns and cities need treatment plants where the waste water is treated and made safe before being released into rivers, lakes and the sea.

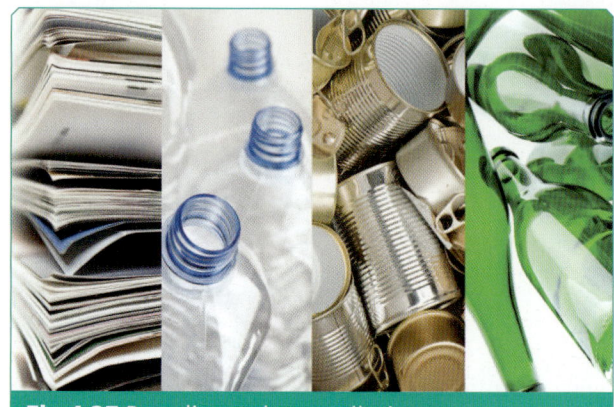

Fig 4.27 Recycling reduces pollution.

In the past in Ireland, waste water and sewage were released directly into rivers, lakes, seas and oceans. This still occurs in many places around the world, particularly in developing countries.

Sewage treatment plants clean waste water by three processes: primary, secondary and tertiary treatments.

- **Primary treatment:** The sewage is physically screened. This removes large objects such as pieces of wood, paper, plastic or metal. The sewage is then transferred to settling tanks. Many of the organic components and suspended solids in the sewage fall to the bottom of the tank as sludge. The sludge is then removed to a separate tank.
- **Secondary treatment:** The water is filtered through large beds of gravel and sand (Fig 4.28). These contain microorganisms which break down the organic effluent into carbon dioxide, water and methane gas. At the end of this stage, the water is usually clean enough to be released into nearby rivers, lakes or the sea.
- **Tertiary treatment:** Whether tertiary treatment is carried out depends on the quality of the water after secondary treatment. Special microorganisms are sometimes added if the phosphate and nitrate levels are high. These microorganisms break down phosphates and nitrates. Chlorine is also often added at the end of the process to kill any pathogenic (disease-causing) microorganisms.

Scrubbers

Scrubbers, which are used by industry, are air pollution control devices that remove any dangerous or polluting gases. Scrubbers use water or other solvents to wash the waste gases before emission. Air pollutants such as dioxins, sulfur and nitrogen dioxides can all be filtered out.

Pollution acts

Governments have introduced many laws to control pollution. Examples include the Environmental Protection Agency Act 1992 and the Air Pollution Act 1987.

Conservation

> **Conservation** is the wise management of our existing natural resources.

The Earth has a finite amount of resources. Over the past few hundred years, we have developed technologies to make use of these resources. Resources are now being used at an astonishing rate. If humans continue to overuse these resources, we will permanently damage many ecosystems.

Ireland was once covered in trees, which were cut down. Today, trees in rainforests are cut down at an alarming rate, often without replanting. The trees are cleared for timber and to make way for cattle farming.

On a local level, these trees help to prevent soil erosion and affect the local climate. On a global level, they absorb much of the carbon dioxide in the atmosphere. They are also home to thousands of undiscovered species, many of which could be lost as trees are felled. This all leads to a reduction in biodiversity. Fig 4.29 (a photograph of the Amazon rainforest taken from space) shows new roads being built and the area of trees that have been cut down.

Fig 4.28 Secondary treatment of sewage.

Fig 4.29 Deforestation in the Amazon rainforest.

Humans have become dependent on fossil fuels to satisfy our ever-increasing demand for energy. Estimates for when oil will run out vary greatly, but the certainty is that in the next 50 or 100 years all the oil wells will run dry. Alternative sources of energy – such as wind, water, solar and nuclear energies – have become more popular in recent years. These provide more efficient ways to meet our energy needs.

We have overfished the oceans to the point that some species are in danger of becoming extinct. It has been estimated that in 1900 there were six times as many fish in the oceans as there are today! Governments around the world have introduced fishing quotas and changes in net sizes to protect fish stocks. The fishing of some species has also been banned.

Conservation is crucial for the survival of our own species and for the planet as a whole.

Waste management

The human population produces vast quantities of waste every year. The average person in a developed country produces between 500 and 750 kg of waste per year! Industry produces even more waste. The agriculture, fishery and forestry industries have developed ways of minimising and managing these wastes

- **Agriculture:** Waste from agriculture includes animal waste such as dung. This is collected and stored in slurry pits until the growing season when it is spread on dry land as a natural fertiliser.
- **Fisheries:** Processing fish for the consumer produces a lot of waste. The waste parts of the fish such as heads and tails are pulped, dried and converted into pig feed. They can also be stored and converted into compost.
- **Forestry:** Forestry agencies ensure forests are maintained by replanting young trees after logging. After trees have been cut down, the branches are collected and used on the forest floor or are converted into wood chippings and saw dust (Fig 4.31) to make particleboards such as chipboard and MDF.

Fig 4.30 Overfishing can have serious consequences for aquatic ecosystems.

Fig 4.31 Wood chippings are used to produce particleboards such as chipboard and MDF.

Problems associated with waste disposal

There are many problems associated with waste disposal. We will look at some common problems below.

- Landfill sites are unattractive, attract vermin and give off unpleasant smells and methane (which contributes to global warming).
- Nuclear wastes stored underground have the potential to leak out and contaminate the soil and water supply.
- Wastes can contain bacteria and other microorganisms that cause disease.
- Wastes can contain toxic chemicals, such as mercury, that can leach into groundwater or can be absorbed by living organisms and be passed along the food chain.
- Waste water can be rich in nutrients such as phosphates and nitrates. These chemicals can cause eutrophication of rivers and lakes. This can kill fish and other animal life in aquatic habitats.

Fig 4.32 Landfill sites are unattractive and attract vermin.

Whatever the type of waste, it is difficult to dispose of it effectively.

Recycling is more widespread now, which deals with a significant proportion of household waste. The remainder is usually incinerated or dumped into landfill.

- Incineration is an effective and quick way of disposing of waste. The heat generated can be converted into electricity. However, many people believe burning waste releases high levels of dangerous gases, such as dioxins.
- Landfill sites (Fig 4.32) have to contain the waste as it decays. Modern landfill sites are now tightly regulated.
    - They must be lined with tough, thick plastic sheets to prevent toxic chemicals seeping into groundwater.
    - They must be layered with soils and gravel to allow proper drainage.
    - They must have sophisticated drainage systems and a methane gas collection system. These systems all prevent contamination of surrounding water supplies and ensure a safe and rapid way to dispose of waste.
- How industrial effluent is disposed of depends on its type. Disposing of dangerous industrial waste, such as acids and bases, can be expensive. Disposal of nuclear waste is also very expensive and extremely hazardous. Only a small number of countries accept nuclear waste. This waste is usually contained in very thick steel and concrete containers and buried deep underground, usually in earthquake-free zones. It will be many thousands of years before this waste is safe.

Waste minimisation

Due to the problems associated with waste disposal, we are continually trying to minimise our waste. Waste minimisation involves the three 'R's.

- **Reduce:** We need to limit the amount of packaging we use. Many supermarkets and food manufacturers are now using less packaging. The Irish government introduced a plastic bag levy (currently at 22c per plastic bag), which has greatly reduced the number of plastic bags produced.
- **Reuse:** Ask yourself whether there is anything that you bought and have finished with that can be reused. For example, clothing can be reused by giving them to charities instead of throwing them away. Plastic shopping bags can be used many times.
- **Recycle:** Most plastics, glass, metal and paper can now be recycled. There are numerous recycling centres around the country and most local authorities ask customers to separate their rubbish for collection and recycling.

Unit 1   Biology: the study of life

Chapter 4   Questions

1. Define the following terms:
   (a) *Ecology*
   (b) *Ecosystem*
   (c) *Biosphere*
   (d) *Habitat*
2. Distinguish between the terms *abiotic* and *biotic*.
3. Give **two** examples of climatic factors that affect a named living organism. Explain what effect each factor might have on the living organism.
4. Give **two** examples of edaphic factors that affect a named organism. Explain what effect each factor might have on the living organism.
5. Name **two** abiotic factors and **two** biotic factors that affect the human population.
6. Where does all the energy in living organisms ultimately come from?
7. What process allows the entry of this energy into living organisms?
8. What is a grazing food chain?
9. Give an example of a simple grazing food chain.
10. Answer the questions in relation to the following food chain:

    Grass → Aphid → Ladybird

    (a) Grass is known as the _____.
    (b) The aphid is called the _____ _____.
    (c) The ladybird is called the _____ _____.
    (d) Where does the grass obtain energy?
    (e) Energy is lost throughout the food chain. What catabolic reaction is responsible for the loss of energy?
    (f) If the ladybirds were removed from the habitat, give two effects this might have on the other two organisms in the food chain.
    (g) Draw a pyramid of numbers for this food chain.

11. The diagram shows a food web. Using the diagram answer the following questions:

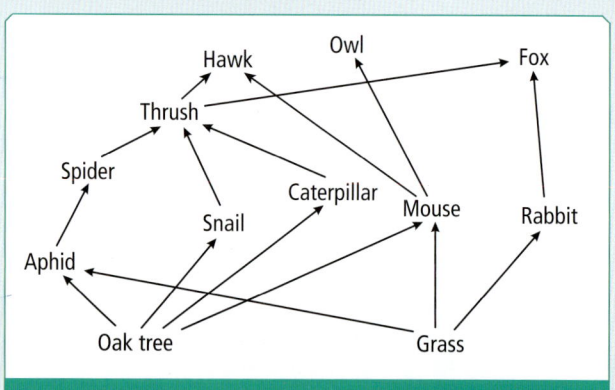

    Fig 4.33 A food web.

    (a) In what kind of ecosystem would you most likely find this food web?
    (b) What is the source of energy for this food web?
    (c) Name a producer.
    (d) Name a primary consumer.
    (e) Name a secondary consumer.
    (f) Name a tertiary consumer.
    (g) Name a top consumer.
    (h) Name a predator and its prey.
    (i) Select and write down a food chain with three trophic levels.
    (j) Select and write down a food chain with four trophic levels.
    (k) If the rabbits, owls and spiders were removed from this habitat, what effects might there be on the other organisms in the food web?

12. What is an ecological pyramid of numbers? Name the group of organisms that are always present at the bottom of a pyramid of numbers.

HL 13. Distinguish between an upright pyramid of numbers and an inverted pyramid of numbers, giving an example for each type.

14 Using the diagram from question 11, draw a pyramid of numbers that:
   (a) Has grass as the producer and the owl as the top consumer.
   (b) Has the oak tree as the producer and the thrush as the top consumer.

HL 15 Give **two** limitations of the use of pyramids of numbers.

16 (a) What do you understand by the term 'niche'?
   (b) What is the niche of a fox?
   (c) If a population of foxes is removed from its habitat by hunting, what effect might this have on its niche?
   (d) Name **two** niches that humans occupy.

HL 17 Suggest a possible ecological explanation for each of the following:
   (a) The numbers of hares in a habitat slowly decrease over a five-year period and then increase.
   (b) Cod fish stocks in the North West Atlantic Ocean collapsed in the early 1990s.
   (c) Most plant growth occurs during the summer months.
   (d) Very few plants are found at high altitudes.
   (e) A flock of birds fly in a V-shaped formation.
   (f) The Wryneck bird migrates from Africa to northern Europe during the spring.
   (g) Birds build nests in tall trees.
   (h) Squirrels bury nuts underground.
   (i) A dead organism decomposes in the soil.
   (j) Farmers use legumes in crop rotations.

18 Distinguish between the terms *population* and *community*.

19 (a) Define *competition*.
   (b) What effect does competition have on the population of a particular species?
   (c) Name **three** factors that plants may compete for in their habitats.
   (d) Name **three** factors that animals may compete for in their habitat.
   (e) Name the **two** types of competition giving a specific example of each type in the living world.

20 (a) What is *predation*?
   (b) Give three examples of predators and their respective prey.
   (c) Explain the importance of predators to the habitat.
   (d) In terms of pyramids of numbers, explain why predator populations are usually small and prey populations are relatively larger.

21 (a) What is *symbiosis*?
   (b) Give **two** examples of symbiosis in the natural world.

22 (a) What is *parasitism*?
   (b) Give an example of a parasite of humans.

23 Describe how the following factors have impacted on the human population:
   (a) War
   (b) Famine
   (c) Contraception
   (d) Disease

24 What is *nutrient recycling*?

25 The carbon cycle has many different aspects.
   (a) In what form is most carbon found in the atmosphere?
   (b) Explain the term *greenhouse gas*.
   (c) Explain how carbon present in the atmosphere and oceans is incorporated into living organisms.
   (d) Name **three** biomolecules present in living organisms that contain carbon.
   (e) Carbon is passed from organism to organism in the food chain. Name the term given to the process of incorporating carbon into the biomolecules of an organism.
   (f) What happens to carbon-containing compounds when a living organism dies?

26 Answer the following questions in relation to the nitrogen cycle:
   (a) What is nitrogen fixation? Name **two** ways in which it occurs.
   (b) Distinguish between nitrification and denitrification.
   (c) Name **two** biomolecules in all living organisms into which nitrogen is incorporated.

27 (a) What is pollution?

(b) Name **one** type of domestic pollution and state its effect on the environment.

(c) Name **one** type of agricultural pollution and state its effect on the environment.

(d) Name **one** type of industrial pollution and state its effect on the environment.

(e) Name **one** human activity that has had a major effect on the ecology of the surrounding area.

(f) Name **two** factors that are used to control pollution.

28 Sewage treatment involves **three** stages. Name and briefly describe each stage.

29 (a) In terms of ecology, what is meant by *conservation*?

(b) Give **two** ways in which conservation is important for humans.

30 Name **one** method of waste management for each of the following industries:

(a) Agricultural

(b) Fishing

(c) Forestry

31 (a) What is *eutrophication*? Explain how it can kill fish.

(b) Other than eutrophication, name **three** problems associated with waste disposal.

(c) Give **one** cause of eutrophication.

32 Waste minimisation involves the three 'R's. What are the three 'R's?

Answer the following multiple-choice questions:

33 A grazing food chain always starts with a:

(a) Primary consumer

(b) Secondary consumer

(c) Producer

(d) Predator

34 A number of individuals of the same species living together in a defined area form a/an:

(a) Community

(b) Population

(c) Ecosystem

(d) Niche

35 The sequence of energy flow through a food chain is:

(a) Primary consumers → higher level consumers → producers.

(b) Primary consumers → producers → higher level consumers.

(c) Producers → higher level consumers → primary consumers.

(d) Higher level consumers → primary consumers → producers.

(e) Producers → primary consumers → higher level consumers.

HL 36 An upright pyramid of numbers is one where:

(a) The bottom of the pyramid is narrow and the top is wide.

(b) The bottom of the pyramid is wide and the top is narrow.

(c) The bottom of the pyramid is the same width as the top of the pyramid.

37 A number of individuals belonging to different species living together in a defined area form a/an:

(a) Community

(b) Population

(c) Ecosystem

(d) Niche

HL 38 Parasitism is where:

(a) An organism catches, kills, and eats another organism.

(b) Two organisms live in close association and at least one of them benefit.

(c) Two organisms live in close association and one of them is harmed.

(d) Two organisms live in close association with both organisms benefiting.

39 The term that describes the relationship between nitrogen-fixing bacteria and a clover plant is:

(a) Competition

(b) Predation

(c) Parasitism

(d) Symbiosis

40 In the carbon cycle, which one of the following factors is not responsible for producing carbon dioxide?

(a) Photosynthesis

(b) Respiration

(c) Volcanic eruptions

(d) Decay

41 During the nitrogen cycle, nitrogen gas is returned to the atmosphere by:

(a) Nitrogen-fixing bacteria

(b) Denitrifying bacteria

(c) Nitrifying bacteria

(d) Bacteria of decay

Chapter 4 Sample examination questions

1 (a) The diagram shows the carbon cycle.

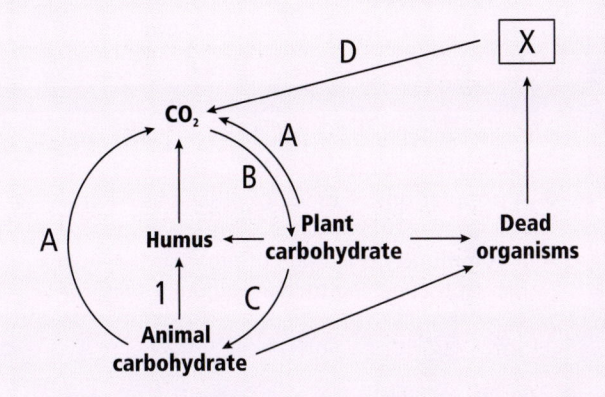

(a) Name the processes A, B, C and D.

(b) Name the substances labelled X.

(c) Why are elements recycled in nature?

(d) Name **one** group of organisms responsible for process 1 in the diagram.

Section A, Question 1 Ordinary Level 2010

HL 2 (a) (i) Distinguish between *contest competition* and *scramble competition* by writing a sentence about each.

(ii) Name a factor, other than competition, that controls wild populations.

(b) What deduction is it possible to make from each of the following observations?

(i) In a particular area the population of a predator did not decline following a big reduction in the population of its main prey.

(ii) Mortality levels resulting from infection by a particular virus tend to decline over the years.

(iii) Where some members of a species remain in the same general area throughout life and some members are migratory, mortality levels tend to be higher in the migratory part of the population.

(iv) There is a greater variety of herbaceous (non-woody) plants in areas where grazing species, such as rabbits, are more plentiful than in areas where grazing species are less plentiful.

(v) In some species of migratory ducks in the northern hemisphere it is found that the wintering grounds of the males lie further south than those of the females.

Section C, Question 10 (a), (b) Higher Level 2011

Chapter 4 Mind map

Ecology is the branch of biology concerned with the study of the interactions of living organisms with each other and with their environment.

Ecosystem: community of organisms that interact with their environment.

Biosphere: region of the Earth where life can be exist.

Habitat: place where an organism lives.

1. **Abiotic factor:** anything that is non-living and has an effect on living organisms in an ecosystem. There are two main types of abiotic factors:
   - **Climatic factors:** anything relating to the weather conditions, such as rainfall.
   - **Edaphic factors:** anything relating to the soil, such as soil pH.
2. **Biotic factor:** anything that is living and has an effect on other living organisms in an ecosystem.

All the energy in living organisms ultimately comes from the Sun.

- A **grazing food chain** shows the sequence of organisms with one species at each trophic (feeding) level.
- A simple food chain is: Grass → Rabbit → Fox
- A **food web** is two or more interconnected food chains.

An **ecological pyramid of numbers** shows the numbers of organisms at each trophic level in a food chain.

- **Niche:** functional role an organism plays in its habitat.
- A **population** is a group of organisms living in a habitat that belong to the same species.
- A **community** is a group of organisms living in a habitat that belong to many different species.

Ecology   Chapter 4

- **Competition** is the struggle between organisms for a resource that is in limited supply.   HL
  - **Contest competition** is the direct fight between two organisms for a resource that is in short supply.
  - **Scramble competition** is the struggle amongst a number of organisms for a resource in short supply and each organism gets a small share of the resource.
- **Predation** is the catching, killing and eating of another organism.
- **Symbiosis** is a biological relationship in which two species live in close proximity to each other and interact regularly in such a way as to benefit one or both of the organisms.
- **Parasitism** is where one organism lives in or on another organism to the detriment of that organism.
- Predator-prey relationships are affected by factors such as camouflage, speed of movement, food availability and size of organism.
- Human population is affected by factors such as war, famine, contraception and disease.

- **Nutrient recycling** is the process of exchanging important elements between living organisms and the environment.
- The **carbon cycle** is the process through which elemental carbon is exchanged between living organisms and their environment.
- The **nitrogen cycle** is the process through which elemental nitrogen is exchanged between living organisms and their environment.

- **Pollution** is any harmful addition to the environment.
- Domestic wastes include solid wastes, liquid wastes and hazardous wastes.
- Agricultural wastes include pesticides, insecticides and slurry.
- Industrial wastes include liquid effluents and gas emissions.

Ecological impact of one human activity: oil spills cause pollution in many coastal habitat around the spill site and can kill many birds and other animals in the habitat.

Pollution can be controlled by **reducing, reusing** and **recycling** waste; sewage treatment; the use of scrubbers by industry; and enforcement of pollution laws.

Sewage treatment consists of three stages:
- **Primary treatment** involves the screening of large debris present in the sewage and the settling of sewage.
- **Secondary treatment** involves the filtration of the water through beds of gravel and sand and allowing bacteria to act on the organic components.
- **Tertiary treatment** involves removing phosphates and nitrates using special types of bacteria. It also involves chlorination to kill pathogenic bacteria.

Conservation is the wise management of our existing natural resources.

Waste management
- Agriculture produces slurry that is spread on land in summer as a natural fertiliser.
- The fishing industry produces waste fish parts that are pulped and dried and used as pig feed or composted.
- The forestry industry produces waste wood that is converted into wood chippings and saw dust. These waste products can then be used to make chipboard.
- Waste minimisation involves **reducing** waste produced, **reusing** materials where possible and **recycling**.

Problems associated with waste disposal
- Landfill sites are unattractive, attract vermin and give off unpleasant smells.
- Nuclear wastes are highly dangerous if they leak out of their containers.
- Wastes can cause disease.
- Wastes can contain toxic chemicals that can get into living organisms causing health problems and death.
- Waste water can be rich in nutrients and cause eutrophication of rivers and lakes.

Chapter 5 The study of an ecosystem

Learning objectives After studying this chapter, you should be able to:
- Identify five animals and five plants in a habitat using identification keys.
- Identify and use various ecological instruments for collecting living organisms from a habitat.
- Carry out a qualitative and quantitative study of plants and animals in a habitat.
- Study three abiotic (non-living) factors present in a habitat.
- Identify an adaptation shown by at least one organism in a habitat.
- Identify the role of organisms from a habitat in energy transfer and construct food chains, a food web and a pyramid of numbers from the organisms in the habitat.

Introduction

There are many different ecosystems surrounding us: woodlands, grasslands, streams, ponds, lakes, rocky seashores, hedgerows, meadows and soils.

There is huge diversity in all ecosystems. Woodlands, forests and marine habitats have the most diverse life forms.

All ecosystems are linked. This means they depend on one another in order to maintain the delicate balance of nature. This is called **interdependence**. If any one factor in an ecosystem is changed, the balance is upset and may take a long time to correct itself.

Fig 5.1 A cape gannet bird diving into water to catch sardines. This is an example of interdependence between two ecosystems.

Practical activity: select and visit one ecosystem

When choosing a habitat to study, you will consider many factors, such as the type of habitats in the areas near your school, access to those habitats, available equipment and the time of year (season). It is best to conduct your ecosystem study between the months of March and May, especially if you are studying woodland or grassland as this is when plants blossom and insect numbers rise. However, it is important to note that to conduct a full study you would have to study the habitat at many different times of the year.

Before you conduct your study, there are a number of important rules that must be followed:
- Obtain permission where necessary – do not just wander onto somebody's land!
- Do not damage any property or any of the plants.
- Leave the property/habitat as you found it.
- Be aware of animals, such as bulls and dogs.
- Any organisms that are captured and taken back to the laboratory must be returned to their habitat.

The study of an ecosystem — Chapter 5

Once you have decided on your ecosystem, there are a number of things the Biology syllabus requires that you do:

- Complete a broad overview of the selected ecosystem, including a description of the ecosystem and habitats and a plan view map of your habitat. Two of the most common – woodland and rocky seashore – are described below.
- Identify any five fauna (animals) and any five flora (photosynthetic organisms) using simple keys.
- Identify a variety of habitats within the selected ecosystem.
- Identify and use various ecological apparatus for collecting organisms in the habitat.
- Conduct a quantitative (counting) study of plants and animals of a sample area of the selected ecosystem.
- Investigate three abiotic factors present in the selected ecosystem.
- Identify one adaptation of any organism in the selected ecosystem.
- Identify the roles the organisms play in energy transfer by constructing food chains, a food web and a pyramid of numbers.
- Analyse and comment on results obtained and discuss any sources of error.

> **NOTE:** Do NOT take any protected species. Species that are protected under the Wildlife Act 1976 and Amendment 2000 are listed in the table below.

PROTECTED SPECIES

Mammals		Amphibians	Reptiles	Invertebrates
Badger	Red squirrel	Natterjack toad	Common lizard	Freshwater crayfish
Bat	Stoat	Common frog	Leatherback turtle	Freshwater pearl mussel
Deer	Otter	Common newt		
Hare	Dolphin			Kerry slug
Hedgehog	Porpoise			
Pygmy shrew	Seal			
Pine marten	Whale			

Practical activity: broad overview of the selected ecosystem and identify any five fauna and any five flora using simple keys

Woodland habitat

There are many woodland ecosystems around Ireland and it should not be difficult to find one near your school. Woodland ecosystems are home to a diverse range of living organisms. This makes them one of the most popular ecosystems to study. Woodlands contain a variety of trees, shrubs and animals (including vertebrates and invertebrates).

Once you have chosen your ecosystem and mapped out your habitat, you must use the collection methods described and identification keys to identify five animals (fauna) and five plants (flora).

Identification keys are usually booklets giving detailed information and photographs and/or drawings of organisms in a particular habitat (Fig 5.3).

You should try to identify organisms you are not familiar with in the habitat rather than choosing organisms that you know very well.

Unit 1 Biology: the study of life

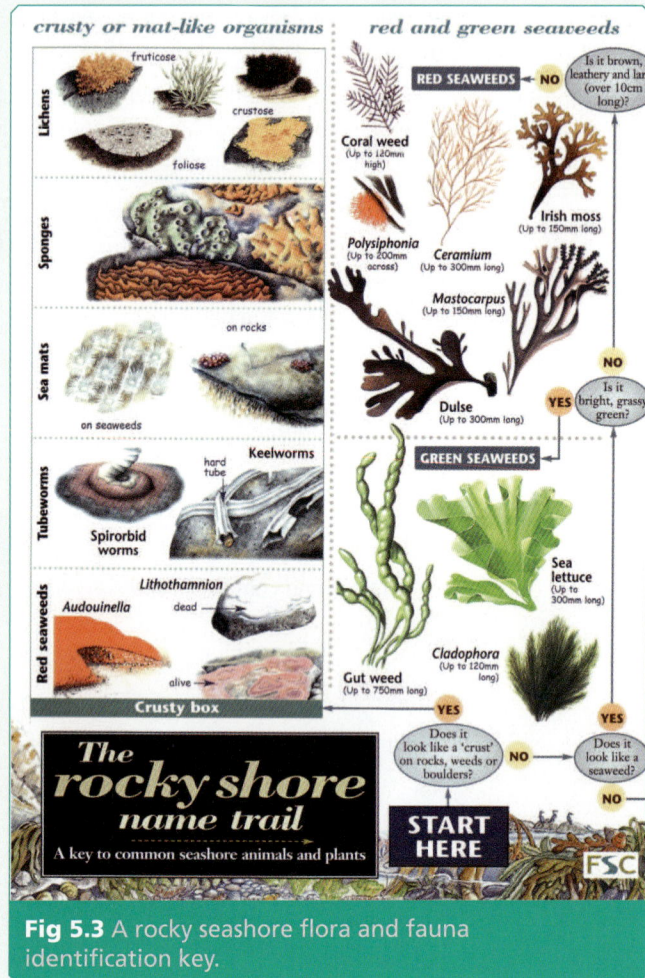

Fig 5.2 A woodland.

Fig 5.3 A rocky seashore flora and fauna identification key.

The table below gives examples of common organisms you may find in a woodland or grassland.

FLORA		FAUNA			
Small plants	**Trees**	**Invertebrates**		**Vertebrates**	
Grass	Beech	Snails	Grasshoppers	Frogs	Rats
Clover	Ash	Slugs	Mites	Rabbits	Ducks
Dock leaves	Hawthorn	Worms	Flies	Hares	Swans
Nettles	Poplar	Woodlice	Wasps	Foxes	Blue tits
Daisies	Aspen	Millipedes	Bees	Red squirrels	Robins
Buttercups	Oak	Centipedes	Ants	Grey squirrels	Blackbirds
Dandelions	Horse chestnut	Springtails	Mayflies	Hedgehogs	Sparrows
Speedwell	Elder	Earwigs	Crane-flies	Badgers	Crows
Lesser celandine	Willow	Ground beetles	Butterflies	Bats	Magpies
Brambles	Whitebeam	Caterpillars	Dragonflies	Moles	Deer
Mosses	Holly	Spiders	Ladybirds	Mice	
Thistles	Sycamore	Aphids			
Ragwort					
Ferns					

The study of an ecosystem   Chapter 5

Fig 5.4A Nettles in a woodland. Nettles have stinging hairs on the edges of their leaves as a protective mechanism.

Fig 5.4B A bee stinging a human finger. During the process of stinging, the bee's abdomen tears open resulting in the death of the bee. Only the female worker bees can sting.

Fig 5.4C Horse chestnuts (also called 'conkers') from the horse chestnut tree. They are mildly poisonous to humans.

Fig 5.4D A red squirrel, which is threatened in Ireland by the larger and stronger grey squirrel.

Unit 1 Biology: the study of life

Seashore habitat

Seashore habitats are also numerous and an excellent choice for schools near the sea. At first glance, seashores do not seem to have a lot of life, but on closer inspection you will find that they are home to a great variety of organisms. The table below shows some of the organisms that might be found on the seashore.

Fig 5.5 A rocky seashore: The rock pools are full of life. Molluscs, crustaceans, marine worms, small fish and algae can all be found on the rocky seashore.

Algae	Echinoderms (marine animals)	Molluscs	Crustaceans	Birds	Other sea organisms
Plankton	Starfish	Cockles	Crabs	Herring gulls	Seagrass
Lichens	Sea urchins	Mussels	Common prawns	Seagulls	Marine worms
Bladder wrack	Sea cucumber	Periwinkles	Barnacles	Storm petrels	Sea anemones
Serrated wrack		Dog whelk	Rock louse	Northern gannet	Sponges
Spiral wrack		Limpets		Roseate tern	Pipefish
		Sea slugs		Grey heron	Sea scorpion
					Common blenny

A

B

C

D

The study of an ecosystem Chapter 5

Fig 5.6

A Seaweed, a type of marine algae, exposed on rocks at low tide.

B Periwinkles, a type of marine snail that live in and around the rocky seashore. They feed on algae.

C A clownfish swimming among snakelocks anemone. Snakelocks anemone lives among seaweed on the rocky seashore. It feeds on small fish and crustaceans, which it catches with its stinging tentacles.

D Limpets are marine snails that attach themselves to rocks using a muscular 'foot'. Within the shell of the limpet is a soft body. The shell offers protection against predators and also prevents drying out during low tide. Limpets feed on algae when the tide is in.

E Sea cucumber on a sandy seabed. It feeds on detritus (dead organic matter) and is related to starfish and sea urchins.

F A satellite image of a phytoplankton bloom around Ireland. Phytoplankton are photosynthetic microscopic algae.

G Sea urchin, a marine invertebrate related to starfish. Sea urchins feed on algae growing on rocks.

Unit 1 Biology: the study of life

Practical activity: identify a variety of habitats from the selected ecosystem

Woodland

Woodlands have many different habitats. Habitats within the woodland include:

- Canopy layer
- Shrub layer
- Ground level
- Leaf litter (detritus layer)
- Deadwood
- Soil

If you choose to study a woodland, grassland or forest ecosystem, you will more than likely study the ground level, leaf litter, deadwood and soil habitats. These are where the greatest range of life forms is found.

- Once you have chosen your habitat or had it assigned by your teacher and/or your ecology instructor, your group should mark it out clearly with ground stakes. You should study only within the marked out area.
- Next, draw a plan view map. This should include a scale, the direction north and a legend, showing where any shrubs or trees are located and showing any nearby roads or rivers that affect the habitat.

Fig 5.8 shows an example of a plan view map of a woodland habitat.

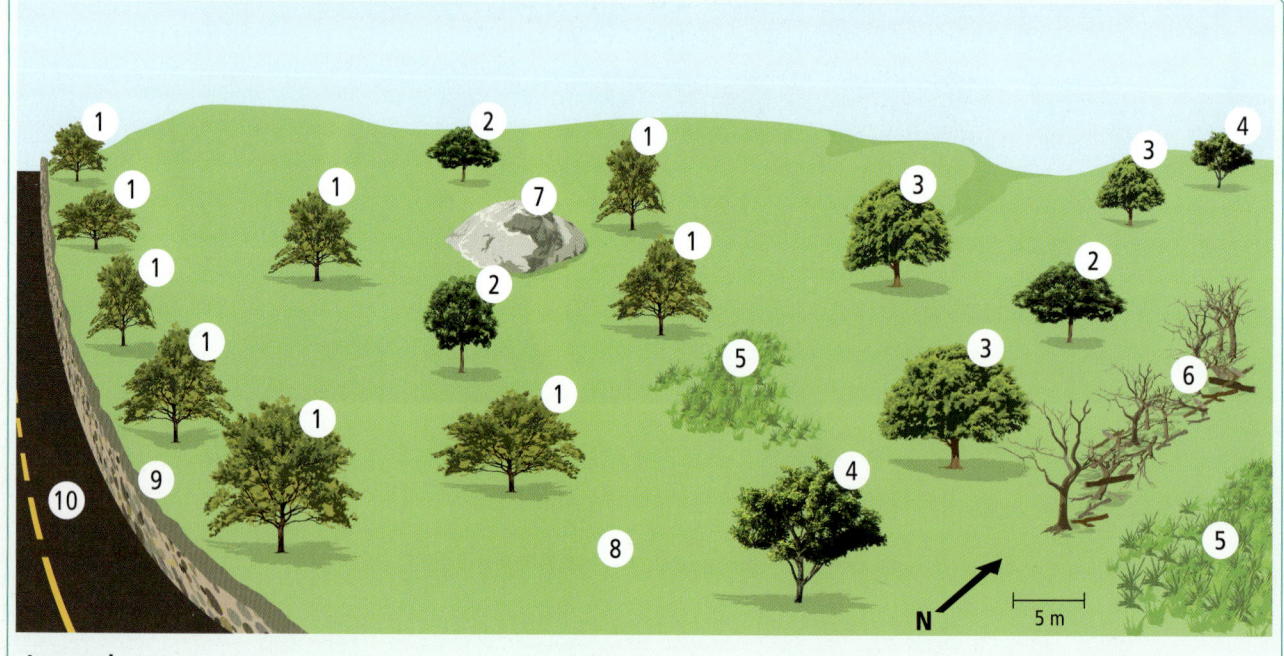

Fig 5.7A A team of scientists collecting and examining insects from the canopy layer of a forest.

Fig 5.7B Fungi and mosses growing on a piece of deadwood.

Legend:
1. Ash
2. Horse chestnut
3. Oak
4. Sycamore
5. Nettles
6. Deadwood
7. Large rock
8. Grass
9. Stone wall
10. Road

Fig 5.8 A plan view map of a typical woodland habitat. The legend numbers and names each element. The map shows the direction of north and a rough scale.

The study of an ecosystem   Chapter 5

Rocky seashore

There are various habitats, or zones, on the rocky seashore. These include the splash zone, intertidal zone, rock pool and littoral zone.

Fig 5.9 shows the typical locations of habitats on a rocky seashore. It also shows the approximate sites of various flora and fauna present on a rocky seashore.

NOTE: If you are studying the littoral zone, you will need to wear wellingtons or preferably waders and be under the proper guidance of your teacher and ecology instructors.

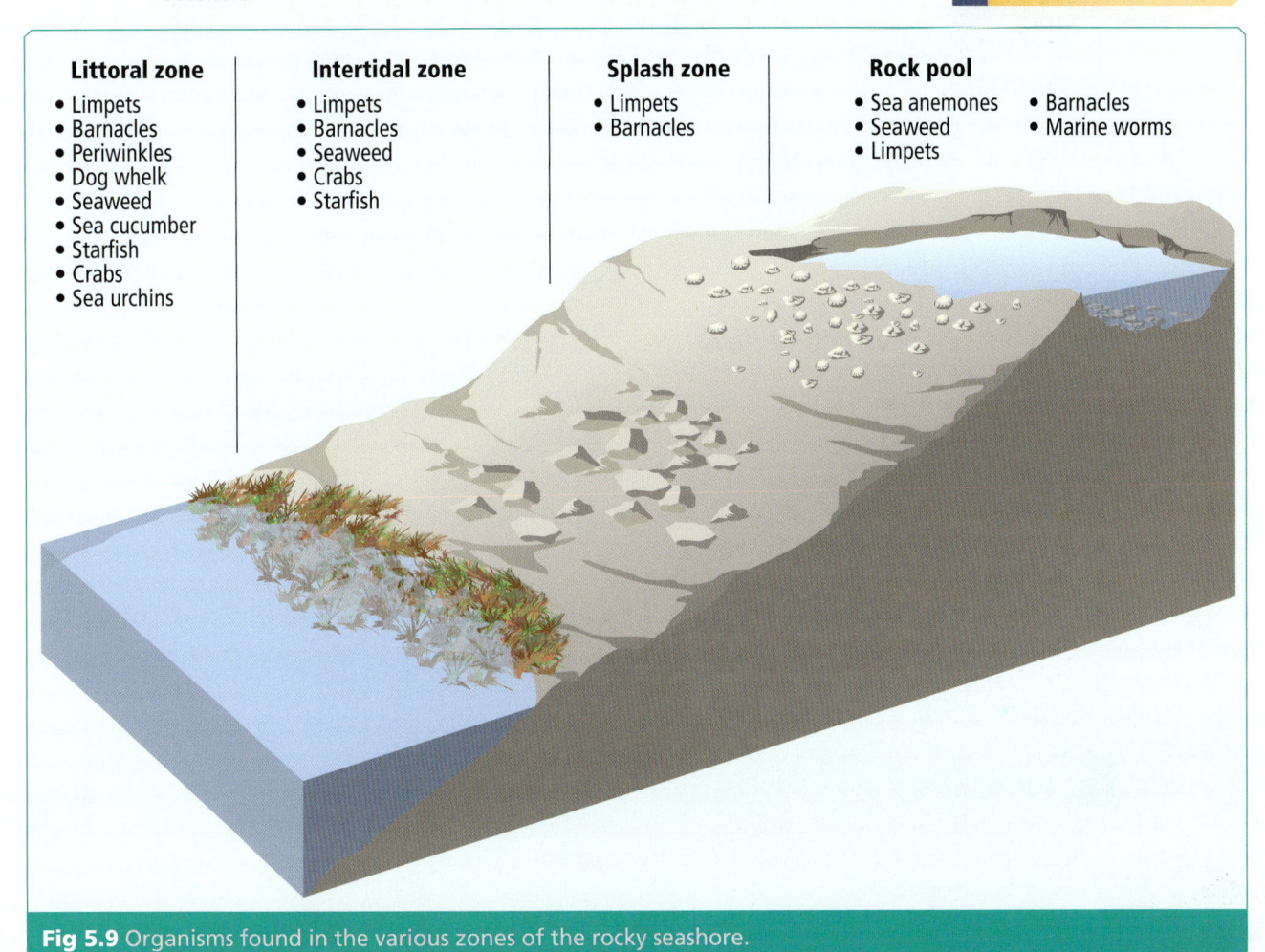

Littoral zone
- Limpets
- Barnacles
- Periwinkles
- Dog whelk
- Seaweed
- Sea cucumber
- Starfish
- Crabs
- Sea urchins

Intertidal zone
- Limpets
- Barnacles
- Seaweed
- Crabs
- Starfish

Splash zone
- Limpets
- Barnacles

Rock pool
- Sea anemones
- Seaweed
- Limpets
- Barnacles
- Marine worms

Fig 5.9 Organisms found in the various zones of the rocky seashore.

If you choose to study the rocky seashore, you should try to visit when the tide is completely out. This is when most of the seashore will be exposed, which means your study will be more comprehensive. It will enable you to get a good idea of the different life forms present in as many different zones of the rocky seashore as possible.

Fig 5.10 A rock pool with an abundance of life.

63

Unit 1 Biology: the study of life

- When you visit the rocky seashore, you will choose a habitat or be assigned one by your teacher and/or ecology instructor.
- Mark out the habitat, using wooden stakes and string or rope. Next draw a plan view map of your habitat. Your map should include a scale, the direction north and a legend, showing the locations of rocks, sand, seaweed and other organisms.

Fig 5.11 shows an example of a plan view map of the rocky seashore habitat.

Legend:

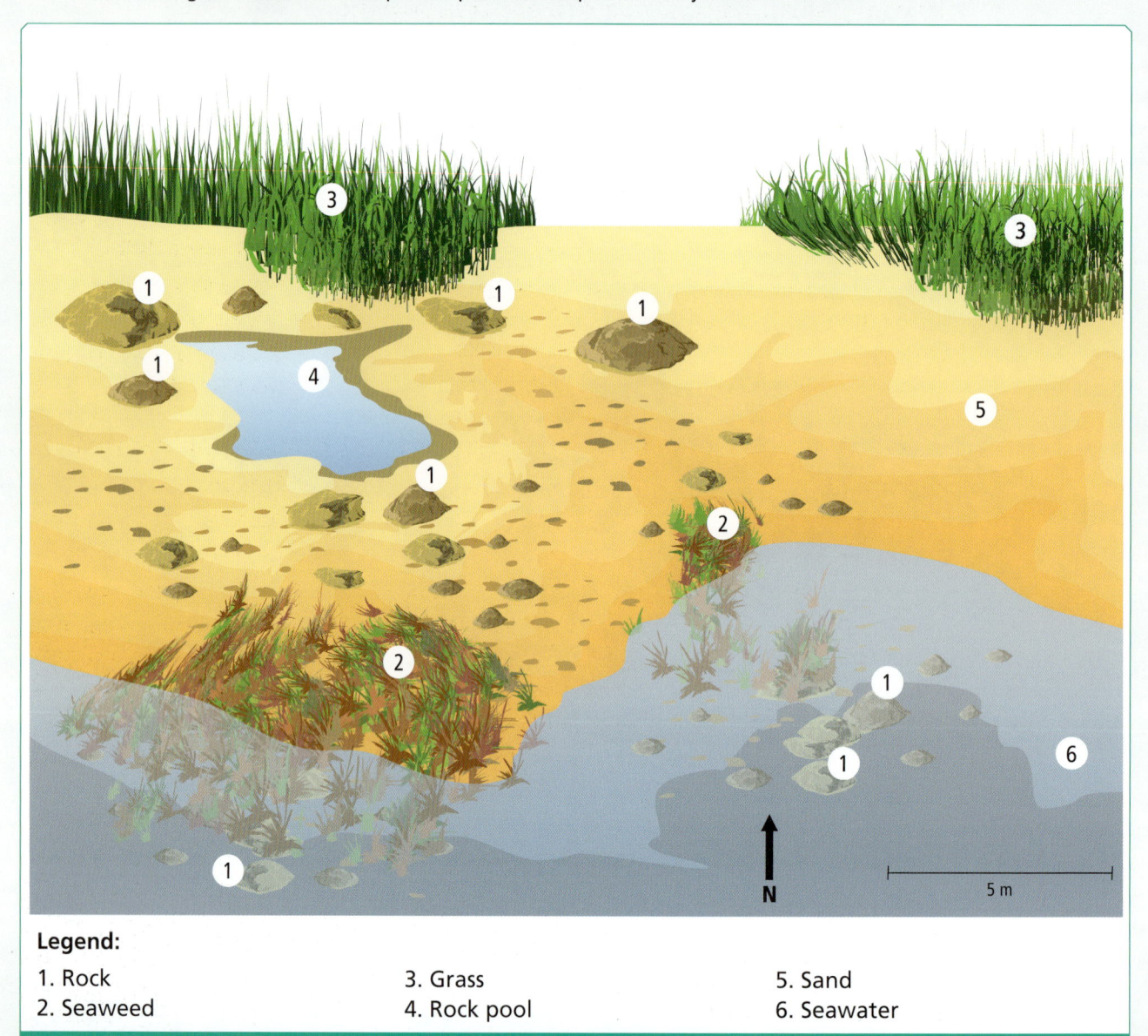

1. Rock
2. Seaweed
3. Grass
4. Rock pool
5. Sand
6. Seawater

Fig 5.11 A plan view map of a typical rocky seashore habitat. The legend numbers and names each element. The map shows the direction of north and a rough scale.

The study of an ecosystem — Chapter 5

Practical activity: identify and use various ecological apparatus for collecting organisms in the habitat

The equipment required will depend on the type of ecosystem you are studying. If you are studying forest, woodland or grassland, then you may use some or all of the following:

- Tape measure
- Spirit level
- Metre stick
- Ground stakes and string or rope
- Bug pot
- Compass
- Stream flow meter (if there is a stream in your habitat)
- Pooter
- Quadrat
- Beating tray
- Cryptozoic trap
- Trowel
- Soil sieve
- Tullgren funnel (if you are planning to sample organisms that live in the soil)
- Soil thermometer
- Air thermometer
- Soil pH meter (or pH test kit)
- Light meter
- Anemometer (if you wish to measure wind speed)
- Pitfall trap
- Mammal traps (if you wish to catch small rodents)
- Sweep net
- Line and belt transects
- Woodland animal and plant identification keys

If you are studying the rocky seashore you may use some or all of the following pieces of equipment:

- Tape measure
- Spirit level
- Metre stick
- Ground stakes and string or rope
- Compass
- Bug pot
- Pooter
- Cryptozoic trap
- Pitfall trap
- Dip net
- Plankton net (if you have access to the littoral zone habitat)
- Light meter
- Air thermometer
- Sand sieve
- Trowel
- Quadrat
- Line and belt transects
- Electrofishing equipment (only available to, and used by, Regional Fisheries Boards)
- Seashore animal and plant identification keys

We will now look at how to use some of this equipment.

Pooter

The pooter is used to catch small animals, such as insects and spiders. The investigator sucks through a tube that has a piece of gauze on the end. The other tube is placed near the animal. The pooter acts like a small vacuum cleaner. The small animals can then be taken back to the lab and identified using a key. You can also transfer the animals to a bug pot with a magnifying glass attached to get a better view.

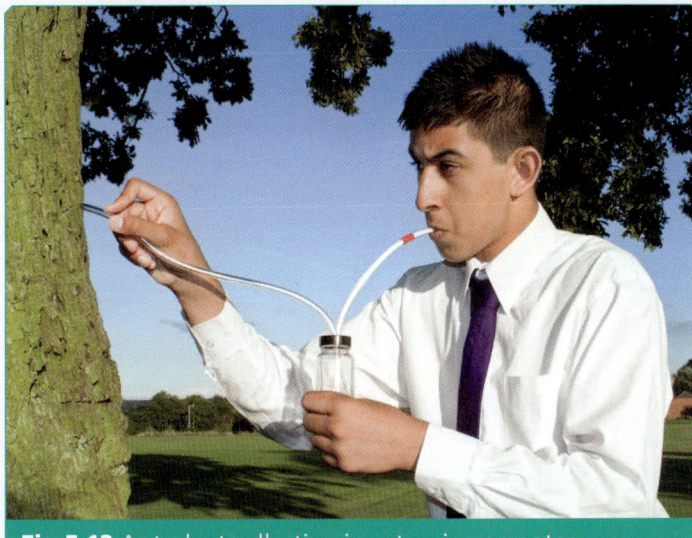

Fig 5.12 A student collecting insects using a pooter.

Pitfall trap

A pitfall trap consists of a pot or jar sunk into the ground so that the rim of the container is level with the ground. It is then covered with leaves or a rock. It is used to catch organisms that live in the leaf litter on the surface of the ground, such as ground beetles, spiders, mites, centipedes, millipedes and earwigs. These animals can then be transferred to the bug pot for a more detailed inspection and identification.

Fig 5.13 A pitfall trap.

Cryptozoic trap

A cryptozoic trap is an old log (deadwood) or stone that has been lying on the ground for a long time. If it is lifted, many organisms will be found underneath, such as woodlice, slugs and different types of arthropods (millipedes). These organisms can then be viewed using the bug pot.

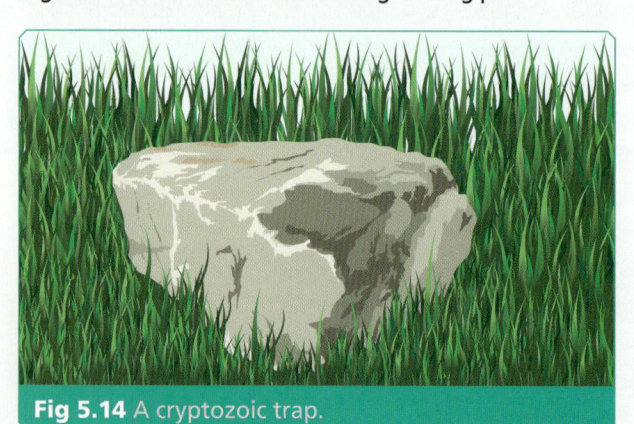

Fig 5.14 A cryptozoic trap.

Mammal trap

Mammal traps are used to capture small mammals. They are used in quantitative studies of fauna in a habitat. Many traps are set in a habitat, such as a woodland. Depending on the species being studied, a set period of time is allowed to pass before the traps are inspected. Once a number of mammals are caught, they are counted and tagged. They are then released back into the same habitat.

A week or two later (depending on the mammal), the same number of mammal traps are reset. The number of mammals caught on the second visit and the number of already tagged mammals are recorded and used to estimate the number of that mammal species in the habitat.

Fig 5.15 A mammal trap.

Beating tray

Beating trays come in various shapes and sizes. They are used to collect insects in the foliage of the shrub layer and canopy layer of trees and bushes.

A pooter and a bug pot are often used along with the beating tray to capture and identify the different species of insects.

Fig 5.16 A beating tray. A pooter is then used to collect the trapped insects.

Sweep net

Sweep nets are used to collect insects and arthropods (spiders) that live in the grass layer and shrub layer of a grassland or woodland ecosystem. They are also mainly used with a pooter and a bug pot.

Fig 5.17 A sweep net.

Electrofishing

Electrofishing uses an electric current to capture fish. The electric current stuns the fish, preventing it from swimming away. The scientist then picks the fish out of the water using a net.

Electrofishing is illegal for normal fishing but is allowed for use by ecologists to determine fish levels in rivers, lakes and seas (Fig 5.18).

Fig 5.18 Ecologists collecting fish using electrofishing.

Plankton net

Plankton are microscopic plants (phytoplankton) and animals (zooplankton) that live in freshwater and marine habitats. Phytoplankton are the producers in marine food chains and food webs. They are important contributors to total photosynthesis on Earth. Zooplankton feed on the phytoplankton. Zooplankton are then eaten by small fish and other forms of sea life.

A plankton net is used to obtain samples of plankton. It is pulled through the water. The plankton are caught in the net and washed down into a small plastic bottle at the bottom of the net. They are then viewed under the microscope, identified and quantified.

Fig 5.19 A plankton net.

Soil sieve

Fig 5.20 A soil sieve.

Soil sieves can be used to extract small animals – such as insects, ants, millipedes, centipedes, woodlice and worms – from the soil.

A number of sieves together can be used to determine the particle sizes present in the soil and to determine how much sand is present, for example.

Tullgren funnel

A Tullgren funnel is used to extract small animals – such as small insects, worms, nematodes, springtails and mites – that live in the soil. A lamp heats the upper layers of a sample of soil. All the living organisms move away from the heat source. Eventually they fall from the lower part of the soil into a container at the bottom.

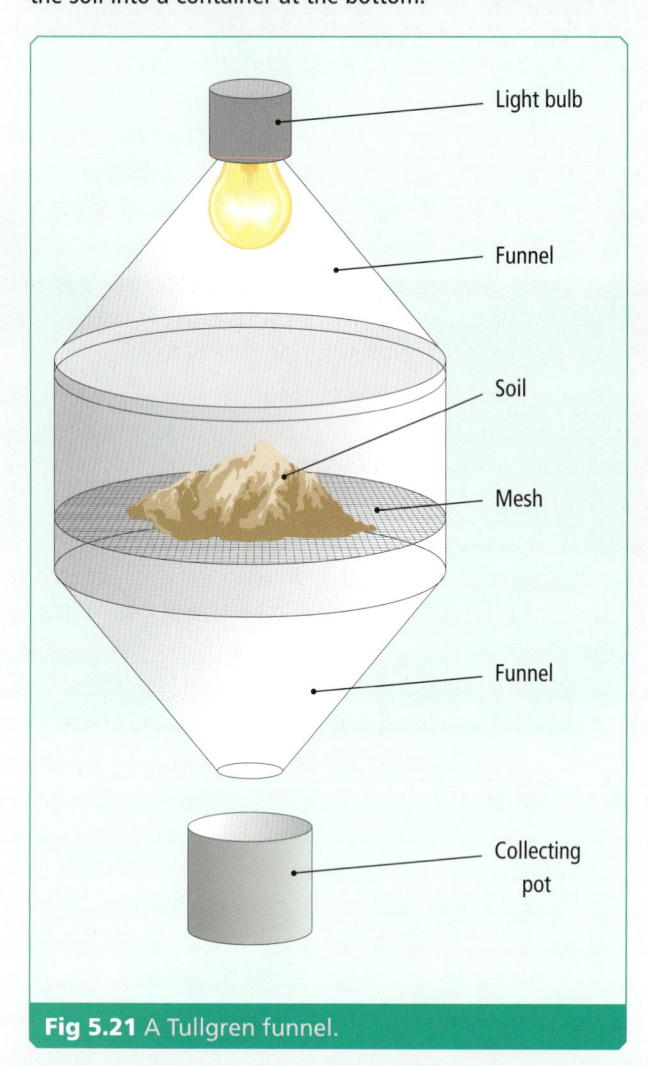

Fig 5.21 A Tullgren funnel.

Spirit level

You may have to calculate the slope of your habitat. Steep inclines may affect the type of organisms that live in the habitat. The direction the incline is facing can also affect the types of organisms present.

You can use a spirit level to calculate the slope.

- Tie a piece of rope to two wooden stakes at either end of the incline (Fig 5.22).
- Use the spirit level to make it horizontal.
- Measure the height from the ground to various positions along the rope.
- Draw a graph showing the different heights.

- To find out the percentage gradient (slope) over the entire length of the habitat, divide the vertical elevation (the 'rise') at the bottom of the incline by the horizontal distance (the 'run') from the bottom of the incline to the top. The percentage gradient is calculated by multiplying by 100.

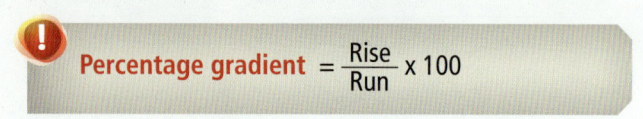

$$\text{Percentage gradient} = \frac{\text{Rise}}{\text{Run}} \times 100$$

The wooden stakes, rope and metre stick can also be used to draw a profile map (Fig 5.22).

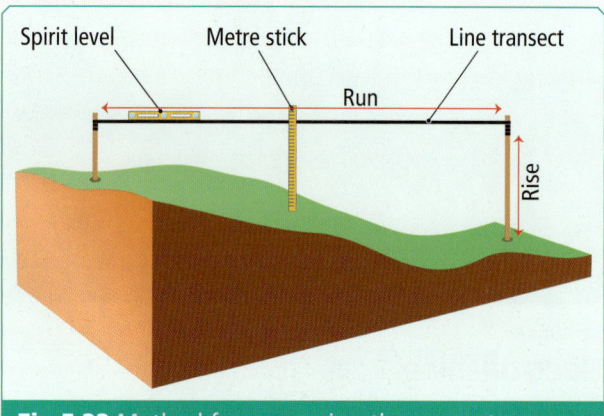

Fig 5.22 Method for measuring the percentage gradient of a habitat.

Anemometer

An anemometer measures wind speed. It is important to measure wind speeds at various locations in your habitat.

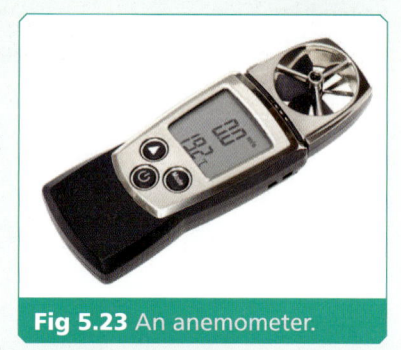

Fig 5.23 An anemometer.

Light meter

Light meters measure light intensity. It is important to measure light intensity at various locations in your habitat.

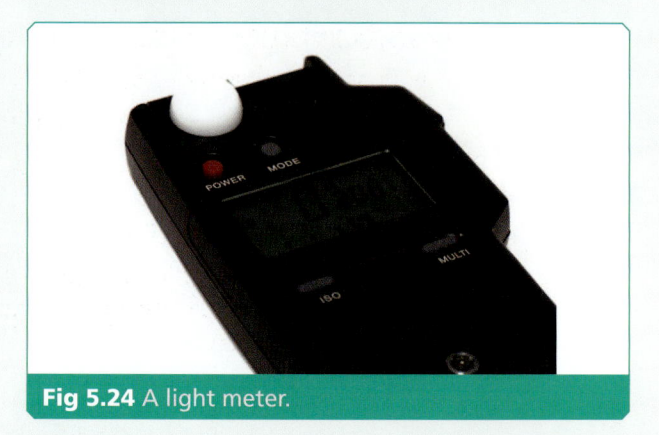

Fig 5.24 A light meter.

The study of an ecosystem Chapter 5

Practical activity: conduct a quantitative study of plants and animals of a sample area of the selected ecosystem

It is important for ecologists to determine plant and animal distribution in ecosystems around the world. This is in order to keep an eye on population numbers of all species and build up an overall picture of food webs of different ecosystems. It is especially important in order to maintain populations of endangered species. There are two main methods used to determine the distribution of organisms in a habitat: qualitative and quantitative methods.

Qualitative method

Qualitative ecological methods simply record whether or not a plant or animal is present.

Your qualitative research of your chosen ecosystem will involve identifying, naming, classifying and sketching five fauna (animals) and five flora (photosynthetic organisms).

Quantitative method

Quantitative ecological methods involve estimating the number of animals or plants in a habitat.

Counting plants and animals in a habitat is usually impractical and often impossible. There are a number of ways of getting an acceptably accurate estimate of the population of a particular species in a habitat.

Your quantitative study of plants will involve estimating the numbers of plants using a quadrat (Fig 5.25). A quadrat is a square frame made from wood or metal. They come in various sizes, including 25 cm^2; 50 cm^2 or 1 m^2.

Fig 5.25 A student conducting a survey using a graduated quadrat.

Quadrats

Quadrats are squares made of metal or wood. However, many are graduated into 16, 25, 64 or 100 squares (Fig 5.25). Graduated quadrats give a more accurate estimate of the quantity and distribution of plants.

Advantages of using quadrats
- It is quick and easy to obtain results.
- Quadrats are widely used by ecologists so results are comparable.
- They give a good general overview of the species of small plants in an ecosystem.

Disadvantages of the use of quadrats
- Quadrats can be used to quantify only very slow-moving animals.
- Quadrats will always indicate that there are no trees or shrubs in woodland habitats.

You will use quadrats to obtain percentage frequency and percentage cover of the five plants identified.

Percentage frequency

Estimating the percentage frequency involves using a simple quadrat that is not graduated and recording the presence or absence of a particular plant species.

> **Percentage frequency** is defined as the chances of finding a given species in a habitat.

A table of results is filled out indicating whether or not the plant species is present. If the quadrat is thrown a number of times (say, ten times) a percentage frequency value can be calculated. For example, if grass was present in all thrown quadrats then grass has a 100 per cent frequency; if dandelions are present in two of the thrown quadrats, then the frequency of dandelions is 20 per cent.

An example of a simple frequency table is shown below. Notice that only five throws were recorded, which means it has a sample size of five. Remember, one of the principles of experimentation is having a large sample size. If the sample size were larger (ten), the results would be more accurate.

Once you have completed the table, draw a graph of the results.

Fig 5.26 Quadrats used for calculating percentage frequency: a quadrat used in a grassland habitat (A); a quadrat used on a seashore (B).

Plant species	1	2	3	4	5	% Frequency
Grass	✓	✓	✓	✓	✓	100
Dock leaf		✓				20
Lesser celandine			✓		✓	40
Thistle	✓		✓			40
Dandelion		✓	✓	✓		60

Percentage cover

> **Percentage cover** is defined as the area of ground occupied by aerial parts of plants.

Percentage cover is usually measured with a graduated quadrat. The greater the number of graduations, the more accurate the percentage cover result.

There are two main ways of calculating percentage cover: the subjective method and the objective method.

Subjective method

In the subjective method, you throw a pencil over your shoulder at random and place the quadrat where the pencil lands. Random selection is one of the principles of experimentation (*see* Chapter 1) and is used to eliminate error due to bias. Otherwise, researchers may either consciously or unconsciously select an area with more vegetation. This is unfair and would lead to unreliable results.

The area of each square of the quadrat covered by each plant species is estimated. The values for each square are added up to give the percentage cover for each species. The quadrat is thrown at random again and percentage cover estimated. This continues for at least ten quadrat throws.

It is subjective, as it depends on the subject. For example, one researcher may say that a particular square of a quadrat is half covered with grass whereas another researcher may say that it is 75 per cent covered.

Objective method

A more accurate way of obtaining percentage cover is by objectively counting the number of times a particular plant species touches a point of intersection (the top left-hand corner of each square) in the graduated quadrat. This method depends less on the researcher as it follows a specific method.

- Count the number of corners that grass touches in the quadrat. For example, grass may have touched 80 corners of a 100 square graduated quadrat. This means that the percentage cover of grass for that one quadrat throw was 80 per cent.
- Then count the number of times the next plant species of interest touches the top left-hand corner and so on. We continue this for the five species of plant identified in the habitat.

Fig 5.27 A graduated quadrat used for calculating percentage cover.

Plant species	1	2	3	4	5	% Cover
Grass	80	75	90	69	92	81.2
Dock leaf	14	21	18	20	16	17.8
Lesser celandine	0	0	4	2	0	1.2
Thistle	0	2	11	0	0	2.6
Dandelion	6	0	2	9	4	4.2

Line and belt transects

Line and belt transects are generally used for sampling a long strip of a habitat, especially where there is a change in some environmental factor such as light intensity, gradient, temperature, soil type or wind speed. They show the biotic effects of abiotic changes, that is, changes in the presence of certain species of plant or slow-moving animals.

A line transect tends to be used in qualitative studies, as it shows the presence or absence of certain species. Belt transects give more detailed results, such as relative numbers of plants and are therefore used in quantitative studies.

Deciding which to use depends mainly on the type of data required and also on any time constraints. For the Leaving Certificate, it is advisable to become familiar with both methods. However, you are required to know about only one of the techniques.

Line transects

Line transects consist of a long piece of string or rope, often with knots at every metre or every 50 cm. The rope is tied to two wooden stakes at either end of the habitat. Line transects are very quick and easy to use to give an overview of the habitat. They are often used on the rocky seashore and can also be used in a grassland or woodland habitat, especially those with gradients and/or changes in environmental factors.

Line transects are useful for studying the effect of changes in light intensity on plant species in the habitat. They can be used from the base of a tree out into a wide open space. This will show that there are changes in the numbers and types of plants as the distance from the tree increases and the intensity of sunlight increases.

Line transect sampling is carried out using one of two methods: continuous sampling or systematic sampling.

- **Continuous sampling:** All of the plants that touch the rope are recorded, along with their position on the transect line. This is a very time-consuming process and the results are not easy to collate and display. Therefore, continuous sampling is usually only done over short distances.

Fig 5.28 A line transect marked off every 50 cm.

- **Systematic sampling:** This is the more widely used method and is much easier to do. The line transect has knots or marks at regular intervals, such as every 50 cm or metre. The presence or absence of plant species at each mark on the line transect is recorded. Systematic sampling can then be repeated at different locations within the habitat. This gives a rough estimate of the percentage cover of plant species. Unlike the quadrat method, systematic sampling includes large trees and bushes in the estimate.

Belt transects

Belt transects are a quantitative survey method. They are particularly useful in rocky seashore habitats, where the distribution of organisms varies widely in a very narrow strip of land.

Belt transects are set up using two long ropes. Shorter ropes are tied between the two longer ropes at regular intervals. Sampling is then carried out in each square of the belt transect. Similarly, belt transect studies can be carried out using quadrats (Fig 5.29), with the quadrat being moved along the area of study. The numbers of each organism are recorded all the way along the belt transect.

Fig 5.29A A graduated quadrat being used as a belt transect in a grassland habitat.

Fig 5.29B A graduated quadrat being used as a belt transect on a rocky seashore.

Quantitative study of animals

Slow-moving animals, such as barnacles and limpets, can be quantified using quadrats. However, most animals in a habitat are fast moving and have to be quantified using the capture-recapture method.

In the capture-recapture method, animals are located and caught using one of the methods listed earlier in this chapter. For example, insects can be caught using pitfall traps, pooters and beating trays. Fast-moving animals can be caught using mammal traps.

- If you are using mammal traps, ensure there is enough food and bedding for the animal until the mammal trap is collected.
- Ensure any mammals caught are handled with care and under the supervision of your teacher and/or your ecology instructor.

For the Leaving Certificate Biology course, it is best to use the capture-recapture method on snails, which are abundant in small woodlands and forests.

Snails live on old trees, which have many crevices that enable the snail to hide from predators. They can be located and collected easily as they leave a distinctive shiny trail.

- Mark the snail's shell.
- Make sure that the mark is not obvious (so as not to make the snails visible to predators) and that it will not wash off in the rain. A permanent, fine-tip black marker is ideal.
- Place the snails back in the same position.
- Record the number of snails caught.

The study of an ecosystem — Chapter 5

- Leave enough time (one week) for the marked snails to redistribute themselves among the population in the habitat.
- On return to the habitat, capture a number of snails.
- Record this number. Count the number of marked snails from the first visit.
- Use the following formula to estimate the number of snails in the habitat.

$$\text{Number of snails} = \frac{\text{Caught 1st} \times \text{Caught 2nd}}{\text{Marked 2nd}}$$

NOTE: 'Caught 1st' refers to the number of snails caught on the first visit.
'Caught 2nd' is the number of snails caught on the second visit.
'Marked 2nd' is the number of marked snails found on the second visit.

Possible errors

Errors occur in all experiments. A large difference will occur between researchers using quadrats, as estimating percentage cover is so subjective. Error in subjective estimates can be as high as 20 per cent, which is unacceptable for detailed and accurate studies such as those of the rainforest or delicate habitats.

Errors also occur when the habitat is studied at only one time of year. In order to conduct a full study of a habitat, it should be studied at different times of the year, such as summer, autumn, winter and spring.

One of the principles of experimentation is to conduct experiments with a large sample size. Not having a large enough sample size in a quantitative study of a habitat is a source of error.

- When using a quadrat, carry out at least ten quadrat counts. This is usually enough to obtain a general estimate of the types and quantities of plants in the habitat.
- In the capture-recapture method, set at least ten mammal traps at each visit.
- If you are counting snails as part of your capture-recapture method, try to collect and mark snails from at least three different trees on your first visit. On your second visit, collect the snails from the same three trees.

Errors also occur in identifying animals and plants. In order to minimise this, use a detailed identification key.

Practical activity: investigate three abiotic factors present in the selected ecosystem

Abiotic factors affect the type of organisms that can survive. Organisms show adaptations to abiotic factors that enable them to survive in their habitat.

Abiotic factors are environmental factors that are non-living.

Abiotic factors include:

- Air temperature
- Soil temperature
- Water temperature
- Salinity (salt content)
- Soil type
- Humus (organic) content of soil
- Soil pH
- Wind speed
- Aspect (direction in which the habitat is facing)
- Slope
- Current
- Wave action
- Degree of exposure

For example, certain plants have adapted to acidic soil (Fig 5.30), some require alkaline soil and some require neutral soil.

Some fish require salt water, some require fresh water and some are capable of living in both!

Certain trees can survive at high altitude on a steep slope (conifers), whereas others require flat land at low altitude with a plentiful water supply (broad-leaf trees).

Most bacteria require oxygen to survive (aerobes); some cannot use oxygen but tolerate its presence (aerotolerant anaerobic bacteria); some use oxygen but do not depend on it (facultative anaerobic bacteria) and some are killed by the mere presence of oxygen (obligate anaerobic bacteria).

Some plants require direct sunlight, some require only small amounts of direct sunlight and some can only live where there is very little direct sunlight.

- Air temperature can be measured using a simple digital thermometer.
- Soil pH is measured using a pH meter or by using universal indicator and a flocculent, such as barium sulphate, that causes the soil particles to form flakes and fall to the bottom of the solution.
- Wind speed can be measured using a digital anemometer.
- Humus content of soil is measured by burning off the organic component and determining the loss in weight using a weighing scales.
- Slope is determined using a line transect, spirit level and metre stick.
- Currents are measured using a stream flow meter.

You must study three abiotic factors in your habitat study.

Fig 5.30 A soil pH meter showing acidic soil.

Practical activity: identify one adaptation of any organism in the selected ecosystem

Adaptations: structural, competitive and behavioural

All living organisms show special adaptations that enable them to survive, prosper and reproduce in their habitat.

Structural examples include:
- Spikes on a hedgehog to protect it from predators.
- Birds' wings that enable flight.
- A cheetah being able to run very fast to catch its prey.
- Pine trees having thin needles to avoid excess water loss on the steep mountainous regions in which they grow.

Competitive examples include:
- The colours of a male duck's feathers contributing to their attractiveness to the female ducks and, therefore, contributing to their ability to reproduce.
- The ability of an organism to camouflage itself increases its chances of surviving predation; for example, grasshoppers are green, making them more difficult to see; caterpillars are also camouflaged.

Behavioural examples include:
- A leatherback turtle making its way to the open ocean as soon as it hatches.
- A spider being able to spin a web to catch its prey (insects).
- Many species of birds singing to attract mates. This increases their chances of reproducing.

The study of an ecosystem **Chapter 5**

> **NOTE** For the Leaving Certificate Biology course, you should be able to name one adaptation shown by one organism you studied as part of your ecology habitat study.

- A commonly studied animal in the woodland habitat is the snail (Fig 5.31). It has a shell to protect itself against predators. It is also camouflaged against its surroundings, making it difficult for predators to pick it out.
- A commonly studied animal on the rocky seashore is the limpet. It also has a shell to protect itself from predators when it is exposed to the air.

Fig 5.31 A garden snail.

Practical activity: identify the roles the organisms play in energy transfer by constructing food chains, a food web and a pyramid of numbers

Energy is transferred from organism to organism via food chains and food webs. As part of your habitat study, you should be able to construct a simple food chain, a food web and a pyramid of numbers from the organisms you found in your habitat. Remember, you must always start with a producer (a green plant).

Fig 5.32 shows a woodland food chain.

Oak tree → Aphid → Spider → Thrush

Fig 5.32 A simple woodland food chain.

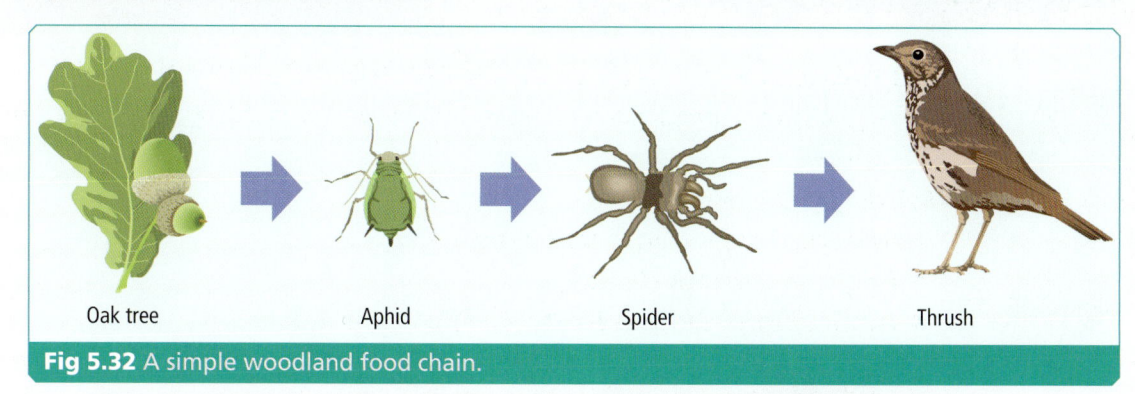

Fig 5.33 shows a pyramid of numbers for a woodland habitat.

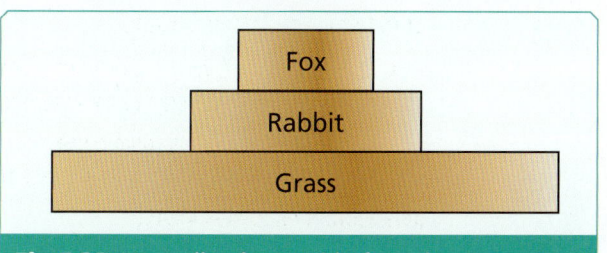

Fox / Rabbit / Grass

Fig 5.33 A woodland pyramid of numbers.

75

Unit 1 Biology: the study of life

Fig 5.34 shows a woodland food web.

Fig 5.34 A woodland food web.

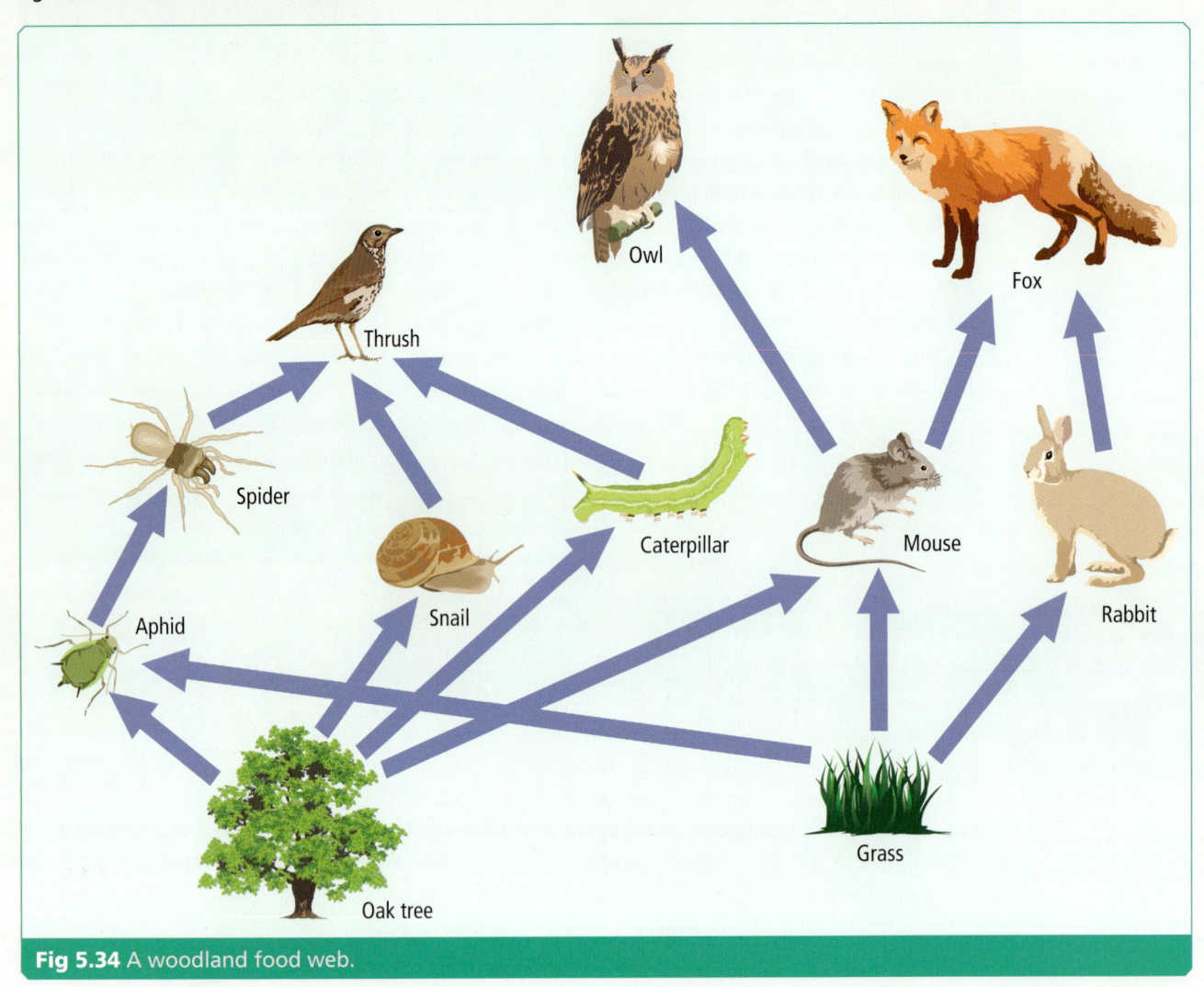

Fig 5.35 shows a food chain from a rocky seashore.

Zooplankton → Barnacle → Dog whelk → Herring gull

Fig 5.35 A rocky seashore food chain.

The study of an ecosystem   Chapter 5

Fig 5.36 shows a pyramid of numbers for a rocky seashore.

Fig 5.36 A rocky seashore pyramid of numbers.

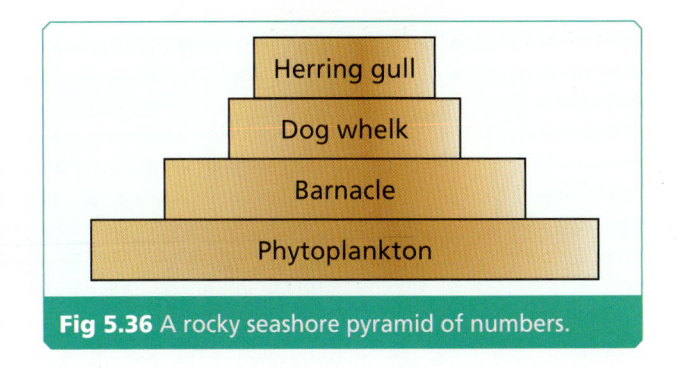

Fig 5.37 shows a rocky seashore food web.

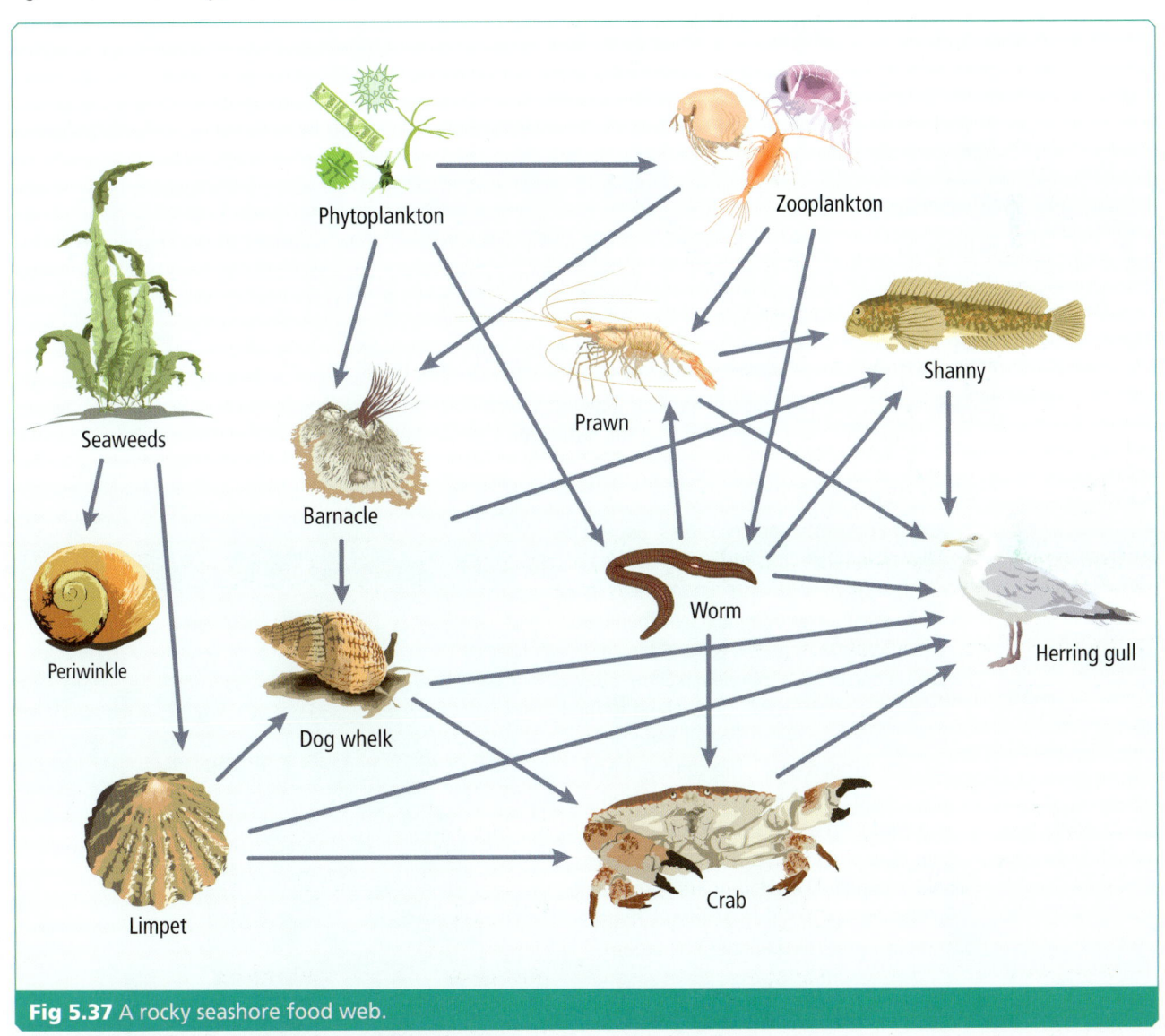

Fig 5.37 A rocky seashore food web.

Analysis and assessment

Once you have completed your habitat study you must analyse your results. This involves asking questions such as:

- Are there any ways in which you could improve upon your habitat study?
- Were there any organisms present that you did not expect to find?
- Were there any organisms not present that you had expected to find?
- In your study of abiotic factors, was there a pattern of organism distribution consistent with a change in the abiotic factor(s) measured?
- Has human activity affected your habitat in any way?
- Was there any pollution in your habitat? If so, did this affect the organisms?
- How many predator-prey relationships can you list from the animals identified in your habitat?
- What might happen if the top consumer were removed?

Local ecological issues

As part of your analysis, you should look at local ecological issues related to your habitat. We will look at some issues below.

Woodland

In the recent past, Ireland's forests and woodlands were cleared to make way for farming. This greatly reduced populations of certain species, particularly trees. The Native Woodland Scheme is one organisation working to eliminate or reduce the number of non-native tree species. Many woodlands around the country are being cleared of non-native coniferous tree species, such as Norway spruce, and being replaced with native trees such as alder, aspen, birch, oak, rowan, willow, elm, beech and ash.

The invasion of the grey squirrel has had a devastating impact on the red squirrel. Conservationists have tried to control the grey squirrel so that the native red squirrel can flourish.

Rocky seashore

- **Beach erosion:** Beach erosion is caused by wave action moving sand along the beach over long periods of time. Entire beaches can be washed away, which can then lead to land erosion. A recent case of beach erosion occurred at a beach in Dingle Bay, County Kerry. In 2008, a new island formed after a sand spit (extension of sand out to sea) was eroded away. The sand spit had a rare sand dune system and was used as a wintering ground for Brent geese and other bird species. These dunes have been completely eroded. There is fear that further erosion will threaten land, houses and businesses in the inner bay area.
- **Seashore pollution:** Oil spills, sewage release, illegal dumping, collection of plastic wastes are all types of pollution that affect our rocky seashores. Pollution affects all organisms in the habitat. Twenty-nine strict criteria must be met before a beach can be given blue flag (pollution free) status.

Fig 5.38 Beach erosion.

Chapter 5 Questions

1. Distinguish between the following:
   (a) *Fauna* and *flora*
   (b) *Producer* and *consumer*
   (c) *Qualitative* and *quantitative*
   (d) *Percentage frequency* and *percentage cover*
   (e) *Subjective estimate* and *objective estimate*
   (f) *Line transect* and *belt transect*
   (g) *Continuous sampling* and *systematic sampling*
   (h) *Phytoplankton* and *zooplankton*
   (i) *Pitfall trap* and *cryptozoic trap*
   (j) *Identification key* and *map scale*

2. Name the ecosystem you studied and answer the following questions:
   (a) Name **three** different habitats within your chosen ecosystem.
   (b) Name **five** flora and **five** fauna you found.
   (c) Briefly describe the structure of **one** flora and **one** fauna from your habitat study.
   (d) Give an adaptation of **one** flora and **one** fauna, which enables their survival in the habitat you studied.
   (e) Name a producer from your habitat.
   (f) Name a consumer from your habitat.

3. Answer the following based on the apparatus you used for your habitat study:
   (a) Name and sketch **five** pieces of apparatus you used.
   (b) Explain how you used each type of apparatus.

4. (a) What are abiotic factors?
   (b) Name **three** abiotic factors you measured in your habitat.
   (c) Explain how you measured the **three** abiotic factors.

5. (a) Name **two** methods for quantifying flora in a habitat.
   (b) Explain the difference between these two methods in terms of:
      (i) Type of quadrat used
      (ii) Subjective or objective
      (iii) Accuracy of estimate
      (iv) Ease of use

6. (a) Name an animal you quantified in your habitat.
   (b) Explain how you quantified the named animal.

7. A student selected a woodland habitat to study and marked out an area of length 20 m and width 5 m. He quantified the number of ferns in his habitat. He obtained the following results:

Quadrat number	Presence/absence
1	
2	
3	✓
4	✓
5	
6	
7	✓
8	✓
9	
10	

   (a) What type of quadrat may have been used for this study?
   (b) Explain why most of the boxes under the heading presence/absence were left blank.
   (c) What is the percentage frequency of ferns in this habitat?
   (d) What does the percentage frequency tell you about the relative abundance of ferns in the habitat?

8. A detailed quadrat study was carried out in which the abundance of the ferns was estimated. The results are shown in the following table:

Quadrat number	Percentage cover
1	0
2	0
3	25
4	50
5	0
6	0
7	75
8	40
9	0
10	0

Unit 1 Biology: the study of life

(a) What type of quadrat may have been used for this study?

(b) There are **two** methods of determining percentage cover.
  (i) Describe each of the **two** methods.
  (ii) Which of the **two** methods is more accurate and why?

(c) What is the total percentage cover for the ferns in this habitat?

9 A capture-recapture experiment was carried out to estimate the number of hares in a grassland habitat. The numbers from the two visits to the habitat were:

First visit: 8 hares

Second visit: 7 hares (of which 3 hares had tags)

(a) Explain how the capture-recapture technique is carried out.

(b) What would have been an appropriate number of traps to set?

(c) Explain how the traps would be set up to minimise discomfort for the hares.

(d) Estimate the number of hares present in the grassland habitat.

(e) Explain why this calculation is only an estimate and not an accurate number for the population.

(f) How could this experiment be made more accurate?

10 At a time when the tide was out, a strip of the seashore from the splash zone down to the bottom of the intertidal zone was sampled for **five** different organisms. A belt transect was used in conjunction with a quadrat. Ten quadrats were used along the strip of seashore. The results are shown in the table below:

(a) What kind of quadrat study was carried out?

(b) What do the results tell us about the distribution of organisms on the seashore?

(c) Calculate the percentage frequency of each of the **five** organisms from the data.

Quadrat number	Limpet	Barnacle	Periwinkle	Bladder wrack	Starfish
1	✓		✓		
2	✓	✓			
3	✓	✓	✓		
4		✓			
5	✓	✓			
6		✓		✓	
7				✓	
8				✓	
9				✓	✓
10				✓	

Chapter 5 Sample examination questions

1 (a) (i) What is meant in ecology by a quantitative survey?
  (ii) What is a quadrat frame?

(b) (i) In the case of a named plant, describe how you would carry out a quantitative survey in the ecosystem that you have studied.
  (ii) Describe how you recorded the results of your survey.
  (iii) Suggest a possible source of error in your study.

Section B, Question 8 Ordinary Level 2006

HL 2 (i) In relation to a study of an ecosystem, distinguish clearly between *qualitative* and *quantitative* surveys by writing a sentence about each.

(ii) How were you able to identify the different plants in the ecosystem that you investigated?

(iii) Describe how you carried out a quantitative survey of the major plant species.

(iv) Give **two** possible sources of error that may have arisen in the course of your survey.

Section C, Question 10 (c) Higher Level 2011

Chapter 5 Mind map

The study of an ecosystem — Chapter 5

> **Woodland and rocky seashore are two commonly studied habitats.**

Flora (photosynthetic organisms) and fauna (animals) are found in both the woodland and rocky seashore habitats.

Woodland habitats include:
- Canopy layer
- Shrub layer
- Ground level
- Leaf litter (detritus layer)
- Deadwood
- Soil

Habitats on the rocky seashore include:
- Splash zone
- Intertidal zone
- Rock pool
- Littoral zone

Choose your habitat, mark it out and draw a plan view map. Your map should include a scale, the direction north and a legend.

Equipment needed for the habitat study includes:
- Pooter
- Pitfall trap
- Cryptozoic trap
- Mammal trap
- Beating tray
- Sweep net
- Plankton net
- Electrofishing equipment
- Soil sieve
- Tullgren funnel
- Spirit level
- Anemometer
- Light meter

- **Qualitative method:** recording the presence or absence of a particular species native to the habitat.
- **Quantitative method:** obtaining an estimate of the numbers of organisms of a particular species native to the habitat. Methods include percentage frequency and percentage cover.
- **Percentage frequency:** the chances of finding a given species in a habitat.
- **Percentage cover:** the area of ground occupied by aerial parts of plants.

- **Line transects:** a long piece of string knotted at regular intervals and placed along the length of a habitat. Useful for habitats with varying conditions, such as a gradient, changes in light intensity, or water/air currents.
- **Continuous sampling:** list all plants present along the transect. **Systematic sampling:** list plants that touch the transect at the regular knots.
- **Belt transects:** placing two long pieces of string or rope along the length of the habitat knotted at regular intervals **or** place one long piece of rope along the length of the habitat and sample the organisms using a graduated quadrat.

Quantitative study of animals
- Record numbers caught.
- Mark animals and place back in habitat.
- After period of time, catch a number of animals and record number.
- Record number with the mark from the first capture.
- Calculate the total number of animals using:

$$\text{Number of animals} = \frac{\text{Caught 1st} \times \text{Caught 2nd}}{\text{Marked 2nd}}$$

Organisms adapt to survive in a particular habitat, for example, snails and limpets have protective shells.

Analysing results, ask questions such as:
- Are there any ways in which you could improve upon your habitat study?
- Were there any organisms present that you did not expect to find?
- Were there any organisms not present that you had expected to find?
- In your study of abiotic factors, was there a pattern of organism distribution consistent with a change in the abiotic factor(s) measured?

You must be able to discuss an ecological issue related to your habitat.

Abiotic factors are non-living environmental factors. They include:
- Air temperature
- Soil temperature
- Water temperature
- Salinity
- Soil pH
- Wind speed
- Slope

Unit 2
The Cell

6	Cell structure	84
7	Diversity of cells	94
8	Movement through cell membranes	99
9	Enzymes	103
10	Energy carriers (HL only)	118
11	Photosynthesis	121
12	Respiration	132
13	The cell cycle	144
14	DNA and RNA	155
15	Protein synthesis	166
16	Inheritance and genetic crosses	171
17	Variation and evolution	193
18	Genetic engineering	203

Chapter 6 Cell structure

Learning objectives After studying this chapter, you should be able to:
- Use a light microscope and be familiar with its parts.
- Describe the function of a transmission electron microscope.
- Describe the structure of a plant and an animal cell and the functions of the organelles present in each.
- Prepare and examine one animal cell and one plant cell, stained and unstained using a light microscope.
- HL ▶ Define *prokaryotic* and *eukaryotic* cells.

Introduction

As we learned in Chapter 2, cells are the smallest unit of living organisms that show the five characteristics of living things. Cells are the basic functional unit of life.

This chapter is about the structure of animal and plant cells. An artist's impression of a typical animal cell (Fig 6.1) and a plant cell (Fig 6.2) are shown below. Note that all animals and plants are multicellular organisms. Therefore, the cells shown in Fig 6.1 are cells that are always part of a tissue (group of similar cells). Note also that many other structures are shown in both diagrams. However, only the important parts related to the Leaving Certificate Biology course are explained below.

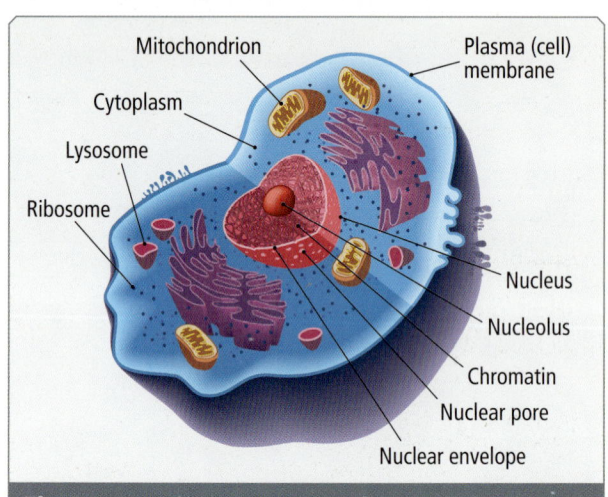

Fig 6.1 An artist's impression of an animal cell.

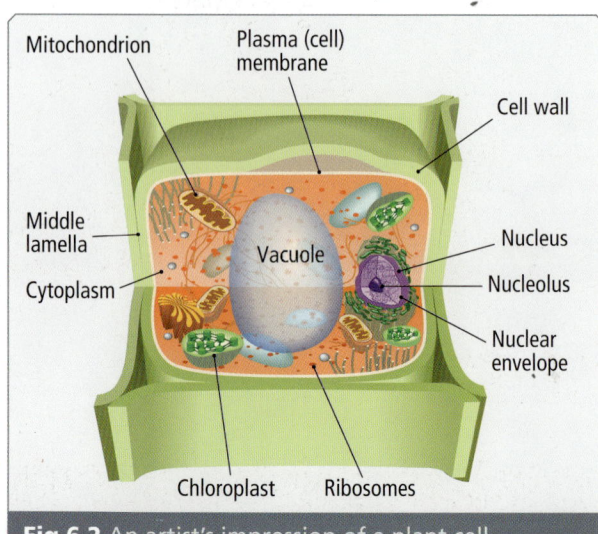

Fig 6.2 An artist's impression of a plant cell.

Ultrastructure of animal and plant cells

Cell components

> An **organelle** is a specialised membrane-bound compartment within a cell that has a specific function.

All cells have organelles and other cell components that enable them to carry out the processes necessary for life. The cell components and organelles common to most cells are listed below.

- **Cell membrane** (made from phospholipids arranged into a bilayer): is the boundary of the cell and controls what enters and leaves the cell. It also maintains the integrity of the cell and holds the contents in.
- **Cytoplasm:** consists of the cytosol (liquid portion of the cell, composed of mostly water) and the organelles. It functions as the medium in which all the chemical processes of the cell occur.
- **Nucleus:** contains the DNA, which is organised into chromosomes. Chromosomes are usually in a thin, thread-like form called chromatin (see Chapters 13 and 14). The nucleus is the control centre of the cell.

It sends chemical signals to all areas of the cell. It has a double membrane (nuclear envelope) separating it from the rest of the cell's contents. There are many **nuclear pores** in the nuclear envelope. These are small holes in the double membrane that allow chemicals to pass in and out of the nucleus.

- **DNA (deoxyribonucleic acid):** is located within the nucleus in structures called chromosomes. DNA contains the genetic code for the manufacture of all proteins needed by the organism.
- **Nucleolus:** is found within the nucleus. There may be more than one nucleolus. They assemble ribosomes, which are then transported to the cytoplasm.
- **Ribosomes** are made from RNA (ribonucleic acid) and are located in the cytoplasm. They are responsible for making the proteins needed by the cell or surrounding cells.
- **Mitochondria:** are the power houses of the cell, and are responsible for carrying out the major metabolic process of respiration (production of energy). They are thought to have originated from bacteria invading more complex cells in the early stages of life on Earth. Mitochondria have their own DNA and can replicate by themselves.
- **Lysosomes:** are organelles that contain enzymes, which are responsible for breaking down any cell debris, viruses, bacteria or worn-out organelles.
- **Chloroplasts** (*apply to plants cells only*): are the organelles responsible for making food using sunlight, water and carbon dioxide. This food is then burned in respiration or stored. Chloroplasts, like mitochondria, are also thought to have originated from bacteria invading complex cells. They also have their own DNA and replicate themselves.
- **Cell wall** (*applies to plants cells only*): is the strong rigid structure responsible for giving plants their strength and shape. It also acts as a protective layer against pathogens.
- **Middle lamella** (*applies to plant cells only*): is cement that binds cell walls together, maintaining the structure of the plant.
- **Large central vacuole** (*applies to plants cells only*): is a large fluid-filled sac that takes up most of the volume of a plant cell. It has many functions, including:
  - Storage of water, food and wastes.
  - Maintaining the shape of the plant cell.
  - Isolating harmful substances.

Microscope

All cells are microscopic, meaning they can be seen only with the aid of a microscope. The light microscope is the most commonly used microscope in biology. The function of any microscope is to magnify small specimens. As part of your course, you will be using the light microscope to view animal cells, plant cells and a thin section of a soft-stemmed (herbaceous) plant (such as geranium).

There are usually four lenses on light microscopes – three objective lenses and one eyepiece lens.

> **NOTE** Light microscopes are also known as compound microscopes.

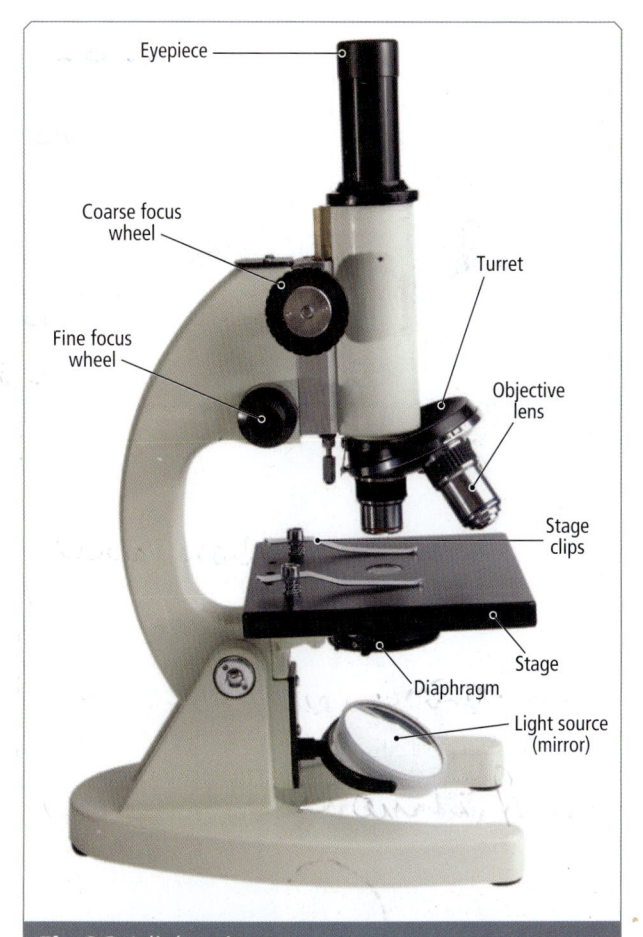

Fig 6.3 A light microscope.

Functions of the parts of the light microscope

- **Eyepiece:** contains the eyepiece lens. The eyepiece magnifies the image. It is through the eyepiece that you view the specimen.
- **Nosepiece/turret:** is the rotatable part of the light microscope that carries the objective lenses.
- **Objective lenses:** collect light directly from the specimen and magnify the image produced. The image is directed to the eyepiece lens for further magnification.
- **Stage:** is where the specimen (usually on a glass slide) is placed.
- **Stage clips:** are used to hold the slide in place.
- **Diaphragm:** controls the amount of light passing up through the hole in the stage.
- **Light source (sometimes a mirror):** shines light up through the hole in the stage and through the specimen.
- **Coarse focus wheel:** makes large adjustments in the clarity of the image (usually by moving the stage up and down)
- **Fine focus wheel:** makes small adjustments to the clarity of the image by moving the stage up and down.

The eyepiece lens is usually a 10x lens, meaning that by itself it magnifies an image ten times. A light microscope usually has three objective lenses, which have various magnifying abilities. The three most common lenses are a 4x, a 10x and a 40x. The total magnification is calculated by multiplying the magnifying power of the eyepiece lens by the magnifying power of the objective lens.

- When the 4x power objective lens is used, the total magnification seen is then 40x.
- When the 10x objective lens is used, the total magnification seen is 100x.
- When the 40x objective lens is used, the total magnification seen is 400x.

Light microscopes can generate a maximum magnification of approximately 1000x. Higher magnification lenses are available, but no greater detail is seen as the wavelength of light is too long.

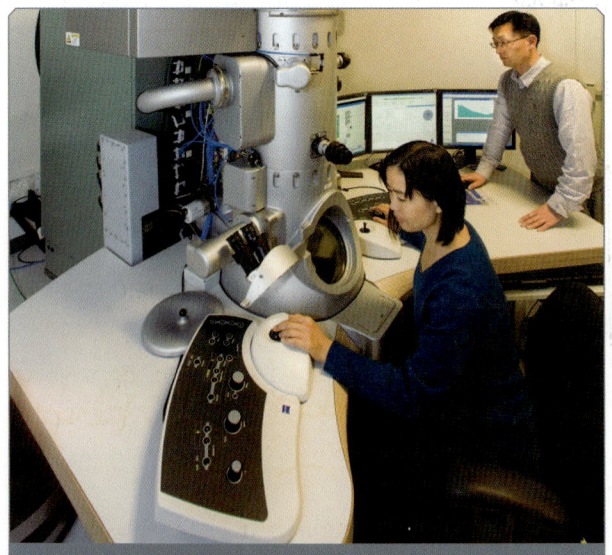

Transmission electron microscope (TEM)

In order to get higher magnifications, we need to use a special type of microscope called a transmission electron microscope. These are extremely powerful microscopes that are capable of magnifying up to 1,000,000 times! They can even view atoms.

Transmission electron microscopes use a particle beam of electrons that strikes the specimen and travels right through it and is diffracted (or deflected) along the way. The electrons are brought into focus using magnets (instead of glass lenses as for light). The image is produced on an electron-detecting screen or photographic film. Fig 6.5 shows a mitochondrion viewed with a transmission electron microscope. An image with this level of detail would be impossible with a light microscope. The colours are put in after the image has been obtained.

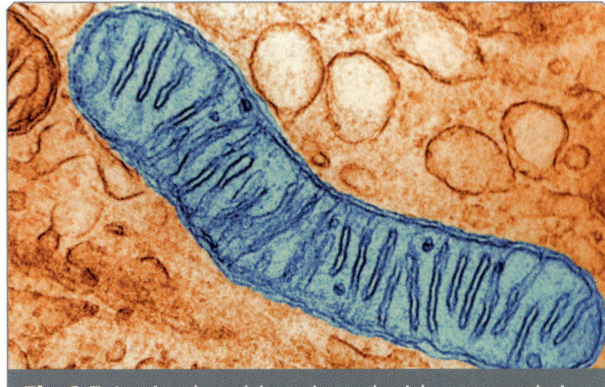

Fig 6.4 A scientist using a transmission electron microscope.

Fig 6.5 A mitochondrion viewed with a transmission electron microscope.

Cell structure   Chapter 6

Practical activity: to be familiar with and use the light microscope

Microscopes are expensive pieces of equipment and must be handled with care. It is very important that you know the procedures for using a light microscope properly.

Method

1. Before turning on the light microscope, ensure the lowest power objective lens (4x) is in position; the stage is at its lowest position and the diaphragm is in the closed position – it is not letting any light through (your teacher or lab assistant will help you).
2. Place the slide on the stage (do not use the clips at this time).
3. Turn the microscope on and slowly open the diaphragm until light appears in the circular field of view through the eyepiece.
4. Ensure the area of the slide you want to magnify is in line with both the hole in the stage and the lowest power objective lens.
5. Looking through the eyepiece and using the coarse focus wheel, slowly and carefully move the stage towards the objective lens until you see an image come into focus.

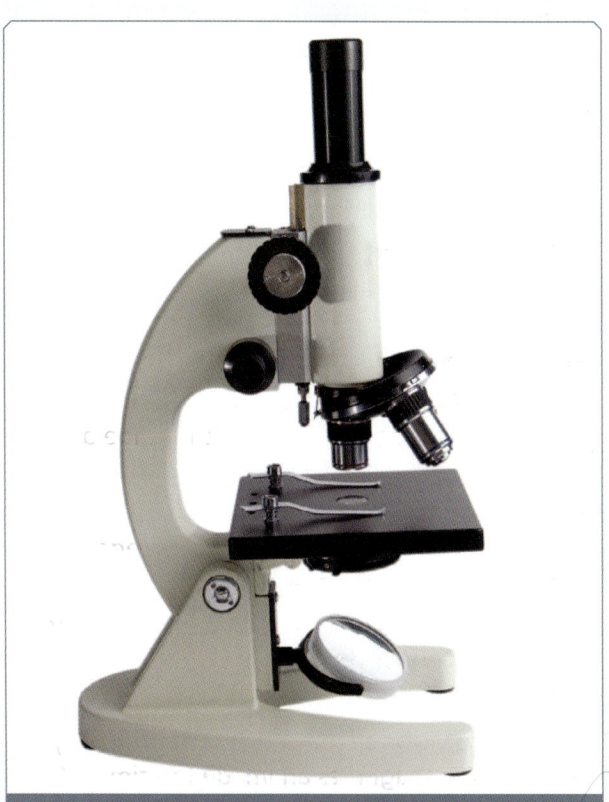

Fig 6.6 A light microscope.

6. When the image starts coming into focus, use the fine focus wheel (if your microscope has one) until the image is clear.
7. At this stage, clip the slide into position. Check the clarity of the image again and refocus using the fine focus wheel if necessary.
8. If you wish to use a higher magnification, switch to the next one up. Do not go straight to the highest power objective lens!
9. As long as you rotate the turret/nosepiece carefully and slowly, the image should still be in focus when you look through the eyepiece. If the image is not clear, then use the fine focus wheel to refocus.
10. You can then switch to the highest power lens by slowly and carefully rotating the turret so that the 40x lens clicks into place.
11. When you have finished viewing the specimen, **do not** remove the slide with the higher power lens in place. You should first move the lowest power lens into position, lower the stage using the coarse focus wheel and then remove the slide carefully. This will prevent damage to the slide and/or the objective lenses.

> **NOTE** Exercise extra care with step 10 as sometimes the highest power lens may not fit above the slide and may damage the slide and/or the objective lens.

Unit 2 The Cell

Practical activity: prepare and examine animal cells (human cheek cells) unstained and stained using the light microscope at 100x and 400x

Animal cells come in many different shapes and sizes. A cheek cell is a typical animal cell that is very easy to obtain, stain and view under the light microscope. You must view cheek cells unstained and stained (using methylene blue). Methylene blue stains tissue by binding to DNA.

SAFETY
Students should wear gloves and a lab coat when handling methylene blue stain.

Method (unstained)

1. Swab the inside of your mouth using a new cotton wool bud.
2. Smear the bud onto a clean glass slide.
3. Place a small drop of water on top of smear (to prevent the cells from drying out).
4. Slowly lower a cover slip using a mounted needle from a 45° angle. This reduces the chances of trapping an air bubble. A coverslip protects the specimen and prevents it from drying out.
5. Before placing the slide on the stage, ensure the light microscope is set up as described in the procedure for using a light microscope.
6. View the cheek cells at 100x and 400x magnifications.
7. Make sketches of both fields of view.

Method (stained)

1. Swab the inside of your mouth using a new cotton wool bud.
2. Smear the bud onto a clean glass slide.
3. Place a small drop of water on top of smear.
4. Place a drop of methylene blue on top of the smear.
5. Leave the stain for 2–3 minutes.
6. Blot off the excess methylene blue using tissue. Do not rub off the smear!
7. Slowly lower a cover slip from a 45° angle using a mounted needle.
8. Before placing the slide on the stage, ensure the light microscope is set up correctly.
9. View the cheek cells at 100x and 400x magnifications.
10. Make sketches of both fields of view.

Results

Fig 6.7A An unstained human cheek cell.

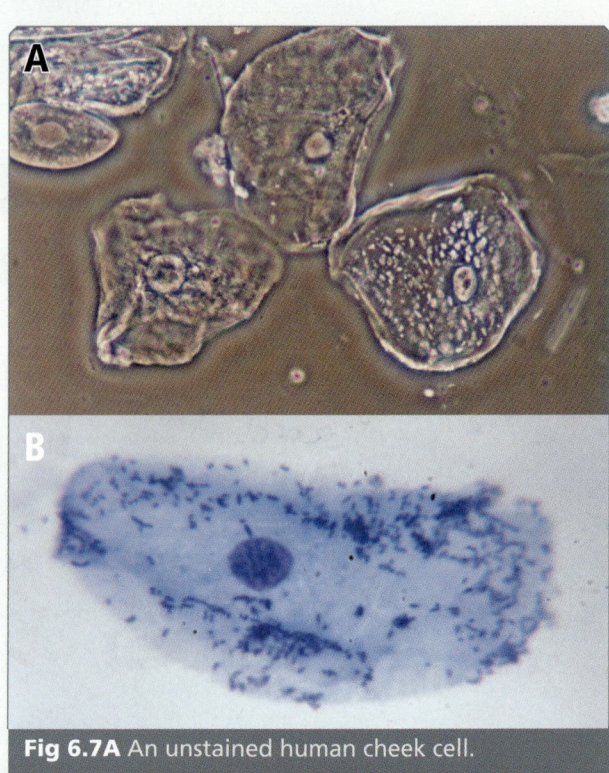

Fig 6.7B A stained human cheek cell. Notice the tiny blue specks – they are stained bacteria. The bacteria come from the mouth.

Cell structure Chapter 6

Conclusion

What did we learn from this practical activity?

- Light microscopes are used to magnify and view small organisms and cells of an organism.
- Lowering the cover slip from 45° prevents bubbles being trapped under the cover slip.
- Staining cells make them much easier to see.

Practical activity questions

1. Explain why cheek cells were used for this practical activity.
2. What stain is used to stain animal cells?
3. Explain how this stain works.
4. Explain why bacteria are always seen with human cheek cells.
5. Why is the cover slip lowered from a 45° angle?
6. With what lens should you first view the animal cells?

HL Prokaryotic cells

> A **prokaryotic cell** is a tiny cell that has neither a membrane-bound nucleus nor membrane-bound organelles.

All bacteria are prokaryotic. This does not mean that bacteria have no DNA. They do have DNA but it is not organised into a membrane-bound nucleus. Bacteria are too small to make having membrane-bound organelles worthwhile. Bacteria range in size from 0.1 to 10 μm (micrometres). They are the only living organisms that are prokaryotic. All other living organisms are eukaryotic.

Eukaryotic cells

> A **eukaryotic cell** is a cell that has a membrane-bound nucleus and membrane-bound organelles.

Eukaryotic cells are much larger than bacteria. They range in size from 10 to 100 μm (micrometres). Therefore it makes structural sense for these more complex cells to compartmentalise themselves. This enables them to keep the many millions of complex chemical reactions that are occurring continuously from interfering with each other. The presence of cell organelles makes for much more efficient metabolism in complex cells.

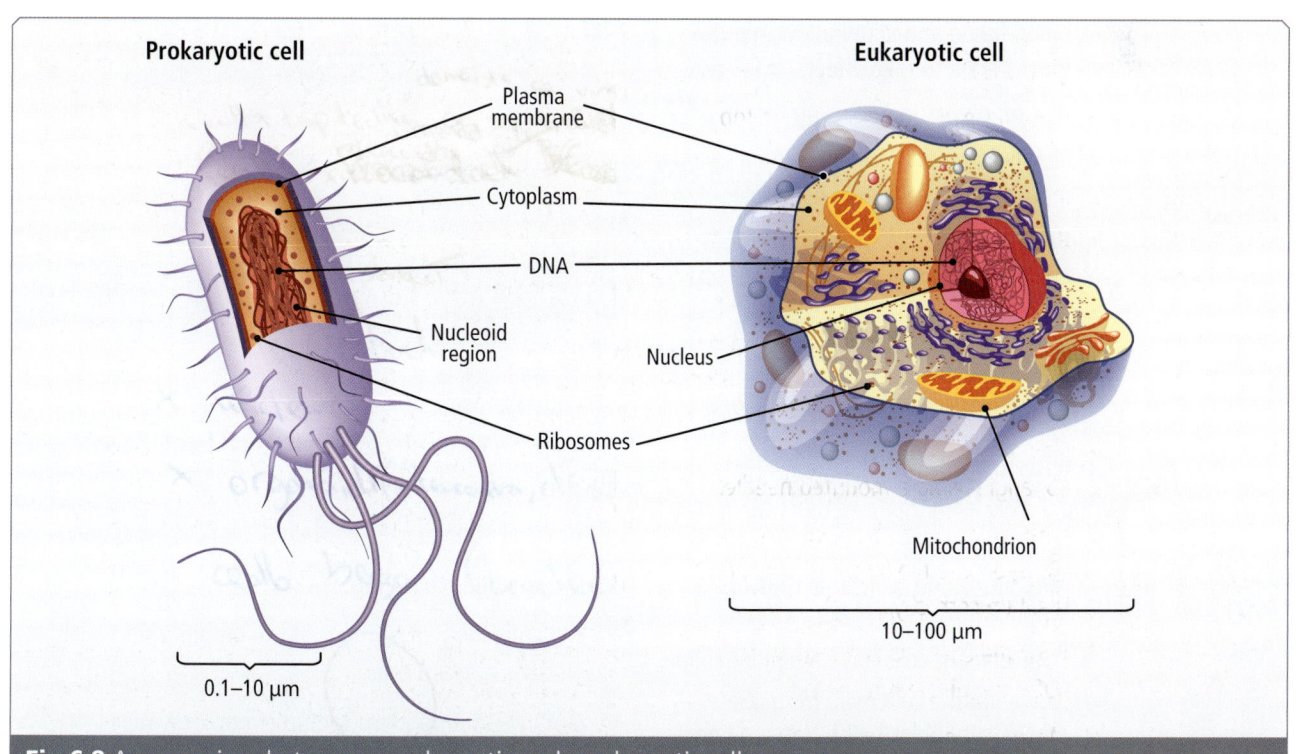

Fig 6.8 A comparison between a prokaryotic and a eukaryotic cell.

Unit 2   The Cell

Practical activity: prepare and examine plant cells (onion cells) unstained and stained using the light microscope at 100x and 400x

Plant cells can be obtained from any plant tissue. It is easy to obtain a single layer of cells from an onion. You must view plant cells, unstained and stained, at 100x and 400x.

Method (unstained)
1. Remove a thin layer of tissue from the inside of an onion.
2. Carefully place this single layer of onion cells on the glass slide and place a drop of water on top of the specimen (to prevent the cells from drying out).
3. Slowly lower a cover slip using a mounted needle from a 45° angle.
4. Before placing the slide on the stage, ensure the light microscope is set up properly.
5. View the onion cells at 100x and 400x.
6. Make sketches of both fields of view.

Method (stained)
1. Remove a thin layer of tissue from the inside of an onion.
2. Carefully place this single layer of onion cells on the glass slide and place a drop of water on top of the specimen.
3. Place a drop of iodine on top of the onion tissue and allow a few minutes for the stain to take effect.
4. Blot off excess iodine using tissue.
5. Slowly lower a cover slip using a mounted needle from a 45° angle.
6. Before placing the slide on the stage, ensure the light microscope is set up properly.
7. View the onion cells at 100x and 400x.
8. Make sketches of both fields of view.

Conclusion
What did we learn from this practical activity?
- Light microscopes magnify small organisms and individual cells of an organism.
- Typical plant cells have a regular shape.
- Lowering the cover slip from 45° prevents bubbles being trapped under the cover slip.
- Staining cells make them much easier to see.

SAFETY

Iodine solution is a mild irritant. Safety goggles, a lab coat and gloves should be worn when handling this product.

Results

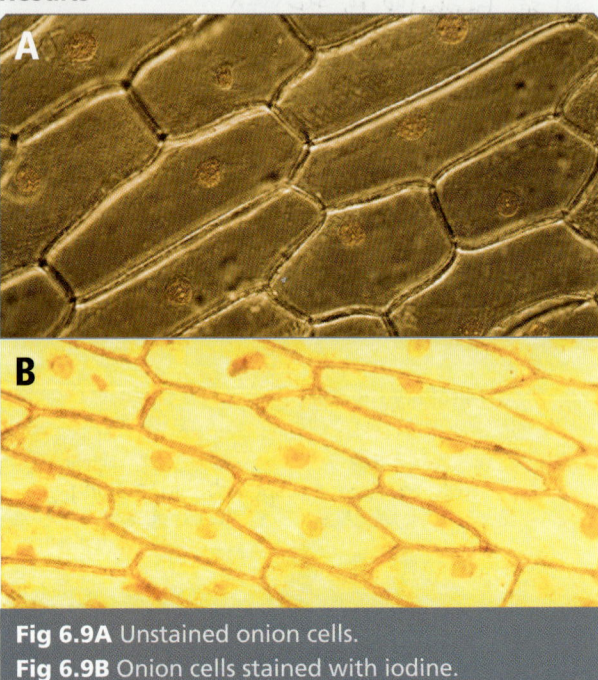

Fig 6.9A Unstained onion cells.
Fig 6.9B Onion cells stained with iodine.

Practical activity questions
1. Explain why onion cells are used for this practical activity.
2. What stain is used to stain plant cells?
3. How does this stain work?
4. Explain why it is important to obtain a single layer of plant cells.
5. Why is it important to add a drop of water?
6. Why is the cover slip lowered from a 45° angle?
7. Which objective lens should you always use first?

Chapter 6 Questions

1. Draw a typical animal cell and a typical plant cell, labelling the following parts where appropriate: *plasma membrane; cell wall, cytoplasm; mitochondrion; chloroplast; nucleus; ribosomes; vacuole.*

2. Draw a table and use it to list the structural differences between animal and plant cells.

3. Give the function of each of the following cell components: *plasma membrane; cell wall, mitochondrion; chloroplast; nucleus; large central vacuole.*

4. What major carbohydrate is responsible for the structure of the cell wall?

5. What major biomolecule is responsible for the structure of the cell membrane?

6. Distinguish between *cytoplasm* and *cytosol*.

7. Where is the DNA located?

8. Answer the following questions in relation to ribosomes:
   (a) Where in the cell are ribosomes mostly found?
   (b) What are ribosomes made from?
   (c) Name the organelle responsible for making ribosomes.
   (d) What is the function of a ribosome?

9. Give **two** differences between the *nuclear envelope* and *cell membrane*.

10. What is a *nuclear pore?* What is the function of a nuclear pore?

11. Name **two** organelles, other than the nucleus, that contain their own DNA. What is the significance of this feature for the named organelles?

12. Answer the following questions in relation to the light microscope:
    (a) Give **two** reasons why it is important to place the lowest power objective lens in position before placing the slide on the stage.
    (b) If the eyepiece lens of a light microscope has a power of 10x and a 40x objective lens is used, what is the total magnification?
    (c) What part of the light microscope do you use to adjust the amount of light entering?
    (d) What is the approximate maximum magnification produced by light microscopes?

13. Copy and complete the following table about light microscopes:

Component	Function
Eyepiece	
Turret	
Objective lens	
	Supports slide
	Holds slide in place
Light source/mirror	
Diaphragm	

14. (a) Explain how a transmission electron microscope (TEM) works.
    (b) Give **one** advantage a TEM has over a light microscope.

HL 15. Distinguish between the terms *prokaryotic* and *eukaryotic*.

16. *Amoeba* (see Chapter 20) is a single-celled organism that uses internal organelles to carry out metabolism. *Amoeba* can be found in fresh water or sea water. Is *Amoeba* prokaryotic or eukaryotic? Explain your answer.

17. Give **one** example of a prokaryotic organism.

Chapter 6 Sample Examination questions

1 (a) Name the parts of the light microscope labelled A and B.

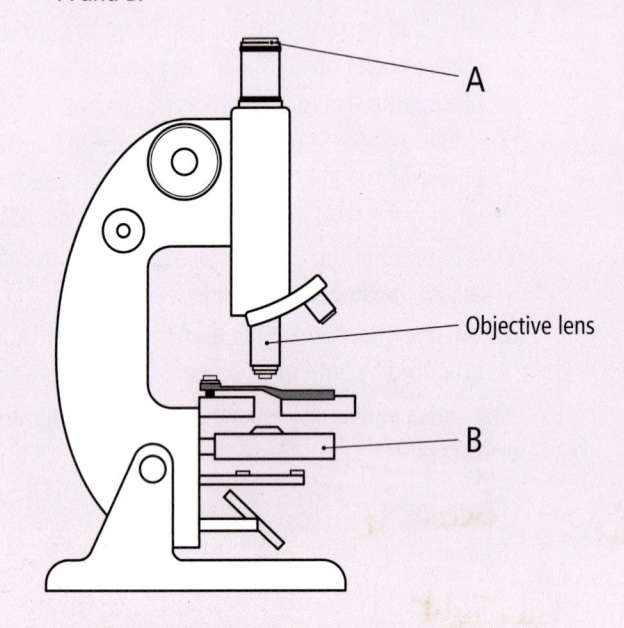

- A
- Objective lens
- B

(b) Answer the following questions in relation to obtaining and staining a sample of plant cells and viewing them under the microscope.

(i) From what plant did you obtain the cells?

(ii) How did you obtain a thin piece of a sample of the cells **and** prepare it for examination?

(iii) What stain did you use on the cells?

(iv) Describe how you applied the stain.

(v) The objective lenses on a microscope are usually labelled 40x, 10x, and 4x. Which objective lens should you begin with when using the microscope?

(vi) Give **one** cell structure that you observed that indicated that the cells were plant cells.

Section B, Question 9 Ordinary Level 2011

HL 2 For which purpose did you use each of the following in the course of your practical studies?

Methylene blue or iodine solution when examining cells with the microscope.

Section B, Question 8 (b)(i) Higher Level 2010

3 (i) State the precise location of the cell membrane in plant cells.

(ii) With what type of cell do you associate with membrane-bound organelles?

(iii) What corresponding term is used to describe bacterial cells?

Section C, Question 14 (c)(i)–(iii) Higher Level 2011

4 (a) State a function of each of the following components of a cell.

(i) Ribosome.

(ii) Cell membrane.

(b) Answer the following questions in relation to the preparation, staining and microscopic observation of a slide of an animal cell.

(i) What type of animal cell did you use? How did you obtain the cell?

(ii) Name the stain that you used. Describe how you applied the stain.

(iii) After staining, a cover slip is placed on the slide. Give a reason for this.

(iv) How did you apply the cover slip? Why did you apply it in this way?

(v) Describe the difference in colour or depth of colour, if any, between the nucleus and cytoplasm when the stained cell was viewed under the microscope.

Section B, Question 8 Higher Level 2006

Chapter 6 Mind map

Cell components
- Cell membrane: maintains cell integrity, controls what enters and leaves.
- Cytoplasm: liquid in which organelles are suspended and medium for metabolism.
- Nucleus: contains the DNA and controls all cell activities.
- Nucleolus: produces ribosomes.
- Ribosomes: make protein.
- Mitochondrion: respiration.
- Lysosomes: engulf viruses, bacteria and cell debris and digest them.
- Chloroplast: photosynthesis.
- Cell wall: maintains cell integrity; supports the structure of cells and tissues; protection.
- Middle lamella: cement that holds plant cells together.
- Large central vacuole: storage.

Viewing animal and plant cells
- Animal cells are stained using methylene blue that specifically stains DNA within the cell.
- Your own cheek cell is an ideal animal cell to use for this practical activity.
- Plant cells are stained using iodine.
- Staining cells makes them easier to see under a light microscope.
- An onion cell is an ideal plant cell to use as they can be easily taken from an onion in the form of a single layer of cells.
- Cover slips must be handled carefully and lowered from a 45° angle to avoid formation of bubbles.

A cell is the basic functional unit of life.

Microscopes
- Microscopes magnify and make visible tiny objects such as living cells.
- Light microscope uses a beam of light to illuminate specimen and magnifies up to 1000x; consists of an eyepiece lens and objective lens.
- To calculate the total magnification of a light microscope, multiply the power of the eyepiece lens with the power of the objective lens.
- Microscopes must be used with due care and attention: always use the lowest power objective lens first, focus and then use the higher objective lenses in turn. When finished always turn to the lowest power objective lens and then remove slide.
- Transmission electron microscope uses a beam of electrons to illuminate specimen and magnifies up to 1,000,000x; the beam of electrons are deflected by specimen, focused using electromagnets and the image is produced on an electron sensor screen.

- **Prokaryotic cells** are tiny cells that have neither a membrane-bound nucleus nor membrane-bound organelles (bacteria). [HL]
- **Eukaryotic cells** are cells that have a membrane-bound nucleus and membrane-bound organelles (human cells).

Chapter 7 Diversity of cells

Learning objectives After studying this chapter, you should be able to:
- Define *tissue, organ and organ system*.
- Name two tissue types from plants and two from animals.
- Name one organ in plants and one from animals.
- Name two animal organ systems.
- Explain tissue culture and give two examples.

Introduction

There are approximately 65 trillion cells in the average human body. There are many different types of cells – approximately 200 different cell types make up the average human body! These cells are grouped into tissues.

Tissues

> A **tissue** is a group of similar cells with a shared function.

NOTE: For Leaving Certificate Biology, you are required to list two animal tissues and two plant tissues only.

Animal tissues

Human and animal tissue types can be broadly categorised into four main groups:

1. Epithelial
2. Muscular
3. Nervous
4. Connective

1 Epithelial tissue

Epithelial tissue consists of a number of types of cells making up the outer and inner coverings of an animal. Human skin is a type of epithelial tissue. Other epithelial tissues include the mucous-producing internal membranes of the nose, mouth and digestive system; the inner lining of the respiratory system; and the inner lining of blood vessels (endothelium).

The function of epithelial tissue depends on its location in the body. Functions include:

- Protection
- Energy storage
- Temperature regulation
- Excretion
- Absorption of nutrients
- Gas exchange

2 Muscular tissue

Muscular tissue in animals is of three distinct types: skeletal, smooth and cardiac.

- Skeletal muscle is voluntary muscle, meaning we have conscious control over it.
- Smooth muscle (muscles in arteries, veins and the digestive system) and cardiac muscle (heart muscle) are involuntary, meaning we have no conscious control over them.

Muscular tissues function in movement.

3 Nervous tissue

Nervous tissue is made up of highly specialised cells with short and/or long projections that are capable of sending electrical impulses. These electrical messages travel around the body of the animal, enabling quick responses to stimuli.

4 Connective tissue

Connective tissue, as its name suggests, connects or binds all other tissues together. It also has other functions. For example, blood is classified as a type of connective tissue that transports substances around the body. Bone, cartilage, tendons and ligaments are other examples of connective tissue that are made of cells embedded in an extracellular (outside the cell) flexible solid. They function in support, protection and movement.

Plant tissues

Plant tissue types can generally be classified into three distinct groups: epidermal, ground and vascular.

1 Epidermal tissue

Epidermal tissue is a layer of cells that make up the outer covering of the plant. They cover the entire plant, from the roots right up to the leaves

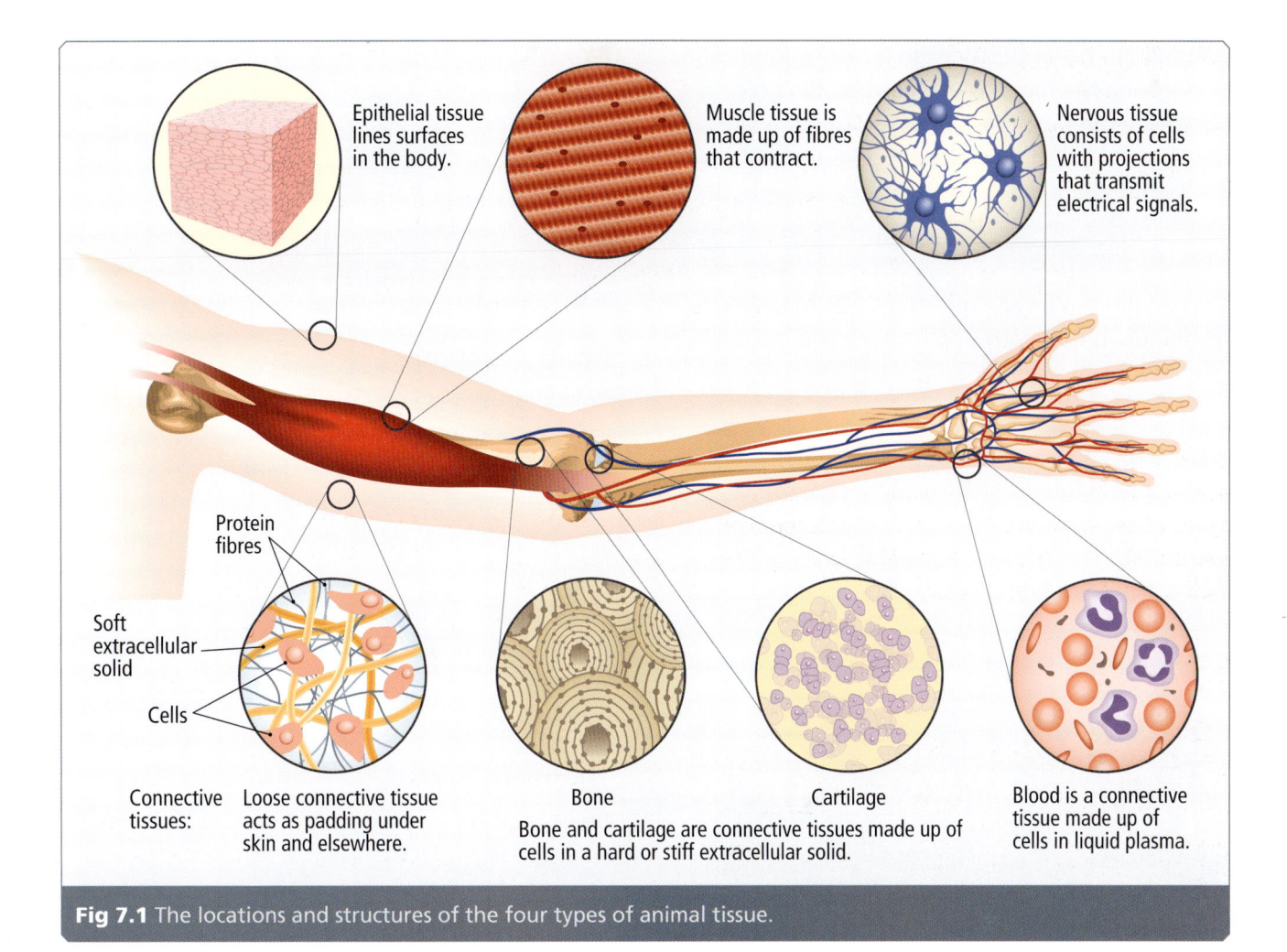

Fig 7.1 The locations and structures of the four types of animal tissue.

(Figure labels: Epithelial tissue lines surfaces in the body. Muscle tissue is made up of fibres that contract. Nervous tissue consists of cells with projections that transmit electrical signals. Connective tissues: Loose connective tissue acts as padding under skin and elsewhere. Protein fibres, Soft extracellular solid, Cells. Bone and cartilage are connective tissues made up of cells in a hard or stiff extracellular solid. Blood is a connective tissue made up of cells in liquid plasma.)

and flowers. The function of epidermal tissue depends on its location. In the aerial parts of the plant, it protects; in the roots it absorbs water and minerals.

2 Ground tissue

Ground tissue is composed of many unspecialised cells that make up the bulk of the plant. The function of ground tissue depends on where it is located within the plant.

- It stores nutrients, such as starch, in storage organs, such as the stem and root. Carrots are an example of a storage organ. They are made up of swollen ground tissue and have lots of starch to enable the carrot plant to survive winter.
- Ground tissue cells present in the leaves of plants function in photosynthesis.
- Ground tissue cells of the root function in transport of water and minerals to the vascular tissue for transport to other areas of the plant.

3 Vascular tissue

The primary function of vascular tissue is the transport of substances around the plant. There are two types of vascular tissue: xylem and phloem.

- Xylem tissue functions in transporting water and minerals from the roots to the aerial parts of the plant. Movement of substances in xylem is always upwards.

Fig 7.2 Veins through a leaf are a type of vascular tissue.

- Phloem tissue functions in transporting food around the plant. Movement within phloem tissue can be either upwards or downwards depending on where the food is needed within the plant.

Tissue culture

Tissue culture is a very important laboratory technique. It has many applications and is used in labs all over the world.

> **Tissue culture** involves growing tissue and/or cells outside of the organism.

Tissue culture is used in cancer research, *in vitro* fertilisation (IVF), skin grafting, vaccine production, and asexual reproduction of plants (micropropagation).

Organs

> An **organ** is a group of tissues joined together to carry out a specialised function.

NOTE For Leaving Certificate Biology, you are required to list one animal organ and one plant organ only.

Animal organs

Animal organs include the heart, lungs, kidneys, stomach and many others.

- The heart pumps blood around the body.
- The lungs bring oxygen into the body for respiration and get rid of carbon dioxide (waste product of respiration).
- The kidneys filter the blood, maintaining waste products at low levels.

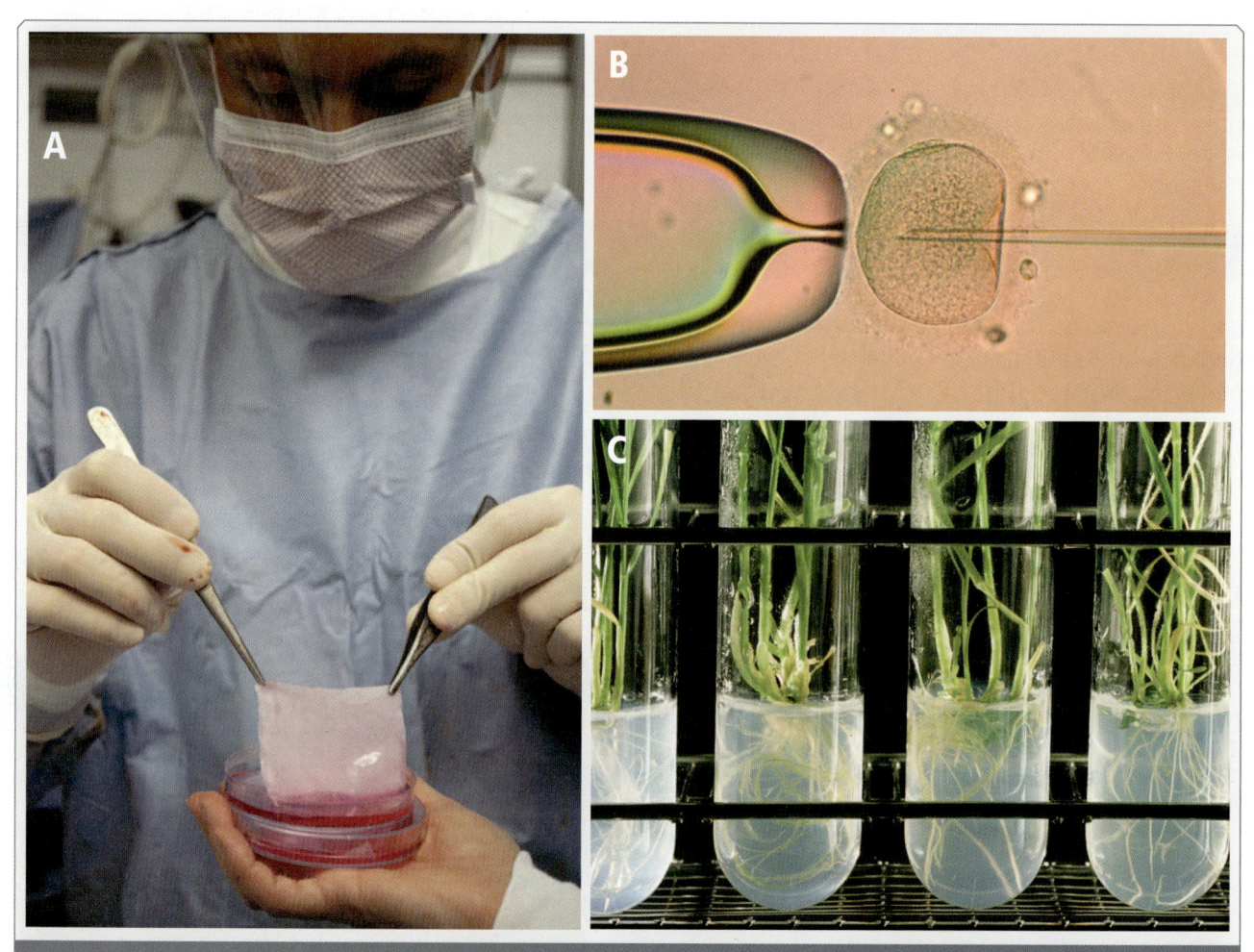

Fig 7.3A Human skin grown in a Petri dish.
Fig 7.3B *In vitro* fertilisation (IVF) – the sperm is being injected into the egg cell.
Fig 7.3C Cereals being grown in a nutrient medium in test-tubes (micropropagation).

Diversity of cells | Chapter 7

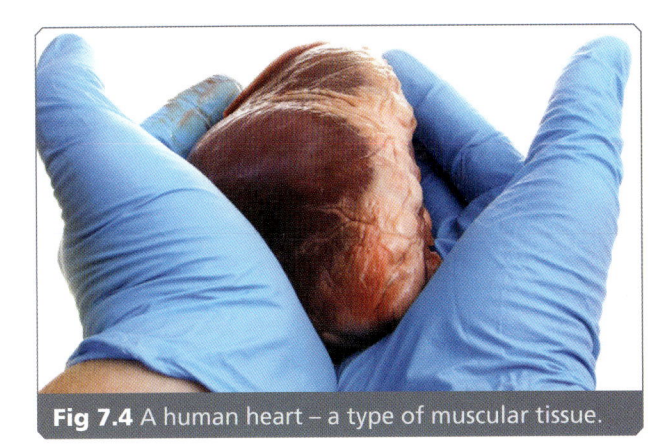

Fig 7.4 A human heart – a type of muscular tissue.

- The stomach kills pathogens (disease-causing microorganisms) present in food by producing acidic conditions. It also functions in chemically and mechanically digesting food.

Plant organs

Plant organs include roots, stems, leaves, flowers and many more.

- The root is responsible for absorbing water and minerals, anchorage of the plant in the ground and sometimes food storage, as in the carrot.
- The stem serves in keeping the aerial parts of the plant supported for photosynthesis and functions in transporting substances up and down the plant.
- The leaf functions in transpiration – the process of losing water from the foliage (*see* Chapter 25), and in photosynthesis.
- The flower functions in sexual reproduction, by the production of gametes (sex cells), fertilisation, seed formation and fruit formation.

Organ systems

> An **organ system** is a group of organs that work together to carry out a number of linked functions.

> **NOTE:** For Leaving Certificate Biology, you are required to list two animal organ systems only.

Major animal systems include the circulatory system (Fig 7.5A), which functions in transporting substances around the body; the digestive system, which functions in breaking down and absorbing food; the excretory system, which functions in getting rid of waste products of metabolism; the reproductive system, which functions in producing gametes that are then used to produce a new individual; the musculoskeletal system, which functions in support and movement; and the nervous system (Fig 7.5B), which functions in sensing and responding to stimuli.

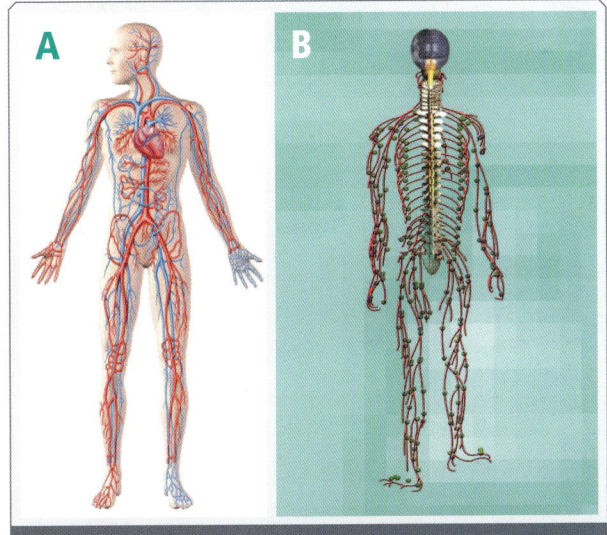

Fig 7.5 The human circulatory system (**A**); the human nervous system (**B**).

Chapter 7 Questions

1. What is a *tissue*?
2. Name **two** types of animal tissue and give **one** function of each type.
3. Name **two** types of plant tissues and give **one** function of each type.
4. (a) What is an *organ*?
   (b) Give **one** example of an animal organ and give its function.
5. Give **one** example of a plant organ and give its function.
6. (a) What is an *organ system*?
   (b) Give **two** examples of organ systems in an animal.
7. (a) What is *tissue culture*?
   (b) Give **two** examples of where tissue culture is used in the scientific/medical community.

Unit 2 The Cell

Chapter 7 Sample examination questions

1 (a) (i) What is a *tissue*?

(ii) Name **two** tissues found in animals.

(b) Tissue culture is used to make a skin graft for patients who have been severely burned.

What is meant by tissue culture?

Section C, Question 11 (a) and (b) (i) Ordinary Level 2007

HL 2 (a) What is a *tissue*?

(b) Name a tissue found in plants.

(c) Give a function of the tissue referred to in part (b).

(d) Name a tissue found in animals.

(e) Give a function of the tissue referred to in part (d).

(f) Explain what is meant by the term *tissue culture*.

(g) Give **one** application of tissue culture.

Section A, Question 4 Higher Level 2010

Chapter 7 Mind map

A **tissue** is a group of similar cells with a shared function.

Two types of animal tissue:
- Epithelial tissue: functions mainly in protection of the animal.
- Muscular tissue: functions in movement.

Two types of plant tissue:
- Epidermal tissue: functions in protection of the plant.
- Ground tissue: functions in support and photosynthesis.

An **organ system** is a group of organs that work together to carry out a number of linked functions.

Two examples of animal organ systems:
- Circulatory system: functions in transporting substances throughout the animal's body.
- Nervous system: functions in transmitting electrical signals around the animal's body.

There are many different types of **cells** in multicellular organisms and they are organised into tissues, organs and organ systems.

- An **organ** is a group of tissues joined together to carry out a specialised function.
- Animal example: the heart transports substances around the animal's body.
- Plant example: the leaf functions in transpiration and photosynthesis.

- **Tissue culture** involves the growth of tissue and/or cells outside of the organism.
- Two examples of use of tissue culture: cancer research and IVF treatment.

Movement through cell membranes
Chapter 8

Learning objectives After studying this chapter, you should be able to:
- Define *diffusion, osmosis* and *turgor*.
- Describe what is meant by *selective permeability*.
- Describe the role of sugar and salt in food preservation.
- Demonstrate osmosis by a practical investigation.

Introduction

> **Osmosis** is the movement of water molecules from a region of high water concentration to a region of low water concentration across a semi-permeable membrane.
>
> **Diffusion** is the passive movement of particles from a region of high concentration to a region of low concentration.

Osmosis is a special type of diffusion. This is because it involves only the movement of water across a semi-permeable membrane.

Diffusion is a type of passive transport. This means no energy is required for it to occur. Think of a can of deodorant being sprayed in a changing room. After a few seconds the smell has diffused to fill the whole room. Molecules will always move (diffuse) to fill all of the available space.

The same occurs in our cells. Water is free to move, unrestricted, across the cell membrane. This movement, called osmosis, has a major effect on our cells. Fig 8.1 shows the effect of water leaving a red blood cell.

If animal cells are placed in a solution with a high amount of dissolved solutes, then they are said to be osmotically challenged. Water will leave the cells by osmosis. This process is called **crenation.** The water is moving down its concentration gradient. Water will always move from where it is abundant to where it is relatively less abundant. This effectively equalises the water pressure.

Conversely, if a cell is placed in a solution with very little dissolved solutes, or none at all, the animal cell is also osmotically challenged and will first swell with water, as it moves into the cell by osmosis, and eventually burst.

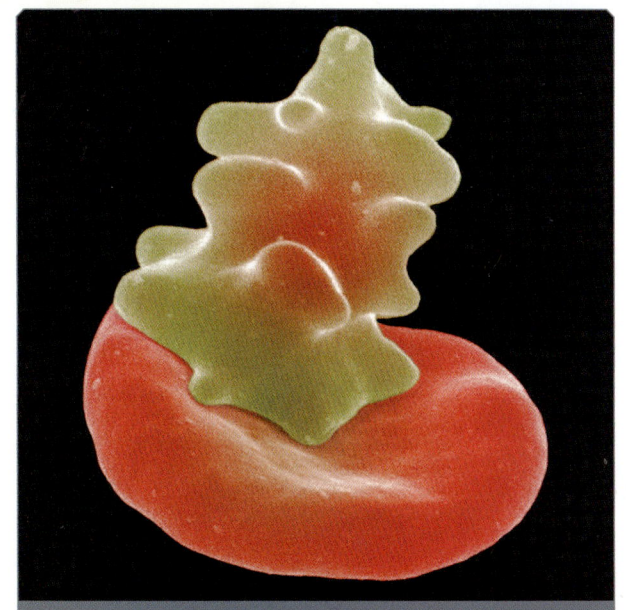

Fig 8.1 Electron microscope image of a red blood cell that has lost water due to osmosis (top) and a normal red blood cell (bottom).

Water is the most important molecule in our cells. As we learned in Chapter 3, water molecules take part in chemical reactions, but also provide the medium in which metabolism occurs. If the water concentration in our cells changes, this will inevitably have an effect (usually a negative one) on the reactions within our cells.

Selective permeability

Not all molecules can pass freely across our cell membranes. Salt, glucose, amino acids and many more concentrations of substances within our cells are tightly controlled. This is because an imbalance of these molecules in the body can kill cells. The control of movement of many biomolecules across the cell membrane is important to the cell's survival. The cell membrane is selectively permeable to control the movement of biomolecules.

Unit 2   The Cell

Applications of osmosis

Osmosis is a key part of our everyday lives. The food industry uses sugars and salts to preserve many foods, which have very long shelf lives as a result. Bacteria and fungi are prevented from growing on the food by osmosis.

Fish and many meats can be salted to preserve them. Jams have a high sugar content. If microorganisms land on these foods, they will lose water by osmosis, shrivel up and die.

Practical activity: to demonstrate osmosis

Osmosis involves the diffusion of water across any semi-permeable membrane, such as Visking tubing. It allows water through but not larger molecules such as sucrose.

Method

1. Cut two equal lengths of Visking tubing and tie both at one end only.
2. Half fill one of the Visking tubes with a known volume of water (control) and the other with the same volume of a 60 per cent sugar solution. A 60 per cent solution means 60 g of the solute (sugar) in 100 ml of water.
3. Tie the other end of both tubes.
4. Measure the mass of both tubes using the electronic balance.
5. Place both tubes in a large beaker of water for at least half an hour or preferably overnight.
6. Reweigh both tubes and record your results in the table.

SAFETY
Use sharp scissors when cutting the Visking tubing. Exercise caution when using the scissors.

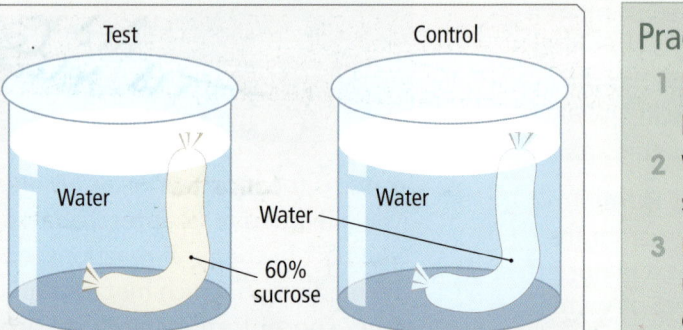

Fig 8.2 Apparatus used to demonstrate osmosis.

Practical activity questions

1. Name a type of membrane that is semi-permeable.
2. What is meant by a 60 per cent solution?
3. Explain why both pieces of membrane used in this practical activity must contain the same volume of solution.
4. Explain the purpose of the control in this practical activity.
5. Describe, in terms of water movement, what happens to the pieces of membrane in this practical activity.
6. Why is sucrose used in this practical activity?
7. Explain why salt is not suitable for this practical activity? (Hint: salt particles are much smaller than sucrose particles.)

Results

	Test		Control	
	Before	After	Before	After
Mass of Visking tube				

Conclusion

What did we learn from this practical activity?

Differences in solute concentration cause movement of water across a semi-permeable membrane (osmosis).

Turgor

> **Turgor** is the pressure of the contents of a cell against its cell wall.

Turgor applies to any organism with a cell wall (all bacteria, fungi and plants). Turgor helps to maintain the shape of the cell. When a plant cell (or bacterial cell) is full of water it is said to be turgid (Fig 8.4). Turgidity is a condition in which the contents of the cell are exerting a pressure on the cell wall, such that the cell wall will not expand any more. It is due to the plant cell containing a more concentrated solution (cytoplasm) than its surroundings. Water will then enter the plant cell due to osmosis. Water is stored in the vacuole, which exerts pressure on the cytoplasm and cell wall. Lack of turgor occurs when a cell with a cell wall loses water by osmosis. It can be most obviously seen in a plant that is wilting (Fig 8.3). A wilted plant's cells have lost too much water. Water is stored mostly in the large central vacuole of the cell. If a plant cell loses water, the central vacuole becomes much smaller. The cell membrane also starts to shrivel inwards away from the cell wall. This process of water loss from a plant cell is called **plasmolysis** (Fig 8.4). Plasmolysis can be reversed by supplying the cell with water.

Fig 8.3 A wilted plant.

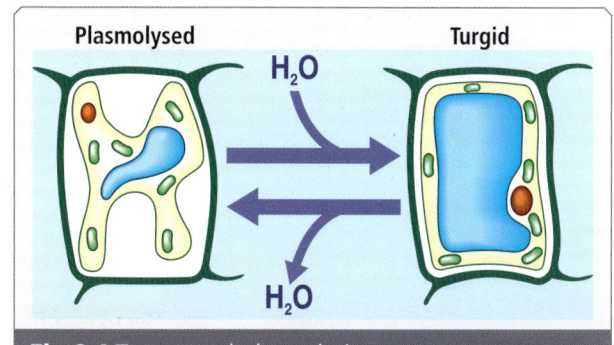

Fig 8.4 Turgor and plasmolysis.

Chapter 8 Questions

1. What is *diffusion*?
2. (a) What is *osmosis*?
   (b) Give **two** applications of osmosis.
3. What is meant by a cell membrane being *selectively permeable*?
4. (a) A red blood cell has been placed into pure water. Explain, using a diagram, what you think will happen to the red blood cell.
   (b) A red blood cell that has been placed in a solution with a very high salt concentration is osmotically challenged. Explain what you think will happen.
5. A student carried out an experiment to demonstrate osmosis and used four cubes of potatoes, all the same size. The four cubes were each placed in solutions of differing concentrations of salt. The weight of each cube before and after was recorded. The table shows the results obtained:

	Concentration of salt solution	Weight before	Weight after
Cube 1	10%	1.1 g	0.8 g
Cube 2	6%	1.2 g	1.1 g
Cube 3	4%	0.9 g	0.9 g
Cube 4	2%	1.1 g	1.4 g

   (a) What does the description of the experiment above tell you about how the student ensured the experiment was fair?
   (b) Explain what has happened to each cube. What process is occurring that contributes to these changes?
   (c) What do the results tell you about the concentration of the cytoplasm of the cells of the potato? Explain.
6. Distinguish between *plasmolysis* and *turgor*.
7. What process has occurred when a plant wilts?

Unit 2 The Cell

Chapter 8 Sample examination questions

1. (a) (i) Define the term *osmosis*.
   (ii) Give an example of osmosis in plants.
   (b) Answer the following questions in relation to practical work you carried out to investigate osmosis.
   (i) Draw a labelled diagram of the apparatus you used in the investigation.
   (ii) Describe how you used this apparatus to carry out the investigation.
   (iii) State the result(s) of your investigation.
   (iv) Briefly explain the result(s) you have given in part (iii).

   Section B, Question 8 Ordinary Level 2009

HL 2. (i) State the precise location of the cell membrane in plant cells.
   (ii) With what type of cell do you associate membrane-bound organelles?
   (iii) What corresponding term is used to describe bacterial cells?
   (iv) The cell membrane is described as being *selectively permeable*. What does this mean?
   (v) Why is diffusion alternatively known as *passive transport*?
   (vi) Osmosis may be described as 'a special case of diffusion'. Explain why.
   (vii) Describe, with the aid of a labelled diagram, how you demonstrated osmosis in the laboratory.

   Section C, Question 14 (c) (i)–(vii) Higher Level 2011

Chapter 8 Mind map

Osmosis is the movement of water molecules from a region of high water concentration to a region of low water concentration across a semi-permeable membrane.

Diffusion is the passive movement of particles from a region of high concentration to a region of low concentration.

Applications of osmosis
- Jam-making
- Salting fish

Practical activity to demonstrate osmosis
- Set up two Visking tubes, one with water (control) the other with a 60 per cent sugar solution.
- Measure the mass of both tubes and place both in a large beaker of water.
- Leave overnight and then re-measure masses.
- The tube with the sugar solution has increased in mass whereas the mass of the control remained constant.

- **Turgor** is the pressure of the contents of a cell against its cell wall.
- When a plant cell is full of water it is said to be turgid.
- Turgidity in plant cells is due to the pressure exerted on the cell wall such that the cell wall will not expand any more.

Enzymes Chapter 9

Learning objectives After studying this chapter, you should be able to:
- Define *metabolism* and *enzyme*.
- Describe the structure and function of enzymes and their role in metabolism.
- Investigate the effect of pH and temperature on the rate of enzyme action.
- HL ◊ Investigate the effect of heat denaturation on the activity of one enzyme.
- ◊ Prepare one enzyme immobilisation and examine its application.
- Describe bioprocessing with immobilised enzymes.
- HL ◊ Define *specificity* and describe the active site theory of enzyme action.
- ◊ Define the terms *optimum activity* and *heat denaturation*.

Introduction

> **Metabolism** is the sum of all the chemical reactions occurring in an organism.

Enzymes are the driving force of metabolism. Enzymes catalyse (speed up) metabolic reactions, such as respiration and photosynthesis, and many other biochemical processes occurring in living cells.

As we learned in Chapter 4 (Ecology), all the energy in a living organism comes from the Sun (**solar energy**).

- This solar energy is transferred from organism to organism via the food chain.
- Solar energy is trapped by the green pigment chlorophyll present in plants.
- Solar energy is used to make glucose (food) in the process of photosynthesis.
- Food can then be stored for future use.

Food is chemical energy which can be released and changed into other forms of energy within the cell (**cellular energy**), such as heat. Respiration is the process in which energy is released from food (*see* Chapter 12).

Cellular energy powers other metabolic activities within cells.

Enzyme structure and function

> **Enzymes** are folded, globular-shaped protein catalysts that speed up reactions without being used up.

As we learned in Chapter 3 (Nutrition), proteins consist of many amino acids joined together. This long line of amino acids folds over on itself to give the three-dimensional shape.

All enzymes are protein. Many enzymes consist of more than one protein, called **domains**. Protein domains interact chemically with each other to give the overall structure of an enzyme.

Fig 9.1 shows the structure of human salivary amylase that digests starch into maltose. It consists of 496 amino acids organised into three separate domains (red, blue and grey).

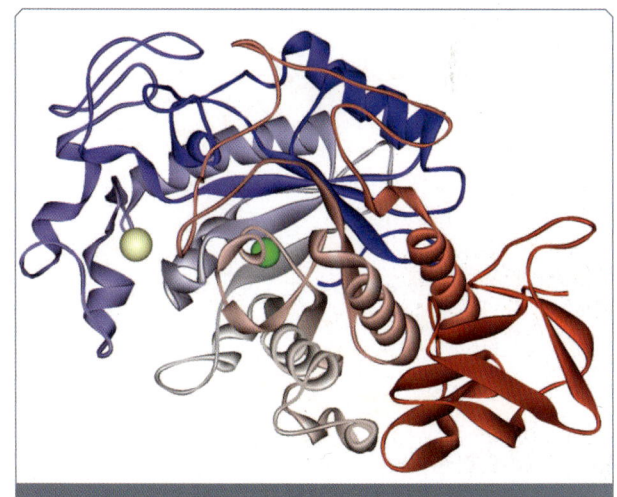

Fig 9.1 A ribbon diagram of salivary amylase.

Without enzymes, life would not exist. Chemical reactions occurring would be under no control. Below is a list of enzymes involved in metabolism.

Examples of enzymes

Some enzymes are involved in breaking down big molecules into smaller ones (catabolism). These are called catabolic enzymes.

- **Amylase** is an enzyme present in saliva and in pancreatic juice that catalyses the breakdown (catabolism) of starch (polysaccharide) into maltose units (disaccharide).
- **Pepsin** is an enzyme present in gastric (stomach) juice that catalyses the breakdown of proteins into peptides.
- **Catalase** is an enzyme present in every living cell that catalyses the breakdown of hydrogen peroxide into water and oxygen gas. It is the fastest-acting mammalian enzyme known.

Other enzymes are involved in building up large molecules from smaller ones (anabolism). These enzymes are called anabolic enzymes.

- **Potato phosphorylase** is an enzyme present in the ground tissue of the potato plant stem that does nearly the exact opposite of amylase. It catalyses the formation of starch from glucose.
- **DNA polymerase** is an enzyme present in all living cells that catalyses the formation of DNA from its constituent molecules (*see* Chapter 14 for details).

NOTE: For Leaving Certificate Biology, you are required to learn about one catabolic enzyme and one anabolic enzyme only.

HL Active site theory of enzyme action

All enzymes have a specific area in their structure called the **active site**.

> The **active site** of an enzyme is the area where the substrate enters and is changed into a product(s).

Active sites are 'specific' as they will only accept one substrate or one set of substrates. Therefore, enzymes show 'specificity' for their substrate(s).

> **Specificity** refers to an enzyme's ability to react with only one substrate.

There are a number of theories of enzyme action, most of which are beyond the scope of the Leaving Certificate Biology course. The theory described here is the active site theory, which involves two models of enzyme action:

1 The lock and key model
2 The induced fit model

1 The lock and key model

The lock and key model of enzyme action was first put forward in 1894 by Emil Fischer. This model states that enzymes have a rigid shape and that the substrate(s) fits into the active site of the enzyme, much like a key fits into a lock. When the substrate(s) arrives in the active site, an enzyme-substrate complex is formed. The enzyme acts on the substrate(s) creating product(s).

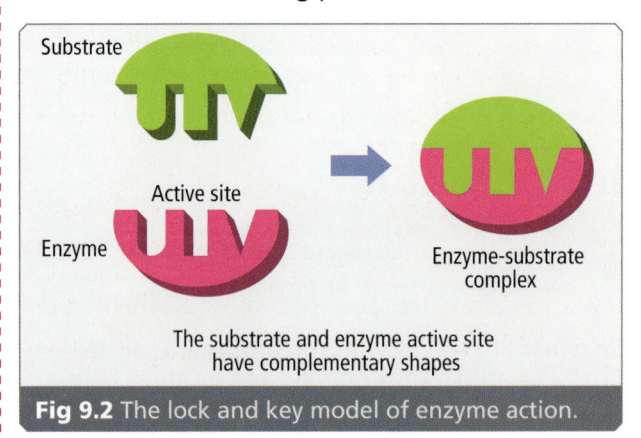

Fig 9.2 The lock and key model of enzyme action.

2 The induced fit model

The induced fit model is the favoured model of enzyme action amongst biologists. It was first suggested in 1958 by Daniel Koshland Jr. It states that the substrate(s) does not fit perfectly into the active site of the enzyme but that the active site is flexible. As the substrate(s) approaches, it 'induces' the active site to change to the correct shape. The substrate(s) can then fit snugly into the active site. An enzyme-substrate complex is formed. The enzyme's active site acts on the substrate(s) to convert it to product(s). The product(s) is released and the active site changes back to its original shape.

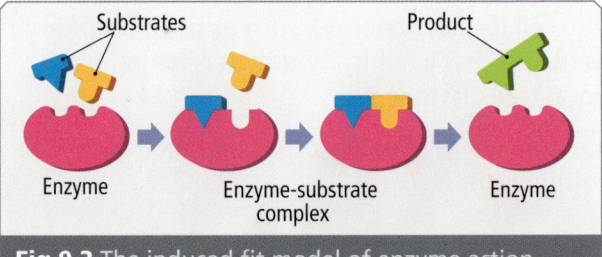

Fig 9.3 The induced fit model of enzyme action.

It is important to note that this model still allows for enzyme specificity – that the enzyme will only act on one substrate or one set of substrates. This means that only one substrate or set of substrates is capable of inducing the active site to take up the required shape.

Factors affecting enzyme action

Enzyme action can be affected by a number of environmental conditions. For the Leaving Certificate Biology course, you need to know only two: **pH** and **temperature**. Enzymes are said to have a specific pH and temperature at which they work best.

pH

The pH of a solution refers to its acidity or basicity (whether it is acidic, neutral or basic). pH ranges from 0 to 14, with any value below 7 being acidic, any value greater than 7 being basic and 7 being neutral.

All enzymes have a pH at which they work best. Even a slight change in the pH will cause enzyme activity to dramatically drop. Changes in pH disrupt the enzyme's shape. If the enzyme's shape is lost, it cannot act on its substrate(s). The shape of an enzyme is lost when the bonds holding the enzyme's domains in position are broken.

Most human enzymes require a pH of 7.4. The pH of animal blood is 7.4 and even a slight change can cause serious health problems. Some animal enzymes require different pH values for optimal activity. For example, pepsin is a stomach enzyme that breaks down proteins into peptides. Because it acts in the stomach, the pH at which it works best is approximately 2.

Temperature

Temperature affects the rate at which enzymes work. Generally, the lower the temperature, the slower enzymes work (this is why we keep food that goes off easily in the refrigerator). The higher the temperature, the faster enzymes work – up to a point. If the temperature rises too high, the enzyme will stop working.

All enzymes have a temperature at which the enzyme works best – this is its optimum temperature (see below). For example, most animal enzymes work best at 37 °C.

Plant enzymes work best between temperatures of 10 and 30 °C, depending on where in the world the plant lives. At low temperatures, the movement of the enzymes and substrates is slow. This means the number of collisions between enzyme and substrate is low, which results in a slow rate of reaction.

As temperature increases, the faster movement of molecules increases the number of collisions. Therefore, the rate of enzyme action is higher. However, when the temperature reaches a certain level, the enzyme will start to lose its shape and cannot act on the substrate(s). The temperature at which enzymes start to lose their shape is over 35 °C for plant enzymes and over 40 °C for animal enzymes.

HL Optimum activity

> **Optimum activity** of an enzyme is the condition(s) under which the enzyme works best.

As mentioned above, all enzymes have a specific pH and temperature at which they work best.

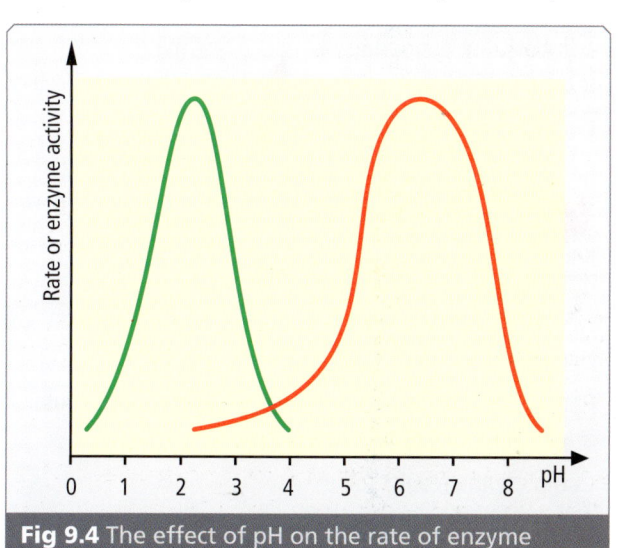

Fig 9.4 The effect of pH on the rate of enzyme action of pepsin (green) and amylase (red).

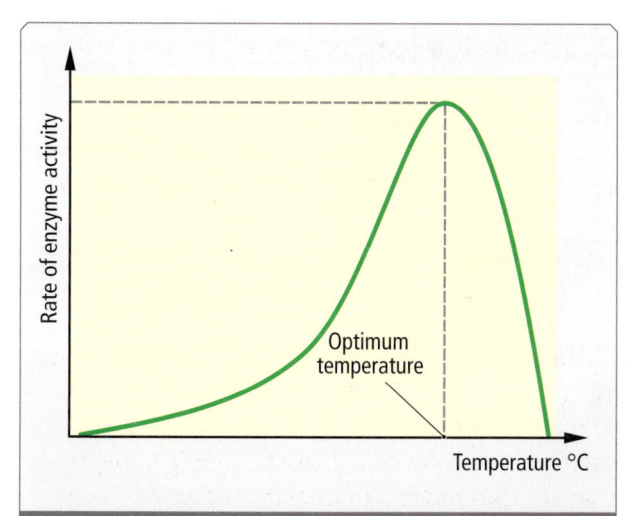

Fig 9.5 The effect of temperature on the rate of enzyme action. Every enzyme has an optimum pH.

These are called the 'optimum' pH and 'optimum' temperature.

Fig 9.4 shows the optimum pH values of pepsin and amylase. Notice how the activity of both enzymes drops dramatically outside a narrow pH range. Fig 9.5 shows a typical rate of enzyme activity versus temperature curve. Notice how the curve (or rate of enzyme activity) drops above a certain temperature. The drops in the curves of both figures are due to the enzyme becoming denatured.

> A **denatured enzyme** is an enzyme that has lost its function due to a change in its shape.

Heat denaturation of proteins

When too much heat is applied to proteins, their shape will change. This change is permanent.

Eggs are high in protein. Egg protein denatures permanently when heated (the albumin of the egg becomes white and opaque). This is called heat denaturation.

All enzymes are protein and are therefore affected by heat in the same way as egg protein. Shape is critical to an enzyme's function. If an enzyme loses its shape due to heat, then the substrate(s) will not fit the active site and the enzyme cannot carry out its function. The enzyme is then said to be denatured.

Practical activity: to investigate the effect of pH on the rate of action of catalase

Catalase is an enzyme present in all living cells. It breaks down the toxic compound, hydrogen peroxide, into the harmless molecules, oxygen and water. Hydrogen peroxide is produced continuously in cells during respiration and as a result of other metabolic processes. Catalase is the fastest-acting mammalian enzyme known. It can act on 40 million molecules of hydrogen peroxide per second!

SAFETY

Hydrogen peroxide is a strong irritant. Wear safety goggles, a lab coat and gloves when handling hydrogen peroxide.

Celery is a good source of catalase. In the following practical activity, washing-up liquid is added to a solution of catalase, followed by the hydrogen peroxide (substrate). Solutions of pH buffer are used to maintain the pH at set values. As the hydrogen peroxide breaks down, bubbles of oxygen will be produced, creating foam as they travel through the washing-up liquid. The faster the catalase works, the more foam is produced. This enables us to make an indirect measurement of the rate of action of the catalase.

Method

1. Set up a large water bath at 25 °C.
2. Take three 100 ml graduated cylinders, and place 1 g of finely chopped celery into each.
3. Add 3 ml of pH 4 buffer to the first graduated cylinder; 3 ml pH 7 buffer to the second; and 3 ml pH 13 buffer to the third.
4. Add **one** drop of washing-up liquid to each graduated cylinder.

   > NOTE: It is important to add one drop only, otherwise too much foam will be produced too quickly.

5. Repeat steps 2, 3 and 4 using separate cylinders, without adding the chopped celery. These will act as controls.
6. Place a test-tube of hydrogen peroxide into the water bath, along with the three graduated cylinders. The apparatus will take a few minutes to reach 25 °C.
7. Copy the results table into your lab book.
8. Record the volume of each graduated cylinder (they should all be the same) and add 1 ml to this value (this allows for the 1 ml of hydrogen peroxide added to each graduated cylinder).
9. Add 1 ml of hydrogen peroxide to each graduated cylinder, while at the same time starting a stopwatch.
10. Record the volumes of foam in each graduated cylinder after 1 minute and again after 2 minutes.
11. Complete the results table.
12. Draw a graph of the results.

Enzymes Chapter 9

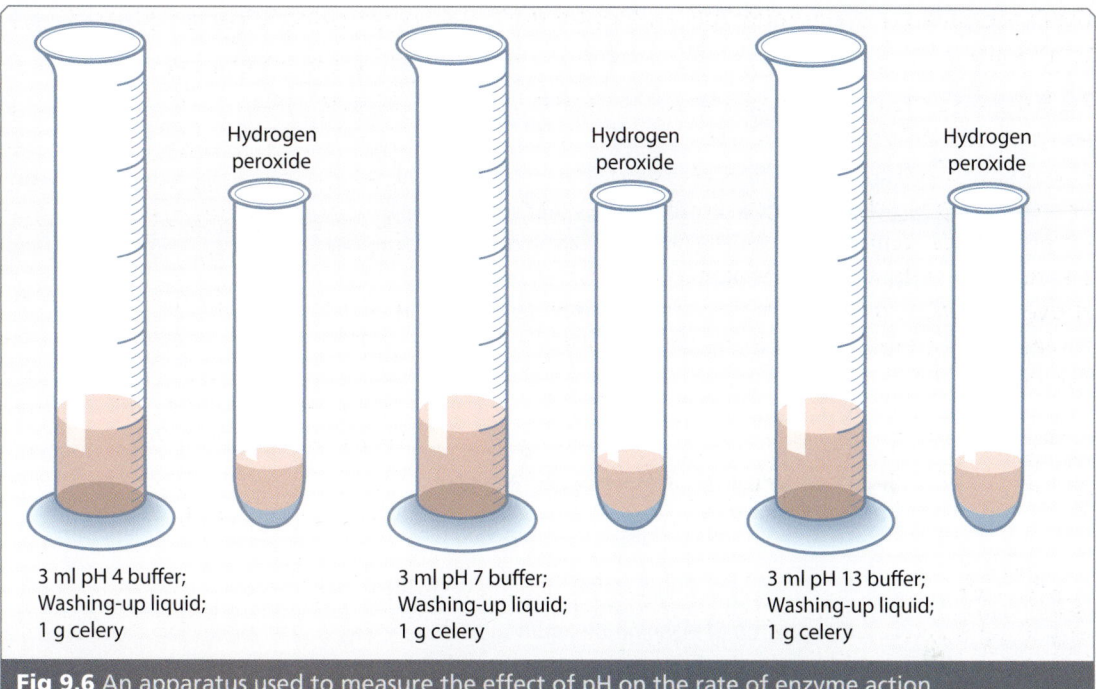

Fig 9.6 An apparatus used to measure the effect of pH on the rate of enzyme action.

Left cylinder: 3 ml pH 4 buffer; Washing-up liquid; 1 g celery
Middle cylinder: 3 ml pH 7 buffer; Washing-up liquid; 1 g celery
Right cylinder: 3 ml pH 13 buffer; Washing-up liquid; 1 g celery

Each cylinder paired with a test tube of Hydrogen peroxide.

Results

pH		Volume in graduated cylinder			Rate of enzyme action
		0 min	1 min	2 min	(2 min vol–1 min vol)
4	Test				
	Control				
7	Test				
	Control				
13	Test				
	Control				

Conclusion

What did we learn from this practical activity?

- pH 7 is the optimum pH for catalase activity.
- Catalase loses its ability to break down hydrogen peroxide outside of the optimum pH.

Practical activity questions

1. Name the enzyme you used.
2. Name the substrate(s) and product(s) of the enzyme you named in Question 1.
3. Name a factor you kept constant in this practical activity.
4. Explain how you kept this factor constant.
5. Explain the procedure you followed to measure the rate of enzyme activity.
6. What was the optimum pH for your enzyme?
7. Give **two** safety precautions you took during this practical activity.

Unit 2 The Cell

Practical activity: to investigate the effect of temperature on the rate of action of catalase

Temperature affects enzyme action. In this practical activity, catalase is kept at various temperatures and the corresponding activity levels are measured. The amount of foam produced from the catalase breaking down hydrogen peroxide into water and oxygen is measured. This is an indirect way of measuring the activity of catalase.

SAFETY
Hydrogen peroxide is a strong irritant. Wear safety goggles, a lab coat and gloves when handling hydrogen peroxide.

Method

1. Set up a number of water baths (beakers maintained at a range of different temperatures will do): set at 0 °C (with ice), 25 °C, 50 °C and 80 °C.
2. Take four 100 ml graduated cylinders and place 1 g of finely chopped celery into each.
3. Add 3 ml of pH 7 buffer to each graduated cylinder.
4. Add **one** drop of washing-up liquid to each graduated cylinder.

> **NOTE:** It is important to add one drop only, otherwise too much foam will be produced too quickly.

5. Repeat steps 2, 3 and 4 using separate cylinders, without adding the chopped celery. These will acts as controls.
6. Place a test-tube of hydrogen peroxide into each water bath, along with the graduated cylinders. The apparatus will take **at least 15 minutes** to reach the correct temperatures.
7. Copy the results table into your lab book.
8. Record the volume of each graduated cylinder (they should all be the same) and add 1 ml to this value (this allows for the 1 ml of hydrogen peroxide added to each graduated cylinder).
9. Add 1 ml of hydrogen peroxide to each graduated cylinder, while at the same time starting a stopwatch.
10. Record the volumes of foam in each graduated cylinder after 1 minute and again after 2 minutes.
11. Complete the results table.
12. Draw a graph of the results.

Results

Temperature (°C)		Volume in graduated cylinder			Rate of enzyme action (2 min vol–1 min vol)
		0 min	1 min	2 min	
0	Test				
	Control				
25	Test				
	Control				
50	Test				
	Control				
80	Test				
	Control				

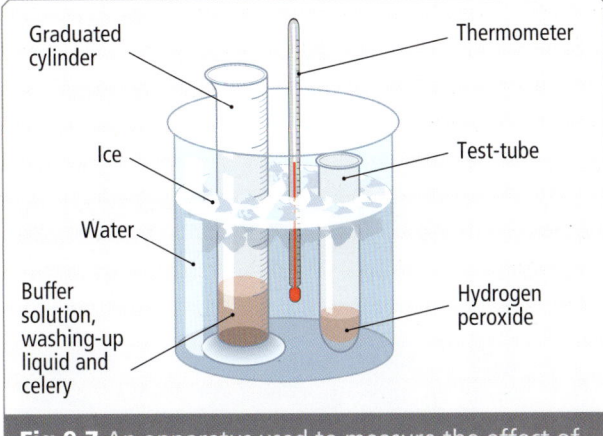

Fig 9.7 An apparatus used to measure the effect of temperature on the rate of enzyme action.

Practical activity questions

1. Name the enzyme you used.
2. Name the substrate(s) and product(s) of the enzyme you named in Question 1.
3. Name a factor you kept constant in this practical activity.
4. Explain how you kept this factor constant.
5. Describe the procedure you followed to measure the rate of enzyme activity.
6. What was the optimum temperature for your enzyme?
7. Give **two** safety precautions you took during this practical activity.

Conclusion

What did we learn from this practical activity?

- 25 °C is the optimum temperature for catalase activity.
- The ability of catalase to break down hydrogen peroxide is reduced outside the optimum temperature.

Practical activity: to investigate the effect of heat denaturation on the activity of catalase

As we have learned, temperature affects the rate of enzyme action. If the temperature is too high the rate of enzyme action drops to zero. The enzyme is then said to be denatured. Even if the temperature is brought back down, the rate of enzyme action remains at zero. This is because denaturation is permanent.

In this practical activity, we will denature the enzyme catalase.

SAFETY
Hydrogen peroxide is a strong irritant. Wear safety goggles, a lab coat and gloves when handling hydrogen peroxide.

Method

1. Take two 100 ml graduated cylinders and place 1 g of finely chopped celery into each.
2. Add 5 ml water to one of the samples of celery and place the graduated cylinder into a boiling water bath for 15 minutes. This step will denature the enzymes within the celery.
3. Allow to cool and filter out the hot water from the boiled celery.
4. Add 3 ml of pH 7 buffer to each graduated cylinder (to both boiled and unboiled celery).
5. Add **one** drop of washing-up liquid to each graduated cylinder.
6. Place the two graduated cylinders of celery and a test-tube of hydrogen peroxide into a 25 °C water bath. Allow 15 minutes for the celery and hydrogen peroxide to reach 25 °C.
7. Copy the results table into your lab book.
8. Record the volume of each graduated cylinder (they should all be the same) and add 1 ml to this value (this allows for the 1 ml of hydrogen peroxide added to each graduated cylinder).

NOTE: It is important to add one drop only, otherwise too much foam will be produced too quickly.

9 Add 1 ml of hydrogen peroxide to each graduated cylinder, while at the same time starting a stopwatch.

10 Record the volumes of foam in each graduated cylinder after 1 minute and again after 2 minutes.

11 Complete the results table.

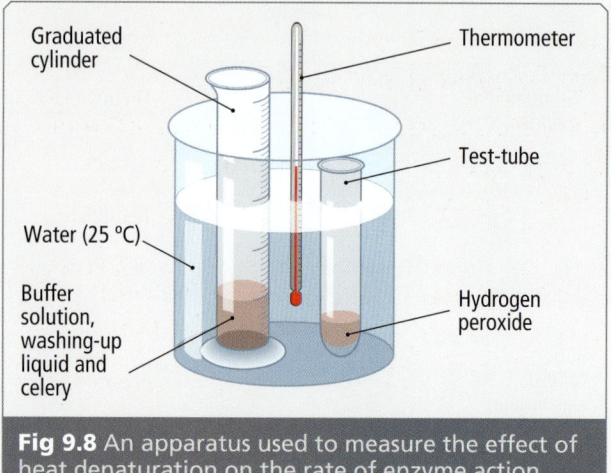

Fig 9.8 An apparatus used to measure the effect of heat denaturation on the rate of enzyme action.

Results

	Volume in graduated cylinder			Rate of enzyme action (2 min vol–1 min vol)
	0 min	1 min	2 min	
Denatured catalase				
Active catalase				

Conclusion

What did we learn from this practical activity?

- The active enzyme showed normal activity and acted on the hydrogen peroxide.
- The denatured enzyme showed no activity. No bubbles of oxygen were produced and hence no foam was produced.
- Boiling an enzyme causes it to become denatured.

Practical activity questions

1 Name the enzyme you used.
2 Name the substrate(s) and product(s) of the enzyme you named in Question 1.
3 Name a factor you kept constant in this practical activity.
4 Explain how you kept this factor constant.
5 Explain the procedure you followed to measure the activity of the enzyme.
6 Explain how you denatured the enzyme.
7 Give **two** safety precautions you took during this practical activity.

Bioprocessing

> **Bioprocessing** is the use of living cells or their components, such as enzymes, to make useful products or to carry out useful procedures.

Bioprocessing is used by many pharmaceutical and food companies. It enables us to produce high quality products very quickly and relatively cheaply. Examples of bioprocessing include:

- The use of yeast (*Saccharomyces* – see Chapter 21) and sugar to produce beer. The yeast cells respire anaerobically to produce alcohol (see Chapter 12).
- The use of *E. coli* bacteria, genetically modified with a human insulin gene. The insulin can then be used to treat type I diabetes (see Chapter 38).
- The use of rennin, an enzyme, to coagulate milk in the cheese-making process.
- The use of glucose isomerase, another enzyme, to convert glucose to fructose, which is a sweeter monosaccharide used in many types of sweets (see Chapter 3).
- The use of proteases in washing powders that break down food stains on clothes.

Immobilised enzymes

Many bioprocesses, including the uses of rennin and glucose isomerase described above, are carried out by immobilised enzymes.

> **Immobilised enzymes** are enzymes that are attached to or trapped in an inert (inactive) insoluble material.

Procedures used for immobilising enzymes

There are three distinct methods of immobilising enzymes: **carrier-binding**, **cross-linking** and **entrapment**.

1 Carrier-binding method

Carrier-binding involves attaching enzymes to a water-insoluble substance such as cellulose or agarose. Enzymes are also attached to man-made substances, such as polyacrylamide gel or porous glass beads.

There are three subtypes of the carrier-binding system:

- **Physical adsorption** is the attachment of the enzyme (usually by hydrogen bonding) to an inert, water-insoluble substance. The immobilised enzyme is very stable.
- **Ionic binding** is where a charged part of the enzyme is attracted to, and binds to, a charged part of the insoluble support. It is also a very stable way of immobilising enzymes.
- **Covalent binding** is where a covalent bond is formed between one part of the enzyme and a part of the insoluble support. This method has the potential to change the structure of the enzyme. Therefore, it is suitable for a limited number of enzymes only.

2 Cross-linking method

The cross-linking method binds the enzymes themselves together covalently. Glutaraldehyde is the most common substance used to carry out cross-linking. Glutaraldehyde acts as the 'glue' between the enzymes.

3 Entrapment method

The entrapment method involves trapping the enzyme in a gel (lattice type) or a membrane (microencapsulation type). This method is more often used to immobilise whole cells rather than free enzymes. Entrapment involves using a gel such as sodium alginate, which is a viscous (thick) polysaccharide obtained from the cell walls of brown algae. Enzymes or cells trapped in the gel are still capable of acting on substrate(s) and producing product(s).

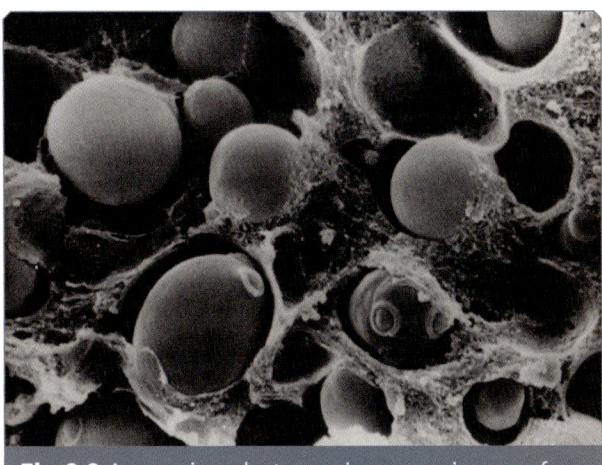

Fig 9.9 A scanning electron microscope image of yeast cells immobilised in calcium alginate beads.

In the practical activity on pages 113–115, we will use the entrapment method to immobilise yeast cells.

Uses of immobilised enzymes

- Immobilised lactase is used to produce lactose-free milk. The immobilised lactase hydrolyses (breaks down using water) lactose into glucose and galactose. This enables lactose-intolerant people to drink milk that has been treated by this enzyme.
- Immobilised rennin is used to coagulate the proteins present in milk in the cheese-making process.
- Immobilised glucose isomerase is used to convert glucose syrups to fructose syrups. Fructose is a sweeter monosaccharide used in many types of sweets.

Advantages of immobilised enzymes

- Most of the immobilisation techniques are gentle, which helps to maintain the function of the enzyme.

- The enzyme does not contaminate the product at the end of the reaction.
- Immobilised enzymes can be reused.
- Immobilised enzymes are more stable.

Bioreactor

All bioprocesses, regardless of whether free enzymes or immobilised enzymes are used, are carried out in a **bioreactor**.

> A **bioreactor** is a vessel in which a product is formed by a cell or cell component, such as an enzyme.

Bioreactors usually have the following components:

- **Feeding pump:** pumps the nutrients or medium into the bioreactor.
- **Submerged aerator:** pumps in gases such as oxygen (if required) and other gases.

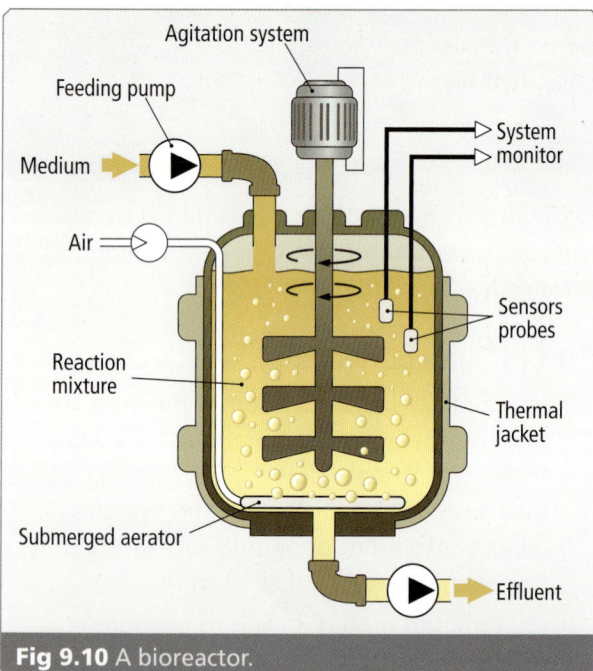

Fig 9.10 A bioreactor.

- **Sensor probes:** used to measure levels of different substances within the bioreactor.
- **Agitation system:** a series of blades that rotate and mix the contents of the bioreactor.

In industry, there are two main ways in which bioprocesses are carried out: **batch cultures** or **continuous-flow cultures**.

1 Batch cultures

A typical batch culture bioreactor consists of a vessel with agitation (stirring) and heating/cooling systems. Batch bioreactors carry out product formation in individual cycles. Each cycle involves a sequence of steps that comes to a definite end. The product(s) is usually withdrawn before too many waste products build up. This is then the end of the cycle. The bioreactor has to be emptied, cleaned and sterilised in preparation for another cycle.

2 Continuous-flow cultures

Continuous-flow culture bioreactors are very similar in structure to batch bioreactors but usually have more sensors. These sensors maintain the correct conditions (temperature, pH, oxygen, carbon dioxide concentrations and so on) throughout the process.

Nutrients, substrates and medium are **continuously** infused into the bioreactor. The reaction inside proceeds at the desired speed and the product(s)/effluent is **continuously** siphoned off at the bottom.

Fig 9.11 A typical bioreactor used in continuous flow cultures.

Enzymes Chapter 9

Practical activity: to prepare one enzyme immobilisation and examine its application

SAFETY
Calcium chloride is an irritant.
Wear safety goggles, a lab coat and gloves when using this substance.

This practical activity involves entrapment as a method of enzyme immobilisation. We will be immobilising yeast cells, which contain the enzyme **invertase**.

We will then examine its application by using both free yeast cells and immobilised yeast cells to convert sucrose (substrate of invertase) into glucose and fructose (products of invertase). We will then compare the products.

Method

1. Dissolve 0.4 g sodium alginate in 10 ml of distilled water to produce a 4% sodium alginate solution. Stir until a smooth paste is formed.
2. Dissolve 2 g dried brewer's yeast in 10 ml of distilled water.
3. Add the yeast suspension to the sodium alginate solution and mix thoroughly.
4. Dissolve 1.4 g calcium chloride in 100 ml of distilled water.
5. Using a 10 ml syringe, draw up the thick yeast/alginate mixture.
6. Add the suspension from the syringe drop by drop into the calcium chloride solution (Fig 9.12). While you are doing this, another member of your group should stir the calcium chloride solution to ensure the sodium alginate beads do not stick together.
7. As soon as the sodium alginate droplets enter the calcium chloride solution, they solidify to form calcium alginate beads.
8. Allow the beads to harden for at least 10 minutes.
9. Strain the beads (Fig 9.13) from the solution using a tea strainer, taking care as calcium chloride is an irritant.
10. Wash the beads at least three times to get rid of any remaining calcium chloride. The beads can be left in the fridge overnight.

NOTE: Be careful not to let calcium chloride come into contact with your skin as it is an irritant.

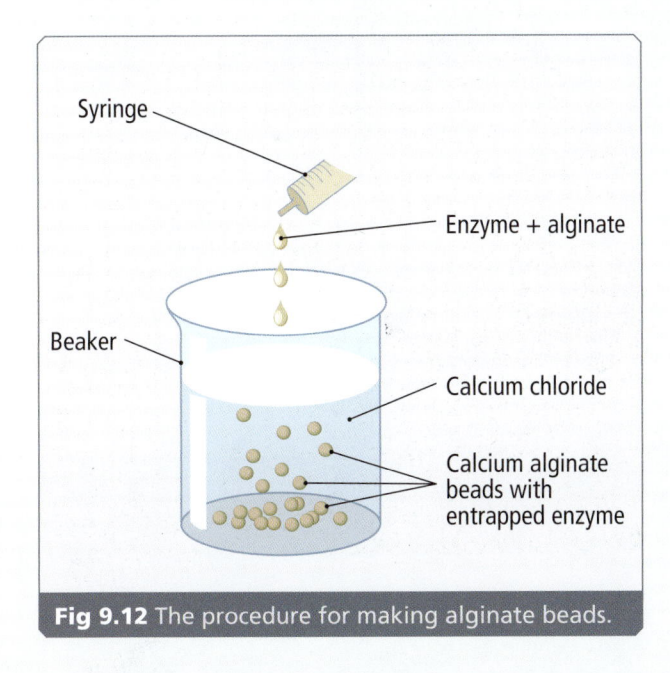

Fig 9.12 The procedure for making alginate beads.

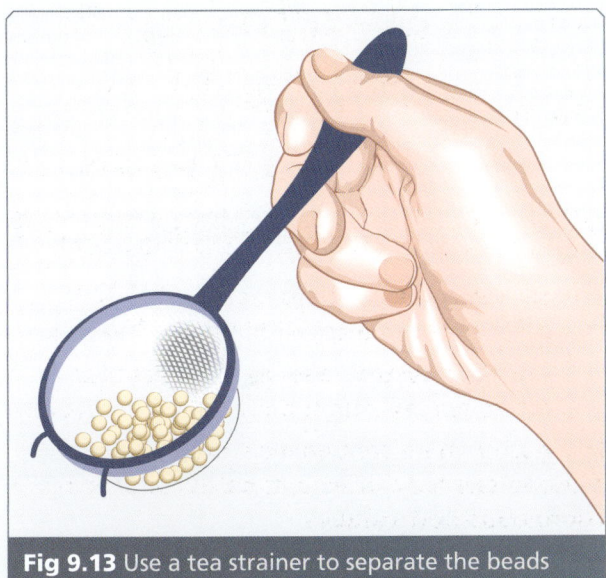

Fig 9.13 Use a tea strainer to separate the beads from the calcium chloride.

11 Place a twisted paperclip at the bottom of a separating funnel and place the beads of immobilised yeast on top. The paperclip prevents any beads blocking the hole at the bottom of the separating funnel.

12 Dissolve 2 g of yeast in 10 ml of distilled water and add this to a second separating funnel. Place the separating funnels in retort stands above beakers.

13 Make up a 1% sucrose solution by dissolving 1g sucrose in 100 ml of distilled water.

14 Heat this solution to approximately 30 °C.

15 Pour 50 ml of sucrose solution slowly into each separating funnel. Start your stopwatch.

16 After 30 seconds, open the tap of both funnels very slightly so that just a trickle of solution comes through (Fig 9.14).

17 Test this solution with Clinistix glucose test strips every 30 seconds.

18 Alternatively, collect a few drops every 30 seconds in separate test-tubes. Use equal volumes of Benedict's solution to test for reducing sugar (see Chapter 3).

19 Keep testing the product every 30 seconds until glucose appears.

20 Compare the free yeast with the immobilised yeast in terms of time taken for glucose to appear in the product and the turbidity (cloudiness) of the product.

21 Complete the table of results.

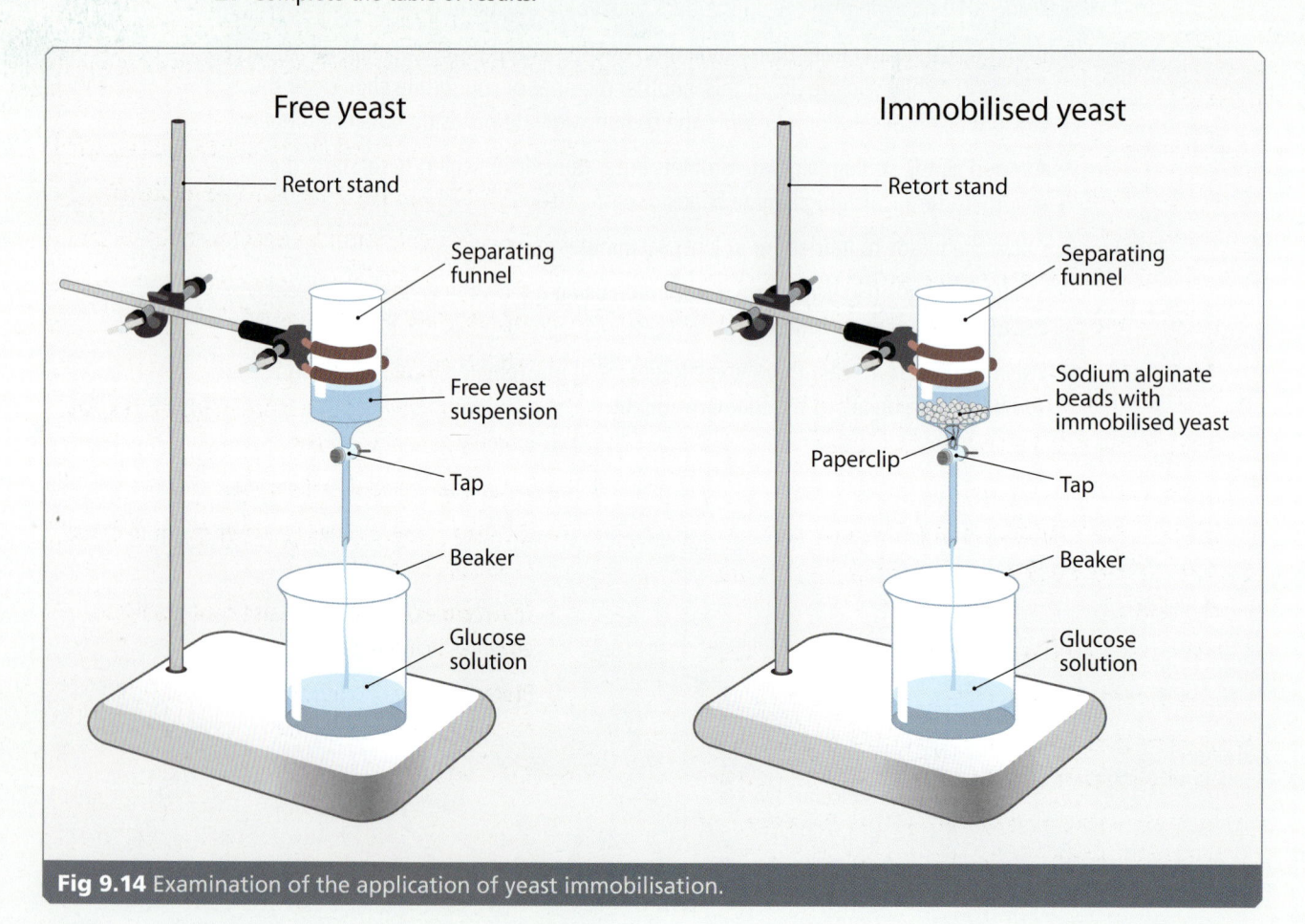

NOTE Clinistix strips test for glucose and turn violet or purple if glucose is present.

Fig 9.14 Examination of the application of yeast immobilisation.

Results

	Free yeast (sucrase)	Immobilised yeast (sucrase)
Time taken (minutes) for glucose to appear		
Cloudiness (turbidity) of product		

Conclusion

What did we learn in this practical activity?

- Immobilising yeast in alginate beads is an effective way to obtain an uncontaminated product.
- Immobilised yeast is unaffected by the immobilisation process.
- Immobilised yeast can carry out the same reactions as free yeast.

Practical activity questions

1. Give the name of the enzyme you immobilised. If it was a cell, give the name of the enzyme of interest within the cell.
2. What method of immobilisation did you use?
3. Explain, in detail, how you carried out the immobilisation.
4. Describe how you showed the application of the immobilised enzyme.
5. Give **two** safety precautions you took during this practical activity.

Chapter 9 Questions

1. Define the following:
   (a) *Metabolism*
   (b) *Enzyme*
2. (a) Distinguish between *catabolism* and *anabolism*.
   (b) Give **one** example of a catabolic enzyme and **one** example of an anabolic enzyme.
3. To what group of biomolecules do enzymes belong?
4. What term is used to describe the shape of:
   (a) An enzyme?
   (b) A structural protein, such as collagen?
5. What is meant by *domains* in terms of the structure of enzymes?
6. Distinguish between the terms *substrate* and *product*.
7. **HL** What is meant by the *active site* of an enzyme?
8. Describe, with the use of diagrams, the lock and key model and the induced-fit model of enzyme action.
9. Name **two** environmental factors that affect enzymes and describe exactly how enzymes are affected by changes in these factors.
10. **HL** What is meant by the *optimum activity* of an enzyme?
11. What is meant by *heat denaturation* of proteins?
12. What property of all enzymes enables scientists to class them as catalysts?
13. Why are enzymes said to be *specific*?
14. (a) What is *bioprocessing*?
    (b) Give **two** examples of bioprocessing and explain why they are of use to us.
15. (a) What is an *immobilised enzyme*?
    (b) Give the **three** main ways in which enzymes may be immobilised.
    (c) Give **two** examples of the use of immobilised enzymes in industry.
    (d) State **two** advantages of using immobilised enzymes over free enzymes.
16. What is a *bioreactor*?

Unit 2 The Cell

Chapter 9 Sample examination questions

1. Enzymes are used in many processes in both plants and animals.
   (i) What is an *enzyme*?
   (ii) Name any **one** enzyme, and its substrate, and its product.
   (iii) The rate of activity of enzymes can be affected by various factors.
   Name any **two** factors that can affect enzyme activity.
   (iv) Enzymes are sometimes immobilised in industrial processes.
   What is meant by the term *immobilised* in relation to enzymes?
   (v) Give **one** advantage of using immobilised enzymes.

   Section C, Question 12 (c) Ordinary Level 2011

HL 2. (a) (i) To which group of biomolecules do enzymes belong?
   (ii) Name a factor that influences the activity of an enzyme.
   (b) In the course of your practical investigations you prepared an enzyme immobilisation.
   Answer the following questions in relation to that investigation.
   (i) Describe how you carried out the immobilisation.
   (ii) Draw a labelled diagram of the apparatus that you used to investigate **the activity** of the immobilised enzyme.
   (iii) Briefly outline how you used the apparatus referred to in (b) (ii) above.

   Section B, Question 9 Higher Level 2009

Chapter 9 Mind map

- Solar energy is the primary source of energy for most living organisms.
- Cellular energy is found in the chemical bonds that bind biomolecules together.

- An **enzyme** is a folded protein that catalyses chemical reactions in living cells without being used up.
- The **active site** of an enzyme is the area where the substrate enters and is changed into product(s).
- **Specificity** refers to an enzyme's ability to react with only one substrate or one set of substrates.
- Enzymes are important to the maintenance of metabolism in all living organisms.
- Catabolic enzymes: amylase, which digests starch into maltose
- Anabolic enzymes: DNA polymerase, which makes DNA in all living cells.

Enzymes are the driving force of metabolism. Metabolism is the sum of all the chemical reactions occurring in an organism.

Enzymes   Chapter 9

The active site theory involves two models: HL
- **Lock and key model:** the active site is the 'lock' that has a rigid, unchanging shape and the substrate(s) is the 'key' that fits the shape of the enzyme exactly. When both come together an enzyme-substrate complex is formed and the enzyme changes the substrate(s) to product(s).
- **Induced-fit model:** the substrate(s) causes the active site to change shape slightly. The substrate enters the active site to become the enzyme-substrate complex. The enzyme then converts substrate(s) to product(s).

- Environmental factors such as pH and temperature affect enzyme function,.
- **Optimum activity** of an enzyme is the condition(s) under which the enzyme works best.   HL
- **Heat denaturation** of protein is when a protein changes shape at a higher temperature.
- A **denatured enzyme** is an enzyme that has lost its function due to a change in its shape.

In investigating the effect of pH on the rate of catalase activity:
- Hydrogen peroxide is added to a mixture of celery, pH buffer (4, 7 and 13) and washing-up liquid, all at 25 °C, and the volume of foam (bubbles) produced per minute is measured for each pH.
- It is found that the reaction at pH 7 produces the most foam. Therefore, pH 7 is the optimum pH for catalase.

In investigating the effect of temperature on the rate of catalase activity:
- Hydrogen peroxide is added to a mixture of celery (contains catalase), pH buffer 7 and washing-up liquid at 0 °C, 25 °C, 50 °C and 80 °C, and the volume of foam (bubbles) produced per minute is measured for each temperature.
- It is found that the reaction at 25 °C produces the most foam (bubbles). Therefore, 25 °C is the optimum temperature for catalase.

In investigating the effect of heat denaturation on catalase activity: HL
- Hydrogen peroxide is added to a mixture of unboiled and boiled celery along with pH 7 buffer and washing-up liquid and the presence or absence of foam (bubbles) is recorded.
- It is found that there is no reaction in the boiled celery (the catalase enzyme was denatured).

- **Bioprocessing** is the use of living cells or their components, such as enzymes, to make useful products or to carry out useful procedures.
- **Immobilised enzymes** are attached to or trapped in an inert insoluble material.

There are three methods of enzyme immobilisation:
- **Carrier-binding:** binding enzymes to a water-insoluble substance in three ways: physical adsorption, ionic bonding and covalent bonding.
- **Cross-linking:** binding enzymes covalently to each other or to other proteins.
- **Entrapping:** trapping the enzyme in a gel or a membrane.
- One use of immobilised enzymes is in the food industry where an immobilised enzyme called glucose isomerase is used to convert glucose syrups to fructose syrups. Fructose is a sweeter monosaccharide.

Advantages of immobilised enzymes include:
- No contamination of the product occurs at the end of the reaction.
- Can be reused.
- Are more stable.

A **bioreactor** is a vessel in which a product is formed by a cell or cell component, such as an enzyme.

In preparing one enzyme immobilisation and examining its application:
- Mix a yeast suspension with a sodium alginate paste and form alginate beads by solidifying using calcium chloride.
- The beads are then exposed to a sucrose solution which the yeast act on and convert to glucose and fructose.
- These reducing sugars are then tested for using Clinistix strips or using Benedict's solution.

117

Chapter 10 Energy carriers (HL only)

HL

Learning objectives After studying this chapter, you should be able to:
- Describe the structure, function and role of ATP.
- Describe the role of NAD$^+$ and NADP$^+$.

Introduction

The major metabolic processes of photosynthesis and respiration involve movement of electrons (e$^-$) and hydrogen ions (protons, H$^+$). The processes of **oxidation** and **reduction** involve transfer of electrons from one molecule to another.

> **O**xidation **I**s **L**oss of electrons.
> **R**eduction **I**s **G**ain of electrons.

An easy way to remember this is by using the underlined letters in the above box which spell out the mnemonic '**OILRIG**'.

Any molecule that loses electrons is said to be **oxidised** and becomes positively charged or less negative; and any molecule that receives electrons is said to be **reduced** and becomes negatively charged or less positive.

In order to understand the detailed study of photosynthesis and respiration, and how energy is transferred from one form to another, it is necessary to learn about three energy carriers found in all living cells, ATP, NADH and NADPH.

> **NOTE** For the Leaving Certificate, you must know what each acronym stands for.

> **ATP:** adenosine triphosphate
> **NAD$^+$:** nicotinamide adenine dinucleotide
> **NADP$^+$:** nicotinamide adenine dinucleotide phosphate.

ATP as an energy carrier

ATP is the most important energy carrier in living organisms. It is the molecule responsible for directly supplying the power for metabolism to occur.

Fig 10.1 shows the structure of ATP. It consists of an adenine base (also present in DNA – see Chapter 14); a five-carbon sugar called ribose (also present in RNA – see Chapter 14); and three phosphates (P).

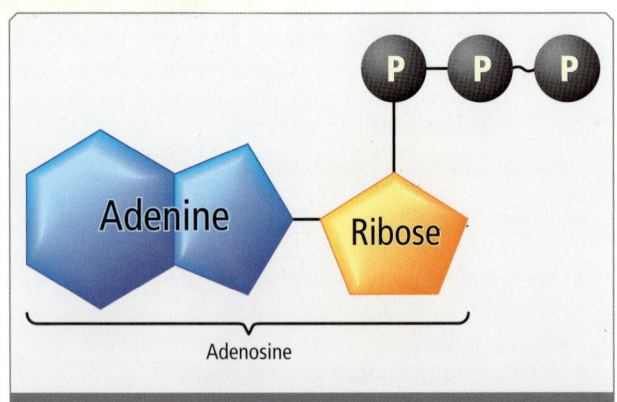

Fig 10.1 The structure of ATP, adenosine triphosphate.

ATP is formed from ADP combining with a phosphate. This is an anabolic reaction (see Chapter 9) and requires energy, which comes from food (glucose). A water molecule is released during the formation of ATP.

> ADP + P + energy → ATP + water

The energy of ATP is stored in the bond between the second and third phosphates (symbolised by the ~). When this bond is broken, energy is released.

> ATP + water → ADP + P + energy

ATP can be thought of as an oil tanker (Fig 10.2) carrying energy (crude oil) from where it was produced (oil well) and refined (oil refinery) to where it is used (combustion engines).

ATP carries energy from where it is produced (mitochondria – see Chapter 12) to where it is needed (for example, protein synthesis – see Chapter 15).

ATP is a high-energy molecule because it is an energy carrier. It is used to power metabolic reactions within cells.

When the third phosphate bond is broken, ADP is formed. ADP stands for adenosine diphosphate.

Fig 10.2 An oil tanker transporting crude oil.

As we will learn in Chapter 12, ATP is formed continuously in the mitochondrion, the power house of the cell, where respiration occurs. A small amount of ATP is also produced during photosynthesis (see Chapter 11).

NAD^+ and $NADP^+$ as high-energy electron and proton carriers

Electrons and protons are very important components in respiration and photosynthesis. In both reactions, electrons gain energy and protons are released in the process. These particles cannot exist by themselves – they are too unstable. Therefore, when they leave one molecule they are transferred to another molecule by the carrier molecules, **NAD^+** (respiration) and **$NADP^+$** (photosynthesis).

Each of these energy carriers can gain one electron (reduction) to become **NAD** and **NADP**. Notice that they now have no charge – they are neutral. They then gain another electron to become **NAD^-** and **$NADP^-$**, respectively. Notice now that each has a negative charge. Hydrogen ions (protons) are positively charged and are attracted towards the NAD^- and $NADP^-$. When hydrogen is taken up by the carriers, they become NADH and NADPH. Note that NADH is used in respiration only and NADPH is used in photosynthesis only.

> **In respiration**
> $NAD^+ + e^- \rightarrow NAD + e^- \rightarrow NAD^- + H^+ \rightarrow NADH$
>
> **In photosynthesis**
> $NADP^+ + e^- \rightarrow NADP + e^- \rightarrow NADP^- + H^+ \rightarrow NADPH$

In both metabolic processes, NADH and NADPH carry the electrons and hydrogen ions to locations where they are required.

- NADH uses its electrons and hydrogen ions to make ATP (see Chapter 12).
- NADPH uses its electrons and hydrogen ions to make glucose (see Chapter 11).

Chapter 10 Questions

HL 1 (a) Distinguish between *oxidation* and *reduction*.
   (b) What has happened to a molecule when it is (i) oxidised and (ii) reduced?

2 What is a proton?

3 (a) What does ATP stand for?
   (b) What is the function of ATP?
   (c) Draw the structure of ATP.
   (d) Give **one** way in which ATP is similar to DNA.
   (e) Give **one** way in which ATP is similar to RNA.
   (f) What bond in ATP is responsible for carrying the energy?

4 Describe how water and energy are involved in the formation of ATP.

5 (a) What does NAD^+ stand for?
   (b) Name a series of reactions in which NAD^+ is used.
   (c) What does $NADP^+$ stand for?
   (d) Name a series of reactions in which $NADP^+$ is used.
   (e) Give the functions of NAD^+ and $NADP^+$.
   (f) With regard to their functions, in what cell organelles might you find NAD^+ and $NADP^+$?

Unit 2 The Cell

Chapter 10 Sample examination questions

HL 1 (a) ATP and NAD⁺ / NADP⁺ play important roles in cell activities.

   (i) Name the substance X, formed by the loss of a phosphate group.
   (ii) The ATP cycle is kept going by Y. What is Y?
   (iii) Suggest a role for NAD⁺ / NADP⁺ in cell activities.

   Section C, Question 12 (a) Higher Level 2009

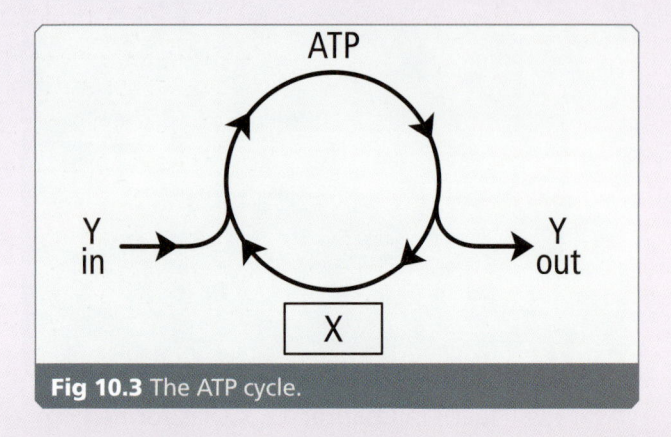

Fig 10.3 The ATP cycle.

Chapter 10 Mind map

Energy carriers

ATP stands for adenosine triphosphate. — HL

- Consists of an adenine molecule, a ribose molecule, and three phosphates.
- A high-energy molecule responsible for carrying energy and powering metabolic reactions within cells.
- When ATP releases its energy in powering a reaction, it is converted to ADP and a phosphate:

   ATP + water → ADP + P + energy

- ADP (adenosine diphosphate) combines with a phosphate during respiration and photosynthesis to form ATP, with the release of water:

   ADP + P + energy → ATP + water

- NAD⁺ stands for nicotinamide adenine dinucleotide. — HL
- NADP⁺ stands for nicotinamide adenine dinucleotide phosphate.
- NAD⁺ and NADP⁺ are molecules responsible for carrying electrons and hydrogen ions from one reaction in a cell to another.
- In respiration the overall reaction for reduction of NAD⁺ is:

   $NAD^+ + 2e^- + H^+ \rightarrow NADH$

- In photosynthesis the overall reaction for reduction of NADP⁺ is:

   $NADP^+ + 2e^- + H^+ \rightarrow NADPH$

Photosynthesis — Chapter 11

Learning objectives After studying this chapter, you should be able to:
- Define and give the balanced chemical equation for *photosynthesis*.
- Describe the locations and roles of chloroplasts and chlorophyll in photosynthesis.
- Describe the formation of carbohydrate in photosynthesis.
- **HL** Describe, in detail, the two stages of photosynthesis: the light stage and dark stage.
- Briefly describe the use of greenhouses in crop growth.
- Investigate the influence of light intensity or carbon dioxide concentration on the rate of photosynthesis.

Introduction

Sunlight is the primary source of energy for life on Earth. The energy in sunlight is trapped in the process of photosynthesis. In this way, light energy is converted to chemical energy. The chemical energy is then passed along the food chain.

Photosynthesis is critical to life on Earth, as without it carbon dioxide levels would rise and oxygen levels would decrease. It is also an important process in the carbon cycle (see Chapter 4).

Organisms that carry out photosynthesis are autotrophic (see Chapters 2 and 3). They include all plants, algae and many forms of bacteria.

Interestingly, about 50 per cent of photosynthesis on Earth occurs in the oceans. Phytoplankton (see Chapter 5), which are collections of microscopic algae in marine habitats, are responsible for producing much of the Earth's oxygen through photosynthesis. Phytoplankton live in the upper layers of the Earth's seas and oceans where light is plentiful.

Photosynthesis

Photosynthesis is a complicated series of chemical reactions and chemical cycles that occur in the chloroplasts of plant cells. The end-product of these reactions is glucose, and oxygen gas is produced as a by-product.

> **Photosynthesis** is the process of producing sugars from carbon dioxide and water using sunlight as a source of energy.

However, these complex reactions can be summarised in one easy-to-remember word equation and balanced chemical equation:

Word equation for photosynthesis

$$\text{Carbon dioxide} + \text{Water} \xrightarrow[\text{Light}]{\text{Chlorophyll}} \text{Glucose} + \text{Oxygen}$$

Balanced chemical equation for photosynthesis

$$6CO_2 + 6H_2O \xrightarrow[\text{Light}]{\text{Chlorophyll}} C_6H_{12}O_6 + 6O_2$$

The chloroplast

Chloroplasts are the organelles in which photosynthesis occurs. All plants and algae have chloroplasts. Photosynthetic bacteria do not have chloroplasts but have the necessary proteins for photosynthesis embedded in their cell membrane.

Fig 11.1A show an image of *Elodea* (Canadian pondweed) with chloroplasts clearly visible. We will be using *Elodea* in an experiment to show how light intensity affects photosynthesis (see pages 127 and 128).

Chloroplasts contribute to the green colour of plants. Notice how the chloroplasts are concentrated around the edge of the cell. This is because the large central vacuole takes up most of the plant cell volume. In leaves, chloroplasts are present mostly in the upper layers of cells of the leaf.

Fig 11.1B shows a sketch of the internal parts of a chloroplast. Notice that chloroplasts have a double plasma membrane. The inner and outer membranes

Unit 2 The Cell

are separated by an intermembrane space. The double membrane is thought to have originated from a **eukaryotic** cell engulfing a bacterium, thus producing a double membrane structure.

The internal part of the chloroplast consists of the stroma (a watery fluid) and stacks of thylakoid membranes collectively called a **granum**. The thylakoid membranes contain the chlorophyll pigments. These are arranged into clusters of pigments called **photosystems** (Fig 11.2).

> **NOTE** The plural of granum is grana.

In photosynthetic bacteria, the machinery that carries out the reactions of photosynthesis are located in the cell membrane.

Requirements for photosynthesis

Photosynthesis is an anabolic process and thus requires an external energy source (sunlight). It also requires the raw materials carbon dioxide, water and the green pigment chlorophyll.

Sunlight

All plants obtain light from the Sun. However, plants are also capable of using artificial light. Sunlight and artificial light sources consist of the seven colours of the rainbow. The chloroplasts of plants specifically use red and blue light for photosynthesis. These colours are absorbed by the chlorophyll molecules. Green and yellow are not used; they are reflected by the chlorophyll molecules. This is why chloroplasts, and hence plants, appear green.

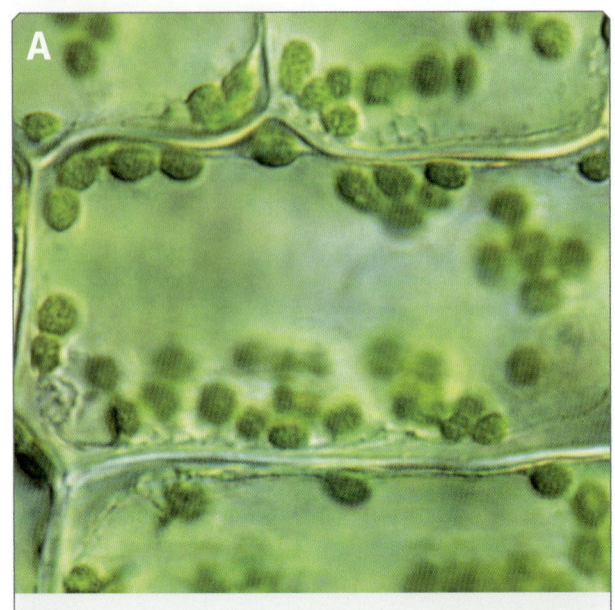

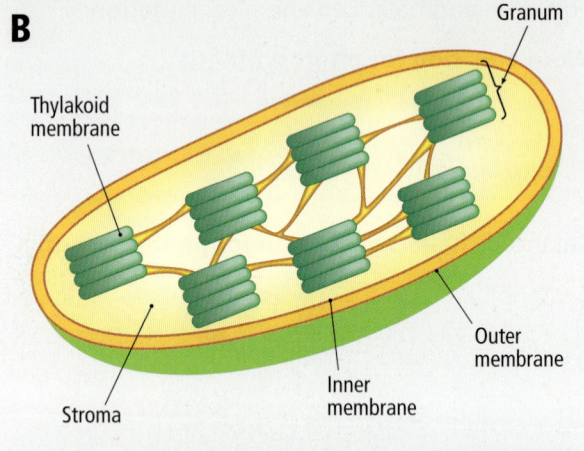

Fig 11.1A Leaf cells from *Elodea*.
Fig 11.1B The structure of a chloroplast.

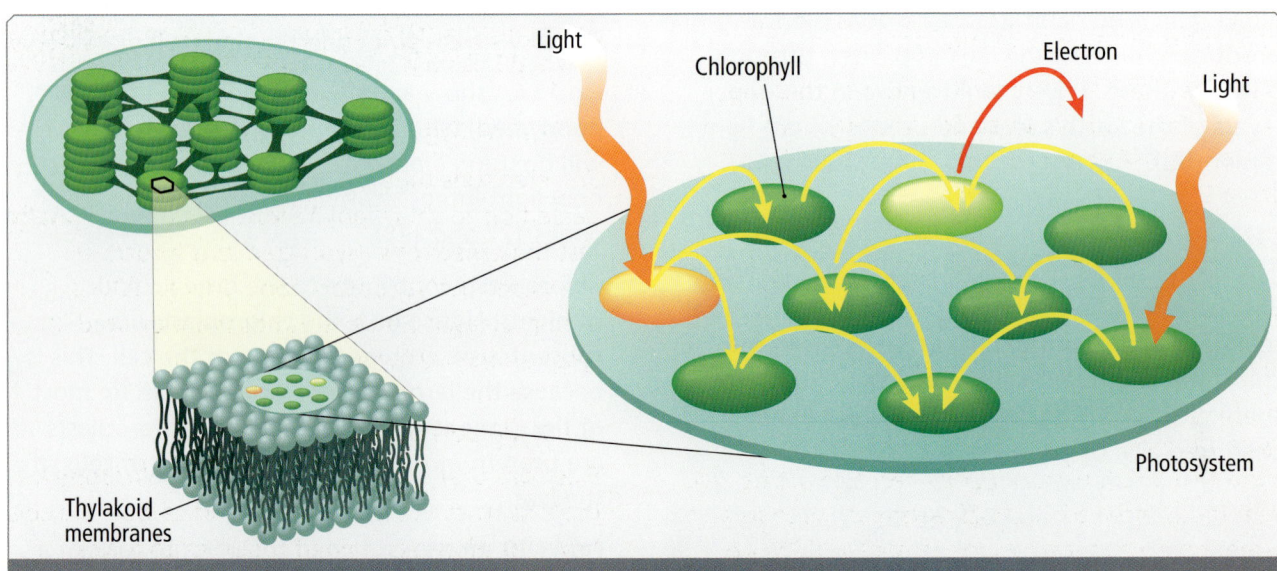

Fig 11.2 A photosystem showing chlorophyll molecules absorbing light energy and transferring the energy onto an electron.

Fig 11.3 Artificial lighting in a greenhouse.

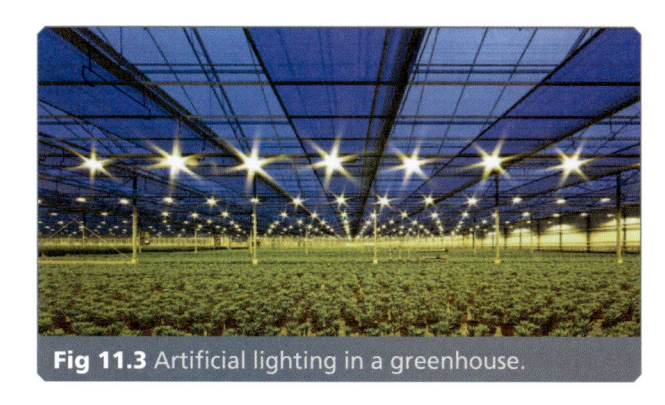

Carbon dioxide

Plants mostly obtain carbon dioxide from the atmosphere. It enters from the atmosphere via the leaf. There are small pores on the underside of all leaves called stomata (singular: stoma). Their opening and closing are controlled by guard cells (see Chapter 25). However, all plants respire, meaning they produce carbon dioxide, which can then be used in photosynthesis. Carbon dioxide is the raw material for the formation of glucose.

Water

Water is obtained from the soil. Water is also a raw material required for the formation of glucose. Horticulturists usually have sophisticated watering systems in their gardens and greenhouses that give the plants the ideal amount of water to maximise growth.

Chlorophyll

Chlorophyll is a green pigment present in the chloroplasts of plant cells. It is responsible for capturing the energy in sunlight.

As we learned in Chapter 3, magnesium is the mineral element required for formation of chlorophyll. Plants need to obtain this mineral from the soil in order to produce chlorophyll.

Human intervention: use of artificial light and carbon dioxide enrichment in crop growth

Many horticulturists use artificial lighting in greenhouses that do not get enough natural light (Fig 11.3). Horticulturists can also artificially manipulate the amount of carbon dioxide in a greenhouse to maximise photosynthesis. Both of these horticultural techniques maximise the growth of plants and crops.

Photosynthesis

1 Absorption of light energy

Chlorophyll molecules absorb sunlight energy. This energy causes electrons to be released from the chlorophyll molecules (Fig 11.5).

2 Photolysis

The energy from sunlight is also used to split water molecules present in the chloroplast. The splitting of water is called photolysis.

The water is split into three components: electrons, hydrogen ions (protons) and oxygen gas (Fig 11.4).

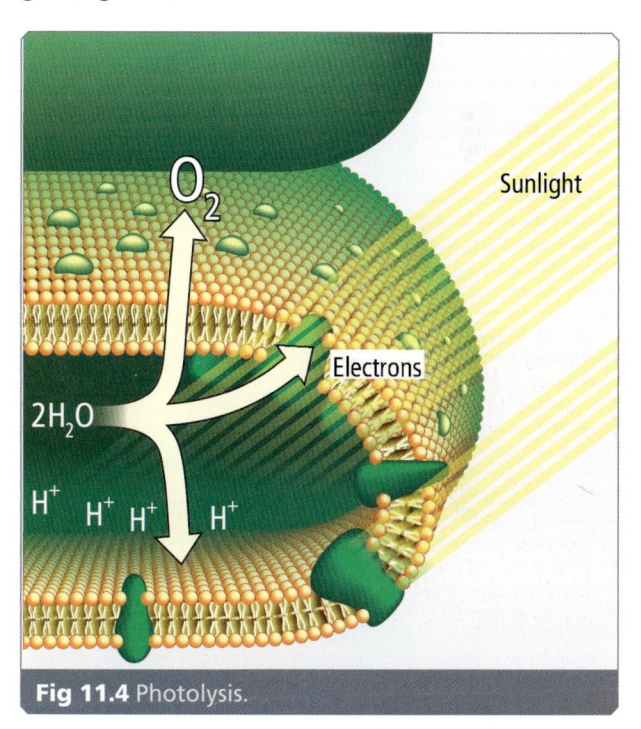

Fig 11.4 Photolysis.

3 Fate of the photolysis products

The electrons that come from photolysis are passed on to chlorophyll molecules that originally lost their electrons. Hydrogen ions (protons) are stored in the proton pool. Oxygen (O_2) is either released into the atmosphere or used in respiration within the leaf.

4 Formation of carbohydrate

Electrons that originally came from chlorophyll, protons from the proton pool and carbon dioxide from the air are all joined together to make carbohydrates. The carbohydrates formed are of the general formula $C_x(H_2O)_y$.

Fig 11.5 The process of photosynthesis.

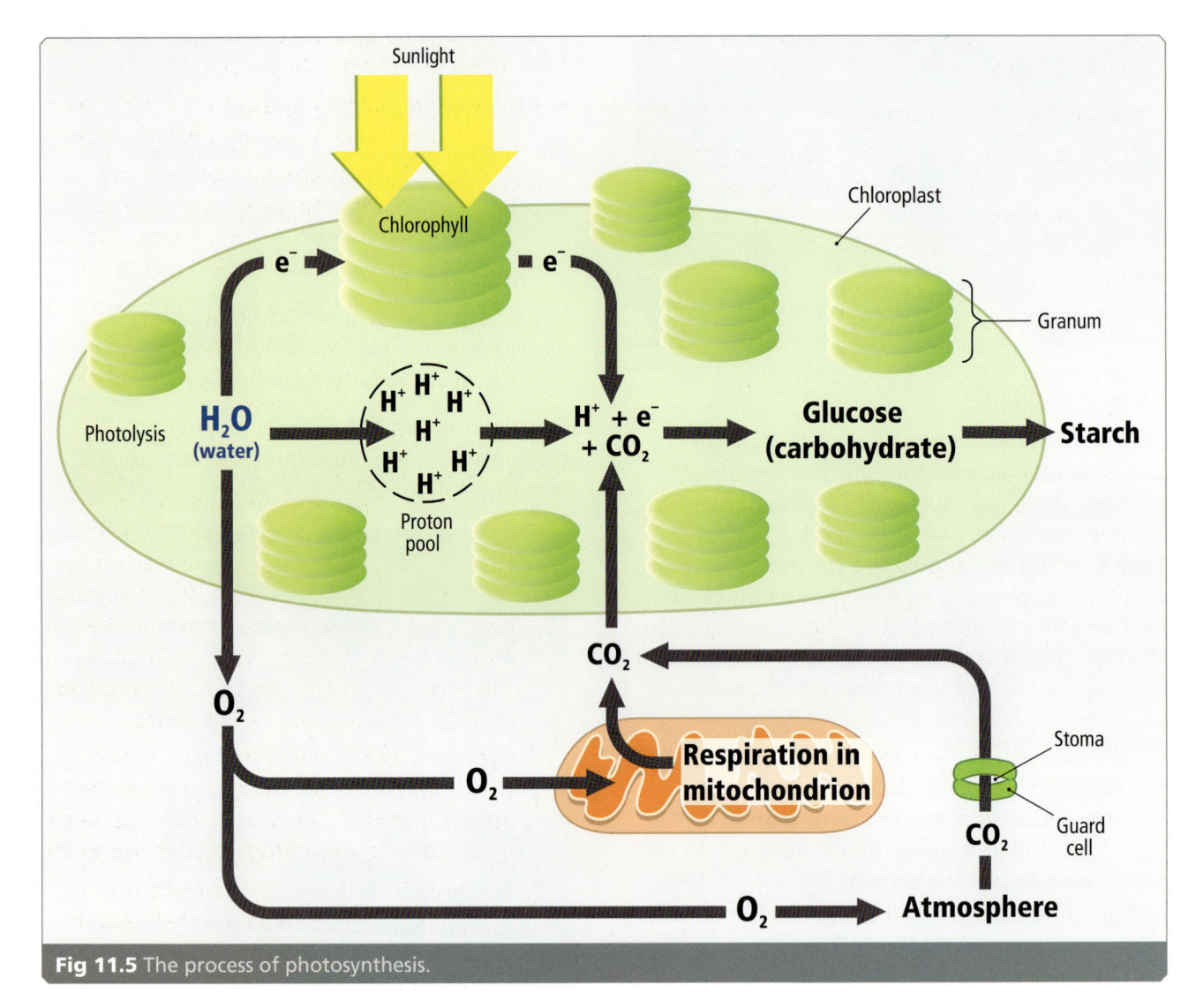

The first carbohydrate produced is glucose ($C_6H_{12}O_6$), which can then be converted into other molecules needed by cells. It can also be stored as starch.

HL Detailed process of photosynthesis

All the reactions of photosynthesis occur in the chloroplast. Many reactions occur in the detailed process of photosynthesis. These reactions can be divided in to two main stages: the **light stage** and **dark stage**. The dark stage is also known as the Calvin cycle, named after Melvin Calvin who discovered it in 1950.

- As its name suggests, the light stage requires light. It is for this reason that it is also called the **light-dependent stage**. The reactions of the light stage require the direct input of energy in the form of sunlight. They occur in the thylakoid membrane of the chloroplast.

- The dark stage does not require light. It is therefore also known as the **light-independent stage**. However, it is important to note here that the dark stage **indirectly** depends on light, as it requires the **products of the light stage** in order for the reactions to occur. The dark stage occurs in the stroma of the chloroplast.

Light stage

The light stage occurs in the thylakoid membrane of the chloroplast and requires sunlight. Photons (small packets of light energy) of light strike a **photosystem** of chlorophyll molecules, which collect the light energy. This energy is directed towards the central chlorophyll molecule of the photosystem, called the **reaction centre chlorophyll** (Fig 11.6).

Electrons are energised in the reaction centre chlorophyll molecule and released. The released electrons can follow one of two pathways:

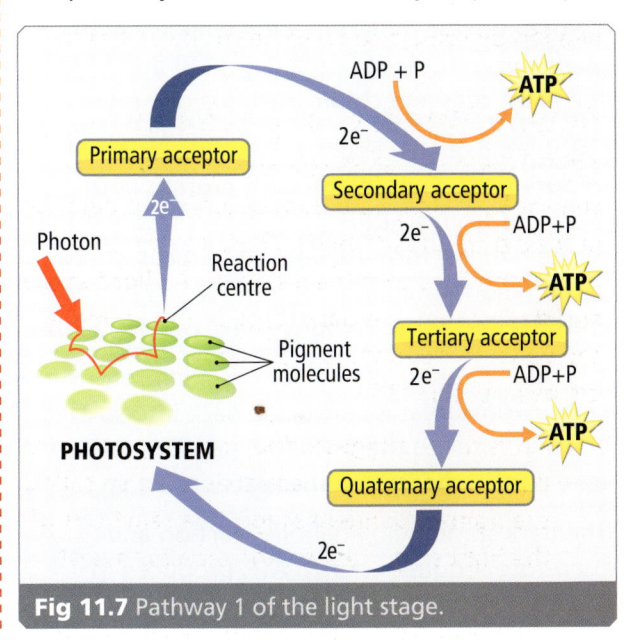

pathway 1 (cyclic pathway) and pathway 2 (non-cyclic pathway).

Pathway 1 (cyclic pathway)

- Electrons are released from the reaction centre chlorophyll molecule and captured by an electron acceptor.
- These electrons have a high level of energy. This energy is released slowly by the passage of the electrons along a series of electron acceptors.
- The electron acceptors use this energy to produce the energy-rich molecule, ATP (adenosine triphosphate) at each step from ADP and a phosphate (Fig 11.7).
- The ATP formed is passed into the stroma of the chloroplast and used in the dark stage.
- Once the electrons have passed through all of the electron acceptors and lost their energy, they are passed back to the same chlorophyll molecule (this is why the process is called 'cyclic').

Pathway 2 (non-cyclic pathway)

- Light strikes a photosystem of chlorophyll molecules, which collect energy and direct it towards the reaction centre chlorophyll molecule of the photosystem.
- Two electrons are released from the central chlorophyll and captured by an electron acceptor.
- The electrons are passed along a series of electron acceptors and lose energy (Fig 11.8).
- This lost energy is used to make ATP from ADP and a phosphate at each step.
- The ATP formed is passed into the stroma of the chloroplast and used in the dark stage.
- The two electrons are then passed onto another photosystem where they are re-energised by sunlight and then captured by $NADP^+$ to become $NADP^-$ (see Chapter 10).
- The first photosystem is still lacking two electrons and these are replaced through the splitting of water (photolysis) by the photosystem.
- Many water molecules are split by many different photosystems. Electrons, oxygen atoms (which join to form oxygen gas, O_2) and hydrogen ions (protons) are formed as a result. The two electrons are taken up by the electron-deficient photosystem; oxygen gas can be used in respiration within the mitochondria of the leaf or be released into the atmosphere; and the protons are stored in the proton pool of the chloroplast.
- Hydrogen ions, in the proton pool of the chloroplast, are positively charged and are attracted towards the $NADP^-$. They are taken up by $NADP^-$ to form NADPH (see Chapter 10).
- The NADPH carries the two electrons and one proton to the stroma, where the dark stage occurs. Note that the two electrons from chlorophyll do not go back to the same chlorophyll molecule. It is for this reason that pathway 2 is called the non-cyclic pathway.

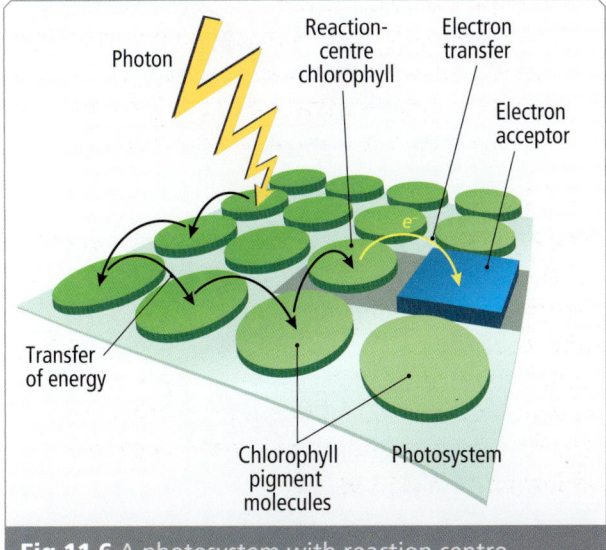

Fig 11.6 A photosystem with reaction centre chlorophyll.

Fig 11.7 Pathway 1 of the light stage.

Fig 11.8 shows the main event of the non-cyclic pathway.

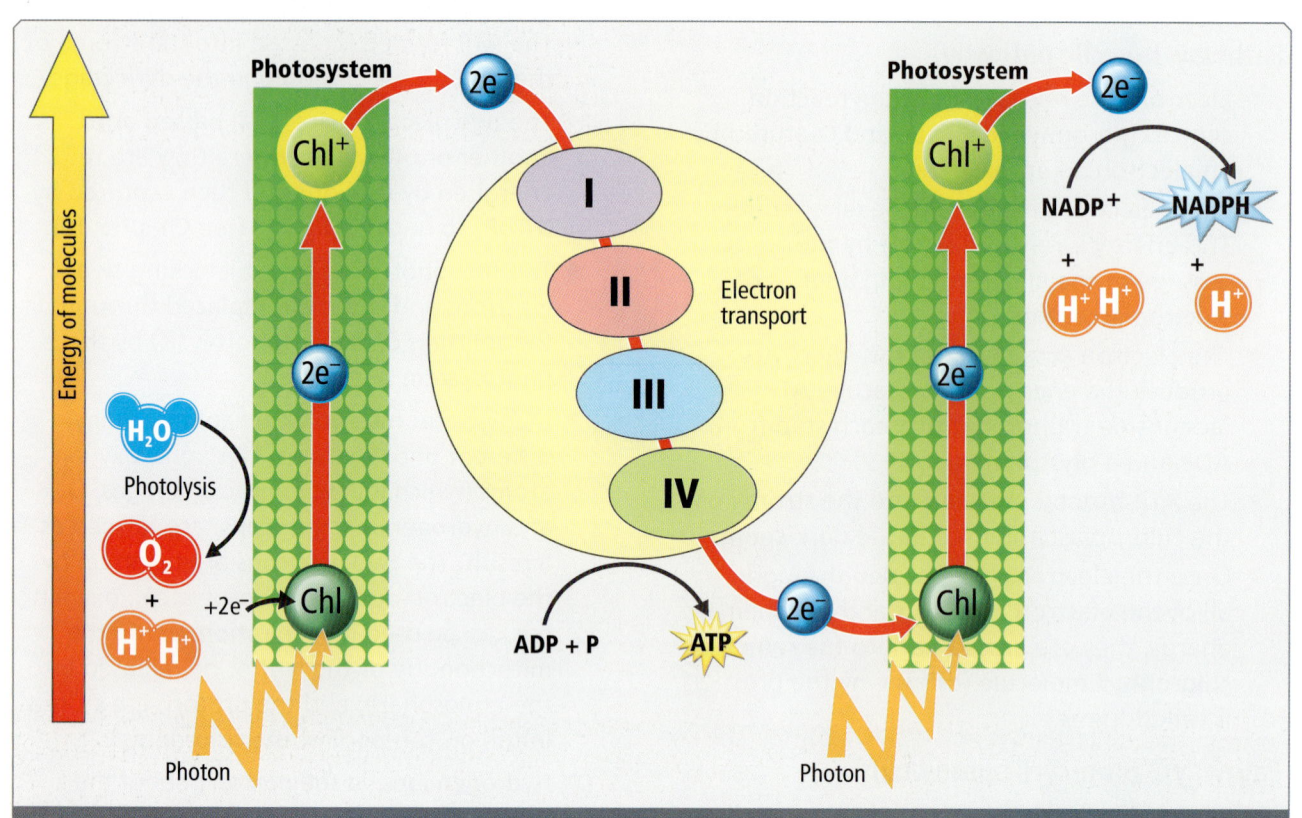

Fig 11.8 Pathway 2 of the light stage. 'Chl' is short for 'chlorophyll'. Chl$^+$ is chlorophyll that has lost an electron.

Dark stage

The dark stage occurs in the stroma of the chloroplast and does not require sunlight. However, the dark stage will not occur unless it receives the products of the light stage: ATP and NADPH.

Carbon dioxide molecules enter the leaves of plant through the stomata (Fig 11.9) and enter the plant cells and chloroplasts via diffusion.

Carbon dioxide is reduced (for explanation of 'reduced' see Chapter 10) with protons and electrons from NADPH. This forms carbohydrates of the general formula $C_x(H_2O)_y$. **Glucose,** a six-carbon monosaccharide, is formed first and then converted to other carbohydrates (see Fig 11.10).

As NADPH donates the electrons and protons to carbon dioxide, it is converted back into NADP$^+$, which returns to the thylakoid membranes to take part in the light stage reactions again.

The dark stage is an anabolic reaction and therefore requires energy. ATP, produced in the light stage, supplies the energy for these reactions. It is broken down into ADP and a phosphate in the process. ADP and phosphate then return to the thylakoid membranes to take part in the light stage once again.

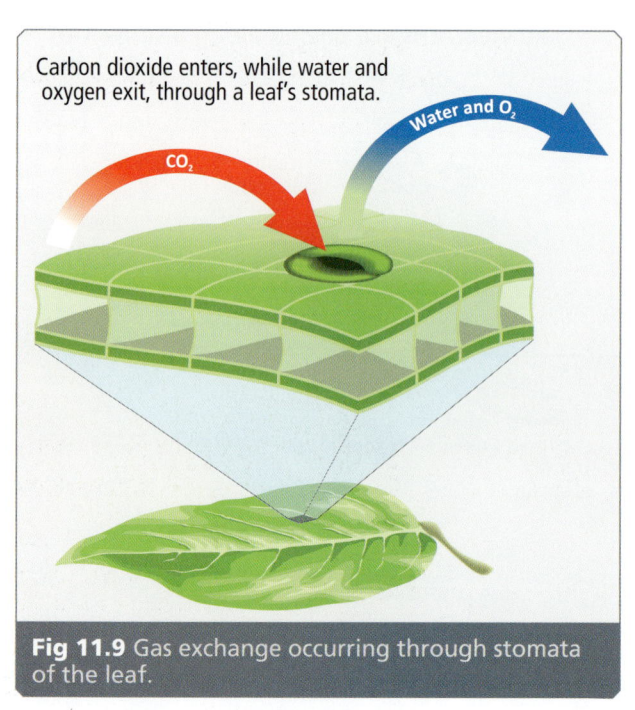

Fig 11.9 Gas exchange occurring through stomata of the leaf.

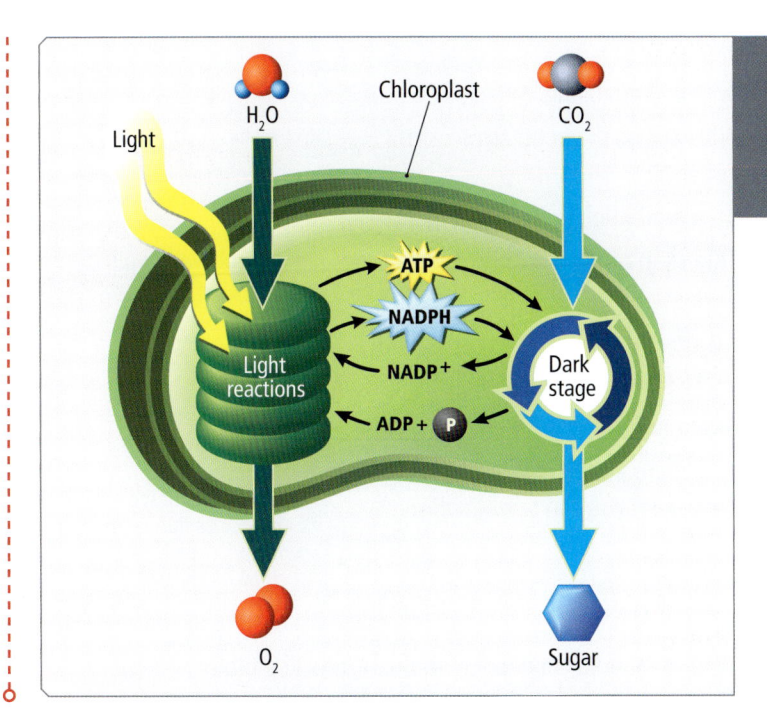

Fig 11.10 Dark stage reactions occurring in the stroma. Notice NADPH gives up electrons and protons to reform NADP$^+$, and ATP is used up in this anabolic reaction, reforming ADP. Both NADP$^+$ and ADP return to the light stage.

Practical activity: to investigate the effect of light intensity OR carbon dioxide concentration on the rate of photosynthesis

The rate of photosynthesis increases with an increase in light intensity, up to a certain point. The point at which the rate does not increase further is the **saturation point.** No matter how much extra light the plant is exposed to, there will be no further increase in the rate of photosynthesis. The rate of photosynthesis can be indirectly measured using a water plant called *Elodea*. It is a type of pondweed commonly used in fish tanks. It belongs to a broad group of water plants commonly known to gardeners as oxygenators. This is because they oxygenate water through the process of photosynthesis.

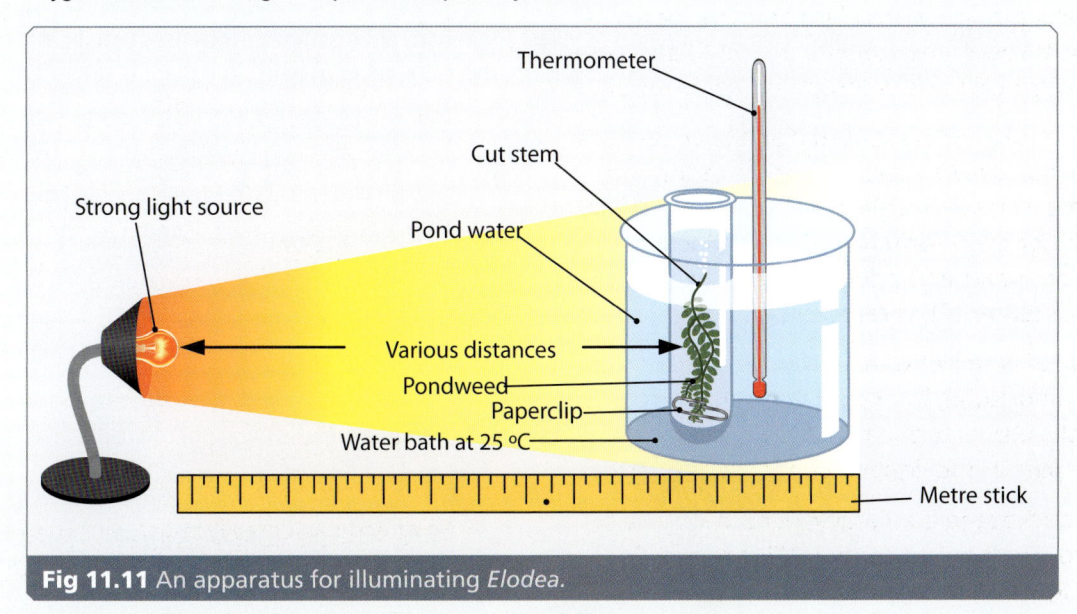

> **NOTE** This practical activity refers only to the effect of light intensity on the rate of photosynthesis.

Fig 11.11 An apparatus for illuminating *Elodea*.

Method

1. Use freshly cut pondweed and cut the stem with a sharp blade.
2. Lightly crush the stem between your fingers. This allows the bubbles of oxygen to be released more easily from the cut end.
3. Pour pond water into a test-tube (do not use tap water unless it has been dechlorinated).
4. Attach a paperclip to the apical (top) part of the stem of *Elodea*. This ensures the piece of pondweed will remain at the bottom of the test-tube.
5. Ensure that the cut end of the stem is pointing upwards.
6. Eliminate as much external light as possible by switching off lights and closing blinds.
7. Place the pondweed 5 cm in front of a fluorescent light source.
8. Allow the pondweed to adjust to its new environment and light intensity for a few minutes. Before you start the experiment ensure you can see bubbles from the cut end of the stem.
9. After adjustment, start the stopwatch and count the bubbles produced in 1 minute.
10. Repeat points 8 and 9 for distances of 20 cm, 40 cm and 80 cm and record the results in a table.
11. Calculate the light intensity for each distance. Light intensity is equal to the inverse of the distance squared ($\frac{1}{d^2}$). Notice from the table below that as the distance from the light source is doubled the light intensity decreases by a factor of four.
12. Draw a graph of the rate of photosynthesis against light intensity. Put light intensity on the x-axis.

> **NOTE:** Note, extreme care must be taken when using the blade.

> **NOTE:** A halogen (fluorescent) light source is preferable to an incandescent light source as fluorescent light has more energy than incandescent light.

Results: effect of light intensity

Distance from light source (m)	0.05	0.1	0.2	0.4	0.8
Bubbles/min (trial 1)					
Bubbles/min (trial 2)					
Bubbles/min (trial 3)					
Average bubbles/min					
Light intensity ($\frac{1}{d^2}$)	400	100	25	6.25	1.56

Notice that if you decide to list your distances in cm, then the light intensity calculation will be $\frac{10{,}000}{d^2}$ because there are 10,000 cm² in 1 m².

Conclusion

What have we learned from this practical activity? The rate of photosynthesis increases with light intensity up to a point, at which the rate of photosynthesis levels off. This is the point at which the plant is saturated with light.

Practical activity questions

1. How did you measure the rate of photosynthesis?
2. Why was an aquatic plant used?
3. Explain the purpose of cutting the stem and crushing it lightly between your fingers before putting it in the pond water.
4. Explain why tap water cannot be used for this experiment.
5. Why must the cut end be pointing upwards?
6. What was the purpose of the paperclip?
7. Explain the importance of eliminating external light.
8. Why is it advisable to use a fluorescent or halogen lamp rather than an everyday (incandescent) light bulb?
9. Why is it important to leave the pondweed in front of the new light intensity for a few minutes before counting the number of bubbles?
10. What is the relationship between the rate of photosynthesis and light intensity?
11. What is meant by light intensity? How is it calculated?
12. When a graph of the relationship is plotted, it levels off. Explain.

Chapter 11 Questions

1. (a) What is *photosynthesis*?
   (b) Write the word equation **and** the balanced chemical equation for photosynthesis.

2. Photosynthesis occurs in the chloroplast. Draw a sketch of a chloroplast, labelling the following structures: *outer membrane, inner membrane, thylakoid membranes, granum* and *stroma*.

3. (a) What is the name of the light-sensitive pigment, present in chloroplasts, that is necessary for photosynthesis?
   (b) What mineral is necessary for its production?
   (c) Name the organelle in which you would find this light-sensitive pigment in leaf cells.
   (d) What is a *photosystem*?
   (e) Explain where exactly in a plant cell you would find a photosystem.

4. Name **four** important requirements for photosynthesis and give each of their source(s).

5. (a) **Photolysis** occurs during photosynthesis. Explain what is meant by the term in bold.
   (b) Name the **three** products of photolysis and give the fates of each.

6. (a) Name the end-product of photosynthesis.
   (b) Give **two** possible fates of this end-product.
   (c) To what group of biomolecules does this end-product belong?
   (d) Give the general formula for this group of biomolecules (*see* Chapter 3).

HL 7. (a) The light stage can be subdivided into pathway 1 and pathway 2. What are the alternative names of the two pathways of the light stage?
   (b) Explain why these pathways have their particular names.
   (c) Where exactly does each of the two pathways occur?
   (d) What do you understand by a high-energy electron?
   (e) What are the products of the two pathways and what are their fates?

8. (a) What is the alternative name for the dark stage?
   (b) Carbon dioxide is involved in the dark stage. Explain how carbon dioxide enters the leaf.
   (c) Give an outline account of all the biochemical reactions of the dark stage.
   (d) Is the dark stage anabolic or catabolic? Explain.

Chapter 11 Sample examination questions

1. The diagram shows part of a section through a leaf.

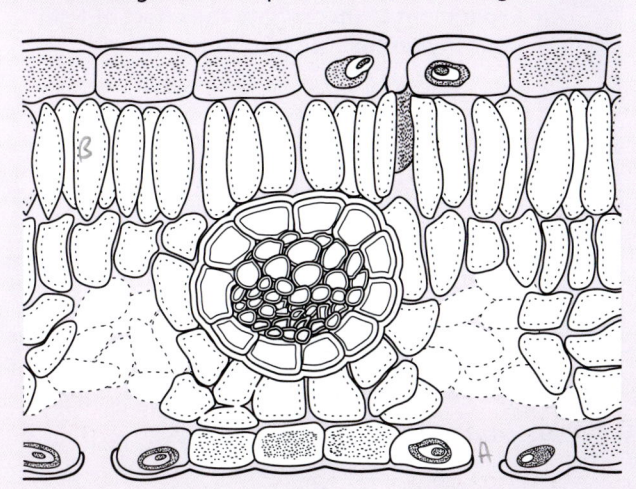

   (a) Use the letter **A** to show a point of entry of carbon dioxide. Name this point.
   (b) Name a gas that **leaves** the leaf at this point.
   (c) Use the letter **B** to show the part of the leaf in which most photosynthesis occurs.
   (d) Name the structures in plant cells in which photosynthesis occurs.
   (e) In addition to carbon dioxide another small molecule is needed for photosynthesis. Name this other molecule.

   Section A, Question 4 Ordinary Level 2006

Unit 2   The Cell

HL 2. (i) Name the openings in the leaf which allow the entry of carbon dioxide for photosynthesis.

(ii) During photosynthesis oxygen is produced.
1. From what substance is oxygen produced?
2. In which stage of photosynthesis is oxygen produced?
3. Give **two** possible fates of oxygen following its production.

(iii) Give an account of the role of each of the following in photosynthesis:
1. ATP 2. NADP

Section C, Question 14 (a) Higher Level 2008

Chapter 11 Mind map

Word equation for photosynthesis

$$\text{Carbon dioxide} + \text{Water} \xrightarrow{\text{Chlorophyll}/\text{Light}} \text{Glucose} + \text{Oxygen}$$

Balanced chemical equation for photosynthesis

$$6CO_2 + 6H_2O \xrightarrow{\text{Chlorophyll}/\text{Light}} C_6H_{12}O_6 + 6O_2$$

Photosynthesis is the process of producing sugars from carbon dioxide and water using sunlight as a source of energy.

Chloroplasts
- The organelles in which photosynthesis occurs.
- Have a double membrane (inner and outer).
- Within the chloroplast is an aqueous liquid (stroma) and stacks of membranes called thylakoids. Each stack of thylakoids is called a granum.

Requirements for photosynthesis
- Light
- Carbon dioxide
- Water
- Chlorophyll

Photosynthesis
- Chlorophyll absorbs sunlight and releases electrons.
- Water molecules are split (photolysis) into electrons, hydrogen ions (protons) and oxygen gas.
- Electrons from water are sent back to chlorophyll; protons are stored in the proton pool; and the oxygen gas is either released into the atmosphere or used in respiration.
- Electrons from chlorophyll and protons from the proton pool, along with carbon dioxide from the air, are combined to make carbohydrates.

Experiment to investigate the effect of light intensity on the rate of photosynthesis
- Cut a piece of *Elodea* and place in a test-tube of pond water.
- Shine a bright light on the pondweed from various distances, counting the number of bubbles produced per minute for each distance.
- The light intensity is calculated by $\frac{1}{d^2}$ (where the distance is measured in metres).
- Plot a graph of the rate of photosynthesis (bubbles per min) against light intensity.

Detailed process of photosynthesis

HL

- Photosynthesis occurs in two stages: light stage and dark stage.
- Light stage consists of two pathways: pathway 1 (cyclic) and pathway 2 (non-cyclic).
- Both pathways occur in the thylakoid membranes of the chloroplast.
- The dark stage (also called the Calvin cycle) occurs in the stroma.

	PHOTOSYNTHESIS		
	Light stage		Dark stage
	Cyclic	Non-cyclic	
Location	Thylakoid membrane	Thylakoid membrane	Stroma
Light requirement	Light-dependent	Light-dependent	Light-independent
Product(s)	ATP	ATP; NADPH; oxygen gas	Glucose

Light stage, Pathway 1 (Cyclic pathway)
- Light strikes a photosystem of chlorophyll molecules, which collect energy and direct it towards the central chlorophyll molecule of the photosystem.
- Two electrons are released from the central chlorophyll and captured by an electron acceptor.
- The electrons are passed along a series of electron acceptors and lose energy.
- This lost energy is used to make ATP from ADP and a phosphate.
- The ATP formed is passed into the stroma of the chloroplast and used in the dark stage.
- The electrons are passed back to the same chlorophyll molecule when they have lost all of their energy.

Light stage, Pathway 2 (Non-cyclic pathway):
- Sunlight strikes a photosystem of chlorophyll molecules, which collect energy and direct it towards the reaction centre chlorophyll molecule.
- The reaction centre chlorophyll releases two electrons.
- The two electrons are captured by an electron acceptor.
- Electrons are passed along a series of electron acceptors and lose energy, producing ATP from ADP and phosphates in the process.
- The ATP is passed to the stroma to be used in the dark stage.
- When the two electrons have lost all their energy in producing ATP, they are then re-energised by light in another photosystem and passed to $NADP^+$, which is reduced to become $NADP^-$.
- Water is split (photolysis) by the photosystem producing more electrons, oxygen gas and hydrogen ions (protons).
- The electrons are taken up by the reaction centre chlorophyll, which returns to its original state ready to absorb more sunlight.
- The oxygen gas is either released into the atmosphere or taken in by the mitochondria for respiration.
- Hydrogen ions are stored in the proton pool. These join with $NADP^-$ to form NADPH, which then travels to the stroma.

Dark stage (Calvin cycle)
- Carbon dioxide molecules enter via stomata.
- Carbon dioxide is chemically joined with protons and electrons from NADPH to form glucose.
- NADPH is broken down into $NADP^+$ in the process.
- $NADP^+$ returns to the thylakoid membranes to take part in the light stage again.
- ATP supplies the energy, being broken down into ADP and a phosphate in the process.
- ADP and phosphate return to the thylakoid membranes to take part in the light stage again.

Chapter 12   Respiration

Learning objectives   After studying this chapter, you should be able to:
- Define and give the balanced chemical equation for *respiration*.
- Describe the two stages of aerobic respiration and their cellular locations.
- Describe the role of the mitochondrion in respiration.
- Define *anaerobic respiration* and make reference to fermentation.
- HL: Describe, in detail, glycolysis, Krebs cycle and the electron transport chain.
- Describe ethanol fermentation or lactic acid fermentation.
- Describe the role of microorganisms in industrial fermentation.
- Prepare and show the production of alcohol by yeast.

Introduction

Respiration is a catabolic reaction carried out and controlled by enzymes. A large molecule (glucose) is broken down (**catabolism**) into smaller molecules (water and carbon dioxide) with the **release** of energy.

> **Respiration** is the enzyme-controlled process of releasing energy from food.

Respiration is an important metabolic process of **all** living organisms. It is needed to produce energy. This energy is then used within the cell(s) of the organism for other metabolic processes such as growth, repair, reproduction (asexual and sexual), movement, response, digestion and excretion.

There are two types of respiration: **aerobic respiration** and **anaerobic respiration**.

Aerobic respiration

> **Aerobic respiration** is the enzyme-controlled release of energy from food *using oxygen*.

Aerobic respiration is the use of oxygen to extract energy from food molecules, such as glucose. It is the more important reaction for many living organisms as it produces more energy than anaerobic respiration. This is because the glucose is completely broken down into the small molecules of water and carbon dioxide.

> **NOTE:** For Leaving Certificate Biology, you must know the balanced chemical equation for aerobic respiration.

Word equation for aerobic respiration

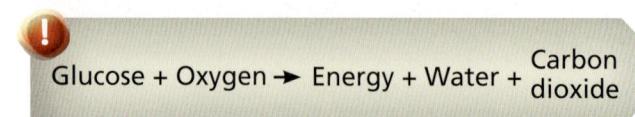

> Glucose + Oxygen → Energy + Water + Carbon dioxide

Balanced chemical equation for aerobic respiration

> $C_6H_{12}O_6 + 6O_2 \longrightarrow$ Energy + $6H_2O + 6CO_2$

The mitochondrion

Aerobic respiration occurs in the mitochondrion (*see* Chapter 6). The mitochondrion is a cell organelle responsible for production of energy.

Like the chloroplast, the mitochondrion has a double-membrane structure (possessing outer and inner membranes). The inner membrane is highly-folded into structures called **cristae**, to allow greater surface area for the enzymes involved in aerobic respiration.

Inside the inner membrane of the mitochondrion is the lumen of the mitochondrion, which contains an aqueous (watery) solution called the **matrix**.

The mitochondrion is thought to have originated from a bacterium that either invaded or was engulfed by a common ancestor of plant and animal cells many billions of years ago!

Fig 12.1 shows the structure of a mitochondrion.

Aerobic respiration is divided into two stages: **stage 1** and **stage 2**.

Fig 12.1 Structure of a mitochondrion.

Fig 12.2 Aerobic respiration.

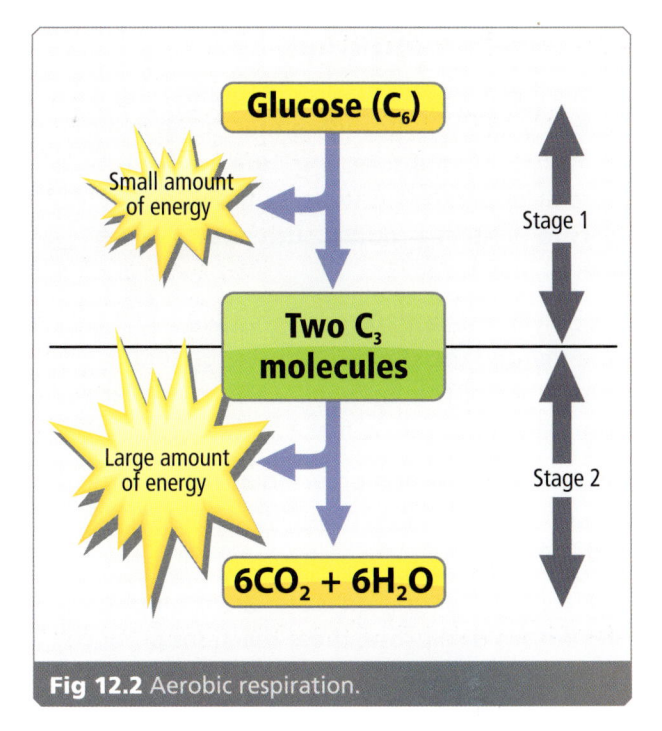

Stage 1

- Stage 1 reactions occur in the cytosol and do not require oxygen. However, it is important to note that stage 1 can occur in the presence of oxygen.
- Glucose, which is a six-carbon molecule (chemical formula: $C_6H_{12}O_6$), is broken down into two three-carbon molecules. A small amount of energy is released from this catabolic reaction. Most of the energy is still present in the two three-carbon molecules.

Stage 2

- Stage 2 reactions occur in the mitochondrion and use the products of stage 1.
- The two three-carbon molecules are moved to the mitochondrion and broken down further to produce water and carbon dioxide. These reactions do require oxygen. If oxygen is absent or is in limited supply, then stage 2 will not occur.
- A large amount of energy is released in the mitochondrion as the molecules are completely broken down.
- Carbon dioxide and water are by-products of stage 2 and are excreted.

Fig 12.2 shows a summary of stage 1 and stage 2 of aerobic respiration.

Anaerobic respiration

> **Anaerobic respiration** is the enzyme-controlled release of energy from food *without oxygen.*

Anaerobic respiration occurs in the cytosol and is also known as **fermentation.** It produces only a very small amount of energy as it does not completely break down the substrate, glucose. This is due to either an absence or a limited supply of oxygen.

There are two types of fermentation: **lactic acid fermentation** and **alcohol fermentation.**

Lactic acid fermentation

Lactic acid fermentation occurs in all animals, many bacteria and fungi. It occurs in the muscles of humans during intense exercise. The muscles do not get enough oxygen during intense exercise and respire anaerobically. This produces lactic acid. Muscle soreness after exercise is due to a build-up of lactic acid.

> **Lactic acid fermentation:**
>
> Glucose → Lactic acid + Small amount of energy

Alcohol fermentation

Alcohol fermentation, as its name suggests, produces alcohol. Alcohol fermentation is the oldest type of bioprocessing. Humans have been using alcohol fermentation for thousands of years to produce products such as beer, wine, vinegar and bread.

It is only in the last 100 years that we have learned the chemical process behind fermentation. This has enabled us to further refine the processes to make better products.

Alcohol fermentation occurs in all plants (when oxygen is limited) and many types of bacteria and fungi.

As alcohol fermentation is also an incomplete breakdown of glucose, these reactions produce very little energy.

Fig 12.3 shows a large vessel in which alcohol fermentation is occurring.

> **Alcohol fermentation:**
>
> Glucose → Alcohol + Carbon dioxide + Small amount of energy

Fig 12.3 Alcohol fermentation is a type of anaerobic respiration.

HL Detailed process of aerobic respiration

As we have already learned, aerobic respiration occurs in two main stages: **stage 1 (glycolysis)** and **stage 2 (Krebs cycle and electron transport chain)**.

Stage 1 (Glycolysis)

- Stage 1 is also called **glycolysis** – '*glyco-*' meaning 'sugar' and '*-lysis*' meaning 'to break'.
- It occurs in the cytosol and is oxygen-independent.
- Glucose is a six-carbon monosaccharide that is broken down in a number of enzyme-controlled reactions to form two three-carbon molecules called pyruvic acid (Fig 12.4).

> **NOTE:** Pyruvic acid is also called pyruvate.

- Because this procedure involves the breakage of chemical bonds, energy is released in the form of high-energy electrons and protons. These are captured by the energy carrier, **NAD$^+$** (*see* Chapter 10). Two **NADH** molecules are formed when four electrons and two protons are released from glycolysis. This is a **reduction reaction.** The NAD$^+$ is said to have been **reduced** to NADH.
- Two molecules of **ATP** are also produced during glycolysis.

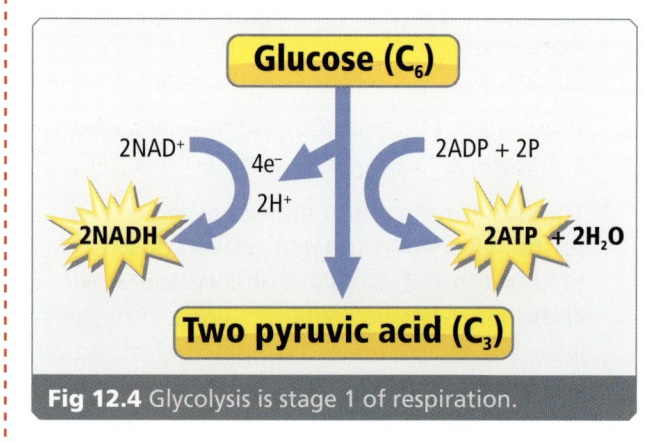

Glucose (C$_6$)

2NAD$^+$ 4e$^-$ 2ADP + 2P
            2H$^+$
2NADH   2ATP + 2H$_2$O

Two pyruvic acid (C$_3$)

Fig 12.4 Glycolysis is stage 1 of respiration.

Stage 2

- Stage 2 occurs in the mitochondrion and is entirely dependent on oxygen. If oxygen is lacking or absent, then pyruvic acid from glycolysis enters the anaerobic respiration pathway.

- Stage 2 is composed of two sets of reactions: **Krebs cycle** and **electron transport chain**.

Krebs cycle

Krebs cycle is named after Hans Adolf Krebs, a German biochemist who discovered the sequence of chemical reactions making up stage 2. In 1953, he was awarded the Nobel Prize for his efforts.

- The Krebs cycle (also known as the citric acid cycle) extracts further energy from pyruvic acid produced in glycolysis. ATP is produced in the process.
- There are two pyruvic acid molecules produced from glycolysis. Therefore, one glucose molecule produces two pyruvic acid molecules. Each pyruvic acid molecule enters a separate Krebs cycle. It is important to note that two Krebs cycles occur for each glucose molecule metabolised in glycolysis.
- Pyruvic acid enters the mitochondria and is converted to **acetyl coenzyme A** (CoA) molecule. Acetyl CoA is a two-carbon molecule, whereas pyruvic acid contains three carbons. Therefore, a carbon is lost in this reaction. It is lost in the form of carbon dioxide, which is excreted by the lungs.
- In addition, because a chemical bond was broken in converting pyruvic acid to acetyl CoA, two high-energy electrons and one proton are released. These are captured by NAD^+ to become NADH.
- Acetyl CoA enters a cycle of reactions by joining with a **four-carbon molecule.**
- When acetyl CoA joins with the four-carbon molecule, a **six-carbon molecule** is formed.
- The **six-carbon molecule** is broken down into a **five-carbon molecule,** which is in turn broken down to the **four-carbon molecule** and the cycle begins again.

> **NOTE** You do not need to know the names of the four-, five- or six-carbon molecules.

- As each of these reactions involves a loss of a carbon, carbon dioxide is produced, which is excreted via the lungs.
- Along this cycle of reactions, chemical bonds are being broken. Therefore, high-energy electrons and protons are being released.

Two electrons and one proton are released at C6 to C5 reaction, forming NADH; and four electrons and two protons are released at the C5 to C4 reaction, forming 2NADH.

- ATP is also formed directly at the C5 to C4 stage of Krebs cycle.

Fig 12.5 shows the reactions that occur in Krebs cycle.

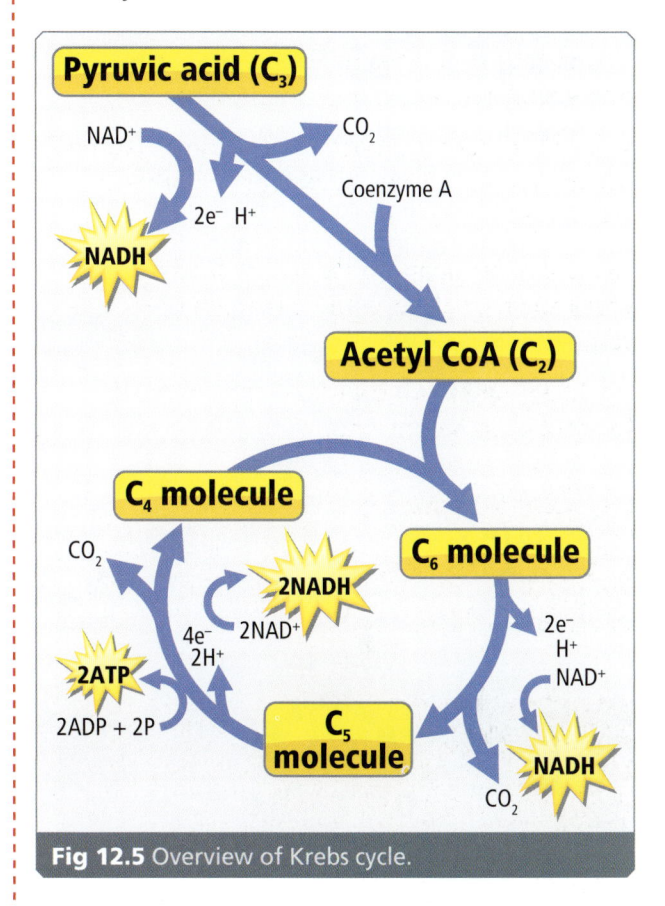

Fig 12.5 Overview of Krebs cycle.

Electron transport chain

As its name suggests, the electron transport chain involves the transfer of electrons along a series of enzymes.

- The electron transport chain is responsible for the vast majority of the ATP formed in aerobic respiration.
- The electron transport chain occurs on the inner membrane of the mitochondrion. The inner membrane is highly folded into cristae, which give a greater surface area. This allows for a higher rate of production of ATP.
- The NADH molecules, formed during glycolysis and the Krebs cycle, are transported to the inner membrane of the mitochondrion

where enzymes take the high-energy electrons and protons from NADH. The NADH becomes NAD^+ in the process (**oxidation**). NAD^+ travels back to glycolysis and the Krebs cycle to be reused.

- The high-energy electrons and protons are used to catalyse the formation of ATP from ADP and a phosphate. Each NADH metabolised in the electron transport chain produces three ATP molecules. ATP goes on to power metabolic reactions, such as growth, repair, movement, digestion, reproduction and excretion.
- Low-energy electrons and protons are left over and are taken up by oxygen gas to form water at the end of the electron transport chain.

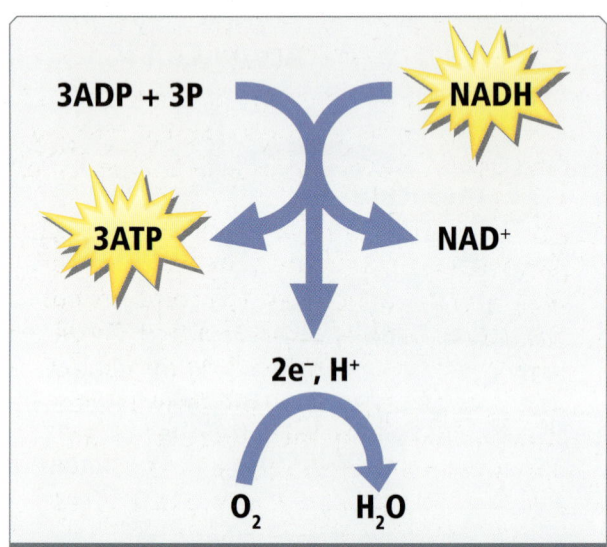

Fig 12.6 Overview of the electron transport chain.

Detailed process of anaerobic respiration

As we have already learned, anaerobic respiration is also called fermentation. It occurs in the cytosol of living cells and occurs without the use of oxygen.

There are two types of fermentation: **lactic acid fermentation** and **ethanol fermentation**. Both types of fermentation begin with glycolysis.

Glycolysis occurs and produces pyruvic acid with the same sequence of reactions as occurs in aerobic respiration (Fig 12.4). The reactions that follow the production of pyruvic acid differ between the two types of fermentation (Fig 12.7).

Lactic acid fermentation

- Pyruvic acid is reduced by NADH and forms lactic acid. In the process the NADH is oxidised (loss of electrons) to NAD^+.
- Pyruvic acid and lactic acid are both three-carbon molecules, so no carbon dioxide is produced.
- Lactic acid fermentation occurs in all animals (when there is a lack of oxygen) and in many bacteria and fungi. Lactic acid formation in humans usually results in muscle soreness.

Ethanol fermentation

- Pyruvic acid is reduced by NADH and forms ethanol (alcohol) and carbon dioxide. NADH is oxidised to NAD^+.
- Ethanol is a two-carbon molecule and pyruvic acid is a three-carbon molecule, so one carbon dioxide molecule is released for every ethanol molecule produced in fermentation.
- Ethanol fermentation occurs in all plants (when there is a lack of oxygen) and many bacteria and fungi.

Fig 12.7 shows an overview of the processes of both lactic acid fermentation and ethanol fermentation, along with glycolysis.

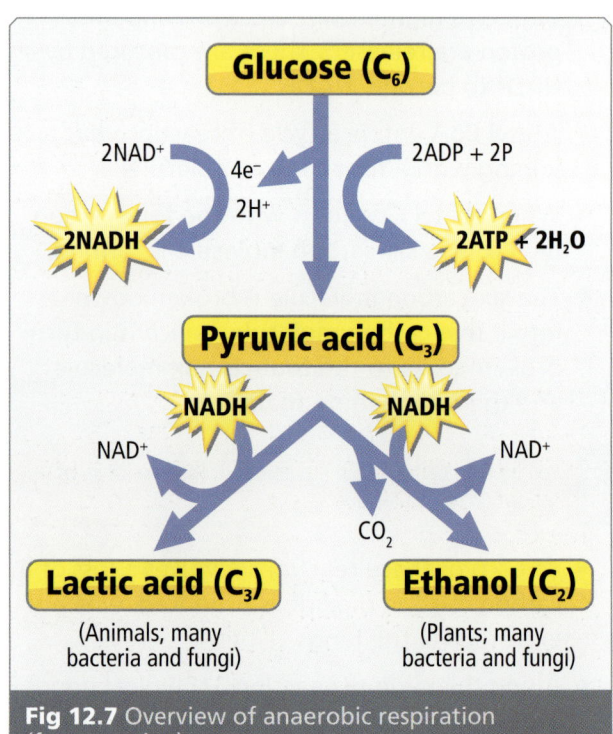

Fig 12.7 Overview of anaerobic respiration (fermentation).

Role of microorganisms in industrial fermentation

Industrial fermentation is a type of **bioprocessing**. In Chapter 9, we learned the definition of bioprocessing.

> **Bioprocessing** is the use of living cells or their components, such as enzymes, to make useful products or to carry out useful procedures.

In industry, fermentation is taken to mean the use of microorganisms to produce products, regardless of whether or not oxygen is present. However, we must remember that scientifically speaking, fermentation is anaerobic respiration.

Common fermentation reactions carried out on a daily basis in industry include:
- Brewing alcoholic beverages and baking bread (using *Saccharomyces cerevicia*).
- Producing dairy products such as yoghurts and cheese (using *Lactobacillus bulgaricus* and *Streptococcus lactis*). The bacteria produce lactic acid, which curdles the milk.
- Making vinegar (using *Acetobacter aceti*).

The microorganisms are grown in a culture that is then placed in a bioreactor along with the substrate(s). In Chapter 9 we learned the definition of bioreactor.

> A **bioreactor** is a vessel in which a product is formed by a cell or cell component, such as an enzyme.

The temperature, oxygen levels (if oxygen is present), carbon dioxide levels, waste product levels are all controlled very tightly and usually electronically.

The microorganisms and substrates are mixed so that action on the substrate is maximised and the reaction will proceed at a faster rate. The mixing is carried out by metal stirrers within the bioreactor that are rotated at a set rate by an agitation system.

The reactions in a bioreactor nearly always create foam due to the gases produced within the reaction mixture. This foam is taken off at the top of the bioreactor either manually or by using a foam breaker. Most industrial bioreactors have many tubes. These carry substances such as substrate(s), gases (such as oxygen via submerged aerator to evenly distribute the gases throughout the mixture), buffers (to maintain pH), water and product(s).

As we learned in Chapter 9 on enzymes, there are two main ways in which industrial fermentation (bioprocessing) is carried out: **batch culture** and **continuous-flow culture**.

1 Batch cultures

- A typical batch culture bioreactor consists of a large steel vessel with agitation and heating/cooling systems.
- Batch bioreactors carry out fermentation reactions in cycles, which involve a sequence of steps that come to a definite end. The product(s) is usually withdrawn before too many waste products build up, that is, before the decline phase of the bacterial growth curve (*see* Chapter 20).
- The withdrawal of product signals the end of the cycle. The bioreactor is emptied, cleaned and sterilised in preparation for another cycle.

2 Continuous-flow cultures

- Continuous flow culture bioreactors are very similar in structure to batch bioreactors but usually have more sensors attached. These sensors function in maintaining the correct conditions (temperature, pH, oxygen and carbon dioxide concentrations and so on) throughout an entire reaction.

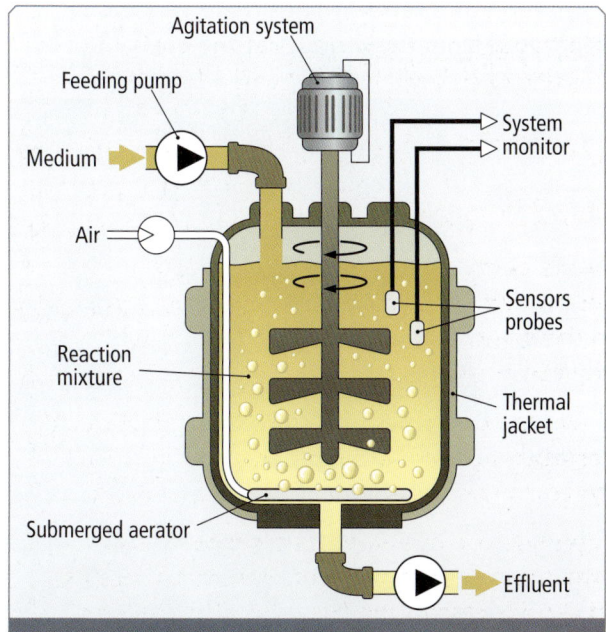

Fig 12.8 The structure of a typical bioreactor used in industrial fermentation.

- Nutrients, substrates and medium are continuously infused into the bioreactor with the reactions proceeding at the desired rate and product(s)/effluent is continuously siphoned off.

Bioprocessing with immobilised cells

We learned about bioprocessing with immobilised cells in Chapter 9. This type of bioprocessing also applies to industrial fermentation. Cells are often immobilised to produce useful products.

Entrapment of cells in a polymer gel, such as alginate, is the most widely studied and used method of cell immobilisation. It has the advantage that it does not damage the cell in any way and substrate(s) can enter and product(s) can leave relatively easily.

Yeast cells are the most commonly immobilised cell due to their use in the industrial fermentation of alcohol. The cells are grown in culture and then mixed with a gel such as sodium alginate. The gel is hardened by adding the cell/gel mixture drop by drop to a solution of calcium chloride. The beads that result contain trapped cells in a solid matrix. As long as the cells are kept in a nutrient medium, they will survive.

The beads containing the immobilised cells are added to the bioreactor and sugars (substrate) are added. The mixture is agitated (mixed) throughout the reaction to maximise the formation of alcohol. The cells are very easily separated from the product at the end of the reaction as they are trapped in the beads. They can be washed and reused.

Fig 12.9 shows an electron micrograph (using a transmission electron microscope) of yeast cells immobilised in calcium alginate.

Uses of immobilised cells

- Immobilised yeast is used in the industrial fermentation of beer, wines and spirits.
- The production of penicillin G uses immobilised *Penicillium* fungal cells trapped in k-carrageenan (a type of polysaccharide from red algae).
- Immobilised *E. coli* are used in water treatment plants to detoxify sewage in waste water.

Advantages of immobilised cells

- Immobilised cells retain their viability. Cell immobilisation is a gentle procedure. The cells are not damaged in any way by the procedure. The cells are simply trapped in a matrix.
- Immobilised cells retain the ability to multiply within the matrix, giving very high cell densities and a more efficient product formation.
- Immobilised cells are easily recovered at the end of the process. Filtration is the usual method of recovering immobilised cells.
- The beads of immobilised cells can be reused following a thorough washing procedure.

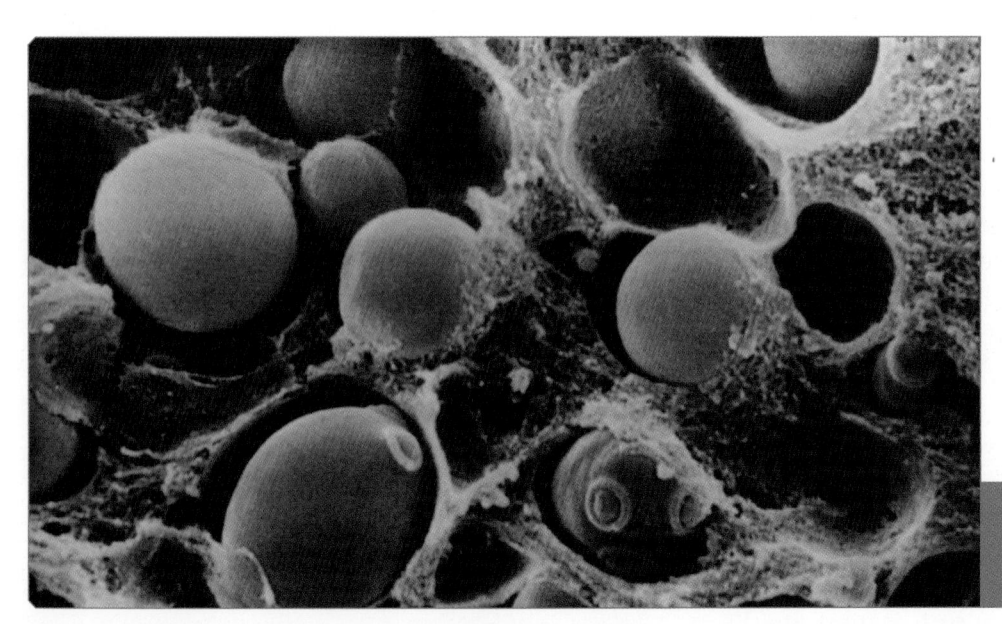

Fig 12.9 An electron micrograph of yeast cells immobilised in calcium alginate beads.

Respiration   Chapter 12

Practical activity: to prepare and show the production of alcohol by yeast

Alcohol is a produced by industrial fermentation on a large scale to satisfy consumer demand.
This experiment shows the basic process behind alcohol fermentation.

You will use immobilised yeast and glucose to produce alcohol. We will then test for the presence of alcohol using the iodoform test for alcohol.

SAFETY
Take care with hot objects after heating and boiling.

Sodium hypochlorite is an irritant and corrosive. This substance should be handled only within a fume cupboard. Wear a lab coat, gloves and safety goggles.

Potassium iodide is non-toxic but can be a mild irritant. It is recommended to wear safety goggles when handling this substance.

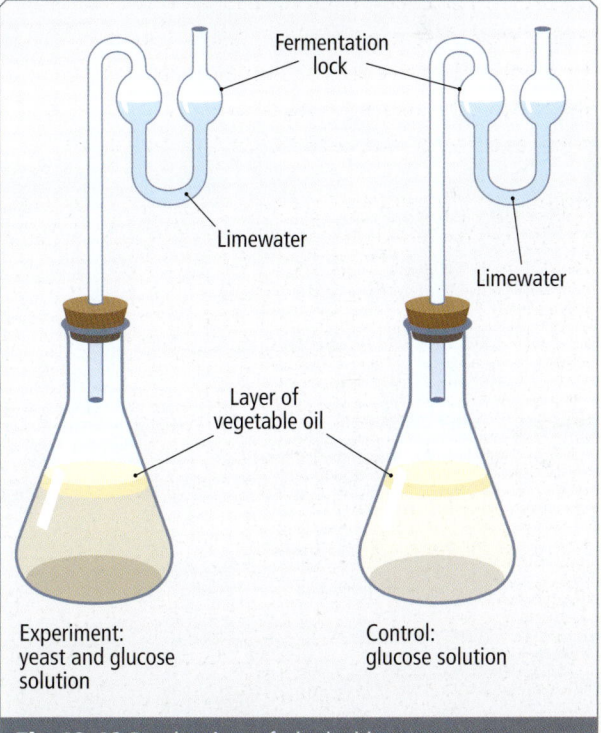

Method

1. Dissolve 50 g glucose powder into 500 ml of distilled water in a conical flask.
2. Slowly bring the glucose solution to the boil using the Bunsen burner, tripod and gauze. This is to sterilise the solution and to remove any oxygen present in the solution.
3. Allow it to cool in the refrigerator or even freezer if there is room.
4. Set up two clean, dry and sterilised conical flasks each with 250 ml of the boiled glucose solution.
5. Add a 5 g sachet of dried brewer's yeast to one of the glucose solutions. The other will remain without yeast (control).
6. Pour a thin layer of vegetable oil on top of the glucose solution. This prevents atmospheric oxygen re-entering the solution.
7. Place a stopper and delivery tube or fermentation lock into the conical flask (Fig 12.10). Place some limewater (test for carbon dioxide) into the fermentation lock.
8. Place the apparatus into a 25 °C water bath or an incubator set at 25 °C.

NOTE Always use a thermometer as thermostats are not always accurate.

9. Incubate the yeast to act on the glucose for two days at 25 °C or for as long as bubbles of carbon dioxide are being produced. Incubate the control flask for the same length of time.
10. Following the fermentation step, filter both solutions using filter paper. This removes the yeast.

NOTE You could also carry out this experiment with immobilised yeast, which would make the filtration step much easier.

Fig 12.10 Production of alcohol by yeast.

Unit 2   The Cell

Testing for alcohol (iodoform test)

1. Place 3 ml of the two filtrates (both test and control) into separate test-tubes.
2. Add 3 ml of potassium iodide solution and 5 ml of sodium hypochlorite solution to each test-tube.
3. Warm the test-tubes gently in a hot water bath for 5 minutes.
4. Allow to cool and record any changes within the test-tubes.
5. Record the results in a table.

Results

The appearance of pale yellow crystals at the bottom of the test-tube is a positive result for the presence of alcohol.

	Iodoform test
Control (glucose + no yeast)	
Test (glucose + yeast)	

Conclusion

What have we learned from this practical activity? Yeast respires anaerobically in an absence of oxygen. Anaerobic respiration results in the production of alcohol.

Practical activity questions

1. In carrying out the practical activity to prepare alcohol using yeast, why was it important to ensure anaerobic conditions?
2. How did you achieve anaerobic conditions?
3. Explain how you maintained anaerobic conditions.
4. What name is given to the type of chemical reaction that occurred in this practical activity?
5. What was the substrate?
6. Name the small gaseous molecule produced as a by-product of the reaction.
7. How did you demonstrate the presence of this small gaseous molecule?
8. How did you know the substrate was all used up?

Chapter 12 Questions

1. (a) What is *respiration*?
   (b) Explain why respiration is important for living organisms.
2. Distinguish between *aerobic respiration* and *anaerobic respiration* in terms of:
   (a) Number of stages
   (b) Cellular locations involved
   (c) Oxygen requirement
   (d) Energy release
   (e) Waste products
3. (a) Write the word equation and balanced chemical equation for aerobic respiration.
   (b) Write the word equations for the **two** types of anaerobic respiration.
4. (a) What is meant by *fermentation*?
   (b) Give **two** examples of fermentation.

HL 5. (a) Distinguish between *oxidation* and *reduction* in terms of electron transfer.
   (b) Name the **two** energy carriers involved in respiration.

(c) Which one of these carriers undergoes oxidation-reduction as part of its role in respiration?

(d) Explain exactly how this energy carrier becomes:
 (i) Oxidised
 (ii) Reduced

6 (a) Name the first stage of aerobic respiration.

(b) Where in the cell does this stage occur?

(c) What are the products of the first stage?

(d) What are the fates of the products of the first stage?

7 The mitochondrion is the site of stage 2 of aerobic respiration:

(a) Draw and fully label the structure of a typical mitochondrion.

(b) Mitochondria are thought to have originated from another organism.
 (i) From what organism are mitochondria thought to have originated?
 (ii) Is this organism a prokaryotic or eukaryotic organism? Give a reason for your answer.

(c) Name the **two** processes that make up stage 2 of aerobic respiration.

(d) Where in the mitochondrion does each of these stages occur?

(e) Outline the events of each of these stages. (You may use diagrams if you wish.)

8 Answer the following in relation to anaerobic respiration:

(a) Under what conditions does anaerobic respiration occur?

(b) Where in the cell does anaerobic respiration occur?

(c) Under what conditions would human muscle start to respire anaerobically?

(d) Name the molecule produced as a result of anaerobic respiration in human muscle.

(e) Name **one** symptom associated with anaerobic respiration in human muscle.

HL (f) Explain, in detail, what happens to pyruvic acid when no oxygen is present.

(g) Oxidation and reduction occur when pyruvic acid is metabolised in anaerobic respiration. Name the molecules involved and state which is reduced and which is oxidised.

9 We learned in Chapter 11 on photosynthesis that the light stage produces energy in the form of ATP. If plant cells can produce energy during photosynthesis, explain why plant cells have mitochondria. (Hint: under what conditions is ATP not produced by photosynthesis?)

10 What is *bioprocessing*?

11 What is a *bioreactor*?

12 Name **two** organisms used in industrial fermentation and for each one name a product produced.

13 (a) What is *cell immobilisation*?

(b) Name a chemical substance commonly used to immobilise cells.

(c) Give an example of an organism commonly immobilised in industrial fermentation.

(d) Give **two** advantages of immobilising cells.

14 (a) Give an outline account of how you would immobilise a named cell using a named immobilising agent.

(b) Give **two** applications of immobilised cells in industry.

Unit 2 — The Cell

Chapter 12 Sample examination questions

1 (a) (i) Identify **X** and **Y** in the following equation which is a summary of aerobic respiration.

$$C_6H_{12}O_6 + 6X \longrightarrow 6Y + 6H_2O$$

  (ii) What is anaerobic respiration?

(b) Answer the following questions in relation to aerobic respiration as a two-stage process.
  (i) Where in the cell does the first stage take place?
  (ii) Does the first stage require oxygen?
  (iii) Comment on the amount of energy released in the first stage.
  (iv) Where in the cell does the second stage take place?
  (v) Does the second stage require oxygen?
  (vi) Comment on the amount of energy released in the second stage.
  (vii) State **two** ways in which the energy that is released is used in the human body.

(c) (i) Describe how you used yeast to produce alcohol (ethanol). Include a labelled diagram of the apparatus that you used.
  (ii) How did you show that alcohol had been produced?

Section C, Question 13 Ordinary Level 2006

HL 2 (a) (i) For what is ATP an abbreviation?
  (ii) What is the role of ATP in cells?

(b) (i) What name is given to the first stage of respiration?
  (ii) Where in a cell does this first stage take place?
  (iii) To what substance is glucose normally converted in this first stage of respiration?
  (iv) Is oxygen required for this conversion?
  (v) Name a compound to which the substance that you have named in (iii) may be converted, in the absence of oxygen.
  (vi) In aerobic respiration, the product of the first stage moves to the mitochondrion. Outline subsequent events in the total breakdown of this product.

Section C, Question 11 (a) & (b) Higher Level 2007

Chapter 12 Mind map

Respiration is the process of releasing energy from food.

Two types of respiration:
- Aerobic respiration: process of release of energy from food using oxygen.

Word equation for aerobic respiration

Glucose + Oxygen → Energy + Water + Carbon dioxide

- Anaerobic respiration: process of release of energy from food without oxygen.

Balanced chemical equation for aerobic respiration

$C_6H_{12}O_6 + 6O_2 \longrightarrow$ Energy $+ 6H_2O + 6CO_2$

Aerobic respiration
- **Stage 1:** oxygen-independent, occurs in the cytosol, releases a small amount of energy after the partial breakdown of glucose.
- **Stage 2:** oxygen-dependent, occurs in the mitochondrion, releases a large amount of energy as glucose is completely broken down into carbon dioxide and water.

Anaerobic respiration
- Also called fermentation.
- Involves only stage 1.
- Oxygen-independent.
- Occurs in the cytosol.
- Releases a small amount of energy.
- Glucose is partially broken down.

Lactic acid fermentation

Glucose → Lactic acid + Small amount of energy

Alcohol fermentation

Glucose → Alcohol + Carbon dioxide + Small amount of energy

Respiration — Chapter 12

Detailed process of aerobic respiration HL
- **Glycolysis (stage 1):** oxygen independent, occurs in the cytosol, glucose (C_6) is broken down to two pyruvic acid (C_3) molecules, two NADH molecules formed, two ATP molecules formed.
- **Krebs cycle and electron transport chain (stage 2):** oxygen dependent, occurs in the mitochondrion.

Krebs cycle (lumen of mitochondrion/matrix) HL
- Pyruvic acid (C_3) molecules are converted to acetyl CoA (C_2) molecules with the production of NADH and the elimination of carbon dioxide.
- Acetyl CoA joins with a C_4 molecule, forming a C_6 molecule. (CoA is released).
- C_6 molecule is broken down to a C_5 molecule producing NADH and eliminating carbon dioxide.
- C_5 is broken down to a C_4 molecule, producing 2NADH and ATP and eliminating carbon dioxide.
- The cycle begins again.

Electron transport chain (inner membrane of mitochondrion/cristae)
- NADH molecules are converted to NAD^+, giving up high-energy electrons and protons.
- ATP is formed from ADP and a phosphate.
- One NADH molecule powers the production of three ATP molecules.
- ATP goes on to power metabolic reactions.
- Low-energy electrons and protons are joined with oxygen to form water.

Detailed process of anaerobic respiration (fermentation) HL
- Also called fermentation.
- Involves only stage 1.
- Oxygen-independent.
- Occurs in the cytosol.
- Releases a small amount of energy.
- Glucose is partially broken down.

Two types:
- **Lactic acid fermentation:** glycolysis occurs (glucose converted to two pyruvic acid molecules). NADH is used up in reducing each pyruvic acid (C_3) to lactic acid (C_3).
- **Alcohol fermentation:** glycolysis occurs (glucose converted to two pyruvic acid molecules). NADH is used up in reducing each pyruvic acid (C_3) to ethanol (C_2). Carbon dioxide is produced.

Role of microorganisms in industrial fermentation
- Industrial fermentation is a type of bioprocessing.
- **Bioprocessing** is the use of living cells or their components, such as enzymes, to make useful products or to carry out useful procedures.
- Fermentation procedures take place in bioreactors.
- A **bioreactor** is a vessel in which a product is formed by a cell or cell component, such as an enzyme.
- Examples of fermentation are: yeast producing alcohol from the anaerobic respiration of sugars, bacteria producing lactic acid in milk, which curdles producing dairy products such as yoghurts and cheese.
- Fermentation and other bioprocesses can be carried out by either **batch culture**: a certain amount of product is formed and collected and the bioreactor is then cleaned and sterilised or **continuous-flow culture**: product is continually collected from the bioreactor with conditions within the bioreactor being strictly controlled.

Bioprocessing with immobilised cells
- **Immobilised cells** are cells that are trapped in a gel, such as calcium alginate.
- Yeast cells are one of the most commonly immobilised cells.
- Yeast is mixed with sodium alginate which is added to a calcium chloride solution drop by drop to solidify the sodium alginate into calcium alginate beads.
- The beads are added to a bioreactor along with the sugars as the substrate. The mixture is agitated and alcohol is formed.
- It is very easy to separate the beads of immobilised cells from the product. They can be washed and reused.

Advantages of the use of immobilised cells
- Gentle procedure – the cells are not damaged.
- Product is separated easily from beads of immobilised yeast at the end of the reaction.
- The beads can be reused.

Preparation of alcohol using yeast
- Add yeast to a cooled boiled glucose solution in a conical flask.
- Place a layer of oil over the mixture to maintain anaerobic conditions.
- Connect flask to a fermentation lock.
- Place the flask into a 25 °C incubator for two days.

In testing for alcohol:
- Filter solution.
- Add 3 ml of filtrate into test-tube.
- Add 3 ml of potassium iodide and 5 ml of sodium hypochlorite.
- Warm test-tube for 5 min.
- Appearance of pale yellow crystals shows the presence of alcohol.

Chapter 13 The cell cycle

Learning objectives After studying this chapter, you should be able to:
- Define the terms *cell continuity, chromosome, gene, homologous pair, haploid, diploid, mitosis, cancer* and *meiosis*.
- Describe the cell cycle under three headings: interphase, mitosis and cell division.
- **HL** Describe the detailed process of mitosis.
- Define *cancer* and give two possible causes.
- Describe the functions of mitosis and meiosis.

Introduction

Cell division is the process of a living cell splitting to form two separate living cells. Cells can increase in number very rapidly. Bacteria can divide every 20 minutes under ideal conditions. By contrast, human cells can divide at a maximum rate of once every few hours.

Cell division gives rise to one of the characteristics of life, which is **cell continuity**.

Cell continuity

> **Cell continuity** refers to living cells arising from living cells of the same type.

Cell continuity is vital in all species to enable growth and for continuity of life (*see* Chapter 2).

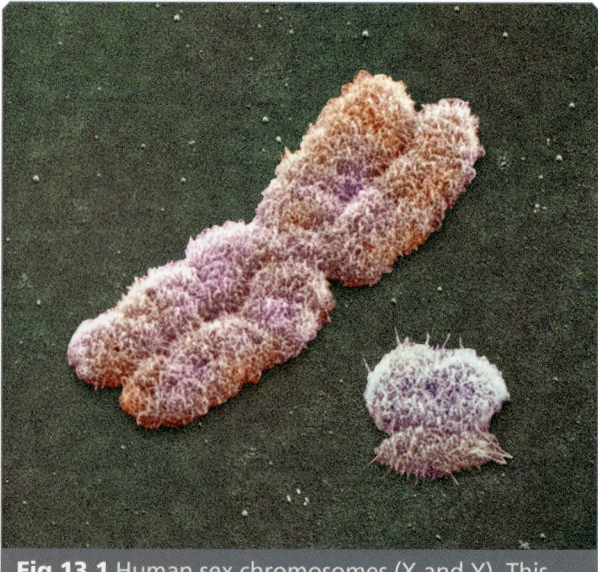

Fig 13.1 Human sex chromosomes (X and Y). This image was obtained using a scanning electron microscope and then using a computer to add the colour.

However, it must be noted that all cells spend the vast majority of their time not dividing. They simply go about their everyday activities.

The **nucleus** is critical to a cell's ability to divide. The nucleus has **chromosomes** that contain all the necessary information for the production of a new cell.

Chromosome

> **Chromosomes** are tightly coiled and highly organised structures of DNA and protein.

Chromosomes are a very efficient means of carrying genetic information. They keep a huge amount of information in a very tiny space – the nucleus.

Chromosomes become visible during cell division. When a cell is dividing, the chromosomes become very thick and condensed. When the cell is not dividing, the chromosomes are very long, thin threads of DNA and protein that are not visible. When they are in the form of long, thin threads they are referred to as **chromatin.**

All species on Earth have their own specific number of chromosomes. For example, bacteria have just one chromosome, pea plants have 14, cats have 38 and humans have 46.

Fig 13.2 shows the 46 chromosomes of a human. It is called a karyotype. Notice that they are organised into pairs. Each member of a pair of chromosomes carries genes controlling the same characteristics.

The first 22 pairs are called autosomal chromosomes (**autosomes**). They carry genes for the everyday functioning of the body's cells.

The 23rd pair is the sex chromosomes, so-called because they control gender. A person is either XX, in which case the person will be female, or XY, in which case they will be male.

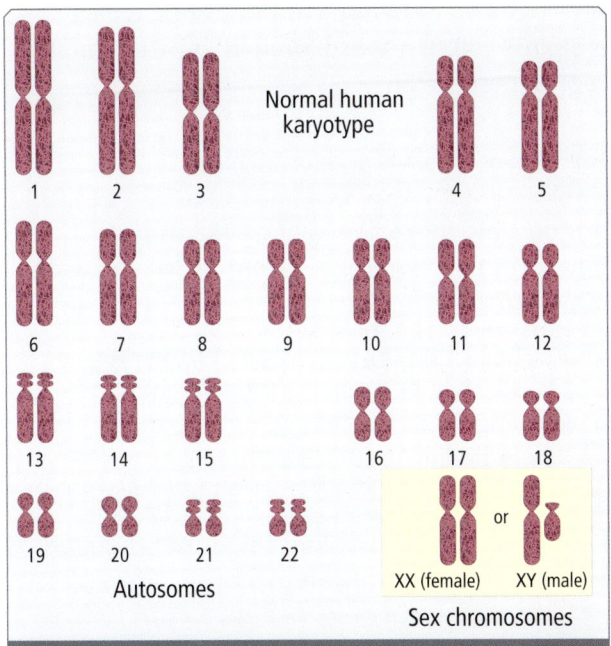

Fig 13.2 Human karyotype of 46 chromosomes. Notice how the chromosomes are arranged in pairs.

Gene

Chromosomes contain **genes**. Genes are the units of inheritance in living organisms, controlling characteristic features of that organism.

All the genes together form the **genome** of an organism. The size of a genome depends on the organism. In general, the more complex the organism, the more genes it needs. There are approximately 30,000 genes in the human genome.

> A **gene** is a short region of a chromosome that contains a code for the production of a protein.

A gene contains a set of instructions for the assembly of a specific sequence of amino acids that make up a protein. Genes are specific – meaning one gene is capable of producing only one type of protein.

Genes control all the features of living organisms, such as height, skin colour, hair colour, weight, number of fingers, gender, and many thousands of other features in humans. Genes also control flower colour, height, chlorophyll production, leaf shape and so on in plants.

Genes control these features by producing proteins such as enzymes, antibodies, hormones, structural proteins, transport proteins and pigments. As a result, genes help to control metabolism.

Homologous pairs

You should notice from Fig 13.2 that chromosomes are arranged in pairs. Humans have 23 pairs. Each pair of chromosomes is called a **homologous pair** ('*homologous*' meaning 'having the same relative position or value').

Homologous pairs carry genes that control the same characteristics. They do not necessarily carry the same genes. For example, one chromosome of a homologous pair might carry the gene for blue eyes, whereas the other chromosome might carry the gene for brown eyes. One gene produces the protein for blue eyes and the other produces the protein for brown eyes. They both control the same characteristic, but give a slightly different product (we will learn more about this in Chapter 16 on inheritance).

The homologous pairs of chromosomes are numbered 1 to 22. Pair number 1 is the longest pair with the most genes. Pair number 22 is the shortest with the least number of genes.

The 23rd pair is not numbered. They are called the sex chromosomes. This is because they carry the genes that determine the sex of the individual. The sex chromosomes also carry genes that control other characteristics unrelated to gender. An example is the gene controlling the ability to see colour and distinguish colours of different shades.

Notice from Fig 13.2 that the Y chromosome is significantly shorter than its homologue, X. The reasons for this are unknown. Due to its shorter length, the Y chromosome is missing a number of genes that are present on the X chromosome (*see* Chapter 16).

Haploid and diploid

The chromosome number of sex cells (egg and sperm) is half the number of a normal body cell (somatic cell).

Sex cells contain one chromosome from each homologous pair. Therefore, in humans, egg and sperm cells contain 23 chromosomes.

Unit 2   The Cell

When a cell has one chromosome from each homologous pair, we say that it has one set of chromosomes and it is called a haploid cell.

The word *'haploid'* is often simply represented as **'n'**. Sperm cells and egg cells are **haploid** cells.

> **Haploid**: one set of chromosomes.

Fig 13.3 shows the 23 chromosomes contained within a sperm cell and the 23 chromosomes contained within an egg cell. Notice a sperm cell can have either an X chromosome or a Y chromosome, whereas an egg cell can only have an X chromosome. It is impossible for an egg cell to have a Y chromosome (we will learn more about this in Chapter 16).

When a sperm cell fertilises the egg, the nuclei fuse together and each set of chromosomes joins together so that the full complement of 46 chromosomes (23 pairs) is re-attained.

Nuclei is the plural of nucleus.

A human cell that has 46 chromosomes, or any cell from any living organism that has its full set (two sets) of paired chromosomes, is called a **diploid cell**. The word 'diploid' is often simply represented as **'2n'**.

> **Diploid**: two sets of chromosomes.

It is possible for certain living organisms to have cells that are triploid (that is, 3n) and even quadraploid (4n).

In Chapter 28 on reproduction in flowering plants, we will learn that a certain tissue in developing seeds is made up of cells that are triploid. They each have three sets of chromosomes.

Knowledge of quadraploid cells is not required for the Leaving Certificate Biology course.

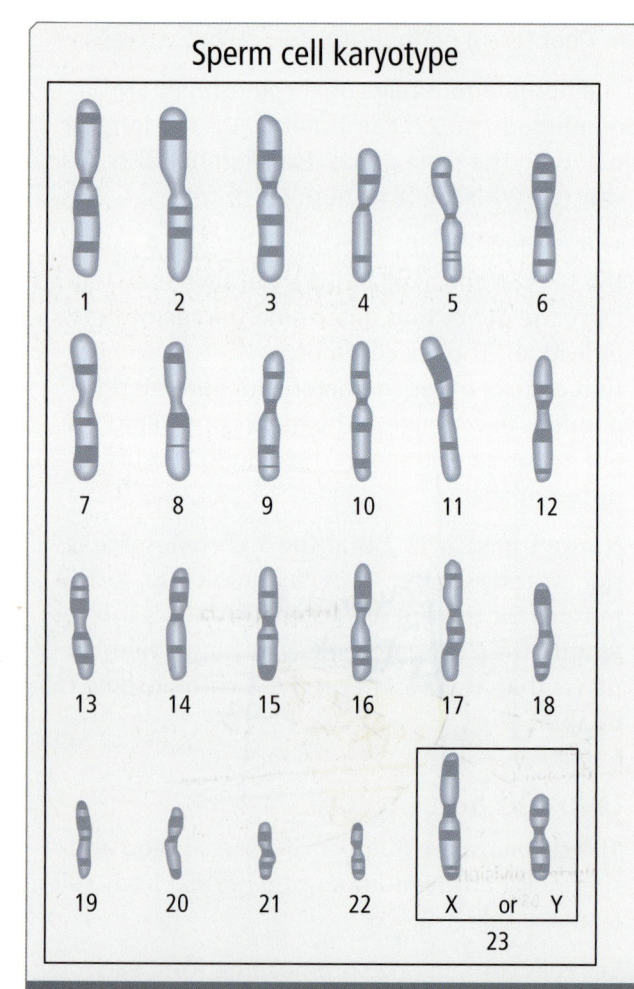

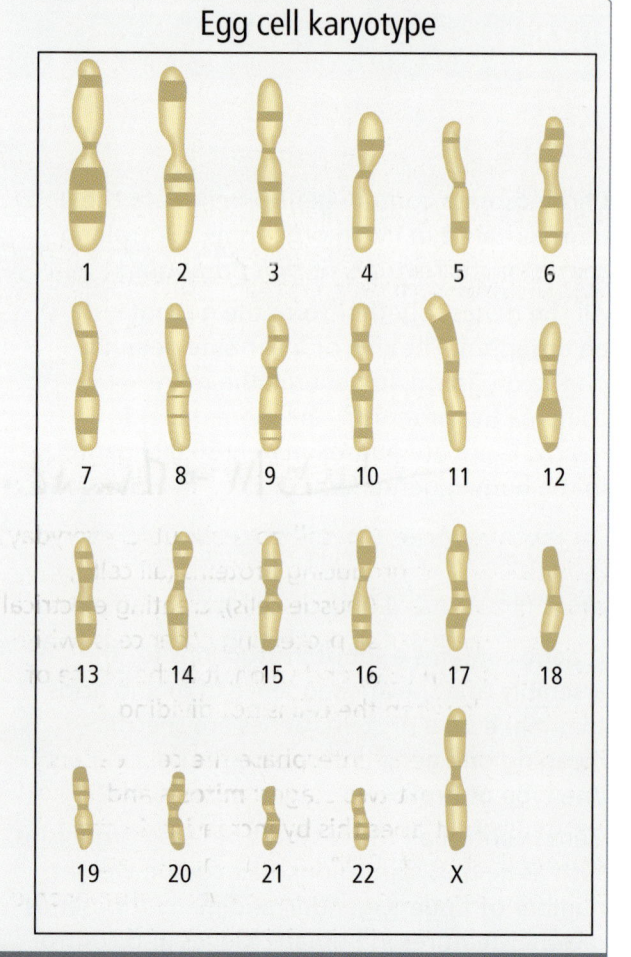

Fig 13.3 Karyotypes of a sperm cell and an egg cell. Notice how the sperm cell can have either an X or a Y chromosome (but not both) and an egg cell can have only an X chromosome.

The cell cycle

The cell cycle consists of three distinct stages: **interphase**, **mitosis** and **cell division**.

1 Interphase

The cell cycle begins with interphase.

> **Interphase** is a long period of the cell cycle during which the cell spends most of its life and carries out its everyday activities.

Fig 13.4 shows a typical cell at interphase. The DNA is elongated within the nucleus **(chromatin)** and the nuclear membrane is intact. Interphase is the portion of the cell cycle in which the cell spends the most time (see Fig 13.6).

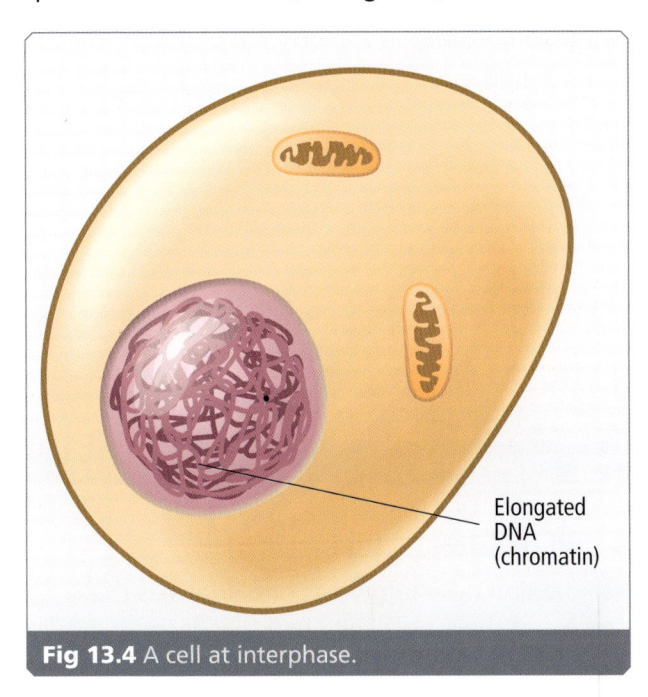

Fig 13.4 A cell at interphase.

During interphase, the cell goes about its everyday activities such as producing proteins (all cells), causing movement (muscle cells), creating electrical impulses (nerve cells), protecting other cells (white blood cells, skin cells) and so on. It is the phase of the cell cycle when the cell is not dividing.

Towards the end of interphase the cell readies itself for the next two stages: **mitosis** and **cell division**. It does this by increasing in size and replicating its DNA so that the nucleus temporarily has four copies of every chromosome. Therefore, at the end of interphase and throughout the next stage (mitosis) a human cell has 92 chromosomes.

2 Mitosis

> **Mitosis** is nuclear division in which the number of chromosomes in the daughter nuclei is the same as in the parent nucleus.

Mitosis consists of four stages: 1, 2, 3 and 4 (Fig 13.6).

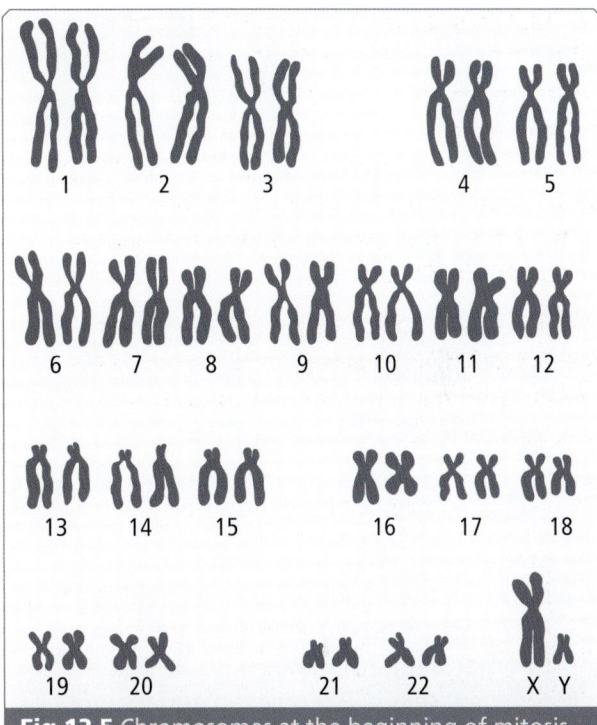

Fig 13.5 Chromosomes at the beginning of mitosis. Notice how each homologous pair now consists of four chromosomes (92 altogether).

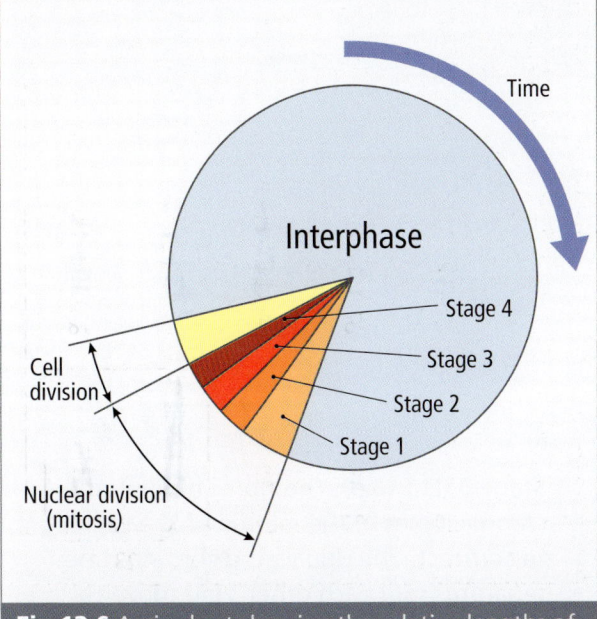

Fig 13.6 A pie chart showing the relative lengths of the stages of the cell cycle.

- **Stage 1** (Fig 13.7): The chromatin condenses and become visible as chromosomes inside the cell. The duplicated chromosomes attach together. The nuclear membrane begins to break up, releasing the chromosomes into the cytoplasm. Fibres form and attach to the chromosomes holding them in specific positions within the cell.

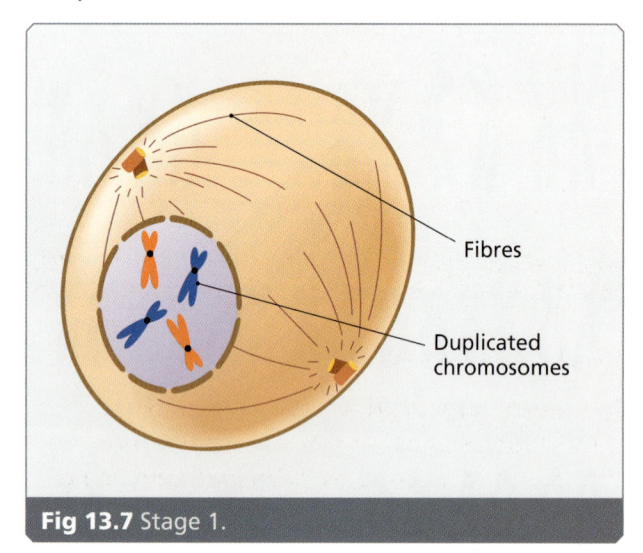

Fig 13.7 Stage 1.

- **Stage 2** (Fig 13.8): Chromosomes line up along the middle of the cell held in position by fibres. The fibres allow the cell to organise the chromosomes so that the two new cells will receive an equal number of chromosomes.

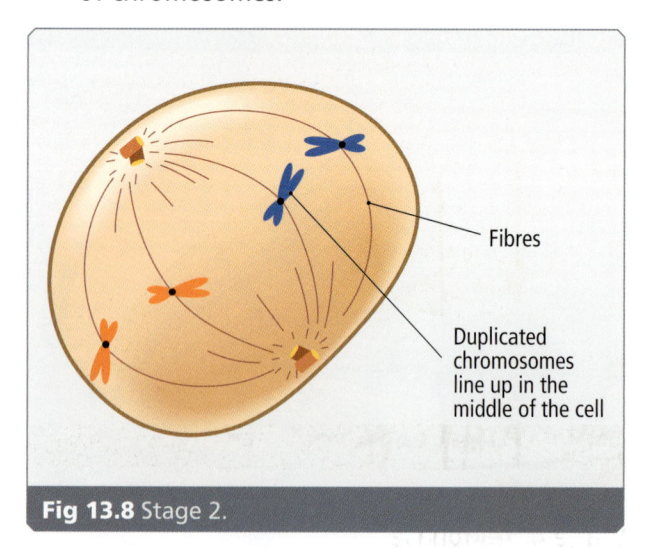

Fig 13.8 Stage 2.

- **Stage 3** (Fig 13.9): The fibres holding the chromosomes in the middle of the cell begin to contract. The duplicated chromosomes separate from each other. Half move to one end, with the other half moving in the opposite direction.

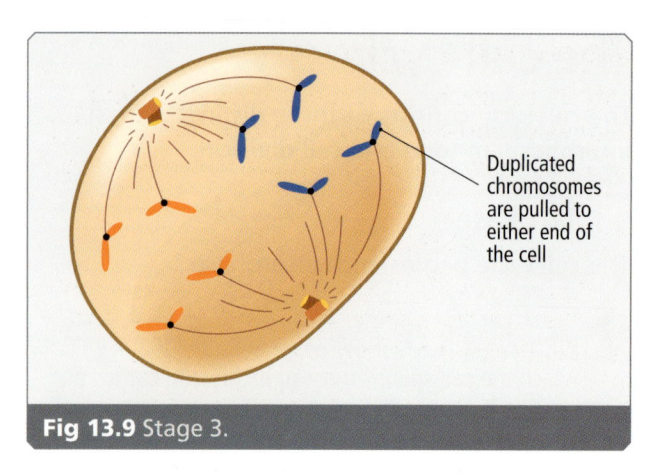

Fig 13.9 Stage 3.

- **Stage 4** (Fig 13.10): The nuclear membrane begins to reform around the chromosomes. The chromosomes unravel and elongate to reform chromatin. The two newly formed nuclei have the same number of chromosomes as the original parent nucleus.

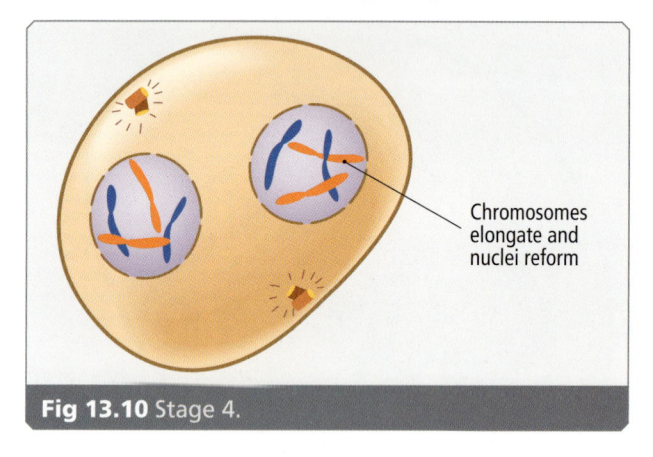

Fig 13.10 Stage 4.

3 Cell division (cytokinesis)

Cell division (also known as cytokinesis) is the process of the whole cell physically dividing in two (Fig 13.11). When two cells have been formed and are independent, the cell cycle is complete and the cell enters interphase once again.

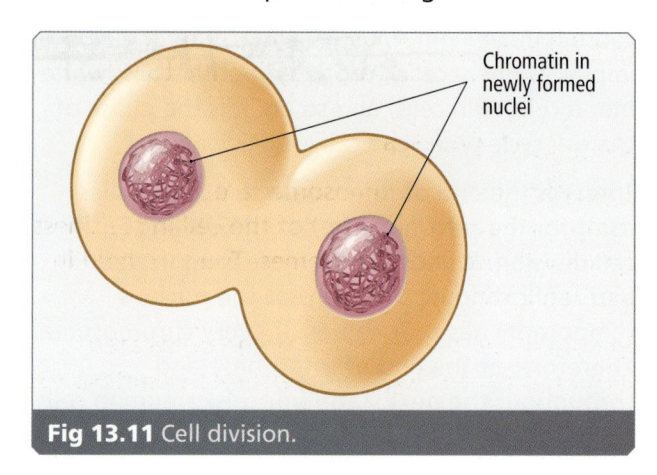

Fig 13.11 Cell division.

HL **Mitosis – detailed process**

Mitosis is a nuclear division. It consists of four relatively short-lived distinct phases (see Fig 13.6): **prophase**, **metaphase**, **anaphase** and **telophase**.

Stage 1: Prophase

In this phase, the chromatin begins to condense into clearly visible chromosomes. The DNA had been duplicated at the end of interphase.

The duplicated chromosomes are attached together by a structure called the **centromere**. The nuclear membrane begins to dissolve, releasing the chromosomes into the cytoplasm.

At the pole of the cell, a structure called the **centriole** produces fibres called **spindle**. Spindle fibres attach to the chromosomes at the centromere.

Fig 13.12 shows a cell at prophase.

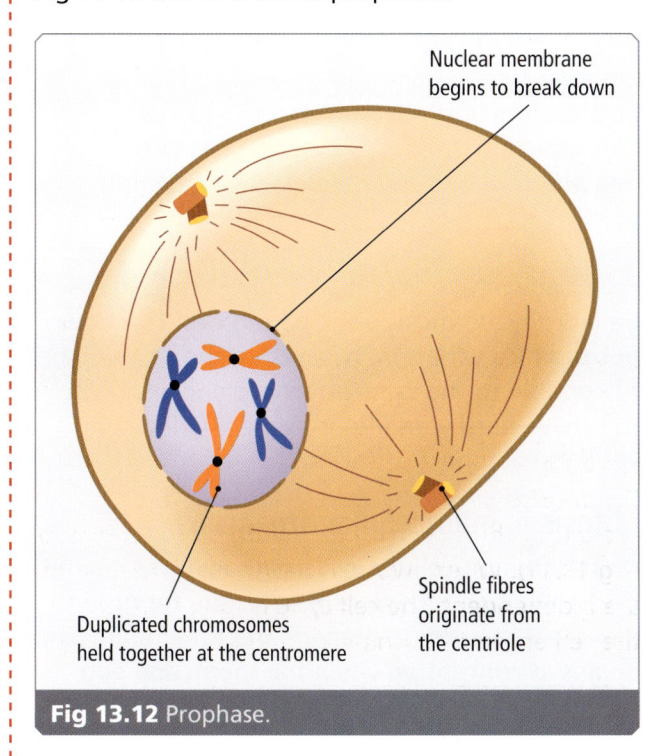

Fig 13.12 Prophase.

Stage 2: Metaphase

In this phase, the chromosomes are lined up along the equator (middle) of the cell in readiness for movement of chromosomes. They are held in position by the spindle fibres.

Spindle fibres help to organise the duplicated chromosomes throughout the stages of mitosis so that each new cell receives the same number of chromosomes.

Fig 13.13 shows a cell at metaphase.

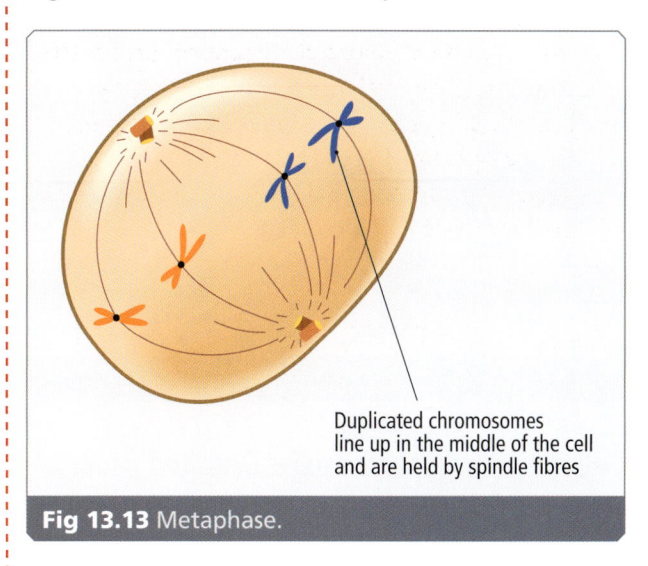

Fig 13.13 Metaphase.

Stage 3: Anaphase

The centromeres holding the duplicated chromosomes together split in two and the chromosomes move apart, with each one going to opposite ends (poles) of the cell.

The spindle fibres contract to move the chromosomes to either pole of the cell.

Fig 13.14 shows a cell at anaphase.

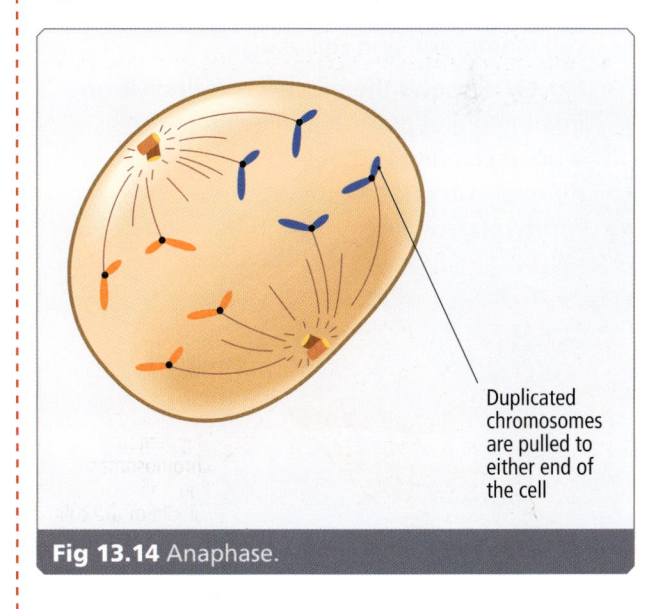

Fig 13.14 Anaphase.

Stage 4: Telophase

Once the chromosomes are at the poles of the cell, the nuclear membrane begins to reform around them. The chromosomes unravel and elongate to reform chromatin. The spindle fibres dissolve away and the cell readies itself for the next stage of **cell division.**

Fig 13.15 shows a cell at telophase.

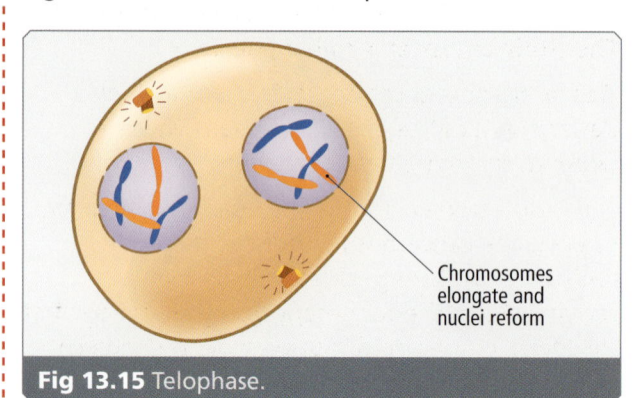

Fig 13.15 Telophase.
Chromosomes elongate and nuclei reform

Cell division (cytokinesis) – Detailed process

The process of cell division differs between animals and plants.

- In animal cells, a **cleavage furrow** forms. A cleavage furrow is an indentation of the cytoplasm that begins on the outside of the cell. Proteins, such as actin and myosin, pull the cell membrane inwards towards the centre of the cell.

- In plant cells, a **cell plate** forms when very small intra-cellular vesicles (small organelles inside the cell) line up along the site of the cell plate. They fuse together, forming a new cell membrane and cell wall.

- Fig 13.16 shows the process of cell division in animal and plant cells. Fig 13.17 shows a plant cell dividing in two following mitosis. You can see the cell plate being formed (arrow).

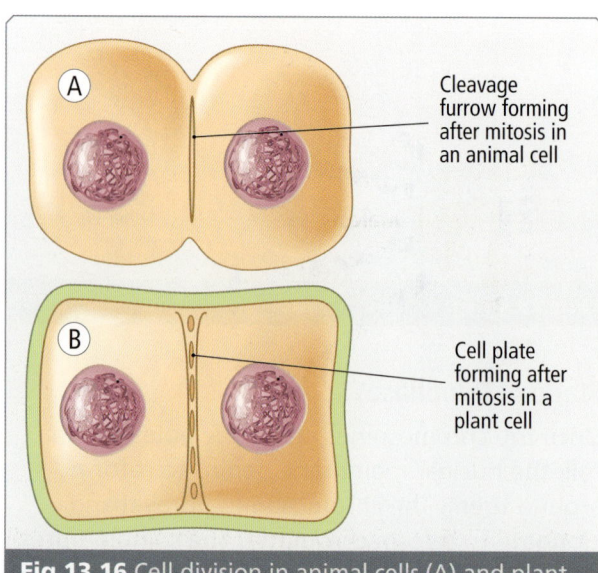

Fig 13.16 Cell division in animal cells (A) and plant cells (B).

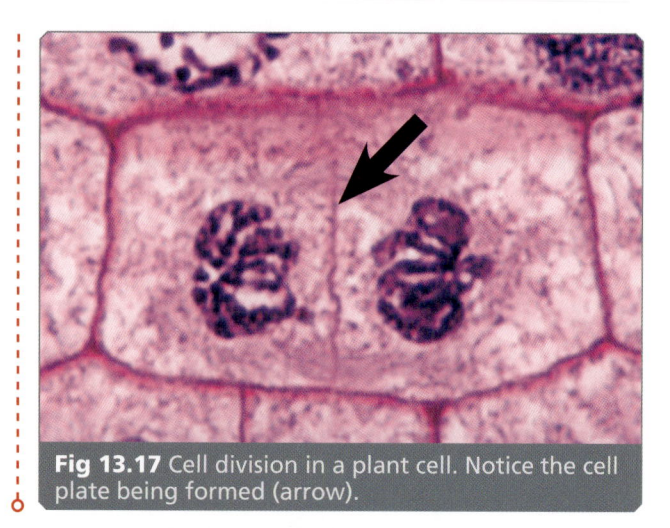

A — Cleavage furrow forming after mitosis in an animal cell
B — Cell plate forming after mitosis in a plant cell

Fig 13.17 Cell division in a plant cell. Notice the cell plate being formed (arrow).

Functions of mitosis

Mitosis and cell division have various functions, depending on the circumstances and type of organism involved.

Mitosis in single-celled organisms

In single-celled organisms, mitosis and cell division function primarily in reproduction. Reproduction by mitosis is asexual, as only one parent is involved. Asexual reproduction by mitosis has the advantage that it can be completed very quickly and efficiently, but has the disadvantage that the daughter cells are genetically identical to the parent cell. This does not produce variation. As a result, the cells will be susceptible to the same infections and less able to survive harsh conditions as there will be no variation amongst offspring.

Mitosis in multicellular organisms

Mitosis in multicellular organisms involves mainly the production of new cells necessary for growth and repair. Mitosis in humans and other animals begins at conception when the sperm and egg cell unite at fertilisation and continues until death. Mitosis occurs in almost every tissue of the body throughout life. For example, the skin replaces itself completely every four weeks. This is possible because of mitosis.

Mitosis also occurs continuously throughout the life of a plant. However, plant mitosis generally occurs at a much slower rate than in animals. This is because plants have a much slower metabolism and do not have to move around to obtain nutrients. Mitosis in plants also functions in growth and repair.

Cancer

Statistically, cancer is a disease that affects one in three of the population at some point in their lifetime. Many cancers are curable, particularly if they are caught and treated early.

> **Cancer** is a group of disorders in which cells lose control over the rate of mitosis and cell division.

Cancer results in the uncontrolled multiplication of cells. Cancer cells are also known as abnormal cells.

Cancer can be of two types: **benign** and **malignant**.

- Benign cancer is where the cancerous (abnormal) cells divide by uncontrolled mitosis and cell division to form a tumour, but do not move or invade other tissues of the body. They stay in one position. In general, they are not life-threatening. However, benign cancer can change to malignant cancer.
- Malignant cancer is where cancerous cells divide by uncontrolled mitosis and cell division and have the ability to leave the tumour. The process of cancerous cells leaving the original tumour is called metastasis. Metastasis, left untreated, is life-threatening.

Causes of cancer

Cancer-causing agents are called **carcinogens**. There are many known carcinogens. Many of these are chemicals and are classified into certain classes – A, B or C – depending on their level of risk.

Other carcinogens are not chemicals but types of energy, such as ultraviolet light.

> **NOTE:** For Leaving Certificate Biology, you need to know only two causes of cancer.

Some common causes are:
- Ultraviolet (UV) light.
- Cigarette smoke.
- Human papillomavirus.
- Radon gas.
- Asbestos fibres.

Carcinogens cause cancer by causing mutations (changes to DNA) in genes.

Most genes, if mutated, do not cause cancer. However, there are certain genes that, when changed by mutations, have the potential to cause cancer. These genes are called oncogenes. The study of cancer is called oncology.

Treatment for cancer occurs in the oncology department of hospitals. Treatment varies depending on the type of cancer.

Types of treatments include surgery to physically remove the cancerous tissue from the body, radiotherapy (killing of cancer cells using radiation) and chemotherapy (using chemicals that specifically target cells that are rapidly dividing).

Meiosis

> **Meiosis** is a type of nuclear division that leads to four daughter cells being produced, each containing half the number of chromosomes as the parent cell.

Meiosis is a very important process for multicellular organisms. It is required for sexual reproduction to occur.

The products of meiosis in humans are the sperm and egg cells. Therefore, meiosis occurs only in one place in the human body: the testes of males and the ovaries of females.

It is involved in gamete (sex cell) formation in all multicellular organisms that reproduce sexually. For example, pollen grains and the egg cell within the ovary of a flower are produced by meiosis.

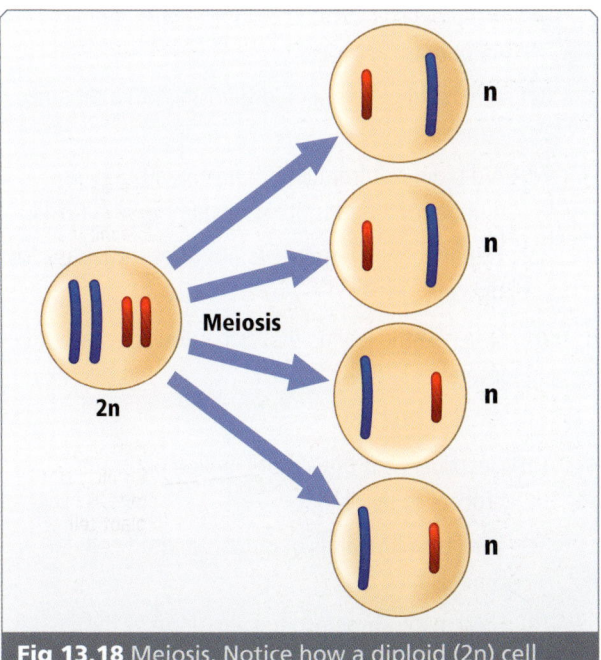

Fig 13.18 Meiosis. Notice how a diploid (2n) cell becomes four haploid (n) cells.

Meiosis is different to mitosis in a number of ways:

- Mitosis only involves division of the nucleus; meiosis involves two rounds of nuclear division.
- Mitosis maintains the number of chromosomes in the daughter cells; meiosis halves the number of chromosomes in the daughter cells.
- Mitosis produces genetically identical cells; meiosis produces variation through rearrangement of the genetic material.
- Mitosis occurs in all living organisms; meiosis occurs only in multicellular organisms.
- Mitosis is used for asexual reproduction in single-celled organisms; meiosis is used for sexual reproduction in multicellular organisms.

Chapter 13 Questions

1. What is meant by *cell continuity*?
2. Distinguish between the following pairs of terms:
   (a) *Chromosome* and *chromatin*
   (b) *Haploid* and *diploid*
   (c) *Mitosis* and *meiosis*
3. What are the **three** stages of the cell cycle?
4. What **two** substances make up a chromosome?
5. (a) What is a *gene*?
   (b) What is the function of a gene?
6. Draw simple diagrams showing each of the following cells:
   (a) A haploid cell from an organism with a diploid number of 8.
   (b) A diploid cell from an organism with a diploid number of 8.
   (c) A haploid cell from an organism with a diploid number of 12.
   (d) A diploid cell from an organism with a diploid number of 4 and is at the beginning of mitosis.
7. (a) Explain why interphase is not a resting phase for the cell.
   (b) Describe the events that occur towards the end of interphase.
8. (a) What is *mitosis*?
   (b) Describe, with the aid of labelled diagrams, the process of mitosis.
   (c) Give **two** functions of mitosis in multicellular organisms.
   (d) How many chromosomes are there at the *beginning* of mitosis in a human cell? Explain why there are this many chromosomes.
9. A cat has a diploid number of 38 chromosomes. How many chromosomes will there be in each of the following cells of the cat:
   (a) Brain cell
   (b) Sex cell
   (c) Skin cell
   (d) Liver cell

HL 10. Answer the following questions on the detailed process of mitosis:
   (a) Name the **four** phases of mitosis in order.
   (b) What is meant by the 'equator' of the cell?
   (c) From what cell component do spindle fibres originate?
   (d) What is the function of spindle fibres?
   (e) Describe what happens during the fourth stage of mitosis.
   (f) What is another name for *cell division*?

11. (a) What is *cancer*?
    (b) Name the **two** main groups of cancer.
    (c) Name **two** causes of cancer.
12. (a) What is *meiosis*?
    (b) Name a location in the human body where meiosis might occur.
    (c) Name a cell that might result from meiosis in humans.
    (d) Give **two** functions of meiosis in the human body.

Chapter 13 Sample examination questions

1 Indicate whether the following are true (T) or false (F) by drawing a circle around T or F in each case.

The cells produced by mitosis are identical.	T F
Meiosis gives rise to variation.	T F
Mitosis always produces four new cells.	T F
Meiosis is never involved in gamete formation.	T F
Single-celled organisms use mitosis for reproduction.	T F

Section A, Question 4 Ordinary Level 2009

2 The diagram shows a stage of mitosis.

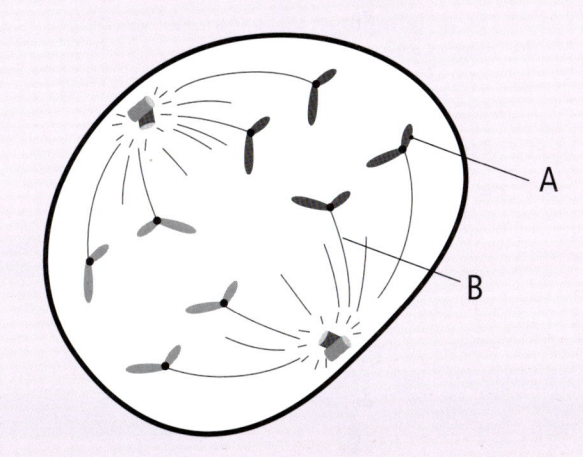

(a) Name A and B.
(b) What is happening during this stage of mitosis?
(c) How many cells are formed when a cell divides by mitosis?
(d) For what purpose do single-celled organisms use mitosis?

Section A, Question 4 Ordinary Level 2005

HL 3 The diagram shows a stage of mitosis.

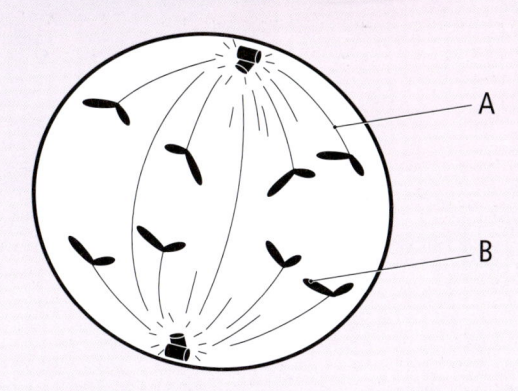

(a) Name this stage of mitosis.
(b) Give a feature from the diagram which allowed you to identify this stage.
(c) Name the parts of the diagram labelled A and B.
(d) What is the function of mitosis in single-celled organisms?
(e) Give **one** function of mitosis in multicellular organisms.
(f) Give **one** location where mitosis occurs in flowering plants.

Section A, Question 5 Higher Level 2009

4 Use your knowledge of mitosis to answer the following questions:

(a) What is the role of mitosis in single-celled organisms?
(b) What medical term is used for a group of disorders in which certain cells lose normal control of mitosis?
(c) Suggest a possible cause of one of the group of disorders referred to in (b).
(d) Name the stage of mitosis in which the chromosomes are located at the equator of the cell and before they begin to separate.
(e) To what are the chromosomes attached in the stage of mitosis referred to in (d)?
(f) Towards the end of mitosis, in what type of cell does a cell plate form?
(g) Give **one** way in which mitosis differs from meiosis.

Section A, Question 2 Higher Level 2011

153

Chapter 13 Mind map

Cell continuity refers to living cells arising from living cells of the same type.

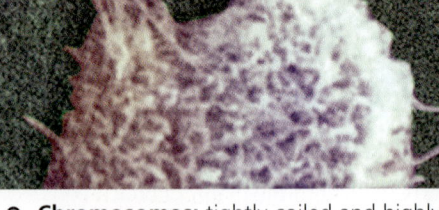

- **Chromosomes:** tightly coiled and highly organised structures of DNA and protein.
- **Gene:** a short region of a chromosome that contains a code for the production of a protein.
- **Haploid:** one set of chromosomes.
- **Diploid:** two sets of chromosomes.

Interphase: a long period of the cell cycle during which the cell spends most of its life and carries out its everyday activities.

- **Mitosis:** nuclear division in which the number of chromosomes in the daughter nuclei is the same as the parent nucleus.
- **Cell division (cytokinesis):** the process of the whole cell splitting into two.

Mitosis

- **Stage 1:** duplicated chromatin condenses and become visible as chromosomes; duplicated chromosomes attach together; nuclear membrane begins to break up, releasing the condensed chromosomes into the cytoplasm; fibres begin to form and attach to the chromosomes.
- **Stage 2:** chromosomes line up along the middle of the cell.
- **Stage 3:** fibres holding the chromosomes contract; duplicated chromosomes separate from each other; half go to one end with the other half going in the opposite direction.
- **Stage 4:** nucleus begins to reform around the chromosomes; chromosomes elongate to reform chromatin; two nuclei have the same number of nuclei as the original parent nucleus.

Mitosis and cell division – detailed process HL

Four distinct stages of mitosis:

- **Stage 1: Prophase:** chromatin condenses and become visible as chromosomes; duplicated chromosomes attach together at the centromere; nuclear membrane begins to break up, releasing the condensed chromosomes into the cytoplasm; spindle fibres begin to form and attach to the chromosomes at points called the centromeres.
- **Stage 2: Metaphase:** chromosomes line up along the equator of the cell.
- **Stage 3: Anaphase:** centromeres holding the chromosomes together break in two; spindle fibres contract pulling the chromosomes to either pole of the cell.
- **Stage 4: Telophase:** nuclear membrane begins to reform around the chromosomes; spindle fibres dissolve and the cell readies itself for the next stage of cell division.

Cell division (cytokinesis):

- Cleavage furrow forms in animals cells.
- Cell plate forms in plant cells.

Functions of mitosis

- In single-celled organisms: reproduction.
- In multicellular organisms: growth; repair.

- **Cancer** is a group of disorders in which cells lose control over the rate of mitosis and cell division.
- Two causes of cancer: UV light; cigarette smoke.

- **Meiosis** is a type of nuclear division that leads to four daughter cells being produced, each containing half the number of chromosomes as the parent cell.
- **Functions of meiosis:** sexual reproduction; genetic variation.

Differences between mitosis and meiosis	
Mitosis	**Meiosis**
Resulting cells have the same number of chromosomes as the parent cell	Resulting cells have half the number of chromosomes as the parent cell
Resulting cells are genetically identical to the parent cell	Resulting cells are not genetically identical to the parent cell
Two new cells result	Four new cells result

DNA and RNA Chapter 14

Learning objectives After studying this chapter, you should be able to:
- Define the terms *heredity*, *gene* and *gene expression*.
- Describe the structure and function of DNA, genes and chromosomes.
- HL ▶ Describe the detailed structure of DNA.
- Describe complementary base pairing in DNA.
- Describe the genetic code and distinguish between coding and non-coding DNA.
- Define *DNA profiling* and *genetic screening* and describe the four stages of DNA profiling as well as two applications.
- Describe the replication of DNA.
- Describe the structure of RNA.
- Describe a practical acivity to isolate DNA from plant tissue.

Introduction

This chapter deals with the structure of DNA and RNA. These are chemicals that are passed on from generation to generation (heredity).

> **Heredity** is the passing on of characteristics/traits from one generation to the next.

DNA is the blueprint needed to make a new organism. It contains all the necessary information to carry out all the vital metabolic processes of life. This information (genetic code) is organised into genes.

Function and structure of genes

As we learned in Chapter 13, genes are the units of inheritance passed on to the next generation.

> A **gene** is a short region of a chromosome that contains a code for the production of a protein.

When a gene produces a protein, **gene expression** has occurred.

> **Gene expression** is the process by which the code in DNA is used to make a protein.

Genes are spread out along the length of a chromosome (Fig 14.1).

Some genes are longer than other genes due to the fact that proteins can be of different lengths/sizes.

- The stretch of DNA where a gene is located is called coding DNA. It is so-called because it contains the code for the production of a protein.
- However, most of the DNA of a chromosome is called non-coding DNA. This is because it is not responsible for producing any proteins (it does not code for any particular protein).
- Non-coding DNA used to be called 'junk DNA'. This term is no longer used because functions for non-coding DNA are slowly being discovered. For example, it is known that some stretches of non-coding DNA function as regulators for gene expression. They control which genes are expressed and the frequency with which they are expressed. They function by turning genes 'on' and 'off'.

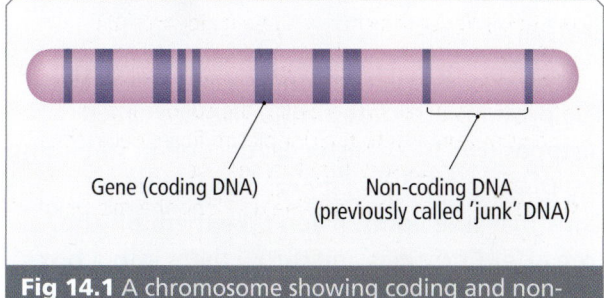

Fig 14.1 A chromosome showing coding and non-coding stretches of DNA.

There are estimated to be approximately 30,000 genes in the human genome, meaning that on average (not taking chromosome size into account) there are about 1,300 genes on each pair of chromosomes.

Remember, homologous chromosomes carry genes that control the same characteristic.

Function and structure of chromosomes

Chromosomes can be circular (as in bacteria) or linear (as in multicellular organisms). Each chromosome is a highly coiled structure composed of a very long molecule of DNA and many millions of separate molecules of protein.

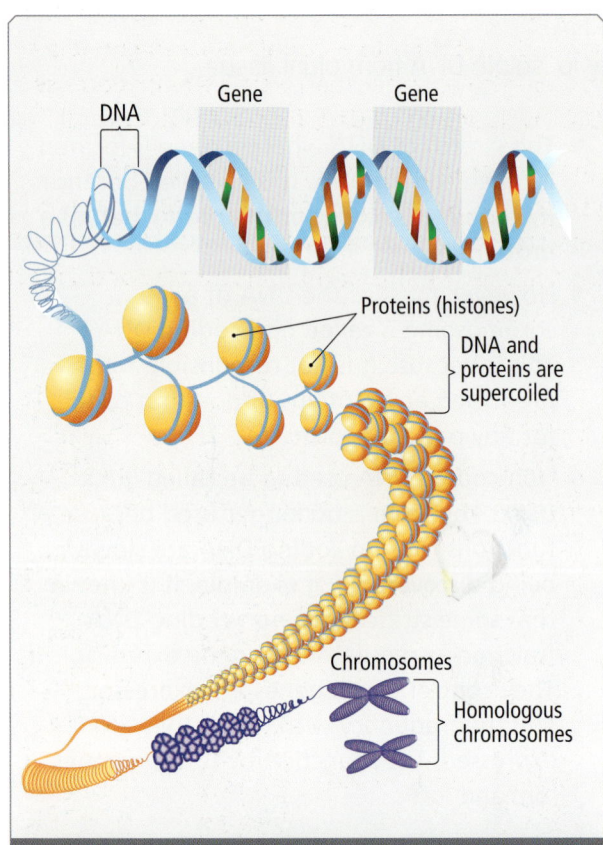

Fig 14.2 The structure of a chromosome showing the DNA and histones.

The proteins associated with DNA are called **histones** (Fig 14.2). Histones function in stabilising the DNA and keeping it organised. Think of Christmas tree lights. If you take them off the tree after Christmas and throw them into a box with the other decorations, they get tangled. If you carefully wind the lights around a piece of cardboard and then place them in the storage box, they will not become tangled and they will be much easier to put up the following year! The piece of cardboard acts like the histones that organise the DNA.

Also, DNA is such a long, slender molecule that without the associated proteins it would easily break into much smaller pieces.

In any one chromosome, 40 per cent is DNA, with protein making up the remaining 60 per cent. We learned in Chapter 13 that chromosomes exist only during mitosis. At all other times, DNA is in the form of **chromatin** (uncoiled DNA).

Fig 14.2 shows how duplicated chromosomes are formed from DNA and proteins. The DNA first replicates itself (at end of interphase) and is wound around the histones, which in turn go through a series of supercoiling steps to give the familiar structure of a duplicated chromosome.

As we learned in Chapter 13, there are 23 pairs of chromosomes in a human diploid cell. The first 22 pairs are called **autosomal chromosomes (autosomes).** Autosomes are responsible for controlling many different characteristics in humans.

The 23rd pair is called the **sex chromosomes** as they are specifically involved in determining the sex of an individual. There are two types of sex chromosome: **X** and **Y**. The X chromosome is much longer than the Y chromosome.

Remember, every person has two sex chromosomes meaning there are two possibilities: **XX** (female) and **XY** (male).

However, there are other genes on the sex chromosomes, which control other characteristics (see Chapter 16).

Basic structure of DNA (deoxyribonucleic acid)

DNA (**d**eoxyribo**n**ucleic **a**cid) is one of two types of nucleic acid (the other type is RNA). DNA consists of two strands (**double-stranded**) attached together by molecules called **bases**. DNA is twisted around on itself to produce a shape called a **double helix** (Fig 14.3).

DNA can be thought of as a ladder made up of stiles (the upright parts) and rungs. The strands of the DNA are the stiles of the ladder. The bases, which attach the strands together, are the rungs of the ladder. Each rung is made up of two bases.

Fig 14.3 Basic DNA structure.

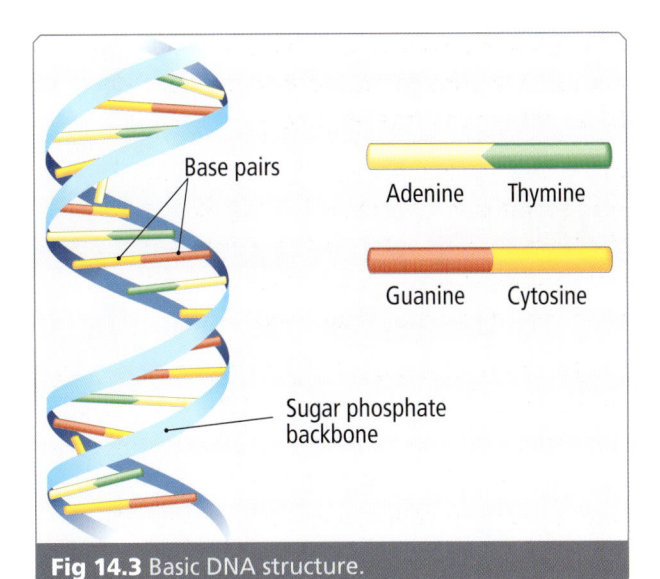

There are four nitrogenous (nitrogen-containing) bases found in DNA: **adenine (A), thymine (T), cytosine (C)** and **guanine (G)**. In each rung, adenine will always be found opposite thymine, and cytosine will always be found opposite guanine (Fig 14.4).

Fig 14.4 The four bases present in DNA. Adenine (A) always joins with thymine (T); cytosine (C) always joins with guanine (G).

Adenine pairs with thymine and cytosine pairs with guanine because of their size and shape. The molecules fit snugly together, much like the pieces of a jigsaw puzzle.

The sequence of these bases determines the function of a stretch of DNA. Many thousands of the bases in sequence make up a gene.

We now know the entire sequence of bases in the human genome. It was completed by scientists all over the world working together on the Human Genome Project. The project started in 1989 and finished in 2000. The researchers planned for the project to take 15 years. They were able to complete it much more quickly because of the rapid advances in DNA technology and DNA sequencing techniques during the 1990s.

The entire haploid human genome – that is, the sequence of bases on 23 chromosomes – numbers just over 3 billion bases. This means that every chromosome contains on average (without taking length of chromosome into account) 130 million base pairs (or 130 million rungs!).

HL Detailed structure of DNA

As already mentioned, DNA is composed of two strands connected together via bases and twisted around on itself into a double helix shape. It is a 'double' helix rather than a single helix because DNA is double-stranded, forming two helices.

The two strands of DNA are composed of phosphates and sugar molecules. The sugar is a five-carbon sugar called **deoxyribose**. Each strand is composed of alternating phosphates and sugars (Fig 14.5).

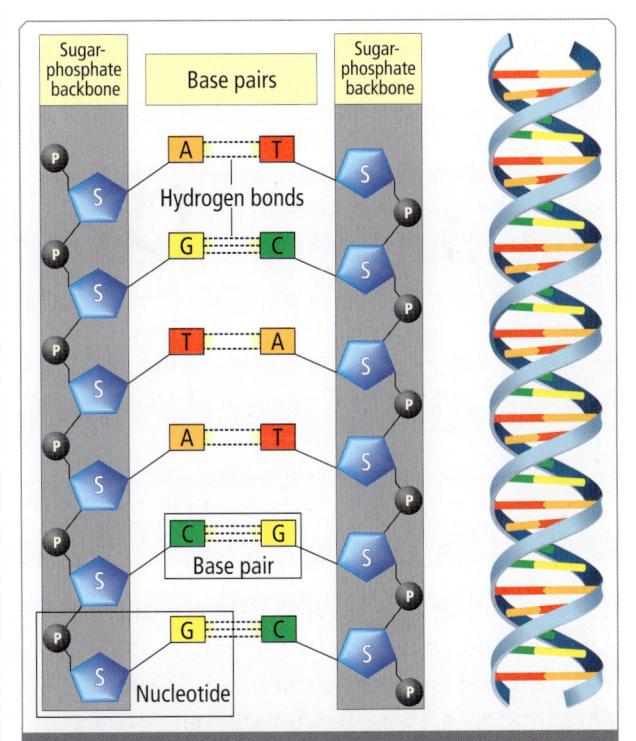

Fig 14.5 Detailed structure of DNA. DNA is made up of units called nucleotides. Each nucleotide is composed of a phosphate, a sugar (deoxyribose) and a base (A, T, C or G).

The two strands are linked by **nitrogenous bases**. 'Nitrogenous' means they each contain the element nitrogen. There are four nitrogenous bases. These are **adenine**

(A), thymine (T), cytosine (C) and guanine (G). Adenine always bonds with thymine and cytosine always bonds with guanine.

The bases join to each other by **hydrogen bonding,** which holds the strands together. Hydrogen bonds are very weak by themselves, but are very strong collectively.

There are two hydrogen bonds between an adenine and a thymine, and there are three hydrogen bonds between a cytosine and a guanine.

The bases are attached to each strand at the sugar, deoxyribose. This sequence of a phosphate bonded to a sugar bonded to a base is called a **nucleotide** (Fig 14.5).

Complementary base pairing

A nucleotide in DNA is composed of a phosphate, a deoxyribose sugar and a nitrogenous base. The only part of a nucleotide that will vary from nucleotide to nucleotide is the nitrogenous base. It can be one of four: adenine, thymine, cytosine or guanine. You must remember that adenine always pairs with thymine with two hydrogen bonds **(A=T)** and cytosine always pairs with guanine with three hydrogen bonds **(C ≡ G)**. This is called **complementary base pairing** because the shapes of adenine and thymine and cytosine and guanine are complementary and fit together perfectly.

Adenine and guanine belong to a large group of biomolecules called **purines**. Caffeine, found in teas and coffees, is an example of an everyday purine. Thymine and cytosine belong to a group of biomolecules called **pyrimidines**.

Replication of DNA

DNA replication occurs towards the end of interphase, when the cell is preparing for mitosis.

Each chromosome must produce an exact copy of itself (Fig 14.6), so that the cell can divide in two and each new cell will receive a copy of each chromosome.

Mechanism of DNA replication

First, the double helix unwinds. An enzyme then opens the two strands, much in the same way a zip works. It does this by breaking the hydrogen bonds between the nitrogenous bases. The bases on the two strands of DNA are then exposed. These act as the template for the production of a new strand.

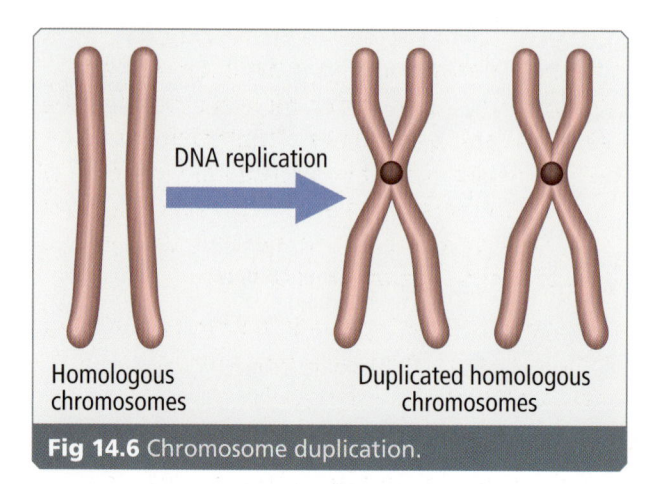

Fig 14.6 Chromosome duplication.

New nucleotides, which enter from the cytosol, are connected to the exposed bases on the 'old' strand. The new nucleotides each contain one of the four nitrogenous bases (A, T, C and G) and are attached, so that base pairing occurs between the bases of the old and new strands (Fig 14.7).

The assembly of the new strands is carried out by the anabolic enzyme, **DNA polymerase** (see Chapter 9).

Each new chromosome consists of one old strand of bases and one new strand.

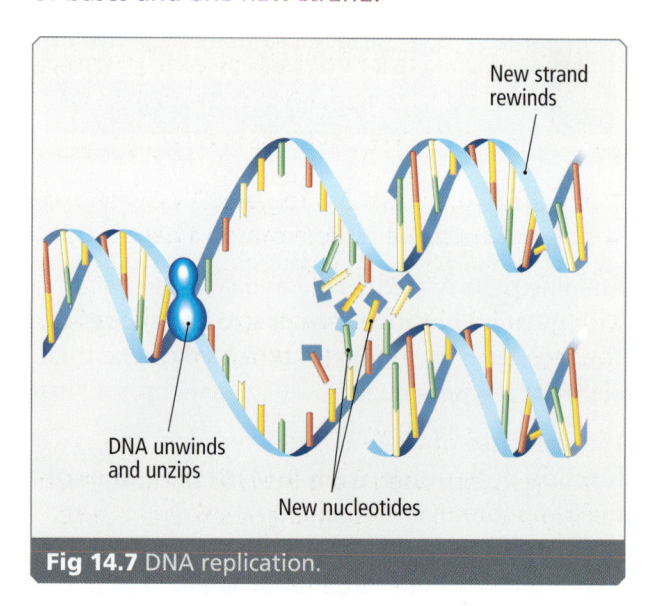

Fig 14.7 DNA replication.

Once DNA replication has finished, the DNA re-associates itself with histones and rewinds, recoils and supercoils into chromosomes. The duplicated chromosomes stay attached together in readiness for mitosis.

DNA and RNA — Chapter 14

Significance of DNA replication

DNA replication is significant because it allows for cell continuity, the process of cells arising from cells of the same type.

DNA has been around since the beginning of life on Earth. It is a unique molecule that has the ability to replicate itself and control the entire cell's activities. It has been passed along from cell to cell with remarkable accuracy. At a molecular level, DNA of all organisms is exactly the same! Only the sequence of bases differs.

For example, DNA is present in both bacteria and humans despite them diverging from a common ancestor billions of years ago!

DNA replication is usually a very accurate process. However, occasionally mistakes occur and the sequence of bases changes. This is how variations develop in a species and ultimately how evolution occurs.

DNA profiling

DNA profiling (also called DNA fingerprinting) is a commonly used technique in hospitals and labs around the world. It has many applications. It is used in scientific research to identify certain species and is used in medicine and in criminology/forensics.

> **DNA profiling** is the method of producing a unique pattern of bands from the DNA of a person so that it can be used for identification purposes.

A tissue sample is needed to get a DNA profile of a person. The tissue sample can be a hair follicle, blood smear or bodily fluid.

DNA profiling involves four steps: **DNA isolation, cutting, separation** and **pattern analysis.**

1 DNA isolation

The DNA is extracted from the cells using a type of detergent. We learned in Chapter 6 that the cell membrane is composed of a type of lipid. Lipids dissolve easily in detergents. When the cell and nuclear membranes are broken, the DNA is released.

2 Cutting

The DNA is in the form of very long threads of chromatin. To produce a profile, these long threads of DNA have to be made more manageable. This is done by 'cutting' them into fragments using an enzyme. As we learned in Chapter 9, enzymes are highly specific. The enzyme that cuts DNA is called a **restriction enzyme.**

Restriction enzymes cut the DNA (Fig 14.8) at a specific base sequence. Wherever this base sequence occurs, the DNA will be cut.

As each person's DNA is different, restriction enzymes cut each person's DNA at different places. Therefore, everyone has a unique mixture of different lengths of DNA fragments.

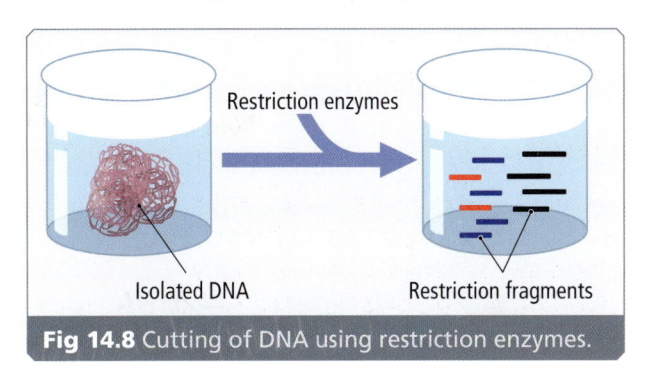

Fig 14.8 Cutting of DNA using restriction enzymes.

3 Separation

The third step involves separating the fragments based on their lengths. This is achieved using a process called **gel electrophoresis.**

Gel electrophoresis is a process in which DNA samples are placed into a porous gel and electric current is applied. This produces an electric field across the piece of gel (Fig 14.9).

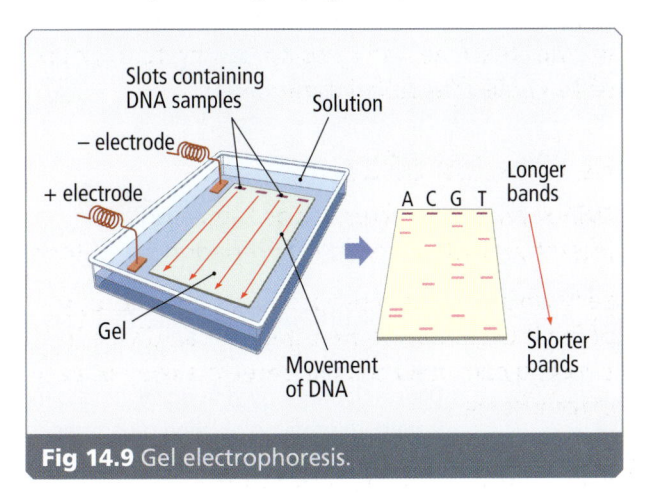

Fig 14.9 Gel electrophoresis.

DNA is a negatively charged molecule and it is therefore attracted to the positive end of the electric field. The DNA samples begin to move across the gel towards the positive end.

The DNA samples are composed of a mixture of different size fragments. The small fragments can move more quickly through the gel than the larger fragments. The DNA fragments are separated out based on their length.

When the process is complete, the gel is stained and exposed to ultraviolet (UV) light. A pattern is seen.

4 Pattern analysis

The fourth and final step is to view the bands of DNA produced by the movement of DNA fragments. The gel is stained and viewed under ultraviolet light. A pattern is seen, such as the one shown in Fig 14.10. An individual's DNA pattern (called a DNA profile) can be compared to another DNA profile to see if there are any similarities or differences.

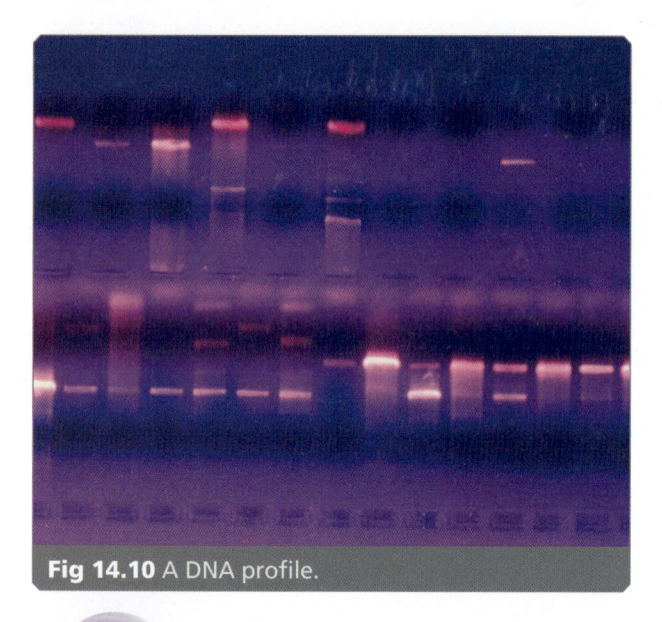

Fig 14.10 A DNA profile.

Genetic screening

Errors do occur in DNA replication. If these errors occur in an important gene, the gene of the resulting cells may not work properly and may not produce a working protein. This is usually not a problem if it occurs in a normal body cell. However, if a mutation occurs in a gamete (sex cell) and this gamete is involved in fertilisation, then the mutated gene will be present in every cell of the resultant offspring. This is when genetic diseases occur.

Genetic screening is a procedure that helps doctors to identify these mutated genes.

> **Genetic screening** is a test of a person's DNA to see if an altered/mutated gene is present.

Genetic screening is often carried out when it is suspected that a person is carrying an altered gene, which may give rise to a genetic disease.

It is also often used along with genetic counselling to assess the risk of a genetic disease being passed on to offspring.

Common genetic diseases that occur in Ireland include **cystic fibrosis** (where there is a build up of mucous in the lungs) and **haemochromatosis** (where there is a build up of iron in the body).

There are ethical issues surrounding the use of genetic screening. For example, with more widespread genetic screening, insurance companies, employers and financial institutions may discriminate against people with a genetic disease or even against people that carry a particular gene for a genetic disease.

Practical activity: to isolate DNA from plant tissue

Isolation of DNA from various tissues is an important biochemical technique and has many applications.

DNA isolation is used in many areas of biological research from DNA profiling of living organisms to genetic engineering (*see* Chapter 18).

In this activity, we will be using everyday household substances to isolate DNA from plant tissue.

SAFETY
Ethanol is extremely flammable and an irritant.
Lab coat, gloves and safety goggles must be worn and this substance should preferably be handled within a fume cupboard.

DNA and RNA   Chapter 14

Method

1. Add 3 g of salt to 10 ml of washing-up liquid and make up to 100 ml with distilled water.
2. Using a sharp knife, finely chop up the onion and add to the salt–washing-up liquid mixture. (Finely chopping the onion ensures a greater surface area for action of the washing-up liquid.)
3. Place the beaker into a hot (60 °C) water bath for 15 minutes, stirring slowly. (This step denatures enzymes that would break down the DNA.)
4. Place the beaker into an ice-cold water bath for five minutes, stirring slowly. (This step prevents the DNA being broken down by the heat.)
5. Pour the mixture from the beaker into a blender and blend for three seconds only.
6. Filter the mixture through coffee filter paper.
7. Take 10 ml of the filtrate and transfer it to a test-tube.
8. Add three drops of a **freshly prepared** protease solution (for example, freshly squeezed pineapple juice) to the test-tube and mix gently by swirling the tube. (This digests and removes the proteins associated with the DNA.)
9. Carefully and slowly pour approximately 10 ml of **ice-cold** ethanol (or ice-cold methylated spirits) down the side of the test-tube so that it forms a layer on top of the filtrate.
10. Leave the test-tube to settle for a few minutes.
11. Observe what happens at the junction between the filtrate and ethanol. (DNA is insoluble in ice-cold ethanol and precipitates as a white substance at the junction between the onion filtrate and ice-cold ethanol.)
12. Using the glass stirring rod, carefully remove any DNA that collects (Fig 14.11).

> **NOTE** Ensure the washing-up liquid is not antibacterial, as this breaks up DNA.
> Salt acts to clump the DNA, which helps in its isolation.
> Washing-up liquid breaks the cell and nuclear membranes, which releases the DNA.

> **NOTE** Blending the mixture breaks down the cell walls.
> Blend for three seconds only as any longer and the DNA itself would be broken down.

> **NOTE** Filtering the mixture removes cell debris, such as cell walls.
> Do not use a lab filter paper as the pores are too small for DNA to get through.

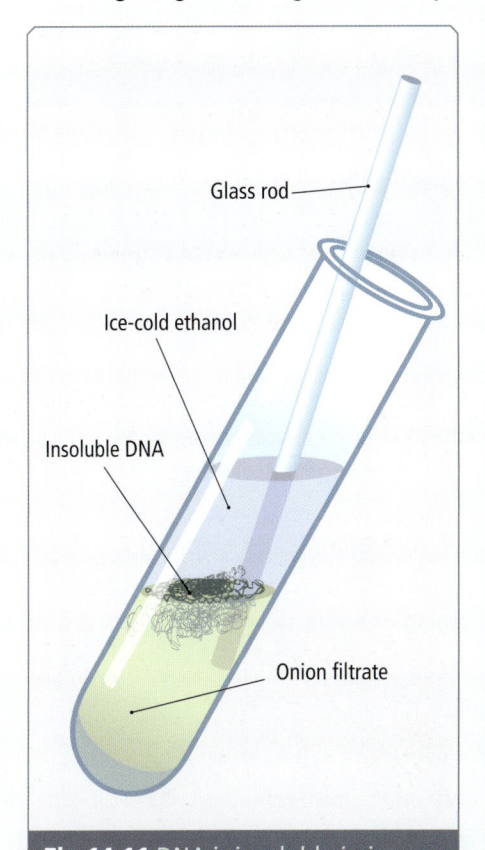

Fig 14.11 DNA is insoluble in ice-cold ethanol.

Results

A white semi-solid substance is seen at the junction between the onion filtrate and ice-cold ethanol.

Conclusion

What did we learn from this practical activity?

- DNA isolation is a procedure that can be carried out using everyday household substances.
- DNA is insoluble in ice-cold ethanol.
- DNA is a white semi-solid substance.

Practical activity questions

1. What plant tissue did you use?
2. What was the purpose of the washing-up liquid?
3. Why did you not use anti-bacterial washing-up liquid?
4. What was the purpose of the salt?
5. Explain the reasons behind the heating and cooling steps.
6. Why was the mixture blended for three seconds only?
7. What was the function of the filtration step?
8. Why was coffee filter paper and not lab filter paper used?
9. Why was it essential to add three drops of the protease enzyme?
10. Explain what problem might occur if the protease enzyme was not freshly prepared.
11. Why did the ethanol added to the boiling tube of filtrate have to be ice-cold?

Structure of RNA (ribonucleic acid)

RNA (ribonucleic acid) is another type of nucleic acid that is mostly found free in the cytoplasm in the form of ribosomes. However, it can also be found in the nucleus.

Ribosomes are composed of RNA. The structure of RNA is similar to DNA. However, there are some notable differences.

RNA is **single-stranded,** meaning it is composed of one strand (like half a ladder) (Fig 14.12).

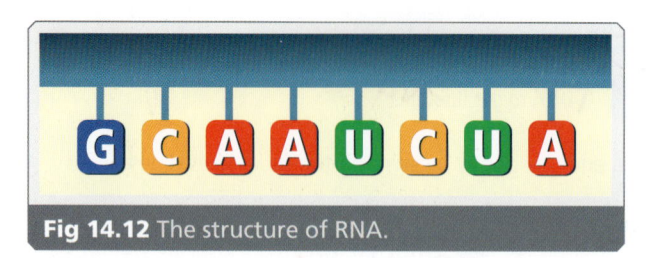

Fig 14.12 The structure of RNA.

RNA has the bases adenine (A), **uracil (U)**, cytosine (C) and guanine (G). You should notice that uracil has replaced thymine. RNA does not have any thymine.

RNA has the sugar **ribose,** whereas DNA had the sugar deoxyribose.

RNA is made using the code in DNA. Therefore, the code of RNA carry is **complementary** to a DNA code. For example, if there is a specific region of DNA that is responsible for producing RNA and the sequence of bases of one strand on the DNA is ATCGGC, then the sequence on the resulting RNA strand will be UAGCCG. Notice how the first letter is U because there is no thymine in RNA. Any cytosines in DNA become guanines in RNA. Guanines in DNA become cytosines in RNA. Also, any adenines in DNA become uracils in RNA and any thymines in DNA become adenines in RNA.

The enzyme that produces RNA is an anabolic enzyme called **RNA polymerase** (see Chapter 15). RNA goes on to function in protein synthesis.

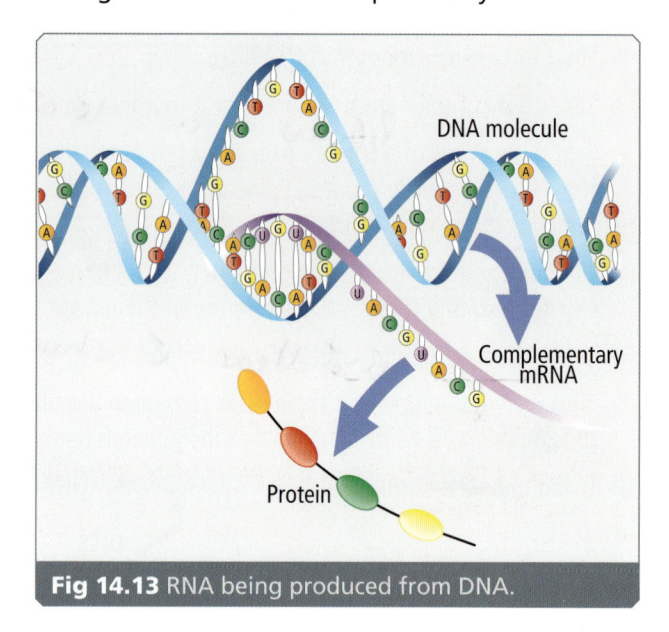

Fig 14.13 RNA being produced from DNA.

Chapter 14 Questions

1. (a) What is heredity?
   (b) What is a *gene*?
   (c) What is *gene expression*?
2. What **two** substances make up a chromosome?
3. (a) Distinguish between *coding* and *non-coding DNA*.
   (b) What is the old name for non-coding regions of DNA?
   (c) Why is this name no longer used?
4. Distinguish between a human haploid cell and human diploid cell in terms of chromosome number.
5. (a) What does DNA stand for?
   (b) What does RNA stand for?
6. Distinguish between DNA and RNA in terms of basic structure, location and function.
7. (a) What is meant by *complementary base pairing*? [HL]
   (b) What kind of bonding holds the bases together?
8. (a) Draw a piece of DNA showing the two strands as phosphates and sugars along with the base sequence ATTCGC on one strand and the complementary sequence on the other.
   (b) Show a nucleotide on your diagram by drawing a box around it.
9. What is the name of the sugar present in DNA?
10. Name the **two** purine bases and the **two** pyrimidine bases present in DNA.

11 (a) Describe, briefly, the steps involved in DNA replication.
   (b) What is the name of the anabolic enzyme involved in DNA replication?
   (c) What is the significance of DNA replication for living organisms?

12 (a) What is *genetic screening*?
   (b) Describe an ethical problem surrounding the use of genetic screening.

Chapter 14 Sample examination questions

1 The diagram represents a part of a DNA molecule. **A** and **C** represent nitrogenous bases.

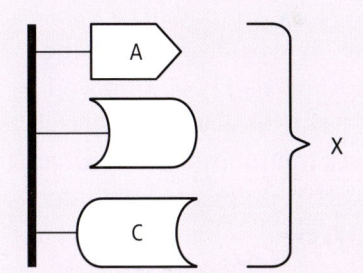

Complete the following in relation to DNA.

(a) Name the nitrogenous bases whose first letters are A and C.

(b) The structure labelled **X** is called a _____.

(c) Where in the cell would you expect to find most DNA?

(d) DNA contains the instructions needed to make protein.
These instructions are called the _____ code.

Section A, Question 5 Ordinary Level 2008

2 (c) (i) Explain, in terms of what happens to body cells, what is meant by the term *cancer*.

(ii) Give two possible causes of cancer.

(iii) Some people choose to be screened to determine their risk of getting a particular type of cancer. What is meant by genetic screening?

(iv) Blood samples taken from a crime scene were put through a process called DNA profiling. During the process, cells were broken down to release the DNA, which was then cut into fragments. The fragments were then separated.

1 What was used to cut the DNA?

2 On what basis were the DNA fragments separated?

3 Give an application of DNA profiling other than solving crime.

(v) The following are the results of the DNA profiling process. Using these results, identify which suspect, A, B or C, committed the crime.

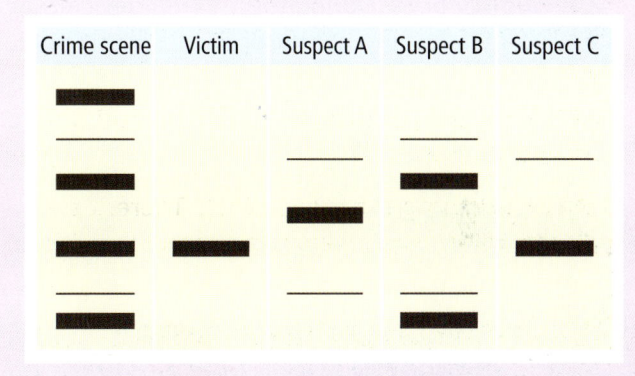

Section A, Question 10 (c) Ordinary Level 2011

HL 3 (a) Copy the diagram into your answer book and then complete it to show the complementary base pairs of the DNA molecule. Label all parts not already labelled.

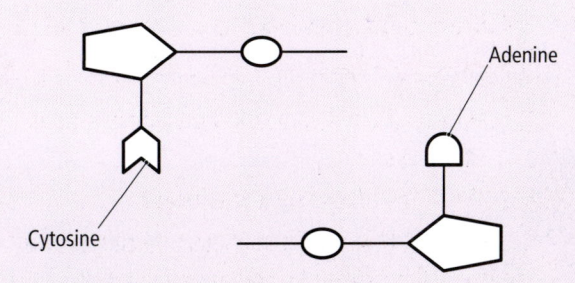

(c) Read the following passage and answer the questions that follow.

> Dolly, the most famous sheep in the world, was cloned in the Roslin Institute in Scotland in 1996.
>
> When this was announced in February 1997 it caused a sensation, because until then many scientists thought that such cloning was impossible.
>
> Such cloning is the production of one or more animals that are genetically identical to an existing animal. This cloning technique is based on the fact that, with the exception of the sperm and the egg, every cell in the body contains in its DNA all of the genetic material needed to make an exact replica of the original body. During the normal development process from embryo to fully-fledged animal, all of the cells in the body are differentiated to perform specific physiological functions.
>
> Before Dolly, the majority view was that such differentiated cells could not be reprogrammed to be able to behave as fertilised eggs.
>
> Dolly was produced by a process known as 'adult DNA cloning', which produces a duplicate of an existing animal. The technique is also known as 'cell nuclear replacement'. During adult DNA cloning, the DNA is sucked out from a normal unfertilised egg cell, using a device that acts somewhat like a miniature vacuum cleaner. DNA that has already been removed from a cell of the adult to be copied is then inserted in place of the original DNA. Following this stage, the cell containing the inserted DNA is implanted in the womb of an animal of the same species, and gestation may begin.
>
> To make Dolly, a cell was taken from the mammary tissue of a six-year-old sheep. Its DNA was added to a sheep ovum (egg) from which the nucleus had been removed. This artificially fertilised cell was then stimulated with an electric pulse and implanted in a ewe.
>
> *Adapted from www.biotechinfo.ie*

(i) What is the difference between a nucleus of an egg cell and that of a somatic (body) cell of an animal?

(ii) Suggest an advantage of producing genetically identical animals.

(iii) Suggest a disadvantage of producing genetically identical animals.

(iv) 'Every cell in the body contains in its DNA all of the genetic material needed to make an exact replica of the original body.' Comment on this statement.

(v) What is the precise meaning of the term 'implanted' in the extract above?

(vi) Suggest a purpose for stimulating the fused egg with an electric pulse.

(vii) What do you think is meant by the phrase 'artificially fertilised cell'?

Section C, Question 13 (a) & (c) Higher Level 2004

Chapter 14 Mind map

DNA and RNA are the chemicals passed on from generation to generation.

- **Heredity** is the passing on of characteristics/traits from one generation to the next.
- A **gene** is a short region of a chromosome that contains a code for the production of a protein.
- **Gene expression** is the process by which the code in DNA is used to make a protein.

- **Chromosomes** are structures made from DNA and protein, found in the nucleus and carry genes that are spread out along its length.
- The sections of DNA, which produce proteins, are referred to as coding DNA.
- The sections of DNA, which do not produce proteins, are referred to as non-coding DNA (formerly known as 'junk' DNA).

- There are 46 chromosomes in a human diploid cell.
- There are 23 chromosomes in a human sex cell.

- DNA stands for deoxyribonucleic acid.
- DNA is a double-stranded structure held together by paired bases and twisted around on itself to form a double helix.
- The bases present in DNA are adenine (A), thymine (T), cytosine (C) and guanine (G).

Complementary base pairing [HL]

- Adenine always pairs with thymine with two hydrogen bonds holding them together.
- Cytosine always pairs with guanine with three hydrogen bonds holding them together.
- Adenine and guanine are purines. Cytosine and thymine are pyrimidines.
- The two strands of DNA are made from alternating units of phosphates and sugars.
- The sugar in DNA is called deoxyribose.
- The bases are attached to the sugars.
- The repeating units that make up DNA are called nucleotides.
- Nucleotides in DNA consist of a phosphate, a sugar (deoxyribose) and a base (A, T, C or G).

DNA replication
- Occurs towards the end of interphase.
- Double helix unwinds and unzips (due to enzyme action).
- DNA polymerase synthesises a new strand by attaching new nucleotides to their complementary positions opposite the old strand.
- Two new chromosomes are formed.

DNA profiling is a method of producing a unique pattern of bands from the DNA of a person so that it can be used for identification purposes.
- DNA is extracted from the tissue sample using detergents.
- The long threads of DNA are cut using restriction enzymes to produce a unique mixture of DNA fragments.
- The mixture of DNA fragments are separated using gel electrophoresis.
- The patterns produced are observed under UV light or stained and compared for identification purposes.

Genetic screening is a test of a person's DNA to see if an altered/mutated gene is present.

Practical activity to isolate DNA from a plant tissue
- Mix finely chopped onion into a salt/washing-up liquid solution and heat for 15 minutes at 60 °C.
- Cool mixture for five minutes in an ice water bath and blend for three seconds.
- Filter the mixture using coffee filter paper.
- Take 10 ml of filtrate and add three drops of protease enzyme.
- Add 10 ml ice-cold ethanol gradually down the side of the test-tube.
- Observe the DNA precipitate out of solution at the junction between the filtrate and ice-cold ethanol.

- RNA stands for ribonucleic acid.
- RNA is found mostly in the cytoplasm in the form of ribosomes.
- RNA is made in the nucleus using the code in DNA and then travels to the cytoplasm where it is involved in making proteins.
- RNA is single stranded.
- RNA has the sugar, ribose.
- RNA has the four bases adenine (A), uracil (U), cytosine (C) and guanine (G).

Chapter 15 Protein synthesis

Learning objectives After studying this chapter, you should be able to:
- Describe the location of and the three stages of protein synthesis: transcription, translation and protein folding.
- HL ▶ Describe the detailed process of transcription, translation and protein folding.
- ▶ Describe the roles of messenger RNA, ribosomal RNA and transfer RNA.

Introduction

> **Protein synthesis** is the making of protein using amino acids and the code in messenger RNA.

Protein synthesis occurs in the cytoplasm on the surface of structures called ribosomes (Fig 15.1). Ribosomes are made from RNA folded over on itself.

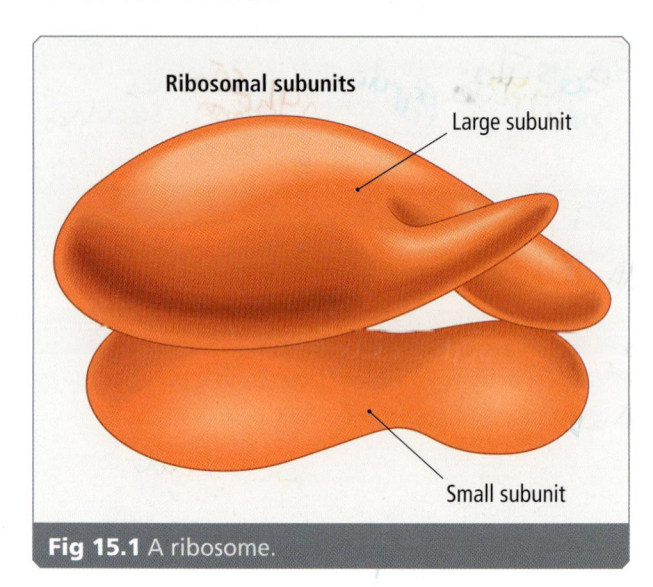

Fig 15.1 A ribosome.

We learned in Chapter 14 that RNA is single-stranded; has the base uracil (instead of thymine); and has the sugar ribose (instead of deoxyribose).

Protein synthesis is continually occurring in living cells at all times. Metabolic processes that make hair, skin, nails, the linings of the digestive and respiratory systems, tissues that make hormones and enzymes, and white blood cells that make antibodies all require continuous protein synthesis.

We learned in Chapter 3 that protein synthesis is an anabolic process – it involves small molecules (amino acids) being joined together to make a large molecule (protein).

Protein synthesis

DNA contains the blueprint or genetic code for protein synthesis. Protein synthesis occurs in the cytosol on the surface of ribosomes. However, DNA does not leave the nucleus during this process. The only time DNA leaves the nucleus is during mitosis and during this stage of the cell cycle the DNA is not available for protein synthesis.

Protein synthesis involves three distinct stages: **transcription**, **translation** and **protein folding**.

1 Transcription

> **Transcription** is the making of mRNA **using** a DNA template.

NOTE It is important to include the word 'using' and not 'from' when defining transcription.

As DNA does not leave the nucleus, the cell must have a messaging system to get the DNA code to a ribosome.

When a cell wants to produce a protein, a chemical message, in the form of RNA, is sent from the nucleus to the ribosome (Fig 15.2). This type of RNA is called **messenger RNA (mRNA)**.

The DNA code (gene) is transcribed (copied) to mRNA, which is then transported out of the nucleus, via nuclear pores, to a ribosome.

2 Translation

> **Translation** is the making of protein **using** the code in mRNA.

NOTE Once again, it is important to include the word 'using' and not 'from' when defining translation.

The mRNA arrives at a ribosome. The ribosome joins amino acids together based on the code (codons) of mRNA (Fig 15.2).

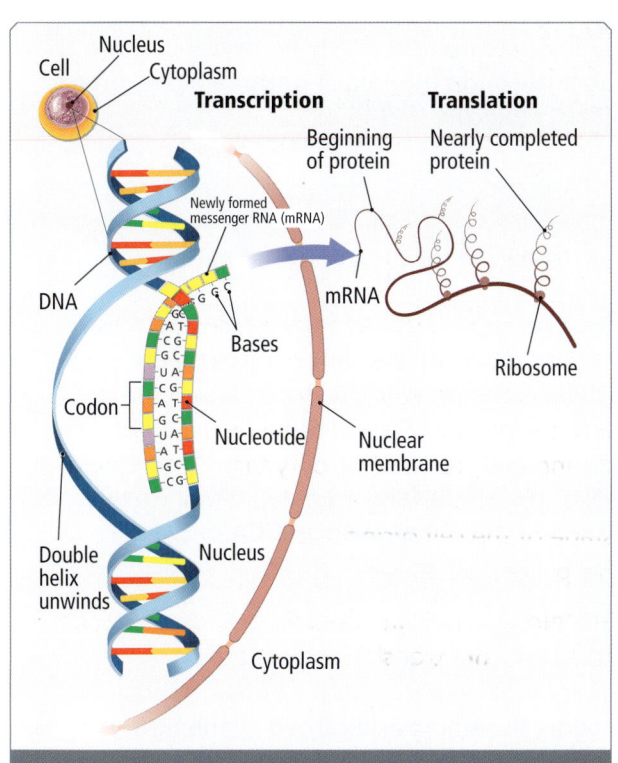

Fig 15.2 Transcription and translation.

3 Protein folding

All proteins have their own characteristic shape. This shape enables them to carry out their specific functions. For example, enzymes need their shape to act on substrate(s); hormones need their shape to bind to receptors on the surface of cells; antibodies need their shape to bind and inactivate foreign invaders, such as bacteria and viruses.

Protein folding is the last stage of protein synthesis (Fig 15.3). A long chain of amino acids has been produced and folds over on itself. It may also attach to other proteins to give the final structure. It is then ready to carry out its function.

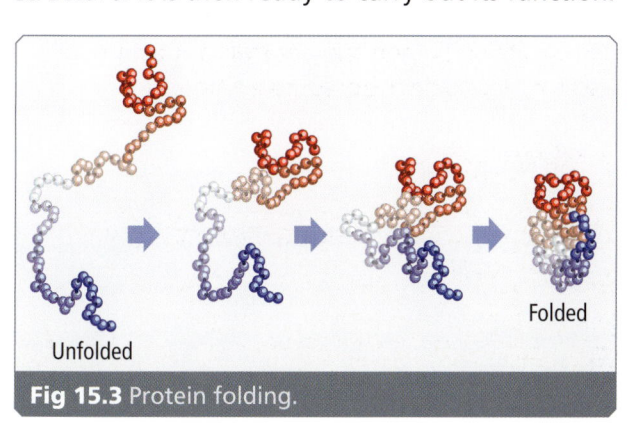

Fig 15.3 Protein folding.

HL Detailed process of protein synthesis

> **NOTE:** HL students must study transcription and translation in greater detail. Students must have an understanding of the molecular functions of DNA, RNA and amino acids in the process of protein synthesis. Even though they are not repeated here, students must also learn the definitions of transcription and translation.

1 Transcription

Transcription occurs in the nucleus. Enzymes unwind and break the hydrogen bonds between the strands of DNA, exposing nucleotide bases only at the site of the gene to be transcribed (Fig 15.4). In this way, transcription is said to be specific. Only the nucleotide bases that control and make up the gene are exposed.

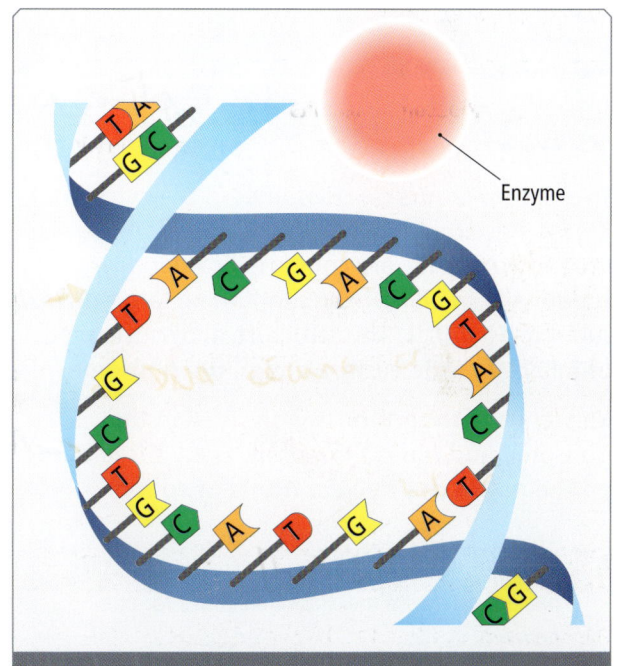

Fig 15.4 An enzyme opening DNA at the site of a gene.

The anabolic enzyme, **RNA polymerase,** synthesises messenger RNA (mRNA) using one of the strands of DNA (Fig 15.5). Free-floating RNA nucleotides from the cytoplasm bond with their complementary nucleotides on the DNA.

> **NOTE:** Remember, that uracil will be complementary to adenine during transcription, as RNA is being formed.

For example, if the sequence of DNA is **ATTGATCTG,** then a piece of RNA made using this piece of DNA will have the sequence, **UAACUAGAC.**

Once the RNA polymerase enzyme has transcribed the entire gene, it detaches from the DNA and moves back to the beginning again, ready for another cycle of transcription.

The newly synthesised piece of mRNA detaches from the RNA polymerase and diffuses from the nucleus out into the cytoplasm, where it interacts with a ribosome.

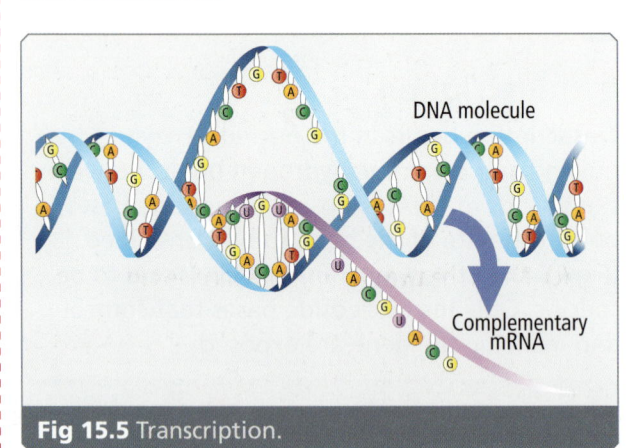

Fig 15.5 Transcription.

2 Translation

Translation occurs on ribosomes in the cytoplasm. Ribosomes are made from RNA, called **ribosomal RNA (rRNA).** They are composed of two RNA subunits: a small rRNA subunit and a large rRNA subunit (Fig 15.1). This structure allows the piece of mRNA to slide easily through the ribosome.

Messenger RNA interacts with rRNA in the ribosome and slides through it. Every three bases on the mRNA are called a **triplet** or **codon.**

> A **triplet** or **codon** is a sequence of three bases present on messenger RNA that codes for one amino acid.

Every codon on mRNA will tell the ribosome to carry out one of the following:

- **Start codon:** A start codon is a sequence of three bases (such as AUG) present on mRNA that tells the ribosome to begin assembling a protein.
- **Amino acid:** Codons follow the start codon and tell the ribosome to add on a specific amino acid.
- **Stop codon:** A stop codon is a sequence of three bases (such as UAG) that tells the ribosome to stop assembling the amino acids and to release the chain of amino acids.

Amino acids are transported to the ribosome by **transfer RNA (tRNA).** Transfer RNA is the third and final type of RNA involved in protein synthesis. Each tRNA molecule carries only one type of amino acid – they are specific. There is an **anti-codon** (sequence of three bases) on each tRNA molecule (Fig 15.6).

> An **anti-codon** is a sequence of three bases present on transfer RNA that will be complementary to a codon present on messenger RNA.

Anti-codons on tRNA molecules interact with codons as the mRNA moves through the ribosome. They will interact only when the anti-codon is **complementary** to the codon. For example, if a codon on mRNA has the sequence **CGU,** then in order for an anti-codon to interact, it must have the sequence, **GCA.**

> **NOTE:** Remember RNA has the base uracil, which is complementary to adenine in RNA.

Every time an anti-codon of tRNA interacts with a codon, the amino acid carried by the tRNA is added to the growing chain of amino acids. Once the tRNA has added on its amino acid at the site of protein synthesis, it is released out into the cytoplasm to pick up another amino acid of the same type.

Fig 15.6 A and B shows the sequence of events in translation.

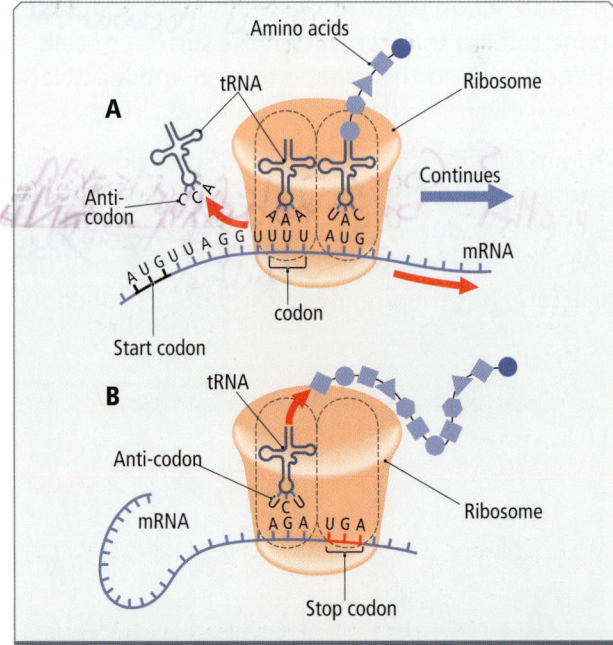

Fig 15.6 The beginning of translation **(A)**; the end of translation **(B)**.

Chapter 15 Questions

1. What is *protein synthesis*?
2. (a) What cell structure is responsible for carrying out protein synthesis?
   (b) What is the cell structure you named in part (b) composed of?
   (c) Where in the cell is the cell structure you named in part (b) mostly located?
   (d) Where in the cell is the cell structure you named in part (b) made (*see* Chapter 6)?
3. (a) Give **two** examples of proteins found in living organisms and give each of their functions (*see* Chapter 3).
   (b) Name the **two** basic shapes of protein and give one example of a protein for each shape (*see* Chapter 3).
4. (a) Define *metabolism* (*see* Chapter 3).
   (b) There are **two** types of metabolism. Name the **two** types of metabolism. To which type does protein synthesis belong? Explain.
5. Name the chemical message that occurs between the nucleus and the site of protein synthesis.
6. (a) What is *transcription*?
   (b) In what cell organelle does transcription occur?
   (c) Name the enzyme responsible for transcription.
   (d) Name the substrate upon which the enzyme you named in part (c) acts.
   (e) Name the product of transcription.
   (f) If the sequence of bases of a gene is **AGG CTA GAT CTA CCT**, give the sequence of bases present on the complementary product of transcription.
7. (a) What is *translation*?
   (b) Where in the cell does translation occur?
   (c) Name the two biomolecules involved in translation.
   HL (d) What is a *codon*?
   (e) What is an *anti-codon*?
   (f) Name the **three** possible events that occur as a result of an anti-codon matching up to a codon during translation.
8. (a) Ribonucleic acid can be subdivided into **three** types. Name the three types.
   (b) Give the function of each type of ribonucleic acid you named in part (a).
9. Explain why it is important for a protein to take up a particular shape after it is made.

Chapter 15 Sample examination questions

1. Complete the following sentence by adding the missing word(s).
   In order to make proteins, DNA is first transcribed as messenger _____.

   Section A, Question 4 (d) Ordinary Level 2007

2. (i) These bases form a triplet code. What is meant by a *triplet code*?
   (ii) The triplet code is transcribed into mRNA. What does this statement mean?
   (iii) To which structures in the cell does mRNA carry the code?

   Section C, Question 13 (b) (ii)–(iv) Ordinary Level 2005

HL 3. The genetic code incorporated into the DNA molecule finds its expression in part in the formation of protein. This formation requires the involvement of a number of RNA molecules. List these RNA molecules and briefly describe the role of each of them.

   Section C, Question 13 (b) Higher Level 2004

Unit 2 — The Cell

4 (i) Explain the terms *transcription* and *translation*.
   (ii) In which structures in the cell does translation occur?
   (iii) How many bases in sequence make up a codon in mRNA?
   (iv) Each mRNA codon specifies one of three possible outcomes during protein synthesis. Name these **three** possible outcomes.
   (v) What does the letter 't' stand for in tRNA?
   (vi) During translation, one end of a tRNA molecule attaches to an mRNA codon. What is usually attached to the other end of the tRNA molecule?

   Section C, Question 10 (b) Higher Level 2010

Chapter 15 Mind map

Protein synthesis is the making of protein using amino acids and the code in messenger RNA.

Protein synthesis

- DNA contains the blueprint or genetic code for the formation of all proteins.
- **Transcription** is the making of mRNA using a DNA template.
- Transcription occurs in the nucleus.
- The mRNA molecule travels to the site of protein synthesis: the ribosome.
- **Translation** is the making of a protein using the code in mRNA.
- The protein takes up its functional shape.

Detailed process of protein synthesis HL

- Enzymes unwind the DNA only at the site of the gene so that the nucleotide bases that make up the gene are exposed.
- Transcription is carried out by the anabolic enzyme, RNA polymerase.
- RNA polymerase joins RNA nucleotide bases together by bonding them to their complementary nucleotide bases present on one strand of the DNA.
- Once synthesised, mRNA leaves the nucleus and travels to the site of protein synthesis: the ribosome.
- The mRNA is composed of hundreds of codons.
- A **codon** is a sequence of three bases present on mRNA that contains the code for one amino acid in a protein.
- The first codon on mRNA specifies a 'start' instruction.
- The last codon on mRNA specifies a 'stop' instruction.
- The codons in-between specify all of the amino acids that make up the protein.
- The mRNA interacts with the ribosome present in the cytoplasm.
- Ribosomes are made from ribosomal RNA.
- Transfer RNA (tRNA) carries an amino acid to the ribosome.
- Transfer RNA molecules contain an anti-codon that is complementary to a specific codon on the mRNA.
- When the codon matches with an anti-codon present on tRNA, the amino acid is added to the protein.
- Transfer RNA molecules continue to interact with the mRNA until the stop codon is reached.
- The stop codon tells the ribosome to disassemble and stop translation.
- The protein is released and takes up its functional shape.

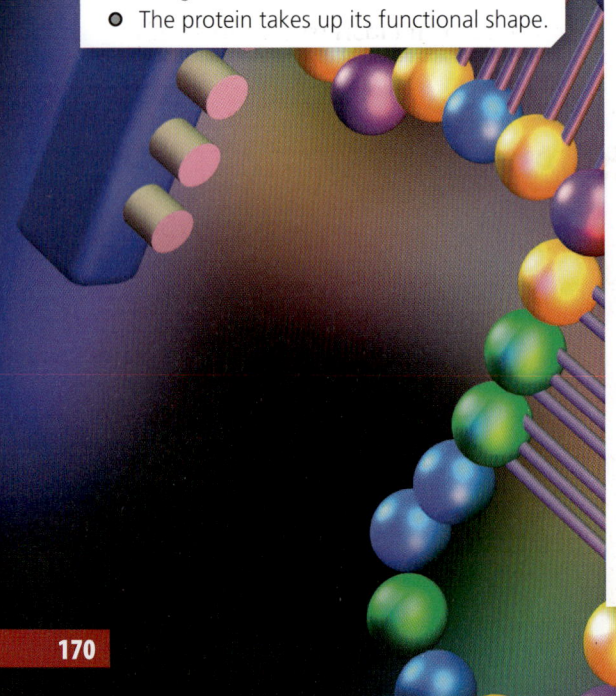

Inheritance and genetic crosses — Chapter 16

Learning objectives After studying this chapter, you should be able to:
- Define a range of terms associated with genetics.
- Describe how single traits/characteristics are inherited to the first generation using monohybrid crosses.
- Describe how gender is inherited using monohybrid crosses.

HL
- Describe the work of Gregor Mendel leading to his two laws.
- Define and explain Mendel's two laws: First Law of Segregation and Second Law of Independent Assortment.
- Describe how two separate unlinked traits/characteristics are inherited to the second generation using dihybrid crosses and the Punnett square technique.
- Define and explain *linkage* and *sex linkage*.
- Compare and explain the change in ratios of possible offspring between non-linked and linked dihybrid crosses.
- Describe the inheritance of the common sex-linked traits: red-green colour-blindness and haemophilia.
- Describe non-nuclear inheritance.
- Read a pedigree study.

Introduction

> **Genetics** is the study of inheritance.
>
> **Inheritance** is the passing on of traits from one generation to the next.
>
> **Traits** are physical and chemical characteristics that a living organism possesses.

When we think of genetics, we think of the colour of our eyes, skin and hair, how tall we are, or how we have similar traits to our parents. Genetics is the study of inheritance and how these traits are passed on.

Continuity of life depends on **inheritance**. In simple organisms, such as single-celled organisms, continuity of life is maintained through **mitosis** (*see* Chapter 13). In more complex plants and animals, this is achieved through **sexual reproduction**. Sexual reproduction is a much more complicated process involving the formation of **gametes** (*see* Chapters 28 and 41).

Gametes

Sexual reproduction depends on the formation of gametes with half the number of chromosomes **(haploid)** as all the other cells in that organism.

> **Gametes** are haploid sex cells.

The importance of the term 'haploid' was explained in Chapter 13.

In humans

In humans, the gametes are the egg cell (produced in the female's ovaries) and the sperm cell (produced in the male's testes). Gametes contain only 23 chromosomes (n or haploid). They are produced by **meiosis** (*see* Chapter 13). This is to ensure that the new individual will have the correct number of chromosomes in all their

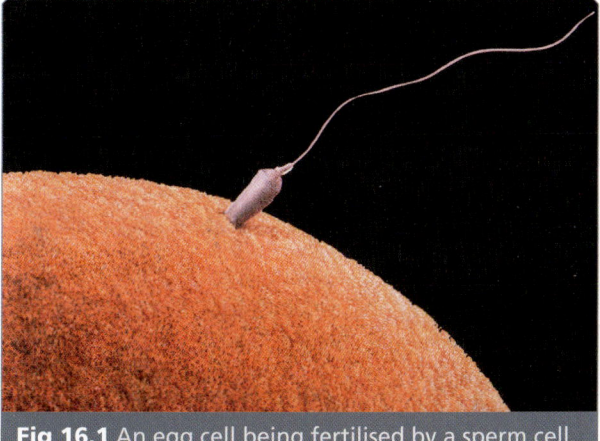

Fig 16.1 An egg cell being fertilised by a sperm cell.

cells. All other cells in the human body contain 23 pairs of chromosomes (2n or diploid); 22 pairs are called autosomes (*see* Chapter 13) and one pair (XX or XY) is called the sex chromosomes.

When the sperm fertilises an egg cell, the nuclei of the two haploid gametes join and the diploid (2n) number of 46 chromosomes is re-attained, so a new individual can develop and grow.

In plants

In plants, the gametes are the egg cell (produced in the ovary of the flower) and the pollen grain (produced in the anther of the flower). Again, the egg cell and pollen grain are haploid (n) sex cells, produced by meiosis, which fuse together during fertilisation to create a diploid (2n) zygote that can then grow and develop into a new plant.

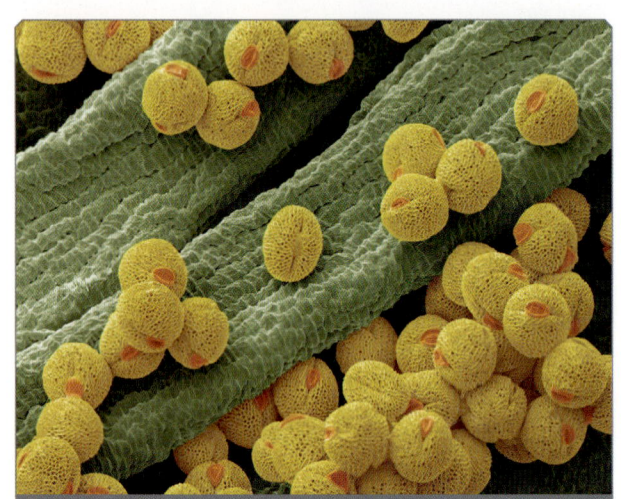

Fig 16.2 Pollen grains – the male gamete of flowering plants.

Fertilisation

Gametes must join together to produce a new individual, in a process called **fertilisation**. The first cell that results from fusion of two haploid gametes is called a **zygote**.

> **Fertilisation** is the fusion of two haploid gametes to produce a diploid zygote.

The gametes carry the genes necessary for inheritance and continuity of life. However, each gamete carries only one copy of each gene, as each gamete is carrying one chromosome from each homologous pair of chromosomes (*see* Chapter 13).

When fertilisation occurs, chromosomes once again exist in the form of homologous pairs. As a result, each cell gets two copies of each chromosome and, therefore, two copies of each gene.

Allele

> An **allele** is a form of a gene where a number of different types of the same gene exist.

Usually only two forms of the same gene exist. Different forms of the same gene are called **alleles**. Alleles can be very different from each other and have very different effects. However, they still belong to the same gene as they control the same characteristic.

For example, brown eyes and blue eyes are very different characteristics. They are controlled by *different* alleles. However, they belong to the *same* gene because they control the same trait – colour of the iris. They are also located at the **same position** or **locus** on homologous chromosomes.

> **Locus** is the position of an allele or gene on a chromosome.

Most genes in living organisms have two or more alleles controlling the outward expression of that gene. These alleles can be the same (**homozygous**) or different (**heterozygous**).

Homozygous and heterozygous

Two alleles can be the same (homozygous) or different (heterozygous).

> **Homozygous:** two alleles are the same.

Homozygous is also often referred to as **pure-breeding**. This is because homozygous organisms produce homozygous offspring when mated together. In other words, there is no variation in the offspring as a result of a cross (sexual reproduction) between two homozygous organisms.

> **Heterozygous:** two alleles are different.

Taking human eye colour as an example, everyone has two alleles controlling eye colour. A person with brown eyes will have two alleles controlling the production of the brown pigment. These alleles could be exactly the same – the person will have two alleles responsible for producing the brown pigment, one on each homologous chromosome. Conversely, they may have two different alleles – they could have one allele responsible for producing the brown pigment on one chromosome and a different allele (such as an allele producing the blue pigment) on the other chromosome. If this is the case, then the person will still have brown eyes.

The reason for this is that the brown allele shows **dominance** over the blue allele. In other words, the blue allele is **recessive** to the brown allele.

Dominance and recessive

In the above example, the allele responsible for giving the individual brown eyes has dominance over the allele that would otherwise give the person blue eyes.

> **Dominance:** where one allele (the dominant one) masks the effect of another allele.

Therefore, we say that the allele responsible for the brown pigment is **dominant** and the allele responsible for the blue pigment is **recessive**.

> **Recessive:** where an allele's effect is only expressed when in the homozygous condition.

We use letters to represent and distinguish between different types of alleles. We use capital letters to refer to dominant alleles and lower case letters to refer to recessive alleles.

- Therefore, a person with brown eyes could have two brown alleles, in which case we describe the person as **'BB'**; or they could have one brown allele and one blue allele, in which case we describe the person as **'Bb'**.
- A person with blue eyes can only be described as **'bb'**. This is because the blue allele is recessive.

Notice that each trait has two letters. These represent the alleles on the two homologous chromosomes. Note also that the alleles are at the same position (**locus**) on homologous chromosomes, as can be seen in the chromosome diagram of Fig 16.3.

- **BB** is also described as being **'homozygous dominant'**, as both alleles are the same and dominant.
- Similarly, **bb** can also be described as **'homozygous recessive'**, as both alleles are the same and recessive.

Genotype and phenotype

The letters representing alleles make up a person's **genotype.**

In the example given above, the person who has brown eyes but carries a blue allele has the genotype, **Bb**. The 'B' symbolises the brown allele; the 'b' symbolises the blue allele.

> **Genotype** is the genetic make-up of an individual.

We can express the letters in the form of a description as well.

In the example given, Bb symbolises a **brown-eyed** individual. This description is called the **phenotype**. A person with the genotype bb has the phenotype blue eyes.

> **Phenotype** is the physical make-up of an individual.

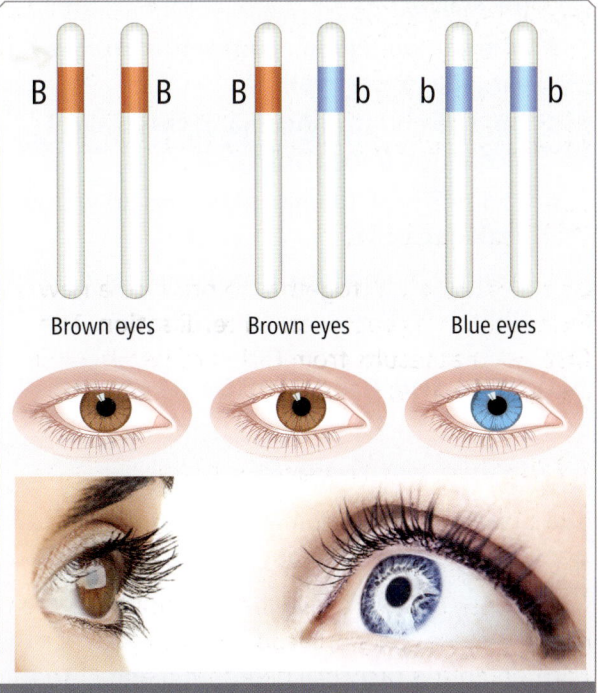

Fig 16.3 Alleles for eye colour located at the same position on homologous chromosomes.

However, the genotype does not have total control over the phenotype. The environment in which we live and are exposed to affects the phenotype. For example, many people will develop a tan when they expose their skin to sunlight. However, if they do not expose their skin to sunlight then no tan (melanin) is produced. Similarly, a person may possess genes that will make them tall. However, if that person is malnourished during childhood then they may not grow to be tall.

Genetic crosses

Monohybrid crosses

Inheritance of single genes in any organism can be studied using **monohybrid crosses**.

> A **monohybrid cross** is a genetic mating between two organisms where one gene is studied.

Examples of characteristics (Fig 16.4) that can be studied using monohybrid crosses include:

1. Ability to tongue roll (**dominant**) versus inability to tongue roll (**recessive**).
2. Cleft chin (**dominant**) versus non-cleft chin (**recessive**).
3. Dimples (**dominant**) versus no dimples (**recessive**).
4. Free ear lobes (**dominant**) versus attached ear lobes (**recessive**).
5. Long second toe (**dominant**) versus short second toe (**recessive**).
6. Widow's peak (**dominant**) versus no widow's peak (**recessive**).
7. Straight thumb (**dominant**) versus curved thumb (**recessive**).

Study of the inheritance of single traits to the first filial generation involving homozygous parents

The **first filial generation** refers to the first generation offspring of any two given parents from any living organisms. Filial generation is usually symbolised by the letter, **F**.

F_1 refers to the first filial generation and F_2 to the second filial generation.

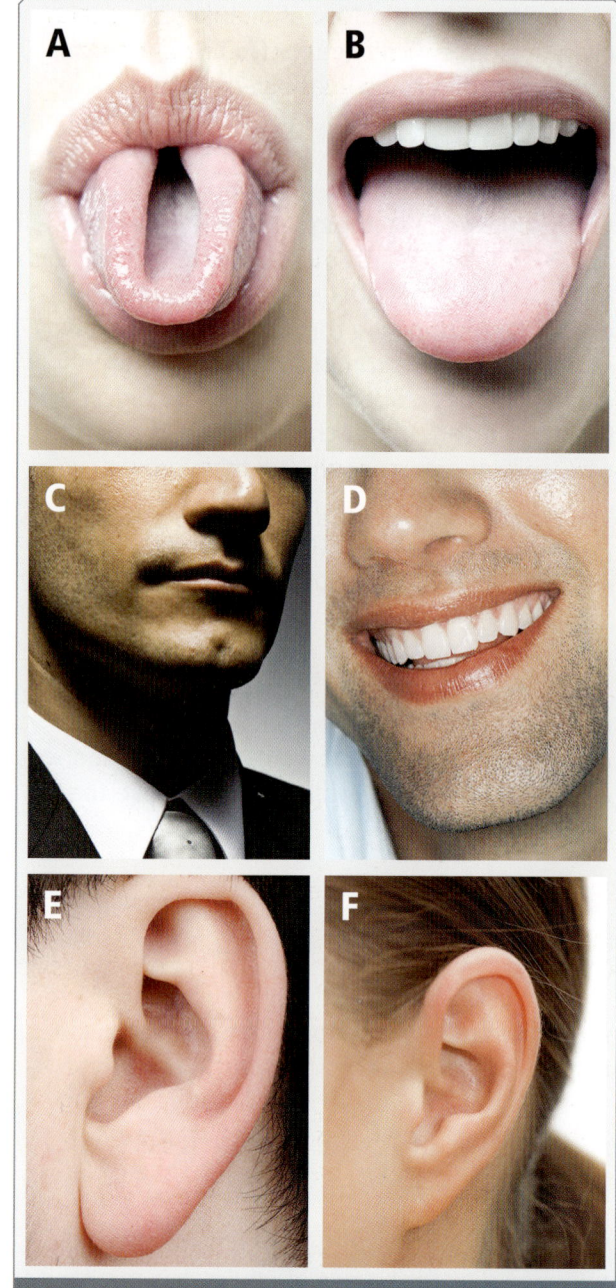

Fig 16.4 Tongue rolling (**A**); inability to tongue roll (**B**); cleft chin (**C**); non-cleft chin (**D**); free ear lobe (**E**); attached ear lobe (**F**).

Study of inheritance is usually carried out by drawing **genetic crosses**.

> A **genetic cross** is a diagram or table showing how characteristics are inherited.

In the first cross, we will look at two parents. One is **homozygous dominant** for brown eyes and the other has blue eyes (**homozygous recessive**).

The brown-eyed parent must have the genotype **BB**. This is because the description of the parents says they are **homozygous** (meaning the alleles are exactly the same) and they are **dominant** meaning that the letters must be capitals.

The second parent must have the genotype, **bb**. We can infer this because the description tells us that brown eyes are dominant to blue eyes.

Therefore, the first part of the genetic cross is:

Brown eyes		Blue eyes	parental phenotypes
BB	x	bb	parental genotypes

Meiosis then occurs, meaning that one chromosome from each homologous pair ends up in each gamete. It is completely random as to which homologous chromosome ends up in each gamete.

This means that for the brown-eyed parent, half of the gametes will get the first '**B**' and the other half of the gametes will receive the other '**B**'. Similarly, with the other parent, half the gametes will receive the first '**b**', with the other half receiving the second '**b**'.

So the second part of the genetic cross is:

```
   BB      x      bb       parental genotypes
  ↙ ↘   Meiosis  ↙ ↘
  B  B   x   b  b           gamete genotypes
```

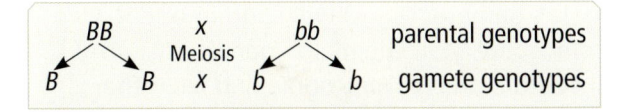

However, in this case there is no point writing two '**B**'s for the gametes of the first parent, as all the gametes from this parent will have the '**B**' allele.

Similarly, two '**b**'s are not needed to describe the gametes of the second parent. All the gametes from this parent will have the '**b**' allele.

So the second part can be written in a much simpler manner:

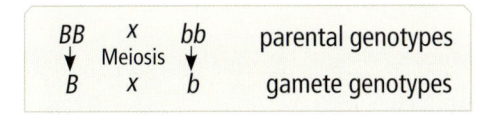

```
BB   x   bb        parental genotypes
 ↓  Meiosis  ↓
 B   x    b        gamete genotypes
```

The next step is **fertilisation**. A gamete from the brown-eyed parent will fertilise a gamete from the blue-eyed parent. Since both parents are homozygous for eye colour, the only possible fertilisation is a brown-eyed allele joining with a blue-eyed allele.

So the next part of the cross is:

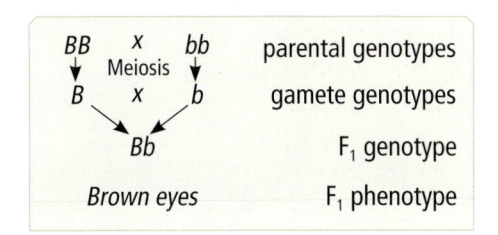

```
BB   x   bb           parental genotypes
 ↓  Meiosis  ↓
 B   x    b           gamete genotypes
      ↘ ↙
       Bb             F₁ genotype
   Brown eyes         F₁ phenotype
```
F_1 genotype
F_1 phenotype

In terms of eye colour, **Bb** is the only possible genotype of the offspring. The phenotype of this genotype is '**brown eyes**'. This is because the offspring have one '**B**' allele, which is dominant to the blue-eyed allele.

This genetic cross can also be written in the form of a **Punnett square** (Fig 16.5):

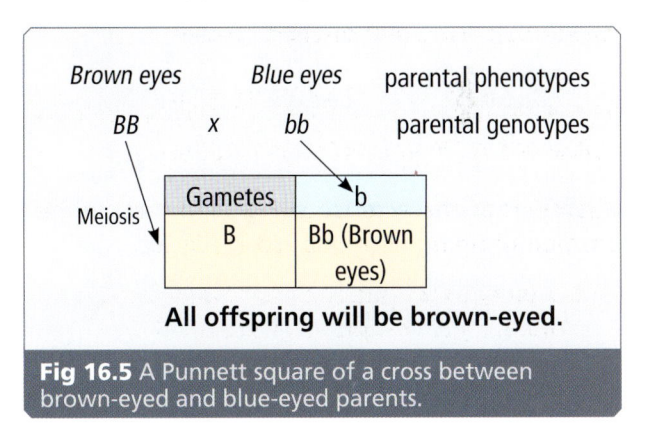

Brown eyes		Blue eyes	parental phenotypes
BB	x	bb	parental genotypes

Gametes	b
B	Bb (Brown eyes)

All offspring will be brown-eyed.

Fig 16.5 A Punnett square of a cross between brown-eyed and blue-eyed parents.

Study of the inheritance of single traits to the first filial generation involving heterozygous parents

In our second cross, we will look at two parents, both **heterozygous** for eye colour. This means that both the parents' genotypes are **Bb**. They both have brown eyes. The first part of the genetic cross is:

Brown eyes		Brown eyes	parental phenotypes
Bb	x	Bb	parental genotypes

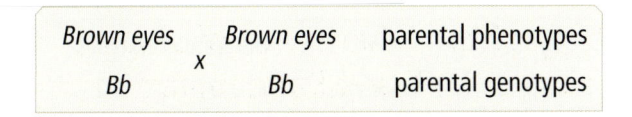

Meiosis occurs, meaning that one chromosome from each homologous pair ends up in each gamete. Again, it is completely random as to which homologous chromosome ends up in each gamete.

This means that for both parents, half of the gametes will get the '**B**' and the other half of the gametes will receive the 'b'. So the second part of the genetic cross is:

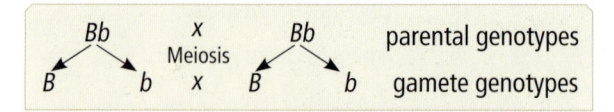

```
Bb      x      Bb       parental genotypes
      Meiosis
B   b   x   B   b        gamete genotypes
```

The next step is **fertilisation**. A gamete from the first parent will fertilise a gamete from the second parent. Again, it is completely random as to which gametes undergo fertilisation. Therefore, we have to write down all the possibilities. In this cross, there will be four possibilities:

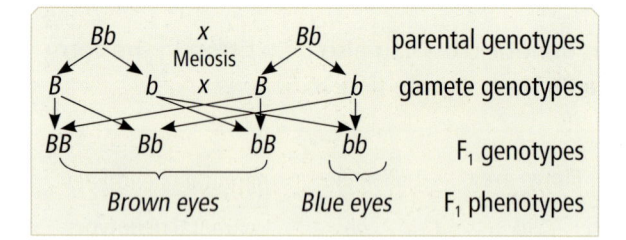

```
Bb        x        Bb       parental genotypes
       Meiosis
B   b    x    B    b         gamete genotypes
BB   Bb   bB   bb            F1 genotypes
 Brown eyes    Blue eyes     F1 phenotypes
```

We can see that one of the genotypes of the offspring is written as **bB**. Strictly speaking there is nothing wrong with this. However, we usually write the capital letter first, regardless of the chromosome position.

We can also see from the offspring that, on average, for every four offspring produced, one of them will be blue-eyed. However, it is very important to note here that if this heterozygous couple had four offspring, it would still be possible for them all to be brown-eyed. This is because fertilisation is a completely random process. Similarly, it would be possible (albeit with a very small chance) for all offspring to be blue-eyed.

As before, we can write this cross in the form of a Punnett square (Fig 16.6). This gives the F_1 offspring in the same way as the arrow diagram.

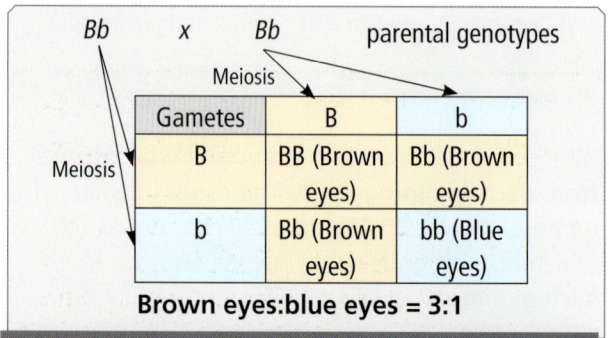

Bb x Bb	parental genotypes	
Gametes	B	b
B	BB (Brown eyes)	Bb (Brown eyes)
b	Bb (Brown eyes)	bb (Blue eyes)

Brown eyes:blue eyes = 3:1

Fig 16.6 A Punnett square of a cross between two brown-eyed parents (both heterozygous).

There is a 75 per cent chance the offspring will have brown eyes and a 25 per cent chance of blue eyes.

Another way of expressing this is in the form of ratios. There is a 3:1 ratio of brown to blue eyes in the F_1 offspring.

Study of the inheritance of gender

We learned in Chapter 13 that chromosomes are arranged in pairs. There is one pair of sex chromosomes that determine gender. In humans, having two **X** chromosomes will give female characteristics and having one **X** and one **Y** chromosome will give male characteristics. Putting this into a genetic cross:

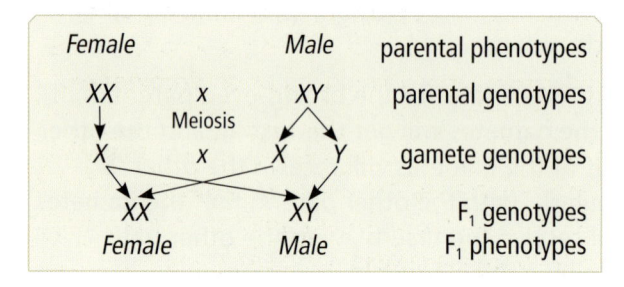

```
Female              Male         parental phenotypes
 XX         x        XY          parental genotypes
         Meiosis
 X          x      X    Y        gamete genotypes
   XX              XY            F1 genotypes
 Female            Male          F1 phenotypes
```

We can see from the above cross that the male determines the sex of the offspring. All of the female's gametes (eggs) will contain one **X** chromosome. Half the male's gametes (sperm) will contain an **X** chromosome and the other half will contain a **Y** chromosome. If an **X** sperm fertilises an egg, then a female results. If a **Y** sperm fertilises the egg, then a male will result.

Once again, it can be easier to represent the genetic cross by means of a Punnett square (Fig 16.7).

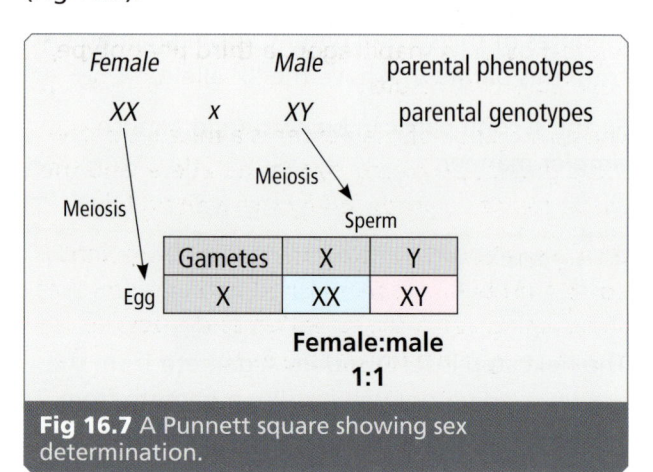

Female		Male	parental phenotypes
XX	x	XY	parental genotypes

	Sperm	
Gametes	X	Y
Egg X	XX	XY

Female:male 1:1

Fig 16.7 A Punnett square showing sex determination.

There is a 50 per cent chance of a female and a 50 per cent chance of a male.

Generally, it is completely random as to which sperm will fertilise the egg. However, for reasons unknown there are always slightly more males born than females. Statistical studies have found the ratio to be 101 males born to every 100 females.

Incomplete dominance

We have learned that different alleles are either dominant or recessive with respect to each other. However, it is possible for different alleles to be equally dominant when paired together. This is where the phenotype produced is a mixture of the phenotypes of the homozygous genotypes.

For example, in the snapdragon plant it is possible to get pink flowers from a cross between a red-flowered snapdragon plant and a white-flowered snapdragon plant. This phenomenon is called **incomplete dominance** or **co-dominance.**

> **Incomplete dominance**: neither allele of an allelic pair is dominant or recessive with respect to each other – they are equally expressed and the resulting phenotype is a mixture, or a blend, of the two.

Another way to define incomplete dominance:

> **Incomplete dominance** occurs when a cross between organisms of two different phenotypes produces offspring with a third phenotype that is a mixture of the parental phenotypes.

Incomplete dominance in plants

An example of incomplete dominance in plants is flower colour in snapdragon plants (Fig 16.8).

If a **red-flowered** snapdragon is crossed with a **white-flowered** snapdragon, a third phenotype, **pink-flowered,** results.

The pink colour of the flower is a mixture of the red pigment, produced by the red allele, and the white pigment, produced by the white allele.

Giving symbols for alleles that are co-dominant poses a problem. As mentioned earlier, dominant alleles are given a capital letter, and recessive alleles are given a lower case letter.

Gene symbols for incomplete dominance generally use the following system: a red-flowered snapdragon plant is **RR** and white-flowered snapdragon is **rr.** The intermediate phenotype, pink, is **Rr.** In the Leaving Certificate it is made clear in the genetic cross when incomplete dominance applies.

Fig 16.8 White **(A)**, red **(B)** and pink **(C)** snapdragon flowers.

Different letters are generally not used to symbolise co-dominance as this would then imply the alleles belong to different genes when in fact they belong to the same gene controlling the same characteristic.

You will notice that the genotype of red-coloured flowers can only be **RR**; white, **rr**; and pink, **Rr**.

Notice that we still use a small letter for white even though it is equally dominant with respect to red. We do this to show that it is a different allele but belongs to the same gene.

- A genetic cross between homozygous parents: Fig 16.9 shows a cross between a red-flowered and white-flowered snapdragon.

Red flower		White flower	parental phenotypes
RR	x	rr	parental genotypes
Meiosis			
Gametes		r (White allele)	
R (Red allele)		Rr (Pink)	

All of the F$_1$ offspring will be pink.

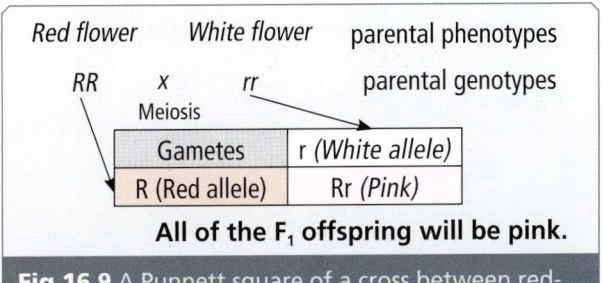

Fig 16.9 A Punnett square of a cross between red-flowered and white-flowered snapdragons.

- A genetic cross between heterozygous parents: Fig 16.10 shows a cross between two pink-flowered snapdragon plants.

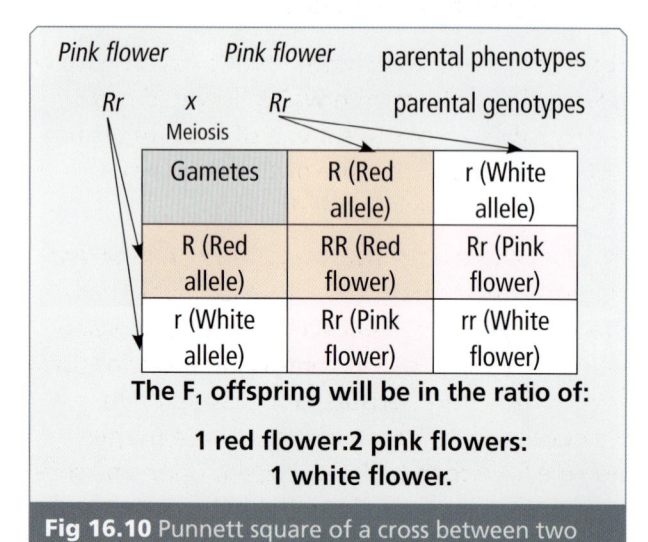

Pink flower	Pink flower		parental phenotypes
Rr	x	Rr	parental genotypes

Meiosis

Gametes	R (Red allele)	r (White allele)
R (Red allele)	RR (Red flower)	Rr (Pink flower)
r (White allele)	Rr (Pink flower)	rr (White flower)

The F$_1$ offspring will be in the ratio of:

1 red flower : 2 pink flowers : 1 white flower.

Fig 16.10 Punnett square of a cross between two pink-flowered snapdragons.

Incomplete dominance in animals

An example of incomplete dominance in animals is coat colour in cattle (Fig 16.12). Red-coated cattle crossed with white-coated cattle have offspring that are neither totally red nor totally white, but an intermediate phenotype consisting of red and white patches. This phenotype is called **roan**.

The gene symbols given for these phenotypes are:

- Red-coated cattle: **RR**
- White-coated cattle: **rr**
- Roan-coated cattle: **Rr**

Again, notice that we still use a small letter for white even though it is equally dominant with respect to red. We do this to show that it is a different allele of the same gene.

- A genetic cross between homozygous parents: Fig 16.11 shows a cross between a red-coated bull and a white-coated cow.

Red coat	White coat	parental phenotypes
RR	x rr	parental genotypes

Meiosis

Gametes	r (White allele)
R (Red allele)	Rr (Roan coat)

All of the F$_1$ offspring will be roan.

Fig 16.11 Punnett square of a cross between a red bull and a white cow.

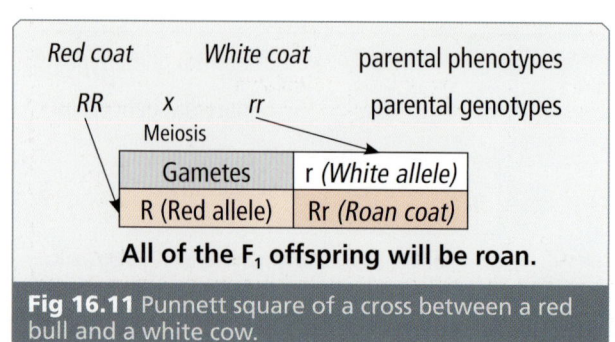

Fig 16.12 A red bull (**A**); white cow (**B**); and roan calf (**C**).

- A genetic cross between heterozygous cattle: Another possible cross in cattle is between roan-coloured cattle. The following shows the possibilities in the offspring of a cross between a roan bull and a roan cow (Fig 16.13).

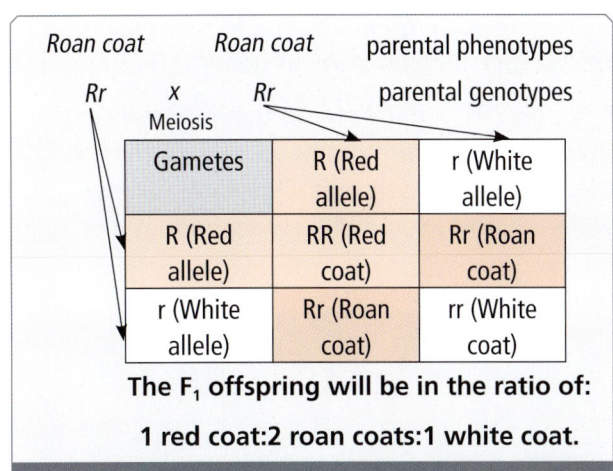

| | Roan coat | Roan coat | parental phenotypes |
| | Rr x | Rr | parental genotypes |

Gametes	R (Red allele)	r (White allele)
R (Red allele)	RR (Red coat)	Rr (Roan coat)
r (White allele)	Rr (Roan coat)	rr (White coat)

The F$_1$ offspring will be in the ratio of:

1 red coat : 2 roan coats : 1 white coat.

Fig 16.13 Punnett square of a cross between a roan bull and a roan cow.

HL Origin of genetics

Work of Gregor Mendel

Born in Germany, Gregor Mendel (Fig 16.15) was an Augustinian monk and an amateur biologist with a background in statistics. He is known as the father of modern genetics for his experimental work on inheritance in pea plants. He conducted all of his experiments on 29,000 pea plants between 1856 and 1863 in the garden of the monastery. He studied **seven** different characteristics in pea plants (Fig 16.14) and demonstrated inheritance patterns.

1 Flower colour (**purple** versus **white**)
2 Flower position (**axial** versus **terminal**)
3 Pea colour (**yellow** versus **green**)
4 Pea shape (**round** versus **wrinkled**)
5 Pod colour (**green** versus **yellow**)
6 Pod shape (**inflated** versus **constricted**)
7 Height (**tall** versus **short**)

For example, Mendel showed that crossing purple-flowered pea plants with white-flowered pea plants did not produce a blend of the two colours. Instead of being a mixture of the two colours, most offspring were purple-flowered.

He did many crosses involving the seven different characteristics in pea plants. He took pure-breeding pea plants that had purple flowers and white flowers, as well as contrasting traits for the seven other characteristics, and crossed them. He noticed that all the pea plants were purple-flowered. He then took the F$_1$ generation and self-fertilised them and noticed that in this case there was a ratio of 3:1 among the F$_2$ offspring. From his results, Mendel came up with the idea of heredity units being passed from one generation to the next. He called these heredity units **'factors'**. These factors are now called alleles. He hypothesised that these 'factors' occurred in pairs, could be the same or different and that they separate during gamete formation. He also hypothesised that each gamete receives only one allele (later discovered as part of meiosis) and that this process occurs at random.

Mendel went on to study how multiple traits in pea plants were inherited simultaneously (dihybrid crosses – see below). He discovered that these traits were inherited independently of one another. That is, the inheritance of one pair of factors had no effect on, and nothing to do with, the inheritance of another pair of factors.

	Flower colour	Flower position	Pea colour	Pea shape	Pod colour	Pod shape	Height
Dominant	purple	axial	yellow	round	green	inflated	tall
Recessive	white	terminal	green	wrinkled	yellow	constricted	short

Fig 16.14 The seven characteristics in pea plants studied by Mendel.

What enabled Mendel to carry out his studies of genetics on pea plants so successfully was that he used pure-breeding (homozygous) pea plants and conducted his experiments with extreme care and detailed planning, preparation and recording of results.

Because Mendel was only an amateur biologist and very little was known about inheritance at the time, many scientists took little notice of his findings. Mendel died in 1884 at the age of 61 without his work being recognised. It was not until the early 1900s that the true value of Mendel's work on pea plants was discovered.

As a result of his work, Mendel came up with two laws of inheritance that are called **Mendel's Laws of Genetics.**

Mendel's First Law of Segregation

> **First Law of Segregation**
>
> Each cell contains two factors for each trait.
>
> These factors separate at gamete formation, so that each gamete contains only one factor from each pair of factors.
>
> At fertilisation, the new organism will have two factors for each trait, one from each parent.

Mendel's Second Law of Independent Assortment

> **Second Law of Independent Assortment:**
> Members of one pair of factors separate independently of another pair of factors during gamete formation.

Explanation of Mendel's First Law

What is happening to the chromosomes at gamete formation?

We learned in Chapter 13 that meiosis is the process a cell undergoes during gamete formation. Each chromosome of a pair of homologous chromosomes must separate from each other – one going into two different cells. This is to ensure that at fertilisation the normal (diploid) numbers of chromosomes is reattained. Mendel did not realise that chromosomes or alleles existed. He called them 'factors'. However, from his results, Mendel came to understand that the factors must separate at gamete formation.

Not only did Mendel realise the importance of these factors separating at gamete formation, but he hypothesised that all pairs of alleles were inherited completely independently of one another.

Fig 16.15 Gregor Mendel (1822–1884).

Explanation of Mendel's Second Law

What is happening to the pairs of alleles at gamete formation?

Mendel's Second Law of Independent Assortment applies to crosses involving more than one gene, that is, two pairs of alleles or even more.

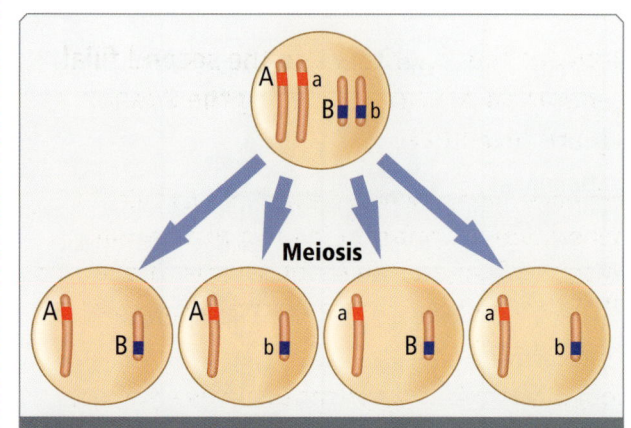

Fig 16.16 Chromosome diagram showing the possible arrangement of alleles in gametes following meiosis involving two traits.

Take, for example, a pair of alleles (**A** and **a**) on one pair of homologous chromosomes and another pair of alleles (**B** and **b**) on a different pair of homologous chromosomes (Fig 16.16). Each new gamete gets one chromosome from each homologous pair (**Mendel's First Law**). Therefore, each gamete has a 50:50 chance of getting each allele.

In this example, there are four possible gametes: **A** with **B** is the first; **A** with **b** is the second; **a** with **B** is the third; and **a** with **b** is the fourth.

The genotypes of the four possible gametes are: **AB**; **Ab**; **aB**; and **ab**.

Notice that in this situation, the third gamete is **aB**. We said before that the capital letter usually comes first, but that is only the case where the letters are the same. If they are different, as in gametes, then it is the allele of the first described chromosome that is listed first regardless of whether it is dominant or recessive.

Without even realising the existence of chromosomes, genes or alleles, Mendel was able to come up with his Second Law of Independent Assortment. He was able to work out what was happening to the factors (alleles) by studying the F_1 offspring and subsequent generations. For example, the ratios he obtained in the F_1 and F_2 offspring led him to conclude that inheritance of the factors was completely down to chance.

However, it was subsequently found that Mendel's Second Law does not apply in all situations (see below).

Dihybrid crosses

Study of the inheritance to the second filial generation of two traits using the Punnett square technique

We have already learned that the first filial generation (F_1) refers to the first generation offspring from a given set of parents. The second filial generation (F_2) refers to the offspring of the F_1 generation.

Looking at this concept another way – you are the F_2 filial generation of your grandparents and your parents are the F_1 filial generation of your grandparents.

In Mendel's experiments, he went on to study two traits at once and how they were inherited through two generations. He studied the ratios of the offspring that resulted. Mendel's crosses can be demonstrated using **dihybrid crosses**.

> A **dihybrid cross** is a genetic mating between two organisms where two separate genes are studied.

One of Mendel's dihybrid crosses involved studying the inheritance of two traits at the same time: height and flower colour in pea plants.

Mendel took two plants that were each **pure-breeding** (homozygous) for height (tall versus short) and flower colour (purple versus white) (Fig 16.17).

Fig 16.17 Purple-flowered (**A**) and white-flowered (**B**) pea plants, similar to the plants studied by Mendel.

Pure-breeding means that if this plant was crossed with another pea plant that was genetically identical, then 100 per cent of the offspring would have the same genotype and phenotype.

Genetic cross between homozygous plants

A pea plant homozygous for both tallness and purple flowers was crossed with a short pea plant with white flowers (Fig 16.18).

Notice here, it is not mentioned that the short pea plant with white flowers was homozygous or pure-breeding. This is because the characteristics, short and white flower, are recessive and will only be expressed in the homozygous condition.

Therefore, it is always taken as given that, when describing an organism with a recessive characteristic, its genotype is always homozygous.

Tall is dominant to short, and purple flower is dominant to white flower. Therefore, let the letter **T** be the allele responsible for the tall characteristic and the letter **t** represent the short characteristic. Let the letter **P** symbolise the allele responsible for purple flowers and the letter **p** represent white flowers.

Therefore, the first part of the cross will be:

Tall, Purple	x	Short, white	parental phenotypes
TTPP		ttpp	parental genotypes

We have learned that gametes get only one chromosome from each homologous pair at meiosis. So, in this dihybrid cross, each gamete will get **two** chromosomes, as there are two pairs of chromosomes listed in the parents. Because of this, each gamete will get two alleles, which means their genotype will have two letters, and those letters will be **different**.

For the tall, purple-flowered pea plant there is only one possible gamete: **TP**. This is because the tall, purple pea plant is homozygous for both characteristics. It does not matter which **'T'** goes with which **'P'**. It is always going to be the same genotype.

Therefore, we simply write the only possible gamete as **TP**.

Similarly, the other parent is also homozygous for both characteristics. Therefore, the only possible gamete genotype will be **tp**.

Tall, Purple	x	Short, white	parental phenotypes
TTPP		ttpp	parental genotypes

Gametes	tp
TP	TtPp (Tall, purple flowers)

All the offspring are tall and have purple flowers.

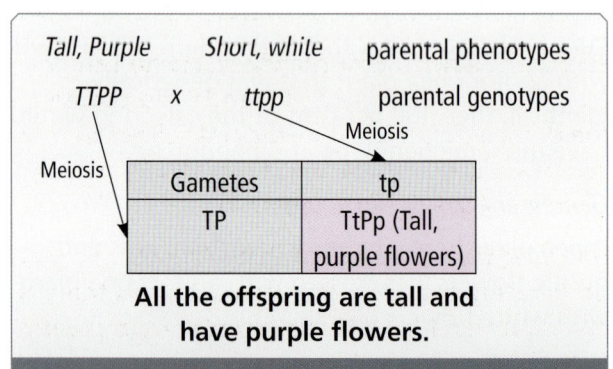

Fig 16.18 A Punnett square of a cross between tall, purple and short, white pea plants.

The gametes will fertilise one another and all the F₁ offspring will have the same genotype because there was only one possible gamete from each parent (Fig 16.18).

The phenotype of the offspring is the same as one of the parents. However, the genotype is different from both parents.

The genotype of all the offspring for these two traits will be heterozygous for both characteristics.

Genetic cross between heterozygous plants

Mendel then went on to self-fertilise the F₁ offspring from the previously mentioned cross. Often geneticists described plants that are self-fertilised as being **'selfed'**. It is a type of inbreeding in plants, whereby members of the same offspring are crossbred, or sometimes one plant is made to fertilise itself.

The following cross shows tall, purple-flowered pea plants, heterozygous for both traits, being self-fertilised (Fig16.19).

Tall, Purple		Tall, Purple		parental phenotypes
TtPp	x	TtPp		parental genotypes

Meiosis

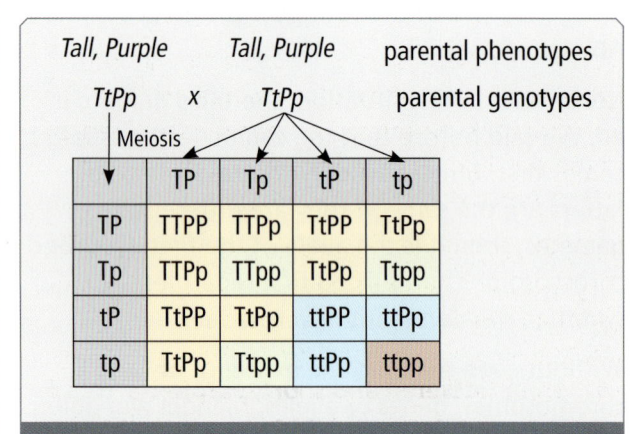

	TP	Tp	tP	tp
TP	TTPP	TTPp	TtPP	TtPp
Tp	TTPp	TTpp	TtPp	Ttpp
tP	TtPP	TtPp	ttPP	ttPp
tp	TtPp	Ttpp	ttPp	ttpp

Fig 16.19 A Punnett square of a cross between two heterozygous tall and purple pea plants.

The ratio from this cross is 9:3:3:1.

- 9: Tall and purple-flowered pea plants.
- 3: Tall and white-flowered pea plants.
- 3: Short and purple-flowered pea plants.
- 1: Short and white-flowered pea plant.

We can see by the colour coding that nine of the possible genotypes are tall and have purple flowers, three are tall with white flowers, three are short with purple flowers, and one is short with white flowers.

The above genetic cross is the most complicated cross you may be asked to do in the exam. It is important to be careful when writing the offspring into the Punnett square.

Another example of a dihybrid cross carried out by Mendel involved a tall, purple-flowered pea plant (heterozygous for both traits) crossed with a short, white-flowered pea plant (Fig 16.20).

The genotype of the heterozygous plant is **TtPp** and the genotype of the short, white-flowered pea plant is **ttpp**.

	tp
	Tall, Purple Short, white parental phenotypes
	TtPp x ttpp parental genotypes
	Meiosis

	tp
TP	TtPp (Tall, purple flowers)
Tp	Ttpp (Tall, white flowers)
tP	ttPp (Short, purple flowers)
tp	ttpp (Short, white flowers)

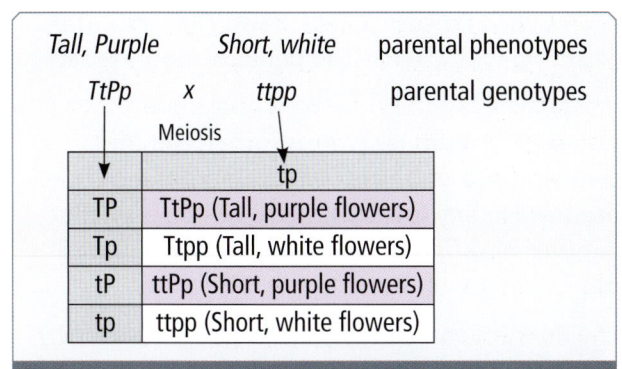

Fig 16.20 Punnett square of a cross between a heterozygous tall and purple pea plant and a short, white pea plant.

Notice that there is only one possible gamete from the homozygous recessive pea plant and four from the heterozygous pea plant. When all of the possible fertilisations are determined a 1:1:1:1 ratio of F_1 offspring results.

Notice that the **tall, purple-flowered** plants and the **small, white-flowered** plants have the same genotypes as the parents, respectively. These plants are called **parental types**. Plants that are **tall, white-flowered** and **short, purple-flowered** are called **non-parental types** (or **recombinants**).

The above cross can also be represented in the form of a chromosome diagram (Fig 16.21).

There are many possibilities of dihybrid crosses with two genes being studied and independent assortment occurring amongst those alleles.

However, at times Mendel's Second Law of Independent Assortment ceases to hold true (*see below*).

Linkage and sex linkage

Mendel was lucky in that the seven characteristics he studied in pea plants all happened to be on separate chromosomes and showed dominant-recessive characteristics – that all the different alleles were either dominant or recessive with respect to each other. He devised his two laws from the results he obtained from studying these seven characteristics.

However, many scientists suspected he deliberately chose these seven characteristics as they showed valid, reproducible results; whereas other characteristics were showing ratios that were not easily explainable. Other characteristics in pea plants would have been linked or even sex-linked (*see below*). Characteristics that are linked

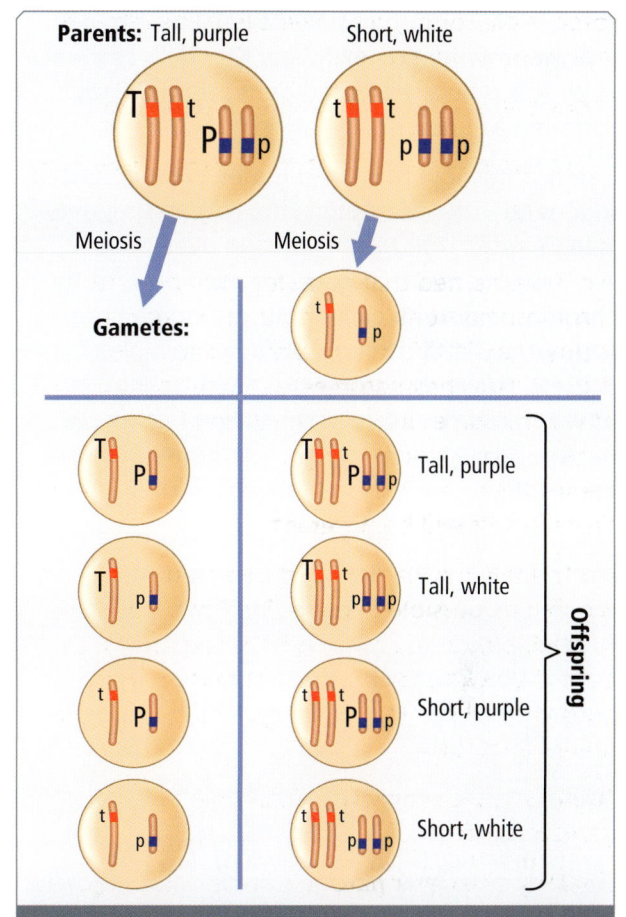

Fig 16.21 Chromosome diagram of a cross between a heterozygous tall and purple pea plant and a short, white pea plant.

together do not follow Mendel's Second Law of Independent Assortment. If Mendel did choose the characteristics, then he did not follow an important step of the scientific method – namely random selection (*see* Chapter 1).

However, there is no proof that Mendel deliberately chose the characteristics; and there is no doubt that Mendel's work contributed greatly to the study of genetics.

Linkage

Linkage refers to the fact that many different genes can be found on the same chromosome.

> **Linked genes** are genes present on the same chromosome.

We learned in Chapter 14 that there are on average 1300 genes on each pair of homologous chromosomes. All these genes could not possibly be inherited independently (as depicted by Mendel's Second Law). Genes that are located on the same chromosomes are called linked genes and, *in general*, **do not** follow Mendel's Second Law. This is because linked genes **tend** to stay together at gamete formation.

Yet, it is possible for linked genes to be inherited independently. This occurs due to **'crossing over'** (see Chapter 17). During crossing over, pairs of homologous chromosomes can swap parts of their chromosomes with each other during gamete formation. This further complicates the inheritance process. However, you **do not** need to know about crossing over for the Leaving Certificate Biology course and it is only mentioned here to demonstrate the true complexity of inheritance.

The previous cross showed a heterozygous pea plant, for both characteristics, crossed with a homozygous recessive pea plant. The ratio of the offspring was 1:1:1:1. The genes were on separate chromosomes (not linked).

However, if a similar cross is carried out, not involving pea plants (as Mendel's studies did not involve any linkage), there will be a smaller number of different gamete genotypes. The ratio of offspring will therefore be different.

The Punnett square and chromosome diagram (Fig 16.22) illustrate why there are fewer gamete genotypes possible. Notice here that T is linked to P and t is linked to p. However, it is also possible for T to be linked to p and t to be linked to P.

Notice in this cross there are **no non-parental types**. This is because the linked alleles stay together at gamete formation. The same letters, genotypes and phenotypes as Mendel's crosses are used in Fig 16.22 for comparison purposes only.

In a dihybrid cross, where both parents are heterozygous for both traits and the traits are not linked, the ratio of the offspring will be 9:3:3:1. However, the ratio changes when the genes are linked. There are fewer possible gamete genotypes (Fig 16.23). Once again, note that the same letters, genotypes and phenotypes as Mendel's crosses are used in Fig 16.23 for comparison purposes. Remember, Mendel's crosses did not involve linked genes.

Tall, Purple   Short, white   parental phenotypes
TtPp   x   ttpp   parental genotypes
              Meiosis

	tp
TP	TtPp (Tall, purple flowers)
tp	ttpp (Short, white flowers)

The ratio of the offspring is 1:1.

Fig 16.22 A Punnett square and chromosome diagram of a cross between a heterozygous organism and a homozygous recessive organism where the genes are linked.

TtPp   x   TtPp   parental genotypes
        Meiosis

	TP	tp
TP	TTPP	TtPp
tp	TtPp	ttpp

Tall, purple-flowered plant: short, white-flowered plant = 3:1.

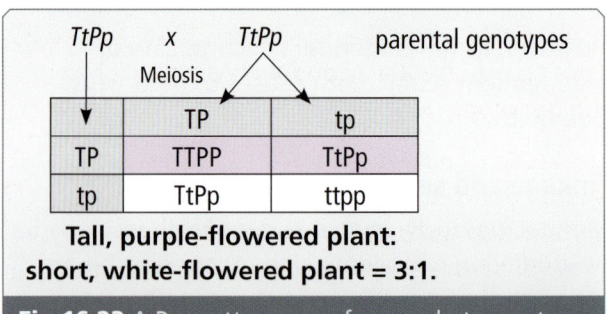

Fig 16.23 A Punnett square of a cross between two heterozygous organisms where the two genes are linked. (T is linked to P and t is linked to p.)

We learned earlier, when looking at Mendel's crosses, that a dihybrid cross between two organisms, heterozygous for both characteristics, results in offspring appearing in the ratio of 9:3:3:1. In the above cross, they are appearing in the ratio of 3:1. Linkage accounts for this difference.

Showing this in the form of a chromosome diagram explains what is happening in greater detail (Fig 16.24).

Inheritance and genetic crosses Chapter 16

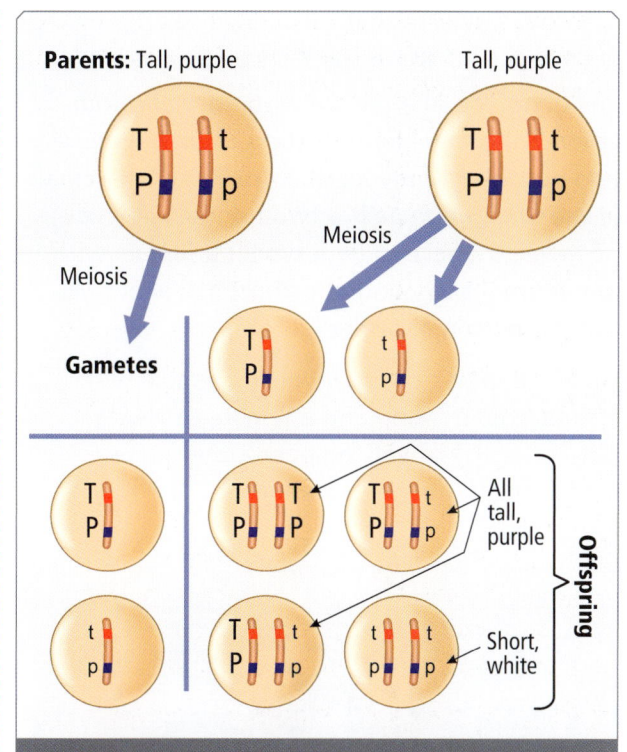

Fig 16.24 A chromosome diagram of heterozygous organisms being crossed when genes are linked.

We learned in Chapter 13 that the Y chromosome is significantly shorter than the X chromosome.

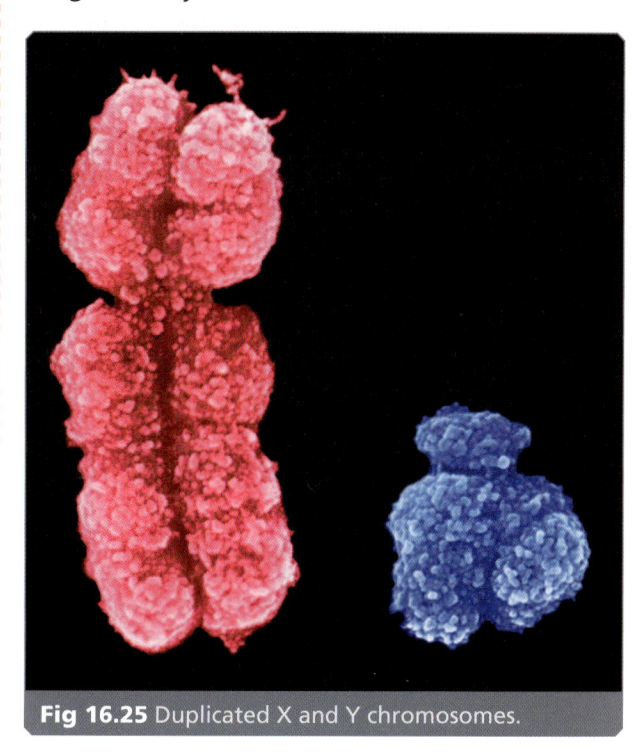

Fig 16.25 Duplicated X and Y chromosomes.

As a result of this, females have two copies of the genes for colour vision and blood clotting, whereas males have only one. A mutation in the colour-vision gene can result in **colour-blindness**. It is a condition that can vary in severity. Most colour-blindness is only mild; complete colour-blindness is very rare. Fig 16.26 shows a test for colour-blindness.

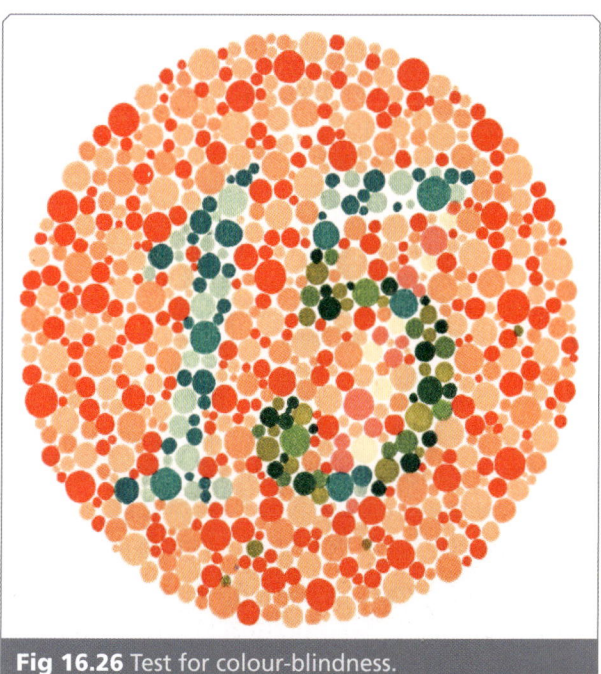

Sex linkage

> **Sex linkage** is where a gene is located on a sex chromosome.

As already mentioned, females have two **X** chromosomes and their genotype is **XX**; whereas males have one **X** and one **Y** chromosome, giving the genotype, **XY**.

Fig 16.25 shows a duplicated **X** chromosome and a duplicated **Y** chromosome. The reason why photographs of chromosomes always show duplicated chromosomes is because this is when they are at their most visible (during mitosis). They are virtually invisible when in the form of chromatin.

The X and Y chromosomes contain genes that control the sex of the individual. However, they also contain other genes that have nothing to do with sex determination. Examples of these genes are the genes for **colour vision** and a gene involved in **blood clotting**.

The unusual characteristic about both of these traits is that they are present on the X chromosome but **not** on the Y chromosome.

Fig 16.26 Test for colour-blindness.

185

A mutation in the blood-clotting gene can lead to an inability to clot blood following a wound or injury, a condition known as **haemophilia** (Fig 16.27).

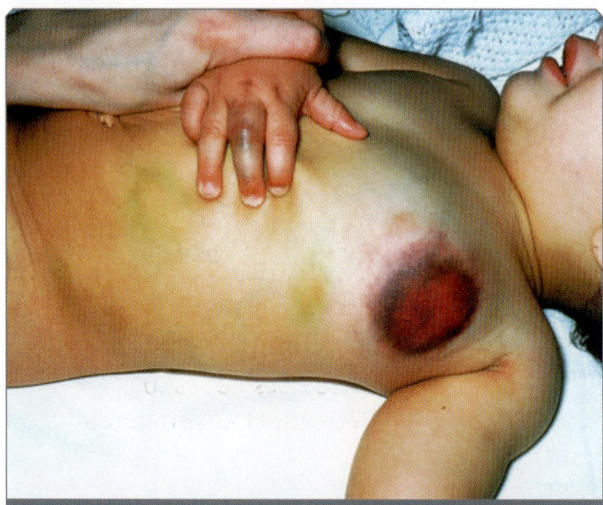

Fig 16.27 A young child suffering from haemophilia.

Figures 16.28 and 16.29 explain how colour-blindness and haemophilia may result. Notice that males are more likely to be colour-blind or haemophiliacs because they have only one copy of each gene.

As we have already learned, sex-linked characteristics in males, such as blood clotting and colour vision, are controlled by only one allele. The **Y** chromosome is missing the alleles for these traits.

Males are 10 to 20 times as likely as females to be colour-blind or haemophiliacs. The incidence of colour-blindness in males is approximately 10 per cent.

> **NOTE**
> For Leaving Certificate Biology Higher Level, you need to be able to show crosses demonstrating how sex-linked characteristics (colour vision and blood clotting) are inherited. These characteristics are usually represented by the letters 'N' and 'n'. 'N' is the normal allele and 'n' is the abnormal (mutated) allele.

Because these alleles are associated with the sex chromosomes, we always write the genotype to include what chromosome the allele is present on. For example, a male who has completely normal colour vision will have a genotype of $X_N Y_-$.

- The **X** and **Y** tell us the individual is male.
- The **'N'** tells us that the **X** chromosome is carrying a normal allele for colour vision.
- The **'–'** tells us that there is no corresponding allele present on the **Y** chromosome.

The genotype of a female with normal colour vision or normal blood clotting could be one of two possible genotypes: $X_N X_N$ or $X_N X_n$. The female in the first genotype has two normal alleles; however, the second genotype is a female with one normal allele and one abnormal allele. We call this person a **'carrier'**.

Fig 16.28 shows a cross involving a male with normal colour vision and a female carrier. Genetic crosses involving haemophiliacs are completed in the usual manner.

	Normal male		Normal carrier female	parental phenotypes
	$X_N Y_-$	x	$X_N X_n$	parental genotypes
	Meiosis ↓		Meiosis	
		X_N	X_n	
X_N		$X_N X_N$	$X_N X_n$	
Y_-		$X_N Y_-$	$X_n Y_-$	

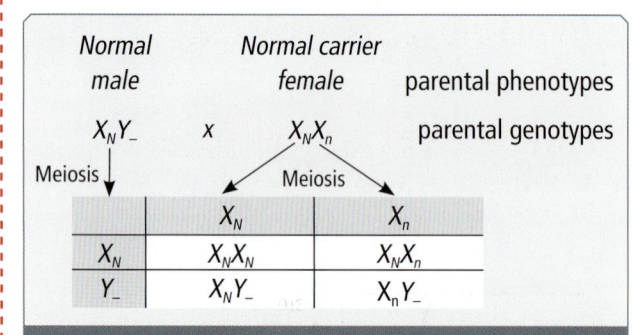

Fig 16.28 A cross between a normal carrier female and a normal male.

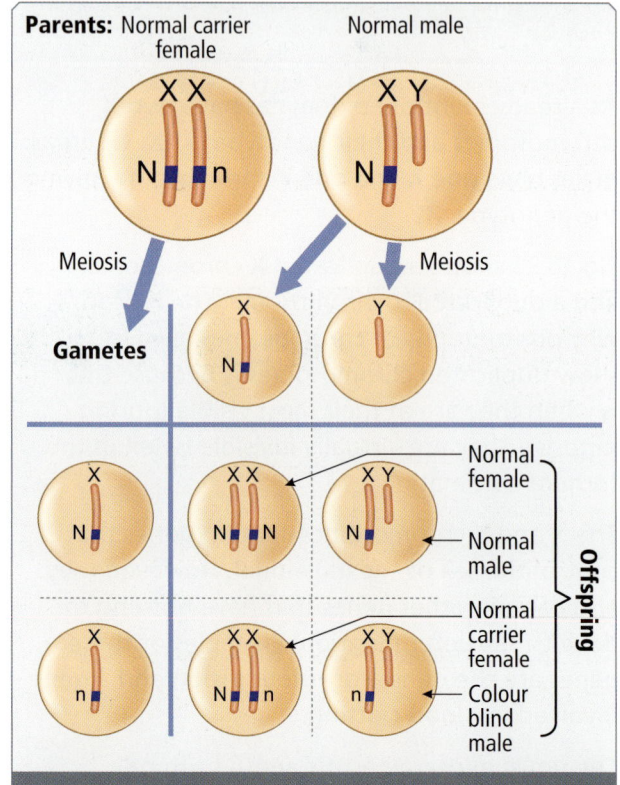

Fig 16.29 A chromosome diagram of a cross between a normal male and a carrier female.

All females will be normal (although 50 per cent will be carriers); 50 per cent of males will be normal and 50 per cent will be colour-blind.

This cross can also be completed using chromosome diagrams (Fig 16.29).

We can then see from the chromosome diagram cross that this couple has a 25 per cent chance of having a colour-blind child.

Pedigree studies

Pedigree studies are often used by geneticists and genetic counsellors for determining and/or explaining inheritance of certain characteristics. Squares and circles are used to represent the male and female individuals, respectively.

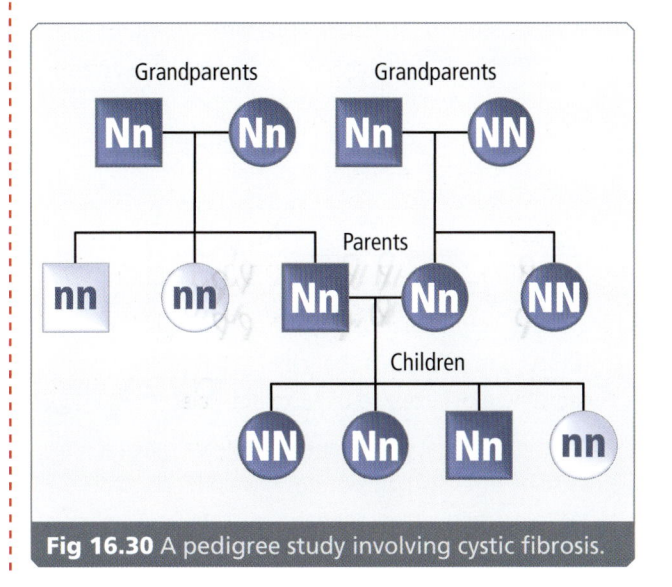

Fig 16.30 A pedigree study involving cystic fibrosis.

Cystic fibrosis (CF) inheritance is often explained using pedigree studies. Fig 16.30 shows a typical pedigree study involving CF. Three of the grandparents are carriers. Some members of the following two generations are affected with cystic fibrosis (shown in white). Unaffected family members are shown in blue. Many of the unaffected family members are carriers.

Non-nuclear inheritance

> **Non-nuclear inheritance** is the passing on of features from one generation to the next without the use of the nucleus.

Non-nuclear inheritance does not follow Mendel's laws of independent assortment and segregation.

Mitochondria and chloroplasts are inherited independently of the nucleus. They have their own DNA. As mentioned in Chapter 6, it is thought that mitochondria and chloroplasts originated from prokaryotes infecting or being engulfed by eukaryotic cells billions of years ago (called the endosymbiosis theory).

Mitochondria are inherited maternally in animals as the cytoplasm of the egg carries the mitochondria. The sperm cell does have mitochondria, but only the nucleus from the sperm cell enters the egg. Therefore, all the mitochondria in the human body are inherited via mothers.

Chapter 16 Questions

1. Genetics is the study of _____.
2. Define the following terms: *gamete, fertilisation*.
3. How many chromosomes are there in a human gamete?
4. Explain the importance of meiosis in sexual reproduction.
5. Define the following terms as used in genetics:
   (a) *Gene*
   (b) *Allele*
   (c) *Locus*
   (d) *Homozygous*
   (e) *Heterozygous*
   (f) *Dominance*
   (g) *Recessive*
   (h) *Genotype*
   (i) *Phenotype*

6 For each of the following genotypes, indicate whether it is homozygous dominant, homozygous recessive, or heterozygous:
   (a) AA homo-dominant
   (b) bb homo-recessive
   (c) Cc heterozygous
   (d) dD hetero dominant
   (e) Ii hetro dominant
   (f) GG homo-dominant
   (g) Kk hetro
   (h) nn homo recessive
   (i) pp homo-recessive
   (j) TT homo dominant
   (k) Yy heterozygous

7 Based on the information given, state the phenotypes of each of the following genotypes:
   (a) Blue flower is dominant to white flower:
      (i) BB Blue
      (ii) bb White
      (iii) Bb Blue
   (b) Tall is dominant to small:
      (i) TT tall
      (ii) tt small
      (iii) Tt tall
   (c) Round seeds are dominant to wrinkled seeds:
      (i) RR round
      (ii) rr wrinkled
      (iii) Rr Round

8 Based on the information given, choose suitable letters and then write down the **genotypes** of each of the following phenotypes:
   (a) Short hair is dominant to long hair:
      (i) Homozygous short hair: _____
      (ii) Heterozygous short hair: _____
      (iii) Long hair: _____
   (b) Free ear lobes are dominant to attached ear lobes:
      (i) Homozygous free ear lobes: _____
      (ii) Heterozygous free ear lobes: _____
      (iii) Attached ear lobes: _____

   (c) Widow's peak is dominant to no widow's peak:
      (i) Homozygous widow's peak: _____
      (ii) Heterozygous widow's peak: _____
      (iii) No widow's peak: _____

9 The ability to roll your tongue is governed by a pair of alleles. A homozygous dominant man who is able to roll his tongue (TT) and his wife who is not able to roll her tongue (tt) had children. Copy the Punnett square below and complete, showing the possible children they might have.

Gametes	

Is it possible for this couple to have a child with the same phenotype as the mother? Explain.

10 Widow's peak occurs in humans when a single dominant allele is inherited. A man and his wife, both of whom have a widow's peak, have a child without a widow's peak. Copy the Punnett square below and complete, showing how this cross is possible.

Gametes	P	p
P	PP	Pp
p	Pp	pp

If this couple have another child, what phenotype is the child most likely to be? Explain. Pp - ½ chance

11 A male black cat and a female white cat have a litter of kittens. All the kittens have a black coat. Explain, using a diagrammatic cross, Punnet square or otherwise, how this could occur.

12 A couple, both of whom have brown eyes, have a blue-eyed son. Answer the following questions relating to this statement:
   (a) Which is the dominant trait? Explain.
   (b) What letter would you use to describe these traits?
   (c) What are the genotypes of the parents?
   (d) Using the Punnett square technique, work out the percentage chance of them having another blue-eyed child.

13 What are *autosomes*?

14 There are _____ pairs of autosomes and one pair of _____ chromosomes in human diploid cells.

15 There are _____ autosomes and one _____ chromosome in human gametes.

16 The female genotype is _____.

17 The male genotype is _____.

18 Explain, using crosses and/or the Punnett square technique, why it is the male that determines the gender of a child.

19 What is unusual about the Y chromosome?

20 (a) Explain what is meant by *incomplete dominance*.

(b) A red-flowered snapdragon plant and a white-flowered snapdragon plant were crossed. All the offspring had pink flowers. Use the Punnett square technique to show the genotype of the offspring produced.

(c) The pink-flowered snapdragons were then self-fertilised and of the resulting 100 offspring, 24 went on to develop red flowers, 49 to develop pink flowers, and 27 to develop white flowers. Using the Punnett square technique, explain how these numbers were attained.

21 A red-coated bull was crossed with a white-coated female. All the offspring had a roan-coloured coat.

(a) What is a roan-coloured coat?

(b) Show by diagrammatic cross how all the offspring came to have this coat colour.

(c) A roan-coated bull was then mated with a roan-coated cow. What is the chance of the calf having a white coat? Explain.

HL 22 (a) Why is Gregor Mendel known as the 'father of modern genetics'?

(b) What nationality was Gregor Mendel?

(c) What was his main career?

(d) Why did Gregor Mendel use pea plants in his genetics studies?

(e) What seven characteristics did he study in these pea plants?

23 Gregor Mendel came up with two laws from all his experiments – the Law of Segregation and the Law of Independent Assortment:

(a) State both laws.

(b) Even though Mendel did not realise that DNA or even chromosomes existed, explain how his laws applies to chromosomes during sexual reproduction.

24 What is a *dihybrid cross*?

25 What is meant by *linkage*?

26 Draw a chromosome diagram showing gamete formation in a cell with the genotype **SsTt** for each of the following conditions:

(a) The genes are **not** linked.

(b) **S** is linked to **T** and **s** is linked to **t**.

(c) **S** is linked to **t** and **s** is linked to **T**.

27 A pure-breeding purple-flowered pea plant with an inflated pod shape is crossed with a white-flowered pea plant with constricted pods.

(a) What would be suitable letters to complete the cross?

(b) Using the Punnett square technique, show the possible gametes and the genotypes and phenotypes of the possible offspring.

(c) What is the ratio of the offspring?

28 Pea plants that produced yellow and round peas were crossed. 320 pea plants were produced from this cross. 182 of the offspring went on to produce yellow and round seeds; 57 went on to produce yellow and wrinkled peas; 63 went on to produce green and round peas; and 18 went on to produce green and wrinkled seeds.

(a) Based on the information given, what type of cross is this?

(b) Which characteristics listed are dominant and which are recessive?

(c) Show by means of the Punnett square technique how these numbers of pea plants were obtained.

(d) Are the genes linked? Explain.

29 (a) What is meant by *sex linkage*?

(b) Name **two** human traits that are sex-linked.

(c) Draw a chromosome diagram for one of the traits you named in part (b), showing a normal male.

(d) Draw a chromosome diagram for one of the traits you named in part (b), showing a carrier female.

(e) Explain why males are more likely than females to suffer from a sex-linked genetic condition.

30 (a) What is meant by *non-nuclear inheritance*?

(b) Name **two** locations in living cells where non-nuclear DNA may be found.

(c) Explain why non-nuclear inheritance is always via females.

Unit 2 | The Cell

Chapter 16 Sample examination questions

1 (a) Explain the following terms, which are used in genetics: *allele, homozygous, genotype*.

(b) (i) Name or draw the sex chromosomes that are present in a human body cell in the case of:
1. A male   2. A female

(ii) Use a Punnet square to show that there is a 50 per cent chance that fertilisation will lead to a male and 50 per cent chance that it will lead to a female.

Section C, Question 11 (a) and (b) Ordinary Level 2006

HL 2 (a) Explain the following terms which are used in genetics: *homozygous, recessive, phenotype*.

(b) In the fruit fly, *Drosophila*, the allele for grey body (**G**) is dominant to the allele for ebony body (**g**) and the allele for long wings (**L**) is dominant to the allele for vestigial wings (**l**). These two pairs of alleles are located on different chromosome pairs.

(i) Determine all the possible genotypes and phenotypes of the progeny of the following cross: grey body, long wings (heterozygous for both) X ebony body, vestigial wings.

(ii) What is the significance of the fact that the two allele pairs are located on different chromosome pairs?

(c) Haemophilia in humans is governed by a sex-linked allele. The allele for normal blood clotting (**N**) is dominant to the allele for haemophilia (**n**).

(i) What is meant by sex-linked?

(ii) Determine the possible genotypes and phenotypes of the progeny of the following cross: haemophilic male X heterozygous normal female.

Section C, Question 11 Higher Level 2008

Chapter 16 Mind map

Genetics is the study of inheritance.

- **Inheritance** is the passing on of traits from one generation to the next.
- **Traits** are physical and chemical characteristics that a living organism possesses.
- **Gametes** are haploid sex cells.
- **Fertilisation** is the fusion of two haploid gametes to produce a diploid zygote.
- An **allele** is a type of gene where a number of different types of the same gene exist.
- The **locus** is the position of a gene on a chromosome.
- **Homozygous:** two alleles are the same.
- **Heterozygous:** two alleles are different.
- **Dominance:** where one allele (the dominant one) masks the effect of another allele.
- **Recessive:** where an allele's effect is expressed only when in the homozygous condition.

- **Genotype:** the genetic make-up of an individual.
- **Phenotype:** the physical make-up of an individual.
- The phenotype is affected by both genotype and the environment.
- **Autosomes** are chromosomes that do not determine gender.
- Sex chromosomes are chromosomes that determine gender.
- A **monohybrid cross** is a genetic mating between two organisms where one gene is studied.

A cross between two heterozygous brown-eyed individuals

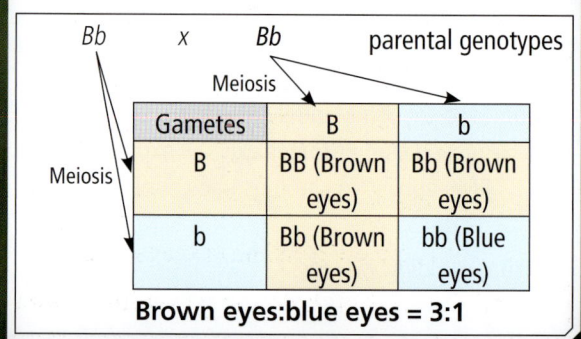

Bb × Bb parental genotypes

Meiosis

Gametes	B	b
B	BB (Brown eyes)	Bb (Brown eyes)
b	Bb (Brown eyes)	bb (Blue eyes)

Brown eyes:blue eyes = 3:1

Inheritance and genetic crosses — Chapter 16

Sex determination

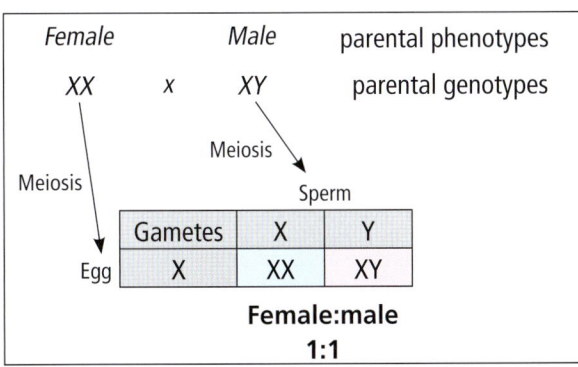

Female × Male — parental phenotypes
XX × XY — parental genotypes

Meiosis (Female) / Meiosis (Male) → Sperm

Gametes	X	Y
Egg X	XX	XY

Female:male 1:1

Incomplete dominance is where neither allele of an allelic pair is dominant or recessive with respect to each other – they are equally expressed and the resulting phenotype is a mixture or a blend of the two.

Incomplete dominance in plants, e.g. snapdragon flower colour

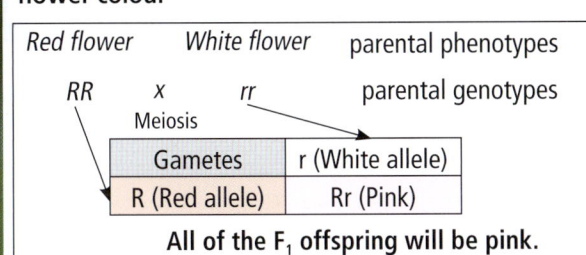

Red flower × White flower — parental phenotypes
RR × rr — parental genotypes
Meiosis

Gametes	r (White allele)
R (Red allele)	Rr (Pink)

All of the F_1 offspring will be pink.

Pink flower × Pink flower — parental phenotypes
Rr × Rr — parental genotypes
Meiosis

Gametes	R (Red allele)	r (White allele)
R (Red allele)	RR (Red flower)	Rr (Pink flower)
r (White allele)	Rr (Pink flower)	rr (White flower)

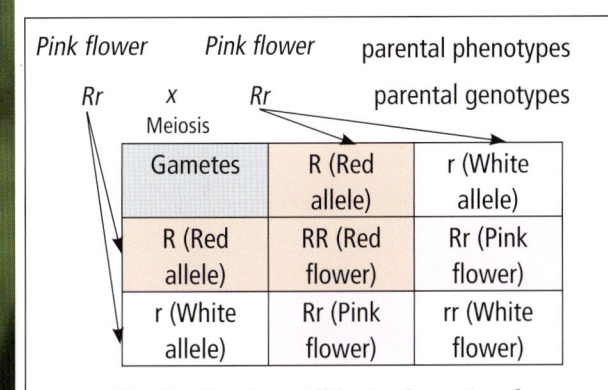

**The F_1 offspring will be in the ratio of:
1 red flower : 2 pink flowers : 1 white flower.**

Incomplete dominance in animals, e.g. coat colour in cattle

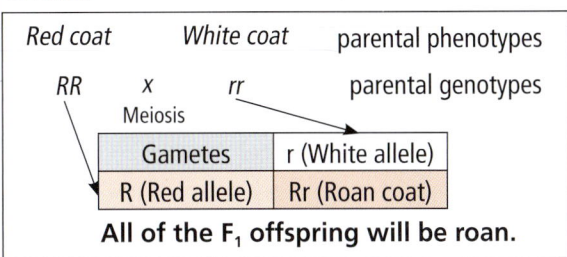

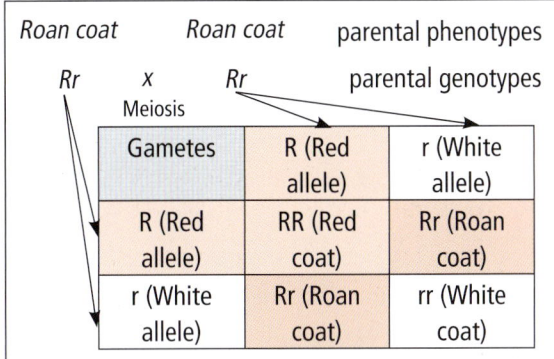

Red coat × White coat — parental phenotypes
RR × rr — parental genotypes
Meiosis

Gametes	r (White allele)
R (Red allele)	Rr (Roan coat)

All of the F_1 offspring will be roan.

Roan coat × Roan coat — parental phenotypes
Rr × Rr — parental genotypes
Meiosis

Gametes	R (Red allele)	r (White allele)
R (Red allele)	RR (Red coat)	Rr (Roan coat)
r (White allele)	Rr (Roan coat)	rr (White coat)

**The F_1 offspring will be in the ratio of:
1 red coat : 2 roan coats : 1 white coat.**

Mendel carried out genetics studies on pea plants. He studied seven different characteristics: [HL]

1. Flower colour (purple versus white)
2. Flower position (axial versus terminal)
3. Pea colour (yellow versus green)
4. Pea shape (round versus wrinkled)
5. Pod colour (green versus yellow)
6. Pod shape (inflated versus constricted)
7. Height (tall versus short)

Mendel's First Law of Segregation [HL]

- Each cell contains two factors for each trait.
- These factors separate at gamete formation so that each gamete contains only one factor from each pair of factors.
- At fertilisation the new organism will have two factors for each trait, one from each parent.
- Explanation: Each chromosome of a pair of homologous chromosomes must separate from each other – one going into two different cells.

Unit 2 — The Cell

- **Mendel's Second Law of Independent Assortment:** HL
Members of one pair of factors separate independently of another pair of factors during gamete formation.
  - Explanation: In a cell with two traits controlled by heterozygous pairs of factors (AaBb) there will be four possible gametes: AB; Ab; aB; ab.

- A **dihybrid cross** is a genetic mating between two HL organisms where two separate genes are studied.
- Pure-breeding tall, purple-flowered plant crossed with a short, white-flowered plant:

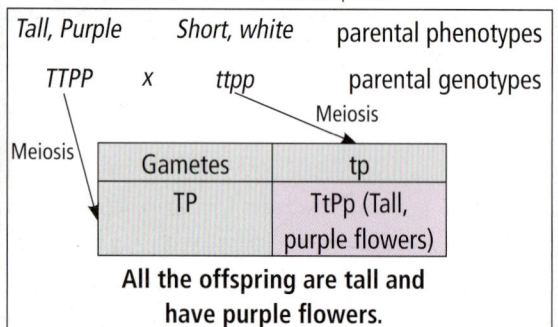

Tall, Purple   Short, white   parental phenotypes
TTPP   x   ttpp   parental genotypes
                 ↓ Meiosis
Meiosis ↓

Gametes	tp
TP	TtPp (Tall, purple flowers)

All the offspring are tall and have purple flowers.

- Two heterozygous tall and purple-flowered pea plants were crossed:

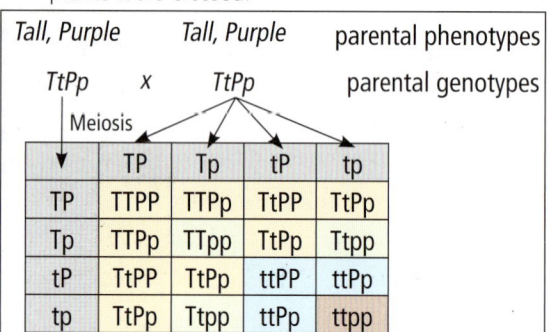

Tall, Purple   Tall, Purple   parental phenotypes
TtPp   x   TtPp   parental genotypes
         ↓ Meiosis

	TP	Tp	tP	tp
TP	TTPP	TTPp	TtPP	TtPp
Tp	TTPp	TTpp	TtPp	Ttpp
tP	TtPP	TtPp	ttPP	ttPp
tp	TtPp	Ttpp	ttPp	ttpp

- 9: Tall and purple-flowered pea plants.
- 3: Tall and white-flowered pea plants.
- 3: Short and purple-flowered pea plants.
- 1: Short and white-flowered pea plants.

Heterozygous tall, purple-flowered pea plant crossed with a short, white-flowered pea plant:

Tall, Purple   Short, white   parental phenotypes
TtPp   x   ttpp   parental genotypes
         ↓ Meiosis

	tp
TP	TtPp (Tall, purple flowers)
Tp	Ttpp (Tall, white flowers)
tP	ttPp (Short, purple flowers)
tp	ttpp (Short, white flowers)

Ratio of offspring is 1:1:1:1.

- **Linked genes** are genes present on the same chromosome. HL
- Mendel's Law of Independent Assortment does not apply to linked genes.
- Heterozygous organism crossed with a homozygous recessive organism and the genes are linked:

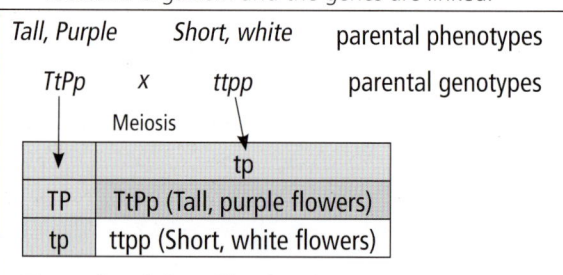

Tall, Purple   Short, white   parental phenotypes
TtPp   x   ttpp   parental genotypes
         ↓ Meiosis

	tp
TP	TtPp (Tall, purple flowers)
tp	ttpp (Short, white flowers)

The ratio of the offspring is 1:1.

- Two heterozygous organisms crossed and the genes are linked:

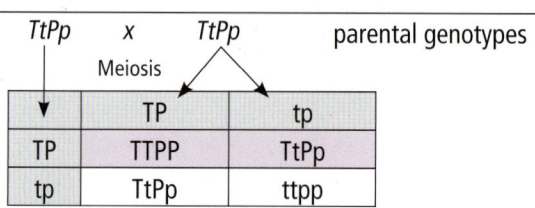

TtPp   x   TtPp   parental genotypes
         ↓ Meiosis

	TP	tp
TP	TTPP	TtPp
tp	TtPp	ttpp

Tall, purple-flowered plant:short, white-flowered plant = 3:1.

Ratio of offspring is 3:1.

- **Sex linkage** is where a gene is located on a sex chromosome. HL
- Colour vision and blood clotting factor are two traits whose genes are sex-linked.

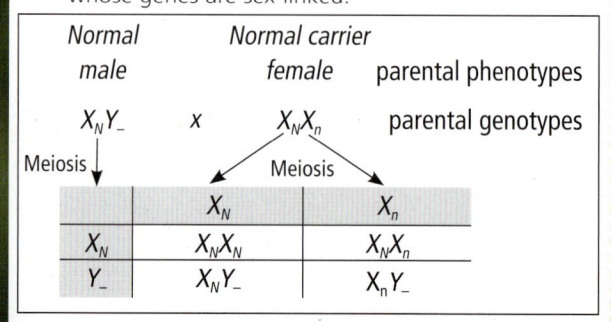

Normal male   Normal carrier female   parental phenotypes
$X_N Y_-$ x $X_N X_n$ parental genotypes
Meiosis ↓   ↓ Meiosis

	X_N	X_n
X_N	$X_N X_N$	$X_N X_n$
Y_-	$X_N Y_-$	$X_n Y_-$

All females will be normal (50 per cent will be carriers). Half the males will be normal and half will be colour blind.

- A **pedigree study** is a diagram of individuals of a family used to determine patterns of inheritance. HL

- **Non-nuclear inheritance** is the passing on of features from one generation to the next without the use of the nucleus. HL

Variation and evolution — Chapter 17

Learning objectives After studying this chapter, you should be able to:
- Define *variation* and describe the ways in which sexual reproduction and mutations cause variation.
- Describe how mutations can occur spontaneously or be induced by mutagens.
- Describe what a mutagen is and give two examples.
- Describe the two types of mutation – gene and chromosome mutations – and name a disease caused by each type.
- Define *evolution*.
- Give a broad outline of Darwin and Wallace's Theory of Natural Selection.
- Describe any one source of evidence in support of evolution.

Introduction

Evolution depends on variation. Without variation evolution would not occur. Variations occur all the time within a population (a group of organisms of the same species). These variations over time eventually give rise to new species. This is the essence of evolution.

Variation

> **Variation** is difference amongst members of the same species.

Variation is an important factor in evolution. Organisms adapt to an ever-changing environment and eventually evolve due to variation.

There are two factors that cause variation: **sexual reproduction** and **mutations**.

1 Sexual reproduction

Sexual reproduction causes variation because it involves meiosis (*see* Chapter 13) and fertilisation. Meiosis involves halving the number of chromosomes. Each gamete receives one chromosome from each homologous pair. It is random as to which chromosome ends up in a gamete. There are 2^{23} (or 8,388,608) possible combinations. When a sperm cell fertilises an egg cell, there are $2^{23} \times 2^{23}$ (or 70,368,744,177,664 – over 70 trillion) possible combinations.

What makes it even more complicated and gives an almost infinite number of different combinations is a process called 'crossing over'. Crossing over occurs in chromosomes before they are distributed to the gametes. Crossing over involves short regions of homologous chromosomes breaking off and swapping places during meiosis.

Therefore, there are an almost infinite number of possible combinations of chromosomes during gamete formation.

> **NOTE** For the Leaving Certificate Biology course, you **do not** need to know about crossing over.

This is why siblings are never identical (unless they are identical twins). The vast majority of us are unique, both chemically and physically. As long as you are not an identical twin, there is no other person like you in the world.

193

2 Mutations

> **Mutation** is a change in the structure or amount of DNA in a cell.

Mutations cause variation because of changes in the genetic material of a cell. Mutations can occur spontaneously or be induced by agents called **mutagens**.

> **Mutagens** are agents that increase the rate of mutations.

Examples of mutagens include cigarette smoke, ultraviolet radiation, X rays, gamma radiation, cosmic rays and radon gas. The birth defects in children born in the years after the Chernobyl nuclear disaster of 1986 were caused by mutagens.

Whether they occur spontaneously or are caused by a mutagen, mutations can be corrected by the cell's DNA repair enzymes. Problems can arise when these mutations are not corrected.

Because mutagens change the structure of DNA, they have the potential to cause cancer. Cancer is caused by abnormalities in the genetic material of a cell. Therefore, we should protect ourselves against mutagens that we have regular contact with, such as ultraviolet light and radon gas. High factor sun cream should be worn in strong sunlight and homes should be tested for levels of radon gas, especially in areas which are known to have high radon levels.

Mutations can be classified under two types.

Gene mutations

> **Gene mutations** are changes in the structure of a single gene.

Gene mutations are also called **point mutations**. They occur when there is a change in at least one base in DNA, sometimes changing the amino acid sequence in the resulting protein.

Sickle-cell anaemia (SCA) is an example of a condition caused by a gene mutation. SCA is a genetic condition resulting from a change in the haemoglobin gene. This change leads to the formation of a deformed haemoglobin protein, which collapses in on itself (Fig 17.1). The whole cell takes on a sickle or crescent shape and it cannot carry as much oxygen. Patients who suffer from SCA need regular blood transfusions.

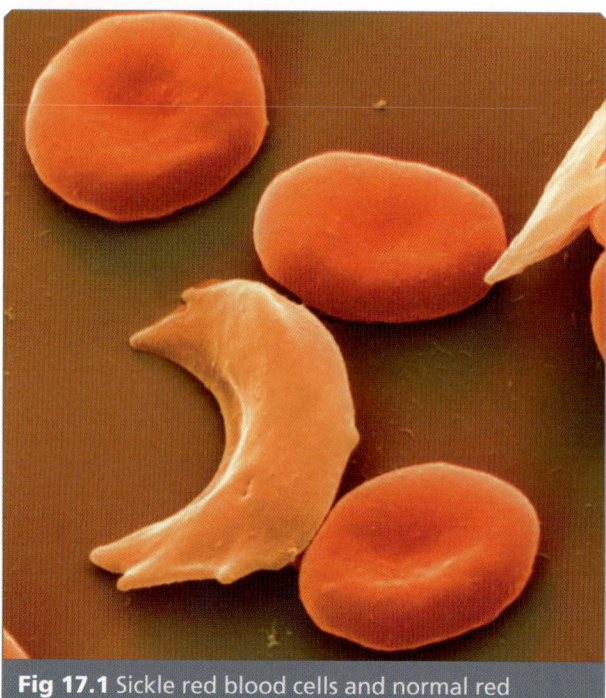

Fig 17.1 Sickle red blood cells and normal red blood cells.

Chromosome mutations

> **Chromosome mutations** are changes in the structure of chromosomes or the number of chromosomes.

For example, a chromosome might break in two, become shorter or longer, or even increase in number.

Down's syndrome (DS) is an example of a condition caused by a chromosome mutation. DS, named after John Langdon Down (a doctor who described the condition in 1866), is a genetic condition caused by the presence of an extra chromosome 21 in all cells of the individual with DS. An error occurs during gamete formation, when a gamete receives two chromosome 21s instead of just one. When the gamete with two chromosome 21s joins with a normal gamete at fertilisation, the resulting diploid zygote has three chromosome 21s. This condition is also called **trisomy 21** (Fig 17.2).

Fig 17.2 Down's syndrome chromosome structure (**A**) and a young girl with Down's syndrome (**B**).

About 5,000 years ago, humans in Europe developed the ability to digest lactose into adulthood. This gave them a selective advantage over people who were lactose-intolerant, as they could drink cow's milk without any adverse effects.

The peppered moth living in England was originally white. This enabled it to avoid predation by camouflaging itself against the light-coloured bark of trees and the light-coloured walls of many buildings. However, when the Industrial Revolution began in the eighteenth century, buildings and trees became blackened with soot and pollution. This gave the dark-coloured moths a selective advantage, as they were better able to avoid predation by birds. The population numbers of dark-coloured moths increased whereas those of white-coloured moths decreased. When pollution levels decreased because of environmental regulations, the white-coloured moth numbers increased once again (Fig 17.3).

Fig 17.3 White-peppered moth and a black-peppered moth.

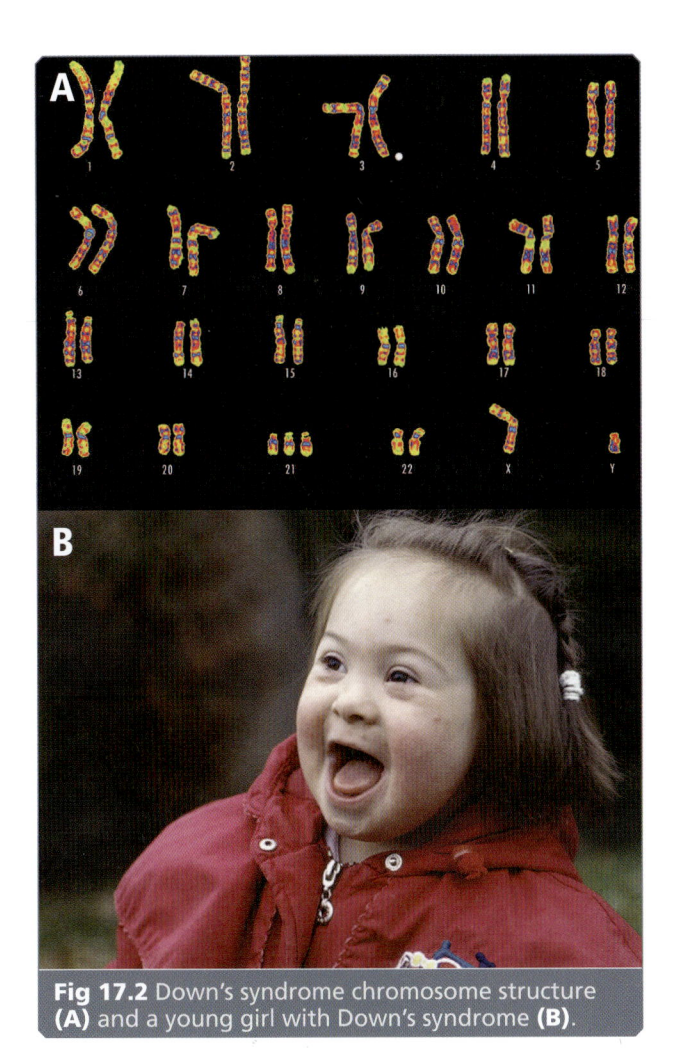

It is important to note that although most mutations harm the living organism and species as a whole, mutations play a very important role in evolution and the adaptation of organisms to new environments.

Without mutations, life would not have developed to be as wonderfully diverse and complex as it is today.

Evolution

> **Evolution** is genetic changes in species, over a long period of time, to produce new species in response to environmental stresses.

When we think of evolution, we think of it occurring over millions of years. However, it is important to realise that evolution can and does occur over relatively short periods of time. For example, bacteria have developed resistance to many antibiotics through changing their DNA or acquiring new DNA over a period of a few years.

Many new changes in a group of organisms over a long period of time will eventually make it so different from the original organisms that it can become a new species.

However, in order to become a new species, the original organism must not be able to produce fertile offspring with a member of the new group. This is an important factor in the formation of new species. This is called **speciation**.

> **Species:** a group of similar organisms that are capable of interbreeding to produce fertile offspring.
>
> **Speciation:** the formation of a new species following many changes in the structure of an organism until the new species cannot interbreed to produce fertile offspring with the original species.

For example, a cross between a male lion and a female tiger produces a **liger** (Fig 17.4). However, ligers are infertile, and therefore a lion and a tiger belong to separate species.

Fig 17.4 A liger – a cross between a lion and tiger.

Similarly, a donkey and a horse can interbreed to produce a **mule** (Fig 17.5). However, mules are infertile. Therefore, a donkey and a horse are also separate species.

Fig 17.5 A mule – a cross between a horse and a donkey.

Theory of natural selection

> **Natural selection** is the process by which particular traits become more common in a population due to that trait being advantageous to the species.

Natural selection relies on heredity, which is the passing on of features from one generation to the next.

Natural selection was first described by Charles Darwin in his 1859 publication, *On the Origin of Species.*

Because of sexual reproduction and random mutations, there is variation in populations of all species. Most of the time, these variations do not affect survival in the habitat. However, occasionally, one variation enables a particular member of a group of the species to reproduce at a faster rate or to survive a changing condition that threatens the existence of the population (Fig 17.6).

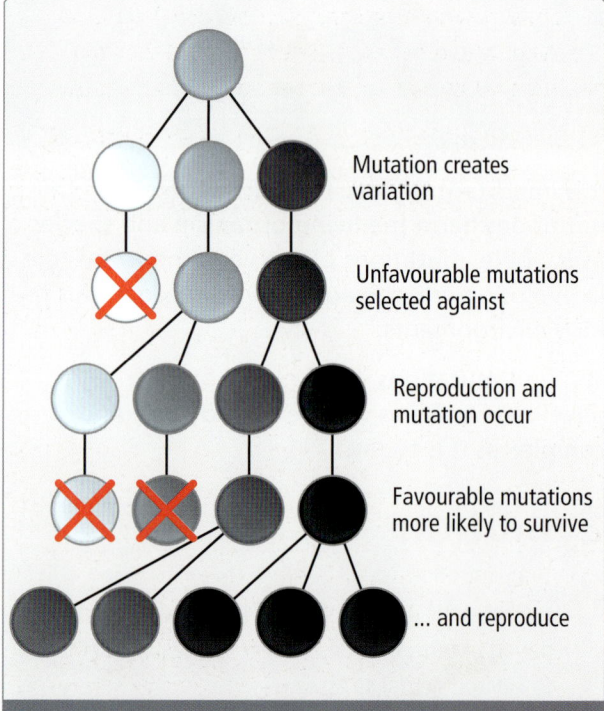

Fig 17.6 Mutations that are favourable are selected through natural selection.

This is natural selection at work – nature selects the most suited organism. The phrase *'survival of the fittest'* sums up natural selection very well. It was first coined by Herbert Spencer after reading Darwin's book.

Examples of natural selection

Sickle-cell anaemia (SCA)

As we have already learned, SCA is a genetic condition where the red blood cells of affected individuals take up a sickle or crescent shape due to a slight change in the structure of haemoglobin. It is a recessive condition, meaning that a person will only suffer from SCA if they are homozygous for the SCA allele. SCA is a devastating condition if untreated. However, even though it is such a debilitating condition (prior to modern medicine), it has remained quite common amongst certain human populations, affecting 1 in 500 black Africans and 1 in 1000 Hispanics.

SCA has continued to affect populations of people in Africa because the heterozygous condition (where the individual is a carrier of the recessive gene, but is unaffected by the condition) confers an increased immunity against malaria, which is very common in Africa. In other words, a person with one recessive allele for SCA and one normal allele has a much greater chance of surviving malaria than someone who has no recessive allele for SCA. Therefore, although having two copies of the recessive allele causes serious disease, being heterozygous for the SCA gene confers a selective advantage in areas where malaria is common.

Development of MRSA

MRSA (multi-resistant *Staphylococcus aureus*) is a deadly bacterium that is resistant to all known antibiotics (Fig 17.7). Since the discovery of penicillin by Alexander Fleming, many other antibiotics have been discovered and used against bacterial infections.

Bacteria reproduce rapidly and most will be killed off easily by a full course of antibiotics. However, misuse and over-prescription of antibiotics and failure to complete the prescribed course are the main reasons bacteria have been able to develop resistance to antibiotics.

Because bacteria multiply rapidly, mutations will occur that may well give one bacterium the ability to resist the effects of the antibiotic. The bacterium with the beneficial mutation is selected because it is 'fit' for its environment. It multiplies and all of its subsequent offspring will have resistance to the antibiotic. If the antibiotic-resistant bacteria get released into the environment, they can cause major health problems.

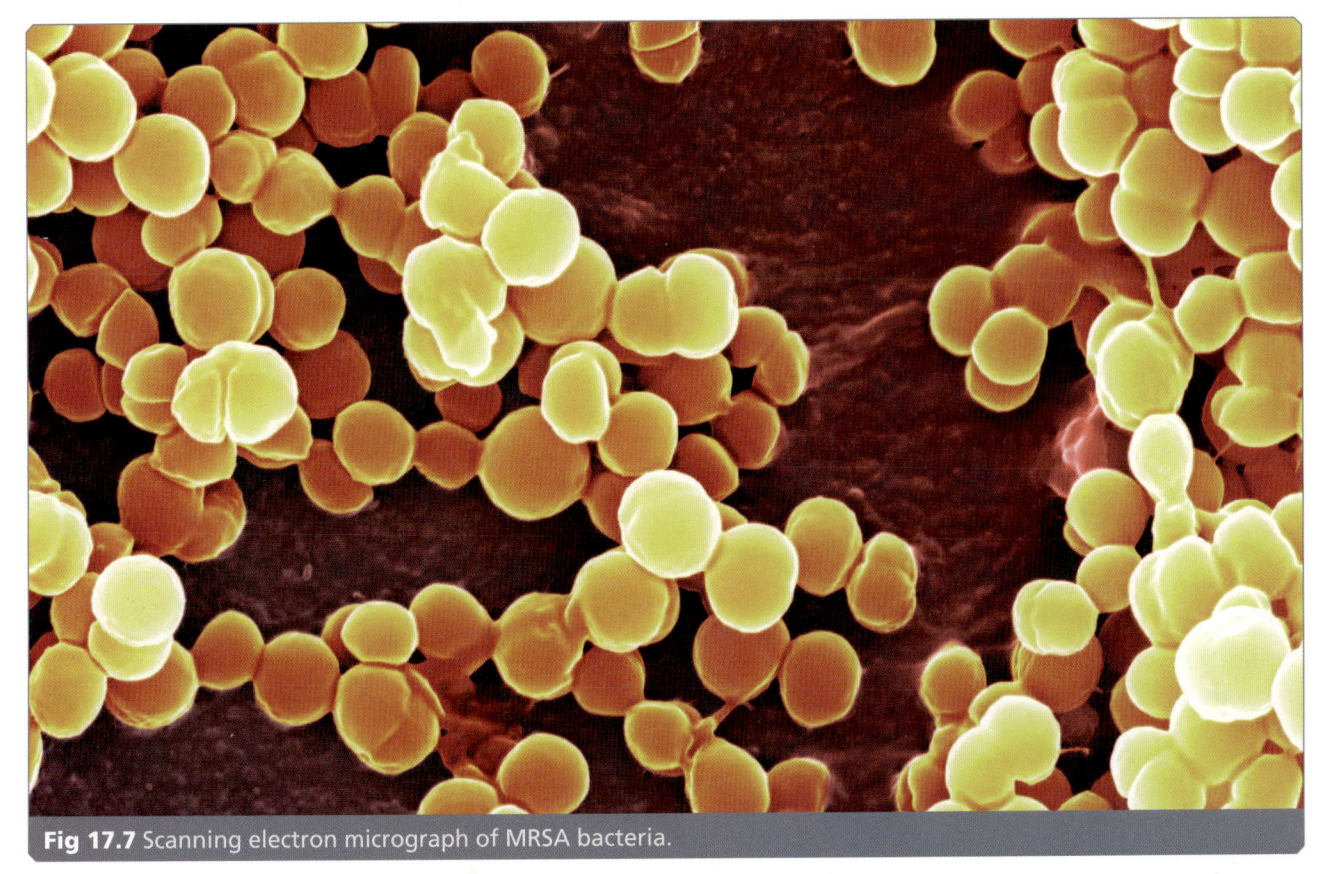

Fig 17.7 Scanning electron micrograph of MRSA bacteria.

Charles Darwin (1809–1882)

Fig 17.8 Charles Darwin (1809–1882).

Charles Darwin was an English naturalist who, along with others, came up with the **theory of natural selection.** Darwin has been given most of the credit for the theory because he was the first to publish a detailed account of it.

Darwin travelled on board the *Beagle* to observe and study the animals of the Galapagos Islands. He published his resulting theory of natural selection in 1859 in his book *On the Origin of Species*.

He concluded that all species originated from a common ancestor many millions of years ago.

Alfred Russel Wallace (1823–1913)

Alfred Russel Wallace was also an English naturalist who independently came up with the same theory of natural selection around the same time as Charles Darwin. His contribution has been recognised, but he received far less credit than Darwin because he did not publish his findings as early.

Darwin's theory of natural selection made a number of observations and conclusions.

Fig 17.9 Alfred Russel Wallace (1823–1913).

Observations

1. Species produce many more offspring than is necessary (overbreeding).
2. There is a limited supply of resources to allow survival of the species.
3. Numbers of species remain relatively constant over long periods of time.
4. All species show variations among their members and these variations are inherited.

Conclusions

1. There is a 'struggle for existence' (*competition*) between species and between members of the same species for food, space, shelter and mates.
2. Organisms most suited to their environment, due to favourable characteristics, will survive and reproduce at a faster rate than those not as well suited.
3. The characteristics that make an organism most suited to its environment will accumulate among the population.

Evidence for evolution and Darwin's theory of natural selection

In the nineteenth century, the scientific world, including Charles Darwin, was well aware of many fossil records showing evolution of species.

However, Darwin realised that there was not enough evidence to write a credible book on his theory of natural selection. He set about obtaining as much evidence as possible to prove his theory.

Some of the ways he proved his theory are outlined below.

> **NOTE** For Leaving Certificate Biology you have to learn about only one piece of evidence in support of evolution.

Palaeontology (study of fossils)

> **Palaeontology** is the study of fossils.
> A **fossil** is the preserved remains of an organism, part of an organism or an imprint left by that organism.

Palaeontology supports the theory of evolution as fossil records show a detailed history of the timeline of evolution and how organisms (including humans) adapted over many millions of years.

Palaeontologists can dig deeper and deeper into rocks to show how the fossils laid down over billions of years change. It has been shown that, over tens of millions of years, the fossilised remains of living organisms have been getting progressively more and more complex in structure. This shows that life has become more complex over time.

Comparative anatomy

> **Comparative anatomy** is the study of similarities and differences in the anatomy of living organisms.

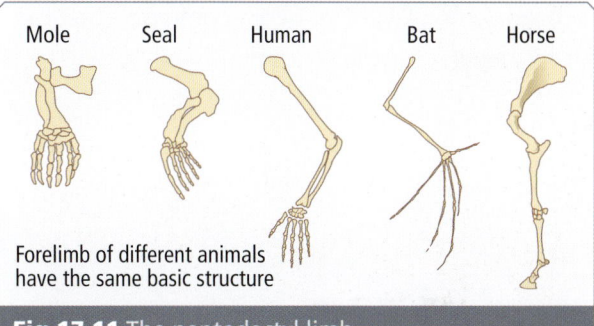

Fig 17.11 The pentadactyl limb.

The pentadactyl limb (meaning an appendage with five digits) is common to many different organisms, such as humans, moles, seals, bats, horses, birds, dolphins and whales (Fig 17.11).

Even though pentadactyl limbs from different organisms can look very different and can have very diverse functions, they are structurally similar. This means that these organisms must have had a common ancestor many millions of years ago.

Darwin used this as his evidence for natural selection.

Fig 17.10 A fossil of a fish.

Comparative embryology

> **Comparative embryology** is the study of similarities and differences in the anatomy of the embryo from different species.

Embryology is the study of the embryo of organisms. The early embryo in many different and diverse organisms is very similar. Darwin used this as evidence that evolution occurred and that all organisms must have had a common ancestor at some point in history.

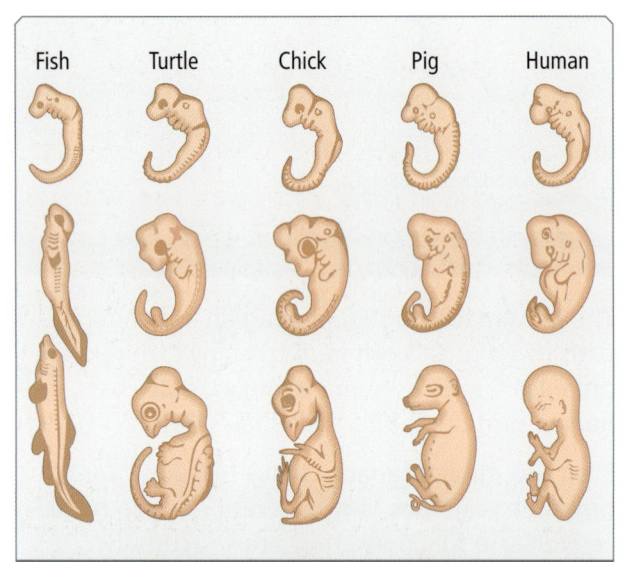

Fig 17.12 Comparative embryology showing the similarities between the early embryos of five different species: fish, turtle, chick, pig and human.

Fig 17.12 shows the remarkable similarities between the early embryos of five organisms: the fish, turtle, chick, pig and human.

As adults, these organisms are structurally completely different. However, a similarity exists in the early developmental stages of many organisms.

Comparative biochemistry

> **Comparative biochemistry** is the study of similarities and differences in the chemistry of living organisms.

Even though Darwin did not mention comparative biochemistry in his book, it still provides very important evidence for evolution.

All living organisms contain DNA as the molecule of heredity (Fig 17.13). The simplest organisms (bacteria) to the most complex life forms (humans) contain DNA.

The basic structure of DNA is **identical** in all life forms. This uniformity in biochemical structure, along with the fact that DNA is a self-replicating molecule, provides strong evidence for evolutionary relationships between even the most diverse organisms.

Similarly, many other chemicals present in our bodies are present in all other life forms, such as proteins, fats, carbohydrates and many more.

Geographical distribution

Darwin studied finches, both at home on the British Isles, and far away on the Galapagos Islands. He discovered that there were 13 different species of finches on the Galapagos Islands that were **not** found anywhere else in the world. He concluded that one species must have originally inhabited the islands and evolved into 13 different species over time. This provided further support for his theory of natural selection.

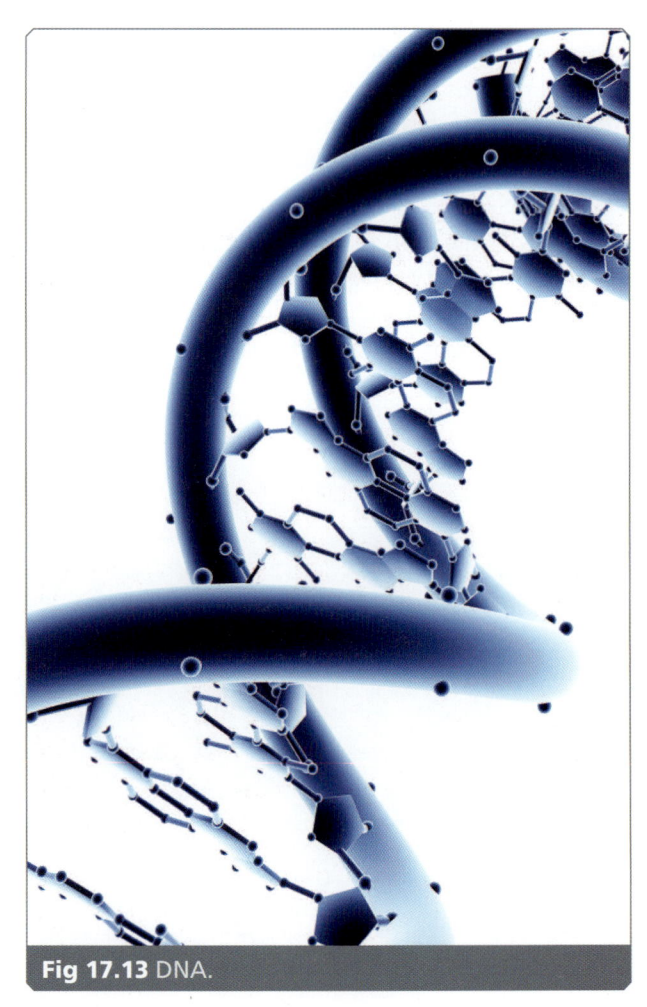

Fig 17.13 DNA.

Chapter 17 Questions

1. What is *variation* and name **two** ways in which it occurs?
2. (a) Name the **two** types of mutations and give an example of a condition associated with each type.
   (b) Name **two** factors that cause the rate of mutations in cells to increase.
3. What is *evolution*?
4. (a) What is a *species*?
   (b) Define the term *speciation*.
5. (a) Explain what is meant by *natural selection*.
   (b) Name the **two** famous naturalists associated with the development of the theory of natural selection.
   (c) Name the book written by one of these famous naturalists.
   (d) Explain why only **one** of the naturalists received most of the credit for the theory of natural selection.
6. Natural selection was subsequently redescribed using the famous phrase '_____ of the _____' by Herbert Spencer.
7. State **four observations** and **three conclusions** made in the theory of natural selection.
8. What is a *fossil*?
9. Detail **one** piece of evidence that supports evolution.
10. Name the islands made famous by the theory of natural selection.
11. No matter where you live you will have hundreds of species of organisms living very close to your home. Name **three** species of living organism that live near you. For each species you name, give **two** adaptive features it possesses that ensures it is suitably 'fit' for its habitat.

Chapter 17 Sample examination questions

1. (i) What is meant by *evolution*?
   (ii) Name **one** of the scientists associated with the theory of natural selection.
   (iii) Give a brief account of the theory of natural selection.
   (iv) Outline the evidence for evolution from any **one** named source.

   Section C, Question 11 (c) Ordinary Level 2008

HL 2. (i) What is meant by the term *evolution*?
   (ii) Name either of the scientists responsible for the theory of natural selection.

   Section C, Question 13 (a) Higher Level 2011

3. (i) Explain the term *species*.
   (ii) Within a species a considerable degree of variation is usually seen.
      1. What is meant by *variation*?
      2. State **two** causes of variation.
   (iii) What is the significance of inherited variation in the evolution of species?
   (iv) State **two** types of evidence used to support the theory of evolution.

   Section C, Question 10 (c) Higher Level 2009

Unit 2 | The Cell

Chapter 17 Mind map

Variation is difference amongst members of the same species.

Evolution is genetic changes that occur over a long period of time in species to produce new species in response to environmental stresses.

Two factors cause variation:
- Sexual reproduction
- Mutations

Mutation is change in the structure or amount of DNA in a cell. There are two ways in which mutations can occur:
- Spontaneous mutations: occur randomly due to mistakes in DNA replication. Two types of spontaneous mutation: gene mutations, e.g. sickle cell anaemia; chromosome mutations, e.g. Down's syndrome.
- Mutations caused by mutagens occur at an increased frequency when compared to spontaneous mutations. They are caused by environmental factors such as cigarette smoke and UV light.

- **Species:** a group of similar organisms that are capable of interbreeding to produce fertile offspring.
- **Speciation:** the formation of a new species following many changes in the structure of an organism until the new species cannot interbreed to produce fertile offspring with the original species.

- **Charles Darwin** (1809–1882) came up with the theory of natural selection.
- **Alfred Russel Wallace** (1823–1913) came up with an almost identical theory around the same time, but failed to publish his results as early as Darwin.

Theory of natural selection
- Natural selection is the process by which particular traits become more common in a population due to that trait being advantageous to the species.
- Darwin's book, *On the Origin of Species,* can be summarised in a number of observations and conclusions:

Observations
- Species overbreed.
- There is a limited supply of resources.
- Populations of species remain constant.
- All species show variations that are inherited.

Conclusions
- There is a 'struggle for existence' between organisms.
- Organisms most suited to their environment will survive and reproduce.
- The most suited characteristics accumulate in the population.

Evidence for evolution
- **Palaeontology:** the study of fossils; for example, fossils showing increased complexity the nearer they are to the surface of a rock formation.
- **Comparative anatomy:** many organisms have a similar structure; for example, the pentadactyl limb of the human, seal, bat and horse.
- **Comparative embryology:** the early embryos of many organisms show similar structures; for example, the early embryos of the fish, turtle, chick, pig and human are structurally very similar.
- **Comparative biochemistry:** many biomolecules show similar structures among many diverse species; for example, DNA is the hereditary material in all organisms and it is structurally similar in all organisms.
- **Geographical distribution:** many organisms are isolated to only one part of the world; for example, Darwin discovered 13 different species of finches on the Galapagos Islands that were not found anywhere else in the world.

Genetic engineering — Chapter 18

Learning objectives After studying this chapter, you should be able to:
- Define *genetic engineering*.
- Describe the five processes of genetic engineering.
- Describe three applications of genetic engineering: one plant, one animal and one microorganism.

Introduction

> **Genetic engineering** is the artificial manipulation and alteration of genes.

Genetic engineering is a relatively new scientific technique. The first organism to be genetically modified was an *E. coli* bacterium in 1973. An antibiotic-resistance gene was inserted into the DNA of *E. coli*. This gave the *E. coli* bacterium, and subsequent generations, the ability to tolerate the presence of an antibiotic called tetracycline. Without the gene, these bacteria were killed by tetracycline.

The following year the first animal (a mouse) was genetically modified. A piece of viral DNA was inserted into a fertilised mouse egg. The scientists showed that as the mouse grew every cell in its body had the piece of viral DNA.

Over the past couple of decades, genetic engineers have found more and more applications for their work, such as in the food industry, agriculture and medicine.

Process of genetic engineering

Genetic engineering involves a series of five important steps:

1 Isolation

> **Isolation** is the process of removing DNA from a cell.

The DNA and gene of interest must be isolated from the cell. DNA is isolated from cells by splitting the cells open using a mild detergent and gentle agitation. Proteases are also added to remove proteins (histones) associated with the DNA.

2 Cutting and ligation

> **Cutting** is the removal of a gene from a piece of DNA using restriction enzymes.

The DNA must be cut open to remove the gene of interest. Another piece of DNA must also be cut open to insert the gene of interest.

Cutting is carried out by **restriction enzymes**. We learned in Chapter 9 on enzymes that all enzymes are specific and will act only on one substrate or one set of substrates. Restriction enzymes will act only on a particular sequence of DNA and cut it open only at that site.

Once the gene of interest has been cut from its position, it is inserted into another piece of DNA called a **vector**.

Fig 18.1 A bacterial plasmid, a commonly used vector in genetic engineering.

> A **vector** is a piece of DNA (such as a bacterial plasmid) that will carry the gene of interest into a host cell.

The vectors used in genetic engineering are usually bacterial plasmids (Fig 18.1), but can also be viruses.

Plasmids are circular pieces of DNA that most bacteria possess in addition to their normal DNA (see Chapter 20). This extra piece of DNA contains a number of additional genes that usually give the bacteria an adaptive advantage, such as an ability to tolerate the presence of antibiotics.

Vectors can also be viruses. Viruses are very good at entering animal and plant cells unnoticed and are therefore excellent tools for transferring new DNA to host cells. A host cell can be another bacterium or a **eukaryotic** cell, such as animal or plant cells.

The same restriction enzyme that is used to cut out the gene of interest is used to cut open the vector DNA (Fig 18.2). Doing this means that the gene of interest will easily fit into the vector DNA because the ends have been cut open by the same enzyme. The exposed pieces of DNA will be complementary (see Chapter 14) and will bind together easily. Another enzyme called **DNA ligase** is responsible for joining the cut ends of the gene with the cut ends of the vector. The process of joining a gene with vector DNA is called **ligation** (Fig 18.2). The new piece of DNA is a combination of the desired gene and a plasmid or piece of viral DNA. This new piece of DNA is called **recombinant DNA**.

> **Ligation** is the joining of a gene to a vector using DNA ligase.
>
> **Recombinant DNA** is a piece of genetically modified DNA that contains DNA from two or more different species.

3 Transformation/transfection/transduction

> **Transformation** is the uptake of recombinant DNA into a bacterial cell.

Transformation is the most commonly used term for transfer of recombinant DNA from one cell to another.

However, strictly speaking, transformation refers to the process of bacteria taking up a recombinant bacterial plasmid (Fig 18.3).

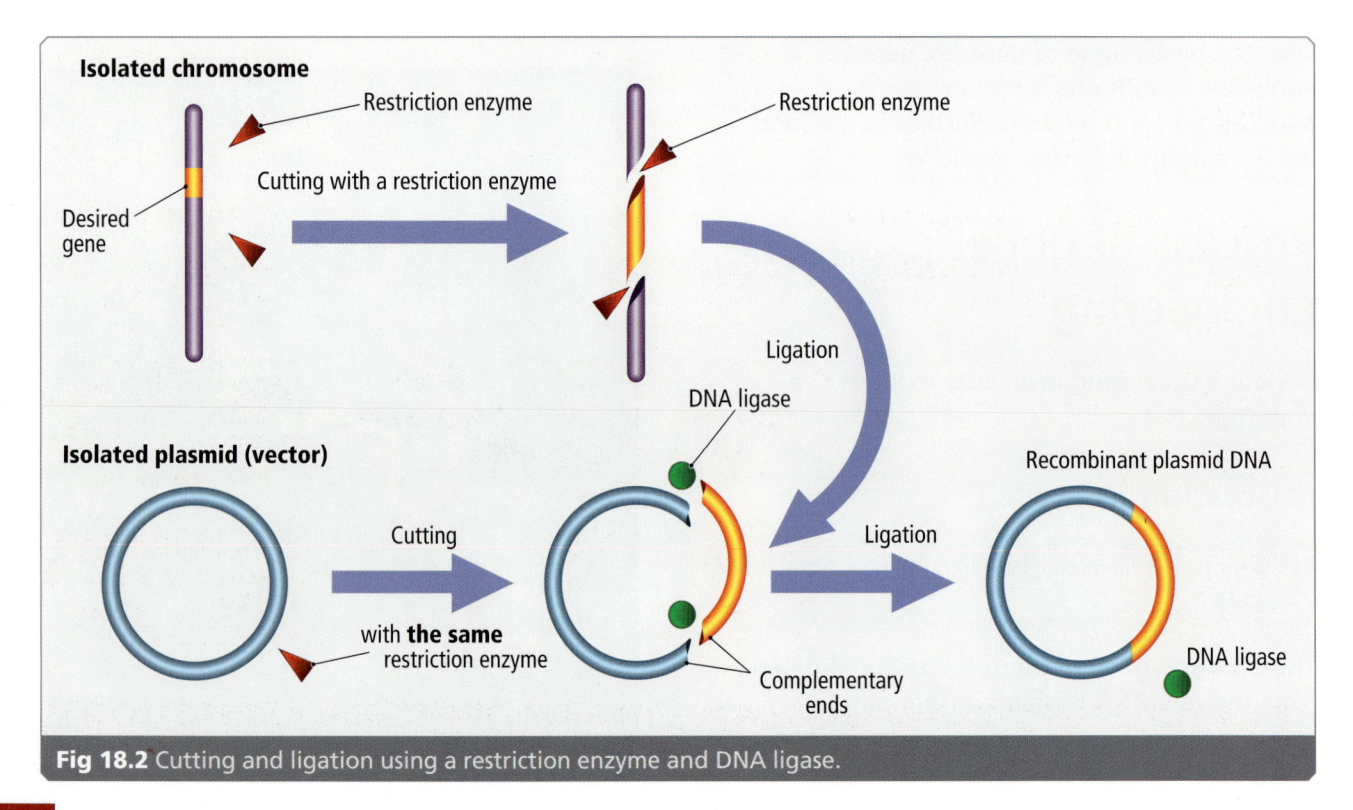

Fig 18.2 Cutting and ligation using a restriction enzyme and DNA ligase.

Genetic engineering Chapter 18

Another two terms often used in genetic engineering are **transfection** and **transduction**.

- Transfection refers to the process of **eukaryotic** cells, such as animal and plant cells, taking up a recombinant bacterial plasmid.
- Transduction refers to the process of any cell taking up a recombinant viral vector or a piece of viral DNA.

4 Selection and cloning

> **Selection** is the process of killing any cells that did not take up the recombinant DNA.

Usually less than 1 per cent of the cells will take up the vector. Therefore, most of the cells do not contain the desired gene. In order to overcome this, a process of selection occurs.

Selection is carried out by killing off the cells that do not have the gene. A vector is usually designed to carry an antibiotic-resistant gene. Any cells that took up the vector will be able to tolerate the presence of an antibiotic. These cells also carry the gene of interest.

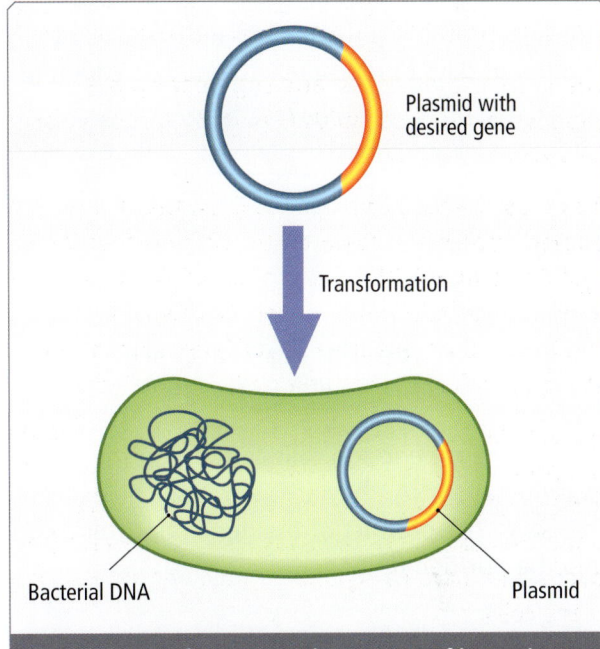

Fig 18.3 Transformation: the process of bacteria taking in a recombinant plasmid.

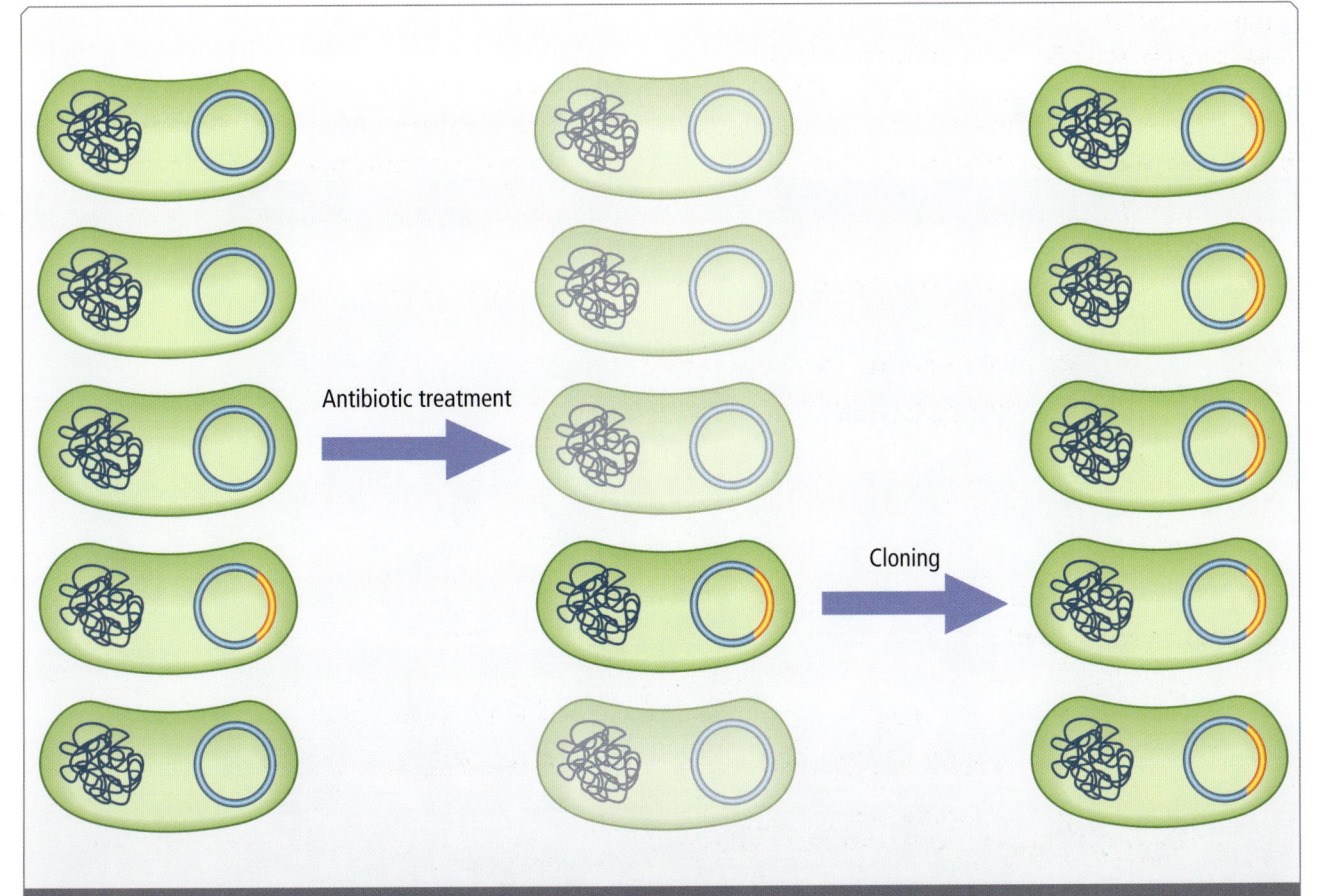

Fig 18.4 Selection and cloning: the cells are exposed to an antibiotic and only those that took up the vector (plasmid) survive. These cells then reproduce to form a large number of cells.

205

During the selection process, all cells are exposed to an antibiotic. Only those that were transformed (took up the vector) will survive. The cells containing the gene are then given a number of days to reproduce themselves **(cloning)**.

> **Cloning** is the process of producing identical copies of a cell.

5 Expression

> **Expression** is the stimulation of a cell to produce the product of a particular gene.

Once there are enough cells containing the recombinant DNA, they are stimulated to express the gene. The product of the gene (a protein) can then be purified if needed.

Applications of genetic engineering

> **NOTE:** For Leaving Certificate Biology, you are required to know three applications of genetic engineering, one each from plants, animals and microorganisms.

1 Plants

Many plants and crops have been genetically modified to make them larger, give higher yields, and be more resistant to disease and herbicides. Genes of interest have been inserted into the plant's genome. These genes make the plant more useful for humans.

Corn grown in Spain has been genetically modified to be herbicide- and insect-resistant (Fig 18.5). Certain corn strains have also been genetically enhanced to express 168 times the normal amount of vitamin A, six times the normal content of vitamin C and twice as much folic acid. (see Chapter 3 for information on vitamins)

2 Animals

Animals have been genetically modified to carry out a variety of functions. The mouse is probably the most regularly used animal in genetic engineering. Genes are routinely 'knocked out' (mutated on purpose) to see what effect it has on the mouse. Scientists can then test various treatments for the diseases generated in the mice. The results are then examined to see if they can be applied to human diseases. This type of genetic engineering will lead to a better understanding of diseases and possibly generate effective treatments.

Fig 18.5 Genetically modified corn.

Mice have also been genetically modified to glow green when exposed to ultraviolet light! The glow is caused by a protein called green fluorescent protein (GFP). GFP was originally discovered in a jellyfish living in the Pacific Ocean. It is hoped that GFP and other fluorescent proteins can be used to highlight cancer cells in the body, which may make it easier to treat.

Fig 18.6 Green mice – they have been genetically modified to express green fluorescent protein that glows when exposed to ultraviolet light.

In 2010, mosquitoes were genetically modified to be resistant to malaria. This may have significant health benefits in the future for people living in regions where malaria is widespread.

3 Microorganisms

Bacteria are vital tools for genetic engineering. They supply scientists with plasmids needed for genetic engineering studies.

E. coli have been genetically modified to carry human genes. This is particularly useful for people who have defective copies of a certain gene (genetic disease).

Patients who lack growth hormone or insulin (type 1 diabetics) can be treated using growth hormone and insulin produced by bacteria.

Biotechnology companies have genetically modified certain strains of *E. coli* bacteria to produce human insulin and human growth hormone. These hormones are then purified and given to patients. The patient's immune system does not react against the hormone because the hormones are human hormones, even though they are produced by bacteria (Fig 18.7).

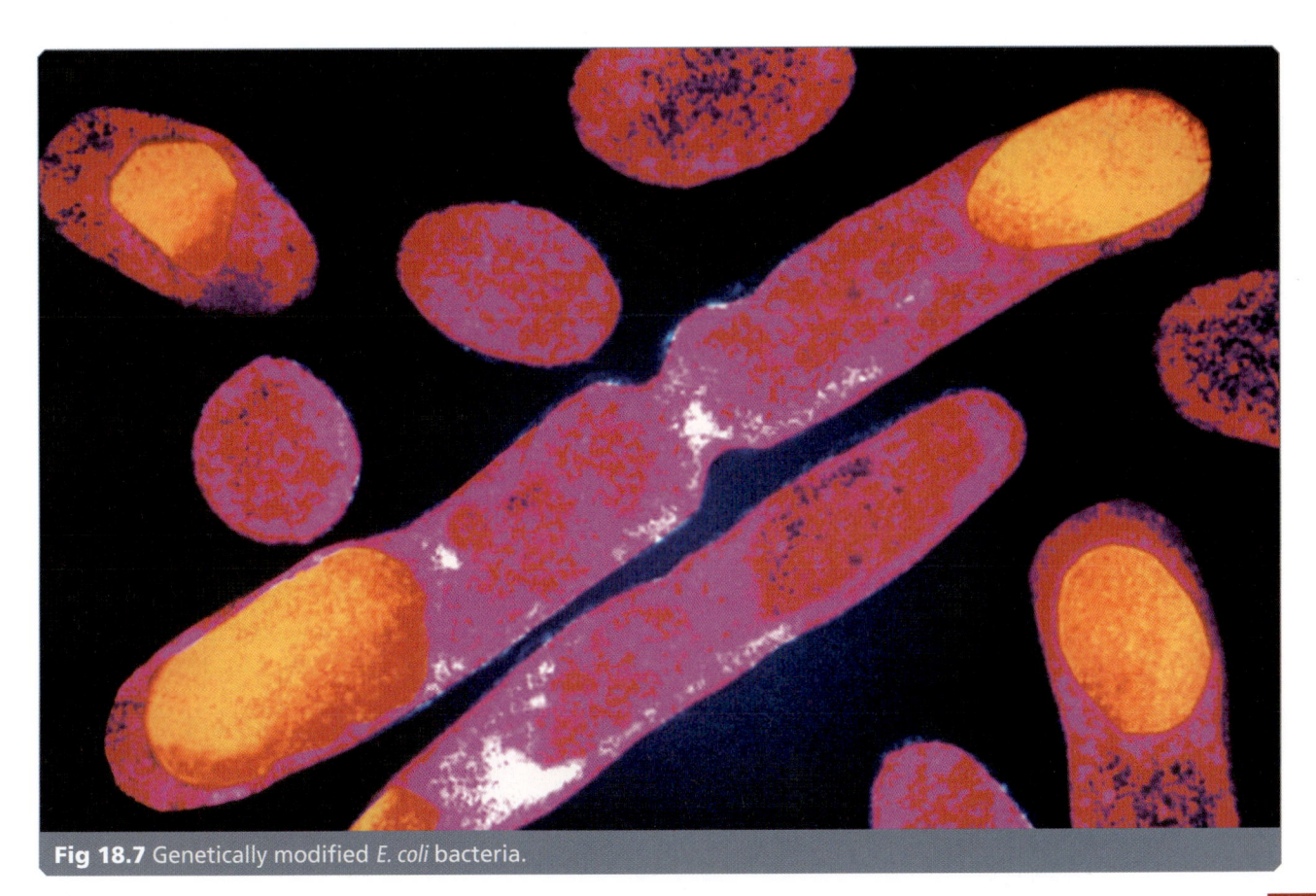

Fig 18.7 Genetically modified *E. coli* bacteria.

Unit 2   The Cell

Chapter 18 Questions

1. (a) What is *genetic engineering*?
   (b) What was the first organism to be genetically modified?
   (c) Name each of the **five** main steps in genetic engineering.
2. (a) What are *histones*?
   (b) How are histones removed from DNA?
   (c) Why do you think it is necessary to remove histones from DNA?
3. Briefly distinguish between *cutting* and *ligation* as they refer to genetic engineering.
4. (a) What are *restriction enzymes*?
   (b) Why is it important to use the same restriction enzyme to cut out a gene of interest from a chromosome and open the vector DNA?
5. What is meant by *recombinant DNA*?
6. (a) What is a *vector*?
   (b) Name **two** types of vector used in genetic engineering.
7. Distinguish between the terms *transformation*, *transfection* and *transduction*.
8. Nearly all bacteria have plasmids.
   (a) What are *plasmids*?
   (b) Give an example of a common gene found on plasmids.
9. (a) Distinguish between *selection* and *cloning* as they refer to genetic engineering.
   (b) Explain why selection is an important step in the process of genetically modifying bacteria.
   (c) Explain how selection is carried out.
10. Give **two** examples of where an expression product of a recombinant gene is purified for treatment of human disease.
11. Give **one** example of genetic engineering in plants and **one** in animals.

Chapter 18 Sample examination questions

1. (i) What is *genetic engineering*?
   (ii) Give **one** example of genetic engineering involving an animal and **one** example involving a plant.

   Section C, Question 11 (c) Ordinary Level 2006

HL 2. (i) What is meant by *genetic engineering*?
   (ii) State **two** applications of genetic engineering, **one** involving a micro-organism and **one** involving a plant.

   Section C, Question 10 (a) Higher Level 2005

3. (a) What is *genetic engineering*?
   (b) Name **three** processes involved in genetic engineering.
   (c) Give an example of an application of genetic engineering in each of the following cases:
      1. A microorganism
      2. An animal
      3. A plant

   Section A, Question 6 Higher Level 2009

Chapter 18 Mind map

Genetic engineering is the artificial manipulation and alteration of genes.

Process of genetic engineering
- **Isolation:** the process of removing DNA from a cell.
- **Cutting and ligation:** Cutting is the removal of a gene from a piece of DNA using restriction enzymes. Ligation is the joining of a gene to a vector using DNA ligase. Recombinant DNA is a piece of genetically modified DNA that contains DNA from two or more different species.
- **Transformation:** the uptake of recombinant DNA into a bacterial cell.
- **Selection and cloning:** Selection is the process of killing any cells that did not take up the recombinant DNA. Cloning is the process of producing identical copies of a cell.
- **Expression:** the stimulation of a cell to produce the product of a particular gene.

Applications of genetic engineering
- **Genetically modified plants:** Foreign genes are inserted into the plant's genome to make the plant more useful to humans; e.g. insect- and herbicide-resistant corn and vitamin A-fortified corn.
- **Genetically modified animals:** Genes can be mutated or 'knocked out' in mice and other animals. This enables the scientist to see what effect the mutation has on the mouse and to design potential treatments. The results are then examined to see if the same applies to humans. This will eventually lead to a better understanding of various diseases.
- **Genetically modified microorganisms:** *E. coli* have been genetically modified to produce human insulin and human growth hormone. These hormones are then purified and given to patients who lack these hormones.

Unit 3
The Organism

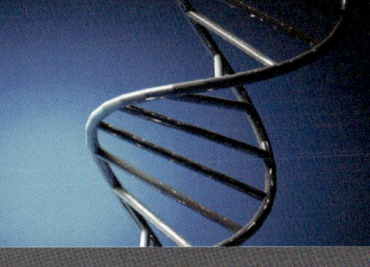

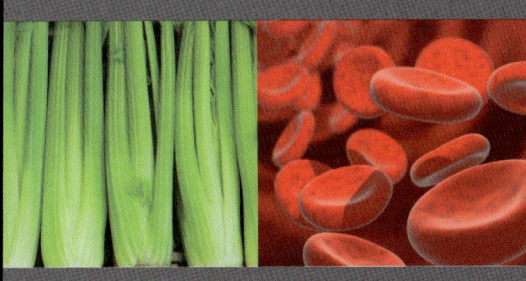

19	Diversity of living organisms 212
20	Kingdom Monera 216
21	Kingdom Fungi 230
22	Kingdom Protista 239
23	Viruses 242
24	Kingdom Plantae 248
25	Nutrition in the flowering plant 260
26	Response in the flowering plant ... 269
27	Vegetative propagation 279
28	Sexual reproduction in the flowering plant 284
29	Homeostasis 304
30	Blood 308
31	The human circulatory system 316
32	The human lymphatic system 332
33	The human digestive system 336
34	The human defence system 351
35	The human breathing system 362
36	Human skin (the integumentary system) 370
37	The human urinary system 374
38	The human endocrine system 383
39	The human nervous system 392
40	The human musculoskeletal system 410
41	The human reproductive system .. 423

Chapter 19 Diversity of living organisms

Learning objectives After studying this chapter, you should be able to:
- Define *taxonomy*.
- Name the five kingdoms of life.
- Describe characteristics of each kingdom.

Introduction

Living organisms are amazingly diverse – from the microscopic bacteria that exist as single cells and reproduce asexually to the largest organisms on Earth, such as the elephant, blue whale and giant sequoia that all consist of trillions of cells working together as a unit. To make it simpler to describe and study living organisms, scientists have devised a system of classification. All living organisms have been classified into one of five groups, called **kingdoms**. **Monera**, **Protista**, **Fungi**, **Plantae** and **Animalia** are the five kingdoms of life.

Classification of organisms is called **taxonomy**. It is a distinct area of biology.

> **Taxonomy** is the study of classification of living organisms.

In the early days of taxonomy, all living things were classified as either plants or animals on the basis of whether or not a cell wall was present.

Monera (Prokaryotae)

Monera, also known as Prokaryotae, include all **bacteria** (*see* Chapter 20). They are listed as the first kingdom as they are the simplest organisms and have been in existence for the longest period of time. They first developed approximately 4 billion years ago and were the only organisms for about 3 billion years!

Bacteria are ubiquitous, meaning they can be found in all areas on Earth. They are by a very long way the most numerous organisms on the planet. It has been estimated that there are more bacteria in an average human mouth (Fig 19.1) than there are people in the world!

It is estimated that there are 5×10^{30} bacteria on Earth, forming a biomass (amount of living

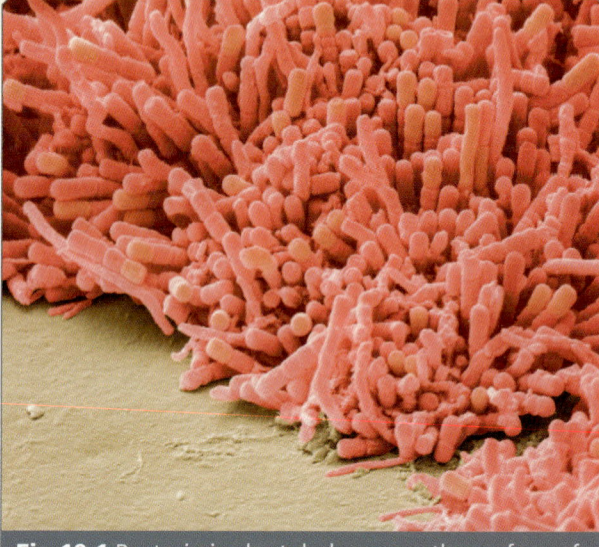

Fig 19.1 Bacteria in dental plaque on the surface of a tooth.

matter) that exceeds the biomass of all the other living organisms put together!

Monera is a very large kingdom currently containing just fewer than 9,000 identified species of bacteria. However, it is thought that the vast majority of bacterial species have yet to be discovered and identified. Estimates of the number of species of bacteria vary widely amongst microbiologists from 3 million to 1 billion!

All members of the Monera kingdom lack a nucleus. They possess DNA, but it is not contained within a membrane-bound nucleus. The Monera kingdom is the only kingdom to also lack membrane-bound cell organelles. They carry out all metabolic processes in the cytoplasm of the cell.

Bacteria are the organisms that keep the carbon and nitrogen cycles going. Hence, they are critically important to the continuation of life on Earth. In the hypothetical scenario of bacteria becoming extinct before other kingdoms, then life would not be sustainable on Earth.

Diversity of living organisms Chapter 19

All bacteria have some common characteristics:
- They all lack a nucleus.
- They all lack membrane-bound organelles.
- They all have a cell wall.
- They all reproduce asexually.

Protista

Kingdom Protista is also known by the name **Protoctista**. Organisms in this kingdom include multicellular algae (such as seaweeds) and single-celled algae (that contribute to plankton), as well as other single-celled organisms (such as *Amoeba* and *cryptosporidium*, Fig 19.2).

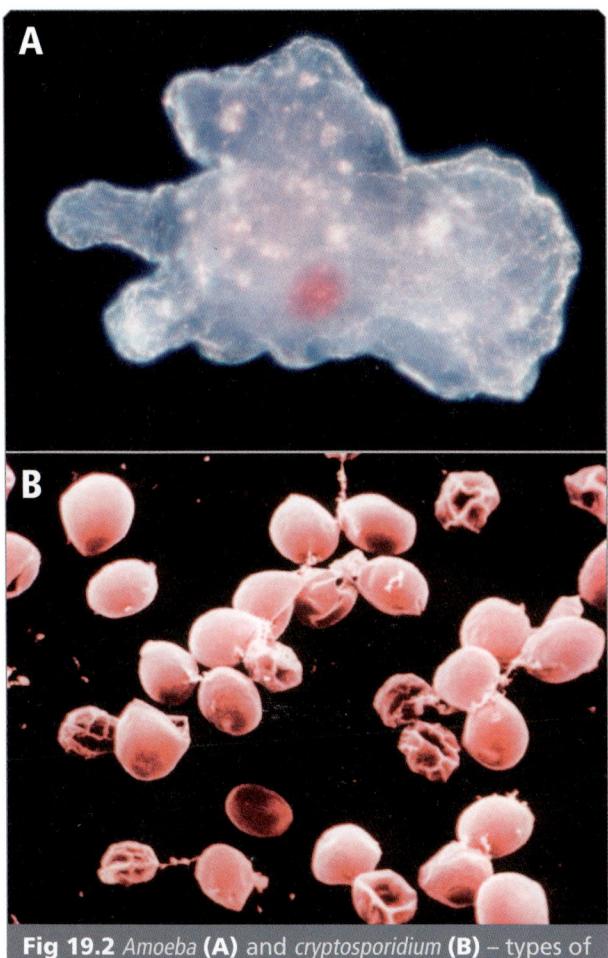

Fig 19.2 *Amoeba* **(A)** and *cryptosporidium* **(B)** – types of protists.

Protists are aquatic-based organisms, found wherever water is present. They are present in soil, rivers, streams, lakes, seas and oceans.

Many protists are autotrophic (make their own food) by photosynthesising. In fact, algae such as plankton in the oceans account for approximately 50 per cent of the photosynthesis on Earth.

Therefore, they are very important organisms in the carbon cycle. Depending on whether they are single-celled or multicellular, protists can reproduce asexually or sexually.

Fungi

Fungi are a diverse group of organisms (Fig 19.3). Examples include moulds (such as bread mould), mildews (such as powdery mildews seen on plants), lichens (such as the white and yellow patches found on rocks), yeasts (such as yeast used in brewing), and mushrooms (such as poisonous and edible mushrooms).

Fig 19.3 Yeast **(A)**; scarlet wax cap fungus **(B)**; and powdery mildew on the leaves of a plant **(C)**.

There are approximately 100,000 identified species of fungus, but there are estimated to be between 1.5 million and 5 million species on Earth. This means there are a large number of species yet to discover and identify.

Despite their diversity, fungi all have some characteristics in common, such as:

- They all have chitin (a type of modified polysaccharide containing nitrogen) in their cell walls.
- They are all heterotrophic (meaning they obtain food from other living organisms).
- They all reproduce by means of spores, either producing the spores by asexual or sexual reproduction.

Many fungi are economically important – yeasts are used in brewing alcohol and baking bread; moulds are used in antibiotic production; and many types of mushroom are edible.

Plantae

Plantae is the taxonomical term for plants. There are between 300,000 and 400,000 documented plant species with many new species discovered and catalogued each year, especially in the rainforests (Fig 19.4).

Fig 19.4 Rainforests, where most biodiversity is present.

The reason for the range of numbers is that many plants on the species list are actually the same species under two or more different names!

Plants have existed for about 500 million years. It is thought that they evolved from photosynthetic algae.

Terrestrial (land) plants evolved from aquatic (water) plants. This enabled other forms of life to inhabit land at around the same time.

Plants all have common characteristics such as:
- They are all multicellular.
- They are all photosynthetic.
- They all have cell walls made from cellulose.
- They all have vacuoles in their cells for storage.
- They can reproduce asexually or sexually.

Animalia

Animalia is the taxonomical term for animals. There are approximately 1,250,000 identified species of animals on Earth with many new species being discovered each year.

The vast majority (almost 1 million) of these are insects.

Fig 19.5 The striped horsefly, a large insect that feeds on farm animals in the USA.

Other examples include amphibians, fish, birds and all mammals (including the human).

Fig 19.6 The bottle-nose dolphin (A) and a chimpanzee (B) – both species of mammal.

All animals have a few common characteristics:
- They are all multicellular.
- They are all heterotrophic.
- They all reproduce sexually.

Diversity of living organisms Chapter 19

Chapter 19 Questions

1. (a) Name the **five** kingdoms of life.
   (b) Name **one** organism from **each** kingdom.
   (c) Which of the five kingdoms do not possess membrane-bound organelles?

2. (a) What is *taxonomy*?
   (b) Name the **two** kingdoms into which all living organisms used to be divided.
   (c) On what basis were the organisms divided?

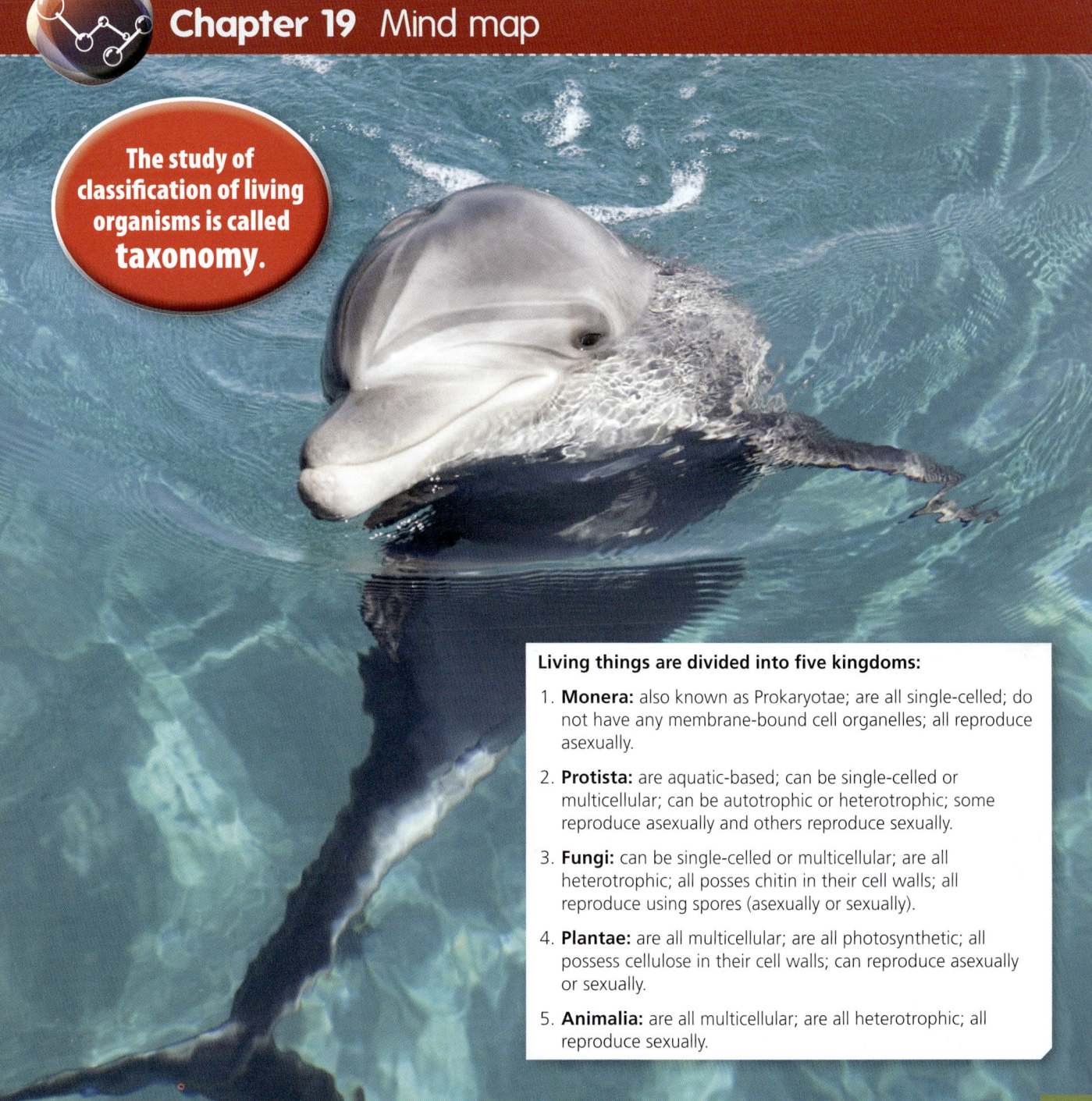

Chapter 19 Mind map

The study of classification of living organisms is called **taxonomy**.

Living things are divided into five kingdoms:

1. **Monera:** also known as Prokaryotae; are all single-celled; do not have any membrane-bound cell organelles; all reproduce asexually.

2. **Protista:** are aquatic-based; can be single-celled or multicellular; can be autotrophic or heterotrophic; some reproduce asexually and others reproduce sexually.

3. **Fungi:** can be single-celled or multicellular; are all heterotrophic; all posses chitin in their cell walls; all reproduce using spores (asexually or sexually).

4. **Plantae:** are all multicellular; are all photosynthetic; all possess cellulose in their cell walls; can reproduce asexually or sexually.

5. **Animalia:** are all multicellular; are all heterotrophic; all reproduce sexually.

Chapter 20 Kingdom Monera

Learning objectives After studying this chapter, you should be able to:
- Describe the wide distribution of bacteria in the environment.
- **HL** Describe the prokaryotic nature of bacteria.
- Draw and label the basic structure of a bacterial cell.
- Describe the functions of the various parts of a bacterial cell.
- Name the three basic shapes of bacteria.
- Describe how bacteria reproduce and form endospores.
- Describe the types of nutrition in bacteria and factors that affect their growth.
- **HL** Describe the growth curve of microorganisms.
- **HL** Describe batch and continuous-flow food processing.
- Name two harmful bacteria and two beneficial bacteria and understand what is meant by the term *pathogenic*.
- Define *antibiotics* and describe their role and potential abuse in medicine.

Introduction

Kingdom Monera is the general name given to the large group of organisms called **bacteria**.

HL All members of the Monera kingdom are **prokaryotes** – meaning they do not have a membrane-bound nucleus or membrane-bound organelles. Bacteria are too small to make it practical to have internal organelles.

Bacteria are single-celled organisms that are present everywhere in the biosphere – air, soil and water (both fresh water and sea water).

Structure of bacteria

All bacteria have a cell wall and cell membrane. The cell wall acts as a protective and structural layer and the cell membrane controls what enters and leaves the cell. Some types of bacteria have an additional layer outside their cell wall called the **capsule**. This acts as an extra layer of protection. Some bacteria also have a tail called a **flagellum** or flagella, which enable movement.

Bacteria are living organisms, so they contain both DNA and RNA. However, they **do not have a nucleus.** The DNA is arranged into a circular chromosome, which is found in an area of the bacterial cell called the **nucleoid**. DNA contains all the genes necessary for the bacterium to live and reproduce. RNA is found mostly in the form of ribosomes in the cytoplasm that function in protein synthesis (*see* Chapter 15).

As well as the nucleoid and ribosomes, bacteria have **plasmids** – extra pieces of DNA that give the bacterium special abilities, such as resistance to an antibiotic.

Fig 20.1 shows the structure of a typical bacterium.

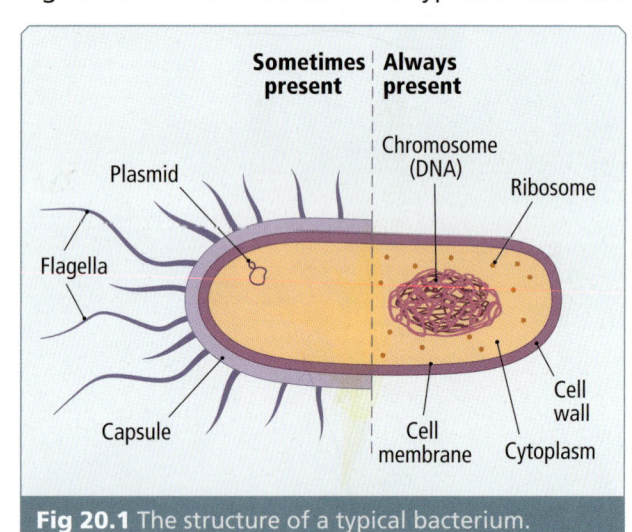

Fig 20.1 The structure of a typical bacterium.

Types of bacteria

Bacteria can be divided into three groups based on their shape: **spherical**, **spiral** and **rod**.

1 Spherical *(coccus/cocci)*

Bacteria that are round in shape are called spherical bacteria, and often have the term *'coccus'* in their name. The plural of *'coccus'* is *'cocci'*. An example of a spherical bacterium is *Staphylococcus aureus,* which is present on our skin naturally.

Fig 20.2 Spherical bacteria.

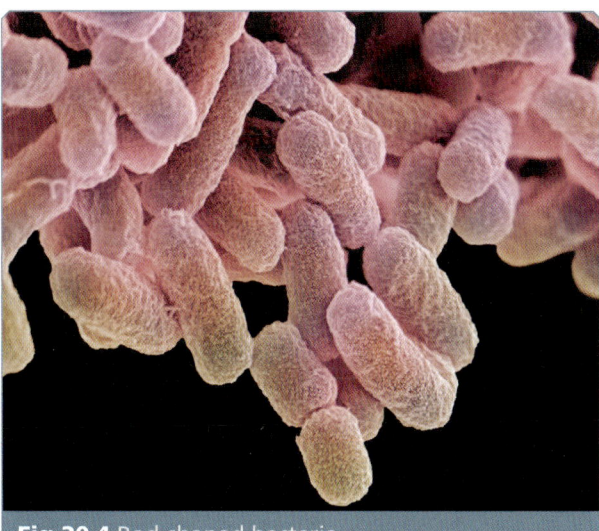

Fig 20.4 Rod-shaped bacteria.

2 Spiral *(spirillum/spirilla)*

Bacteria that are spiral in shape often have the term *'spirillum'* in their name. The plural of *'spirillum'* is *'spirilla'*. An example of a spiral bacterium is *Helicobacter pylori*, a bacterium that infects the stomach and duodenum and causes ulcers.

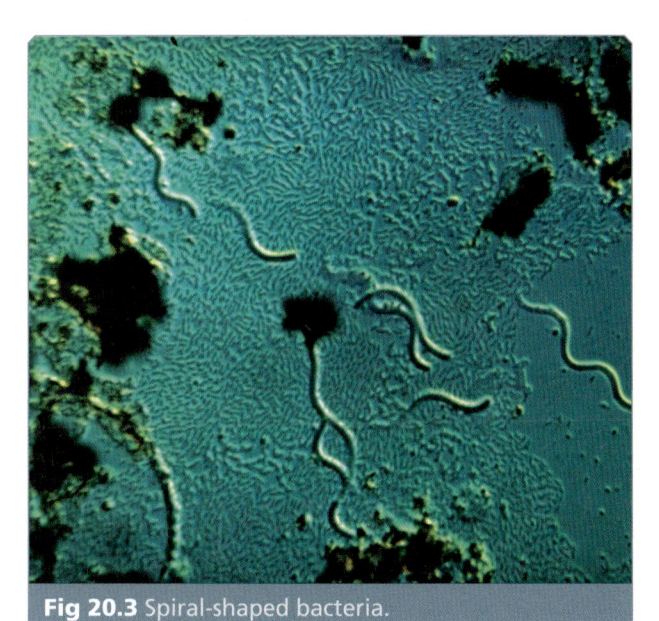

Fig 20.3 Spiral-shaped bacteria.

3 Rod *(bacillus/bacilli)*

Bacteria can also be rod-shaped, and often have the term *'bacillus'* in their name. The plural of *'bacillus'* is *'bacilli'*. An example of a rod-shaped bacterium is *Escherichia coli*, more commonly known as *E. coli*, which is a bacterium present naturally in our digestive systems, sometimes causing disease.

Bacterial reproduction

Bacteria are single-celled organisms and therefore do not have complex ways of reproducing. Bacteria reproduce asexually by a process called **binary fission** (Fig 20.5).

Binary fission

> **Binary fission** is asexual reproduction in bacteria.

- Binary fission begins with DNA replication.
- The cell then increases in size.
- The two identical pieces of DNA move to opposite ends of the cell.
- Cytokinesis (cell division) occurs when the cell membrane and cell wall pinch towards the centre of the cell.

Under ideal conditions, the whole process of binary fission can occur every 20 minutes. This means one bacterium could become 2^{72} after just 24 hours. That is 4,722,366,482,869,645,213,696 bacteria (4.7 billion, trillion)!

This rapid rate of division is one of the reasons why bacteria are able to evolve so rapidly. Mutations occur at random in bacteria all the time. This gives many opportunities to produce better, *'fitter'* bacteria that are more suited to their environment.

However, achieving 2^{72} bacteria in 24 hours is unrealistic. This is because in actual bacterial habitats, conditions are only occasionally ideal.

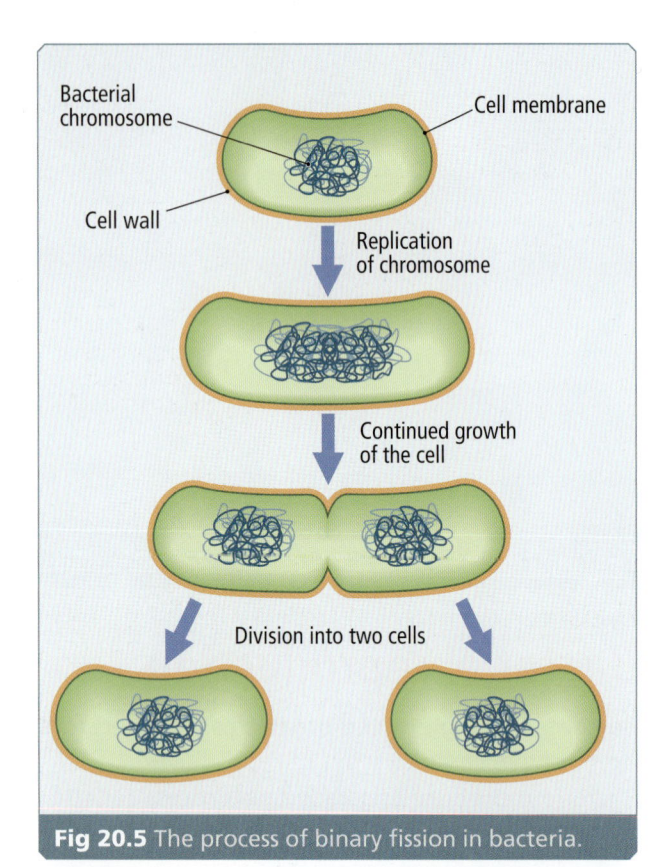

Fig 20.5 The process of binary fission in bacteria.

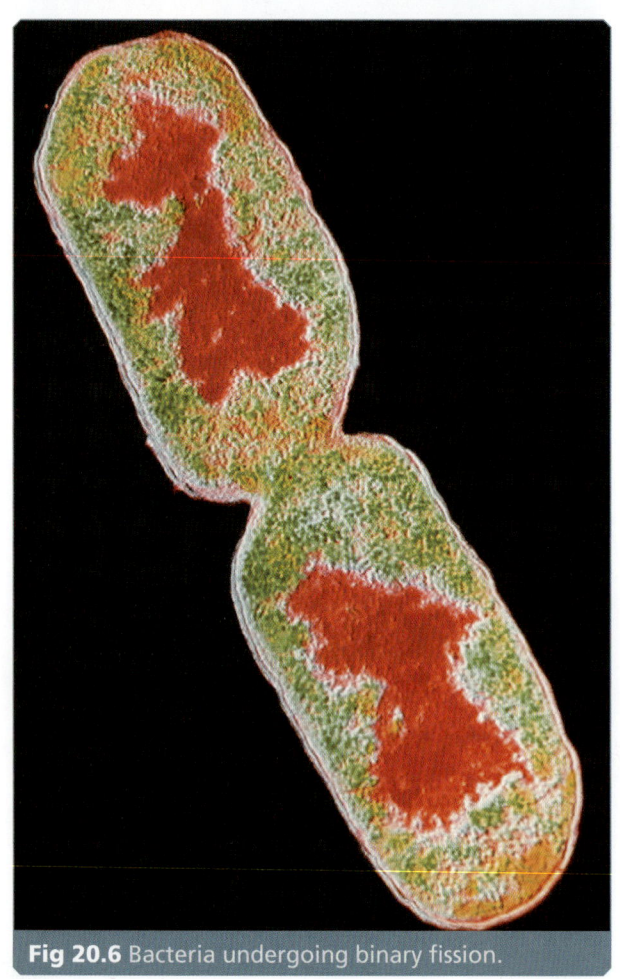

Bacterial reproduction and death comes at a cost – the build-up of waste products and toxins. These limit bacterial growth. There is also always a finite food supply. When the food supply runs out and toxins build up, the level of bacterial reproduction (binary fission) slows down. Bacterial death increases. Eventually, most of the bacteria die and only a few bacteria survive. The ones that do survive form endospores that can survive harsh conditions.

Endospore formation

> An **endospore** is a thick and tough-walled, dormant and dehydrated bacterial cell formed during unsuitable conditions.

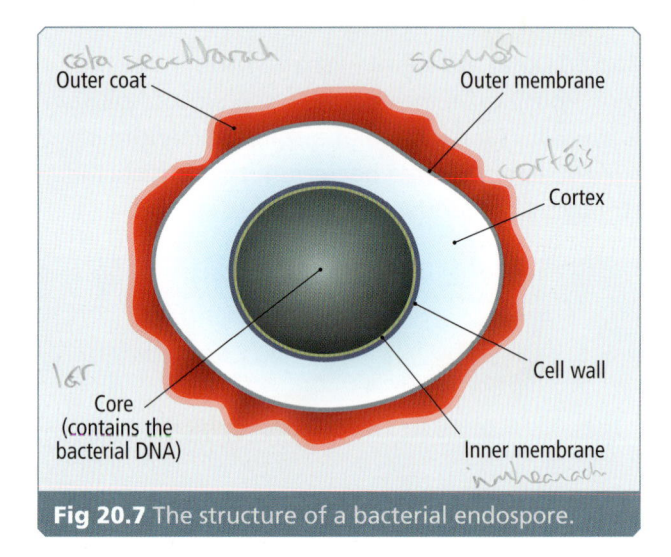

Fig 20.7 The structure of a bacterial endospore.

Fig 20.6 Bacteria undergoing binary fission.

Process of endospore formation

- Conditions become less favourable for the bacterium – nutrients begin to run out.
- The cell undergoes asymmetrical binary fission (one cell is larger than the other). This type of division is called **polar division**.
- The smaller cell is engulfed by the larger cell (this all happens within the original cell wall).
- A thick wall, called the cortex, begins to form around the engulfed cell.
- An outer coat forms around the cortex as an extra layer of protection from harsh conditions.
- The endospore matures; the larger cell holding the endospore degenerates; and the endospore is released (Fig 20.8).

Fig 20.8 The process of endospore formation in bacteria.

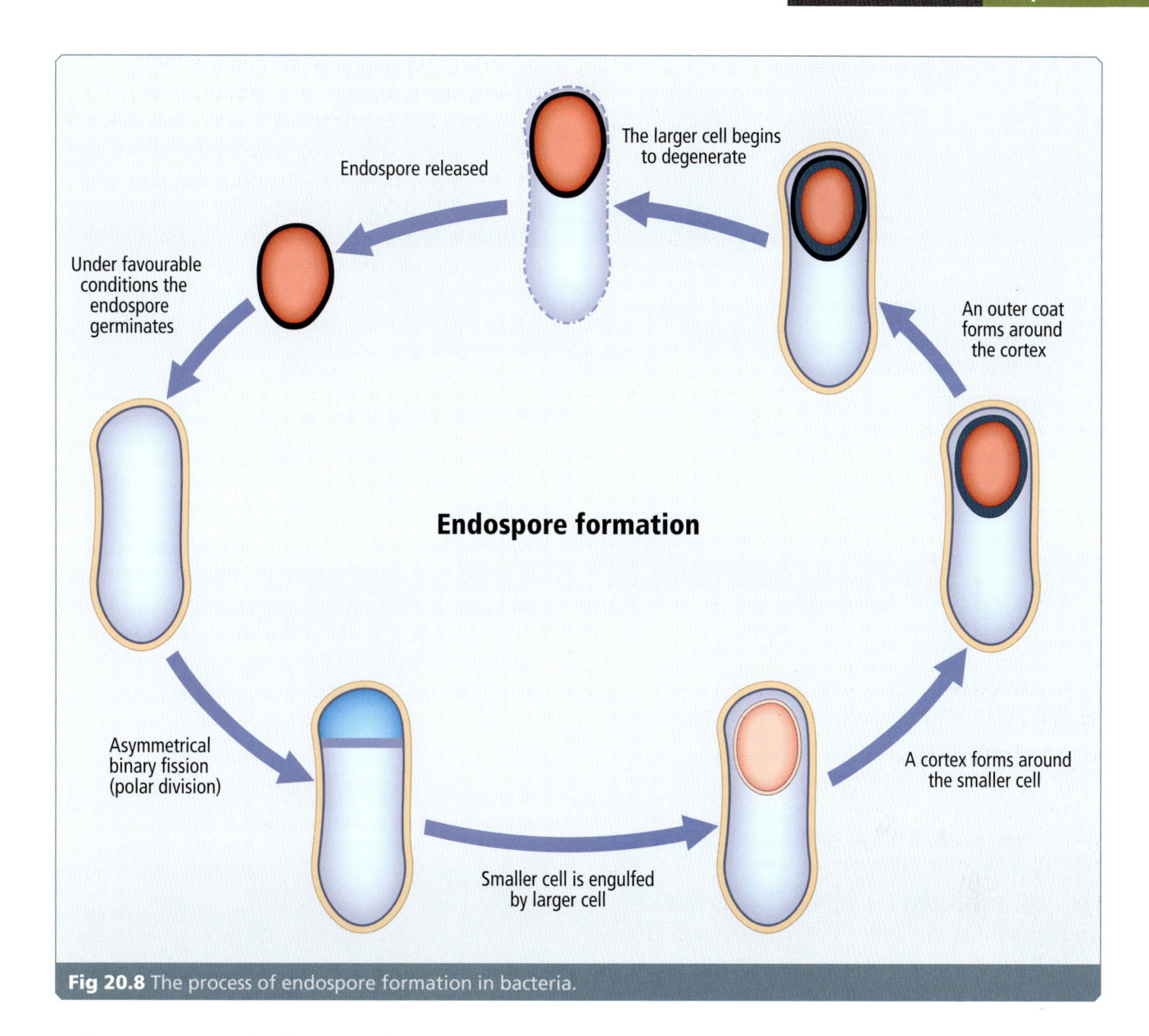

Endospores can survive for a very long time.

Endospores germinate when conditions become favourable again – when there are enough water and nutrients present. The endospore absorbs water and the tough wall and cortex breaks open, releasing the new cell which reproduces by binary fission.

Nutrition in bacteria

Nutrition is the way in which organisms obtain and use food.

There are two ways in which bacteria obtain their food: **autotrophic nutrition** and **heterotrophic nutrition**.

1 Autotrophic nutrition

Autotrophic nutrition in bacteria is where the bacteria produce their own food.

There are two subtypes of autotrophic nutrition:

- **Chemosynthesis:** Nitrifying bacteria are chemoautotrophs that convert ammonia to nitrates as part of the nitrogen cycle (see Chapter 4).
- **Photosynthesis:** Purple-sulfur bacteria are an example of a photosynthetic species. They convert carbon dioxide into carbohydrates using light (see Chapter 11).

2 Heterotrophic nutrition

> **Heterotrophic nutrition** in bacteria is where bacteria obtain their food and nutrients from other living organisms.

There are two subtypes of heterotrophic nutrition:

- **Saprophytic nutrition:** Bacteria that feed off dead organic matter, for example, bacteria of decay.
- **Parasitic nutrition:** Bacteria that feed off living organisms, for example, *E. coli*. The bacterium is the **parasite** and the organism that the bacterium feeds off is called the **host**.

Factors affecting bacterial growth

Temperature

Bacteria are living organisms with enzymes. Enzymes are affected by temperature (*see* Chapter 9). If the temperature is too low (as in a refrigerator or freezer), the enzymes do not interact with their substrate as much and reactions are much slower.

However, there are bacteria that can survive and carry out metabolism and reproduction at temperatures below the freezing point of water! These bacteria are called cryophiles. They have a special type of cell membrane that remains fluid even below 0 °C. The cell produces a type of protein antifreeze that ensures their cytoplasm remains fluid and no ice forms.

Fig 20.9 A volcanic hot spring where thermophiles can be found.

Conversely, if the temperature is too high the enzymes lose their three-dimensional structure and become inactive (a process called **denaturation**). Therefore, a bacterial cell with denatured enzymes will die. However, there are bacteria that actually require high temperatures to survive. These bacteria are called thermophiles (bacteria that live and grow at temperatures between 60 and 80 °C) and hyperthermophiles (bacteria that live and grow at temperatures between 80 and 120 °C).

Oxygen concentration

Most bacteria require oxygen to survive. This is because they need oxygen to produce ATP during respiration. These are **aerobic bacteria**.

However, there are many types of bacteria that are killed by oxygen (**obligate anaerobic bacteria**); and bacteria that cannot use oxygen, but tolerate its presence (**aerotolerant anaerobic bacteria**); and bacteria that can use oxygen but do not depend on it (**facultative anaerobic bacteria**).

pH

Enzymes are affected by pH, which means bacterial reproduction will be affected by pH.

Fig 20.10 An acidic river, the Rio Tinto, in southwestern Spain. Bacteria and algae are able to survive in the river with pH values as low as 2.

Most bacteria require a neutral pH to survive. However, there are bacteria that can live in very acidic environments (acidophiles) and in very alkaline environments (alkaliphiles).

Despite these extreme environments, these bacteria manage to maintain their cytoplasm at near neutral.

Fig 20.11 Mono Lake, Eastern California, has a pH of 10 and is three times as salty as sea water! Yet many organisms live there, including alkaliphiles.

External solute concentrations

The water content of a bacterium depends directly on the environment in which it finds itself. For example, if its environment suddenly becomes very concentrated with sugars or salts, then water will move out of the bacterial cell, by osmosis, into its environment. This causes the bacterium to shrivel up and die. This is the principle at work in salting food, storing foods in syrup or maintaining a high sugar content such as in jams (Fig 20.12).

Fig 20.12 Jams have a long shelf-life due to their high sugar content.

Pressure

Fluid (air and water) pressure affect all organisms. Almost all animals and plants have to live within quite a narrow pressure range, otherwise the function of their organ systems is disrupted.

Bacteria and other microorganisms can live at a very large range of pressures. For example, bacteria are found at extreme ocean depths (10 km deep) where water pressure is enormous. They have adapted to these pressures.

High fluid pressures are used in the food industry to sterilise foods. This process is known as High Pressure Processing (HPP). The high pressure causes the cell walls of the bacteria to collapse and break, releasing the contents. HPP is used for foods that would otherwise lose quality and characteristic flavours and texture through heat treatment.

HL Growth curve of microorganisms

Microorganisms go through a series of phases in their life cycle, or growth curve (Fig 20.13):

1. **Lag phase:** This is where the microorganisms are adjusting to the conditions. A new substrate could be present, which takes some time to adjust to. Microorganisms have to produce the enzymes needed to break it down.

2. **Log phase:** Once the microorganisms have fully adjusted, the substrate is digested very quickly and microorganism reproduction (binary fission) is exponential (very rapid).

3. **Stationary phase:** Nutrients begin to run out. Waste products and harmful toxins begin to build up. This kills microorganisms until the rate of binary fission equals the rate of death.

4. **Decline phase:** The nutrients have almost run out and toxins and wastes are at high levels. Death of the microorganisms is now much greater than reproduction.

5. **Survival phase:** The survival phase is where some microorganisms produce endospores that enable long-term survival. However, this stage does not apply to all forms of microorganisms because not all form endospores.

Fig 20.13 Growth curve of microorganisms.

Fig 20.14 Yakult, a yoghurt drink that has beneficial bacteria, such as *Lactobacillus casei*.

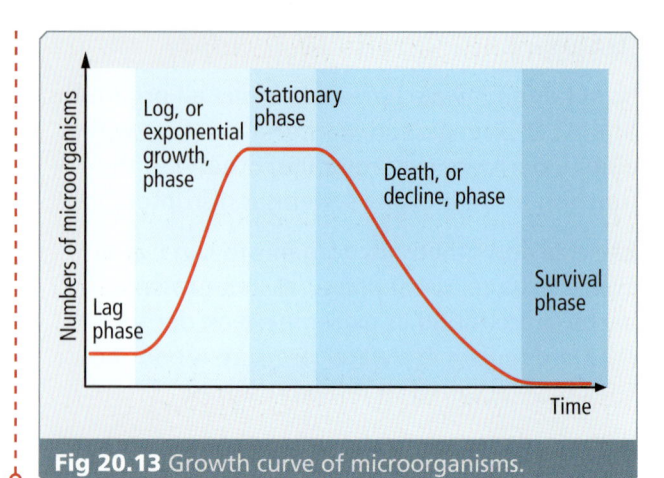

Economic importance of bacteria

Bacteria are very important in our lives and in the well-being of life on Earth. They keep the cycle of life going by contributing to nutrient recycling (*see* Chapter 4), such as the carbon and nitrogen cycles. Without bacteria, these cycles would come to a halt.

Beneficial bacteria

Beneficial bacteria are those that are directly useful to humans in everyday life.

> **NOTE:** For Leaving Certificate Biology, you must be able to give **two** examples of useful bacteria.

Two examples are **lactic acid bacteria,** such as *Lactobacillus casei*; and **bacteria used in genetic engineering,** such as *E. coli*.

1 Lactic acid bacteria (*Lactobacillus casei*)

Lactic acid bacteria are very important in the food industry. They are responsible for curdling milk to make dairy products, such as butters, cheeses and yoghurts (Fig 20.14).

Lactic acid bacteria are also present naturally in our intestines. They produce lactic acid, which helps the growth of desirable bacteria (instead of harmful bacteria).

Yoghurts contain *Lactobacillus casei*. Many yoghurt products claim to contain 'good bacteria'. While it is true that there are good bacteria in these products, these bacteria are present in all milk products!

2 Bacteria of the large intestine (*E. coli*)

We often hear of *E. coli* bacteria causing serious illness in humans, but most strains are harmless and are actually useful.

Many strains live naturally in our large intestine, producing vitamins (B group vitamins and vitamin K). These bacteria are in a symbiotic relationship with the person. The bacteria have shelter and food and the person receives vitamins.

Other strains are used in genetic engineering (*see* Chapter 18). Human insulin has been inserted into *E. coli* bacteria so that it can be produced on a large scale for type I diabetics.

Harmful bacteria

Harmful bacteria are also known as **pathogenic** bacteria, which means they have the ability to cause disease.

> **NOTE:** For Leaving Certificate Biology, you must be able to give **two** examples of pathogenic bacteria.

We will examine four examples of pathogenic bacterium below.

1 Strep throat bacteria (*Streptococcus pyogenes*)

This bacterium causes sore throat and scarlet fever (Fig 20.15).

2 Tuberculosis bacteria (*Mycobacterium tuberculosis*)

Tuberculosis (TB) is a serious infection of the lungs (Fig 20.16). Symptoms include pain in the chest, persistent coughing and coughing up blood. If left untreated, it is usually fatal.

Kingdom Monera Chapter 20

3 Meningitis bacteria *(Neisseria meningitidis)*

Meningitis is a serious condition that usually requires immediate hospital treatment.

Symptoms include a severe headache, a stiff neck, fever, an inability to tolerate light, and a rash that does not disappear when pressed with a glass (Fig 20.17).

Treatment involves intravenous injections (injections directly into the bloodstream) of antibiotics.

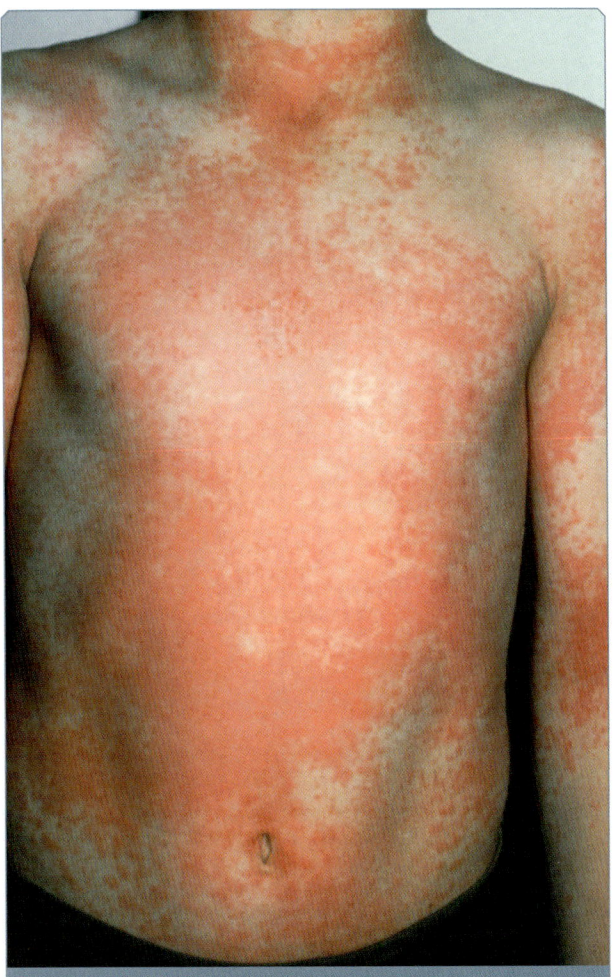

Fig 20.15 The effects of scarlet fever, which is caused by the bacterium *Streptococcus pyogenes*.

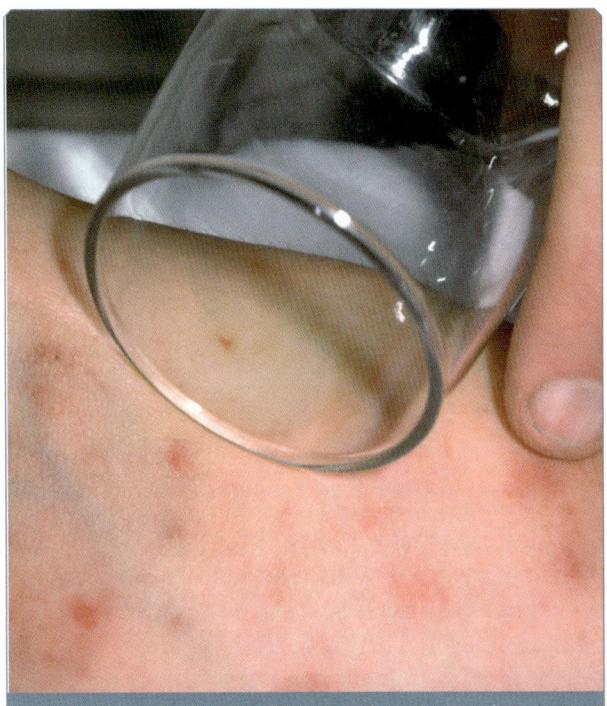

Fig 20.17 A rash that does not disappear when pressed with a glass is associated with bacterial meningitis.

4 *E. coli* bacteria *(Escherichia coli)*

In summer 2011, bean sprouts (Fig 20.18) were blamed as the most likely source of an *E. coli* infection outbreak that killed 25 people in Germany, and smaller numbers elsewhere. Many people were left with severe complications, such as kidney failure and nerve damage.

The *E. coli* strain proliferated in the gut of the infected people and released a toxin. This toxin was absorbed into the bloodstream and damaged the kidneys.

As a result of the outbreak, scientists and doctors advised people to cook all their vegetables well before eating them.

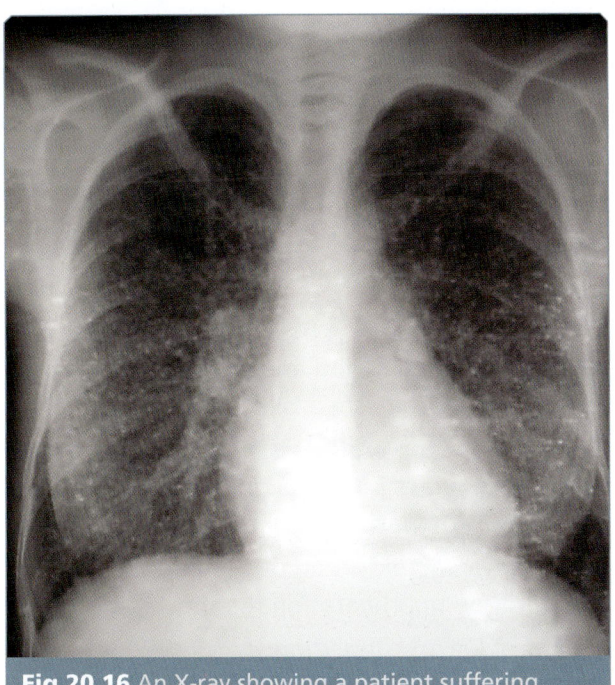

Fig 20.16 An X-ray showing a patient suffering from TB.

Fig 20.18 Bean sprouts.

Fig 20.19 A rash associated with MRSA infection.

Antibiotics

> **Antibiotics** are chemicals produced by microorganisms that prevent the growth of, or kill, other microorganisms.

Antibiotics are used to treat conditions such as those listed in the harmful bacteria section above.

The most commonly used antibiotic is **penicillin,** which was discovered in 1928 by Alexander Fleming (*see* Chapter 1). Antibiotics, such as penicillin, affect bacteria and other microorganisms only and have no effect on viruses. Therefore, conditions such as flu and colds are not treated with antibiotics.

Overuse of antibiotics

Overuse of antibiotics has led to the emergence of antibiotic resistance among bacterial strains such as MRSA (*methicillin-resistant Staphylococcus aureus*), which is resistant to all known antibiotics (Fig 20.19).

Resistance occurs when one bacterium in a population develops a mutation that enables it to avoid the effects of an antibiotic or to develop the ability to break down the antibiotic. This one resistant bacterium is then able to multiply, producing a new colony of resistant bacteria that has a competitive advantage over sensitive (non-resistant) bacteria. All bacteria that are sensitive to the antibiotic are killed off.

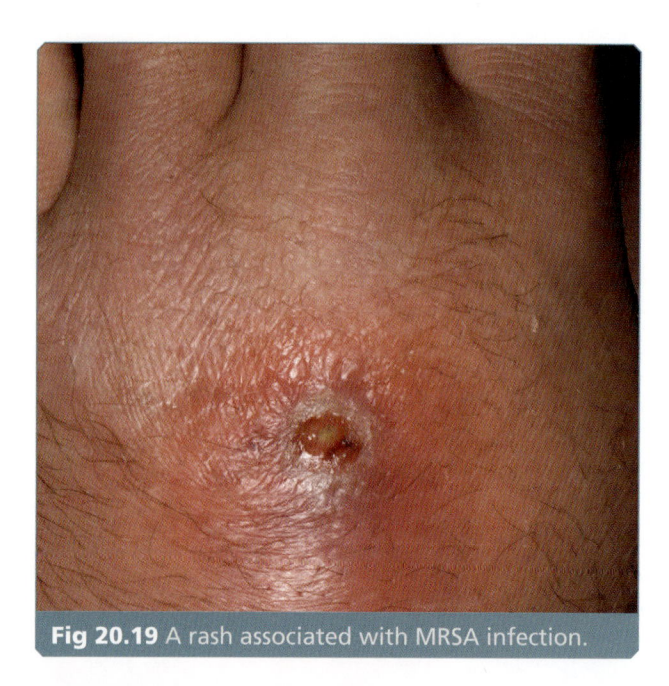

HL Food processing

> **Food processing** is the process of taking raw ingredients and converting them to food fit for consumption.

There are a range of food processing techniques used by the food industry. In this chapter, we will look at food processing with bacteria, of which there are two main types: **batch food processing** and **continuous-flow food processing.**

Both occur in large stainless steel bioreactors.

1 Batch processing

Batch processing is where only a measured amount of nutrients are added to a bioreactor. The bioreactor is then inoculated with a culture of bacteria, which are allowed to grow.

- The bacteria act on the substrate and go through the lag, log and stationary phases of the microorganism growth curve.
- Generally the product is removed before the decline phase is reached in order to limit the amount of waste products present.
- The bioreactor is then washed, cleaned and sterilised in preparation for another batch.

Batch food processing is much more widely used than continuous-flow food processing as it is a simpler process and less expensive.

Examples of food stuffs made by batch food processing are yoghurt and alcoholic beverages.

2 Continuous-flow processing

Continuous-flow processing is much more complicated and expensive than batch processing.

Nutrients are continuously added to the bioreactor; the bacteria are maintained in the log phase of growth; and product is continuously removed from the bioreactor.

This technique requires sophisticated bioreactors capable of maintaining the most ideal environment for the bacteria.

An example of a food stuff produced by continuous-flow food processing is single-cell protein, which is used in feeding livestock.

Fig 20.20 Stainless steel bioreactor in which batch food processing occurs.

Chapter 20 Questions

1. To which kingdom do bacteria belong?

HL 2. (a) Explain why bacteria are considered to be 'prokaryotic'?

    (b) Which organelles within eukaryotic cells are thought to have originated from bacteria?

3. (a) Draw the structure of a typical bacterial cell and label the following structures: *cell wall, cell membrane, cytoplasm, ribosomes, DNA, plasmid.*

    (b) Give the function of the following bacterial structures: *cell wall; ribosomes; plasmid.*

    (c) In what area of biology are plasmids used by biologists?

    (d) Some bacteria have a capsule outside of the cell wall. What is the function of the capsule?

    (e) Flagella are often present on the outside of bacterial cells. What is the function of flagella?

    (f) What name is given to the area within a bacterial cell where DNA is found?

    (g) Bacteria do not have any cell organelles. Where within the cell do you think aerobic respiration might occur? Refer to Chapter 12.

4. Name the **three** shapes of bacteria and make a sketch of each type.

5. Bacteria reproduce by _____ _____. This is a type of _____ reproduction.

6. (a) Describe the process of bacterial reproduction with the aid of diagrams.

    (b) Describe the process some bacteria go through when conditions become unsuitable for growth.

7 (a) Define *nutrition*.

(b) There are **two** types of nutrition in bacteria. Copy and complete the following table:

Types of nutrition	Subtypes	Examples of bacteria
	1. 2.	1. 2.
	1. 2.	1. 2.

8 Name **two** factors that affect growth of bacteria and state how bacteria respond to changes in these factors.

9 (a) Draw a growth curve of microorganisms showing all **five** phases.

(b) Describe what is happening to the microorganisms at each phase.

10 (a) Name **two** beneficial bacteria and their beneficial effects.

(b) Name **two** harmful bacteria and their harmful effects.

11 (a) What are *antibiotics*?

(b) Give **one** example of an antibiotic.

(c) Antibiotics were discovered completely by accident. Who discovered the first antibiotic and explain how it was discovered (*see* Chapter 1).

(d) Explain how some bacteria have become resistant to antibiotics.

12 What is a *bioreactor*?

HL 13 (a) What is food processing?

(b) Distinguish between batch food processing and continuous-flow food processing.

(c) Give **one** example of a food produced by **each** type of food processing.

Answer the following multiple-choice questions:

14 Bacteria belong to kingdom:
 (a) Monera
 (b) Protista
 (c) Fungi

15 Bacteria do not have a:
 (a) Ribosomes
 (b) Cell wall
 (c) Cell membrane
 (d) Nucleus

16 Bacteria reproduce asexually by:
 (a) Polar division
 (b) Binary fusion
 (c) Binary fission
 (d) Polar fission

17 Antibiotics are chemicals produced by:
 (a) Protozoans
 (b) Fungi
 (c) Plants
 (d) Animal cells

Chapter 20 Sample examination questions

1 (a) The diagram shows a typical bacterial cell.

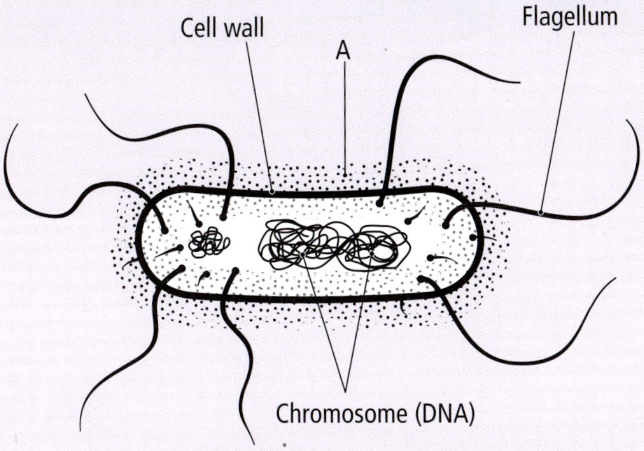
Cell wall
A
Flagellum
Chromosome (DNA)

(i) Some bacteria have a layer outside the cell wall (labelled **A** in the diagram). Name this layer and state its function.

(ii) Name a structure, other than **A**, which is not found in all bacteria.

(b) The table below shows ways in which bacteria obtain their food. Study the table and then answer the questions that follow.

Autotrophic	Heterotrophic
Photosynthetic	Parasitic
Chemosynthetic	Saprophytic

(i) Distinguish between *autotrophic* and *heterotrophic* nutrition.

(ii) What is *saprophytic* nutrition?

(iii) Why are saprophytic bacteria important in nature?

(iv) Briefly explain *chemosynthesis.*

(v) What term is used for the organism from which a parasite obtains its food?

(vi) Give examples of **two** harmful bacteria.

Section C, Question 13 (a) and (b) Ordinary Level 2007

HL **2** The diagram shows a bacterial growth curve.

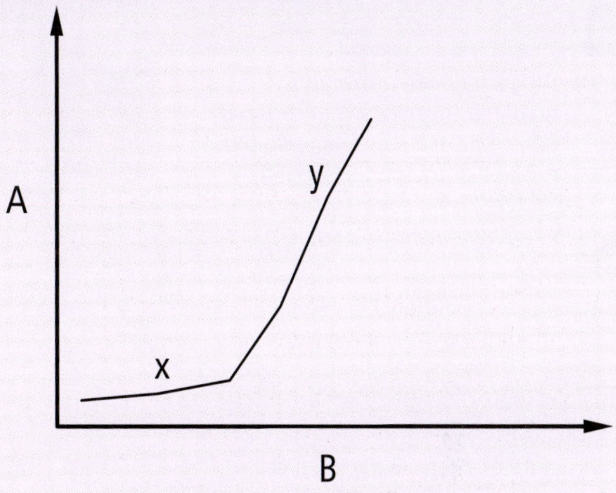
A
y
x
B

(i) **A** and **B** represent the labels on the axes. What does each of them stand for?

(ii) What term is applied to the part of the curve labelled **x**? What is happening during **x**?

(iii) What term is applied to the part of the curve labelled **y**? What is happening during **y**?

(iv) Copy the diagram into your answer book and continue the curve to show the next phase.

Explain why you have continued the curve in this way.

(v) Distinguish between batch and continuous-flow food processing using microorganisms in the food industry.

Section C, Question 15 (c) Higher Level 2008

Unit 3 | The Organism

Chapter 20 Mind map

- All bacteria are prokaryotes – meaning they are single-celled and do not have a membrane-bound nucleus or membrane-bound organelles. **HL**

Bacteria belong to the kingdom of Monera

Bacteria can be found everywhere in the biosphere: land, air and water.

Structure of a typical bacterial cell
- **Capsule:** only present in some types of bacteria. It functions as an extra layer of protection.
- **Flagellum:** tail-like structure that enables movement.
- **Cell wall:** maintains both the shape and integrity of the bacterium.
- **Cell membrane:** maintains the integrity of the bacterium and controls what enters and leaves the cell.
- **Nucleoid:** contains the DNA of the bacterium.
- **Ribosomes:** carry out protein synthesis.
- **Cytoplasm:** fluid of the cell, where all chemical reactions occur.
- **Plasmid:** circular piece of DNA present in most bacteria. It contains extra genes (e.g. antibiotic-resistance genes).

Types of bacteria
- Spherical (*coccus*): spherically-shaped bacteria; e.g. *Streptococcus aureus*.
- Spiral (*spirillum*): spiral-shaped bacterium; e.g. *Helicobacter pylori*.
- Rod (*bacillus*): rod-shaped bacterium; e.g. *Escherichia coli*.

Bacterial reproduction
- Reproduction in bacteria is asexual. It is called **binary fission.**
- Binary fission involves the cell increasing in size, replicating the DNA and plasmid, moving the replicated structure to either end of the cell, cell wall and cell membrane pinching inwards, and finally cell division.

- **Endospore:** thick and tough-walled, dormant and dehydrated bacterial cell formed in unsuitable conditions.
- Under harsh conditions some bacteria have evolved a mechanism to survive – endospore formation. Forming an endospore involves:
  1. Nutrients begin to run out.
  2. Asymmetrical binary fission occurs.
  3. The smaller cell is engulfed by the larger cell.
  4. The engulfed cell forms a tough wall.
  5. The tough, walled cell is released to become and endospore.

Kingdom Monera — Chapter 20

Nutrition is the way in which organisms obtain and use food.

1. **Autotrophic nutrition:** bacteria produce their own food.
   - Chemosynthesis; e.g. nitrifying bacteria.
   - Photosynthesis; e.g. purple-sulfur bacteria.
2. **Heterotrophic nutrition:** bacteria obtain their food from other living organisms.
   - Saprophytic nutrition; e.g. bacteria of decay.
   - Parasitic nutrition; e.g. *E. coli*.

Factors affecting growth of bacteria
- Temperature
- Oxygen concentration
- pH
- External solute concentration
- Pressure

Growth curve of microorganisms HL
- **Lag phase:** bacteria are adjusting to their new environment.
- **Log phase:** bacteria multiply exponentially.
- **Stationary phase:** nutrients are beginning to run out and bacteria begin to die – rate of bacterial death equals rate of bacterial reproduction.
- **Decline phase:** the rate of bacterial death has overtaken the rate of bacterial reproduction due to build up of toxins and very little nutrients left.
- **Survival phase:** only some bacteria will survive as endospores.

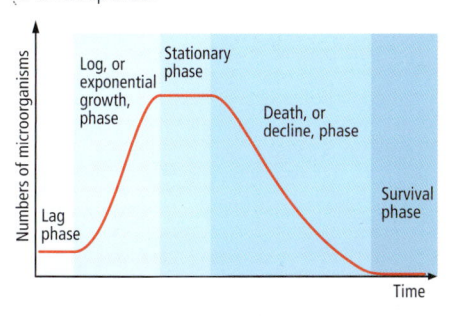

Economic importance of bacteria

1. **Beneficial effects of bacteria**
   - Dairy products: lactic acid bacteria are used in food processing to turn milk into dairy products such as yoghurt, cheeses and butter.
   - Production of vitamins and human insulin: *E. coli* live in the human large intestine and produces vitamin K and some B group vitamins. *E. coli* has been genetically engineered to produce human insulin.
2. **Harmful effects of bacteria**
   - Strep throat: Strep throat is caused by *Streptococcus pyogenes*.
   - Tuberculosis: Tuberculosis is caused by *Mycobacterium tuberculosis*.

- **Antibiotics** are chemicals produced by microorganisms that inhibit the growth of, or kill, other microorganisms.
- Overuse of antibiotics is the primary reason that many bacteria are becoming resistant to a wide range of antibiotics.
- Methicillin-resistant *Staphylococcus aureus* (MRSA) is resistant to every known antibiotic.

Food processing is the process of taking raw ingredients and converting them to food fit for consumption.
- **Batch food processing:** for example, yoghurt production.
- **Continuous-flow food processing:** for example, production of single-cell protein used in animal feed.

Chapter 21 Kingdom Fungi

Learning objectives After studying this chapter, you should be able to:
- Describe the wide distribution of fungi in the environment.
- Name the features that distinguish fungi from other kingdoms.
- HL Describe the eukaryotic nature of fungi.
- Describe the type of nutrition in fungi and name saprophytic and parasitic forms of fungi.
- Describe yeast under the headings of structure and reproduction.
- Describe *Rhizopus* under the headings of structure and reproduction.
- Describe the economic importance of fungi (beneficial and harmful).
- Describe edible and poisonous fungi with examples of each and methods of distinction.
- Describe procedures for handling microorganisms using aseptic technique and containment and disposal techniques.
- Grow leaf yeast using agar plates and controls.

Introduction

Fungi are a diverse group of heterotrophic living organisms. There are **no** autotrophic fungi. They can be single-celled or multicellular and can be found living in most areas of the biosphere (air, soil and water).

HL All fungi are eukaryotic in nature. This means that all of their cells possess a membrane-bound nucleus and membrane-bound organelles.

Most fungi have haploid nuclei as the main part of their life cycle. Fungi include microscopic fungi, such as yeasts, and large fungi, such as mushrooms.

The study of fungi is called mycology and scientists who study fungi are called mycologists.

Fungi make up their own kingdom of living organisms. The main factors that distinguish them from other kingdoms are:

- Their cell walls are made from a polysaccharide called **chitin** (as opposed to cellulose in plants).
- They are all heterotrophic and they **do not** possess chlorophyll.

You would be forgiven for thinking that mushrooms (the most visible and familiar types of fungi) belonged to the plant kingdom or that they have similar characteristics to plants. However, surprisingly, genetic studies have revealed that fungi are more closely related to animals than to plants!

Fungi, like bacteria, play critical roles in our everyday lives. They carry out important roles in the carbon and nitrogen cycles as they are decomposers – breaking down dead organic matter and releasing nutrients back into the environment.

Fig 21.1 Artist's fungi, *Ganoderma applanatum*, found mostly in North America living on tree trunks **(A)**; *Candida*, a common nail fungus **(B)**; the werewere-kokako, a blue mushroom found in New Zealand **(C)**.

Fungi have been used as a food source for a long time. Mushrooms and truffles can be eaten by humans, and yeasts have been used for fermentation and baking bread for thousands of years. Mushrooms are an excellent source of vitamin D. The vitamin D content of mushrooms can be increased greatly by exposing them to sunlight!

Fungi are also used to produce antibiotics to treat serious bacterial infections and have saved millions of lives since Alexander Fleming accidentally discovered penicillin in 1928.

Nutrition

> **Nutrition** is the way in which an organism obtains and uses its food.

All fungi are **heterotrophic,** meaning that they obtain their nutrients from other organisms. There are two types of heterotrophic nutrition in fungi: **saprophytic** and **parasitic**.

- **Saprophytic fungi:** Saprophytic fungi obtain their food from dead organic matter. They decompose the dead organism, releasing the nutrients into the soil; for example, fungi of decay.
- **Parasitic fungi:** Parasitic fungi obtain their nutrients from a living host; for example, Athlete's foot. The living host is usually harmed.

Yeast (Saccharomyces cerevisiae)

Yeast is best known for its use in brewing beer and in baking bread.

Structure of yeast

Yeast is a single-celled (unicellular) fungus. Like all fungi, yeast has cell walls made from chitin. They have a granular cytoplasm containing vacuoles.

Reproduction of yeast

Yeast reproduces asexually by mitosis in a process more commonly known as **'budding'**.

- A small extension of the cell occurs during budding. The 'bud' fills with cytoplasm.
- The nucleus divides by mitosis and eventually moves into the bud.
- The new cell formed can remain attached to the parent cell and form a string of yeast cells that remain attached to each other, eventually forming a colony. Alternatively, they can break away from the parent cell giving single-celled yeast (Fig 21.2).

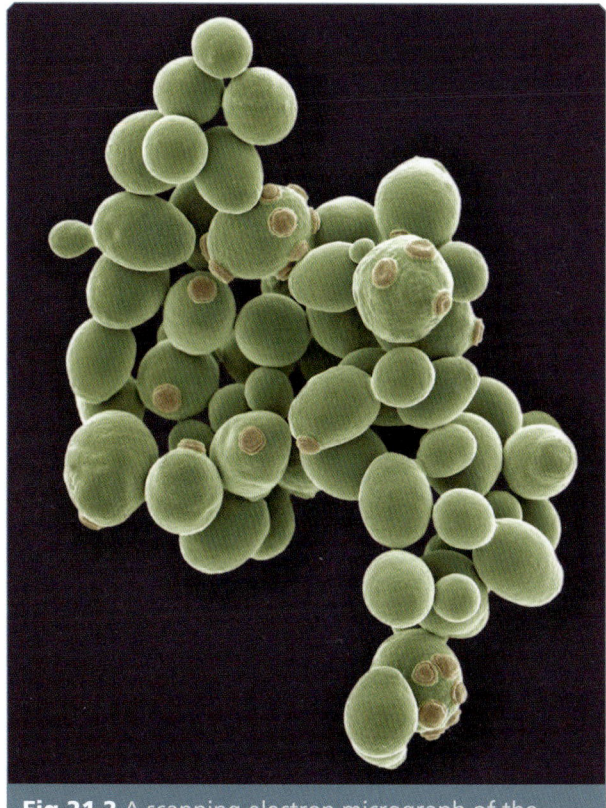

Fig 21.2 A scanning electron micrograph of the structure of yeast.

The particular yeast species, *Saccharomyces cerevisiae,* is responsible for metabolising carbohydrate into alcohol and carbon dioxide. Yeast has been used for thousands of years in the process of baking bread and brewing alcohol.

Rhizopus (common bread mould)

Rhizopus (common bread mould) is a **saprophytic** fungus feeding off dead organic matter, such as bread.

Structure of *Rhizopus*

Rhizopus, as with most fungi, consists of microscopic, tubular, thread-like structures called **hyphae**.

- The hyphae spread out in all directions during growth.
- Some hyphae grow upwards, and are called **sporangiophores.**
- At the end of each sporangiophore is a structure called the **sporangium,** supported by the **apophysis** and **columella.** The sporangium holds the **spores** that are eventually released as part of **asexual reproduction.**
- Hyphae that grow horizontally along their substrate are called **stolons.**
- Hyphae that grow down into a substrate are called **rhizoids.** Rhizoids have three main functions:
    1 They anchor the fungus to its substrate.
    2 They release digestive enzymes into the substrate.
    3 They absorb nutrients from the substrate as it is digested.

All the hyphae together are called a **mycelium.** All the cells in a mycelium are haploid.

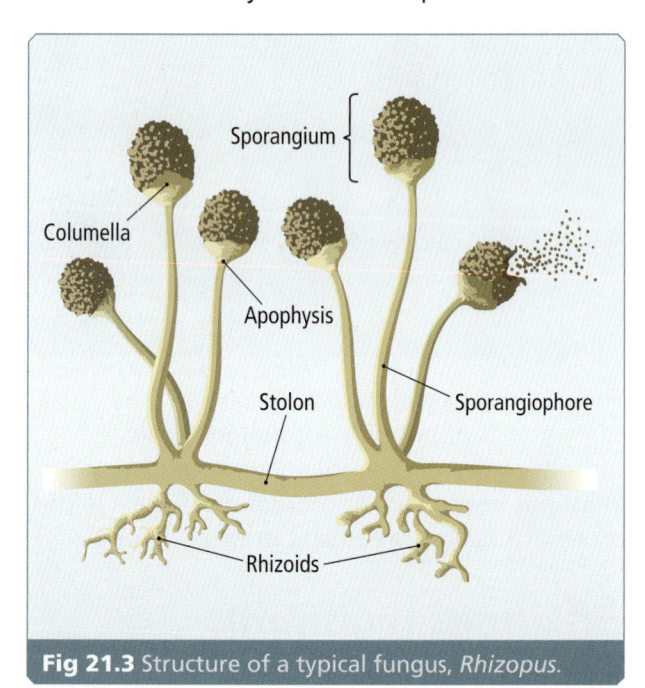

Fig 21.3 Structure of a typical fungus, *Rhizopus*.

Reproduction of *Rhizopus*

Rhizopus can reproduce asexually and sexually.

Asexual reproduction

Asexual reproduction is by means of **sporulation** – the production of spores. This process occurs within the sporangium by mitosis. The spores form tough, resistant walls that enable them to survive for a period of time after being released.

The spores are released when the sporangium is fully mature. They travel on air currents and eventually settle on new substrates and germinate into a new fungus.

Sexual reproduction

Sexual reproduction occurs when nutrients are running out. It is a method of survival. Two compatible hyphae grow close together. The two hyphae must be of opposite strains: a **plus (+)** strain and a **minus (−)** strain.

Swellings, called **progametangia,** develop opposite each other on opposing hyphae. They are held in place by suspensors (*see* Fig 21.5) Eventually the progametangia fuse to form a **gametangium,** where many haploid cells enter from both hyphae. They meet and fuse to form **diploid cells.**

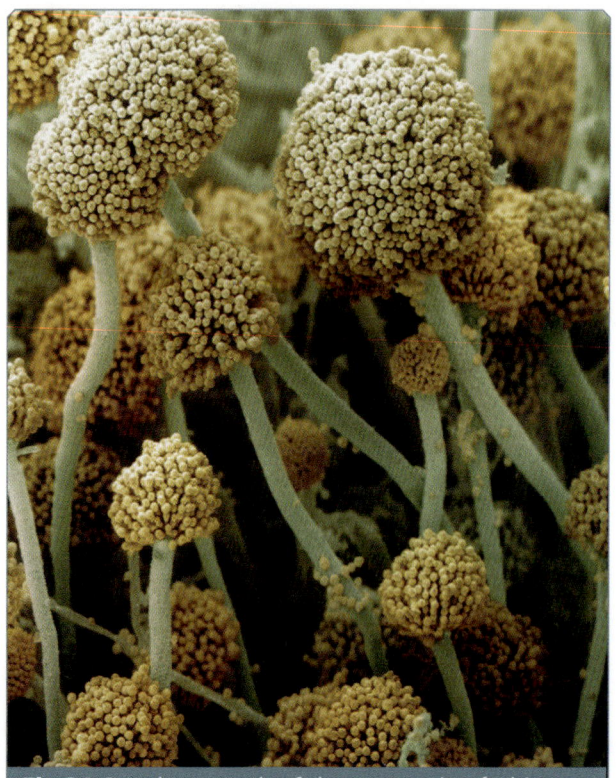

Fig 21.4 A photograph of the sporangia of *Rhizopus*.

The gametangium forms a tough wall around itself and becomes a **zygospore.**

The zygospore is resistant to harsh conditions. When suitable conditions arise, the zygospore **germinates by meiosis,** to form a new mycelium (Fig 21.5).

Kingdom Fungi **Chapter 21**

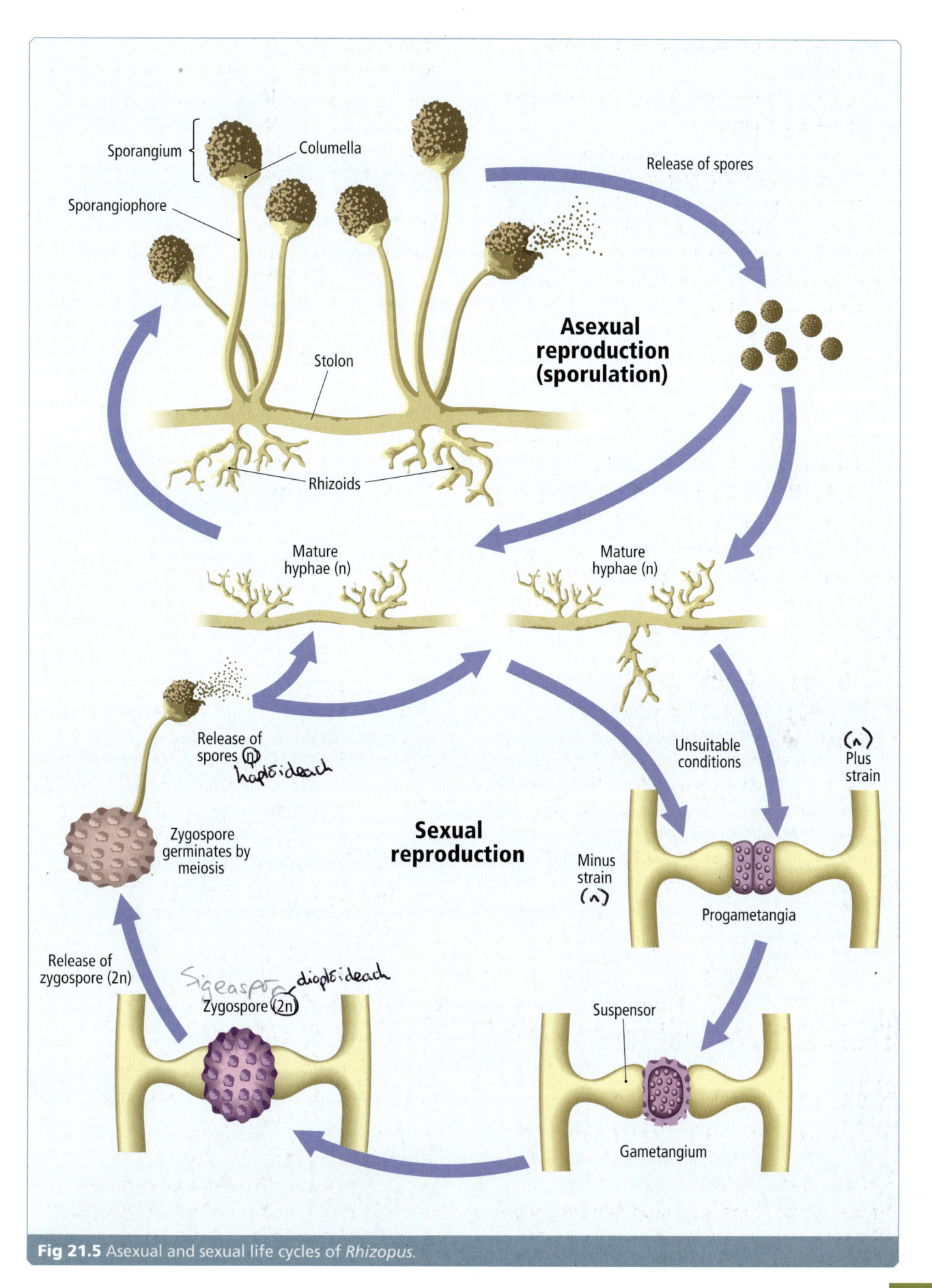

Fig 21.5 Asexual and sexual life cycles of *Rhizopus*.

233

Unit 3 The Organism

Practical activity: to investigate the growth of leaf yeast using agar plates and controls

Yeasts can be found almost everywhere – in the air, soil and water. They can also be found in symbiotic relationships with other organisms.

One such symbiotic relationship is leaf yeast living on the underside of leaves, especially older leaves.

In this laboratory activity, we will attempt to grow leaf yeast from leaves collected from a local habitat. Ash tree leaves are ideal.

The best time of year to conduct this activity is in September when the leaves are still on the trees and the leaf yeast will be most numerous.

Laboratory procedures when handling microorganisms

When working with any microorganisms care should be taken, as the microorganisms should be considered to be hazardous unless proven otherwise.

Aseptic technique should be followed at all times when handling potentially dangerous microorganisms. This maintains **asepsis**.

Precautions to be taken when handling microorganisms:

- Always wear a lab coat.
- Wash your hands before and after every practical activity involving microorganisms.
- Wear protective latex or nitrile gloves where appropriate.
- Wear safety glasses where appropriate.
- Keep hands away from your face during practical activities.
- Clean the bench thoroughly before and after use and swab with a disinfectant such as 70% ethanol or Milton.
- Clean and sterilise all glassware involved in the experiment before and after use by placing in an autoclave or a pressure cooker at 120 °C for 15 minutes. If using plastic, sterilise the dishes after the experiment by immersing the dishes in a disinfectant solution for 24 hours. The plastic can then be disposed of in normal waste bins.
- Sterilise agar by placing it in an autoclave or pressure cooker for 15 minutes at 120 °C. Make sure you use containers and lids that can withstand the pressure and temperatures used in autoclaves.
- When using Petri dishes and other containers, open very slightly and for the shortest possible time to avoid contamination and maintain asepsis.
- If using forceps or an inoculating loop (circular piece of metal wire), use a flame to sterilise them before and after use.

> **Aseptic technique** (asepsis) is a procedure where contact with, or contamination by, microorganisms is avoided.
>
> **Sterile** is a state of being free from microorganisms.

Method

1. Ensure aseptic technique is followed throughout this experiment.
   Make up agar solution by dissolving 1.5 g of nutrient agar in 100 ml of distilled water.
2. Sterilise the agar by boiling it.
3. Carefully pour just enough agar to cover the bottom surfaces of three sterile Petri dishes. Two of these dishes will act as controls.
4. Allow the agar to set solid – which takes between 10 and 15 minutes.
5. Obtain old leaves from a local park or your garden.

> **NOTE:** When taking the leaves, wear gloves so as not to contaminate the leaf with any fungi that might be present on your skin. Place the leaves in a plastic bag until you get back to the lab.

6 Disinfect one of your leaves by swabbing/rubbing it thoroughly with a disinfectant solution, such as Milton or an alcohol-based solution.

7 Using some petroleum jelly, attach the disinfected leaf (**control**) inside the lid of the Petri dish with the underside of the leaf facing towards the agar (Fig 21.7). The leaf **should not** touch the agar in case there are any bacteria or other fungi surviving on the leaf. Bacteria will be transferred very easily to the agar if the leaf is touching it.

8 The other leaf is placed in the lid of the other Petri dish **without disinfecting it.** Once again, ensure that no part of the leaf is touching the agar as this will cause other organisms (such as bacteria) to grow very quickly on the agar and compete with the leaf yeast.

NOTE: When placing the leaves, open the dishes for as little time as possible to avoid outside contaminants – remember the agar is sterile.

9 Leave the third agar dish without a leaf – this is also a control, acting as a comparison to the other two.

10 Seal the dishes with parafilm – this ensures the dishes are not accidently opened when moving them.

11 Place the dishes upside-down in an incubator set at 25 °C. Leaving the dishes upside-down ensures that no condensation will form in the lid of the dishes.

12 Observe the dishes daily to investigate if growth of leaf yeast has occurred.

Results
- If leaf yeast has grown on the agar, it will appear as one or more small, round pink colonies (Fig 21.6).
- The controls should not have any colonies growing.

Conclusion
What did we learn from this practical activity?
- Leaf yeast grows on the underside of older leaves.
- Leaf yeast can be grown on agar in the laboratory and forms small, round pink colonies.

Fig 21.6 Pink colonies of leaf yeast growing on agar.

Fig 21.7 Petri dish with leaf in position above the agar.

Practical activity questions

1 In the practical activity to grow leaf yeast, what growth medium did you use?

2 Explain the importance of sterilising the growth medium before putting the leaves into the Petri dishes.

3 Why do you think it is better to use older leaves for this practical activity?

4 Explain the importance of a control in this practical activity.

5 Explain how you set up the controls for this practical activity.

6 Name **one** safety procedure you carried out in the course of completing this practical activity.

7 Explain why it was necessary to have the underside of the leaf facing the growth medium.

8 Explain why it is necessary to leave the dishes upside-down in the incubator.

9 What were your results for this practical activity?

10 Explain how you carefully disposed of the Petri dishes at the end of the experiment.

Economic importance of fungi

Beneficial effects of fungi

- Yeast is used to brew alcoholic beverages and to bake bread.
- Many different fungi are used to produce antibiotics, such as penicillin and cephalosporin, to treat bacterial infections.
- Some mushrooms are edible. For example, button mushrooms (Fig 21.8) and truffles.
- Mould is used in the production of certain cheeses, such as blue cheese and Roquefort.

Fig 21.8 Button mushrooms – a type of edible fungus.

Harmful effects of fungi

- Some fungi are parasites. For example, Athlete's foot is a fungal infection of the skin between the toes and ringworm is a fungal infection of the skin.
- Some are highly poisonous. For example, the death cap (*Amanita phalloides*) and the destroying angel (*Amanita bisporigera*). These mushrooms cause death approximately four days after being eaten. They contain a toxin that causes liver failure. Good mushroom guidebooks should be consulted if looking for edible mushrooms and, if there is any doubt of the species it belongs to, the mushroom should not be eaten.
- Some fungi are responsible for spoiling food. For example, *Rhizopus* causes bread mould.

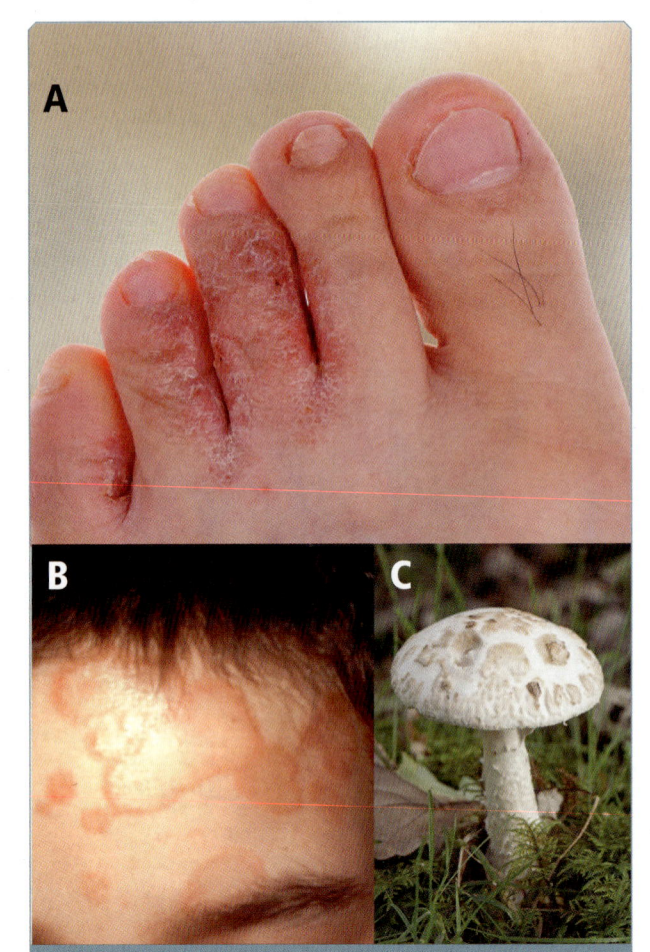

Fig 21.9 Athlete's foot, a fungal infection of the soft skin between the toes **(A)**; ringworm, a fungal infection of the skin **(B)**; the death cap fungus (*Amanita phalloides*) **(C)**.

Chapter 21 Questions

HL 1 (a) Explain why fungi are considered to be 'eukaryotic'?

(b) Give **two** distinguishing features between fungi and plants.

2 There is only **one** main way in which fungi obtain their food. Copy and complete the following table:

Type of nutrition	Subtypes	Examples of fungi

3. (a) What is the other name for common bread mould?
   (b) What are *hyphae*?
   (c) Name the **three** types of hyphae in the common bread mould.
   (d) Give **one** function of **each** of the three types of hyphae.
   (e) What is a collection of hyphae called?
   (f) Draw the structure of common bread mould and label the following structures: *sporangium; sporangiophore; stolon; rhizoids; apophysis; columella*.
   (g) Describe how the common bread mould reproduces asexually.
   (h) Describe the sequence of events that occur when the common bread mould undergoes sexual reproduction.
4. (a) Give the other name for yeast.
   (b) Give **two** everyday uses for yeast.
   (c) Explain what is meant by **'budding'** in relation to yeasts.
5. (a) Name **two** beneficial fungi and how they are beneficial.
   (b) Name **two** harmful fungi and the way in which they are harmful.

Chapter 21 Sample examination questions

1. The diagram shows a yeast cell, which is undergoing asexual reproduction.

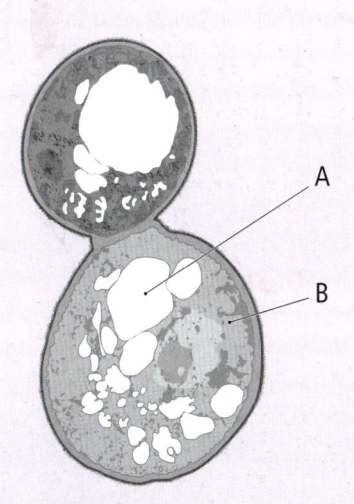

   (a) Name **A** and **B**.
   (b) What type of asexual reproduction is shown in the diagram?
   (c) Which type of division, mitosis or meiosis, is involved in this form of reproduction?
   (d) If yeast cells are kept under anaerobic conditions, alcohol (ethanol) and another substance are produced.
      (i) What are anaerobic conditions?
      (ii) Name the other substance produced.

   Section A, Question 6 Ordinary Level 2006

HL 2. The diagram below shows part of the mycelium of the fungus *Rhizopus*.

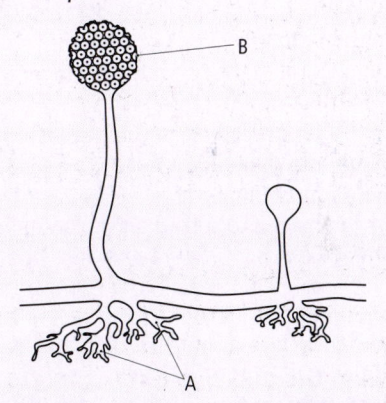

   (i) Give the name **and** state a function of the part labelled A.
   (ii) Name part B **and** explain why the reproduction associated with it is asexual.
   (iii) The nutrition of *Rhizopus* is described as being *saprophytic*.
      1. What does the term *saprophytic* mean?
      2. Explain the importance of saprophytic nutrition in the overall scheme of nature.
   (iv) Saprophytic nutrition is a form of *heterotrophic* nutrition. What does the term *heterotrophic* mean?
   (v) Name another form of nutrition employed by some fungi.
   (vi) Give **two** examples of harmful members of the kingdom fungi.

   Section C, Question 15 (c) Higher Level 2011

Unit 3 — The Organism

Chapter 21 Mind map

All fungi are eukaryotic: all of their cells possess a membrane-bound nucleus and membrane-bound organelles. **HL**

Fungi are eukaryotic.

- Fungi are heterotrophs. There are no autotrophic fungi.
- Fungi have cell walls made from chitin.

- Fungi are either saprophytic or parasitic.
- Saprophytic fungi are those that feed off dead organic matter (e.g. mushrooms and moulds).
- Parasitic fungi are those that feed off a living host (e.g. Athlete's foot and ringworm).

Rhizopus (common bread mould)
- *Rhizopus* is a multicellular, saprophytic fungus that causes food to spoil – especially bread.
- *Rhizopus* consists of thin, tubular, thread-like structures called hyphae.
- There are three types of hyphae: sporangiophores, stolons and rhizoids.
- Sporangiophores grow vertically upwards and produce sporangia at their tips.
- Sporangia are structures that produce and hold the spores for asexual reproduction.
- Stolons are horizontally-growing hyphae, which enable the fungus to spread and colonise new substrates.
- Rhizoids grow down deep into the substrate, anchoring the fungus to the substrate, releasing enzymes into the substrate for digestion and absorb the nutrients.
- All the hyphae together are called the mycelium.

Asexual reproduction
- Asexual reproduction in *Rhizopus* is by means of spores, which are released from the sporangium.

Sexual reproduction
- Two hyphae, of opposite strains (plus and minus), grow close together.
- Swellings occur on each strand opposite one another. These are called progametangia.
- The progametangia join together to form a gametangium.
- Nuclei move into the gametangium and fertilisations occur.
- Diploid nuclei form. The gametangium becomes the zygospore.
- The zygospore is a tough, walled structure capable of surviving harsh conditions.
- The zygospore will germinate when suitable conditions are present.

- Yeast (*Saccharomyces cerevisiae*) is a single-celled fungus.
- Yeast reproduces asexually by means of budding.

Economic importance of fungi
- **Two beneficial fungi:** button mushrooms – edible; yeast – used in brewing and baking.
- Two harmful fungi: death cap – highly poisonous; *Rhizopus* – causes food to spoil.

Practical activity to investigate the growth of leaf yeast using agar plates and controls
- Take two leaves or parts of leaves, sterilise one (control).
- Place both leaves in separate Petri dishes attached to the lid using petroleum jelly.
- Incubate at 25 °C for a few days.
- View Petri dishes for pink colonies.

Kingdom Protista Chapter 22

Learning objectives After studying this chapter, you should be able to:
- Draw and label the structure of an *Amoeba* and describe the functions of the various parts.

Introduction

Protista (also called Protoctista) is a diverse kingdom of living organisms. They comprise mostly single-celled microorganisms but do include multi-cellular organisms, such as seaweeds.

HL All protists are eukaryotic in nature. This means that all of their cells possess a membrane-bound nucleus and membrane-bound organelles.

Protists continue to pose a problem for taxonomists as there is great variation among different members of the kingdom.

Some protists are heterotrophic cells (for example, *Amoeba*; plural: amoebae) that survive by capturing and ingesting prey (Fig 22.1); some are autotrophic cells that photosynthesise (for example, algae); whilst others are parasitic cells (for example, water moulds).

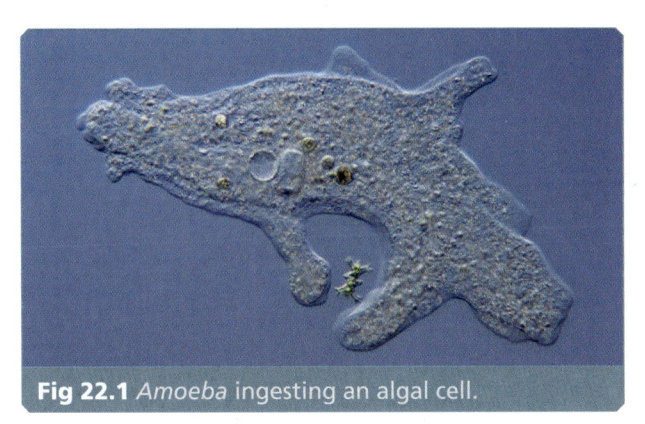

Fig 22.1 *Amoeba* ingesting an algal cell.

As a result of this diversity there may be, in the future, another kingdom or even kingdoms, added to the five kingdom classification of living organisms.

Cryptosporidium is another example of a protist. *Cryptosporidium* infected the water supply of Galway in March 2007, making many people ill with cryptosporidiosis. Symptoms included diarrhoea, stomach cramps and a mild fever. Some infected people had no symptoms.

The council advised the local population to boil the water for drinking, food preparation and brushing teeth.

After five months, the water supply was finally given the all-clear on 20 August 2007.

Officially, 240 people are known to have contracted the disease; however, experts say the true figure could be as high as 5,000. Fortunately, no one died from the outbreak.

Amoeba

All amoebae are single-celled organisms and belong to Kingdom Protista. They can live in freshwater streams, rivers, ponds and lakes as well as in marine habitats (seas and oceans). They feed on other protists, such as algae, but also on bacteria and single-celled fungi.

Cell structure

Amoeba has no definite shape due to the constant flow of the cytoplasm (Fig 22.2). The cytoplasm is composed of a thin, viscous (firm) outer layer called **ectoplasm** and a very fluid, watery **endoplasm**.

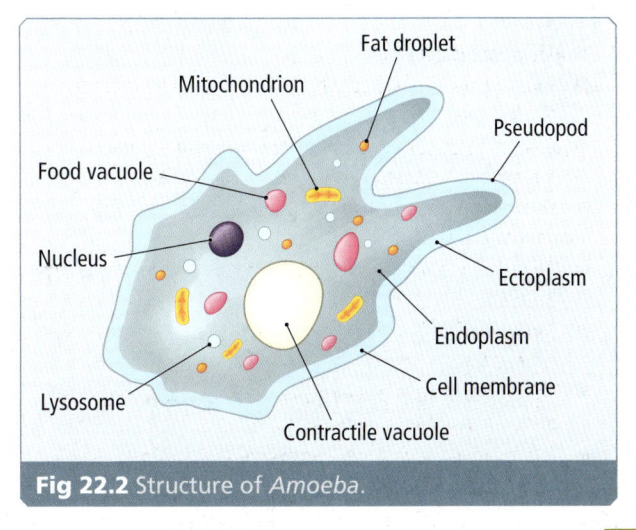

Fig 22.2 Structure of *Amoeba*.

Unit 3   The Organism

Pseudopods (false feet) are extensions of the ectoplasm and endoplasm.

The endoplasm of *Amoeba* also contains a number of sub-cellular structures or cell organelles such as mitochondria, food vacuoles, lysosomes, fat droplets and contractile vacuoles. Amoebae do not possess chloroplasts as they are not photosynthetic.

Functions of cell and sub-cellular structures

- The **cell membrane** is made up of a phospholipid bilayer (*see* Chapter 5) and is responsible for retaining the contents of the cell, controlling what enters and leaves the cell, and allowing diffusion of gases (oxygen and carbon dioxide) and water.
- The **nucleus** controls all the metabolic activities of the cell.
- **Fat droplets** store fat as an energy reserve for use during times when food is not readily available.
- **Food vacuoles** secrete a mixture of acids and digestive enzymes that kill and digest the prey.
- **Pseudopods** enable movement of *Amoeba*, usually in the direction of prey. The more fluid endoplasm flows into the pseudopod as the *Amoeba* moves. *Amoeba* engulfs prey by extending its pseudopods around the prey (Fig 22.1); much in the same way that white blood cells (*see* Chapter 34) engulf bacteria.
- All freshwater amoebae have **contractile vacuoles** for osmoregulation. Water is continually moving into freshwater *Amoeba* by osmosis. This poses a serious threat to the integrity of the *Amoeba*. If the water is not removed, the cell will burst.
  - Contractile vacuoles collect the excess water that builds up in *Amoeba*. They do this by actively transporting the water from the cytoplasm into the contractile vacuole.
  - Eventually the contractile vacuole grows large enough to fuse with the cell membrane and the excess water is released (Fig 22.3).
  - Marine amoebae (present in the sea and oceans) do not possess contractile vacuoles as there is no osmotic gradient present between the inside and outside of the cell. This is due to the high salt concentration of the sea.

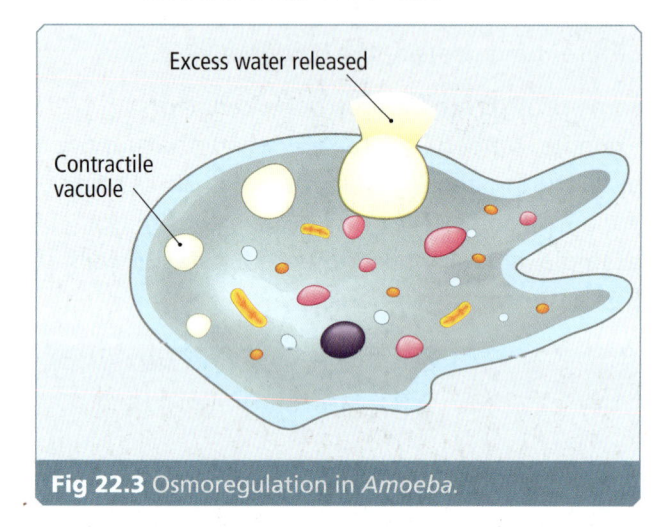

Fig 22.3 Osmoregulation in *Amoeba*.

Chapter 22 Questions

1. (a) To what kingdom does *Amoeba* belong?
   (b) Name **two** habitats where amoebae might be found.
   HL (c) Explain how *Amoeba* is classified as being a eukaryote.
2. (a) Draw a diagram of an *Amoeba* labelling the following structures: *pseudopod; endoplasm; ectoplasm; food vacuole; contractile vacuole; nucleus.*
   (b) Distinguish between *ectoplasm* and *endoplasm*.
   (c) Distinguish between a *food vacuole* and a *contractile vacuole*.
3. (a) Explain, in detail, how *Amoeba* catches and digests its prey.
   (b) Give an example of an organism *Amoeba* might prey on.

4 (a) Define *osmosis*.
   (b) Using your knowledge of osmosis (Chapter 8), explain why marine *amoebae* do not need a contractile vacuole.
   (c) Freshwater amoebae are continuously posed with a problem.
      (i) What is this problem?
      (ii) Explain with the aid of a labelled diagram how *Amoeba* overcomes this problem.
      (iii) If a marine *Amoeba* was placed in fresh water what might happen?

5 (a) Considering what you learned in *Unit 2 The Cell*, how do you think *Amoeba* reproduces?
   (b) What type of reproduction does *Amoeba* undergo?

6 State a similarity between *Amoeba* and a white blood cell.

Chapter 22 Sample examination questions

HL

1 The diagram shows the structure of *Amoeba*.

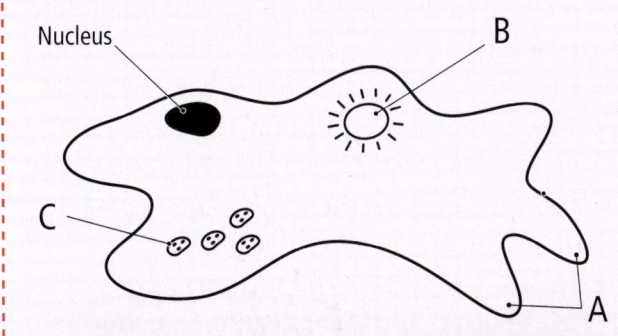

(a) Name the parts labelled **A**, **B** and **C**.
(b) To which kingdom does *Amoeba* belong?
(c) Is the cell of *Amoeba* prokaryotic or eukaryotic?
(d) Give a reason for your answer to part (c)
(e) Give **one** function of A in *Amoeba*.
(f) 1. Give **one** function of B in *Amoeba*.
    2. Suggest **one** reason why B is more active in freshwater amoebae than in marine amoebae.

Section A, Question 3 Higher Level 2010

Chapter 22 Mind map

Amoeba is a member of Kingdom Protista.

- All protists are eukaryotic: all of their cells possess a membrane-bound nucleus and membrane-bound organelles.
- It is single-celled with a complex cytoplasm (firm outer ectoplasm and fluid inner endoplasm).
- It is a water-based organism (can be found in fresh water or sea water).
- It feeds and moves using its pseudopods.
- It is a cell with food vacuoles (for digestion) and contractile vacuoles (for osmoregulation).

Chapter 23 Viruses

Learning objectives After studying this chapter, you should be able to:
- Describe the problem of defining viruses as living or non-living.
- Describe the basic structure and variety of shapes of viruses.
- Describe viral replication.
- Describe two examples of harmful viruses and one example of a beneficial use of a virus.

Introduction

The study of viruses is called **virology.** Viruses are extremely small and are measured in nanometres (nm). One nanometre is one billionth of one metre! Viruses measure 20–300 nm in diameter.

Viruses are not cells. They are composed of protein with a piece of DNA or RNA inside. They are infectious particles, meaning they enter living cells. They are so small they can be seen only using an **electron microscope** (see Chapter 6).

Famous scientists, such as Louis Pasteur and Edward Jenner, could not find the causative agents (viruses) responsible for *rabies* and *smallpox* because these agents were so small. Dmitry Ivanovsky finally discovered viruses in 1892 using a special filter, invented by Charles Chamberland. This filtered out all bacteria but let viruses through.

Viruses are **obligate parasites,** meaning they can only replicate themselves within a host cell.

Are viruses living or non-living?

Scientists are still debating a complete definition of 'life', and until that definition is decided we cannot say for sure whether viruses are living or non-living.

A broad definition is that in order for an organism to be defined as living it must possess the five characteristics of living things which are:

1. Organisation
2. Nutrition
3. Excretion
4. Response
5. Reproduction

It can be argued that viruses demonstrate only two of these characteristics – organisation and response.

- They demonstrate organisation because they consist of an organised protein coat and **either** DNA **or** RNA (never both), and sometimes possess an envelope made of lipids.
- They demonstrate response because they respond to the surface antigens of living cells by attaching to proteins and either injecting their DNA/RNA or entering as a whole virus.
- They **do not** show nutrition as they do not metabolise food for energy production.
- They **do not** show excretion as there are no direct waste products from viruses.
- They **do not** show reproduction because reproduction is the ability to propagate oneself, independently, within the species, either by asexual or sexual reproduction. Viruses use a host's nucleus and protein synthesis machinery to replicate themselves.

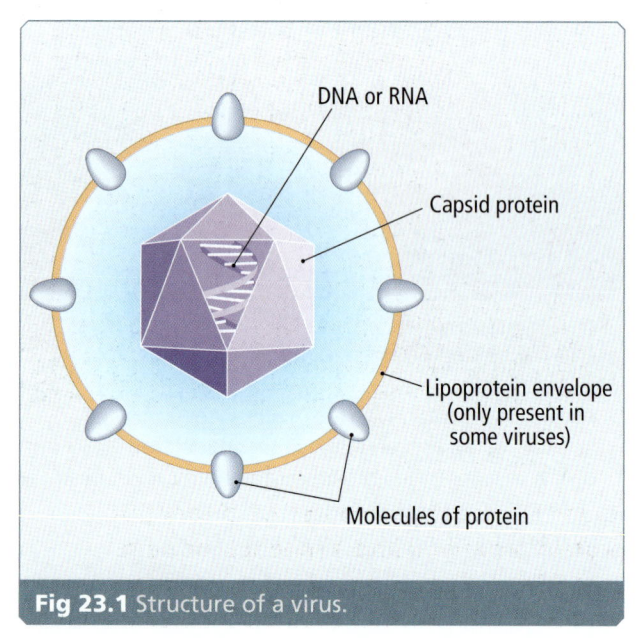

Fig 23.1 Structure of a virus.

Basic structure of a virus

A typical virus consists of a protein coat, called a **capsid,** along with a single piece of **either** DNA **or** RNA. Viruses are the only biological entities not to contain both DNA and RNA.

Some viruses also have an outer layer of lipid (fat) and protein called a lipoprotein envelope, around the virus. This enables it to enter and leave cells much more easily. This is because the cell membrane of living cells is made from lipid and protein (see Chapter 6).

Shapes of viruses

Viruses are classified based on their shape:

1 Rod-shaped virus (tightly packaged helix)

Fig 23.2 shows the tobacco mosaic virus (TMV). This rod-shaped virus consists of proteins organised into a helical shape with DNA located in a groove within the helical structure. Under the electron microscope TBV appear rod-shaped, which is why they are classified as rod-shaped viruses.

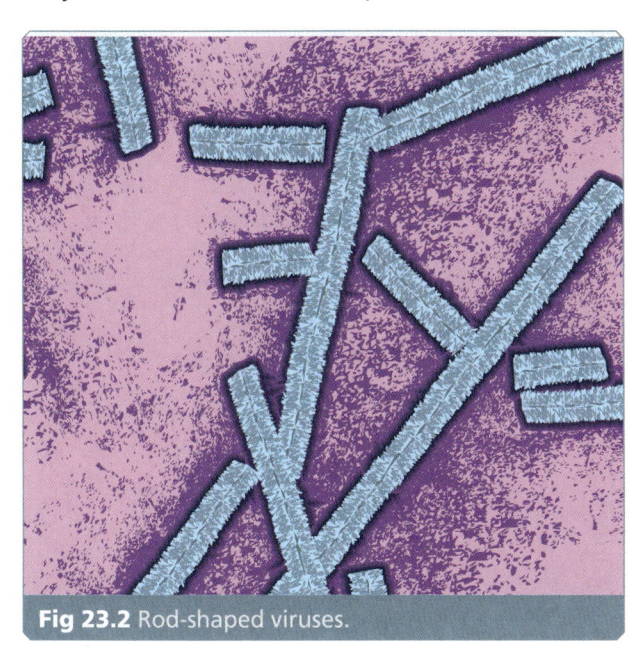

Fig 23.2 Rod-shaped viruses.

2 Round virus

Round viruses are composed of 20 identical proteins arranged into a spherical protein coat. Many round viruses have a lipid envelope surrounding the protein coat. Examples of round viruses are the rhinovirus, which causes cold and flu; and picornavirus, which causes hepatitis A.

Fig 23.3 shows the structure of a round virus.

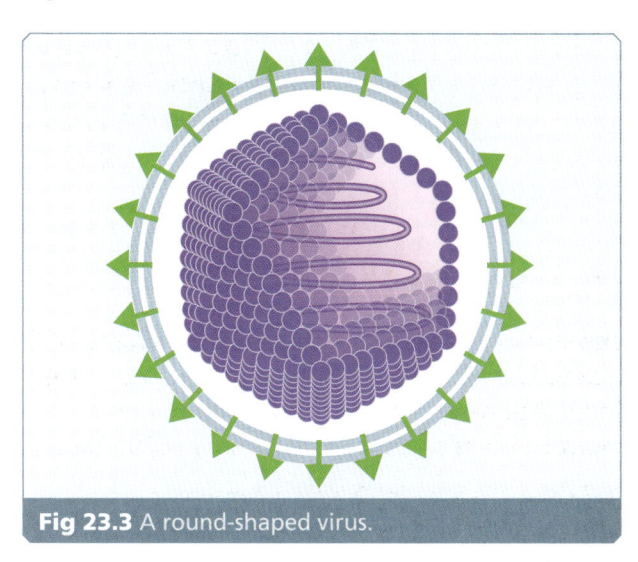

Fig 23.3 A round-shaped virus.

3 Complex virus

Complex viruses are a large group of viruses with a variety of shapes. However, the most common type is the **bacteriophage.** Bacteriophages, as their name suggests, infect bacteria.

Fig 23.4 shows the structure of a bacteriophage.

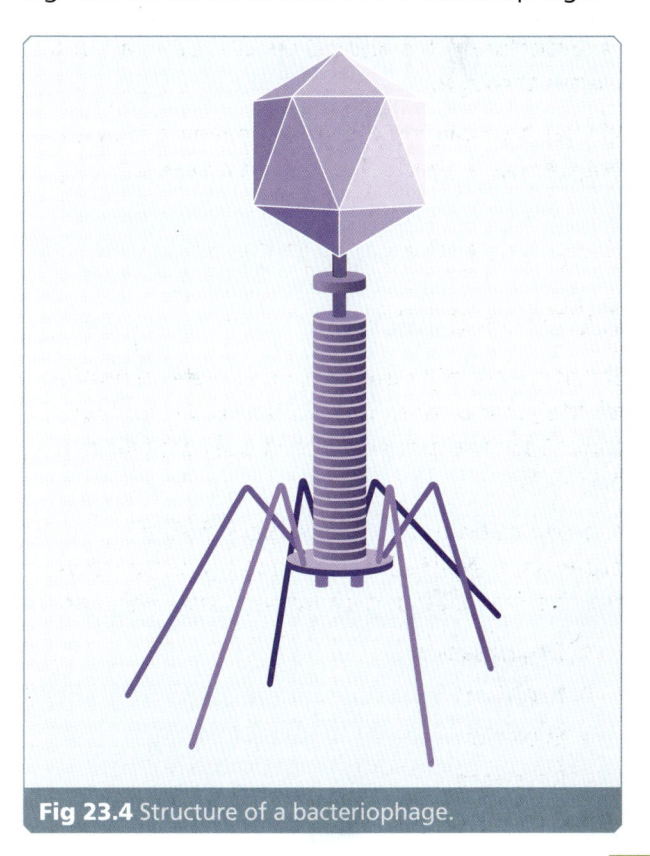

Fig 23.4 Structure of a bacteriophage.

Timthriall Litric
Timthriall Lisogéaneach

Replication of viruses

Viruses are **obligate parasites,** meaning they need to be within a host cell in order to remain viable and to replicate.

Viruses are totally dependent on a host cell. There are a number of stages involved in the process of viral replication. Fig 23.5 shows the sequence of events.

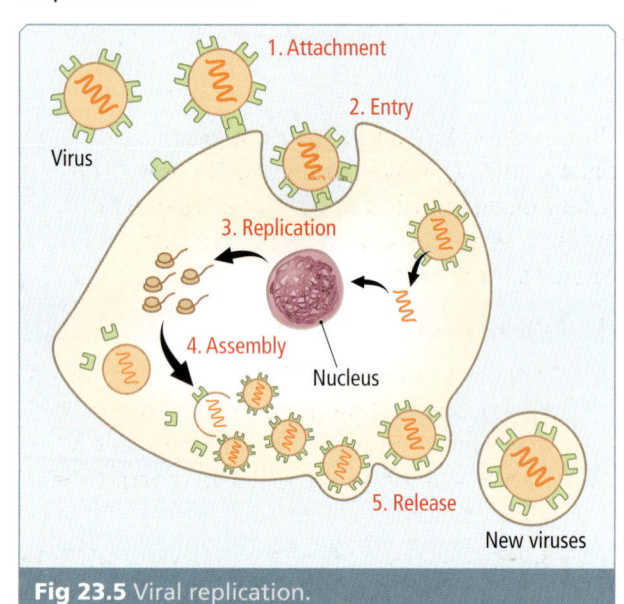

Fig 23.5 Viral replication.

1 **Attachment:** The virus binds to complementary proteins on the surface of a host cell. Viruses cannot attach to any cell they like. The cell has to have the correct proteins on its surface. Even within an organism, a virus might only be able to attach to certain types of cells. For example, the flu virus is capable of infecting only the cells of the nasal cavity and throat.

2 **Entry:** The whole virus may enter the cell or, in the case of complex viruses, inject the DNA **or** RNA into the host cell.

3 **Replication:** The virus or virus DNA/RNA takes over the nucleus of the host cell and its ribosomes. The virus uses the host cell's nucleus and ribosomes to make new viral proteins and viral DNA or RNA.

4 **Assembly:** Thousands of new viruses are pieced together by the host cell.

5 **Release:** New viruses are released from the host cell to go on to infect more cells. They can be released by bursting the host cell open (killing it in the process) or by diffusing out or budding through the cell membrane.

Economic and medical importance of viruses

> **NOTE:** For Leaving Certificate Biology, you need to know two examples of harmful viruses and one beneficial use of viruses.

Humans

Viruses cause many millions of deaths per year. Therefore, there is a moral incentive and also a financial incentive to work to control viral infections.

The World Health Organisation and biotechnology companies are investing a lot of money in the fight against diseases such as AIDS.

Harmful human viruses include:

1 HIV (human immunodeficiency virus), which causes AIDS (acquired immunodeficiency syndrome).
2 Flu virus, which causes colds and flu.

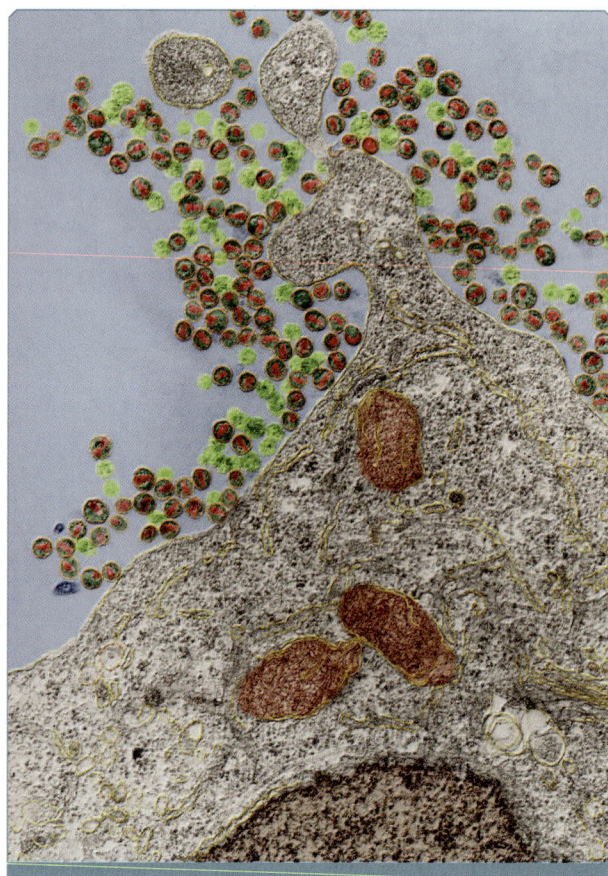

Fig 23.6 Human immunodeficiency viruses (HIV), the causative agent of AIDS, attaching to a white blood cell.

3. Paramyxovirus, which causes measles.
4. Polio virus, which cause poliomyelitis – a condition that can sometimes be fatal or can paralyse the patient's limbs.
5. Hepatovirus, which causes hepatitis – an inflammation of the liver.
6. Mumps virus, which causes mumps – a condition where the salivary glands swell.
7. Rabies virus, which causes rabies in humans. It is contracted when bitten by an infected animal. Rabies is always fatal if the person does not receive treatment before the onset of symptoms.
8. Varicella zoster virus, which causes chicken pox in children and shingles in adults.

Biotechnology and drug companies have used many of these viruses to produce vaccines. Vaccines exist for flu, measles, polio, mumps, chicken pox and shingles. However, only some of these vaccines are widely distributed among the population. Researchers continue to work on a vaccine for HIV. This is a very difficult task, as the HIV virus hides within the cells of the immune system and mutates regularly.

Animals

Viruses also infect animals. This can have an effect on our food supply if animals have to be destroyed as a result of a viral infection. It can also have health consequences if the virus also has the ability to infect humans.

Harmful animal viruses include:

1. Foot and mouth virus: affects livestock. It causes a fever in the animals for about three days, followed by blisters in the mouth and feet. The foot blisters may cause the animal discomfort when walking. The foot and mouth crises of 2001 and 2007 had a big impact on the agriculture industry. Most cases occurred in Britain, but Ireland was affected with one confirmed case in Co. Louth in 2001. Luckily there were no confirmed cases in Ireland in 2007. During a foot-and-mouth outbreak, all animals in an infected area are culled (killed) and movement of livestock is forbidden. This is to prevent further spread of the disease. Foot and mouth can infect humans, but it is not fatal.
2. Swine flu: a viral infection that originated in pigs. It produces flu-like symptoms in pigs. However, in the winter of 2009–2010, swine flu infected humans and a number died as a result of respiratory complications.
3. Rabies: an animal virus that can infect humans. It causes encephalitis (inflammation of the brain) and death soon thereafter. It is widespread in wild canine animals on continental Europe.

Plants

Viruses can infect and damage plants – particularly the leaves of plants. This costs the food industry billions of euros per year, which makes it economically important to carry out research into plant viruses.

Harmful plant viruses include:

1. Tobacco mosaic virus (TMV): causes billions of dollars worth of damage to tobacco plants each year. It leaves a characteristic yellow mottling pattern on the leaves – hence the name 'mosaic'.

Fig 23.7 Mosaic disease of a plant.

2. Tomato mosaic virus: infects the leaves of tomatoes.
3. Lettuce mosaic virus: infects the leaves of lettuces.

Unit 3 — The Organism

Viruses and genetic engineering

Some viruses have been very beneficial in scientific and medical research. Many types of viruses are used as **vectors** to transfer genes to cells (*see* Chapter 18). It is hoped that some of these viruses may be used in gene therapy in the future. For example, it is hoped that viruses will be able to deliver a functioning gene to the correct location in the body for treating diabetes and cystic fibrosis – two genetic diseases where genes have mutated.

Examples of viruses used in genetic engineering are:

1. SV40 virus – used in cancer research.
2. Adeno-associated virus (AAV) – used in gene therapy research to deliver useful genes to tissues that lack a gene or a product of the gene.

Viruses as a potential substitute for antibiotics

Research into bacteriophages (viruses that infect and kill bacteria) is increasing. It is hoped that they can be used as anti-bacterial agents. In the future, bacteriophages may be used for cleaning surgical equipment, sterilising food, and treating bacterial infections in humans and plants.

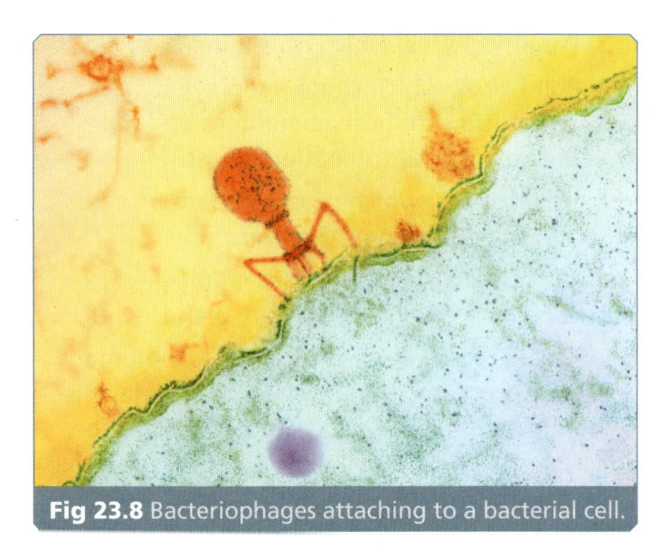

Fig 23.8 Bacteriophages attaching to a bacterial cell.

Viruses and the immune system

Viruses are unaffected by antibiotics. In most viral infections, the body's immune system overcomes the virus by producing antibodies against it. The body is then immune from future infections involving this virus. If the same virus does infect the body again, the person will have no symptoms as antibodies are produced very quickly by the immune system (*see* Chapter 34) and the virus is eliminated. Serious viral infections, such as swine flu, shingles, and AIDS are treated with anti-viral agents such as interferon and azidothymidine (**AZT**). However, the body must still produce antibodies in order to get rid of the virus.

Chapter 23 Questions

1. What is the study of viruses called?
2. What is the approximate size of a virus?
3. Explain why viruses are called *obligate parasites*.
4. Explain the problem in determining whether viruses are living or non-living.
5. Draw and label the typical structure of a virus.
6. Name the **three** basic shapes of viruses and make a sketch of each shape.
7. Viruses replicate, they do not reproduce. Give a detailed account of the process of viral replication.
8. Name **two** viruses that are harmful and state how they are harmful.
9. Name **one** virus that is beneficial and state how it is beneficial.
10. Explain why antibiotics are not used to treat colds and flu.
11. Name **two** substances that are used to treat serious viral infections, such as AIDS and swine flu.

Chapter 23 Sample examination questions

1. (i) Explain why it is difficult to classify viruses as living organisms.
   (ii) Give the **two** main chemical components of a virus.
   (iii) Briefly describe how viruses replicate.
   (iv) Give **one** way in which viruses are beneficial and **one** way in which they are harmful.

   Section C, Question 12 (c) Ordinary Level 2009

HL 2. (i) Comment on the difficulty of defining viruses as living organisms.
   (ii) What are the **two** main biochemical components of a virus particle?
   (iii) Name **two** diseases caused by viruses.
   (iv) Give an example of a beneficial application of a virus.
   (v) What is an antibiotic?
   (vi) Antibiotics should not be prescribed for a person suffering from a viral infection. Suggest a reason for this.

   Section C, Question 14 (b) Higher Level 2007

Chapter 23 Mind map

Viruses are extremely small, non-cellular, infectious particles.

- The study of viruses is called virology.
- Viruses are obligate parasites, meaning that they need a host cell in order to replicate and remain viable.
- There is a problem in describing viruses as either living or non-living as they do not possess all the five characteristics of living things.
- Viruses are composed of a protein coat (capsid) and a piece of genetic material (DNA or RNA, but **not** both).
- Some viruses also have an envelope made from lipid.
- Three common viral shapes are round, rod and complex.

Replication of viruses
- **Attachment:** virus binds to receptors on the surface of a cell.
- **Entry:** virus either injects its DNA/RNA or the whole virus enters.
- **Replication:** virus takes over the cell's nucleus and uses it to produce copies of itself.
- **Assembly:** viruses use the cell's machinery to make new viruses.
- **Release:** new viruses are released by the cell bursting open or by budding from the cell.

Economic and medical importance of viruses
- **Harmful viruses:** HIV (human immunodeficiency virus) causes AIDS (acquired immunodeficiency syndrome); influenza virus causes colds and flu.
- **Beneficial viruses:** adeno-associated virus (AAV) is used in genetic engineering research.

Chapter 24 Kingdom Plantae

Learning objectives After studying this chapter, you should be able to:
- Identify the root, stem, leaf, flower, seed and vascular structures and describe their functions.
- Define the term *meristem* and describe its location in the root and shoot.
- Locate dermal, ground and vascular tissues in longitudinal and transverse sections of root and stem.
- Describe the structure and functions of xylem and phloem.
- Distinguish between dicotyledons and monocotyledons in terms of type of stem, arrangement of flower parts, arrangement of vascular bundles, and seed leaf numbers.
- Prepare and examine microscopically the transverse section of a dicotyledonous stem.

Introduction

Plants are multicellular, autotrophic organisms capable of producing their own food via photosynthesis (see Chapter 11).

Plants are an incredibly diverse kingdom of organisms. They consist of organisms as diverse as mosses, ferns, conifers and flowering plants.

This chapter is about flowering plants. This group of plants includes all grasses, small plants, shrubs, bushes and most trees. They are all flower, seed, and fruit-producing plants. Flowering plants, also called **angiosperms,** are the most diverse and numerous of all divisions of the plant kingdom.

Flowering plants can be divided into two general but distinct groups:

1. Monocotyledonous plants (monocotyledons)
2. Dicotyledonous plants (dicotyledons)

The '-cotyledonous' part of the above terms comes from the word 'cotyledon'.

> A **cotyledon** is an embryonic seed leaf.

The cotyledon is used as a direct food source by some young plants and others use it to produce food in photosynthesis. Once true leaves start to grow and photosynthesise the cotyledon(s) is/are no longer needed.

- Monocotyledonous (*monocot* for short) plants have one cotyledon in their seeds.
- Dicotyledonous (*dicot* for short) plants have two cotyledons in their seeds.

There are other differences between monocot and dicot plants, which we will look at throughout the chapter.

Types of tissue in flowering plants

Plant tissue is generally divided into three broad categories:

1. **Dermal (or epidermal) tissue:** This is the outer covering of the plant. It protects the plant. In the roots, the dermal tissue is specialised to absorb water and minerals from the soil. In the leaves, it is specialised to secrete a waxy cuticle that prevents excess water loss.

2. **Ground tissue:** This is the most common tissue and makes up the bulk of a plant. Its functions depend on where it is located within the plant. Functions include:
   - Support
   - Photosynthesis
   - Storage of water and food

3. **Vascular tissue:** There are two types:
   - **Xylem tissue:** This functions in transporting water and dissolved minerals up to the aerial parts of the plant.
   - **Phloem tissue:** This functions in transporting food up and down the plant – or to wherever it is needed.

All three categories of tissue are to be found throughout the entire plant.

> **NOTE:** Meristematic tissue (meristem) develops into each of the three tissue types in plants.

> ❗ The **meristem** is composed of unspecialised cells that are continuously dividing by mitosis.

Meristematic tissue is found in the shoot and root tips. It is also found in all buds (growth points of the plant). A more detailed account of their locations is given in the sections below.

Structure of flowering plants

We learned in Chapter 2 that organisation is a characteristic of life. We have seen above that plant cells are organised into tissues: dermal, ground and vascular. These tissues are organised into organs, which are in turn organised into systems. All flowering plants consist of two main systems: a **shoot system** and a **root system.** The shoot system is always above ground and consists of the following plant organs: stem, branches, petioles, leaves, buds, flowers, seeds and fruits. The root system consists of many roots (primary and secondary or lateral roots) branching in many different directions in search of minerals and water.

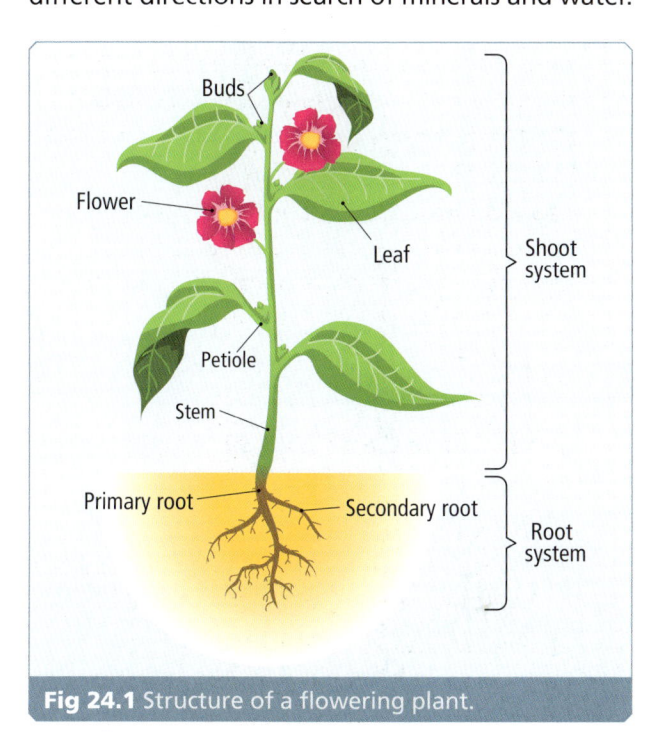

Fig 24.1 Structure of a flowering plant.

Shoot system

The shoot systems of flowering plants vary in size depending on the species – ranging from a few millimetres high to over 100 m high! The shoot has many functions in the life cycle of a flowering plant. Its overall functions include:

1. Photosynthesis
2. Reproduction (both sexual and asexual)
3. Storage of food
4. Support
5. Gas exchange
6. Transport

Stem

The stem of plants can have a variety of functions. The main function is in support and transport. The stem holds up the aerial parts to enable photosynthesis and sexual reproduction to occur. The stem is also responsible for growth. It continuously produces new tissue, increasing in size. It also allows for transport of materials up and down the plant.

Stems, if green in colour, can take part in photosynthesis. In certain plants such as asparagus and potatoes, stems can also store food. Stems of monocots are usually herbaceous, meaning they are green in colour and capable of photosynthesis. Stems of dicots are usually woody, meaning they have a thick bark that is not capable of photosynthesising.

Stem structure

The stem is divided into different regions called **nodes** and **internodes.**

- Nodes are the points on the stem where new branches and leaves develop.
- Internodes are the regions between nodes where no branching occurs (Fig 24.2).
- The stem also has lenticels along its entire length. Lenticels function in gas exchange.

> ❗ **Lenticels** are small pores on a stem that function in gas exchange.

Locations of plant tissues in the stem

Internal stem structure depends on whether the plant is a monocot or dicot. In all plants, the vascular tissues are arranged in bundles.

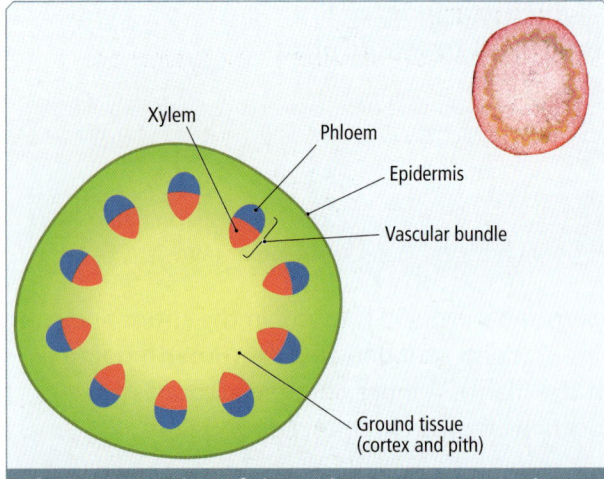

Fig 24.2 Locations of nodes and internodes in a plant.

Fig 24.4 Location of tissues in a transverse section of a dicot stem. Xylem tissue is on the inside of each vascular bundle.

Fig 24.5 shows the locations of the three plant tissues in a longitudinal section of a stem.

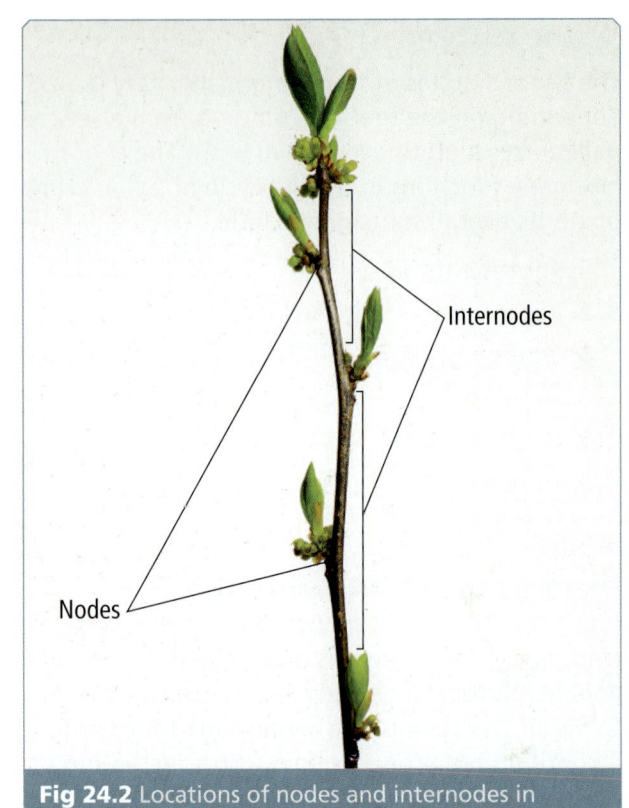

- In monocots, the vascular bundles are arranged at random (scattered) throughout the stem (Fig 24.3).
- In dicots, the bundles are arranged in a circle (Fig 24.4).

The tissue surrounding the vascular bundles is ground tissue. This type of tissue makes up the vast majority of a plant. In the centre of the stem, the ground tissue is called the **pith.** The outer region of ground tissue within the stem is called the **cortex.**

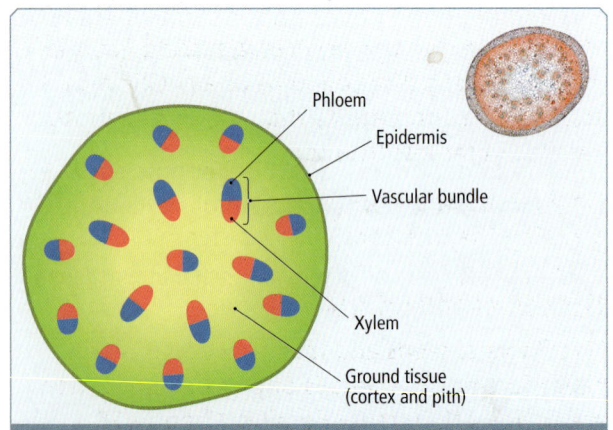

Fig 24.3 Location of tissues in a transverse section of a monocot stem. The xylem is on the inside of each vascular bundle.

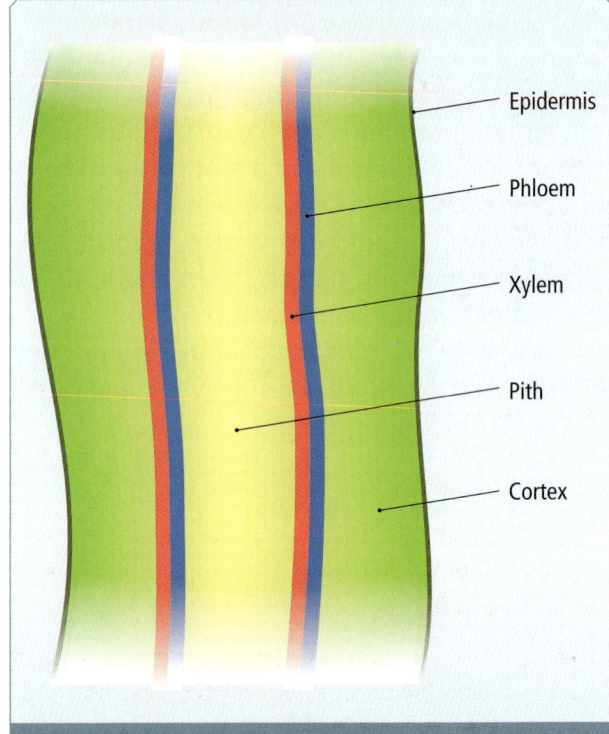

Fig 24.5 Location of vascular tissues in a transverse section of a dicot stem.

Leaf

The leaf is an organ specialised to make food. It contains **chlorophyll** (green pigment) that captures the energy in sunlight to make food in the process of photosynthesis (*see* Chapter 11).

It also functions in **transpiration**, the loss of water from the leaf.

Leaf structure

Fig 24.6 shows the structure of a typical broad-bladed leaf.

Fig 24.6 Basic external structure of a leaf.

Fig 24.7 Leaf venation: reticulate (**A**) versus parallel (**B**).

Leaves are thin structures with a large surface area. This enables them to carry out photosynthesis and transpiration very efficiently.

The edge of the leaf is called the **leaf blade** (or **lamina**). The leaf is attached to the stem or branches by a **leaf stalk** (or **petiole**). The leaf also has veins running through it, which are the vessels through which water and minerals travel. The veins are composed of the vascular tissues, xylem and phloem.

Fig 24.8 shows the positions of xylem and phloem in a leaf. Xylem is always on the top side of the leaf with phloem below.

There are two types of venation in plants: **parallel** and **reticulate (net)** venation (Fig 24.7A and B).

- Nearly all monocots (such as grass) have parallel venation. Leaves with parallel venation have veins that run the entire length of the leaf.
- Nearly all dicots have reticulate or net venation. Dicot plants have broad leaves that show net venation. They have a **midrib** and veins that branch out from it (Fig 24.6).

The internal area of the leaf has many air spaces to allow gas exchange and evaporation of water **(transpiration** – see Chapter 25).

On the underside of the leaf are thousands of tiny apertures (small openings) called **stomata** (singular: stoma). They allow gas exchange (see Chapter 25). **Guard cells** control the opening and closing of the stomata. The leaf also acts as an excretory organ for the plant. During daytime, the plant photosynthesises and produces oxygen gas – most of which is not needed. Therefore, oxygen is released (excreted) through the stomata. At night, the plant respires and does not photosynthesise. It produces carbon dioxide as a product of respiration. This is excreted via the stomata.

The leaf also has a waxy cuticle secreted by the epidermal cells. The presence of a cuticle and stomata are adaptations that help the plant to control water loss (transpiration).

Fig 24.8 shows a transverse section of a leaf showing the locations of the various tissues.

Flower, seed and fruit

The flowers, seeds and fruit function in sexual reproduction. The details of plant reproduction are dealt with in more detail in Chapter 28.

In this chapter, we will describe the difference between flowers of monocots and dicots.

Unit 3   The Organism

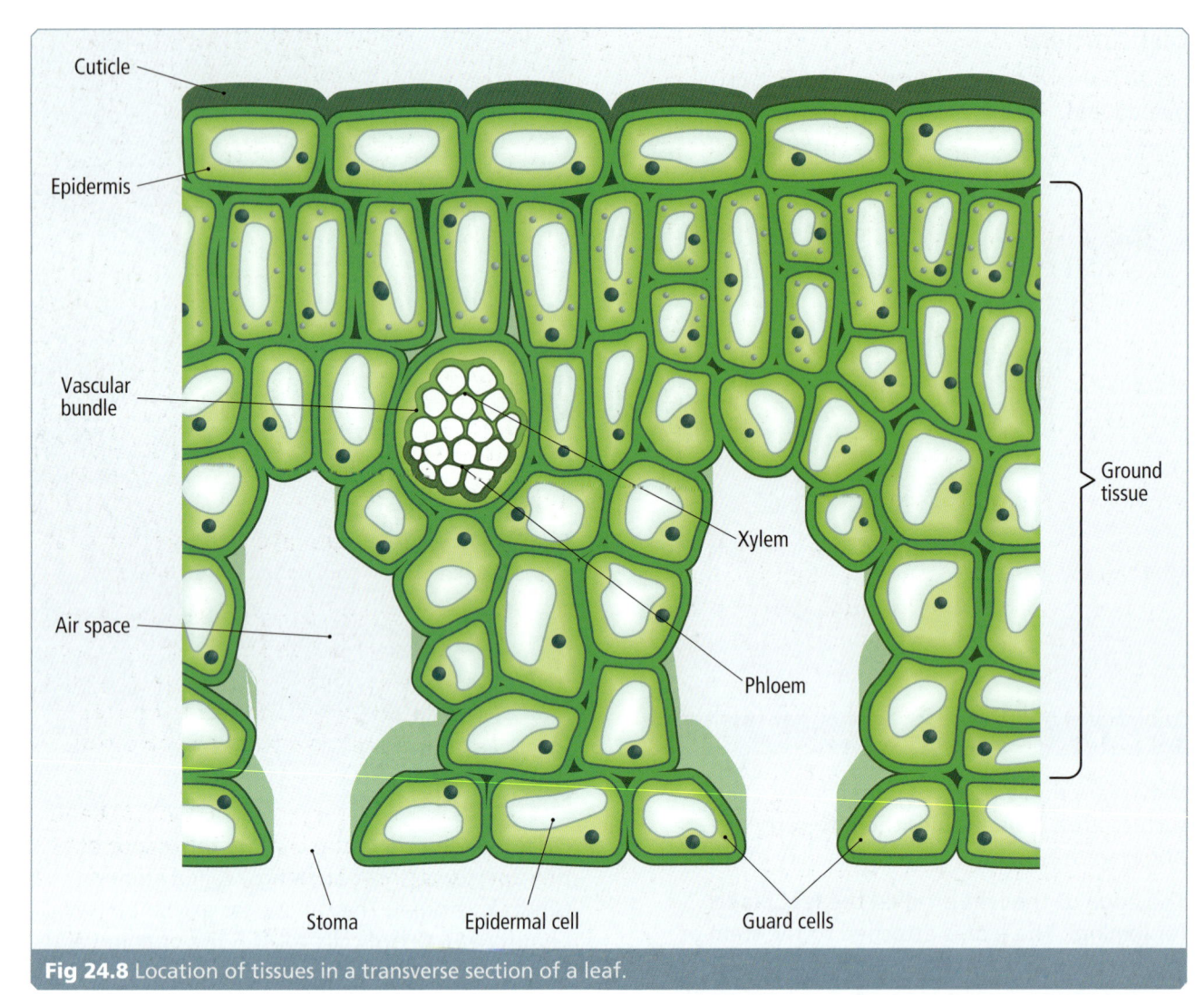

Fig 24.8 Location of tissues in a transverse section of a leaf.

The arrangement of flower parts between monocots and dicots differ.

- Monocots have flower parts arranged in multiples of three. This means that there can be three, six, nine (or any multiple of three) petals, anthers and stigmas in monocot flowers.
- Dicots have flower parts arranged in multiples of four or five, meaning flower parts such as petals, anthers and stigmas can be present in lots of four, eight, 12 and so on; or, if in multiples of five, then five, 10, 15 and so on (see Fig 24.9).

Bud

> A **bud** is an undeveloped shoot.

Buds can develop into a new stem, branch, leaf or flower. Buds contain meristematic tissue (meristem).

Fig 24.9 Monocot flower (**A**) versus a dicot flower (**B**).

Fig 24.10 Location of axillary buds.

Fig 24.11 An apical bud.

Fig 24.12 An adventitious bud.

There are three types of bud:

1. **Axillary buds** are present at the **axil** of the leaf (junction between the petiole and stem) and may develop into a new branch, petiole and leaf, or flower. A leaf bud is an example of an axillary bud (Fig 24.10).
2. **Apical buds** are present at the tip of the plant or at the tip of a branch. They can also develop into various plant organs, such as a leaf, flower or new branch. A flower bud is an example of an apical bud (Fig 24.11).
3. **Adventitious buds** can be present anywhere on the plant, including the stem, branch, root or even leaf.

   Pruning a plant stimulates the development of adventitious buds on the stem or branch. They are stimulated to develop when an apical bud has been cut off. Plants are pruned when a horticulturist wants to thicken the plant (make a plant bushier) by stimulating more branch formation.

Root system

The root system is a network of underground branches that have various functions depending on the plant:

1. Anchorage of the plant in the soil.
2. Absorbing water and minerals.
3. Transport of absorbed water and minerals to the shoot system.
4. Storage of food.
5. Support.

NOTE: Roots can also grow above ground. See adventitious roots below.

Types of root systems

Root systems can be grouped into three general categories:

1. **Tap root system:** The young root that first emerged from the seed during germination thickens. Many smaller roots grow from this main root. Examples of plants with a tap root system are the dandelion and carrot plants (Fig 24.13).

   Most dicots have tap roots. Fig 24.13 A and B shows two plants (dandelion and carrot) with a tap root system.

Fig 24.13 Examples of tap root systems: dandelion (**A**); and carrot (**B**).

2. **Fibrous root system:** The young root withers away and roots begin to emerge from the young shoot. Many roots of the same size emerge and extensive branching occurs. Examples of plants with a fibrous root system include grasses, clovers and marigold.

   Most monocots have fibrous roots. Fig 24.14 shows grasses, clovers and marigold with fibrous roots.

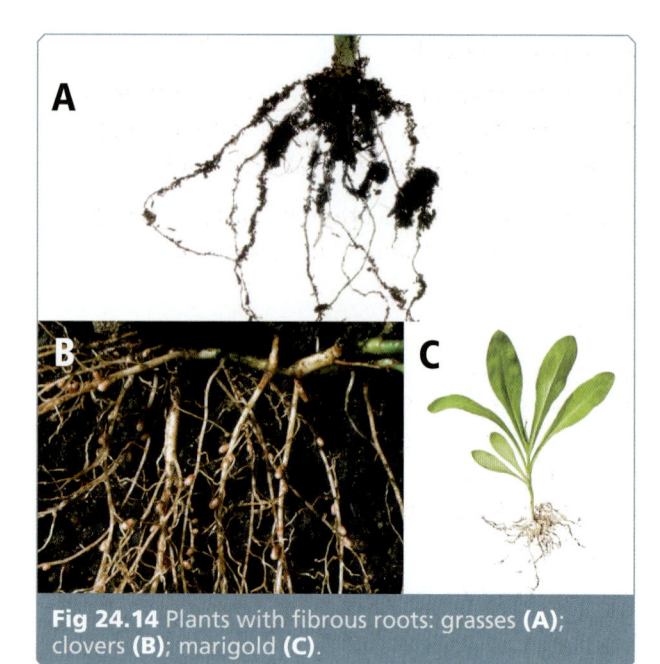

Fig 24.14 Plants with fibrous roots: grasses (A); clovers (B); marigold (C).

3. **Adventitious root system:** Adventitious roots are related to fibrous roots and grow from unusual places on a plant. They can emerge from anywhere on the stem or branches depending on the plant species. Ivy and bayan trees are examples of plants with an adventitious root system.

There are many subtypes of adventitious roots with many functions that you do not need to know for the Leaving Certificate Biology course.

Fig 24.15 Adventitious roots of the ivy plant (which uses the roots to attach to another tree or to a wall) (A); adventitious roots of the bayan tree (B).

Root structure

All roots have the same general structure, consisting of four zones:

1. **Zone of protection:** consists of a *root cap* to protect the meristematic tissue during growth.
2. **Meristematic zone:** consists of meristematic tissue (meristem) undergoing rapid cell division (mitosis).
3. **Zone of elongation:** newly produced cells increase in size.
4. **Zone of differentiation:** cells specialise by becoming ground tissue cells, epidermal cells and xylem and phloem.

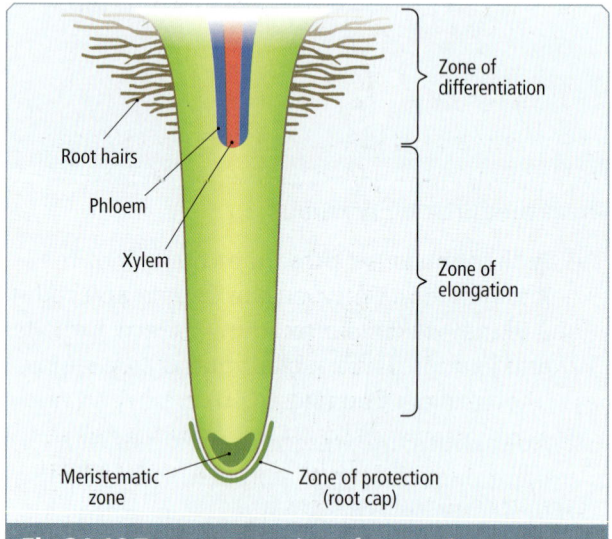

Fig 24.16 Transverse section of a root tip.

The mature root has all three types of tissue arranged as shown in Fig 24.17.

Notice how the xylem and phloem are arranged differently to their arrangement in the stem.

An easy way to remember the structure of vascular tissue in the root is that the xylem is always the 'X' shape in the root.

Root hairs are extensions of the epidermis and act to increase surface area for absorption of water and minerals.

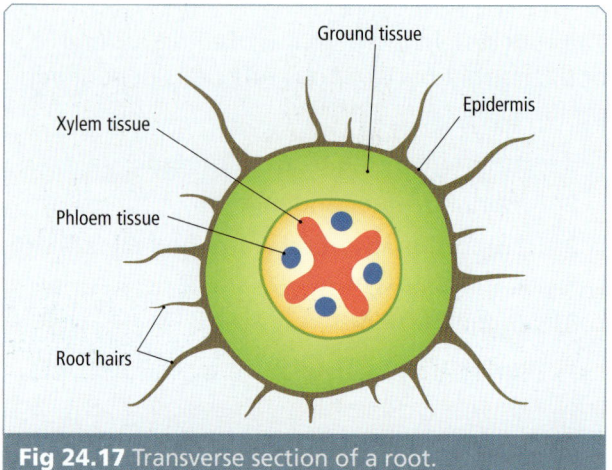

Fig 24.17 Transverse section of a root.

Vascular tissue

Xylem

Xylem transports water and minerals from the roots to the foliage. Xylem is a dead tissue. The cells that make up xylem lose their cytoplasm early in development to become hollow cells capable of holding and transporting water and minerals. There are two types of xylem: **vessels** and **tracheids.**

1 Xylem vessels

Xylem vessels are hollow cells connected end to end. During development, the end walls break down to leave a continuous tube.

The walls of the vessels are kept rigid and prevented from collapsing by a substance called **lignin**. Lignin forms a spiral around the wall of the vessel. Lignin is the substance that gives wood its strength. The walls of xylem vessels also have **pits** that enable water movement between different vessels. Fig 24.18 shows a longitudinal section through xylem tissue.

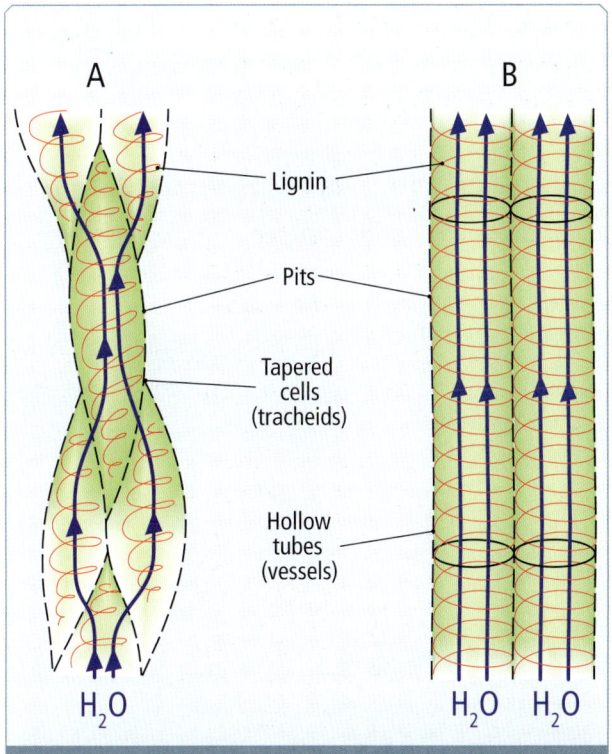

Fig 24.18 Longitudinal section of xylem tracheids (A) and xylem vessels (B). Lignin is present in both types of xylem (red spiral).

2 Xylem tracheids

Xylem tracheids are also hollow cells. However, they have tapered ends and are connected to other tracheids by pits in their side walls.

The walls of tracheids are also reinforced with lignin to prevent them from collapsing.

Phloem

Phloem is a living tissue that transports food molecules (such as sugars) around the plant. Water and minerals always travel upwards through the xylem. However, food can travel either upwards or downwards to wherever it is needed.

Phloem consists of two types of cells: **sieve tube cells** and **companion cells**.

1. The sieve tube cells have cytoplasm, but do not have a nucleus. They are long, tubular cells with end walls. Their end walls become porous during development and are called **sieve plates.**
2. The companion cells function in maintaining the sieve tube cells.

Fig 24.19 shows a longitudinal section through phloem tissue.

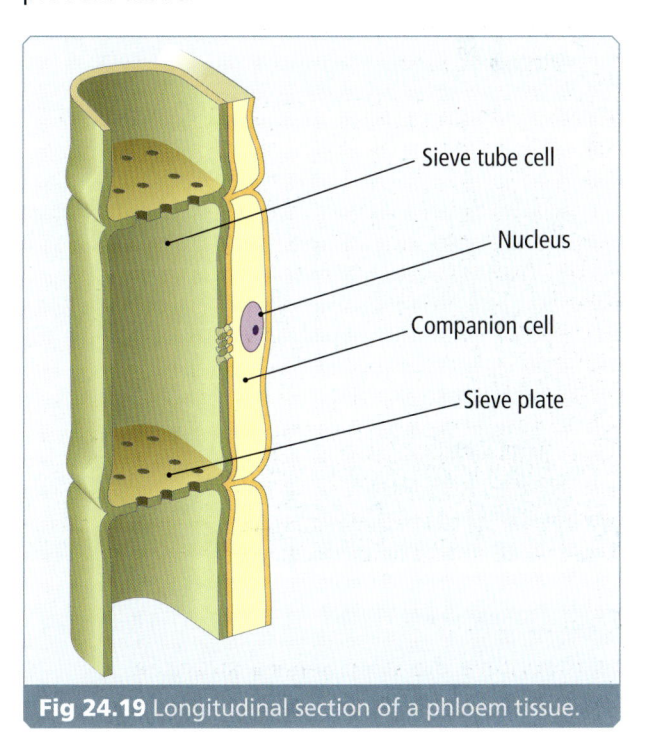

Fig 24.19 Longitudinal section of a phloem tissue.

Unit 3 The Organism

Practical activity: to prepare and examine microscopically the transverse section of a dicot stem (100x, 400x)

A dicot stem has vascular bundles arranged in a ring or circle (Fig 24.4). The vascular bundles can be seen quite clearly under the light microscope.

A herbaceous stem is used for this experiment as it is easier to cut through. Suitable plants for this activity include the busy Lizzy, geranium and begonia.

SAFETY
Extreme care must be taken when using the knife to cut sections.

Method

1. Cut out a section of stem from the internode (between two nodes) using a backed blade. Do not take sections at the nodes as the vascular tissue will be arranged in an irregular manner.
2. Cut a triangular-shaped slit along the length of a carrot and place the internode stem of the dicot stem into the slit in the carrot. This supports the herbaceous stem while cutting thin sections and makes cutting easier.
3. Wet the blade before cutting as this will enable you to slice through the stem much more easily.
4. Cut away from your fingers (your teacher will show you the correct method for cutting).
5. Take care to cut the thin sections at right angles, avoiding wedge-shaped sections or overly thick sections. The sections must be thin to allow light through, but also to prevent the coverslip from breaking when placed over the section.
6. Transfer the thin sections to a clock glass of water (this prevents the sections from drying out). Use a paintbrush to transfer the sections as it picks up the delicate sections without damaging them.
7. Place a section on a glass slide and add a drop of water to the section. This prevents the section drying out under the heat of the microscope light.
8. Carefully lower a coverslip from a 45° angle. This avoids air bubbles from being trapped.
9. Turn on the microscope and view under low power (100x).
10. Identify the vascular bundles.
11. Switch to high power (400x).
12. Sketch the structure of the dicot stem as seen in the field of view under low power and high power and label fully.

Results

Fig 24.20 shows a typical dicot stem (dandelion). This stem has been stained to make the xylem and phloem within each vascular bundle visible.

Fig 24.20 Transverse section through a dicot stem (100x).

Conclusion.

What have we learned from this practical activity?

Dicotyledonous plants have vascular bundles arranged in a circle within the stem.

Practical activity questions

1. What is a herbaceous stem? Explain why a herbaceous stem was used in this practical activity.
2. Name the plant you used.
3. Distinguish between a node and an internode. Why did you cut an internode section of stem?
4. Describe a method of supporting the herbaceous dicot stem during cutting.
5. Why did you wet the blade before cutting?
6. Why was it important to avoid wedge-shaped sections?
7. How did you prevent the sections from drying out?
8. How did you prevent the formation of air bubbles in the section?
9. In what way were the vascular bundles arranged?

Chapter 24 Questions

1. What is another name for flowering plants?
2. Name the parts labelled A to E on Fig 24.21.

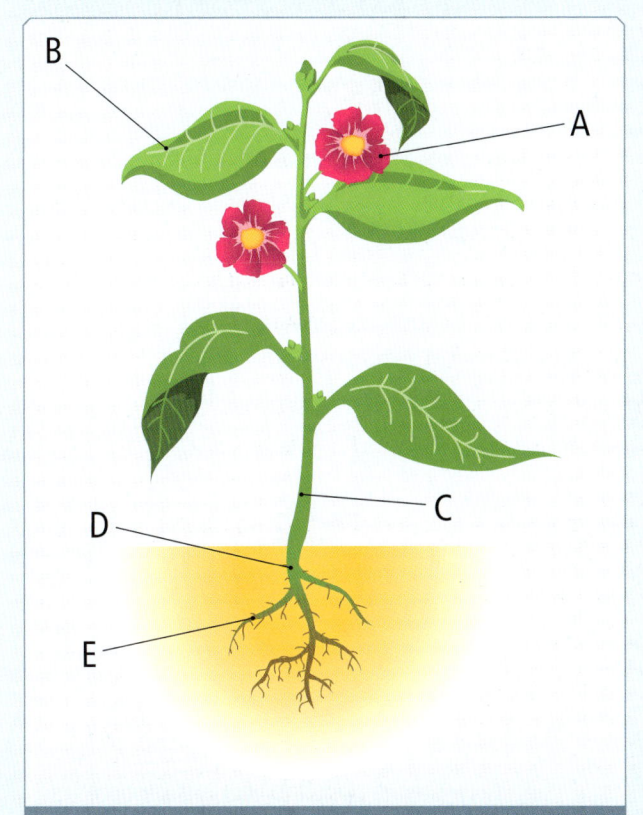

Fig 24.21 Structure of a flowering plant.

3. Name a plant that is not a flowering plant.
4. Distinguish between *monocotyledonous* and *dicotyledonous* plants in relation to:
   (a) Numbers of seed leaves
   (b) Flower part arrangement
   (c) Leaf venation
5. Name the **three** types of tissues in plants and their respective functions.
6. Distinguish between *xylem* and *phloem* in terms of function.
7. What is the function of cotyledons in flowering plants?
8. Name **three** structures that are part of the shoot system.
9. Give **three** functions of the shoot system.
10. What is a *lenticel* and what is its function?
11. Distinguish between the terms *herbaceous* and *woody*.
12. Distinguish between a *node* and an *internode*.
13. (a) Draw transverse sections of monocot and dicot stems and label the following structures: *xylem; phloem; vascular bundle; epidermis; cortex;* and *pith*.
    (b) Draw a longitudinal section of a dicot stem.
14. (a) What is the main function of the leaf?
    (b) What pigment is found in the leaves of a plant?
    (c) Give **three** ways in which a leaf is adapted to carry out its functions.
    (d) Draw a cross-section of a leaf showing the exact positions of xylem and phloem.
15. (a) What is a *bud*?
    (b) Name the **three** different types of bud.
16. (a) Give **three** functions of a root system.
    (b) Name and give the function of the parts labelled A to F on Fig 24.22 of a transverse section of a root.

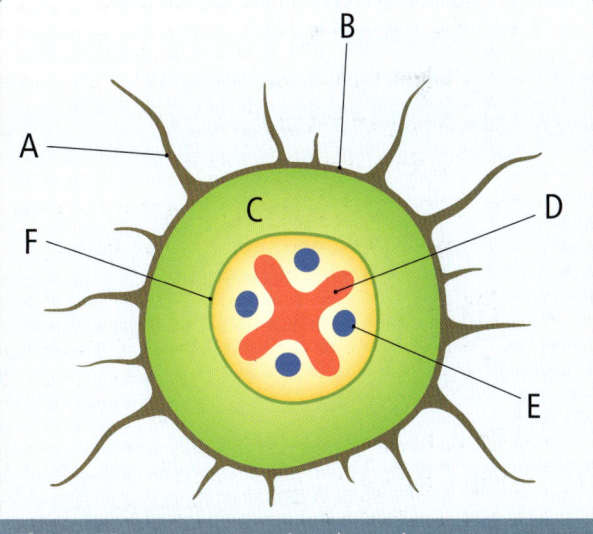

Fig 24.22 Transverse section through a root.

17. Draw a diagram of a xylem vessel and xylem tracheid, labelling the locations of lignin and pits. What is the function of the lignin and pits?
18. Draw a diagram of a phloem companion cell and sieve tube cell. Explain the importance of companion cells.
19. Give **two structural** differences between xylem and phloem.

Unit 3   The Organism

Chapter 24   Sample examination questions

1 The photograph below shows the tissues in a **transverse** section of a dicotyledonous (dicot) stem.

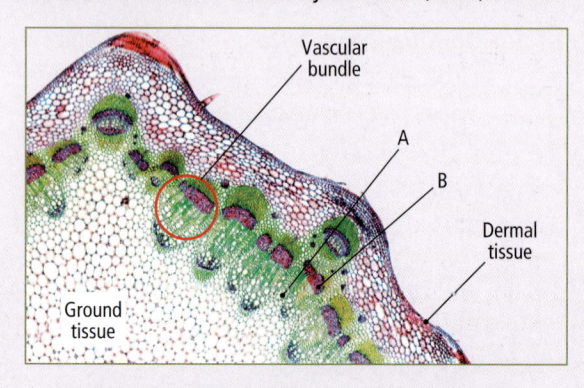

(i) Give **one** feature shown in the photograph that allows you to identify the section as a stem and not a root.

(ii) Name the **two** vascular tissues, A and B, found in a vascular bundle.

(iii) Draw a labelled diagram to show a **longitudinal** section of tissue B. Include the following labels in your diagram: sieve tube; sieve plate; companion cell.

(iv) Give **one** function of **each** of the following:
   1. Dermal tissue.
   2. Ground tissue.

(v) 1. In which of the vascular tissues does water transport occur?
   2. State **one** way in which this tissue is adapted for water transport.
   3. In which direction does this transport take place?

Section C, Question 14 (a) Ordinary Level 2009

2 The diagrams are of two tissues of a flowering plant.

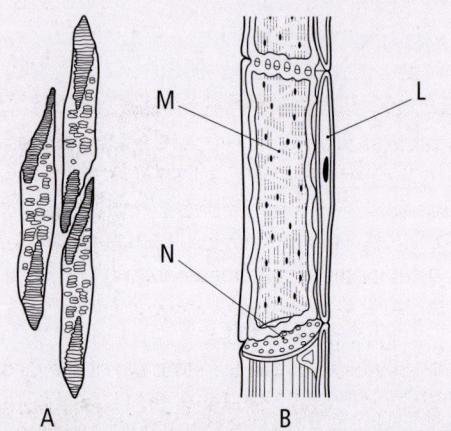

(i) Identify tissues A and B.
(ii) To which tissue type do A and B belong?
(iii) Identify cells L and M and part N in tissue B.
(iv) Name a substance transported in tissue A.
(v) Name a substance transported in tissue B.
(vi) Tissue A has another function in addition to transport. What is this other function?
(vii) Where in a young root would you find tissues A and B?

Section C, Question 14 (b) Ordinary Level 2006

HL 3 The diagram shows part of a transverse section through a dicotyledonous stem.

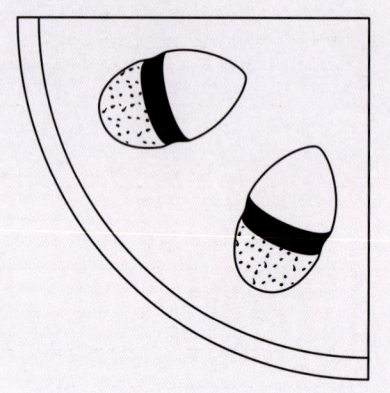

(i) Copy the diagram into your answer book and identify each of the following by placing the appropriate letter on your diagram: phloem P, ground tissue G, xylem X, dermal tissue D.

(ii) In which of the tissues that you have identified are sugars mainly transported?

(iii) State a function of D.

(iv) In the course of your practical work you cut and observed a transverse section of a stem. Answer the following in relation to that procedure.
   1. What did you use to cut the section?
   2. How did you support the stem while you were cutting the section?
   3. How did you transfer the section to a microscope slide?

(v) State **one** way in which a transverse section through a monocotyledonous stem differs from the one that you cut.

Section C, Question 14 (c) Higher Level 2006

258

Chapter 24 Mind map

Flowering plants are the most diverse and numerous of all divisions of the plant kingdom.

- The **shoot system** is made up of stem, branches, petioles, leaves, flowers and buds.
- The **root system** is made up of primary roots and secondary (or lateral) roots.

Flowering plants can be divided into two groups: monocotyledonous and dicotyledonous plants.
- A **cotyledon** is an embryonic seed leaf.
- **Monocotyledons** have one cotyledon. Monocots are usually herbaceous (green).
- **Dicotyledons** have two cotyledons. Dicots are usually woody.

Types of plant tissue and functions

Tissue		Functions
Dermal		Protection
		Absorption
Ground		Support
		Photosynthesis
Vascular	Xylem	Transport water and minerals
		Support
	Phloem	Transport food

Stem
- Stems have lenticels (small pores that allow gas exchange).
- Stems have nodes (where branches originate) and internodes.
- Internal stem structure consists of epidermal, ground and vascular tissues.
- Vascular bundles are arranged randomly in monocots and in a circle in dicots.

Leaf
- Organ that carries out photosynthesis.
- Thin, flat structure.
- Green with the pigment chlorophyll.
- Many air spaces throughout its internal structure.
- Stomata with guard cells.
- Veins present.

A **bud** is an undeveloped shoot. There are three types:
- Axillary buds
- Apical buds
- Adventitious buds

Root
- Absorption of water and minerals.
- Anchorage of the plant to the ground.
- Storage of food.
- Support.
- Transport of water and minerals to the stem.

Three types of root system
- Tap root system, e.g. dandelion.
- Fibrous root system, e.g. grass.
- Adventitious root system, e.g. ivy.

Four zones
- Zone of protection
- Meristematic zone
- Zone of elongation
- Zone of differentiation

Differences between xylem and phloem

Xylem		Phloem	
Vessels	Tracheids	Sieve tube cell	Companion cell
Hollow tubes with pits	Tapered cells with pits	Contains cytoplasm but no nucleus and has sieve plates	Contains cytoplasm and nucleus (supports the sieve tube cell)
Lignin	Lignin	No lignin	No lignin
Dead tissue	Dead tissue	Living tissue	Living tissue

Monocots versus dicots

Monocots	Dicots
Vascular bundles arranged randomly in stem	Vascular bundles arranged in a circle in the stem
Narrow leaves with parallel venation	Broad leaves with net (reticulate) venation
Flower parts usually in sets of three or multiples of three	Flower parts usually in sets of four or five or multiples of fours or fives

Practical activity to prepare and examine a transverse section of a dicot stem
- Suitable plants include busy Lizzy, geranium, begonia.
- Cut a very thin section using a wet blade.
- Place the cut sections in water.
- View sections under low power (100x) first and then higher power (400x).
- Sketch and label the structure of the dicot stem.

Chapter 25 Nutrition in the flowering plant

Learning objectives After studying this chapter, you should be able to:
- Describe the absorption and transport of water, carbon dioxide, minerals and the products of photosynthesis through a plant.
- Name one example of a root, stem and leaf modification as a food storage organ.
- **HL** Outline the cohesion-tension model of water transport in xylem tissue.

Introduction

All plants are **photosynthetic** – a type of autotrophic nutrition. They contain chlorophyll, a green pigment responsible for capturing the energy of light (see Chapter 11).

In order for photosynthesis and other metabolic processes to occur, plants require water, carbon dioxide, oxygen and minerals.

Water and mineral uptake by the roots

Water is one of the raw materials needed for photosynthesis to occur. It is also the medium in which many metabolic reactions take place. Water enters a plant at the roots. The root system is specifically designed to absorb water and transport it very quickly to where it is needed.

As we learned in Chapter 24, the roots are composed of root hairs, ground tissue (cortex), and xylem and phloem. The root hairs, cortex and xylem are involved in water and mineral uptake.

Minerals are water soluble. They are vital to the health of the plant and are needed in many different metabolic reactions. For example, magnesium is required in the formation of chlorophyll molecules and calcium is needed for the formation of the middle lamella, the cement that holds the plant cells together (see Chapter 3).

Other soluble substances absorbed by the roots include nitrates and phosphates, which are essential for DNA replication (see Chapter 14) and protein synthesis (see Chapter 15).

Water and mineral uptake by the roots is also helped by fungi. Fungi in the soil are composed of long hyphae (see Chapter 21), which intertwine with the roots of plants. This increases the surface area for absorption of water and minerals.

- Water first enters the root hairs by osmosis. We learned in Chapter 8 that osmosis is the diffusion of water molecules from a region of high water concentration to a region of low water concentration, across a semi-permeable membrane.
- Water in the soil is less concentrated with solutes than water in the cytoplasm of the root cells. Therefore, water moves across the root hair membrane by osmosis.
- Root hairs are extremely small extensions of the root epidermal cells. They have thin walls and a large surface area, maximising uptake of water and minerals.
- Once the water has entered the root hair it diffuses across the root cortex (ground tissue) towards the xylem.

Water and mineral transport through the plant

Water builds up in the xylem, creating **root pressure.** Root pressure pushes the water molecules up the xylem vessels and tracheids.

However, root pressure is not strong enough to push water up to the top of tall trees. The maximum measured root pressure in a plant is only enough to raise water 7 m high in the plant. Another factor is responsible for enabling water to be moved up to great heights – **transpiration.**

> **Transpiration** is the loss of water vapour from the aerial parts of a plant.

Transpiration helps to keep water moving upwards through the plant. Each water molecule pulls on the rest behind. This force is transferred the entire length of the xylem tissue. The movement of water upwards through a plant is called the **transpiration stream.**

Nutrition in the flowering plant **Chapter 25**

Fig 25.1 Movement of water through a plant (transpiration stream).

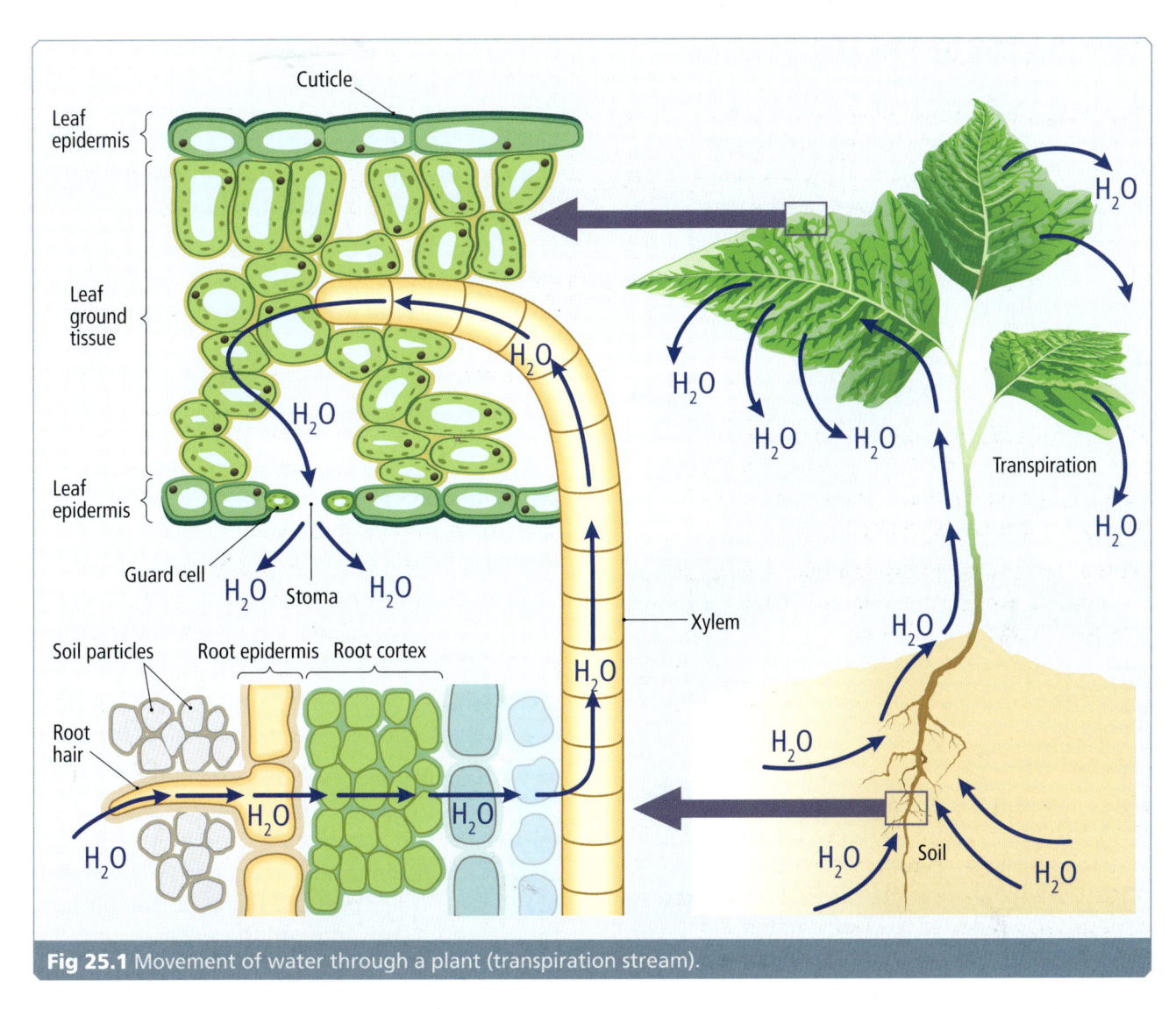

> A **transpiration stream** is the movement of water through a plant.

The transpiration stream is kept going by a number of factors:

- Osmosis
- Root pressure
- Transpiration

As we learned in Chapter 24, excess water loss is controlled by the waxy cuticle on the upper and lower surfaces of the leaf and by the opening and closing of the stomata on the underside of the leaf. If the plant has lost too much water, as happens during high temperatures, the stomata will close. Stomata also close at night as there is no photosynthesis occurring.

HL Water and mineral uptake by the roots – detailed process

Mineral uptake is vital to the health of the plant and is needed for many different metabolic reactions. As already mentioned, minerals dissolve in water and are absorbed into the root hairs along with water by **passive transport**. However, minerals are also taken up by **active transport**. This requires energy in the form of ATP. Minerals are moved from the soil into the root hair against their concentration gradient (or moving from low concentration to high concentration). This is because the minerals are often more concentrated within the root hairs than in the soil.

Active transport of minerals into the root also helps to draw water into the root more efficiently by osmosis.

Cohesion-tension model of water transport in xylem tissue

Plants move water upwards against the force of gravity. The taller the plant, the more difficult it is to transport the water upwards. Large trees, such as the giant sequoia (Fig 25.2), can reach heights of 115 m. Giant sequoias can lose over 1000 L of water on a hot day!

Fig 25.2 Giant sequoias can grow to 115 m high. Water can still be transported up to these great heights.

The mechanism of water transport through the xylem is still not fully understood, but two Irish scientists are credited with the most widely accepted model.

Henry Dixon and **John Joly** were two scientists from Trinity College Dublin, who proposed the cohesion-tension model of water transport through the xylem. They proposed this model in their 1894 research publication entitled *On the ascent of sap*.

Fig 25.3 Henry Dixon was one of the two Irish scientists who proposed the cohesion-tension model of xylem transport.

In their model, they proposed that water evaporates from the aerial parts of the plant (transpiration) creating a 'pull' or **'tension'** between the water molecules (hydrogen bonding) in the xylem tissues. This force is transferred all the way down the plant to the roots.

They hypothesised that the tension was due to **cohesion** between the water molecules. Hydrogen bonding holds the water molecules together.

> **Cohesion** is the sticking together of water molecules due to hydrogen bonding.

They also proposed that **adhesion** helps water move through the plant. Adhesion of water occurs if you pour water out of a jug. There will be droplets of water on the inside walls of the jug.

> **Adhesion** is the sticking of water molecules to the sides of the xylem vessels.

Water tends to weakly bond with the walls of the xylem vessels, making it easier to travel up the plant.

As we have learned, **root pressure** also contributes to upwards movement of water through a plant. Water enters the root by osmosis and builds up within the cortex and xylem tissues of the root. Water pressure builds up and **pushes** the water upwards through the xylem tissues. However, this force is only strong enough to push water up to a maximum height of 7 m. Therefore, the pull of transpiration is the most significant contributor to water movement in tall trees such as the giant sequoias (Fig 25.2). It is so great that the circumference of tree trunks reduces during the daytime, when transpiration is greatest. The tree's circumference returns to normal at night when transpiration stops. Lignin prevents the xylem tissue from completely collapsing under the force of transpiration.

Finally, **active transport** of minerals also helps to move water up through a xylem vessel or tracheid due to water moving with minerals by osmosis.

Control of transpiration

Transpiration is indirectly controlled by the waxy cuticle on the upper and lower surfaces of the leaf. The waxy cuticle prevents too much water loss from the plant. However, the rate of transpiration can be directly controlled by

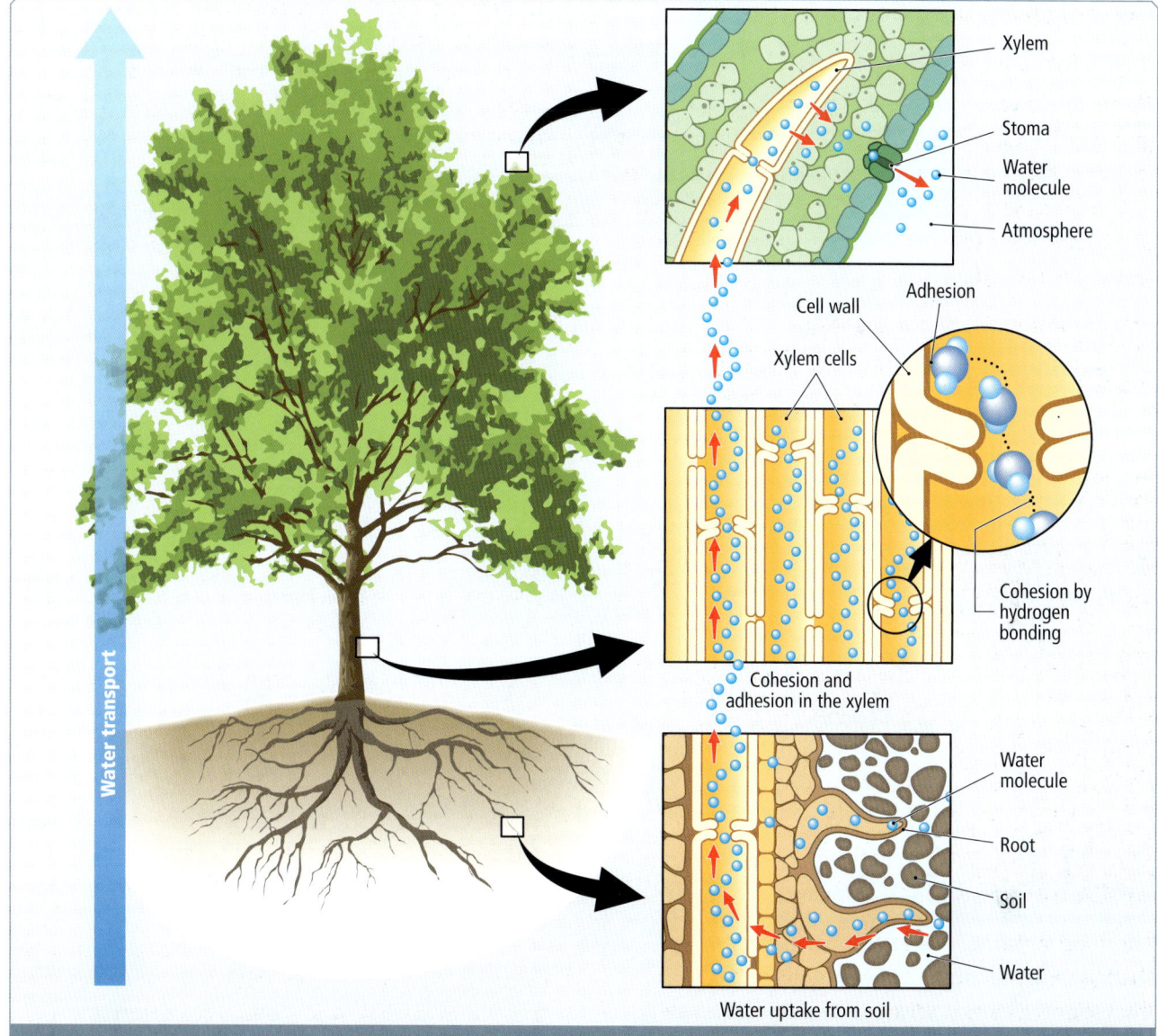

Fig 25.4 Cohesion and adhesion are important factors in the movement of water upwards in plants.

the **stomata,** which are tiny pores found on the underside of the leaf (see Chapter 24).

Stomata consist of two **guard cells** capable of separating from each other to create an entry to the air spaces within the leaf (Figs 25.5 and 25.6). Stomata can open and close in response to certain environmental conditions.

Carbon dioxide uptake

Plants produce carbon dioxide continuously through respiration. However, plants use far more carbon dioxide than they produce. This carbon dioxide is used in photosynthesis.

Carbon dioxide taken in by chloroplasts comes from two sources: respiration within the mitochondria of the leaf and from the atmosphere.

Atmospheric carbon dioxide enters the leaf through the stomata (Fig 25.6). It diffuses into the ground tissue of the leaf, where most of the chloroplasts are located. Here it takes part in photosynthesis (see Chapter 11) – the process of reducing carbon dioxide into glucose.

Stomatal opening and closing

Stomata open and close in response to changes in environmental conditions. In general, stomata close by night and open by day. However, it is important to note that light does not directly cause the opening and closing of stomata.

High water levels can stimulate the stomata to open and low water levels stimulate the stomata to close.

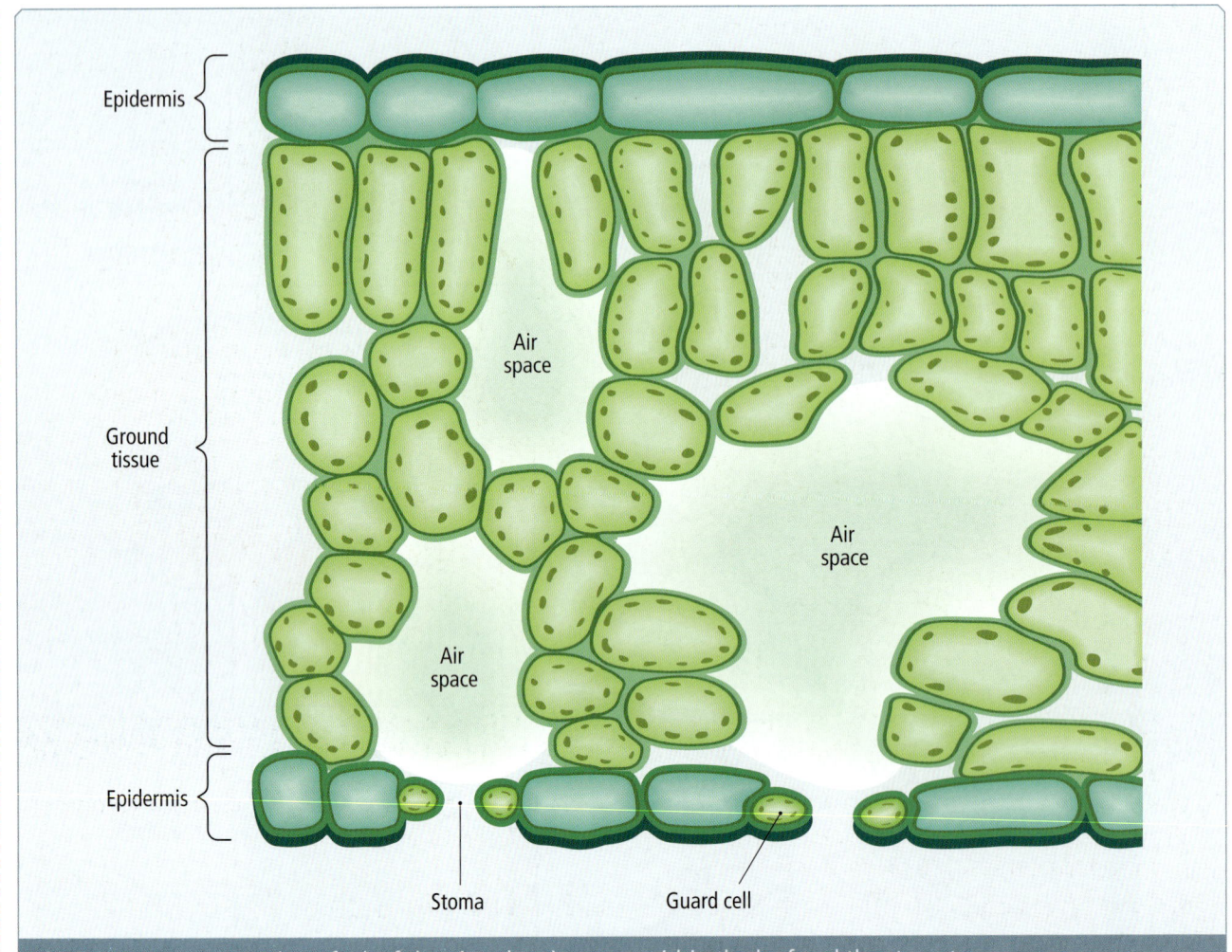

Fig 25.5 Transverse section of a leaf showing the air spaces within the leaf and the stomata.

Other environmental conditions also affect the opening and closing of stomata. For example, windy conditions cause an increase in transpiration, meaning the plant will lose water at a faster rate. The stomata close to prevent too much water loss. Calm conditions will cause the stomata to open.

Guard cells control the opening and closing of the stoma by controlling their turgidity (see Chapter 8). The walls of the guard cells are thicker on the inside than outside (Fig 25.7). When the guard cells become turgid (swollen with water), they curve away from one another due to the uneven thickness of their cell walls. This causes a gap (stoma) to form between the two cells.

When the guard cells lose water (and become flaccid), their cell walls remain together, keeping the stoma closed.

Fig 25.6 A stoma on the underside of a leaf.

Carbon dioxide: a controlling factor in gas exchange

Low levels of carbon dioxide (during the day) stimulate the stomata to open, whereas high levels of carbon dioxide (during the night) stimulate the stomata to close.

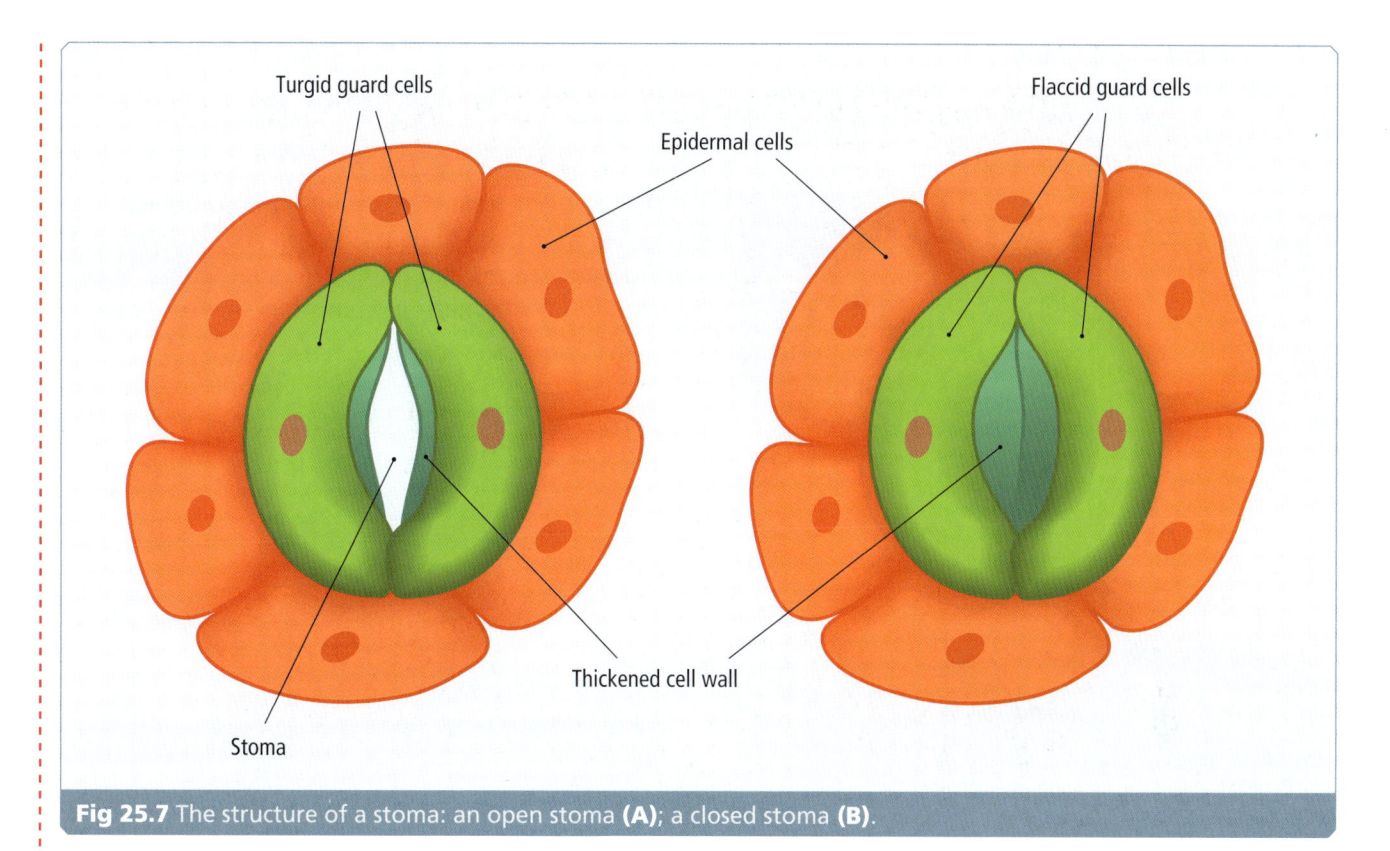

Fig 25.7 The structure of a stoma: an open stoma (**A**); a closed stoma (**B**).

Photosynthesis during the day maintains lower levels of carbon dioxide – keeping the stomata open. This allows more carbon dioxide to enter from the atmosphere.

As light fades into night, photosynthesis stops and carbon dioxide levels increase, due to respiration within the leaf cells. Higher levels of carbon dioxide cause the stomata to close.

Transport of the products of photosynthesis

Oxygen is a by-product of photosynthesis. There are two fates of oxygen. It is either released into the atmosphere or used within the leaf cells for respiration.

Glucose is produced directly by photosynthesis and can be used immediately in respiration. However, most of it is converted to starch for storage within the cell or converted to sucrose for transportation to other areas of the plant (via phloem tissue).

We learned in Chapter 24 that carbohydrate (in the form of sugars) and other food molecules are transported around the plant via phloem sieve tube cells. The sucrose can then be converted to either starch for storage or glucose for respiration in other areas of the plant.

Excretion in plants

Plants do not excrete as much as animals. Photosynthesis and a much slower metabolic rate mean excretion is not as important in plants.

However, plants do excrete oxygen during photosynthesis and carbon dioxide at night during respiration via the stomata of the leaves.

Modified plant food storage organs *Feach Ich 280*

Starch can build up in specific groups of tissues of a plant. These tissues are storage organs. They help the plant to survive the harsh conditions of winter and also to reproduce asexually (*see* Chapter 27).

Root storage organ

The tap roots of carrots (Fig 25.8) and parsnips are examples of food storage organs. They become swollen during the summer months when the foliage of the plant is photosynthesising. Glucose produced in photosynthesis is converted to sucrose and transported to the root, where it is converted to starch and stored. This enables the plant to survive winter. These are used extensively as a food for human consumption.

Fig 25.8 Modified tap roots (carrots).

Stem storage organ

Potatoes (Fig 25.9) are formed from underground stems, not roots. The potato storage organ is known as a **tuber**. The underground stem swells with food produced by the foliage of the potato plant during the summer.

Fig 25.9 Modified stems: potato **(A)** and asparagus **(B)**.

The formation of tubers by the potato plant is a method of asexual reproduction as well as a method of surviving the winter.

The foliage of the potato plant is highly toxic to humans. If potatoes are left out in the sun, the skin turns green due to the formation of chlorophyll. Toxic compounds called glycoalkaloids are formed, which if eaten, can make a person sick.

Another commonly eaten food that is a modified stem is asparagus (Fig 25.9).

Leaf storage organ

Onions and garlic are examples of modified leaves that swell with starch. The leaf storage organ of onions and garlic are called bulbs. They are used for human consumption.

Fig 25.10 Modified leaf (onions).

Petiole storage organ

Celery and rhubarb are examples of modified petioles (leaf stalk) that have become swollen with starch and act as a food reserve for the plant. The leaves of celery can be eaten, but the leaves of rhubarb are toxic to humans.

Fig 25.11 Modified petiole (celery).

Chapter 25 Questions

1. Name **one** characteristic that **all** plants have in common.
2. What is meant by *autotrophic nutrition*?
3. Name **four** essential substances required by all plants.
4. (a) What is *transpiration*?
   (b) What is meant by the transpiration stream?
5. Give an outline account of the process of movement of water up the stem of a plant by including the key words: *osmosis, root pressure* and *transpiration*.
6. **HL** Name the **two** scientists who proposed the cohesion-tension transport model of water and mineral transport through xylem tissue.
7. (a) Explain what *'cohesion'* refers to.
   (b) Explain what 'tension' refers to.
8. Name **two** other factors that contribute to the model of water transport.
9. Explain how the movement of water upwards through a tree is brought about by both **push** and **pull** forces.
10. Explain why the diameter of large tree trunks becomes slightly smaller during the day.
11. (a) What are stomata?
    (b) Draw a diagram of a stoma labelling the following: *stoma; guard cells, epidermal cells*.
    (c) Name **two** situations in which stomata will close.
    (d) How does carbon dioxide from the atmosphere get to the site of photosynthesis after entering through the stomata?
12. Label A to G on the following diagram.

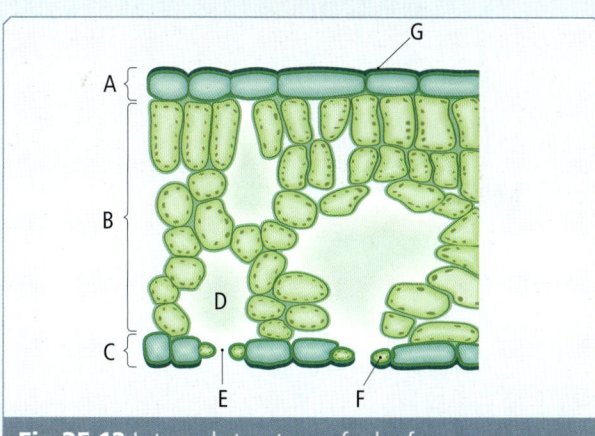

Fig 25.12 Internal structure of a leaf.

13. (a) Name a source of carbon dioxide other than the atmosphere.
    (b) **HL** Explain the effect of carbon dioxide on the opening and closing of the stomata.
    (c) Name another factor that can control opening and closing of the stomata.
14. Give **two** possible fates for oxygen after it is produced in photosynthesis.
15. Give **two** possible fates for glucose after it has been produced in photosynthesis.
16. Name **one** example of a vegetable produced by each of the following:
    (a) Root (b) Stem (c) Leaf
17. What biomolecule is present in large quantities in the vegetables you have named above?

Chapter 25 Sample examination questions

1. Water is vital for the survival of living things. Plants absorb water from the soil.
   (i) Through which microscopic **structures** does water enter a plant from the soil?
   (ii) By what **process** does water enter a plant?
   (iii) Name the **tissue** that water travels through in a plant.
   (iv) Draw a labelled diagram of one cell of the tissue referred to in (iii) above.
   (v) Name **one** process that causes water to move upwards in a plant.
   (vi) Consider that night has fallen and the plant is in darkness. Suggest what will happen to the **amount** of water moving through the plant **and** give a reason for your answer.

   Section C, Question 15 (a) (i)–(vi) Ordinary Level 2010

Unit 3 The Organism

HL 2 (a) The diagram shows part of the under surface of a leaf as seen through the microscope. A is an aperture (small opening). B and C are cells.

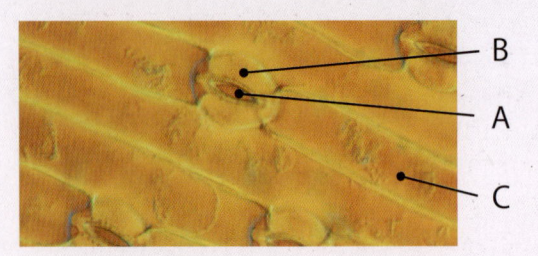

(i) Name A, B, C.
(ii) What is the function of A?
(iii) Name a factor that influences the diameter of A.
(iv) Name the apertures (small openings) in stems that are equivalent to A.

(b) In some species of flowering plants the leaves are modified for the storage of food.

(i) Name a plant in which the leaves are modified for food storage.
(ii) Name a carbohydrate that you would expect to find in the modified leaves of the plant that you named above.
(iii) Name a type of modified stem that functions in food storage.

Section A, Question 4 Higher Level 2004

Chapter 25 Mind map

All plants are photosynthetic (autotrophic).

Water and mineral uptake
- Water is absorbed into root hairs by osmosis.
- Water moves through the cortex and into the xylem tissue via diffusion.
- Water builds up in the xylem tissue, creating root pressure.
- Root pressure causes the water to move up the xylem tissue.
- Transpiration occurs, pulling the water molecules up the xylem tissue.

- **Transpiration** is the loss of water vapour from the aerial parts of a plant.
- **Transpiration stream** is the movement of water throughout the plant.

Water and mineral uptake – detailed process (cohesion-tension model of xylem transport) HL
- Dixon and Joly proposed this model in 1894.
- Water travels upwards through a plant by:
  - Root pressure.
  - Active transport of minerals contributing to osmosis.
  - Adhesion of water molecules to the walls of the xylem tissues.
  - Cohesion of the water molecules by hydrogen bonding.
  - Transpiration.

- **Mineral uptake:** Minerals dissolve in water and enter the root hairs by passive transport (diffusion) but can also be actively transported into the root.
- **Carbon dioxide uptake:** Carbon dioxide is produced in respiration and enters the leaf through the stomata. Carbon dioxide diffuses into the chloroplasts where it is converted to glucose in photosynthesis.

Control of stomatal opening and closing

Stomata open	Stomata close
When there is a plentiful supply of water	During water shortages
During calm weather conditions	During windy conditions
When carbon dioxide levels decrease HL	When carbon dioxide levels increase HL

Transport of the products of photosynthesis
- Oxygen can be used in respiration or released into the atmosphere.
- Glucose can be used in respiration or converted to starch and stored.
- Glucose can also be converted to sucrose and transported to other areas of the plant (via phloem).

Modified plant food storage organs
- **Tap root:** swells with starch, e.g. carrot and parsnip.
- **Tuber (modified stem):** swells with starch, e.g. potato and asparagus.
- **Bulb (modified leaf):** swells with starch, e.g. onion and garlic.

Response in the flowering plant — Chapter 26

Learning objectives After studying this chapter, you should be able to:
- Define the terms *stimulus, response, tropism, phototropism, geotropism, thigmotropism, hydrotropism* and *chemotropism*.
- Name examples of phototropism and geotropism.
- Define *growth regulator* and describe how it is transported; describe combined effect and give examples of growth promoters and growth inhibitors.
- Name any two uses of growth regulators.
- Investigate the effect of IAA (indoleacetic acid) growth regulator on plant tissue.
- Describe four anatomical or four chemical adaptations shown by plants for protection.
- HL ▶ Describe auxin as a growth regulator under the headings of production site(s), function and effects.
- ▶ Explain the mechanism of plant response to any one external stimulus.

Introduction

Plants show all five characteristics of living things (biological organisation; nutrition, excretion, response and reproduction). This chapter deals with **response**. Plants respond to the following stimuli: light, day length, temperature, chemicals and gravity. Plants also respond to touch.

> A **stimulus** is anything that causes a response in an organism.

A plant responds to these stimuli by doing one of the following:
- Growth (either towards the stimulus or away).
- Production of enzymes.
- Production of growth regulators.
- Absorption of nutrients.
- Transport of nutrients around the plant.
- Photosynthesis.
- Movement.

> A **response** is the activity of an organism or a part of an organism as a result of a stimulus.

The main response shown by plants is growth. Growth is regulated in a plant by **growth regulators**. Growth regulators can stimulate growth or inhibit growth.

> A **growth regulator** is a chemical that controls growth in a plant.

Growth regulators are transported around the plant in vascular tissue. They are produced in the meristematic regions of the plant, such as the growing tips of the shoots and roots. Growth regulators can be growth promoters at one particular concentration or growth inhibitors at another concentration (*see* experiment below). Different combinations of growth regulators can have varying effects.

An example of a growth regulator that promotes growth is auxin. However, in very high concentrations, auxin can inhibit growth – the mechanism of this growth inhibition is unknown. Other growth regulators, such as **abscisic acid** and **ethene**, specifically inhibit growth. Combinations of growth regulators can have more pronounced effects on plants than their individual effects. This is called the **combined effect** and refers to the use of two or more growth regulators to inhibit or promote growth in plants. It is used by horticulturists and farmers.

Tropism

> A **tropism** is a growth response of a plant to a stimulus.

Tropisms can be either positive or negative. A positive tropism is when a plant grows towards the stimulus and a negative tropism is when a plant grows away from the stimulus.

Tropisms are an adaptive advantage for plants in that they allow plants to obtain the most favourable growing conditions.

There are **five** main tropisms: **phototropism, geotropism, thigmotropism, hydrotropism** and **chemotropism**.

1 Phototropism

> **Phototropism** is the growth of a plant in response to light.

Fig 26.1 Phototropism.

An example of phototropism is when a plant bends towards a window. The shoots of plants show positive phototropism, meaning they will always grow towards a source of light. The shoots contain the foliage (leaves) – the photosynthesising parts of the plant. It is advantageous for the shoot to grow towards light as the more light the plant obtains, the greater the rate of photosynthesis and, therefore, the greater the growth of the plant.

Roots are negatively phototropic, meaning they grow away from light. This is advantageous to the plant as the roots will stay below the soil where water and minerals are located.

2 Geotropism

> **Geotropism** is the growth of a plant in response to gravity.

An example of geotropism is the way in which roots of plants grow downwards after germination. Roots show positive geotropism (Fig 26.2B), meaning they will grow in the direction of gravity. This is advantageous to the plant as growth downwards will result in the plant obtaining more water. The shoots of a plant are negatively geotropic (Fig 26.2A), meaning they will grow in the opposite direction to gravity.

This is an advantage as light comes from above, meaning growth away from gravity (upwards) will result in the plant obtaining more light.

Fig 26.2 Negative geotropism **(A)**; positive geotropism **(B)**.

3 Thigmotropism

> **Thigmotropism** is the growth of a plant in response to touch.

The prefix *'thigmo'* comes from the Greek word for 'touch'. Certain types of adventitious roots (*see* Chapter 24) can be positively thigmotropic. For example, ivy sends out adventitious roots from its stems to attach to walls or other plants, such as trees (see Fig 24.15A). Certain types of shoot can also be positively thigmotropic. The pink clematis plant (Fig 26.3B) produces thin stems (tendrils) that reach out and hook onto and wrap around the stems of other plants. Most roots are negatively thigmotropic. Negative thigmotropism allows the root to find the path of least resistance through the soil.

4 Hydrotropism

> **Hydrotropism** is the growth of a plant in response to water.

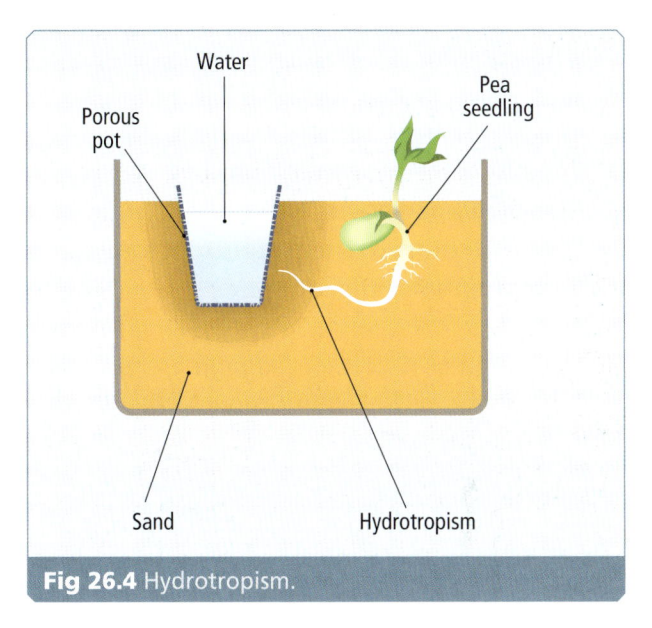

Fig 26.4 Hydrotropism.

Roots are positively hydrotropic (Fig 26.4). They grow towards a source of water.

5 Chemotropism

> **Chemotropism** is the growth of a plant in response to chemicals.

Plants will grow towards fertilisers, such as phosphates and nitrates. Another type of chemotropism is the formation of the pollen tube (see Chapter 28) following pollination of a flower. The pollen tube burrows its way down the female carpel (stigma and style) towards the ovary. The pollen tube is guided by chemical signals.

HL Auxin

As we have already learned, auxin is a growth promoter. There are many different types of auxin. A common example is indoleacetic acid (IAA).

Production sites

IAA is produced in the meristematic tissues of apical, lateral and adventitious buds, as well as in root tips. It is also produced in developing seeds.

Fig 26.3 Thigmotropism (A); pink clematis (B), a plant that demonstrates thigmotropism.

Functions and effects of IAA

IAA functions in:

- Stimulating cell elongation.
- Stimulating cell division in meristematic regions of the plant.
- Formation of xylem and phloem cells.
- Apical dominance, whereby auxin from the apical meristem diffuses down the stem, inhibiting the growth of branches.
- Delaying ripening of fruit.
- Tissue culturing by stimulating root formation.
- Phototropism and geotropism.

The primary functions of IAA are in cell elongation and cell division. At high concentrations, however, IAA can inhibit growth, especially in the roots.

Cell elongation plays a key role in the tropisms. Stems bend towards light and roots bend towards gravity due to cell elongation.

IAA causes apical dominance, whereby the apical (top) meristem produces auxin that diffuses down the stem inhibiting side branching. As the plant grows taller, the auxin further down the stem becomes less concentrated and has less of a negative effect on side branching. This allows lower branches to grow more strongly than branches above them.

In horticulture, side-branching is often stimulated to 'thicken' a plant. This pruning involves removing the apical meristems. It removes the source of IAA and thereby the inhibition on side branching.

IAA is also produced by developing seeds and causes the surrounding ovary to swell with food. It also prevents early ripening of fruit.

Mechanism of phototropism

Shoots bend towards light as a result of cell elongation on the shaded side of the stem. As we have already learned, cell elongation is caused by auxins, such as IAA.

IAA is produced in the apical meristem. Scientists do not know the mechanism by which it diffuses down the shaded side and not the light-exposed side of the stem. The fact that the cells on the shaded side elongate means that bending of the stem occurs in the direction of the light (Fig 26.5).

Uses of plant growth regulators

> **NOTE**: For Leaving Certificate Biology, you have to know only two uses of plant growth regulators.

- Certain auxins, such as **naphthalene acetic acid (NAA)** and **indolebutyric acid (IBA)**, are used as commercial rooting powders (substances that stimulate roots to grow).
- Other types of auxin, such as **2,4-dichlorophenoxyacetic acid (2,4-D)**, are used as synthetic (man-made) weed-killers.
- **Gibberellins** are used to increase the size of fruits.
- **Ethene** is used as a ripening agent for fruit.

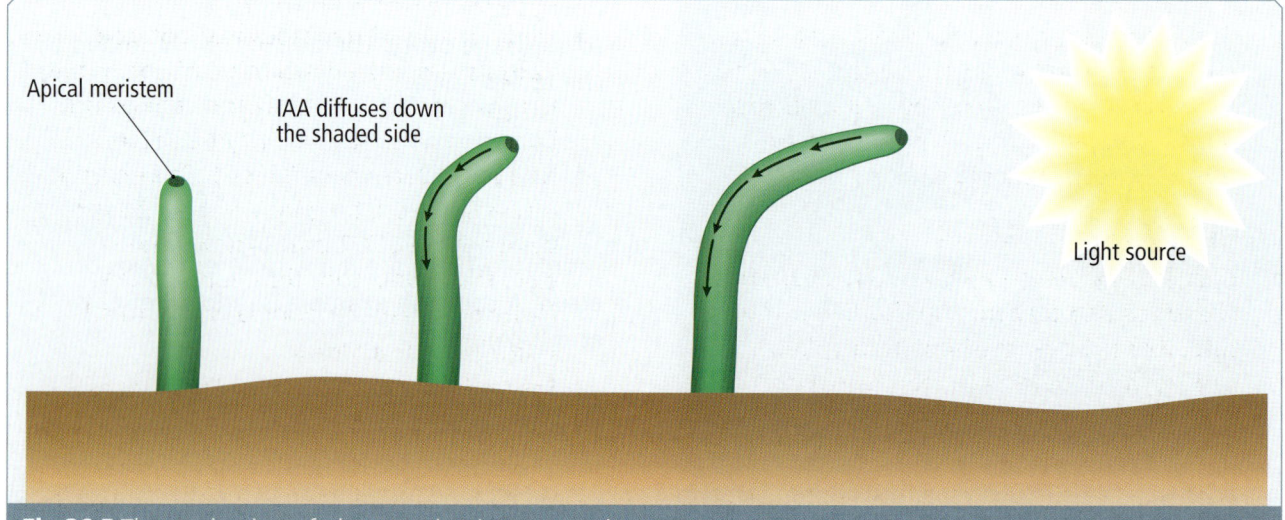

Fig 26.5 The mechanism of phototropism in a young shoot.

Plant adaptations for protection

Plants have adapted to the habitats in which they live over many millions of years. Plant adaptations can be grouped into two areas: **anatomical** and **chemical** adaptations.

> **NOTE:** For Leaving Certificate Biology, you must know four anatomical or four chemical adaptations for protection in plants.

Anatomical adaptations

- All plants have an epidermis. This epidermis has adapted over time in many plants. Bark is a type of epidermis that protects trees. Thorns, spines, needles and stinging hairs on the epidermis of some plants, bushes and shrubs are other adaptations that protect species from predators. The thick waxy cuticle present on leaves is an extra layer of protection for the plant – both against pathogens and loss of water.
- All plants have guard cells in the epidermal layer that prevent excess water loss.
- Cacti have evolved to grow no leaves in order to survive harsh desert conditions. Their stem swells to store water and is green to photosynthesise. Cacti also have spines to discourage animals from eating the plant for its high water content.
- Some plants have flowers that open during the night (for example, Casablanca lily and evening primrose) when pollinators (insects) are more active.
- Conifer trees have adapted to live at high altitudes or on the sides of mountains where there is less water. They have thin, narrow, needle-like leaves with few stomata to prevent excess water loss.

Chemical adaptations

- Corn lily is a poisonous plant (Fig 26.6) that sheep used to graze on. In the 1950s, it was discovered that something in the plant was causing birth defects in the sheep. One of the birth defects was cyclopia, which is caused by an alkaloid called cyclopamine.
- Alkaloids are a group of compounds produced by many herbaceous plants to protect against herbivores, such as insects and animals.

Fig 26.6 The poisonous corn lily causes birth defects in sheep.

However, many insects and animals, including humans, have developed mechanisms to detoxify these poisons. Examples of some common alkaloids that are poisonous but tolerated to certain extents by humans are cocaine, nicotine, caffeine and morphine.

- Poison ivy produces a chemical called urushiol to protect the plant from herbivores. Even brushing against the plant will cause an allergic skin rash in humans.
- In conifers, chemicals called monoterpenes accumulate in the leaves and branches. These chemicals are toxic to certain insect herbivores, such as beetles.
- Some species of tomatoes and potatoes have developed a mechanism of combating herbivores such as insects and caterpillars. They produce a special enzyme called threonine deaminase 2 (TD2). This enzyme is released from the plant when attacked by herbivores. TD2 breaks down the essential amino acid, threonine, in the herbivores' diet. Threonine is vital to all organisms for growth.
- Spotted knapweed is a weed that takes over an area wherever it grows. It does this by producing a phytotoxic chemical called catechin, which kills all other plants around it. It is hoped that catechin can be used as a completely natural weed-killer.

Practical activity: to investigate the effect of indoleacetic acid (IAA) growth regulator on plant tissue

IAA is an auxin. It is a growth promoter in plants stimulating both root and shoot growth. It is produced by meristematic cells of the shoot, root, bud and young leaf. It stimulates growth at low concentrations and inhibits growth at high concentrations.

> **SAFETY**
> Indoleacetic acid is an **irritant** and **potentially toxic compound.** It must be handled with extreme caution. Lab coat, gloves and safety goggles must be worn when using the powdered form.
>
> It is recommended to weigh and dilute IAA using a fume cupboard. When diluted, it poses less of a risk.
>
> Ethanol is **highly flammable** and **harmful** to internal organs.

Method

1. Familiarise yourself with the method before proceeding as it is quite detailed.
2. Dissolve 0.1 g (100 mg) of IAA in 3 ml of ethanol.
3. Add distilled water to the solution of IAA and ethanol. Bring the volume to 1 L.
4. Label eight Petri dishes A to H.
5. Label eight small plastic bottles in the same way.
6. Using a syringe, add 10 ml of the IAA stock solution (100 ppm) to the first bottle.
7. Using another syringe add 9 ml of distilled water to each of the next seven bottles.
8. Using a dropper, remove 1 ml of the IAA solution from the first bottle and add it to the second bottle. Place the cap on the second bottle and mix thoroughly.
9. Using a **different dropper,** remove 1 ml of solution from the second bottle and add it to the third bottle. Place the cap on the third bottle and mix thoroughly.
10. Using a different dropper each time, repeat the serial dilution for the fourth, fifth, sixth and seventh bottles.
11. Discard 1 ml of solution from the seventh bottle. Each bottle (A to G) now contains 9 ml of IAA solutions, **each of a different concentration**.
12. Each bottle differs in concentration by a factor of 10 (see tables below).
13. Bottle H is the control which contains no IAA – only 9 ml of distilled water.
14. Place a circular acetate grid inside the lid of each dish.
15. Place **five** radish seeds along a grid line in each dish.
16. Place a filter paper on top of the seeds in each dish.
17. Using the appropriate droppers, add 2 ml of each solution to its corresponding dish. Use the dropper to press gently on the damp filter paper, to reduce the trapped air.
18. Place cotton wool on top of the filter paper in each dish.
19. Add the remaining 7 ml of each solution to the cotton wool in the appropriate dish. Leave for a few minutes, until the cotton wool absorbs all of the solution.
20. Place the base of the Petri dish over the cotton wool.
21. Secure the lid and base using tape or parafilm.
22. Stack the dishes together so that the lines of seeds are all parallel to one another.
23. Secure all the dishes together using tape.

NOTE: IAA is first dissolved in ethanol because it does not easily dissolve in water.

NOTE: On completing point 3 you will have a stock solution with a concentration of 100 mg/L. This concentration can also be expressed as 100 ppm (parts per million). This solution will be diluted in preparing each Petri dish.

24. Place the dishes in an incubator set at 25 °C. Stand the dishes on their edge with the lines of seeds in the horizontal position. This is to ensure the roots will grow down along the acetate grid and the shoots will grow upwards.
25. Leave the dishes in the incubator for two to three days.
26. Measure the length of the roots and shoots of the seedlings in each dish by using the acetate grids or a ruler and record.
27. Calculate the average length of the roots and shoots in each dish and record.
28. Calculate the percentage stimulation or inhibition of root and shoot growth for each dish using the following formula:

$$\% \text{ stimulation or inhibition} = \frac{\text{Avg length} - \text{Avg length of control}}{\text{Avg length of control}} \times 100$$

29. Draw a graph of percentage stimulation and inhibition of root and shoot growth against IAA concentration, putting IAA concentration on the horizontal axis.
30. Replicate the experiment or compare your results with other groups in the class.

Results

Copy the following tables into your lab notebook and complete.

Concentration of IAA		Length of roots (mm)					Average length (mm)	Percentage stimulation or inhibition
ppm	mg/L	Seed 1	Seed 2	Seed 3	Seed 4	Seed 5		
0 (control)	0 (control)							
10^{-4}	0.0001							
10^{-3}	0.001							
10^{-2}	0.01							
10^{-1}	0.1							
$10^0 = 1$	1							
10^1	10							
10^2	100							

Concentration of IAA		Length of shoots (mm)					Average length (mm)	Percentage stimulation or inhibition
ppm	mg/L	Seed 1	Seed 2	Seed 3	Seed 4	Seed 5		
0 (control)	0 (control)							
10^{-4}	0.0001							
10^{-3}	0.001							
10^{-2}	0.01							
10^{-1}	0.1							
$10^0 = 1$	1							
10^1	10							
10^2	100							

Unit 3   The Organism

Conclusion
What did we learn from this practical activity?

IAA stimulates root growth at low concentrations and inhibits root growth at higher concentrations. At higher concentrations, shoot growth is stimulated.

Practical activity questions

1. What type of seeds did you use in your practical activity?
2. Describe how you prepared IAA.
3. Explain why you had to prepare IAA in this way.
4. Why are a number of seeds placed in each Petri dish and not just one?
5. What is the purpose of placing the Petri dishes on their side in the incubator?
6. Describe the results you obtained in your practical activity. If your results were not as expected can you explain the reasons behind them?
7. Give **one** safety precaution you took during this practical activity.

Chapter 26   Questions

1. Distinguish between the terms *'stimulus'* and *'response'*.
2. (a) What is a *growth regulator*?
   (b) Name **two** environmental factors that affect the growth of plants.
3. (a) What is a *tropism*?
   (b) What is the benefit to a plant of having tropisms?
4. (a) Name the **five** types of plant tropisms.
   (b) Give **one** example of a positive tropism and **one** example of a negative tropism.

   HL (c) Describe the mechanism of **one** of the tropisms you named above.
5. Give **two** uses of plant growth regulators.
6. (a) Where in a plant is auxin produced?
   (b) IAA is an example of an auxin. What does IAA stand for?
   (c) Give **two** functions of IAA.
   (d) Name **two** effects of the above functions.
7. Name **two** growth inhibitors and give their respective functions.
8. Plants, like all other organisms, are subject to the stresses of their environment. They have to adapt to survive. Give **two** anatomical and **two** chemical adaptations plants have developed to survive in their habitats.
9. Broad bean seeds were germinated in the dark, and then treated as shown in Fig 26.7.

   Three pots of newly germinated broad beans were placed next to a window.

   Pot 1: broad beans had no treatment.

   Pot 2: broad beans had their apical meristems completely covered with aluminium foil.

   Pot 3: broad beans had their apical meristems removed completely.

   (a) Which pot is the **control?** Explain why.
   (b) What will be seen in the control?
   (c) What was the idea behind covering the apical meristems in pot 2 and cutting the apical meristems off in pot 3?
   (d) Explain what will happen to the broad beans in pots 2 and 3.

Fig 26.7 Broad bean plantlets.

Chapter 26 Sample examination questions

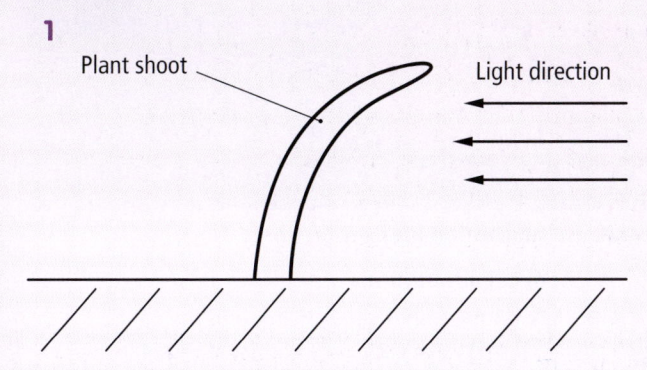

1

Plant shoot — *Light direction*

(a) Give the term used for the growth response shown by the plant shoot in the diagram above.
(b) Why is this growth response of benefit to plants?
(c) Name the group of substances that controls such responses.
(d) Name the tissue through which the substances named in (c) are transported in the plant.
(e) Name another growth response found in plants.

Section A, Question 6 Ordinary Level 2009

HL 2 The graph shows the effect of varying auxin concentration on the roots and shoots of a plant.

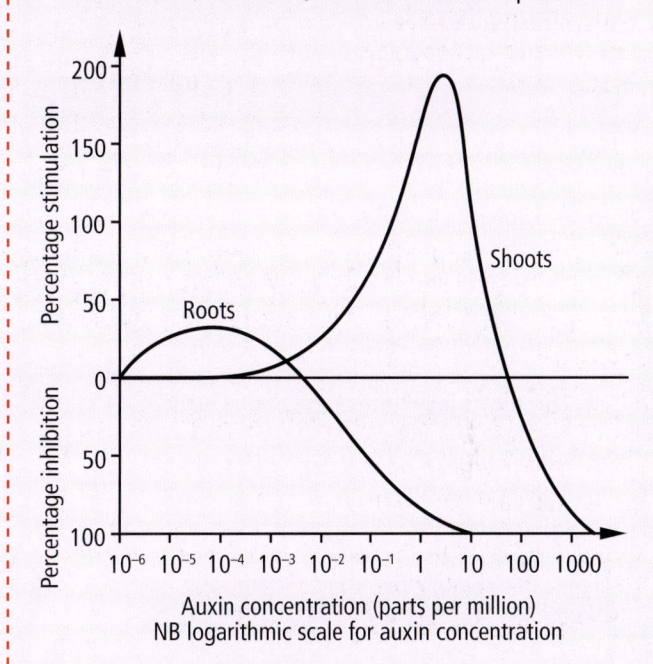

(i) What is an auxin?
(ii) At what approximate auxin concentration does the root receive maximum stimulation?
(iii) At what approximate auxin concentration does the shoot receive maximum stimulation?
(iv) What is the effect on the root of an auxin concentration of 10^{-2} parts per million?
(v) Give **two** examples of uses of synthetic (man-made) auxins.
(vi) Describe **three** methods used by plants to protect themselves from adverse external environments.

Section C, Question 14 (b) Higher Level 2005

Unit 3 The Organism

Chapter 26 Mind map

Response in the flowering plant

- A **stimulus** is anything that causes a response in an organism.
- A **response** is the activity of an organism or a part of an organism as a result of a stimulus.

- A **growth regulator** is a chemical that controls growth in a plant.
- A **tropism** is a growth response of a plant to a stimulus.
- **Phototropism** is the growth of a plant in response to light.
- **Geotropism** is the growth of a plant in response to gravity.
- **Thigmotropism** is the growth of a plant in response to touch.
- **Hydrotropism** is the growth of a plant in response to water.
- **Chemotropism** is the growth of a plant in response to chemicals.

Auxin   HL
- Production sites: meristematic regions of the plant.
- Functions and effects: stimulates cell elongation, cell division, and xylem and phloem formation; inhibits the growth of side branches (apical dominance); delays fruit ripening; stimulates root formation; involved in phototropism and geotropism.

Mechanism of phototropism   HL
- Light illuminates one side of the stem.
- IAA is produced in the meristematic tissue of the shoot tip and diffuses down the shaded side of the stem.
- This causes cell elongation on the shaded side only.
- As a result the stem bends towards the light.

Uses of plant growth regulators
- Rooting powder: naphthalene acetic acid (NAA) and indolebutyric acid (IBA) are used as commercial rooting powders.
- Weed-killer: 2,4-dichlorophenoxyacetic acid (2,4-D) is used as a synthetic weed-killer.
- Fruit: gibberellins are used to increase the size of fruits.
- Fruit ripening: ethene is used as a ripening agent for fruit.

Plant adaptations for protection

Anatomical adaptations
- Bark on trees and woody plants and the cuticle on leaves prevent entry of pathogens and prevent excess water loss.
- Thorns, spines, needles, and stinging hairs are present on the epidermis of some plants and protect against predators.
- Guard cells prevent excess water loss.
- Cacti have no leaves; their stems storing water. Cacti also have spines to discourage predators.
- Casablanca lily and evening primrose have flowers that open only at night when pollinators (insects) are more active.
- Conifer trees have narrow, needle-like leaves with few stomata to prevent excess water loss.

Chemical adaptations
- Corn lily produces a poisonous compound called cyclopamine.
- Poison ivy produces a poisonous chemical called urushiol.
- Conifers produce poisonous chemicals called monoterpenes.
- Tomatoes and potatoes produce an enzyme called threonine deaminase 2 (TD2), which breaks down the essential amino acid threonine.
- Spotted knapweed is a weed that produces a poisonous chemical called catechin, which is toxic to most other plant species.

Practical activity to investigate the effect of indoleacetic acid (IAA) growth regulator on plant tissue
- Set up eight Petri dishes and label A to H.
- Carry out a serial dilution, whereby the concentration is reduced by a factor of ten each time.
- Place an acetate grid in the lid of each Petri dish along with five radish seeds in a row and filter paper on top.
- Place cotton wool in each dish and add remaining solution.
- Close the dishes and tape together.
- Incubate for two to three days.
- Record the lengths of roots and shoots and compare.

Vegetative propagation — Chapter 27

Learning objectives After studying this chapter, you should be able to:
- Define *vegetative propagation*.
- Describe vegetative propagation from each of the following plant parts: stem, root, leaf, bud.
- Describe any four methods of artificial vegetative propagation.

Introduction

The variety of flowering plants is truly astonishing. They come in all shapes and sizes and in almost every colour.

There is also great diversity in the shapes of flowers. Some are very small, while others are extremely large.

The time of year flowers appear also varies. Some flowers appear very early in the year (as early as January), such as the daffodil. However, most flowers appear in spring and early summer. Fig 27.1 shows some of the more unusual flowers.

All flowering plants reproduce sexually (*see* Chapter 28). However, many flowering plants can also reproduce asexually. Reproduction is one of the five characteristics of living things.

> **Asexual reproduction** is the production of a new individual from one parent. The new individual is genetically identical to the parent.

Asexual reproduction has the advantage of being a faster method of reproduction because the new individual does not have to grow from a single cell.

Also, plants resulting from asexual reproduction bear flowers and fruits much faster than plants from seeds (sexual reproduction). Asexual reproduction has the disadvantage of producing plants that are all genetically identical to one another. The genetically identical plants will all be at risk from the same diseases as a result.

Asexual reproduction in plants is called **vegetative propagation**.

> **Vegetative propagation** is asexual reproduction in plants.

There are two main types of vegetative propagation:
1. Natural vegetative propagation
2. Artificial vegetative propagation

Fig 27.1 The variety of flowering plants.

Natural vegetative propagation

1 Stem

New plants can arise from the stem. For example, strawberry plants send out long horizontal stems, called **'runners'** or **stolons.** When sufficiently far away from the parent plant, the runner sends out a shoot and root. A new, but genetically identical, strawberry plant is formed (Fig 27.2).

Fig 27.2 Strawberry runners – a type of asexual reproduction.

2 Root

New plants can also arise from roots. Trees that have been cut down often send out new shoots from underground roots. Raspberries and many shrubs, such as holly, grow their roots away from the parent plant and then send up a shoot, called a **root sprout** or **'sucker'** (Fig 27.3).

Fig 27.3 Root sprouts.

3 Leaf

Asexual reproduction by leaf is rare, but does occur in some plants, such as the **Devil's backbone** (*Kalanchoe daigremontiana,* Fig 27.4). This is a poisonous plant native to Madagascar.

Little plantlets develop on the edges of its leaves and drop off when fully developed. The roots grow and take hold in the soil and a new plant is produced that is genetically identical to the parent plant.

Fig 27.4 *Kalanchoe daigremontiana*, a plant that reproduces by leaf asexual reproduction.

4 Bud

Buds are present over most areas of a plant. However, only some buds have the ability to produce a new individual plant. An example of a bud that produces new plants is the axillary (lateral) buds of an onion bulb (Fig 27.5).

Onion bulbs consist of a short underground stem surrounded by modified leaves. The leaves become swollen with starch. In between the leaves are axillary buds. Each axillary bud grows, using the stored starch from the modified leaves, into a new onion plant.

Vegetative propagation — Chapter 27

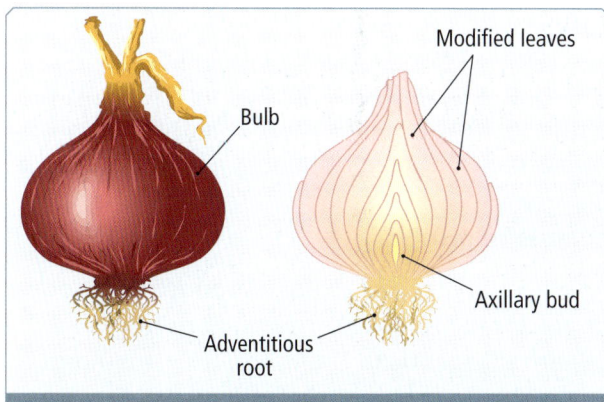

Fig 27.5 The structure of an onion bulb.

Artificial vegetative propagation

Artificial vegetative propagation is used by gardeners and farmers to propagate plants rapidly.

1 Cutting

> **Cutting** is the process of removing a small piece of a parent plant and encouraging it to grow into an independent plant.

Some cuttings can be potted straight into soil and will take root within a few weeks. Other cuttings require special treatment, such as special soils and rooting powder. **IBA** is an example of rooting powder used for cuttings (*see* Chapter 26).

Often it is recommended to place a plastic bag over the fresh cutting and to remove some leaves as this will limit water loss from the foliage and improve the cutting's chances of survival.

Fig 27.6 Cuttings placed in a pot covered with plastic to conserve water (**A**); a cutting potted with rooting powder that stimulates root formation over a number of weeks (**B**).

2 Layering

> **Layering** is a process in which a stem of a parent plant is bent down into the soil and encouraged to grow into an independent plant.

Layering is used more by recreational gardeners than by horticulturists or farmers as it does not produce large numbers of plants in the same way cuttings do. Layering is also only useful for plants with long stems such as climbing plants, for example, clematis.

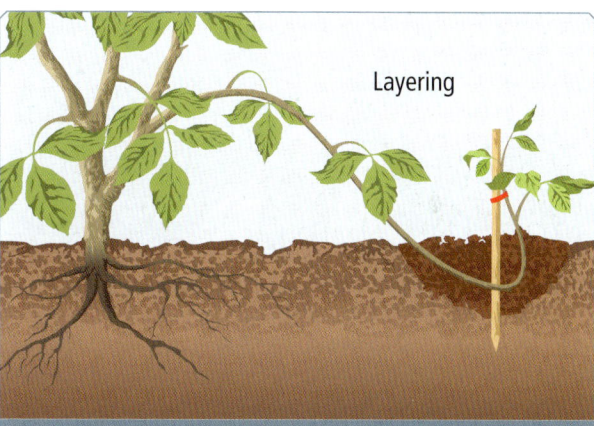

Fig 27.7 Layering is a process of bending a long stem into the soil surrounding a plant. Eventually, a new root and shoot forms.

3 Grafting

> **Grafting** is a process in which the shoot system (scion) of one plant is joined to the root system (stock) of another.

Grafting is especially useful for eating-apple trees. The **scion** (shoot system) of the eating-apple tree is attached to the **stock** (root system) of a crab apple tree. This produces better quality eating apples as the crab apple tree has a better root system than an eating-apple tree.

Grafting is also used in rose plants to produce healthy, large, brightly coloured roses. The strong, large root system of a wild rose plant, that ordinarily produces small roses, is grafted onto the shoot system of a flowering rose plant, which ordinarily has a weak, small root system, but produces large roses. This maintains the roses' qualities year after year and reduces the chances of having a poor yield in any one particular year.

Unit 3 The Organism

Tissue culturing is expensive, labour intensive and requires special equipment and expertise. It is used only when a large number of plants is required. However, the advantage is that it is a very effective way of obtaining a high yield. It is also a very fast method of producing a large number of plants.

As with all types of asexual reproduction, another disadvantage is that all the resultant plants are genetically identical. Therefore, they are more vulnerable to the same diseases.

Fig 27.8 Grafting, where the good properties of two separate plants are combined. A scion (shoot system) is 'grafted' to a stock (root system).

4 Tissue culturing (micropropagation)

> **Tissue culturing** (also called micropropagation) is the growth of a large number of plantlets in a nutrient medium from small tissue samples.

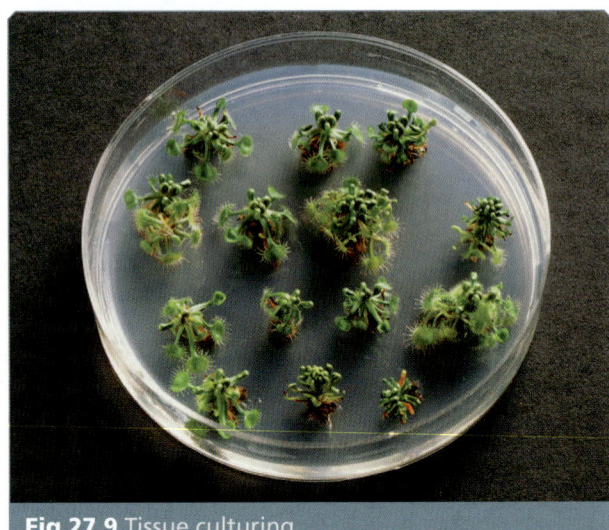

Fig 27.9 Tissue culturing.

NOTE Comparison of reproduction by seed (sexual) with vegetative propagation (asexual) is described at the end of Chapter 28.

Chapter 27 Questions

1 Define *asexual reproduction*.
2 Distinguish between *natural* and *artificial vegetative propagation*.
3 (a) Name the **four** types of natural vegetative propagation and give **one** example of a plant for each type.
  (b) Name the **four** types of artificial vegetative propagation.
4 What is a *cutting*?
5 Describe how *layering* is used to propagate plants.
6 Distinguish between a *scion* and a *stock*.
7 (a) What is *micropropagation*?
  (b) Give **two** advantages and **two** disadvantages of micropropagation.

Chapter 27 Sample examination questions

1 (i) What is *vegetative propagation*?

(ii) Give **one** example of vegetative propagation and state whether it involves a stem, a root, a leaf or a bud.

(iii) How does vegetative propagation differ from reproduction by seed? (Answer this question after studying Chapter 28.)

(iv) Artificial propagation is widely used in horticulture. Give **two** examples of artificial propagation.

(v) Suggest **one** advantage and **one** disadvantage of artificial propagation.

Section C, Question 15 (b) Ordinary Level 2005

HL 2 (i) In relation to flowering plants explain what is meant by *vegetative propagation*.

(ii) Clones are genetically identical individuals. Are the products of vegetative propagation clones? Explain your answer.

(iii) Give **two** examples of natural vegetative propagation that involve different parts of a plant.

(iv) Describe **two** techniques of artificial vegetative propagation that are used for flowering plants. Suggest a benefit of artificial propagation.

Section C, Question 14 (b) Higher Level SEC Sample Paper (2003)

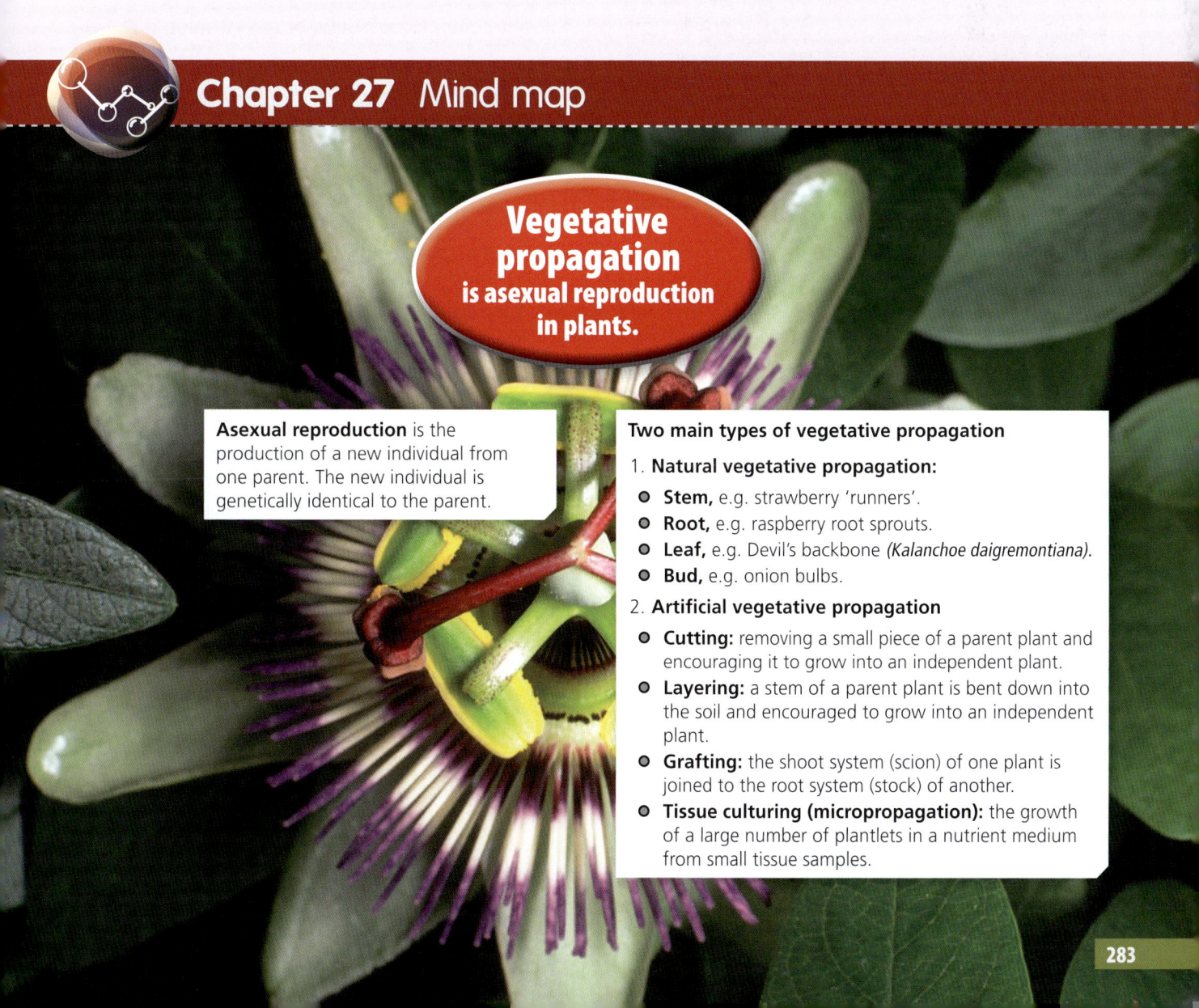

Chapter 27 Mind map

Vegetative propagation is asexual reproduction in plants.

Asexual reproduction is the production of a new individual from one parent. The new individual is genetically identical to the parent.

Two main types of vegetative propagation

1. **Natural vegetative propagation:**
   - **Stem,** e.g. strawberry 'runners'.
   - **Root,** e.g. raspberry root sprouts.
   - **Leaf,** e.g. Devil's backbone *(Kalanchoe daigremontiana)*.
   - **Bud,** e.g. onion bulbs.

2. **Artificial vegetative propagation**
   - **Cutting:** removing a small piece of a parent plant and encouraging it to grow into an independent plant.
   - **Layering:** a stem of a parent plant is bent down into the soil and encouraged to grow into an independent plant.
   - **Grafting:** the shoot system (scion) of one plant is joined to the root system (stock) of another.
   - **Tissue culturing (micropropagation):** the growth of a large number of plantlets in a nutrient medium from small tissue samples.

Chapter 28: Sexual reproduction in the flowering plant

Learning objectives After studying this chapter, you should be able to:
- Describe flower structure and function.
- Describe that pollen grains produce male gametes and the embryo sac produces the egg cell and polar nuclei.
- HL ▸ Describe pollen grain development from microspore mother cells.
- ▸ Describe embryo sac development from megaspore mother cells.
- Define *pollination* and describe the various types of pollination.
- Define *fertilisation* and describe the second fertilisation.
- Describe seed structure and function.
- Distinguish between monocotyledons and dicotyledons.
- Describe fruit formation.
- Describe the four types of fruit and seed dispersal.
- Define and state the advantages of *dormancy*.
- Describe seedless fruit production.
- Define *germination* and state the factors necessary for germination.
- Describe the stages of seedling growth.
- Investigate the effect of water, oxygen and temperature on germination.
- Use starch agar or skimmed milk plates to show digestive activity during germination.

Introduction

> **Sexual reproduction** is the production of a new individual from two parents. The new individual is genetically different to both parents.

Sexual reproduction involves the formation of gametes. Gametes in plants are the male pollen grain (produced in the anther) and the egg cell (produced in the ovary). When the male gamete fertilises the egg cell, a diploid zygote is formed that goes on to develop into a seed enclosed within a fruit.

Structure and function of flowers

The function of flowers is sexual reproduction. Even though there is an amazing diversity in the flowers of plants, the basic structure of the flower remains the same. All flowers have the following structures: **carpel (stigma, style, and ovary), stamen (anther and filament), sepal, petal** and **receptacle** (Fig 28.1).

- The carpel is the female part of the flower, and is composed of the stigma, style and ovary. Flowers usually have a number of carpels. The stigma is a sticky part of the carpel where pollen grains are trapped. The style is a stalk that places the stigma in a position most likely to trap pollen grains. The ovary contains one or more ovules that, following fertilisation, will develop into the seeds. Each ovule contains an **embryo sac,** the structure in which the egg cell and **polar nuclei** develop.

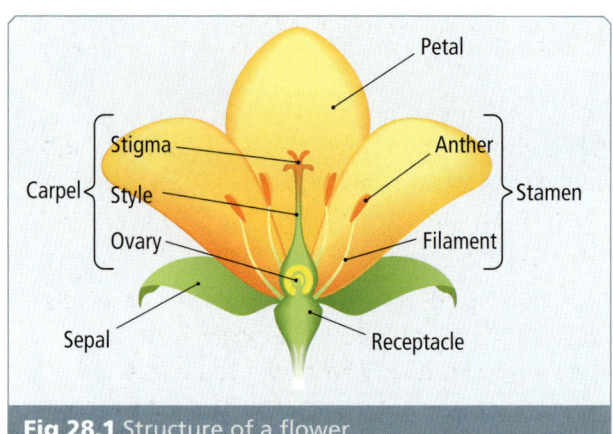

Fig 28.1 Structure of a flower.

- The stamen is the male part of the flower, and is composed of the anther and filament. Flowers usually have many stamens. The anther is an organ in which pollen grains develop. When the pollen is mature, the anther breaks open easily – either by wind action or by being broken open when an insect brushes past. Each pollen grain contains the male gamete. The filament is a stalk that places the anther in a position most likely to result in the pollen grains being transferred away from the flower.
- Sepals protect the developing flower before it blooms.
- The petals in brightly coloured flowers attract insects, and are called insect-pollinated flowers. Petals can also be very small and green.
- The receptacle is the organ from which the flower develops and functions in supporting the flower following blooming.

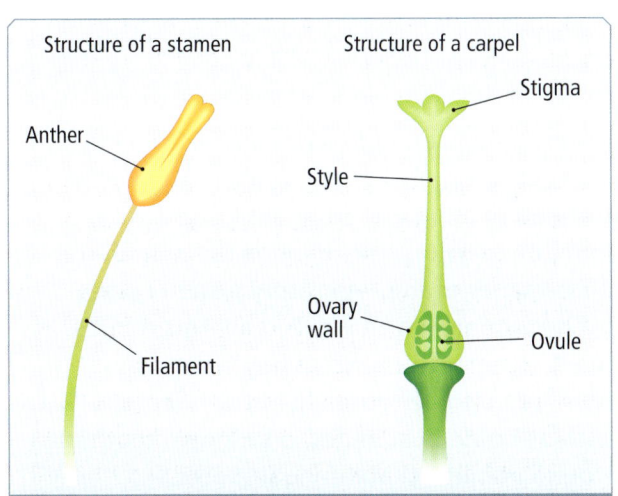

Fig 28.2 The reproductive organs in flowers: stamen and carpel.

Gamete formation (HL)

Embryo sac development

Cells within the ovule start out **diploid**. These are called **megaspore mother cells**. They are called 'megaspore' because they eventually give rise to the egg cell, which is a very large cell.

The megaspore mother cell undergoes **meiosis** to produce **four haploid daughter cells**. These cells are immature. Three eventually die, with the remaining one going on to develop into the embryo sac. The nucleus of the new haploid cell undergoes **three rounds of mitosis**, but no cell division.

We learned in Chapter 13 that mitosis is a type of cell division in which the numbers of chromosomes are maintained. Therefore, if a diploid cell divides by mitosis, the resulting cells will remain diploid with the same numbers of chromosomes. Similarly, if a haploid cell undergoes mitosis, the resulting cells will remain haploid.

Following the three rounds of mitosis, without cell division, the haploid cell has **eight haploid nuclei.** This is because the first round of mitosis produced two nuclei from one. The second round produced four nuclei from two and the third round of mitosis produced eight nuclei from four. The eight new nuclei are arranged as shown in Fig 28.3.

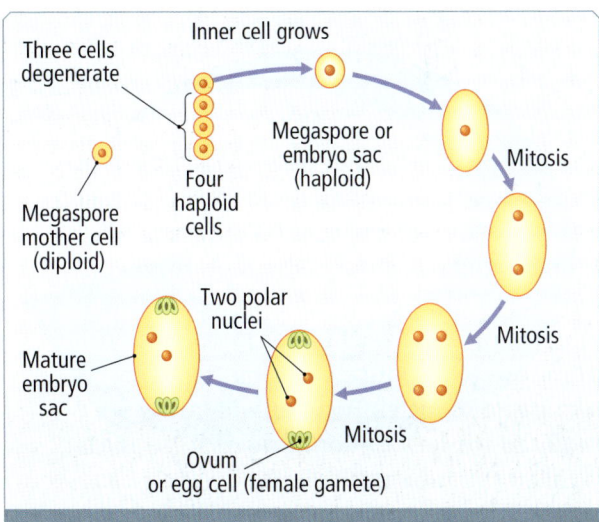

Fig 28.3 Embryo sac development.

All but two nuclei form cell membranes. One of the six newly formed cells becomes the egg cell (female gamete). Two more cells, which are smaller than the central egg cell, stay close to the egg cell. Three cells remain at the top of the embryo sac. The two nuclei that did not form cell membranes remain in the centre of the embryo sac and are known as the **polar nuclei**. The embryo sac remains in this condition until fertilisation.

Pollen grain development

Pollen grain development occurs within the anthers of the flower. The anther is supplied with nutrients by the vascular strand (Fig 28.4). Cells within the chambers of the anther start out **diploid**. These are called **microspore mother cells**. They are called 'microspore' because once the pollen grains are fully formed, they are much smaller than the egg cell. They are supplied with food from a layer inside the anther called the **tapetum**.

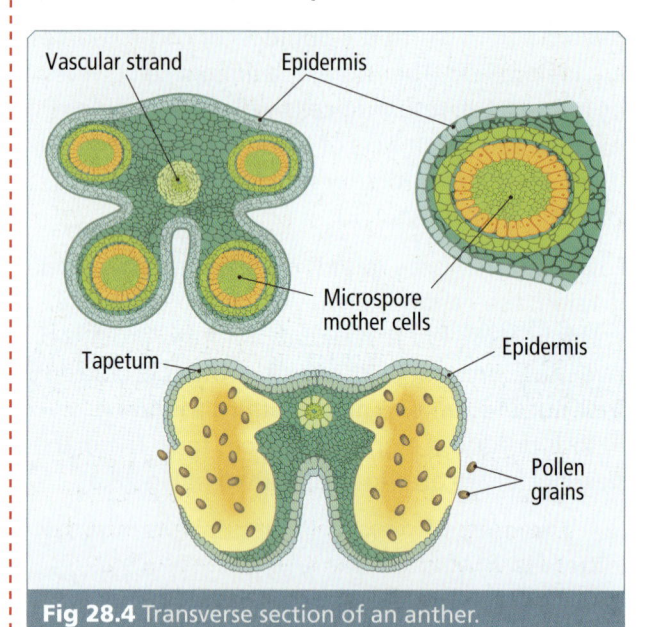

Fig 28.4 Transverse section of an anther.

The microspore mother cells divide by **meiosis** to produce **four haploid daughter cells,** called a tetrad. None of the cells degenerate. All four haploid daughter cells go on to the next stage of pollen grain development. The haploid cells each undergo one round of mitosis (without cell division) to form two haploid nuclei. Two haploid nuclei are required for fertilisation. One of these nuclei is called the **tube nucleus** and the other is called the **generative nucleus.**

The pollen grain then matures to form a tough inner and outer wall called the **intine** and **exine,** respectively. The exine of pollen grains varies depending on the species: it can be smooth or have many different textures.

The mature pollen is released when the thin epidermis layer (Fig 28.4) breaks open. Pollen grains come in all shapes and sizes (Fig 28.6). Some are small, smooth and round, whereas others are large, irregular shaped and sticky. Some pollen grains can also possess spines on their surface.

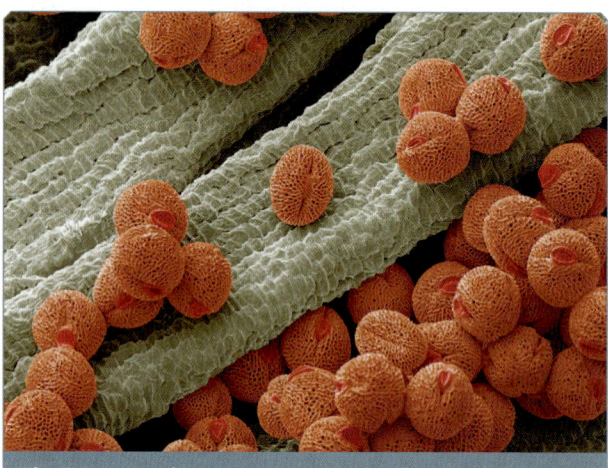

Fig 28.6 An electron micrograph of some of the various shapes of pollen grains.

Pollen is small enough to be inhaled directly into our lungs. As a result, pollen can become trapped in our air passages and cause an immune reaction. The immune reaction in the air passages of the respiratory system causes inflammation, which is called **allergic rhinitis,** more commonly known as **hay fever.** Hay fever can also be caused by other allergens such as house dust, mites, duck down feathers (found in pillows) and fungal spores.

Fig 28.5 Pollen grain development.

Fig 28.7 Hay fever (allergic rhinitis).

Pollination

> **Pollination** is the transfer of pollen from the anther to the stigma of a flower of the same species.

Fig 28.8 Pollen being carefully taken from a flower.

There are two types of pollination: self-pollination and cross-pollination.

> **Self-pollination** is the transfer of pollen from the anther to the stigma of the same plant.
>
> **Cross-pollination** is the transfer of pollen from the anther to the stigma of a different plant but of the same species.

Cross-pollination is much more desirable for the plant than self-pollination as cross-pollination creates variation. Plants resulting from cross-pollination show stronger growth than plants resulting from self-pollination.

Self-pollination will generally only occur when a plant has failed to cross-pollinate with another plant of the same species.

There are two types of cross-pollination:

1. **Animal pollination:** The pollen grains are physically carried by animals from one flower to another. Most animal pollination is carried out by insects, but other animals such as birds can also contribute. Examples of flowers that are pollinated by animals include any brightly coloured flower such as the rose, tulip, dandelion, lily and pink clematis.

Fig 28.9 Animal (insect)-pollination. A bee obtains nectar from the flower and inadvertently carries pollen away on its body.

2. **Wind pollination:** The pollen grains travel on air current from one flower to another. Examples of wind-pollinated plants include all grasses and cereals, and trees such as hazel, sweet chestnut and conifers.

Fig 28.10 Wind-pollination. The anthers of wind-pollinated flowers tend to be very large and produce a large amount of pollen.

Structure of animal-pollinated flowers

Animal-pollinated flowers tend to have large petals that are brightly coloured to attract insects. They also tend to be scented and have **nectar,** a sugary solution at the base of flowers. The anthers are usually firmly attached to the base of the filaments and are located within the flower. This is to maximise the chances of the insects brushing against the anthers when they are collecting the nectar.

Animal-pollinated flowers generally produce less pollen than wind-pollinated flowers. The insects efficiently transfer pollen from one flower to another, so there is no need to produce large amounts of pollen.

Pollen from animal-pollinated flowers tends to be larger than the pollen from wind-pollinated flowers. It can also be sticky and spiny to allow easy attachment to the surface of an insect.

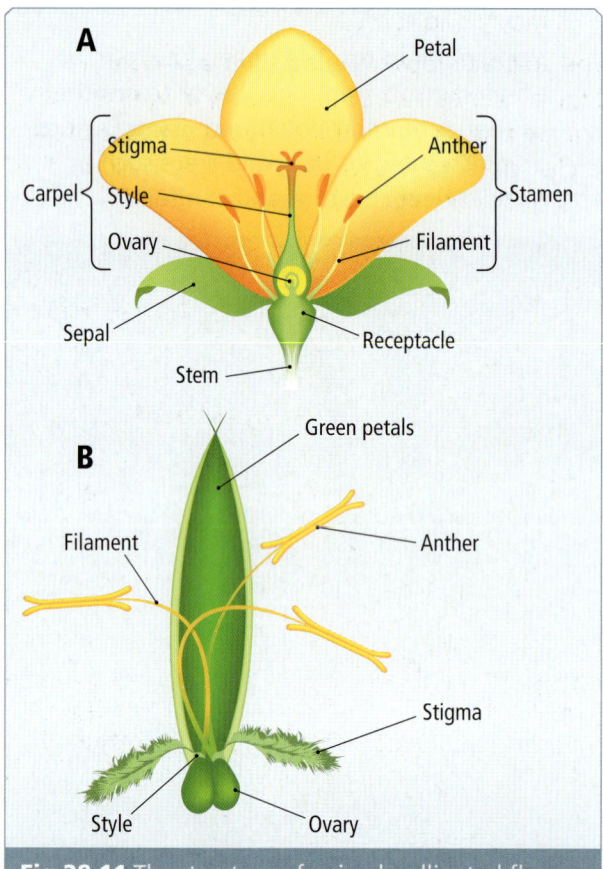

Fig 28.11 The structure of animal-pollinated flowers (A) and wind-pollinated flowers (B).

Structure of wind-pollinated flowers

Wind-pollinated flowers tend to have small green petals. There is no advantage to a wind-pollinated plant having brightly coloured petals. They are not scented and do not have any nectar.

The anthers are usually very large, outside the flower and loosely attached when fully mature. This allows the pollen to be released easily in the wind.

The stigmas are also large, outside the flower and feathery to increase the chances of catching pollen.

Wind-pollinated flowers have to produce huge quantities of pollen to ensure their pollen is transferred to another flower that may be some distance away. Their pollen tends to be very small, light and smooth, so it can be carried easily on wind currents.

Fertilisation

> **Fertilisation** is the union of a haploid male gamete with a haploid female gamete to form a diploid zygote.

Once the pollen grain has landed on the stigma, chemical signals stimulate the formation of a pollen tube. A pollen tube is a structure through which the male gametes move on their way towards the egg.

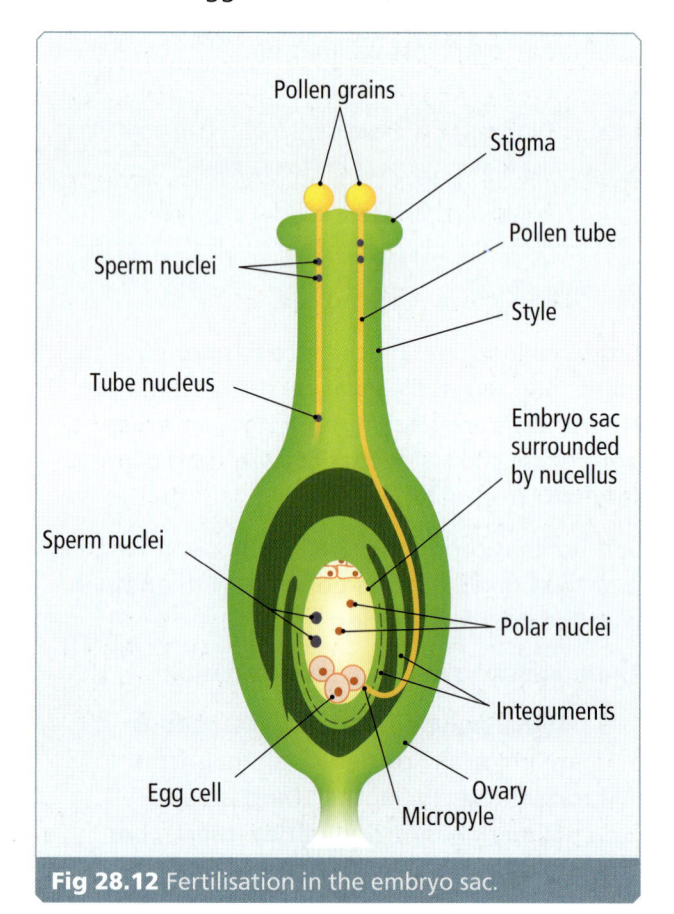

Fig 28.12 Fertilisation in the embryo sac.

There are two nuclei in a pollen grain, one called the **tube nucleus** and the other called the **generative nucleus**.

Sexual reproduction in the flowering plant   Chapter 28

- The tube nucleus is responsible for forming the pollen tube. The tube nucleus moves down through the stigma and style and enters the ovary at the micropyle (a small opening in the ovule), guided towards the egg by chemotropism. Once the pollen tube is fully formed, the tube nucleus degenerates, as it is no longer needed.
- The generative nucleus enters the pollen tube and makes its way towards the ovary. As it travels through the pollen tube, it undergoes another round of **mitosis** to form **two sperm nuclei**. Both sperm nuclei are **haploid**.
- The sperm nuclei enter the ovule and the embryo sac. One fertilises the egg cell to become a **diploid zygote**. The zygote immediately starts dividing by mitosis to become the **plant embryo**.

Second fertilisation

The second sperm nucleus enters the embryo sac. It fuses with the **two polar nuclei** forming a **triploid (3n) nucleus,** which goes on to form **endosperm**. The young embryo uses the endosperm as a food source during development and/or during germination.

The two fertilisations that occur within the embryo sac are often called a 'double fertilisation'.

Seed structure and function

The fertilised egg divides by mitosis to become a young plant embryo and seed leaves called **cotyledons**. We learned in Chapter 24 that a cotyledon is an embryonic seed leaf.

The embryo is an immature plant which will grow into a new mature plant when ideal conditions are present. The embryo consists of a young radicle, which will go on to form the root, and a young plumule, which will go on to form the shoot.

> The **radicle** is the embryonic root.
> The **plumule** is the embryonic shoot.

The embryo of monocots has one cotyledon (seed leaf), whereas the embryo of dicots has two cotyledons.

The triploid endosperm swells with food (lipids, proteins and carbohydrates) by absorbing the inner layer of the ovule, called the **nucellus**. As the seed matures one of two things happens:

1. The cotyledons absorb all of the endosperm to give what is called a **non-endospermic** seed, which is common to dicots, such as broad beans, peanuts and sunflowers.
2. The cotyledons absorb only a small amount of the endosperm to give what is called an **endospermic** seed. Endospermic seeds are nearly always monocots, such as maize and corn.

The embryo stops growing after a period of time and enters a dormant stage, in which it will remain until germination. The walls of the ovule (called the **integuments**) dry out and become the wall of the seed **(testa)**.

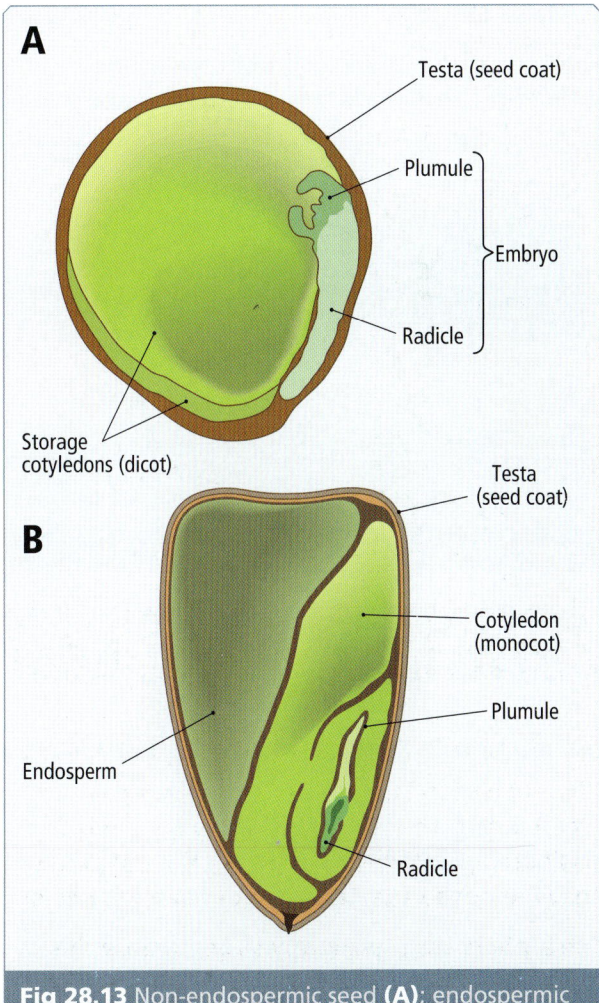

Fig 28.13 Non-endospermic seed **(A)**; endospermic seed **(B)**.

Fruit formation

Fruit formation occurs after fertilisation at the same time as seed development. The flower parts are no longer needed following fertilisation and die away.

True fruits

Fruit formation involves the **ovary** swelling with food and sometimes water. Fruits that swell with water as well as food are called succulent fruits, and include apricots, plums, peaches and oranges. Other fruits that swell with food only are called dry fruits, and include beans, nuts and grains. In both succulent and dry fruits, the ovary wall becomes the fruit wall, called the **pericarp**.

False fruits

You might have noticed that common fruits such as apples, pears and strawberries were not in the above list of succulent fruits. This is because they are false fruits.

False fruits do not develop from the ovary. Instead the **receptacle** swells with food and water.

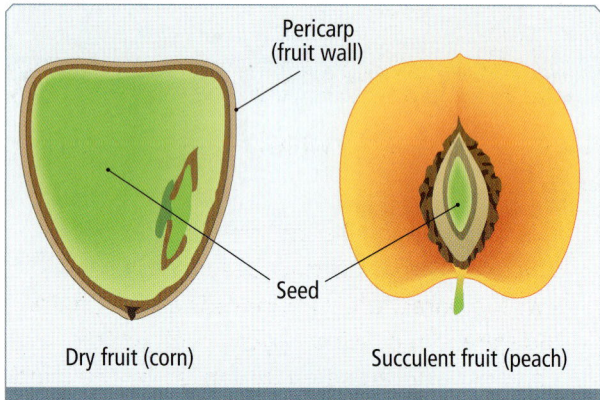

Fig 28.14 Dry and succulent fruit structures.

Fig 28.15 An apple is a false fruit (it develops from the receptacle of the flower).

Advantage of fruit formation

Whether the fruit is true or false, fruit formation is an advantage to the plant. It protects the seeds until they are ready to germinate. Fruits also attract animals, which eat the fruit and disperse the seeds away from the parent plant.

Seedless fruits

Seedless fruits are fruits formed without seeds (Fig 28.16 A and B). It is nicer to eat seedless versions of some fruits, such as seedless grapes. Seedless fruits also have a longer shelf life. As a result, seedless fruits are commercially more valuable than seeded fruits.

Fig 28.16 Seedless water melon (**A**) and seedless oranges (**B**).

Seedless fruits are formed in two ways: **genetic manipulation** and **auxin treatment**.

1. Genetic manipulation can occur naturally, or is more commonly induced by horticulturists.
   - **Natural genetic manipulation:** Occasionally plants produce seedless fruits due to changes in their chromosome numbers that cause the egg cell and/or pollen grains to become unviable and seeds do not develop.
   - **Artificial genetic manipulation:** This is similar to natural genetic manipulation, but is induced artificially. Special breeding programmes are carried out to change the numbers of chromosomes in the offspring. In this way, the gametes become unviable and seeds do not develop.

2 Auxin treatment is where the horticulturist or farmer sprays the plants with auxins. This stimulates the ovary to swell with food before fertilisation has occurred. Tomatoes and cucumbers are examples of fruits produced in this way. Auxin treatment also has the effect of making the fruits much bigger than they would be otherwise.

Ripening of fruit

Fruit ripens over time. Bananas turn from green to yellow to black as they ripen. Similarly, tomatoes turn from green to red as they ripen. Many fruits start out green and turn to their characteristic colour as they ripen.

Ethene is a gas important in the ripening of fruit, both naturally and artificially. Ethene ripens fruit by making the cell walls less rigid.

Ethene is also responsible for leaf fall in autumn, a process called abscission.

Fruit stored in a closed plastic bag ripens more quickly. The bag traps the ethene that the fruit produces naturally, speeding up the ripening process.

Fig 28.17 Bananas ripening.

Fruit and seed dispersal

Dispersal is the transfer of seeds and fruit away from the parent plant.

Dispersal is advantageous to a plant as it:
- Prevents competition between the parent plant and offspring.
- Allows the plant to colonise new habitats.
- Increases chances of survival.

Fig 28.18 Animals help in the dispersal of seeds.

There are four ways in which plants disperse their seeds and fruits:

1 **Wind dispersal:** Dandelion plants and sycamore trees produce seeds and fruits with a parachute of hundreds of light hairs (dandelion) or wings (sycamore), which means they can be easily carried by the wind.

Fig 28.19 shows the structure of these seeds.

Fig 28.19 Dandelion 'parachute' **(A)** and the winged seeds of the sycamore **(B)**.

2 **Water dispersal:** Coconut trees and water lilies produce fruits that can float on water. They are carried by water currents until they find a suitable place to grow (Fig 28.20).

Fig 28.20 Coconut (A) and water lily (B) fruits.

3 **Animal dispersal:** Many plants rely on animals to disperse their fruits. Animals eat the fruit, the seeds pass through the digestive system and are subsequently egested (released in the faeces) possibly in another habitat. Animals can also carry the fruit on their fur, for example, goose grass and burdock fruits are dispersed in this way (Fig 28.21).

Fig 28.21 Goose grass (A) and burdock (B) fruits.

4 **Self dispersal:** Pea pods are an example of a plant that self-disperses its seeds (Fig 28.22). When the pod dries out, it splits open very quickly. This causes the seeds (peas) to shoot out.

Fig 28.22 Self-dispersal of peas.

Dormancy

> **Dormancy** is a resting period for the seed when it undergoes no growth.

Dormancy is another adaptation flowering plants have developed. It is advantageous to plants for the following reasons:

- It allows time for seed dispersal.
- It allows time for embryo development within the seed.
- It allows the plant to avoid harsh winter conditions.
- It allows the plant time to fully develop before the following winter.
- It allows germination in the springtime to be staggered to maximise survival of plants from each seed.

Dormancy is brought about by growth regulators in the seed that prevent growth and germination. The main growth regulator responsible for dormancy is abscisic acid. You may notice the similarity with the word 'abscission'. It was thought that abscisic acid caused abscission. However, it was subsequently discovered that ethene causes abscission. Dormancy growth regulators, such as abscisic acid minimise metabolic activities during harsh environmental conditions.

There are many different types of dormancy. They are complicated by the fact that plant scientists have not agreed on a classification system for the different types of dormancy. Seeds go into and stay in dormancy for a range of different reasons that often overlap.

Seeds enter dormancy and remain dormant for one or a combination of the following reasons:

- The temperature has decreased.
- Day length has decreased.
- Rainfall has decreased or increased (depending on the species).
- Abscisic acid levels are high within the seed.
- Growth promoter levels are low within the seed.

Dormancy in agriculture and horticulture

Breaking dormancy and stimulating germination in seeds sometimes poses a problem for gardeners and farmers. All seeds of a particular species are genetically unique and germinate at different times of the year or may not germinate at all even when exposed to certain conditions.

Gardeners and farmers often carry out certain procedures on the seeds to maximise germination and to ensure all the seeds germinate at the same time. These procedures include:

- **Scarification:** This involves slightly damaging the seed coat to allow oxygen and water in. It also allows the young plant to break through the testa. It may involve rubbing seeds on sandpaper or soaking in hot water or even acid.
- **Pre-chilling:** This involves storing seeds at cold temperatures for a certain period of time, depending on the species.
- **Heating:** This involves exposing the seeds to a certain amount of heat to stimulate germination. Some species of seed show a higher rate of germination following a fire!
- **Treatment with growth regulators:** This involves adding a plant growth regulator, such as gibberellin, to the seed to stimulate germination.

Germination

> **Germination** is the regrowth of a plant embryo after a period of dormancy when environmental conditions are suitable.

Fig 28.23 Germination of a red clover plant.

The embryo consists of a radicle, a hypocotyl, cotyledon(s), epicotyl and plumule. There is also endosperm present. Germination involves the reactivation of metabolism, and the emergence of the **radicle** and **plumule through the seed coat (testa).**

Three general conditions **must** be met before germination can occur:

1. The embryo must be alive (viable).
2. Any factors maintaining dormancy and/or preventing germination must be overcome.
3. Ideal environmental conditions must exist for germination – water, oxygen and a suitable temperature.

Even if the above three general conditions are satisfied, some seeds, for unknown reasons, may not germinate. Seeds can remain dormant in the soil for many years before germinating. Recently, a 32,000-year-old frozen seed belonging to a flowering plant native to Siberia was germinated. It has grown into a healthy plant producing flowers and seeds of its own. Previously, the oldest known seed that had been successfully germinated was a 2000-year-old Judean Date Palm tree seed found in Israel.

External and internal conditions have to be just right for the regrowth of the embryo. For example, if the levels of abscisic acid are too high within the seed, germination will not occur no matter how ideal the external conditions are in the environment.

As already mentioned above, the three environmental conditions that are essential for all seeds to germinate are the presence of oxygen, presence of water and the presence of a suitable temperature.

1. **Oxygen:** This is required for aerobic respiration (*see* Chapter 12), with the subsequent metabolic reactions relying on the energy produced by aerobic respiration.
2. **Water:** This is the medium in which all metabolic reactions occur. Water even takes part in some metabolic reactions, such as digestion. Digestion is the first set of reactions that occur in a germinating seed. Water is also required to wash away the inhibitors that maintain seed dormancy.

3. **Suitable temperature:** This is needed for metabolic reactions such as respiration, digestion and protein synthesis. All metabolic reactions are controlled by enzymes. As we learned in Chapter 9, enzymes are affected by temperature. This is one of the reasons that germination will occur only when a suitable temperature is reached.

Digestion in a germinating seed

Germination begins with digestion of the food reserves in the cotyledons and/or the endosperm. The lipids (oils) must be digested to fatty acids and glycerol; the carbohydrate (starch) must be converted to glucose; and the protein must be converted to amino acids.

Digestion allows for the embryo to grow. Digestion is a catabolic reaction and requires water. The biomolecules produced (fatty acids, glycerol, glucose and amino acids) are moved into the growing embryo.

These food reserves (in the cotyledons and/or endosperm) are used to enable the young plant to push its way through the soil. Once above soil level, photosynthesis can take over as the source of food.

Respiration in a germinating seed

Once food molecules have been mobilised from the food stores (cotyledons and/or endosperm) to the embryo, respiration occurs. This creates the energy needed for anabolic reactions. Growth involves anabolic reactions, such as the formation of DNA and protein for each new cell produced. As the food reserves are used up during the process of germination, the **dry weight** of the seed **decreases.**

> ! The **dry weight** of the seed is the mass of the seed minus the water.

Dry weight is calculated by placing the seeds, at various stages of germination, into an oven at 100 °C overnight. The seed is weighed once cooled.

Once the young plant shoot moves above soil level and starts to photosynthesise, the biomolecules (glucose) needed for respiration to occur are produced and the dry weight of the seedling **increases** once again.

Stages of seedling growth

A seedling is a young plant that has just germinated. There are two types of seedling growth: **epigeal** and **hypogeal.**

1 Epigeal

The term *'epigeal'* means 'growing above ground'. In the context of germination, epigeal refers to the fact that the cotyledon(s) move above the ground during germination and start to photosynthesise (Fig 28.24).

Firstly, the seed absorbs water and swells. The **radicle,** which is the embryonic root, emerges from the seed after about three days.

The radicle grows down towards gravity (positively geotropic). Water and minerals are absorbed from the soil.

The part of the embryo just below the cotyledon(s), but above the radicle, is called the **hypocotyl.** The hypocotyl begins to grow rapidly. One of two things happens (depending on the plant) as a result of this growth:

1. The cotyledon(s) are pulled out of the seed coat and move above the ground to photosynthesise. The testa is left behind in the soil.
2. The entire seed is pushed above ground with the cotyledons still enclosed in the testa. Eventually, the testa falls away, leaving the cotyledon(s) to photosynthesise.

Fig 28.24 Epigeal germination in the sunflower plant.

In both cases, the plumule is protected by the cotyledon(s). Once the cotyledon(s) are above the soil, they start photosynthesising, producing food which is transported to all areas of the new seedling for growth.

The plumule is exposed when the cotyledon(s) separates. The part of the embryo just above the cotyledon(s), but below the plumule, is called the **epicotyl**. The epicotyl begins to grow (positive phototropism and negative geotropism) and leaves are formed.

2 Hypogeal

In hypogeal germination, the cotyledon(s) remains below the soil. The epicotyl grows rapidly and pushes the plumule above the soil, leaving the cotyledon(s) behind.

The plumule grows upwards (positive phototropism and negative geotropism), leaves are produced and photosynthesis occurs.

The cotyledon(s) remain within the testa below the soil.

Comparison of reproduction by seed with vegetative propagation

Many plants use both methods of reproduction. However, there are advantages and disadvantages to both methods. These are outlined in the table below.

Fig 28.25 Hypogeal germination in the broad bean plant.

Seed reproduction (sexual)		Vegetative propagation (asexual)	
Advantages	Disadvantages	Advantages	Disadvantages
Produces genetic variation	Complex process relying heavily on environmental factors	Simple process not so reliant on environmental factors	Offspring are genetically identical to parents
Seeds can be dispersed widely, reducing competition	Wasteful process, using a lot of energy	Efficient process with little waste of energy	Offspring will grow very near to parent plant, creating competition
Good chance of surviving a harsh winter	Long period of growth required to reach maturity	Relatively short period of growth to reach maturity	May be killed by a harsh winter
Seed bank of dormant seeds are produced	Slow reproductive rate	Fast reproductive rate	No dormant structures are produced

Unit 3   The Organism

Practical activity: to investigate the effect of water, oxygen and temperature on germination

This experiment can be done using Petri dishes and an anaerobic jar, if available, or more simply using boiling tubes. It is better to use boiling tubes rather than test-tubes for this experiment, as it is easier to get cotton wool into and out of them.

Rapidly germinating seeds such as radish, mustard or cress seeds are ideal for this experiment.

Method

1. Label four boiling tubes A, B, C and D.
2. Add a small but equal amount of cotton wool to each.
3. Add four radish (or other suitable) seeds to each boiling tube.
4. Add the same amount of water to tubes A and B.
5. Add some cool boiled water to tube C so that the seeds are totally submerged.
6. Add a small amount of vegetable oil on top of the water in tube C only.
7. Leave tube D dry (without water).
8. Place tubes A, C and D in an incubator set at 25 °C.
9. Place tube B in a refrigerator (at 4 °C).
10. Leave the tubes for two to three days.
11. Copy and complete the following results table:

NOTE: Boiled water contains no dissolved oxygen.

NOTE: Adding vegetable oil prevents re-entry of oxygen to the water.

Tube	Conditions present	Condition absent	Result
A	Oxygen Water Warmth	None (control)	
B	Oxygen Water	Warmth	
C	Water Warmth	Oxygen	
D	Oxygen Warmth	Water	

Conclusion

What did we learn from this practical activity?

- Boiling water removes dissolved oxygen.
- Water, oxygen and a suitable temperature are necessary for germination.

Practical activity questions

1. Describe **two** ways in which you ensured the practical activity was fair.
2. What plant did you use? Explain why you chose this plant.
3. Explain how you eliminated each environmental factor in setting up this practical activity.
4. What were your results?

Sexual reproduction in the flowering plant Chapter 28

Tube A: contains all three factors (CONTROL)

Tube B: contains water, oxygen but is placed in the fridge.

Tube C: contains water and a suitable temperature, but no oxygen

Tube D: contains oxygen and a suitable temperature, but no water

Fig 28.26 Experiment to investigate the three factors necessary for germination.

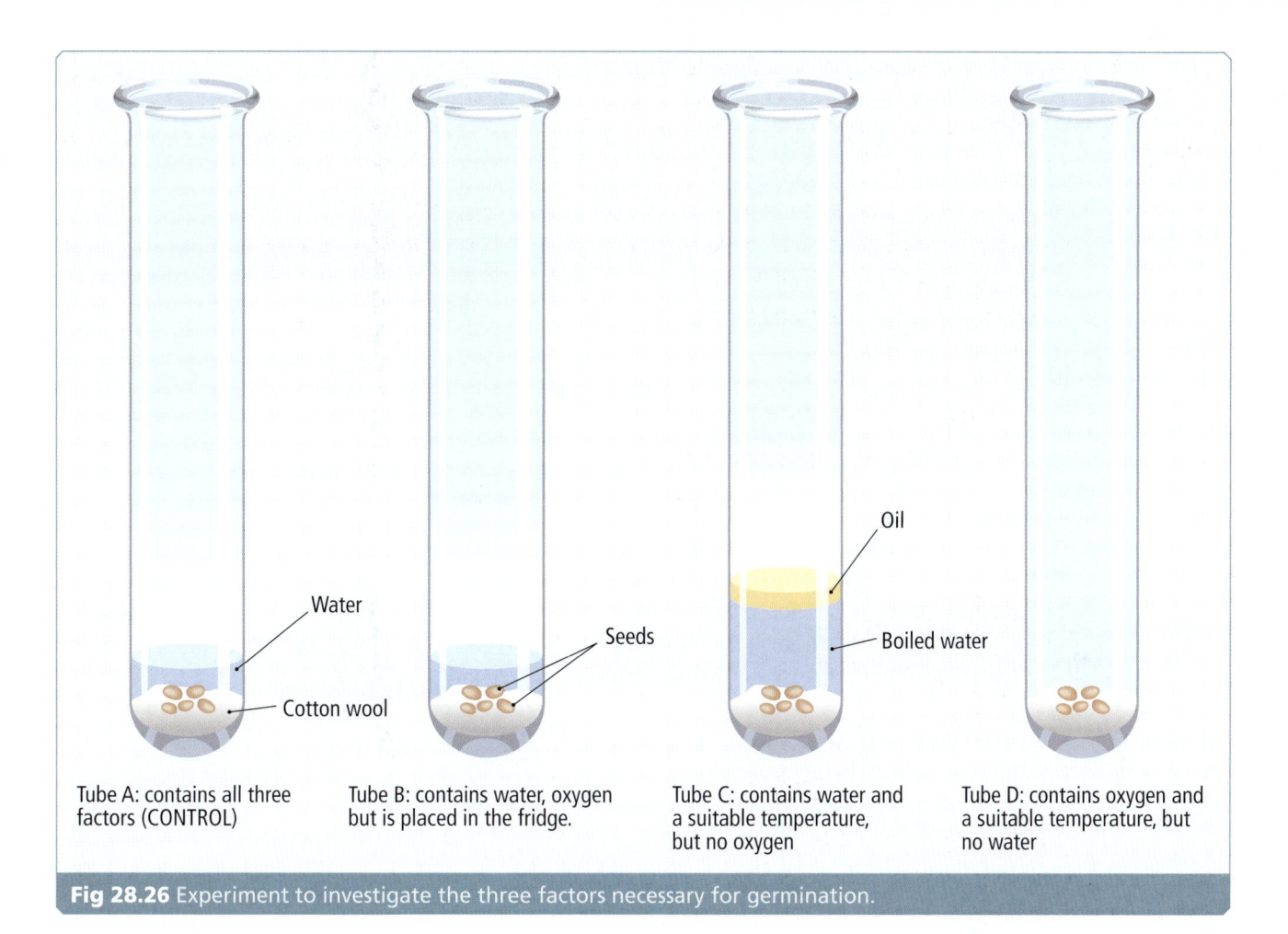

Practical activity: to use starch agar or skimmed milk plates to show digestive activity during germination

This experiment involves using either starch agar plates or skimmed milk plates. In the following experiment, we will use starch agar plates.

Germinating seeds contain various enzymes that are active in mobilising stored foods such as starch. One of these enzymes is amylase, which digests starch to maltose. Therefore, the starch in the starch agar plates will be broken down by a germinating seed.

Broad bean seeds are ideal for this practical activity.

To make the starch agar for this practical activity, dissolve 1.5 g of nutrient agar and 1 g of starch into 100 ml of water, sterilise the mixture, pour into sterilised Petri dishes and allow to set by cooling for 15 minutes.

Method

1. Soak four broad bean seeds in water for 48 hours. This stimulates germination.
2. Disinfect your bench.
3. Kill two of the seeds by boiling them for 10 minutes (control).
4. Cut all seeds (living and dead) in half using a backed blade.

SAFETY
Be extremely careful when cutting the seeds in half as the seeds can easily slip during cutting.

NOTE: Do not worry if the seed coats peel off during boiling. Do not try to put them back on.

5. Sterilise all seeds (living and dead) by dipping them into a dilute alcohol solution or dilute disinfectant solution for 10 seconds.
6. Sterilise forceps by dipping them in a dilute alcohol/disinfectant solution or by flaming them in a Bunsen flame.
7. Use the sterilised forceps to take the living and dead seeds and place them into the starch agar plates, with the **cut side facing the agar.** Place the living seeds into a dish labelled 'test' and the dead seeds into another dish labelled 'control'.

> **NOTE** When placing the seeds into the starch agar plate, open the plates only a small amount so as to minimise the chances of bacteria and fungi growing.

8. Store the dishes in a 25 °C incubator for three days.
9. Remove the seeds after the incubation period and add iodine solution.
10. Allow the iodine to soak into the agar for a few minutes and then pour off any excess.
11. Record the results.

Results

The area the seeds were positioned will be one of two colours: either blue-black, showing the presence of starch, or yellow-red, showing the absence of starch.

Dish	Iodine test
Test (live seeds)	
Control (boiled seeds)	

Conclusion

What have we learned from this practical activity?

- Germinating seeds digest and use up starch.
- Boiling seeds denature the enzymes necessary for digestion (the seeds are killed).

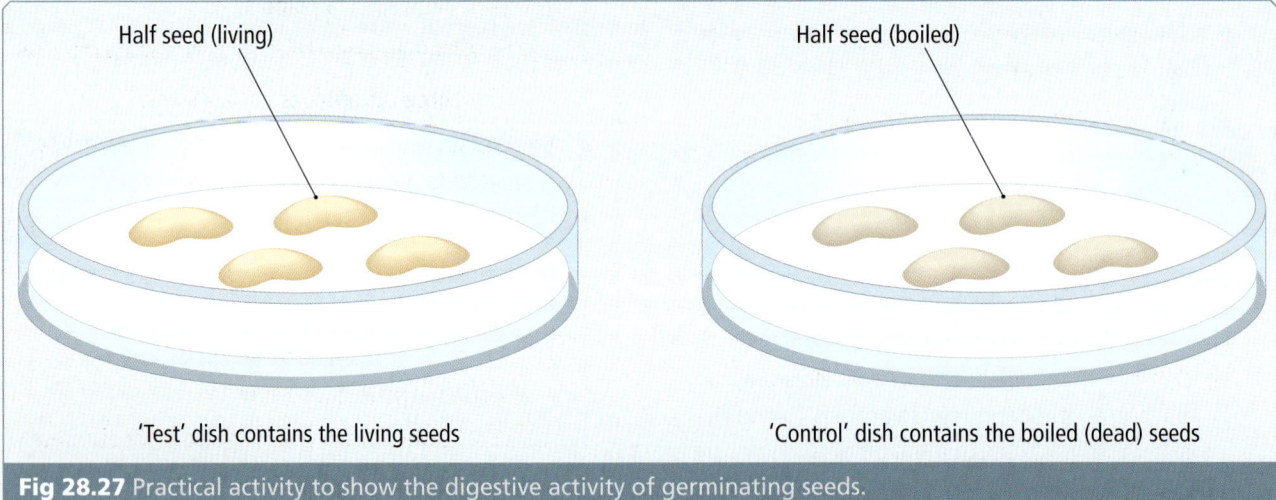

Fig 28.27 Practical activity to show the digestive activity of germinating seeds.

Practical activity questions

1. How did you prepare the starch agar/skimmed milk plates?
2. What seeds did you use?
3. Explain the importance of soaking the seeds for 48 hours before carrying out the practical activity.
4. Explain why you boiled some of the seeds.
5. Explain the importance of sterilising all the seeds before placing them into the starch-agar/skimmed milk plates.
6. Explain how you tested to see if the germinating seeds digested the starch/milk.

Chapter 28 Questions

1. Draw the structure of a typical animal-pollinated flower and label the following: *sepal; receptacle; ovary; stigma; style; anther; filament; petal.*

HL 2. Answer the following in relation to embryo sac development:
   (a) Explain why the diploid cells within the ovary are called *megaspore mother cells.*
   (b) Explain the importance of *meiosis* and *mitosis* in embryo sac development.
   (c) Explain how, in a mature embryo sac, there are eight haploid nuclei present.
   (d) Where are the polar nuclei located within the embryo sac?

3. Answer the following in relation to pollen grain development:
   (a) Explain why the diploid cells within the ovary are called *microspore mother cells.*
   (b) Explain the importance of *meiosis* and *mitosis* in pollen grain development.
   (c) Distinguish between *tube nucleus* and *generative nucleus.*
   (d) Distinguish between *intine* and *exine.*

4. What is *hay fever*?

5. (a) Define *pollination.*
   (b) Distinguish between *cross-pollination* and *self-pollination.*
   (c) Name the **two** methods of cross-pollination.
   (d) Describe, with the aid of a labelled diagram, the events that occur immediately following pollination up to the point of fertilisation.

6. (a) Explain what is meant by the 'second fertilisation'.
   (b) What are the products of second fertilisation?
   (c) Explain how chemotropism contributes to fertilisation.

7. (a) Distinguish between the following:
      (i) *Radicle* and *plumule*
      (ii) *Endospermic* and *non-endospermic seeds*
      (iii) *Monocotyledonous* and *dicotyledonous*
   (b) Give **one** example of an endospermic seed and **one** example of a non-endospermic seed.
   (c) From which flower structure does the seed develop?
   (d) From which flower structure does the seed coat (testa) develop?

8. (a) Distinguish between true fruits and false fruits, giving **one** example in each case.
   (b) Give **two** ways in which seedless fruits can be formed.
   (c) Give **one** advantage to flowering plants of fruit production.
   (d) Name the growth regulator responsible for fruit ripening.

9. (a) Define *dispersal.*
   (b) Give **four** ways in which dispersal occurs and name **one** plant that demonstrates each type.
   (c) Name **three** reasons why dispersal is advantageous to a plant.

10. (a) In relation to seeds, what is meant by *dormancy*?
    (b) Give **three** advantages of dormancy.
    (c) Explain why a good knowledge of dormancy is useful to gardeners and farmers.

11. (a) Define *germination.*
    (b) Name **three** important biomolecules stored in a seed.
    (c) What **two** important metabolic processes occur in a germinating seed?
    (d) What **three** environmental factors are absolutely required for germination?
    (e) Give an account of the general sequence of events in germination.
    (f) Name the two types of *seedling growth* and give a brief description of both types, giving **one** example of a plant that germinates by each method.

12. Give **three** advantages of reproduction by seed and **three** advantages of reproduction by vegetative propagation.

Chapter 28 Sample examination questions

1. (i) What is meant by *fertilisation*?

   (ii) Name the part of the flower in each case:
   1. Where fertilisation occurs.
   2. That becomes the fruit.

   (iii) Each seed is made up of an <u>embryo</u>, a food store and a seed coat (testa). One function of fruit is to aid <u>dispersal</u>.

   Explain **each** of the underlined terms.

   Blackberries   Sycamore fruit

   (iv) By which method is **each** of the fruits shown above dispersed?

   (v) What term is given to the growth of an embryo into a plant?

   (vi) In order for this growth to be successful, certain environmental conditions must be present. Name any **two** of these conditions.

   Section C, Question 14 (c) Ordinary Level 2010

HL 2. (a) Give a role for **each** of the following parts of a flower: sepals, anther, stigma.

   (b) (i) Describe the development of pollen grains from microspore mother cells.

   (ii) What is meant by the term *fertilisation*?

   (iii) Give a brief account of the process of fertilisation in flowering plants.

   (c) (i) What is meant by the *dormancy* of seeds?

   (ii) Give **one** way in which the dormancy of seeds is of benefit to plants.

   (iii) Suggest **one** way in which a knowledge of dormancy is useful to farmers and gardeners.

   (iv) Water, oxygen and a suitable temperature are all required for the germination of seeds.

   In the case of **each** of these factors, describe its effect on the process of germination.

   (v) Which part of the embryo in a germinating seed gives rise to each of the following parts of the seedling?
   1. The root
   2. The shoot

   Section C, Question 13 Higher Level 2010

Chapter 28 Mind map

Sexual reproduction is the formation of a new individual from two parents. The new individual is genetically different from the parents.

Structure of a flower
- **Carpel** is the female part of the flower and comprises:
  - **Stigma:** traps pollen.
  - **Style:** holds stigma in a position to trap pollen.
  - **Ovary:** where the egg cell is produced.
- **Stamen** is the male part of the flower and comprises:
  - **Anther:** pollen is formed here.
  - **Filament:** holds anther in a position to release pollen.
- **Sepals:** protect the flower when it is in the bud.
- **Receptacle:** structure from which the flower develops and supports the flower.
- **Petals:** protect flower and attract insects.
- The **pollen** grain contains the male gamete.

Embryo sac development   HL
- Occurs within the ovule.
- The food supply is a thin layer called the nucellus.
- Meiosis occurs in the megaspore mother cells producing four haploid cells.
- Three degenerate and one forms the embryo sac.
- Nucleus of embryo sac undergoes three rounds of mitosis producing eight haploid nuclei.
- Two become the polar nuclei.
- One of the membrane-bound haploid nuclei forms the egg cell.

Pollen grain development
- Occurs within the anther.
- The food supply is a thin layer called the tapetum.
- Microspore mother cells divide by meiosis to form a tetrad of four haploid cells.
- Pollen grains mature by forming a tough wall made up of an intine and an exine layer.
- The haploid nucleus divides by mitosis to form two haploid nuclei – one is called the tube nucleus and the other is the generative nucleus.

- **Pollination:** the transfer of pollen from anther to stigma of a flower of the same species.
- **Self-pollination:** the transfer of pollen from anther to stigma of the same plant.
- **Cross-pollination:** the transfer of pollen from the anther to the stigma of a different plant but of the same species. Cross-pollination is more desirable as it creates variety and the seeds show stronger growth during germination.
- There are also two methods of pollination:
  - **Animal pollination:** pollen grains are physically carried by animals (such as insects) from one flower to another.
  - **Wind pollination:** pollen grains travel on air current from one flower to another.

Animal-pollinated flowers	Wind-pollinated flowers
Large, brightly coloured petals	Small, green petals
Nectar present and flower is often scented	No nectar present and no scent
Anthers and stigmas are small and inside flower	Anthers and stigmas are large and usually outside the flower
Anthers are firmly attached to filament	Anthers are usually loosely attached to filament
Small amounts of pollen produced that is usually large, sticky or spiny and heavy	Large amounts of pollen produced that is usually small, smooth and light

Fertilisation
- Tube nucleus forms the pollen tube.
- The generative nucleus follows the tube nucleus and divides by mitosis to form two sperm nuclei.
- **Fertilisation** is the union of a haploid male gamete with a haploid female gamete to form a diploid zygote.
- Sperm nuclei enter the embryo sac and one fertilises the egg cell.
- **Second fertilisation:** the other sperm nucleus fuses with the two polar nuclei. This forms a triploid endosperm.

Seed development

- The embryo continues to develop and then enters a dormant stage until suitable conditions for germination arrive.
- The embryo consists of a radicle, a hypocotyl, cotyledon(s), epicotyl and plumule. There is also endosperm present.
- The endosperm is sometimes completely used up by the embryo, with food reserves transferred to the cotyledon(s) – in which case the seed is called a non-endospermic seed (e.g. broad bean). Non-endospermic seeds are nearly always dicotyledonous.
- Endosperm can also exist alongside the cotyledon(s), in which case the seed is an endospermic seed (e.g. corn). Endospermic seeds are nearly always monocotyledonous.

Fruit

- Fruit formation occurs after fertilisation.
- Involves the ovary swelling with food (true fruits, e.g. grape) or the receptacle swelling with food (false fruits, e.g. apple).
- Seedless fruit occur when fruit formation occurs without fertilisation.
- This can be caused by two main methods:
  - Genetic manipulation, both natural and artificial.
  - Spraying with auxins.
- Ripening of fruit is caused by ethene – a gas released by fruit. It works by softening the cell walls. Ethene is a growth inhibitor and also causes leaf fall in autumn.

Dispersal is the transfer of seeds and fruit away from the parent plant. Dispersal is advantageous to a plant as it:

- Prevents competition between the parent plant and offspring.
- Allows the plant to colonise new habitats.
- Increases chances of survival.

There are four ways in which plants disperse their seeds and fruits:

1. **Wind,** e.g. dandelion and sycamore.
2. **Water,** e.g. coconut trees and water lilies.
3. **Animal,** e.g. plants that produce succulent fruits attract animals to eat them.
4. **Self,** e.g. pea pod dries out, splits open and the seeds (peas) shoot out.

Dormancy is a resting period for the seed when it undergoes no growth. Dormancy is advantageous to a plant because it:

1. Allows for dispersal.
2. Allows time for the embryo to develop.
3. Allows the plant to avoid the harsh environmental conditions of winter.
4. Allows the plant time to fully develop before the following winter.
5. Allows germination to be staggered to maximise survival.

Sexual reproduction is the formation of a new individual from two parents. The new individual is genetically different from the parents.

Seeds enter dormancy and remain dormant for one or a combination of the following reasons:

- Temperature has decreased.
- Day length has decreased.
- Rainfall has decreased or increased (depending on the species).
- Abscisic acid levels are high within the seed.
- Growth promoter levels are low within the seed.

Sexual reproduction in the flowering plant — Chapter 28

Farmers and gardeners use the following procedures to cause germination in seeds:

- **Scarification:** slightly damaging the seed coat to allow oxygen and water to enter.
- **Pre-chilling:** storing seeds at cold temperature
- **Heating:** exposing the seeds to a certain amount of heat.
- Adding plant **growth regulators** such as gibberellins.

Germination is the regrowth of a plant embryo after a period of dormancy when environmental conditions are suitable. There are three external environmental conditions that are essential for all seeds to germinate:

1. Presence of oxygen
2. Presence of water
3. Presence of a suitable temperature

Practical activity to investigate the effects of water, oxygen and temperature on germination

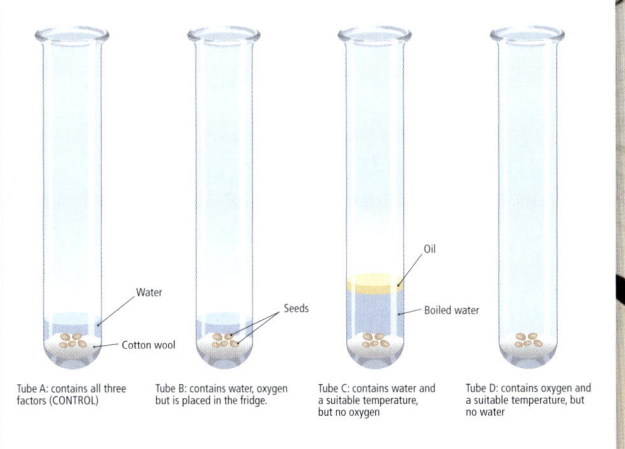

Tube A: contains all three factors (CONTROL)
Tube B: contains water, oxygen but is placed in the fridge.
Tube C: contains water and a suitable temperature, but no oxygen
Tube D: contains oxygen and a suitable temperature, but no water

The seeds in tube A germinate, whereas seeds in the other tubes do not germinate.

- Digestion occurs in a germinating seed when food reserves from the cotyledon(s) and/or the endosperm are mobilised to the growing embryo.
- Lipids (oils) are digested to fatty acids and glycerol.
- Carbohydrate (starch) is converted to glucose.
- Protein is converted to amino acids.

Practical activity to use starch agar plates to show the digestive activity of germinating seeds

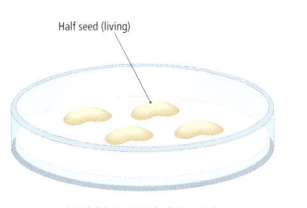

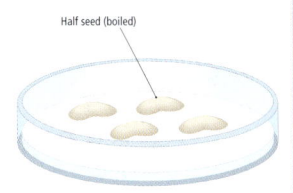

'Test' dish contains the living seeds
'Control' dish contains the boiled (dead) seeds

- The living seeds digest the starch (when iodine is added the colour remains a yellow red colour).
- The dead seeds do not digest the starch (when iodine is added the colour turns blue-black).

Stages of seedling growth

1. **Epigeal**
   - The seed absorbs water and swells.
   - Radicle emerges and grows down.
   - The hypocotyl starts to grow rapidly.
   - The cotyledon(s) are pulled out of the seed and pushed above ground.

   OR

   - The entire seed is pushed above soil level.
   - The plumule is protected by the cotyledon(s).
   - The cotyledon(s) open and photosynthesise.
   - The plumule starts to grow rapidly producing leaves.

2. **Hypogeal**
   - The epicotyl grows and pushes the plumule above the soil, which grows rapidly, producing leaves.
   - The seed, with the cotyledon(s), remains below the soil.

Seed reproduction	Vegetative propagation
Complex process	Simple process
Wasteful of energy	Energy efficient
Long period of growth required	Short period of growth required
Produces genetic variation	Offspring are genetically identical
Dispersal reduces competition	No dispersal
Survives harsh winters	May not survive winter
Seed bank produced	No dormant structures are produced
Slow reproductive rate	Fast reproductive rate

303

Chapter 29 Homeostasis

Learning objectives After studying this chapter, you should be able to:
- Define *homeostasis*.
- Distinguish between an *endotherm* and an *ectotherm*.
- Describe the importance of homeostasis for living organisms.

Introduction

> **Homeostasis** is the maintenance of a constant internal environment.

Homeostasis enables organisms to function in a wide variety of environmental conditions. Bodily functions continue despite changes in the environment.

Temperature regulation

Maintaining the correct temperature is very important to many living organisms, as metabolism depends on temperature. Metabolism will slow down or even stop in living organisms if the temperature of the cells is not maintained above a certain level.

In plants

Plants can survive in a range of temperatures. Many can survive extremely cold conditions (below 0 °C) and at temperatures above 40 °C. If the plant is too hot, it may increase transpiration in order to cool itself.

In animals

Animals can also resist quite wide temperature fluctuations (changes). For example, some types of insect can produce their own antifreeze (glycerol) to enable them to survive harsh winters. Most animals, however, maintain their body temperatures above freezing at all times.

All animals can be classified into two groups based on the way they regulate their temperature: **endotherms** (formerly called warm-blooded) and **ectotherms** (formerly called cold-blooded).

> **Endotherms** are those animals that maintain a constant internal body temperature despite fluctuations in external temperature.

> **Ectotherms** are animals that cannot maintain a constant internal temperature. Their temperature fluctuates with the environmental temperature.

In all animals, the main organs that control homeostasis are the brain, liver, kidneys, lungs and skin.

Endothermic animals (such as mammals and birds) maintain a constant internal body temperature: mammals at 37 °C and birds at 40 °C. They can do this independently of environmental conditions. The main source of heat in endotherms is metabolism within the internal organs, such as the liver and brain. Metabolism is controlled by the hormone thyroxine (*see* Chapter 38). Therefore, internal temperature is affected by levels of the hormone thyroxine.

Ectothermic animals (such as insects, spiders, amphibians and reptiles) do not maintain their body temperature at a constant value. Their internal body temperature varies with environmental temperature.

Some ectotherms can control their body temperature using their environment; for example, reptiles will often rest in a sunny area to warm themselves up. Then, when they are sufficiently warm they move to a shaded area.

Fig 29.1 A green iguana basking in the sun to warm itself.

Ectotherms tend to be much less active in colder conditions, whereas an endotherm may be fully active.

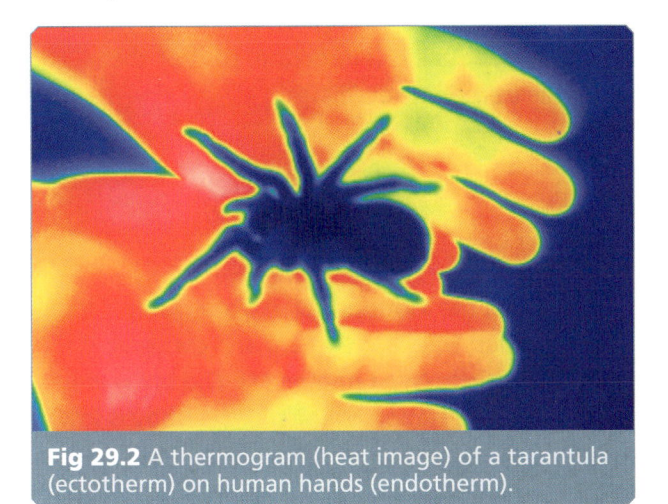

Fig 29.2 A thermogram (heat image) of a tarantula (ectotherm) on human hands (endotherm).

Cooling down

However, environmental conditions do also have an effect on endotherms. Sweating (Fig 29.3), rapid breathing and vasodilation (widening of blood vessels) help to cool the body when it is too hot. Cooling occurs when water evaporates from the skin during sweating (perspiration). Heat is also lost very effectively through blood vessels during breathing and vasodilation.

Fig 29.3 Perspiration is an effective way of losing heat, thereby maintaining homeostasis.

Warming up

Shivering, goose bumps, vasoconstriction, and secretion of thyroxine help to warm the body up when it is too cold.

- Shivering is the alternate contraction and relaxation of skeletal muscles. This generates heat.
- Goose bumps are caused by small muscles under the surface of the skin (see Chapter 36). They are connected to hair follicles. When contracted, they cause the hairs to rise up. Raised hairs trap a layer of air close to the skin.

Fig 29.4 Goose bumps.

- Vasoconstriction is the contraction of the muscles surrounding arterioles (see Chapter 31). This prevents blood flow to certain areas of the body. When the body's temperature drops, even slightly, vasoconstriction occurs in the arterioles of the skin. This prevents heat loss through the skin. The blood is kept deeper within the body, thereby conserving as much heat as possible.
- Secretion of thyroxine affects all cells in the body by raising their metabolic rate (see Chapter 38). This has the effect of raising the body's temperature.

Temperature regulation in endotherms comes at a price – a major increase in energy consumption. Endotherms consume huge amounts of energy keeping their bodies at the correct temperature.

Most animals have a layer of hair or fur covering their bodies (humans being one of the very few exceptions). The fur traps a thin layer of air next to the skin. This helps to keep the animal warm.

Ectotherms require much less energy. As a result, reptiles do not eat as regularly as endotherms. Some species of snake can survive without food for over six months!

pH regulation

Internal pH must be tightly controlled in all organisms.

- In animals, the blood pH must be kept close to 7.4. If the pH of the blood drops (becomes more acidic) due to an increase in carbon dioxide levels in the bloodstream, animals respond by increasing their breathing rate (getting rid of carbon dioxide) and by excreting hydrogen ions via the kidneys (see Chapters 35 and 37, respectively).
- Plants do not have the same direct mechanisms for controlling their internal pH. The pH of the soil determines whether or not a particular plant will grow. However, plants demonstrate chemotropism and the roots will grow to soil areas that are alkaline, acidic or neutral depending on its needs.

Glucose levels

Maintaining blood glucose levels within a narrow range (approximately 1 g/L) is vital to the health of an animal. If the glucose blood concentration falls too low, it can cause coma and death; whereas if it goes too high, it can cause irreparable damage to blood vessels, nerves and the kidneys.

Glucose levels in the blood are controlled by two hormones: **insulin,** which is released when glucose levels are too high (such as after a meal); and **glucagon,** a hormone released when glucose levels are too low (such as when an organism is hungry). Both hormones are released by the hormone-producing (endocrine) part of the pancreas (see Chapter 38).

Water and salt balance (osmoregulation)

In mammals, the kidneys will excrete water if there is too much in the bloodstream and conserve it if there is too little (see Chapter 37). The brain will also create a sensation of thirst if the body is low in water. All these homeostatic mechanisms are controlled by hormones (see Chapter 38).

In plants, if water levels are too low, the stomata will close and roots will grow (hydrotropism) in search of water.

Calcium levels

Calcium is critical for maintaining healthy teeth and bones in animals. It is also required for muscle contraction.

If blood calcium levels decrease, the **parathyroids** (glands in the neck) secrete **parathormone** that increases calcium levels (see Chapter 38). If calcium levels are too high then parathormone levels decrease.

Chapter 29 Questions

1. Define *homeostasis*.
2. Give **three** ways in which homeostasis is important to living organisms.
3. How do plants control their temperature?
4. What is normal body temperature for:
   (a) a human?
   (b) a bird?
5. (a) Distinguish between an *endotherm* and an *ectotherm*, giving **one** example in each case.
   (b) Give **one** advantage of endothermic temperature regulation over ectothermic.
   (c) Name **three** ways in which an endotherm can control its internal temperature.
6. What is the normal pH level of blood in animals?
7. What is *osmoregulation*?

Chapter 29 Sample examination questions

1 (i) The human being is an endotherm. What does this mean?

(ii) What is the main source of body heat in endotherms?

(iii) What happens to the small arteries (arterioles) in the skin when the external temperature drops?

Section C, Question 15 (a) (ii), (iii), (v) Ordinary Level 2006

HL 2 (i) What is an *endotherm*?

(ii) What word is used to describe animals which are not endotherms?

(iii) Suggest an advantage of being an endotherm.

Section A, Question 4 (a) Higher Level 2011

Chapter 29 Mind map

Homeostasis is the maintenance of a constant internal environment.

The advantage of homeostasis is that normal cellular and bodily functions continue despite changes in the environment.

Temperature regulation in organisms is either ectothermic or endothermic.
- **Ectothermic temperature regulation:** a living organism's internal body temperature varies with their environment, e.g. insects.
- **Endothermic temperature regulation:** a living organism's internal body temperature is kept constant despite wide changes in external temperatures, e.g. humans.

Temperature regulation
- In animals, temperature is regulated through a variety of mechanisms such as sweating, rapid breathing, shivering, vasoconstriction and vasodilation.
- In plants, temperature is regulated through increasing or decreasing transpiration.

- In animals, blood pH levels must be maintained at 7.4 as all enzymes are affected by pH.
- In plants, pH levels are maintained by plants being able to grow only in certain soil types (acidic, alkaline or neutral).

In animals, blood glucose levels are maintained at specific levels (approximately 1 g/L) by two hormones: insulin and glucagon.

Osmoregulation is the control of water levels in the body. When there is too much water, it is excreted by the kidneys.

Calcium levels are sensed by the parathyroid gland and controlled by parathormone.

Chapter 30 Blood

Learning objectives After studying this chapter, you should be able to:
- Describe that blood is a tissue and name the four components of blood.
- Describe the function of each part of the blood.
- Describe the role of haemoglobin.
- **HL** Describe the structure of red blood cells – their lack of a nucleus and mitochondria and describe their affinity for oxygen.
- Describe the four main blood types: A, B, AB and O.
- Describe the Rhesus factor as an additional blood type.

Introduction

Blood is a fluid tissue composed of cells in watery liquid called plasma. Blood is circulated around the body in a network of blood vessels. It is composed of **plasma, white blood cells, platelets** and **red blood cells.**

The average human has 5 L of blood, and this accounts for approximately 8 per cent of body weight (5 kg). Every millilitre of human blood contains approximately 5 million red blood cells, 8,000 white blood cells and 300,000 platelets!

The primary function of blood is transport. It transports oxygen, carbon dioxide, water, nutrients, hormones, wastes and blood cells around the body. Blood also fights infection, preventing entry of pathogens by clotting, temperature regulation, and tissue pH regulation.

Composition of blood

Plasma

Plasma, the liquid portion of the blood, makes up about 54 per cent of the volume of blood. When a blood sample is taken and the blood cells are removed, plasma is left behind. It is a straw-yellow liquid composed of 92 per cent water, with dissolved salts, sugars, lipids and proteins (such as antibodies and hormones) making up the rest.

Red blood cells

Red blood cells (also known as **erythrocytes**) make up approximately 45 per cent of the volume of blood. Red blood cells are made in the red

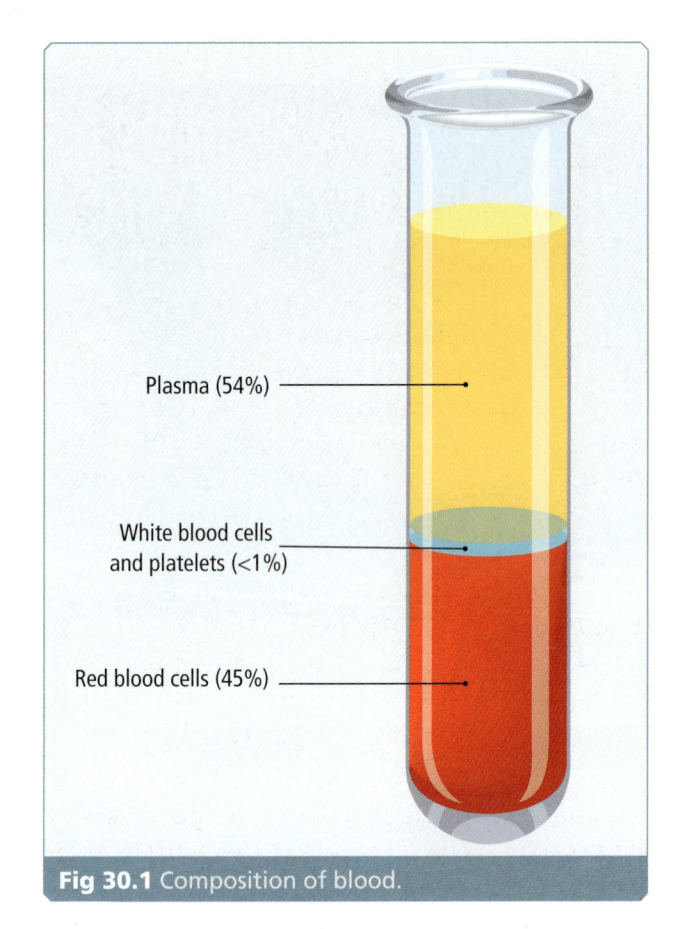

Fig 30.1 Composition of blood.

- Plasma (54%)
- White blood cells and platelets (<1%)
- Red blood cells (45%)

bone marrow of long bones, such as the femur. They have a unique disc-like shape. Both sides of the disc are a concave shape. This shape is called **'biconcave'** (Fig 30.3).

Red blood cells are involved in transporting oxygen around the body. Blood that is rich in oxygen – that is blood leaving the lungs – is bright red. Blood that is deficient in oxygen – blood in veins and blood entering the lungs – is dark red.

Red blood cells do not respire as their only function is to transport oxygen.

Blood | Chapter 30

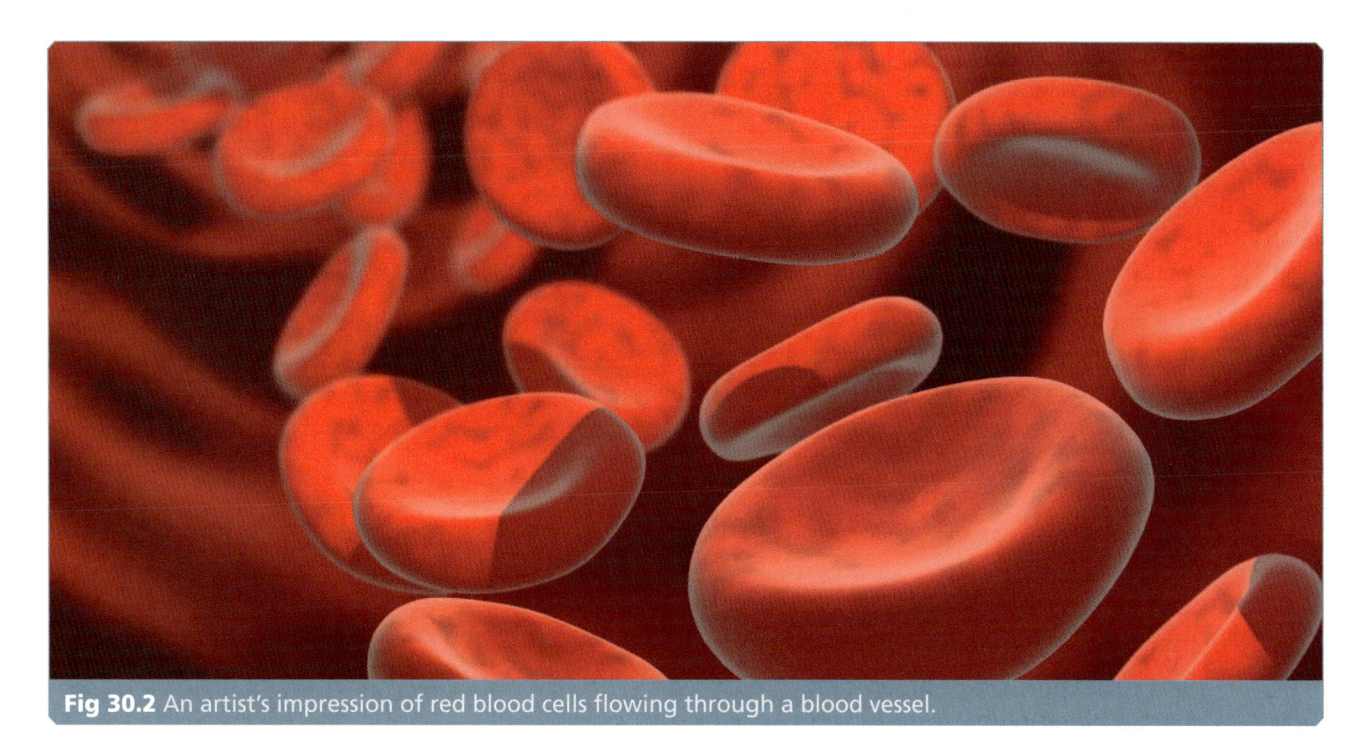

Fig 30.2 An artist's impression of red blood cells flowing through a blood vessel.

Red blood cells live for approximately 120 days before being broken down in the liver. The liver breaks down the haemoglobin into pigments called **bilirubin** and **biliverdin.** These pigments are then sent to the gall bladder where they are secreted into bile (*see* Chapter 33) and released into the digestive tract.

Haemoglobin

Haemoglobin is a red pigment, made from protein. It gives red blood cells their colour. It is responsible for carrying oxygen.

Haemoglobin is a globular protein with a haem (iron-containing) group. The haem group is responsible for carrying oxygen. Each haemoglobin protein is capable of carrying four oxygen molecules. When haemoglobin is carrying oxygen, it is called **oxyhaemoglobin.** It picks up the oxygen molecules in the lungs and releases it into the tissues after travelling in the bloodstream. Once it has released its oxygen, oxyhaemoglobin is converted back to **deoxyhaemoglobin.**

Red blood cells – detailed study

Red blood cells have a unique affinity for oxygen. As mentioned above, haemoglobin is responsible for carrying oxygen. Red blood cells absorb oxygen in the lungs, where oxygen is plentiful and release it in the tissues of the body, where

HL it is relatively less plentiful. They are the only complete cells that do not possess a nucleus,

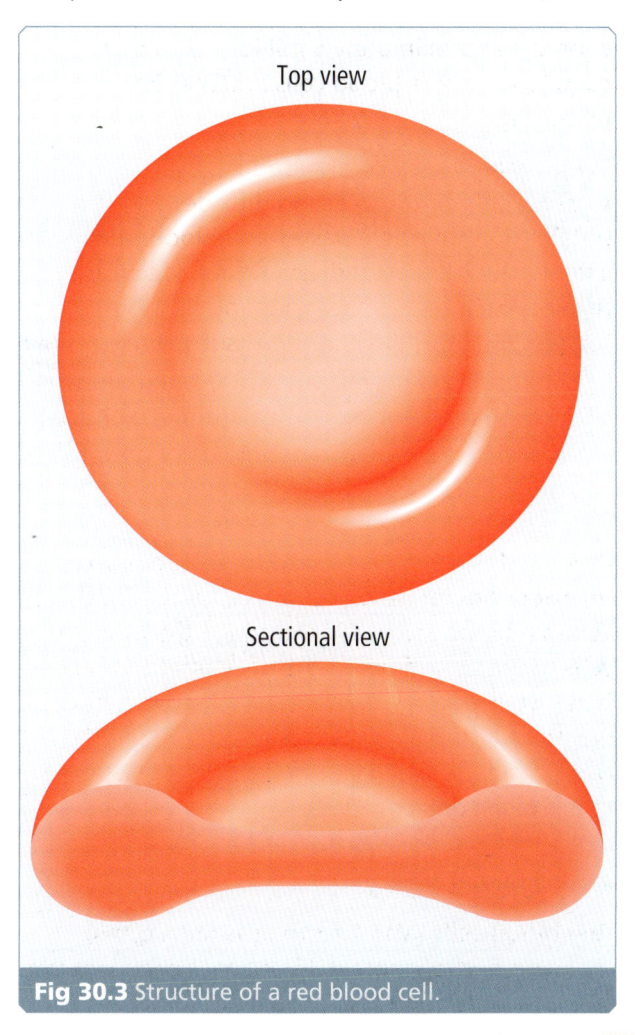

Top view

Sectional view

Fig 30.3 Structure of a red blood cell.

309

which they lose during development. The fact that red blood cells have no nucleus and have a biconcave shape (Fig 30.3) enables them to be smaller than average cells and fit through the very small capillaries (microscopic blood vessels). Their unique shape also gives a greater surface area for oxygen to diffuse in and out.

As mentioned above, red blood cells do not respire. This is because they do not have mitochondria. This gives even more room for carrying oxygen and for squeezing through capillaries.

Blood groups

There are currently 30 recognised blood grouping systems in humans, of which the **ABO system** is the most important.

Everybody belongs to a certain blood group. Your blood group depends on the type of proteins on the surface of your red blood cells.

The ABO blood group system was discovered by Austrian Karl Landsteiner in 1900. It consists of four blood types (Fig 30.4):

- A
- B
- AB
- O

The letters for each blood type originate from the type of molecule present on the surface of the red blood cells.

- People who are blood group **A** have a molecule on the surface of their red blood cells that stimulates **anti-A antibodies** if their blood is injected into people belonging to the **B** or **O** blood groups.

- Similarly, people who are blood group **B** have a molecule on the surface of their red blood cells that stimulates **anti-B antibodies** if their blood is injected into people belonging to the **A** or **O** blood groups.

- People belonging to the **AB** blood group posses **both** molecules on the surface of their red blood cells.

- People belonging to the **O** blood group have neither **A** nor **B** molecules on the surface of their red blood cells.

This means that people who are blood group **A** can receive blood transfusions from other group **A** people. They can also receive blood transfusions from blood group **O** people (see below).

Similarly, blood group **B** people can receive blood transfusions from people who are group **B** or group **O**. However, if an **A** group person receives **B** blood or vice versa, then antibodies will be made against the foreign molecules causing the cells to break open. This is called a **haemolytic transfusion reaction** and can be fatal.

AB blood group people can receive blood transfusions from people belonging to either group **A** or group **B**. They can also receive blood from people who belong to blood group O. People belonging to the **AB** blood group are called **universal recipients,** as they can generally receive blood transfusions from any blood group.

Group **O** people do not have any molecules that stimulate formation of antibodies. Therefore, people belonging to group **O** can donate blood to any other blood group. Therefore, group O people are called **universal donors.**

The ABO blood system

Blood type (genotype)	Type A (AA, AO)	Type B (BB, BO)	Type AB (AB)	Type O (OO)
Red blood cell surface proteins (phenotype)	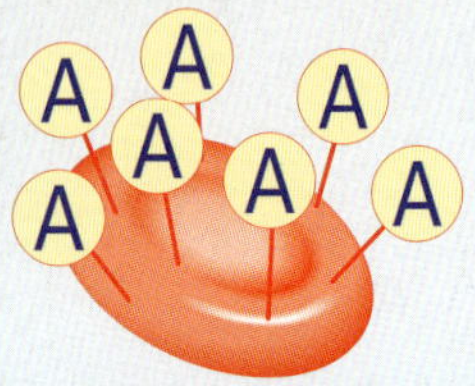	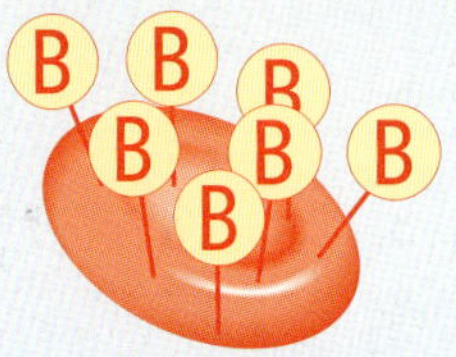	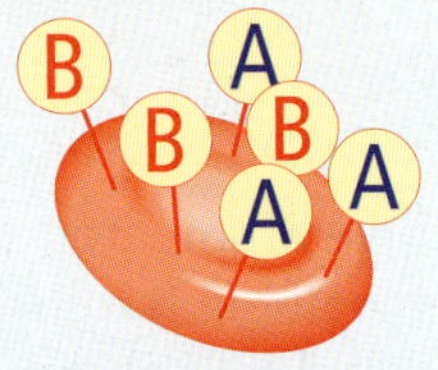	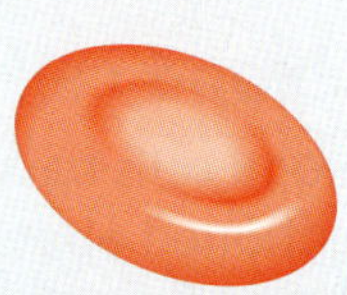

Fig 30.4 The ABO blood group system consisting of four blood types, A, B, AB and O.

However, people who are blood group **O** can only receive blood from others that are also blood group **O**. Fortunately, blood group **O** is the most common human blood group, so there is rarely a lack of this blood group.

Inheritance of blood groups

Inheritance of blood groups is Mendelian in nature (*see* Chapter 16).

- This means that a person who belongs to blood group **A** can have one of two possible genotypes – **AA** or **AO** – since **A** is *dominant* to **O**.
- Similarly, people belonging to blood group **B** can be **BB** or **BO**.
- People who belong to the **AB** blood group have the genotype **AB**.
- People belonging to blood group **O** all have the genotype OO as it is *recessive* to all other blood types.

As already mentioned, blood group **O** is the most common blood group, especially in Ireland, followed by **A**, then **B** and **AB**.

It has been found that blood group **O** people have a statistically smaller chance of getting certain cancers. The reasons for this are unknown.

Donating blood

Blood transfusions are carried out every day in hospitals. Many emergency surgeries would not take place without donated blood. This makes it very important for people to donate blood. When you donate blood, you know that you will have helped someone.

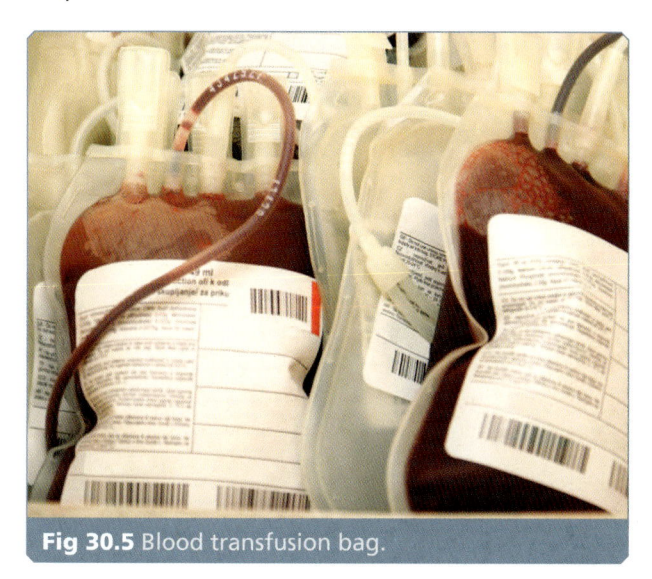

Fig 30.5 Blood transfusion bag.

The Rhesus factor

Blood transfusions are not as simple as using the ABO blood grouping system to ensure a patient is getting the correct blood type. For a successful blood transfusion, the blood must also match according to the **Rhesus blood grouping system**. It is called *'Rhesus'* because it was first discovered in the Rhesus monkey.

A person either has or does not have the Rhesus factor (Rh). If it is present on the red blood cells, then the person is said to be Rhesus-positive **(Rh+)**; if the person does not have it then they are Rhesus-negative **(Rh–)**.

- A person who is Rh+ can donate only to Rh+ people, but can receive blood from either Rh+ or Rh– people.
- Rh– people can receive blood only from Rh– people but can donate to either.

Rhesus incompatibility (Fig 30.6) can occur during pregnancy, when the mother is rhesus-negative and the baby is rhesus-positive. The mother's immune system can react and produce antibodies against the baby's rhesus-positive blood. These

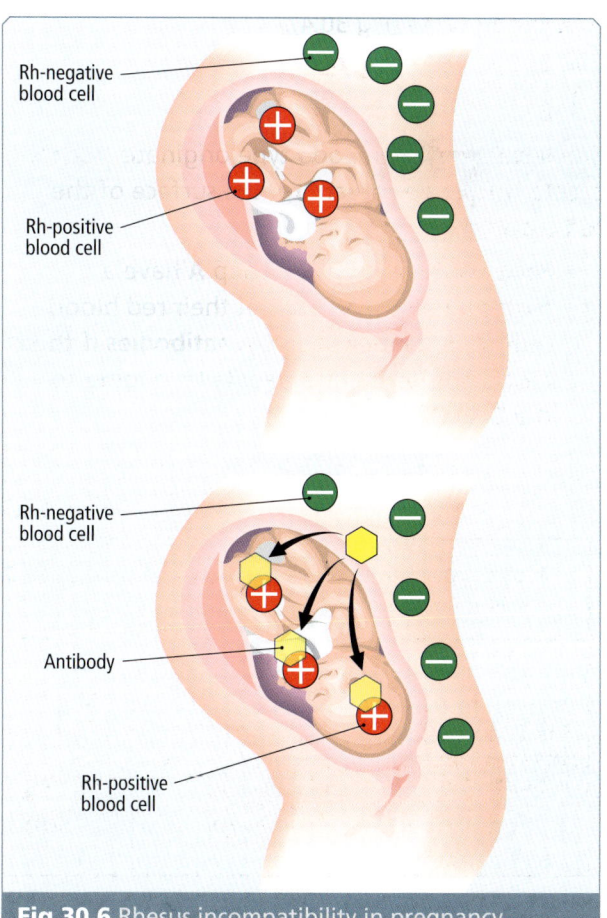

Fig 30.6 Rhesus incompatibility in pregnancy.

antibodies can diffuse through the placenta into the baby, where they react to the baby's red blood cells causing anaemia in the baby.

Rhesus incompatibility is usually not a problem for the first baby. However, any subsequent rhesus-positive babies may be seriously harmed by the mother's antibodies. Rhesus incompatibility complications rarely occur in the western world now due to screening of pregnant women. Rhesus-negative mothers are given treatments to prevent them producing antibodies against the baby's blood. This helps to ensure that subsequent pregnancies will be healthy even if the first baby is rhesus-positive.

White blood cells

White blood cells and platelets make up the remainder 1 per cent of blood volume. They are involved in defence mechanisms within the body. White blood cells are round cells with a large nucleus. They attack foreign invaders in a variety of ways (see Chapter 34).

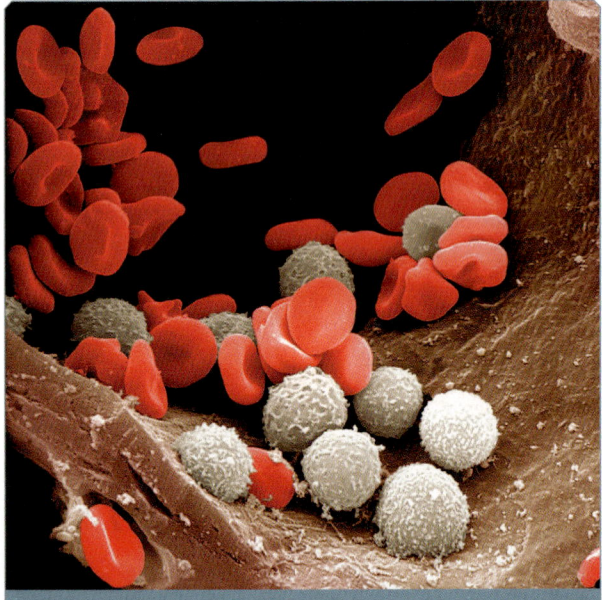

Fig 30.7 A scanning electron micrograph of a blood vessel with red blood cells and white blood cells.

HL White blood cells (also known as leucocytes) are produced in the bone marrow and are involved in the immune response of animals. They are of two main types:

1 **Monocytes** are a large group of white blood cells that mature into more specific types of white blood cells, such as macrophages. They are involved in recognising anything that is foreign. They ingest the foreign particle in a process called **phagocytosis.** In general, monocytes tend to have a kidney-shaped or notched nucleus (Fig 30.8).

2 **Lymphocytes** are involved in more specific defences within the body and specifically recognise individual pathogens, **producing antibodies** against them. This inactivates and immobilises the pathogen. There are many different types of lymphocytes (see Chapter 34). Lymphocytes tend to have a large round nucleus that takes up most of the volume of the cell (Fig 30.9).

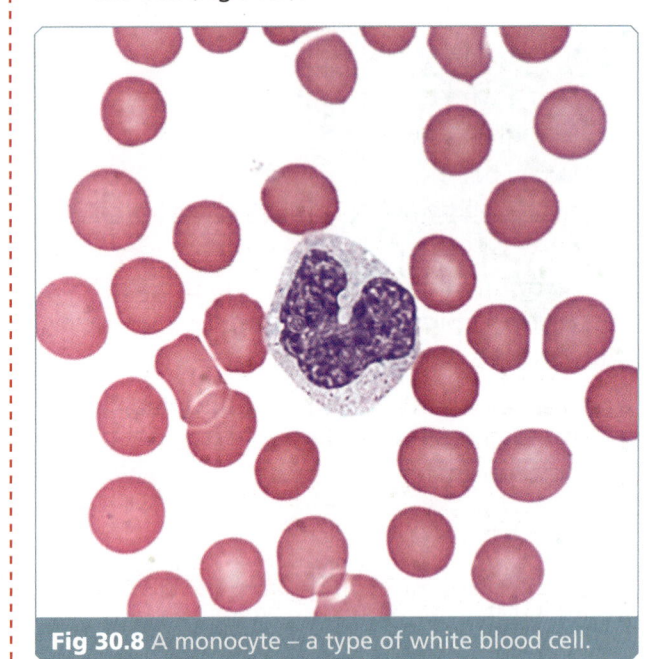

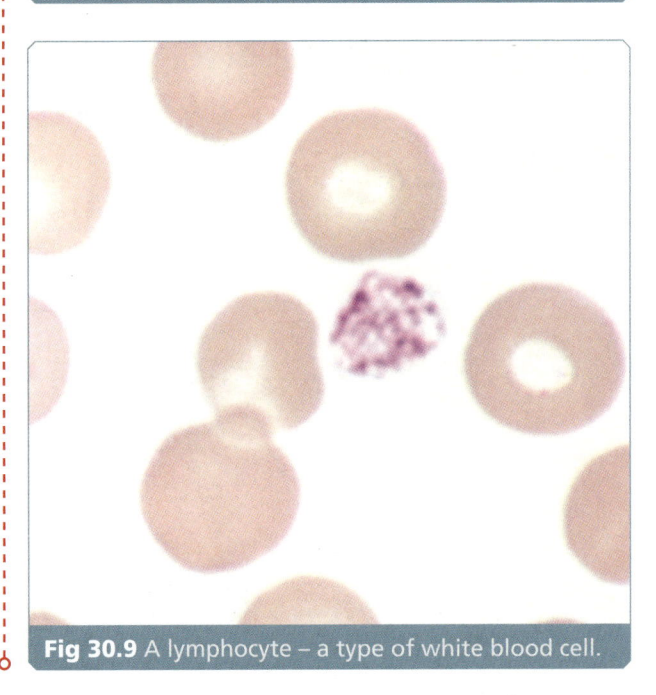

Fig 30.8 A monocyte – a type of white blood cell.

Fig 30.9 A lymphocyte – a type of white blood cell.

Platelets

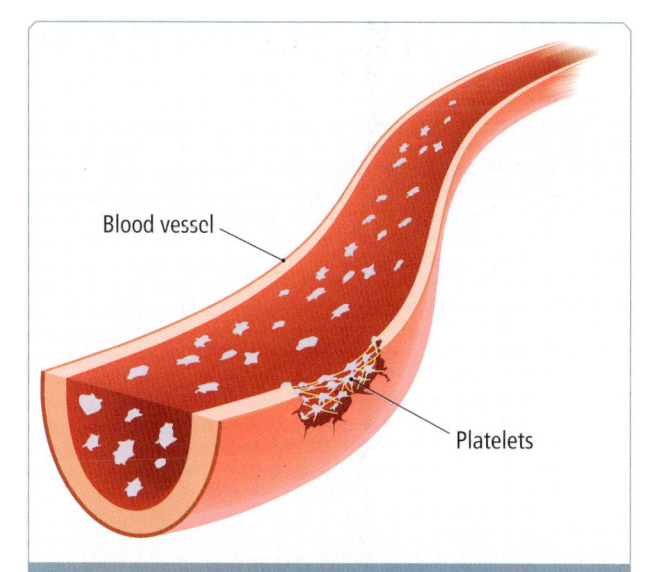

Fig 30.10 Platelets involved in healing a wound.

Platelets (also known as thrombocytes) are small irregular-shaped cell fragments that do not have a nucleus. The average lifespan of a platelet is just seven days.

Platelets are essential in **blood clotting**. In this way, platelets help to prevent blood loss and entry of pathogens into the body via a wound.

However, sometimes they may form an unwanted clot, especially deep within the veins of the legs (Fig 30.11). This condition, called **deep vein thrombosis (DVT),** occurs more frequently in older people but can affect people of any age. DVT is usually brought on by sitting still in one position for extended periods of time, such as on a long haul flight. The blood clot can move from the vein and travel to the lungs, where it causes a serious, potentially life-threatening condition called **pulmonary embolism**.

This is why it is recommended to take regular breaks to walk around on both flights and long car journeys and to wear flight socks.

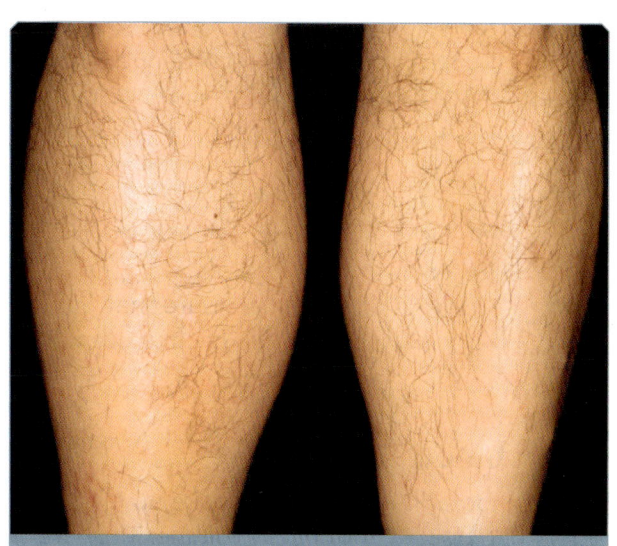

Fig 30.11 Deep vein thrombosis causes swelling around the site of the clot.

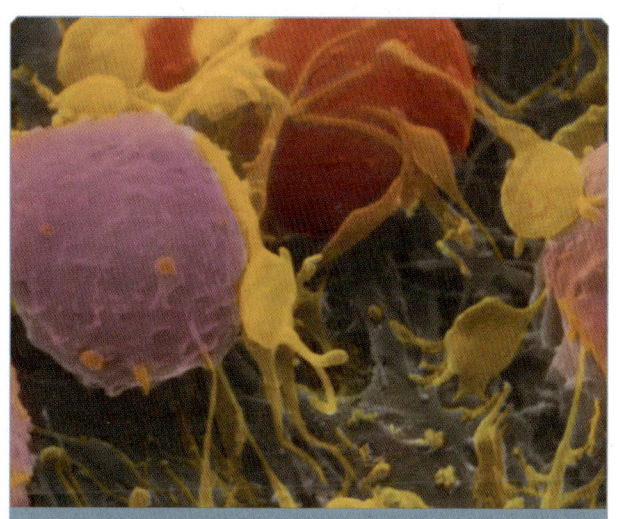

Fig 30.12 A scanning electron micrograph of platelets involved in blood clotting.

Unit 3 The Organism

Chapter 30 Questions

1. Name the **four** main components of blood and give **one** function for each component.
2. Name **two** types of protein present in the blood.
3. (a) Explain why blood is considered a type of tissue.
   (b) What tissue type does blood belong to? (Hint: *see* Chapter 7).
4. What percentage of the volume of blood is:
   (a) Plasma? (b) Red blood cells?
5. (a) What group of biomolecules does haemoglobin belong to?
   (b) What is the function of haemoglobin?
   (c) Distinguish between *oxyhaemoglobin* and *deoxyhaemoglobin*. In terms of:
      (i) Oxygen content.
      (ii) General locations in the circulatory system.
      (iii) Colour.
   (d) Explain what happens to haemoglobin when it is broken down.
   (e) Where do the broken-down products of haemoglobin end up?

HL 6. (a) Sketch the structure of a red blood cell showing its unique shape.
   (b) Explain why red blood cells have this shape and name **one** other unique characteristic of red blood cells.

HL 7. Distinguish between a *monocyte* and a *lymphocyte* in terms of structure and function.

8. What is *deep vein thrombosis* and how is it caused?
9. (a) What are *platelets*?
   (b) Where are platelets produced?
   (c) What is the function of platelets?
10. (a) Approximately how many different blood grouping systems are known in humans?
    (b) What is the main blood grouping system in humans?
    (c) There are four main blood types in this blood grouping system. List them in order of frequency in the population.
11. Give **one** reason why hospitals need a constant supply of blood donors.
12. A man and his wife have four children, each with a different blood type. Give:
    (a) The possible genotypes of the father and the mother. in terms of their blood types
    (b) The genotypes of the possible gametes produced.
    (c) The genotypes and phenotypes of the four children.
13. (a) What is the *Rhesus factor*?
    (b) Why is Rhesus incompatibility a problem for some pregnant women?

Chapter 30 Sample examination questions

1. (a) Name the liquid part of blood.
   (b) Give **two** components of this liquid.
   (c) Complete the following table in relation to blood cells:

Cell	One function
Red blood cell	
White blood cell	
Platelet	

   Section A, Question 5 Ordinary Level 2009

HL 2. (i) State a precise location in the human body at which red blood cells are made.
   (ii) State **two** ways in which red blood cells differ from typical body cells, e.g. from the cheek lining.

   Section C, Question 13 (a) Higher Level 2006

Chapter 30 Mind map

Blood is a fluid tissue composed of cells in watery liquid called plasma.

Blood consists of four major components:
- Plasma
- Red blood cells
- White blood cells
- Platelets

- Plasma is the liquid portion of the blood, making up 55 per cent of blood by volume.
- Plasma consists of 92 per cent water with dissolved salts, sugars, lipids and proteins making up the rest.
- Plasma's main function is transport.

Red blood cells are:
- Small, disc- and biconcave-shaped cells without a nucleus or mitochondria. **HL**
- Red in colour due to haemoglobin. They function in transport of oxygen around the body.

The Rhesus factor is a protein present on the surface of a person's red blood cells. A person is either rhesus-positive or rhesus-negative.

White blood cells are round cells with a large nucleus. They are responsible for fighting infections.

They are also known as leucocytes. **HL**

There are two main types:
1. Monocytes: recognise any foreign particles and engulf and destroy them.
2. Lymphocytes: specifically recognise individual pathogens and produce specific antibodies against them.

Platelets are also known as thrombocytes and are required for the clotting mechanism of blood. They function in preventing blood loss and entry of pathogens into the body via a wound.

- There are four main blood groups in humans
  - A
  - B
  - AB
  - O
- O is the most common, followed by A, B and AB.
- O group people are known as universal donors as they can donate their blood to any of the other blood groups.
- AB is known as the universal recipients as they can receive blood from any of the other groups.
- Blood groups are determined by the presence/absence of molecules on the surface of red blood cells.

Chapter 31 The human circulatory system

Learning objectives After studying this chapter, you should be able to:
- Describe what is meant by organisational complexity of the human.
- Describe the structure and organisation of the human circulatory system and its associated organs.
- Describe the role of skeletal muscles and valves in the movement of blood through veins.
- Describe the two-circuit circulatory system: pulmonary and systemic circuits.
- Draw the structure of the heart, associated blood vessels and the main pathways of blood circulation, including the hepatic portal system.
- Describe the structure and function of the hepatic portal system.
- Describe how the cardiac artery supplies blood to the heart.
- Describe the heartbeat and how it is controlled by the pacemaker.
- HL State the functions and locations of the SA and AV nodes.
- Describe the heart cycle: systole and diastole periods.
- Define *pulse* and *blood pressure*. State the average human pulse rate, average human blood pressure and name the instrument used to measure blood pressure.
- Describe the effect of smoking, diet and exercise on the circulatory system.
- Dissect, display and identify the various parts of a sheep's heart.
- Investigate the effect of exercise on the pulse rate (heart rate) of a human.

Introduction

We learned in Chapter 2 that organisation is one of the characteristics of life. The human body and other animal bodies show a large amount of organisational complexity. This is seen in the number of different organ systems that make up the bodies of animals. This chapter deals with the circulatory system. The circulatory system of a human consists of a complex network of blood vessels, along with the heart and blood.

Open and closed circulatory systems

The human circulatory system is an example of a closed circulatory system. This means that the blood flows continuously in a network of totally enclosed blood vessels. The blood never leaves the blood vessels (Fig 31.2).

In contrast, an open circulatory system allows the blood to flow out of its vessels and surround tissue cells before flowing back to the heart via pores in the heart called ostia (Fig 31.2). There are no veins in an open circulatory system.

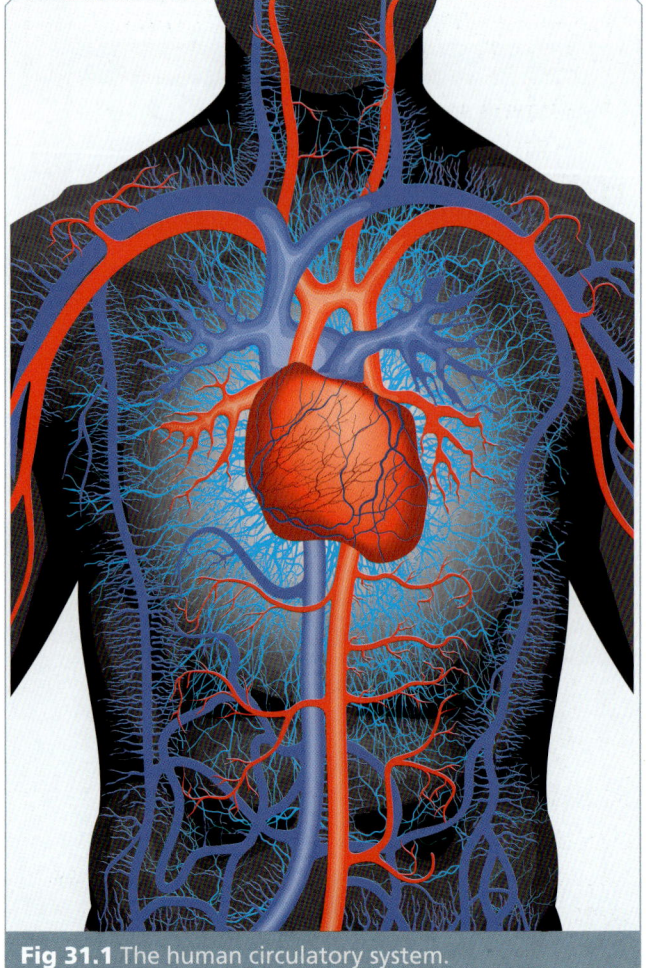

Fig 31.1 The human circulatory system.

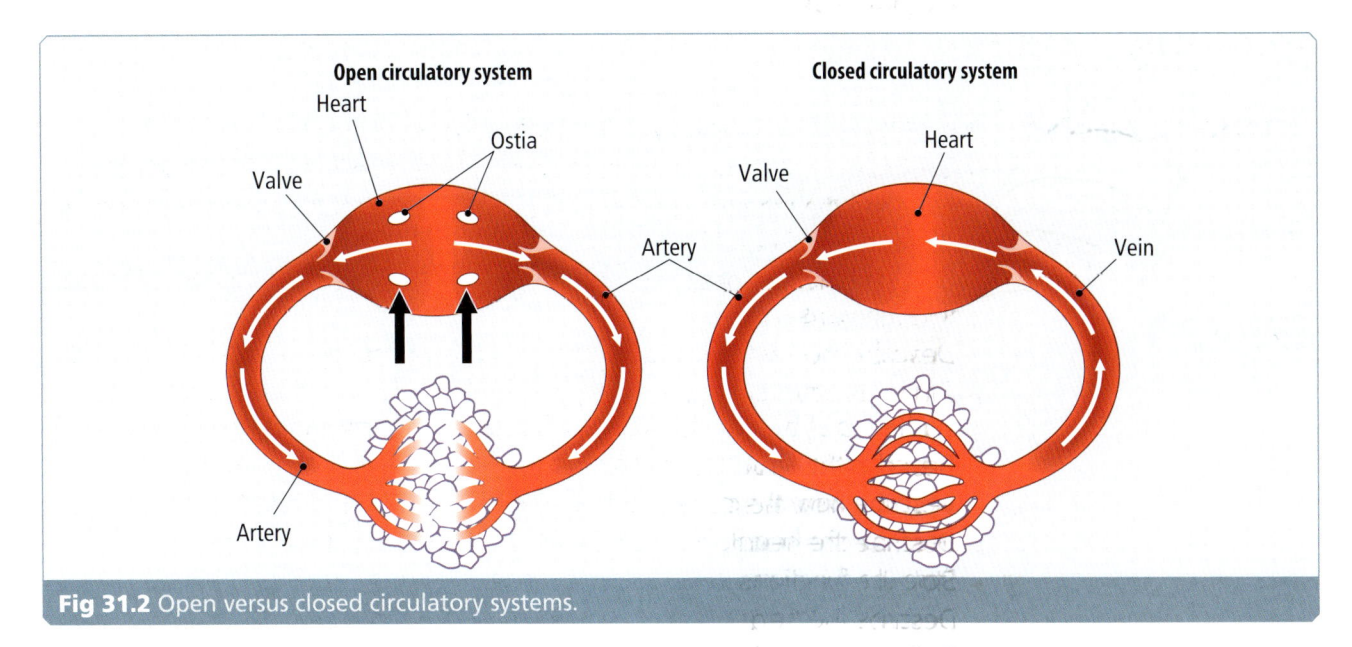

Fig 31.2 Open versus closed circulatory systems.

Most invertebrates have an open circulatory system. Examples of organisms with an open circulatory system are insects, spiders, beetles and worms.

Closed circulatory systems are an adaptation to an increase in body size. All vertebrates and some invertebrates have closed circulatory systems.

Characteristics of a closed circulatory system include:

- Oxygen is delivered to all tissues without blood having to leave blood vessels.
- It allows faster delivery of oxygen and nutrients and withdrawal of wastes. This allows for longer periods of activity.
- It also enables the body to control what areas of the body receive blood. For example, during physical activity blood flow increases to the muscular system and is taken away from the digestive system. This is not possible with an open circulatory system.

Human circulatory system

The human circulatory system consists of:

- Blood vessels.
- Blood (see Chapter 30).
- Heart.

Blood vessels

Closed circulatory systems contain three main types of blood vessels. These vessels are: **arteries**, **veins** and **capillaries**.

Artery

> An **artery** is a blood vessel that carries blood away from the heart in powerful pulses. It has a thick wall, small lumen and no valves.

In general, arteries carry **oxygenated** blood away from the heart. However, there is one exception: the pulmonary artery carries **deoxygenated** blood away from the heart to the lungs.

Arteries have to have very thick, tough, but elastic walls to be able to withstand the pressure of the blood flowing in pulses from the heart (Fig 31.3). The outer layer is made from collagen (connective tissue) and the inner layers are made of elastic tissue and muscle. This muscle contracts involuntarily (without conscious control) and pushes the blood along.

Muscles that contract involuntarily (without the person having to think about it) are called **smooth muscles** (see Chapter 40).

The innermost layer of arteries is a single layer of cells called the **endothelium**.

The space through which blood flows in an artery is called the **lumen**. The lumen of an artery is small, compared to that of a vein.

Arteries carry blood to smaller blood vessels called **arterioles**.

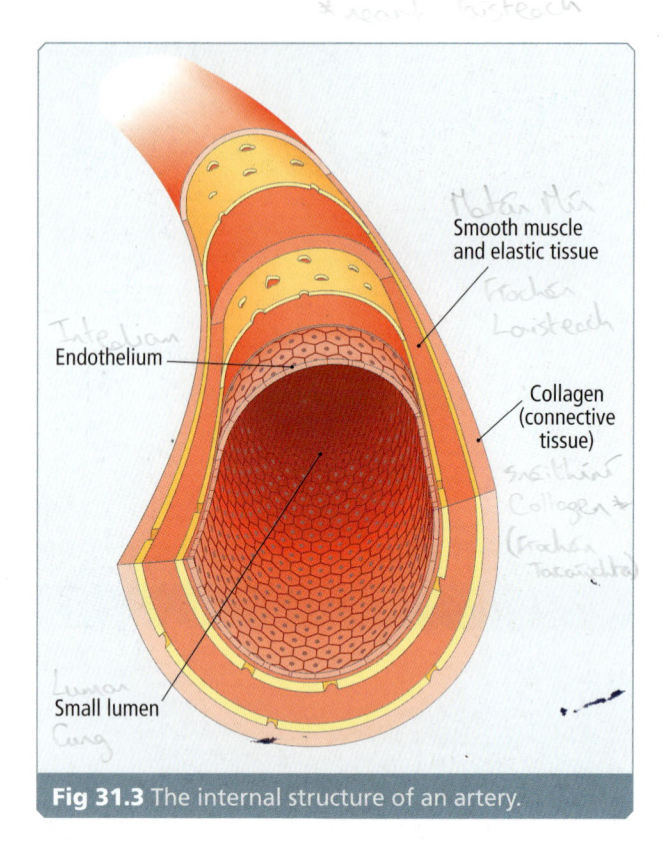

Veins have a similar structure to arteries, except the wall is much thinner. This is because the blood pressure in veins is much lower. The innermost layer is a single layer of cells called the endothelium. There is a layer of elastic tissue and smooth muscle that helps to push blood along the veins by contracting. There is also an outer layer of collagen (Fig 31.4). Skeletal muscles, especially in the legs, also help to move blood along.

Veins have a large lumen and possess valves to prevent the backflow of blood. Veins receive their blood from venules, which in turn receive their blood from **capillaries**.

Vein problems

The smooth muscle of veins is not always enough to push the blood along back to the heart. Blood can pool in the veins of the legs and can clot due to lack of movement. This condition is called **deep vein thrombosis (DVT)**. This is why it is important to move around regularly or wear 'flight' socks (Fig 31.5) when on a long journey, such as long-haul flights or long car journeys.

The valves within the veins can begin to fail with age. Blood is not moved along as effectively. This can cause pooling of blood in some of the veins, especially in the legs. These are called varicose veins.

Fig 31.3 The internal structure of an artery.

Vein

> A **vein** is a blood vessel that carries blood towards the heart in an even flow. It has a thin wall, large lumen and valves.

In general, veins carry **deoxygenated** blood **towards** the heart. However, there is one exception: the pulmonary vein carries **oxygenated** blood towards the heart from the lungs.

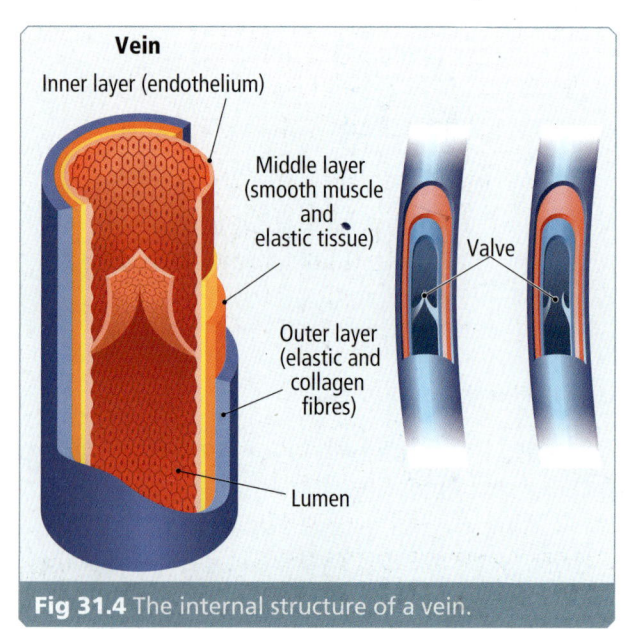

Fig 31.4 The internal structure of a vein.

Fig 31.5 'Flight' socks are worn on long journeys to reduce the risk of deep vein thrombosis.

Capillary

> A **capillary** is a blood vessel with a wall one cell thick that carries blood from arterioles to venules through tissues, releasing nutrients and taking away wastes.

Capillaries receive blood from arterioles and transfer the blood on to venules (Fig 31.6). Capillaries have tiny lumens when compared to other blood vessels. Only a single-file of red and white blood cells can fit through the smallest capillaries!

Because capillaries are so small, they can be found in every single tissue in the body. They deliver food and oxygen and take away waste products of metabolism very efficiently. This is possible because their walls are only one cell thick (**endothelium**). This allows rapid diffusion of molecules in and out of the capillary. Even white blood cells can leave a capillary by squeezing between the endothelial cells lining the capillary. They then work their way into infected or damaged tissues.

A summary of the structures of arteries, veins and capillaries is shown in the table below:

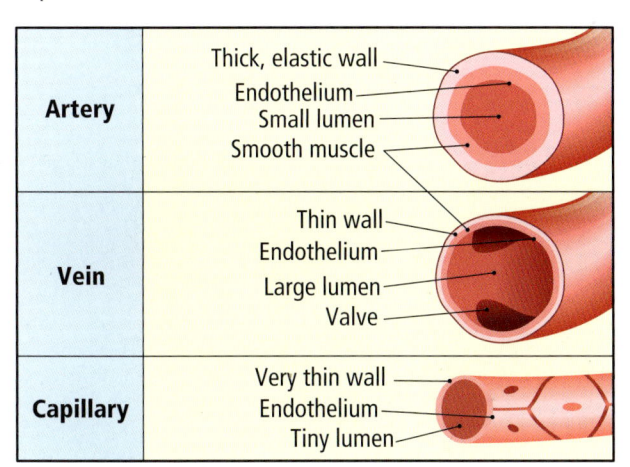

Artery	Thick, elastic wall / Endothelium / Small lumen / Smooth muscle
Vein	Thin wall / Endothelium / Large lumen / Valve
Capillary	Very thin wall / Endothelium / Tiny lumen

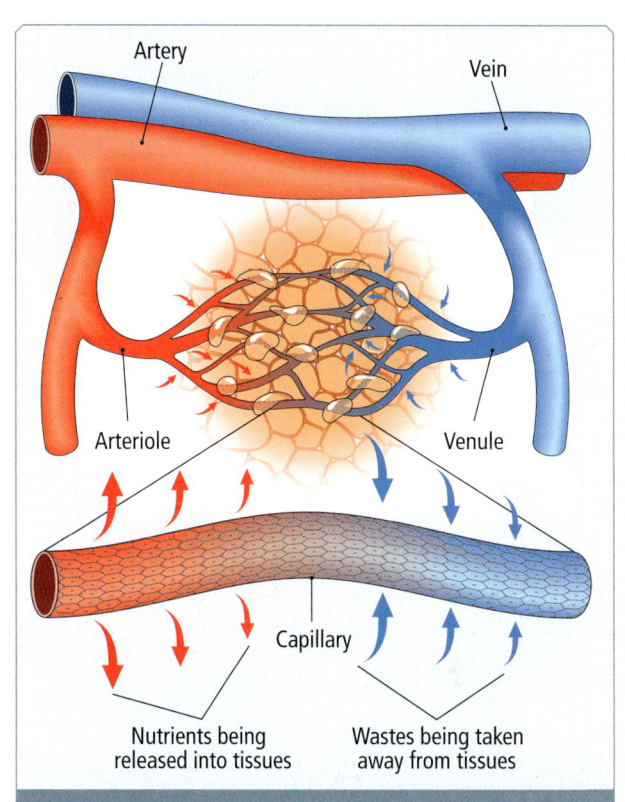

Fig 31.6 The flow of blood from arterioles to venules via capillaries.

Systemic circuit and pulmonary circuit

The human circulatory system consists of two circuits: **systemic** and **pulmonary**.

- The systemic circuit is a network of blood vessels that supplies blood to all of the major organs and tissues of the body, except the lungs.
- The pulmonary circuit is a network of blood vessels that carries blood to the lungs.

Both circuits begin and end at the heart (Fig 31.7). These two circuits are often referred to as a **double circulation**.

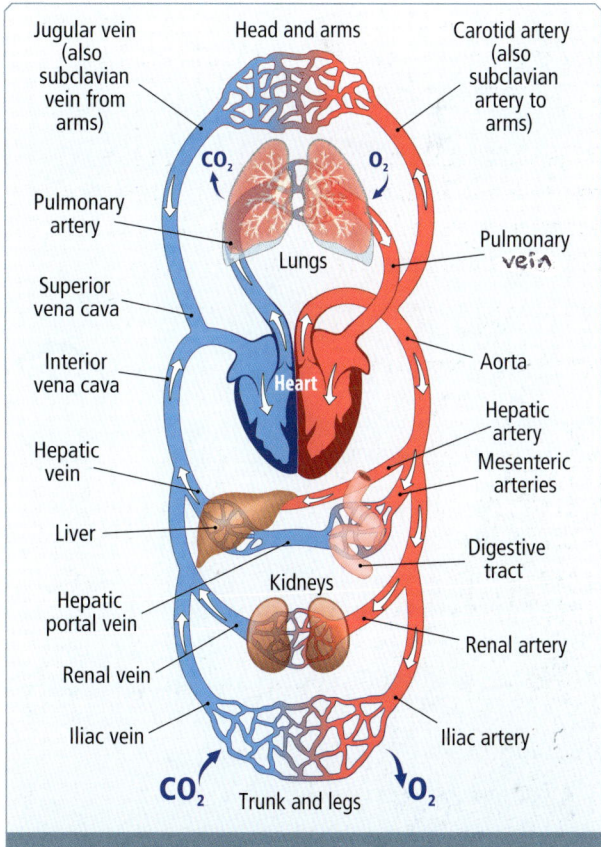

Fig 31.7 Structure of the pulmonary and systemic circulatory systems.

The heart itself is a double pump with a right and left side, separated by a structure called the **septum**. The heart has a front side that is more rounded than the back side. The left side of the heart is also firmer than the right side. This is because the muscle on the left side is thicker than the right side. The right-hand side of the heart takes deoxygenated blood from the body and sends it to the lungs (pulmonary circuit) to be reoxygenated. The left side receives blood from the lungs and sends it out to the whole body (systemic circuit).

The systemic circuit is a much larger and longer circuit than the pulmonary circuit. The aorta (part of the systemic circuit) branches as soon as it leaves the heart.

All of the branches of the aorta supply blood to the major organs of the body.

- The first branch is a very small artery called the **coronary artery.** This carries blood to the heart muscle itself (Fig 31.8 and 31.9). Other branches of the aorta carry blood to the head and also to the lower half of the body.

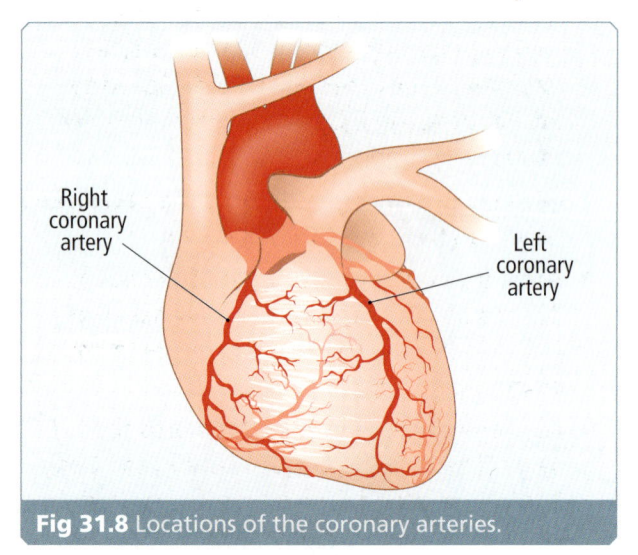

Fig 31.8 Locations of the coronary arteries.

- The **hepatic artery** carries blood to the liver; the **renal arteries** carry blood to the kidneys; a group of arteries called the **mesenteric arteries** carry blood to the small and large intestines; the **carotid arteries** supply blood to the head; the **subclavian arteries** supply blood to the arms; and the **iliac arteries** carry blood to the legs.

Blood flows back to the heart via veins. A number of major veins converge to carry blood into the superior and inferior vena cavae (singular: vena cava).

- The **coronary vein** drains the heart muscle of blood into the vena cava.
- The **hepatic vein** carries blood away from the liver; the **renal veins** carry blood away from the kidneys; the **jugular veins** carry blood from the head; the **subclavian veins** carry blood from the arms back to the heart; and **iliac veins** carry blood away from the legs (Fig 31.10).

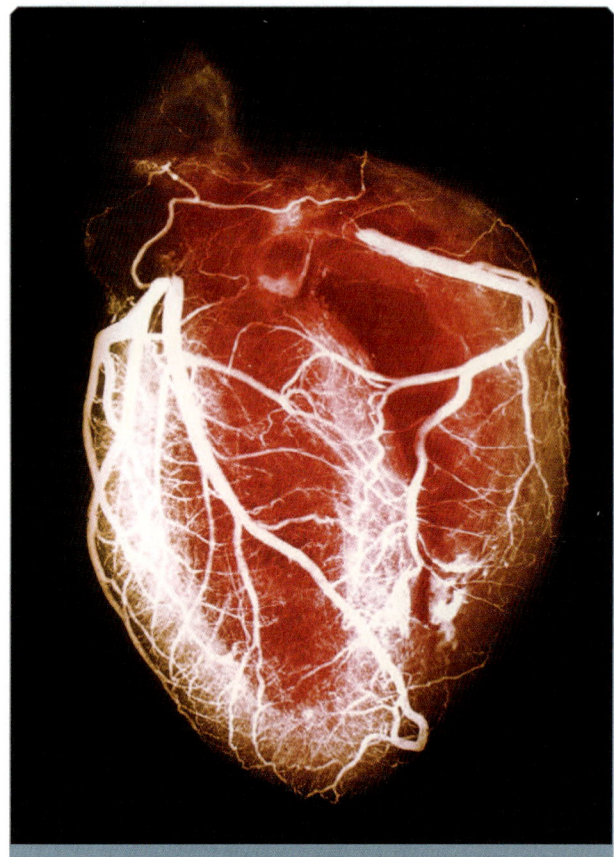

Fig 31.9 An angiogram of a healthy human heart, showing healthy coronary arteries (white).

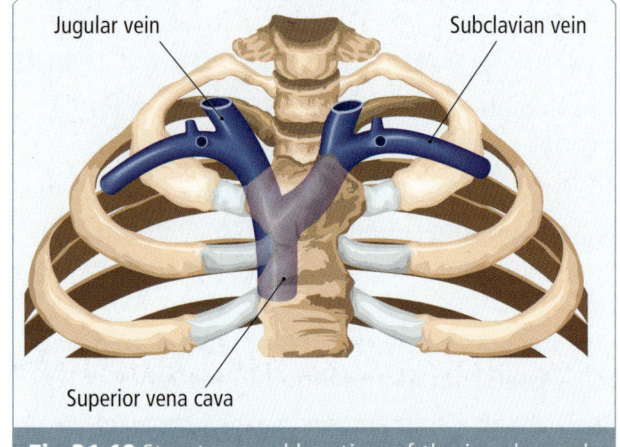

Fig 31.10 Structure and location of the jugular and subclavian veins.

Portal system

> A **portal system** is a network of capillaries in one organ or tissue joined to another network of capillaries in another organ or tissue via a vein or veins.

An example of a portal system is the **hepatic portal system**. In this portal system, the capillaries of the small intestine absorb nutrients into the bloodstream and carry them to the liver via the **hepatic portal vein,** where it branches out into another network of capillaries in the liver.

The liver detoxifies any harmful substances in the nutrient-rich blood. It also stores useful nutrients the body may need.

Once the liver has filtered the incoming blood from the digestive system, it releases it to the body via the **hepatic vein,** which carries the blood back to the heart via the inferior vena cava.

Structure of the heart

The heart is an organ located in the chest cavity, slightly to the left of the sternum (breast bone). It is protected by the breast bone and rib cage. The heart is composed mostly of **cardiac muscle**. This is a special type of muscle that is slow to tire.

Fig 31.11 Structure of a human heart.

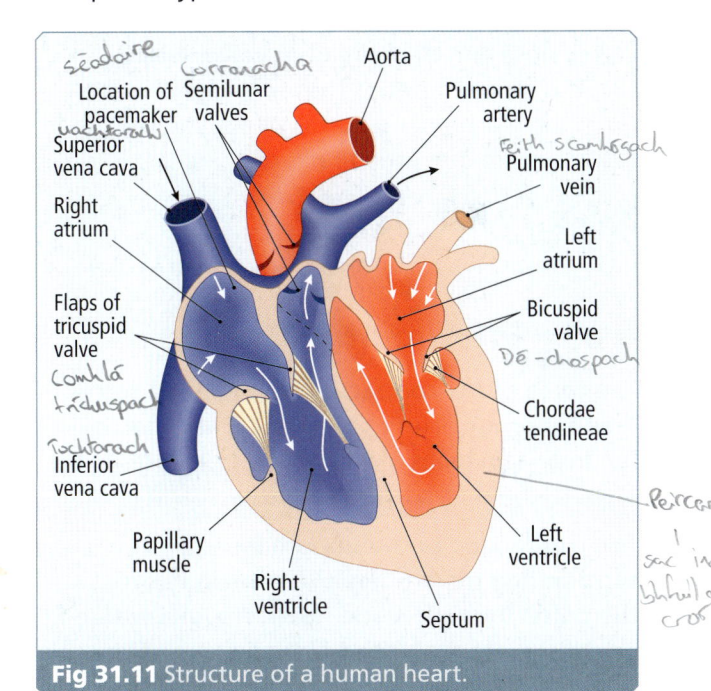

Fig 31.11 shows the major parts of the heart that you have to be able to identify for the Leaving Certificate Biology exam.

The heart is a double pump composed of a right side and a left side.

- The septum separates the two sides of the heart. Each side is split into two chambers: the **atrium** (plural **atria**) and the **ventricle.**
- The left side of the heart is a stronger pump than the right. This is because it has to pump blood all around the body **(systemic circuit)**, whereas the right side pumps blood the short distance to the lungs **(pulmonary circuit)**.
- The right and left atria are located above the ventricles and separated from them by valves. The left valve is called the **bicuspid** and the right valve is the **tricuspid.**

> **NOTE** An easy way to remember on which side each valve is located is to look at the start of each word. Tricuspid starts with 'tRI'. The second and third letters are 'r' and 'i', which are the first two letters of the word 'right'. In this way, we can remember that the tricuspid valve is located on the right-hand side of the heart. The bicuspid, therefore, belongs to the left-hand side.

- The bicuspid and tricuspid valves are the biggest valves in the body and are held in place by tendons, called **chordae tendineae**. These tendons are attached to the ventricle walls by a small muscle, called the **papillary muscle.**
- At the top of the right atrium is the **pacemaker**. It controls the rate of the heartbeat.
- There are four major arteries attached at the top of the heart: **vena cavae** (superior and inferior), **pulmonary artery, aorta** and **pulmonary veins.**
- The vena cavae carry blood towards the heart. They are the largest veins in the body. Both direct blood flow into the right atrium. The superior vena cava carries blood from the head, and the inferior vena cava carries blood from the lower half of the body.
- The pulmonary artery carries blood away from the heart towards the lungs. It is the only artery in the body that carries deoxygenated blood. The pulmonary artery has a valve called the **semilunar valve** at the point where it leaves the heart. This prevents the backflow of blood into the right ventricle.
- The pulmonary veins carry blood back to the heart from the lungs and direct it into the left atrium.

- Finally, the **aorta**, which is the largest blood vessel in the body, carries blood away from the heart to all areas of the body, except the lungs. The aorta also has a semilunar valve at the point where it leaves the heart. This prevents the backflow of blood into the left ventricle.
- The **septum** keeps deoxygenated blood separate from oxygenated blood.

The cardiac (heart) cycle (stages of the heartbeat)

The heartbeat (also referred to as the **cardiac or heart cycle**) consists of a number of stages. It is controlled by the **pacemaker**.

The pacemaker is located in the top of the right atrium wall. The pacemaker is **nervous tissue** that sends out electrical signals. The heart muscle (cardiac muscle) contracts in response to the signals.

Atrial contraction

The atria are the first two chambers to contract. As they contract, the bicuspid and tricuspid valves open. The contraction and opening of the valves together move blood from the atria into the ventricles.

Ventricular contraction

The electrical signal from the pacemaker then reaches the ventricles, which contract. This closes the bicuspid and tricuspid valves. As the ventricles contract, the semilunar valves open and blood flows into the major arteries: the pulmonary artery and aorta.

HL The cardiac (heart) cycle (stages of the heartbeat) – detailed process

There are two pacemakers: the **sinoatrial node** (SA node) and the **atrioventricular node** (AV node). The SA node is located in the top wall of the right atrium. The AV node is located between the right atrium and ventricle. Both nodes are composed of nervous tissue.

The nodes are completely independent of the nervous system. This means that the heart can beat by itself, without direct connection to the nervous system.

The stages of the heartbeat can be described under two headings: **atrial systole** and **ventricular diastole** and **ventricular systole** and **atrial diastole**.

1 Atrial systole and ventricular diastole

Firstly, the atria receive blood from the major veins (vena cavae and pulmonary veins) entering the heart. The SA node sends an electrical signal that spreads throughout the nerves within the cardiac muscle. As a result, the atria contract and both the bicuspid and tricuspid valves open. Blood flows into the ventricles. Atrial contraction is also called **atrial systole**. While the atria are in systole, the ventricles are in **diastole** (relaxation).

2 Ventricular systole and atrial diastole

After the ventricles have received blood from the atria, the AV node receives a signal from the SA node. It then sends an electrical signal that spreads throughout the nerves within the cardiac muscle of the ventricles. This causes **ventricular systole**. As a result, the bicuspid and tricuspid valves close and the semilunar valves open. Blood is pumped out of the ventricles into the pulmonary artery and aorta. Whilst the ventricles are in systole, the atria are in diastole (Fig 31.12).

Pulse

> A **pulse** is the alternate contraction and relaxation of an artery as blood passes through.

The force of the contraction of the heart forces blood through arteries in **pulses**. Pulses can be felt in certain areas of the body where arteries are close to the skin, such as at the wrist and neck.

The contraction of the smooth muscle surrounding the arteries also contributes to the pulse. Because blood flows in spurts within arteries, there is no need for valves.

However, there are valves in veins. This is because blood flows continuously in veins rather than in spurts. As a result, without valves blood could flow backwards.

The human circulatory system   Chapter 31

Fig 31.12 Stages of the heartbeat.

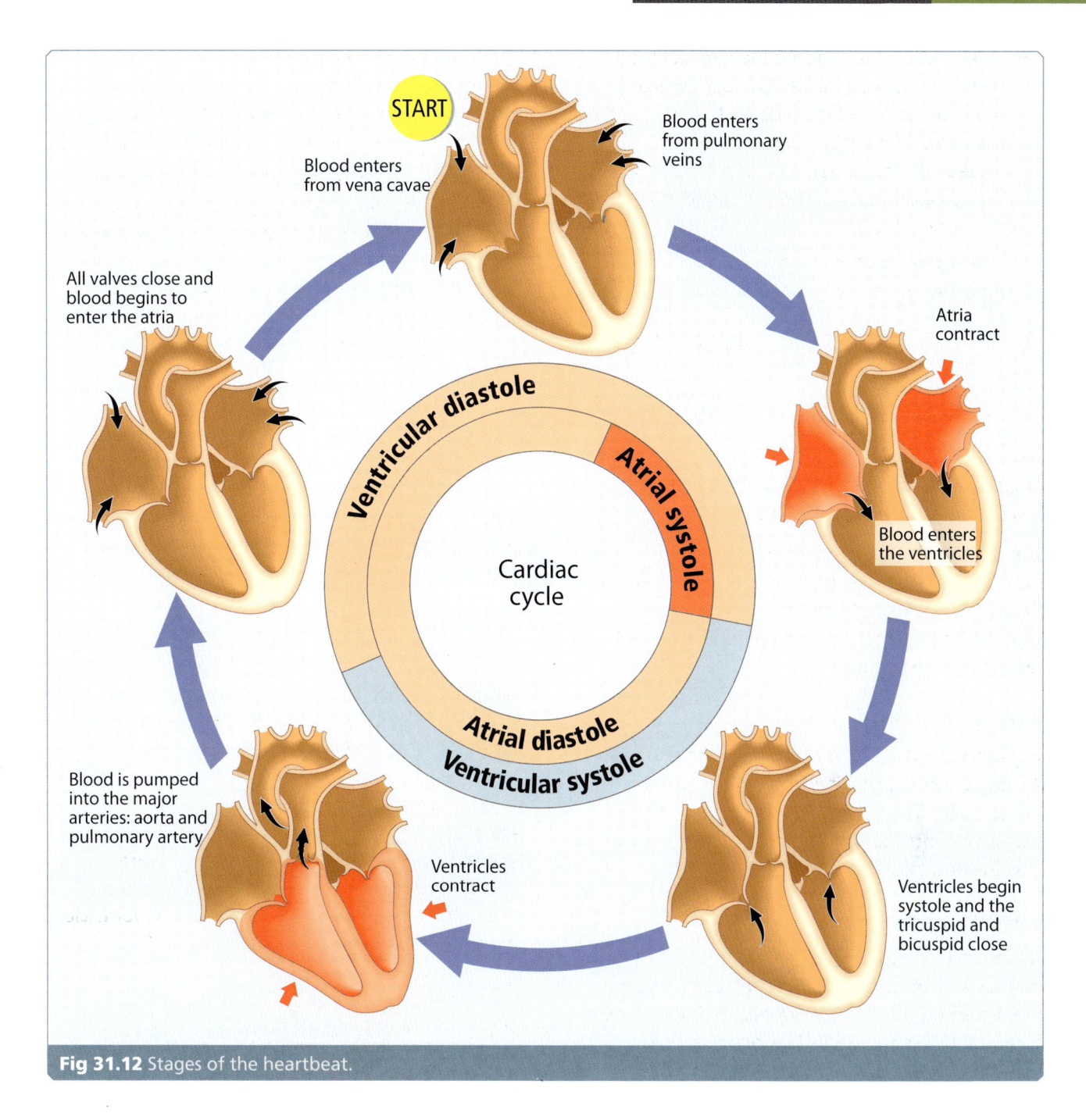

Varicose veins (Fig 31.13) can occur when the valves are not working properly. This allows the blood to pool within the vein. They are most often seen in the legs of older people. They can be very painful and can even become infected.

Blood pressure

> **Blood pressure** is the force blood exerts on the walls of blood vessels.

Blood pressure is highest in the arteries due to contraction of the heart. As blood flows away from the arteries to arterioles, capillaries and venules, the pressure decreases. Blood pressure is lowest in the veins.

Blood pressure is always expressed as two numbers. This is because blood pressure changes as the heart contracts and relaxes.

When the heart beats (contraction), the blood pressure is highest. When it is relaxing, the pressure is lower. The higher value is called **systolic pressure** and the lower value is called **diastolic pressure**.

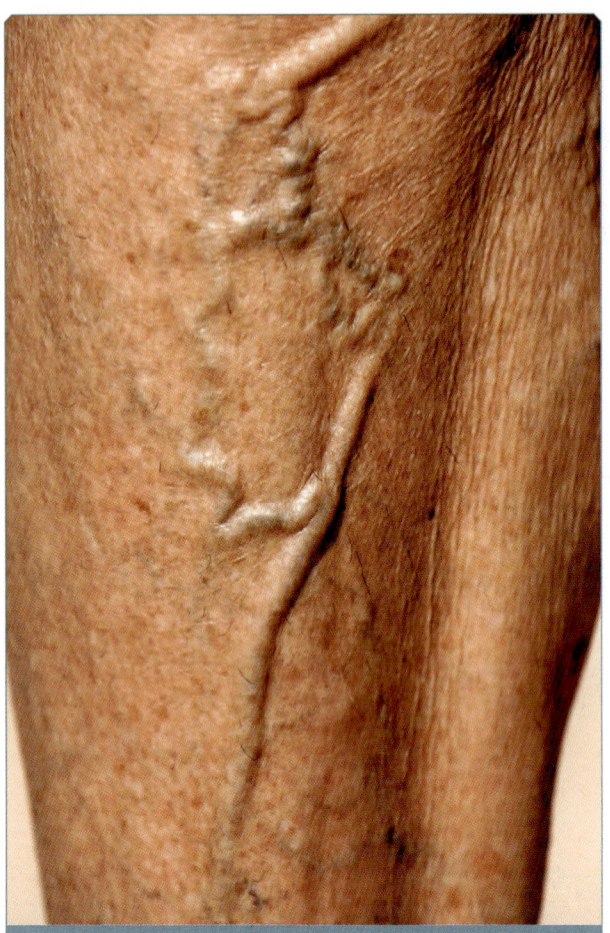

Fig 31.13 Varicose veins in a leg.

This means that systolic pressure is 120 mmHg and diastolic pressure is 80 mmHg. The unit of pressure is expressed as mm of Hg (mercury). This means that the systolic blood pressure is enough to hold up a column of mercury that is 120 mm high and diastolic pressure can hold up an 80 mm column of mercury.

High blood pressure is a common disorder of the circulatory system. Blood pressure is generally considered high if it is anything above 150/110 mmHg. Having high blood pressure increases the risks of having a heart attack and/or stroke.

Hardening or narrowing of arteries is another circulatory system disorder. It is caused by the build-up of fatty tissue on the inside of blood vessels. This condition is called **atherosclerosis.** It increases blood pressure even further and thereby increases the risk of heart attack and/or stroke.

Fig 31.15 A build-up of fatty deposits on the inside of an artery (atherosclerosis).

Blood pressure is measured using a **sphygmomanometer** (Fig 31.14). Medical professionals usually measure blood pressure by placing a strap around the upper arm and measuring the pressure required to stop blood flow through the major artery in the upper arm.

Normal blood pressure for an adult human is **120/80 mmHg.** We say this as '120 over 80'.

Effects of smoking, diet and exercise on the circulatory system

Smoking

Cigarettes are highly addictive due to the number of addictive chemicals they include. **Nicotine** is one of the most addictive drugs and causes an increase in heart rate. This can also cause an increase in blood pressure. Over a long period of time, smoking can lead to heart disease and stroke, as well as various types of cancer (see Chapter 13).

All cigarette manufacturers must now place a clearly visible sign on their packaging stating at least one serious effect of smoking on the body (Fig 31.16).

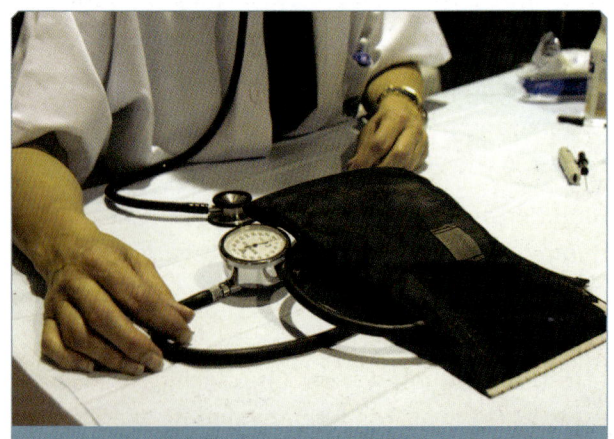

Fig 31.14 Sphygmomanometers are used to measure blood pressure.

The human circulatory system   Chapter 31

Fig 31.16 Smoking has a harmful effect on the circulatory system.

Diet

Diet has a major effect on the circulatory system. A diet high in saturated fats increases blood pressure and atherosclerosis.

A diet high in salt also increases blood pressure. The brain tries to keep the concentration of the bloodstream the same at all times (homeostasis). If salt levels in the blood increase, the brain responds by stimulating thirst. Water is taken in, increasing blood volume (without an increase in volume of the circulatory system). This causes blood pressure to rise.

Patients with heart disease are often given **diuretics** to decrease blood pressure. They work by decreasing blood volume.

Fig 31.17 A 'full Irish' breakfast. This meal is high in saturated fats that cause atherosclerosis.

Exercise

Exercise stimulates an increase in heart rate and blood pressure. However, it increases the strength of the heart and promotes healthy arteries and veins. Long-term effects of exercise include a stronger heart and healthier arteries, veins and capillaries. Exercise also helps to lower blood pressure.

Fig 31.18 Exercise strengthens the heart and keeps the blood vessels healthy.

Unit 3 The Organism

Practical activity: to dissect, display and identify an ox's or a sheep's heart

Method

Your teacher will supply you with a sheep's heart. They are similar in size to a human heart.

> **NOTE** The experiment described involves a sheep's heart. The process is the same for an ox's heart.

> **SAFETY**
> Extreme caution must be taken with the scalpel, mounted needle and scissors.
> Wear a lab coat and gloves.

1. Wash the heart well with water over a wash basin. This removes any blood clots that may block your view of internal structures.
2. Place the heart on a dissection board.
3. Distinguish between the left and right sides of the heart. The left side will feel much firmer than the right. This is because the left side of the heart has to pump blood all around the body.
4. Distinguish between the front and back sides of the heart. The back side will be more flat than the rounded front. Place the heart on its back, flat side (Fig 31.19).
5. Identify the coronary artery on the front surface of the heart.
6. Identify the four major arteries at the top of the heart (Fig 31.20).
7. Examine the flaps of tissue on the top of the heart. These ear-like flaps are the auricles.
8. Notice the large opening on top of the heart next to the right auricle. This is the opening to the superior vena cava, which brings blood from the top half of the body to the right atrium.
9. There is a smaller opening further down the heart on the left-hand side. This is the inferior vena cava, which brings blood from the lower part of the body.
10. Next to the left auricle, you will find the pulmonary vein, which brings blood from the lungs into the left atrium.
11. In the centre of the heart at the top is the largest blood vessel in the body, the aorta. This takes oxygenated blood from the left ventricle to the rest of the body.
12. Find the pulmonary artery, which takes blood from the right ventricle to the lungs. It is just behind and slightly to the left of the aorta.
13. The aorta branches into many arteries on leaving the top of the heart.
14. Draw a labelled diagram of the external structure of the heart.
15. Turn the heart so that it is lying on its front surface. Make an incision using dissecting scissors or a scalpel by cutting into the superior vena cava down through the walls of the right atrium and ventricle, as shown by the right-hand dotted line in Fig 31.20.
16. Open up the incision and identify the right atrium, right ventricle, tricuspid valve, papillary muscles and chordae tendineae (Fig 31.21).
17. Insert a probe down through the pulmonary artery. It should come through to the right ventricle. Leaving the probe in place, cut up through the wall of the pulmonary artery. Identify the semilunar valve that prevents backflow of blood into the right ventricle.

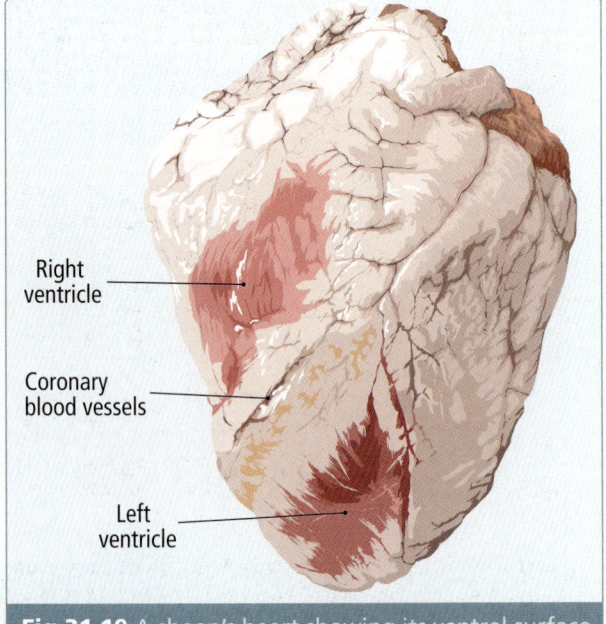

Fig 31.19 A sheep's heart showing its ventral surface

18 Make another incision, using the scissors, at the left auricle at the base of the superior vena cava down through the wall of the left atrium and left ventricle, as shown by the left-hand dotted line in Fig 31.20.

19 Open up the incision and identify the left atrium, left ventricle, the bicuspid valve, papillary muscles and chordae tendineae (Fig 31.22).

20 Insert a probe down through the aorta. It should come through to the left ventricle.

21 Leaving the probe in place, cut up through the wall of the aorta. Identify the semilunar valve that prevents backflow of blood into the left ventricle.

22 Label as many structures as possible using pins and labels.

23 Sketch the internal structure of the heart and label all the structures.

Conclusion

What have we learned from this practical activity?

- The left ventricle has a much thicker wall than the right ventricle. This is because the left ventricle must pump blood into the systemic circuit (around the body).
- The coronary artery is on the front surface of the heart.
- There are four major arteries at the top of the heart: aorta, pulmonary artery, vena cava and pulmonary vein.
- There are four internal chambers in the heart separated by valves and the septum.

Practical activity questions

1 Distinguish between the front and back surfaces of the heart by briefly describing each.

2 On which side is the coronary artery found?

3 Which side of the heart is stronger and why?

4 Name the **four** major arteries located at the top of the heart.

5 What type of muscle is the heart made from?

6 Explain why it is important to make two incisions on either side of the heart rather than making one incision in the centre of the heart.

7 Give **two** safety precautions you took during this practical activity.

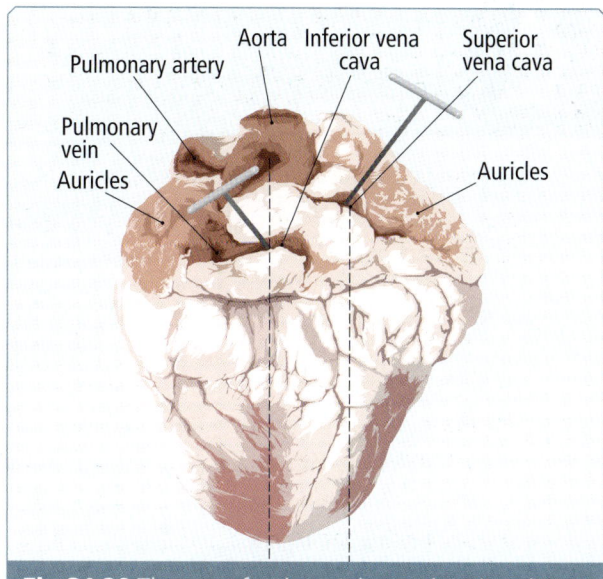

Fig 31.20 The top of a sheep's heart showing the major arteries and the auricles (viewed from the back).

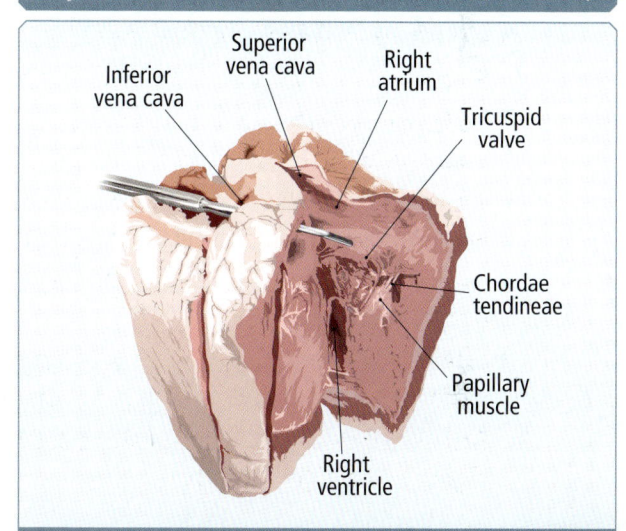

Fig 31.21 The internal structure of a sheep's heart viewed from the back with the right side of the heart dissected open.

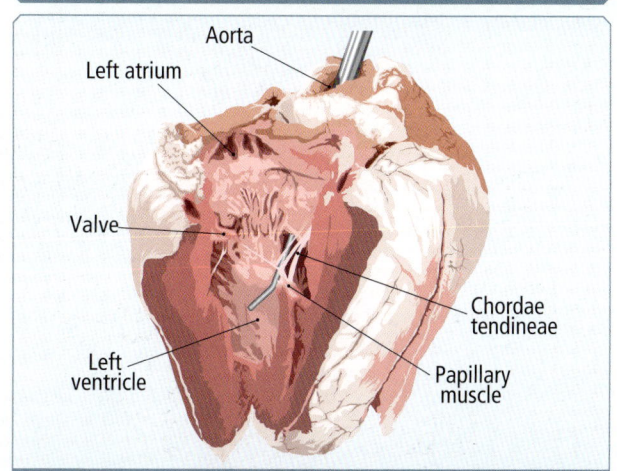

Fig 31.22 The internal structure of a sheep's heart viewed from the back with the left side of the heart dissected open.

Unit 3   The Organism

Practical activity: to investigate the effect of exercise on pulse rate

Pulse rate is the same as your heart rate as each pulse is caused by one contraction of the heart.

Measuring your heart rate involves using your index finger and middle finger to count the number of pulses at the wrist or on the neck over the course of one minute.

Everyone's resting heart rate will be different. The average resting heart rate in humans is approximately 70 beats per minute (bpm).

Very fit athletes will have very low resting heart rates; for example, cyclist Miguel Indurain had a resting heart rate of 28!

> **NOTE** The syllabus states that you have to do either this activity or the activity to investigate the effect of exercise on breathing rate (page 366).

> **NOTE** You can also count for 15 seconds and multiply the result by four. Do not use the thumb as it has its own pulse.

Method

1. Measure your pulse rate three times while at rest. Calculate your average pulse rate.
2. Walk slowly for 3 minutes and measure your pulse rate.
3. Walk briskly for 3 minutes and measure your pulse rate once again.
4. Finally, run for 3 minutes and measure your new pulse rate.
5. You can also see the effect of vigorous exercise on pulse rate by running as fast as you can for 3 minutes.
6. Copy and complete the results table below.

> **NOTE** If you have access to a heart rate monitor you will be able to see the effect exercise has on your heart rate in real time. Also some heart rate monitors come with software that enables you to download the data to a computer and view the results in a graph.

Results

	Pulse rate (bpm)
Resting	
Walking slowly	
Walking briskly	
Running	

Conclusion

What have we learned from this practical activity?

- Average resting pulse rate in humans is approximately 70 beats per minute.
- Exercise increases pulse rate.

Practical activity questions

1. Explain how you measured pulse rate.
2. If you measured your pulse rate manually, why is it important that you did not use your thumb?
3. Explain why, following exercise, it is more accurate to measure your pulse rate over the course of 15 seconds, and multiply by 4, rather than counting for 1 minute.

Chapter 31 Questions

1. Distinguish between an *open* and *closed* circulatory system. Give **one** example of an organism belonging to each group.
2. What type of muscle is the heart made from and what special characteristic does this muscle have?
3. Draw a cross-section of an artery, a vein and a capillary, labelling the following where applicable: *collagen*; *smooth muscle*; *endothelium*; *lumen*.
4. Copy and complete the following table:

	Direction of blood flow	Structure
Artery		
	Carries blood towards the heart	
		One cell thick (endothelium)

5. What is meant by *double circulation* in reference to the circulatory system of vertebrates?
6. (a) Draw the internal structure of a human heart labelling the following structures: *right atrium*; *left atrium*; *right ventricle*; *left ventricle*; *septum*; *bicuspid valve*; *tricuspid valve*; *vena cava*; *pulmonary artery*; *aorta*; and *pulmonary vein*.
   (b) Place an X on your drawing showing where the pacemaker is located.
7. (a) What type of tissue is the pacemaker?
   (b) What is the function of the pacemaker?
8. (a) What is a *portal system*?
   (b) Give **one** example of a portal system.
9. Describe the process of the cardiac cycle.

HL 10. Answer the following in relation to the detailed process of the cardiac cycle:
   (a) The pacemaker consists of two nodes: the SA node and the AV node. What do these letters stand for?
   (b) State exactly where each node is located in the heart.
   (c) Explain what *atrial systole* is and how it occurs.
   (d) Describe what happens during atrial systole.
   (e) Explain what *ventricular systole* is and how it occurs.
   (f) Describe what happens during ventricular systole.

11. (a) What is a *pulse*?
    (b) Why is a pulse not felt in a vein?
12. (a) What is *blood pressure*?
    (b) How is blood pressure measured?
    (c) What is normal blood pressure for an adult human?
13. State the specific effects the following have on the human circulatory system:
    (a) Smoking.
    (b) Diet.
    (c) Exercise.

Chapter 31 Sample examination questions

1. (a) Name the blood vessel referred to in each of the following cases:
      (i) The vein connected to the lungs.
      (ii) The artery connected to the kidneys.
      (iii) The vein that joins the intestine to the liver.
   (b) The following questions relate to the human heart.
      (i) Give the precise location of the heart in the human body.
      (ii) What structure(s) protects the heart?
      (iii) Name the upper chambers of the heart.
      (iv) Name the valve between the upper and lower chambers on the left-hand side.
      (v) What is the average resting human heart rate?

(vi) Give **two** factors which cause an increase in heart rate.
(vii) Name the blood vessels that bring oxygen to the heart muscle.
(viii) Explain why the walls of the lower chambers of the heart are thicker than the walls of the upper chambers.

(c) **Copy the table below into your answer book** and use your knowledge of blood vessels and the information in diagrams A, B and C to complete the table. Some boxes have been filled as examples.

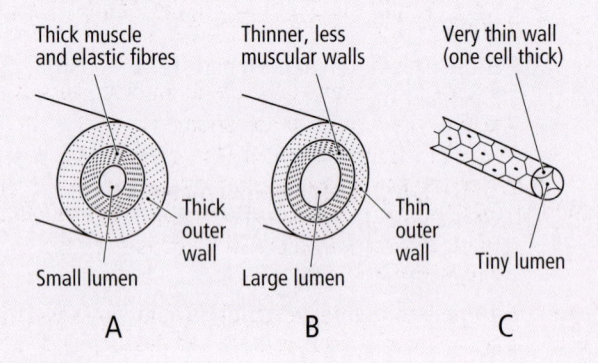

A — Thick muscle and elastic fibres, Thick outer wall, Small lumen
B — Thinner, less muscular walls, Thin outer wall, Large lumen
C — Very thin wall (one cell thick), Tiny lumen

Vessel	A	B	C
Name		Vein	
Lumen	Small		
Wall			
Direction of blood flow			
Valves present			

Section C, Question 13 Ordinary Level 2009

HL **2** (a) The human circulatory system has two circuits.
   (i) Give the name of each of these circuits.
   (ii) Which of these circuits involves the pumping of blood by the left ventricle?
(b) (i) Write a short note on **each** of the following:
      1. Pulse.
      2. Blood pressure.
   (ii) Comment on the effect of **each** of the following on the circulatory system:
      1. Diet.
      2. Exercise.
   (iii) Give **two** ways, other than colour, in which a red blood cell differs in structure or composition from a typical body cell such as one in the cheek lining.
   (iv) What is the role of the SA (sinoatrial) and AV (atrioventricular) nodes in the heart?
   (v) Give the **precise** locations of **both** the SA and the AV nodes in the heart.

Section C, Question 13 (a) and (b) Higher Level 2009

Chapter 31 Mind map

The circulatory system of a human consists of a complex network of blood vessels, along with the heart and blood.

- The human circulatory system consists of two circuits: systemic circuit and pulmonary circuit.
- The **systemic circuit** carries blood to and from all parts of the body, other than the lungs.
- The **pulmonary circuit** carries blood to and from the lungs.

Three types of blood vessels
- **Artery:** a blood vessel that carries blood away from the heart in powerful pulses; has a thick wall, small lumen and no valves.
- **Vein:** a blood vessel that carries blood towards the heart in an even flow; has a thin wall, large lumen and valves.
- **Capillary:** a blood vessel with a wall one cell thick (endothelium) and carries blood from arterioles to venules through tissues releasing nutrients and taking away wastes.

- **Open circulatory system:** a system of blood vessels where blood leaves the vessels and flows around cells, e.g. insects.
- **Closed circulatory system:** a system of blood vessels where blood flows within blood vessels, e.g. humans.

The human circulatory system — Chapter 31

Structure of the heart
- The heart is a double pump made from cardiac muscle that is slow to tire.
- The heart consists of four chambers: left and right atria and ventricles; separated by a wall of muscle called the septum; bicuspid, tricuspid and semilunar valves; papillary muscles; chordae tendineae; vena cava; pulmonary artery; aorta; pulmonary vein; pacemaker; coronary artery and vein.
- Front of heart is rounded and back of heart is flatter.

Portal system: a network of capillaries in one organ or tissue joined to another network of capillaries in another organ or tissue via a vein or veins, e.g. hepatic portal system connecting the digestive system with the liver.

Heartbeat
- The pacemaker sends a signal to the atria which contract.
- Blood flows into the ventricles, forcing the bicuspid and tricuspid valves to open in the process.
- The pacemaker sends another signal to cause the ventricles to contract.
- This causes the bicuspid and tricuspid valves to close and the semilunar valves to open as blood flows out into the aorta and pulmonary artery.

Heartbeat: detailed process   *HL*
- The pacemaker of the heart is composed of the sinoatrial (SA) node and the atrioventricular (AV) node.
- The SA node is located in the top wall of the right atrium.
- The AV node is located between the right atrium and right ventricle.
- The SA node sends a signal to the walls of the atria, causing them to contract (atrial systole).
- The bicuspid and tricuspid valves open as blood flows into the ventricles.
- The ventricles are relaxed (diastole).
- The AV node receives the signal from the SA node and creates another signal, which is sent to the walls of the ventricles.
- The ventricles contract (ventricular systole).
- The bicuspid and tricuspid valves close and the semilunar valves open as blood flows out of the heart into the aorta and pulmonary artery.
- When the ventricles are in systole the atria are in diastole.

Pulse
- A pulse is the alternate contraction and relaxation of an artery as blood passes through.
- A pulse can be found anywhere an artery is near to the surface of the skin, e.g. wrist and neck.

Blood pressure
- The force blood exerts on the walls of blood vessels.
- Measured using a sphygmomanometer.
- Normal blood pressure is 120/80 mmHg.

The effects of smoking, diet and exercise on the circulatory system
- Smoking increases heart rate. This puts a greater strain on the circulatory system and raises the risk of a heart attack and stroke.
- Diets rich in saturated fat increase atherosclerosis, blood pressure and the risk of a heart attack and stroke.
- Exercise increases pressure on the circulatory system and increases the strength of the heart in the long term.

Practical activity to dissect, display and identify an ox's or a sheep's heart
- Identify the front from the back surface.
- Place heart on the back surface.
- Identify the four major arteries on top of the heart.
- Place the heart on its front surface and make two incisions from each auricle down either side of the heart.
- Open up the chambers and identify each of the four chambers, the valves, papillary muscles, tendons and septum.

Practical activity to investigate the effect of exercise on pulse rate
- Measure the average pulse rate at rest by counting the number of pulses at the wrist per minute.
- Walk slowly and measure pulse rate again.
- Walk briskly and measure again.
- Finally, exercise vigorously and measure the pulse rate.
- Notice that pulse rate increases as the intensity of exercise increases.

Chapter 32 The human lymphatic system

Learning objectives After studying this chapter, you should be able to:
- Describe the composition, formation and function of lymph.
- Describe the structure and functions of lymph nodes and lymph vessels.

Introduction

The lymphatic system is part of the immune system and is directly linked to the circulatory system. The lymphatic system consists of many lymph vessels and lymph nodes that have many functions.

The lymphatic system can be thought of as a type of circulatory system as it collects excess fluid surrounding cells and returns it to the blood. This fluid is called **interstitial fluid**, also known as **extracellular fluid**.

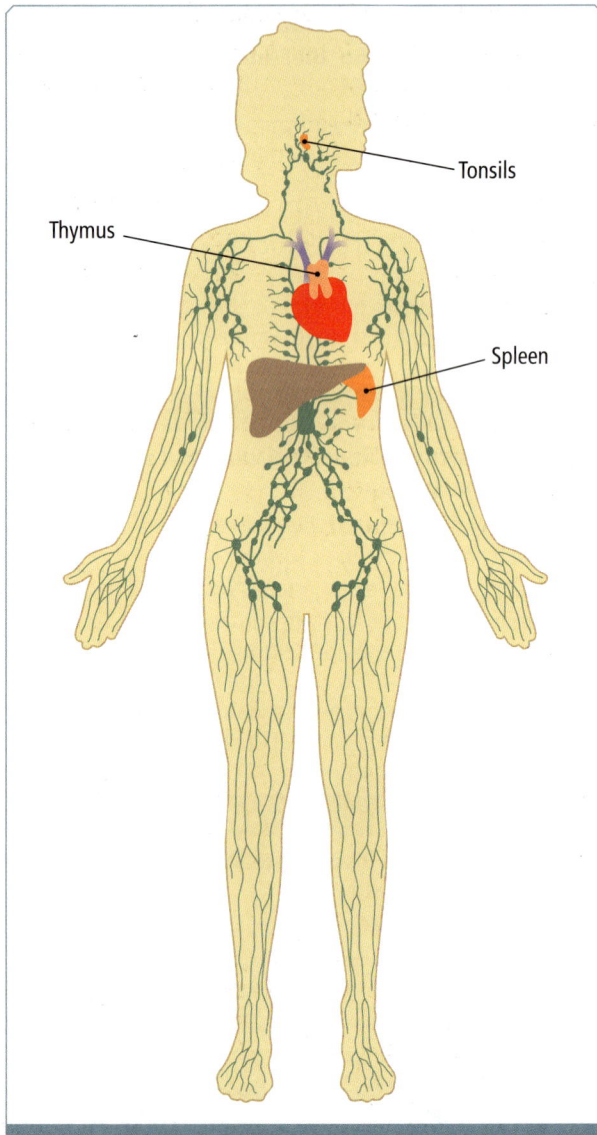

Interstitial fluid is formed by plasma leaking from the capillaries. We learned in Chapter 31 that capillaries have very thin walls. As a result, fluids can leak very easily through their walls into the spaces surrounding cells. The plasma leaks due to the blood pressure in the capillaries. Most interstitial fluid (90 per cent) diffuses back into the bloodstream to reform plasma. The remaining 10 per cent is collected by the lymph vessels. Interstitial fluid in the lymphatic system is called **lymph**.

> **Lymph** is a clear liquid that is collected from around cells and is transported by the lymphatic system back to the bloodstream.

Structure of the lymphatic system

The lymphatic system consists of **lymph, lymph vessels, lymph nodes, spleen, tonsils, adenoids, lacteals** and **thymus**.

> **Lymph vessels** are narrow, dead-ending tubes that transport lymph and are present in every tissue and organ throughout the body.

The walls of lymph vessels in tissues are one-cell thick **(endothelium)** to allow diffusion. Other lymph vessels have thicker walls and have valves to prevent backflow of lymph. Lymph is transported in the same way blood is transported in veins. All lymph vessels throughout the body join together and carry lymph back to the bloodstream at the **subclavian veins,** the place where the lymphatic system joins with the blood circulatory system.

Fig 32.1 The lymphatic system.

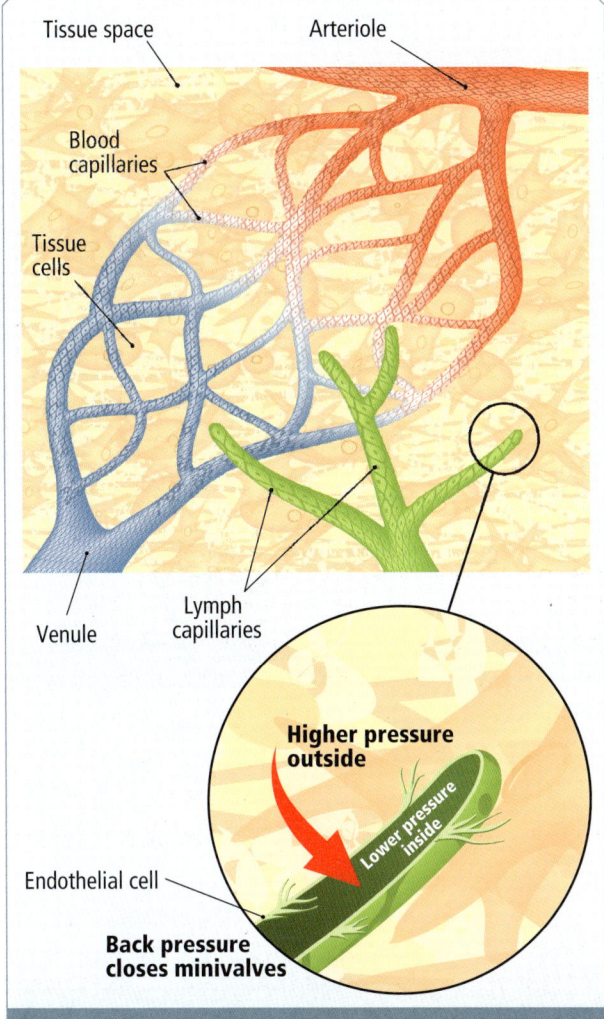

The human lymphatic system   Chapter 32

Fig 32.2 The structure of lymph vessels.

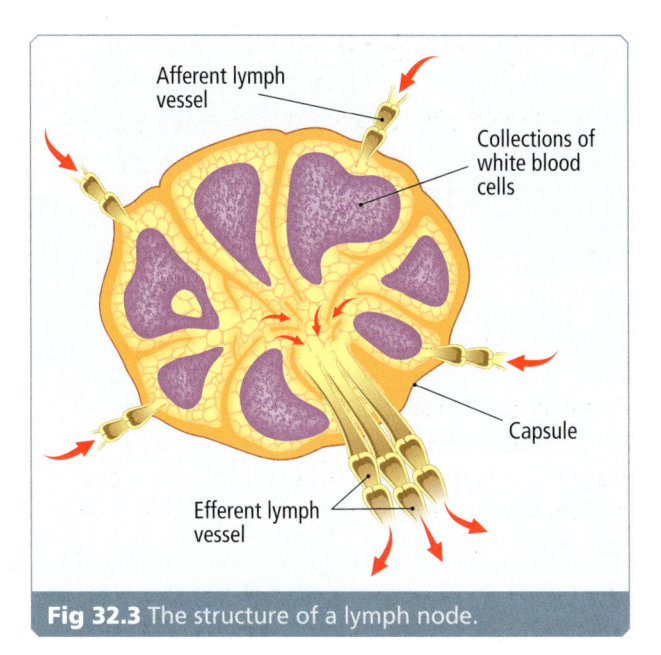

Fig 32.3 The structure of a lymph node.

Within the lymph node are collections of specialised white blood cells (see Chapter 34) that filter any harmful particles out, such as bacteria, viruses and abnormal cells.

The **spleen** (to the left of the stomach), **thymus** (just below the sternum in the chest), **adenoids** (back of the nose), and **tonsils** (either side of the throat) are also part of the lymphatic system.

Spleen

The spleen is a lymphatic organ (Fig 32.4) located just to the left of the stomach. It produces lymphocytes and antibodies. It also filters bacteria, viruses and abnormal cells.

Subclavian veins are so called because they are located just beneath the collar bones (clavicles).

The lymphatic system also consists of **lymph nodes** (Fig 32.3), which are mostly concentrated in the digestive system, groin, armpits and neck areas.

> **Lymph nodes** are small spherical-shaped organs of the lymphatic system that contain many white blood cells.

Lymph nodes have an outer wall called the capsule with afferent lymph vessels carrying lymph in and efferent lymph vessels carrying lymph out.

> **NOTE** 'Afferent' refers to a vessel carrying a body fluid **towards** an organ/tissue; 'efferent' refers to a vessel carrying a body fluid **away** from an organ/tissue.

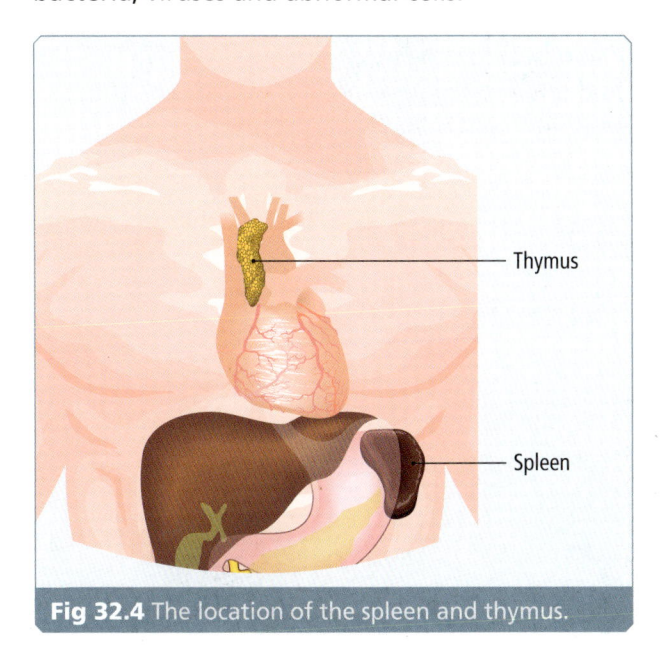

Fig 32.4 The location of the spleen and thymus.

333

Injury to the abdomen or ribs can rupture the spleen, and in severe cases it may have to be removed. The spleen is not essential for life, but it is thought to play an important role in fighting and preventing some serious infections.

Thymus

The thymus gland is a specialised organ belonging to the immune and lymphatic systems. It is located just in front of the heart and below the sternum. It functions in producing mature lymphocytes (*see* Chapter 34).

Adenoids and tonsils

The adenoids are located at the very back of the nose. The tonsils are located towards the back of the mouth on either side.

Sometimes both the adenoids and tonsils become inflamed and enlarged. Swollen adenoids can obstruct breathing through the nose, especially in children. In severe and chronic cases they may have to be removed. Similarly, tonsils may become regularly infected (tonsillitis) and may have to be removed.

Neither the adenoids nor the tonsils are essential for life; but, like the spleen, they are thought to decrease the chances of contracting some types of serious infections.

Functions of the lymphatic system

In addition to collecting excess interstitial fluid and returning it to the bloodstream, the lymphatic system has other functions.

> **NOTE** For Leaving Certificate Biology, you must know any three functions of the lymphatic system.

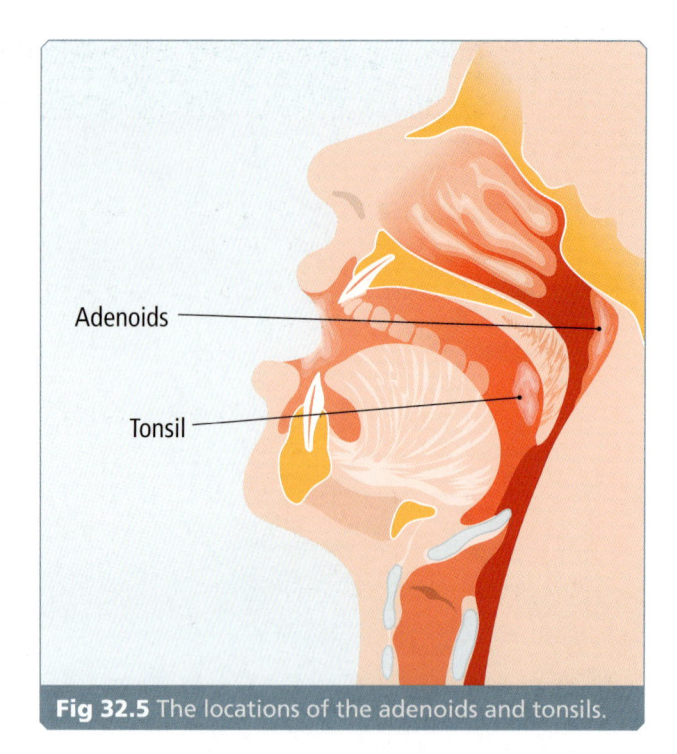

Fig 32.5 The locations of the adenoids and tonsils.

- It filters lymph through lymph nodes. Lymph can contain bacteria and viruses and cell debris (old parts of cells). White blood cells present in lymph nodes remove these unwanted components of lymph.
- It absorbs fat from the small intestine. Lymph vessels and lymph nodes are present throughout the wall of the digestive system. The lymph vessels branch into specialised vessels called lacteals (*see* Chapter 33). Lacteals absorb lipids after digestion.
- It is responsible for maturation of certain types of white blood cells. White blood cells called lymphocytes mature and become fully active in the thymus (*see* Chapter 34).
- It fights infections. White blood cells recognise foreign invaders (bacteria and viruses) and react against them by producing antibodies (*see* Chapter 34).

Chapter 32 Questions

1. (a) The lymphatic system is closely linked to **two** other systems. Name these systems.
   (b) Why can the lymphatic system also be considered a type of circulatory system?
2. (a) What is a *lymph vessel*?
   (b) Give **two** ways in which lymph vessels are similar to veins.
3. (a) What is *interstitial fluid*?
   (b) How is interstitial fluid formed?
4. Distinguish between *plasma* and *lymph*.
5. (a) What are *lymph nodes*?
   (b) Where in the body might you find lymph nodes?
   (c) What is the function of lymph nodes?
6. Apart from lymph nodes, name **three** other organs that are part of the lymphatic system and give each of their functions.
7. Where does the lymphatic system join with the blood circulatory system?
8. Give **three** functions of the lymphatic system.

Chapter 32 Sample examination questions

1. The lymphatic system is another series of vessels carrying fluid in the body. Give any **two** functions of the lymphatic system.

   Section C, Question 13 (b) (vii) Ordinary Level 2011

HL 2 (i) Describe the structure of the lymphatic system.
   (ii) Give an account of **three** functions of the lymphatic system.

   Section C, Question 13 (c) Higher Level 2006

Chapter 32 Mind map

The lymphatic system is part of the immune system.

- The lymphatic system consists of lymph, lymph vessels, lymph nodes, spleen, tonsils, adenoids, lacteals and thymus.
- It transports lymph in the same way veins transport blood.
- **Lymph** is a clear liquid that is collected from around cells and is transported by the lymphatic system back to the bloodstream.
- Lymph vessels are narrow tubes that transport lymph.
- **Lymph nodes** are small round organs of the lymphatic system that contain white blood cells.
- The lymph enters the bloodstream at the subclavian veins.

Functions of the lymphatic system
- Transports lymph back to the bloodstream via the subclavian veins.
- Filters lymph through the lymph nodes.
- Absorbs fat from the small intestine.
- Responsible for maturation of certain types of lymphocytes.
- Fights infections.

Chapter 33 The human digestive system

Learning objectives After studying this chapter, you should be able to:
- Define the terms *carnivore*, *herbivore* and *omnivore*.
- Define *digestion* and describe the need for digestion and a digestive system.
- Describe the process of nutrition under the following headings: ingestion, digestion, absorption and egestion.
- Describe the structure and function of the parts of the human digestive system.
- Distinguish between *mechanical* and *chemical digestion* and state the structures, organs and substances involved in each.
- Describe two roles of symbiotic bacteria in the human digestive system.
- Describe the benefits of fibre in the diet.
- Describe the basic structure of the small intestine and large intestine in relation to their functions.

Introduction

We have already learned that all organisms are either autotrophic or heterotrophic, that is, they either make their own food or obtain it from other living organisms.

Plants and some bacteria demonstrate autotrophic nutrition. There are two types of autotrophic nutrition: photosynthetic (plants and some bacteria) and chemosynthetic (bacteria only).

All animals, fungi and some bacteria demonstrate heterotrophic nutrition. In fungi and heterotrophic bacteria, there are two types of nutrition: parasitic nutrition and saprophytic nutrition.

All animals are **herbivores, carnivores** or **omnivores.**

> A **herbivore** is an animal that eats only plant material.
> A **carnivore** is an animal that eats only animal material.
> An **omnivore** is an animal that eats both plant and animal material.

Nutrition in the human

We have already learned that nutrition is the way in which organisms obtain and use food. Humans obtain food from both plant and animal sources and are therefore, omnivores. However, most animals are either herbivores or carnivores.

Many people choose to be herbivores, or vegetarians, and do not eat animal products.

Fig 33.1 Herbivore (**A**); carnivore (**B**); and omnivore (**C**).

Stages of nutrition

There are four main stages to the process of nutrition in animals: **ingestion, digestion, absorption** and **egestion.**

1 Ingestion

> **Ingestion** is the process of taking in food.

2 Digestion

> **Digestion** is the breaking down of food into its constituent molecules, which can be absorbed into the bloodstream.

There are two types of digestion: **mechanical** and **chemical**.

- Mechanical digestion involves the action of teeth, the rhythmical contractions of the gut and churning of the stomach to break food down into smaller particles. Mechanical digestion enables chemical digestion to occur more efficiently.
- Chemical digestion involves the action of enzymes present in digestive juices and acid produced by cells lining the stomach to break down food into even smaller molecules.

3 Absorption

> **Absorption** is the passage of single biomolecules from the gut into the cells lining the gut.

Once the biomolecules have been broken down into their basic constituent molecules, they are small enough to pass directly into cells lining the gut. Absorption can be either **passive** (no energy is needed) or **active** (requiring energy).

4 Egestion

> **Egestion** is the getting rid of undigested material.

The undigested material is called **faeces**. It is usually brown in colour, semi-solid in nature and has a characteristic unpleasant odour. Egestion usually occurs one to three times a day.

Digestion in the human

Digestion is an important component of nutrition for all heterotrophs.

Heterotrophs obtain their food from other organisms. This food is in the form of large biomolecules. They need to be broken down in order to be absorbed into the bloodstream and tissues where the molecules are needed.

There are two types of digestion: mechanical and chemical (*see* below). Both types occur in almost all animals. However, in organisms such as heterotrophic bacteria, protists and fungi and a very small number of animals, chemical digestion is the only type.

Organisms that demonstrate only chemical digestion usually engulf their food and chemically digest it within the cells, or they secrete enzymes to digest their food outside of their cells and then absorb it.

Most animals have a digestive system. The digestive system mechanically and chemically breaks down food. The ability to mechanically digest food enables animals to ingest complex food stuffs.

Enzymes (chemical digestion) then break down the food molecules into their basic constituent molecules. For example, starch is broken down into maltose molecules.

The digestive system in animals is an evolutionary adaptation so that every cell does not need digestive enzymes and can concentrate on other functions.

Structure of the human digestive system

The human digestive system is composed of a number of different organs. The digestive system is a very long continuous tube system. It starts at the **mouth** (also known as the **oral** or **buccal cavity**) and ends at the **anus**.

The digestive system is also known as the **'gut'** or **alimentary canal**.

It is composed of the **oral cavity** and associated glands (**salivary glands**); **pharynx**; **oesophagus**; **stomach**; **duodenum** and associated organs (**liver, gall bladder** and **pancreas**); **bile duct, small intestine (ileum); appendix; caecum; large intestine (colon); rectum** and **anus** (Fig 33.2).

You should note that there are sphincters (types of muscle) between each major section of the alimentary canal. Sphincters control the movement of food through the various sections of the digestive system. There are sphincters entering and leaving the stomach; at the junction between the small intestine and large intestine; and the anus itself is a sphincter.

The internal surface of the gut is made of specialised epithelial cells. Therefore, the alimentary canal is continuous with the outside of the body (as the skin is also a type of epithelial tissue).

The internal lining of the digestive system has various functions depending on its location along the alimentary canal. For example, the cells lining the stomach are specialised to secrete hydrochloric acid and protein-digesting enzymes, whereas the cells lining the large intestine are specialised for absorption of water, vitamins and minerals.

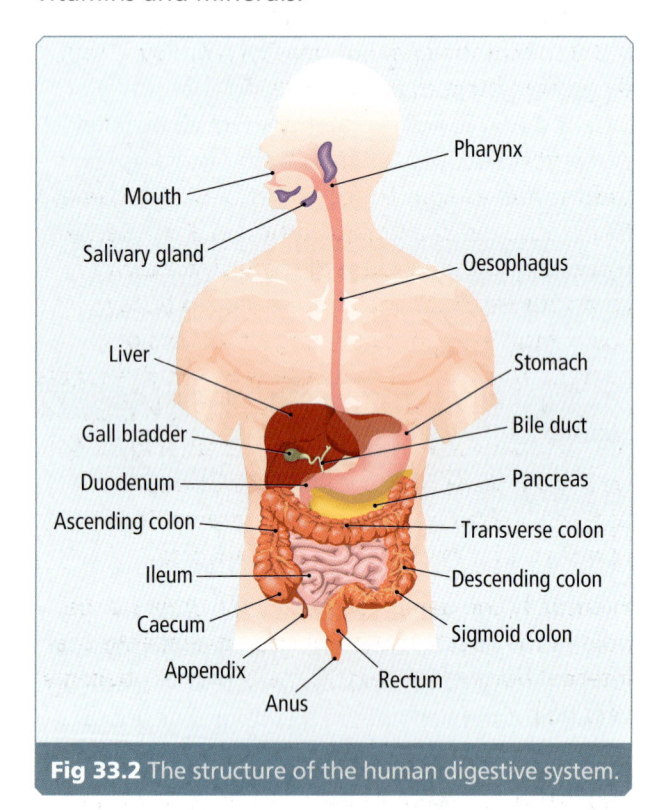

Fig 33.2 The structure of the human digestive system.

Digestion involves the **mechanical** and **chemical** breakdown of food.

Mechanical breakdown of food

Mechanical digestion involves the mouth, teeth, tongue and stomach. The muscles lining the mouth, along with the tongue, mix the food with saliva and move it around the mouth helping to break it up. The mouth and tongue also move the food into positions where the teeth can break the food down further.

Salts are produced by the liver and stored in the gall bladder as bile salts. They are involved in mechanical digestion. They emulsify (break up) lipids physically. This is not a chemical reaction, which is why it is classified as a type of mechanical digestion. Salts are also produced by the pancreas (sodium hydrogen carbonate). Sodium hydrogen carbonate neutralises the acid that enters the duodenum from the stomach.

The organs involved in mechanical digestion are described in greater detail below.

Chemical breakdown of food

Chemical digestion involves the use of enzymes, acid, water and salts to help with the digestive process.

Enzymes (see Chapter 9) are protein catalysts that break down food into smaller particles. For example, the salivary glands produce amylase; the stomach produces pepsin; and the pancreas produces lipase (and other enzymes).

Water helps with the hydrolysis of large molecules into smaller molecules (see Chapter 3).

The organs that produce the chemicals necessary for chemical breakdown of food are described in more detail below.

Oral cavity (mouth)

The oral cavity, or mouth, is where food enters **(ingestion)** and is mixed with **saliva.** Saliva is stimulated whenever food enters the mouth. It can even be stimulated by the sight or smell of food. Saliva is produced by the **salivary glands** of the mouth. It consists of **water, mucous, salts** and the **enzymes, amylase** and **lysozyme.**

Water and salts help to dissolve the food particles and enable the enzymes to work on the substrates. Amylase acts on starch converting it to maltose. Lysozyme is an enzyme that breaks open bacterial cell walls, killing the bacteria in the process. Tears also contain lysozyme.

The tongue is another important organ associated with the digestive system. It plays a role in ingestion, mechanical digestion, tasting and swallowing.

Food is mixed with saliva and mechanically digested by the teeth and tongue. A ball of soft food, called a **bolus,** is formed. The bolus is swallowed with help from the tongue.

During swallowing, the epiglottis closes over the **glottis** (see Chapter 35) to ensure the bolus travels down the oesophagus and not the windpipe.

Teeth

Physical digestion is also carried out by the teeth. They break solid food up into small pieces, making it easier to swallow and easier for enzymes to act on it.

There are four different types of teeth based on their shape and function. There are eight **incisors**, four **canines**, eight **premolars** and 12 **molars** giving a total of 32 teeth in a fully formed, healthy adult human mouth.

The human dental formula shows the number and type of teeth in a full set of teeth.

$$2(I\tfrac{2}{2}; C\tfrac{1}{1}; PM\tfrac{2}{2}; M\tfrac{3}{3})$$

The first '2' in the dental formula represents the two sides of the mouth. Each letter represents each type of tooth from the front of the mouth to the back. The numbers are expressed as fractions, with the upper number representing the number of teeth on the upper jawbone and the lower number representing the number of teeth on the lower jaw bone.

Incisors

Incisors are chisel-shaped teeth with a sharp edge. They are designed for **cutting** through food.

Canines

Canines are pointed teeth. They are usually very long in carnivores, but are smaller in humans as a result of a change in the human diet over many thousands of years. Their pointed shape makes them useful for **gripping** and **tearing** through food.

Premolars and molars

Premolars and molars have very similar shapes. They all have **cusps**. These allow **grinding** and **crushing** of food. This breaks the food up into very fine particles.

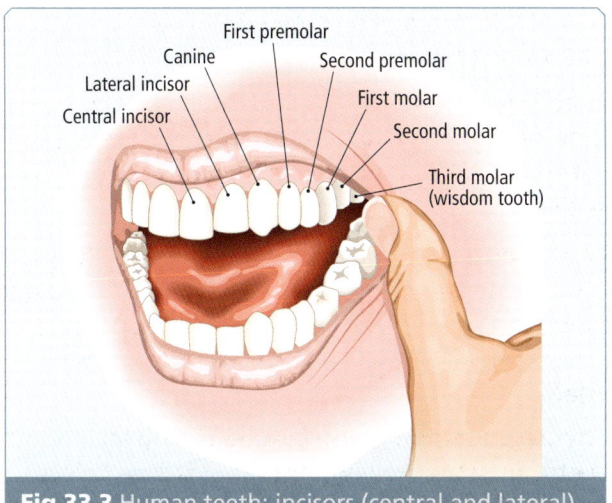

Fig 33.3 Human teeth: incisors (central and lateral), canines, premolars and molars.

Most adults have fewer than 32 teeth, as four of the molars are called wisdom teeth.

Wisdom teeth are the last teeth to break through the gums. They start to break through at around age 20. However, they rarely grow normally through the gums. They will often grow at an angle within the gum (called 'impacted' wisdom teeth) and cause pain in the other molars nearby. If they become impacted (made visible by X-ray), they often have to be removed.

Tooth decay

Despite the availability of better dental hygiene, tooth decay is still a major problem. Poor dental hygiene and the modern diet are significant contributors to the incidence of tooth decay. Foods high in sugar allow large numbers of bacteria to grow. When bacteria act on the sugars in the mouth, lactic acid is produced. It is this acid that corrodes the enamel of the teeth (Fig 33.4), creating cavities. If the teeth are not cleaned properly, bacteria can lodge themselves in the cavities and make the decay even worse.

Eventually the dental cavity can become a large hole in the tooth. If the hole penetrates into the internal parts of the tooth, the tooth can become very painful.

It is recommended that we floss once per day and brush our teeth twice a day to prevent the formation of dental cavities.

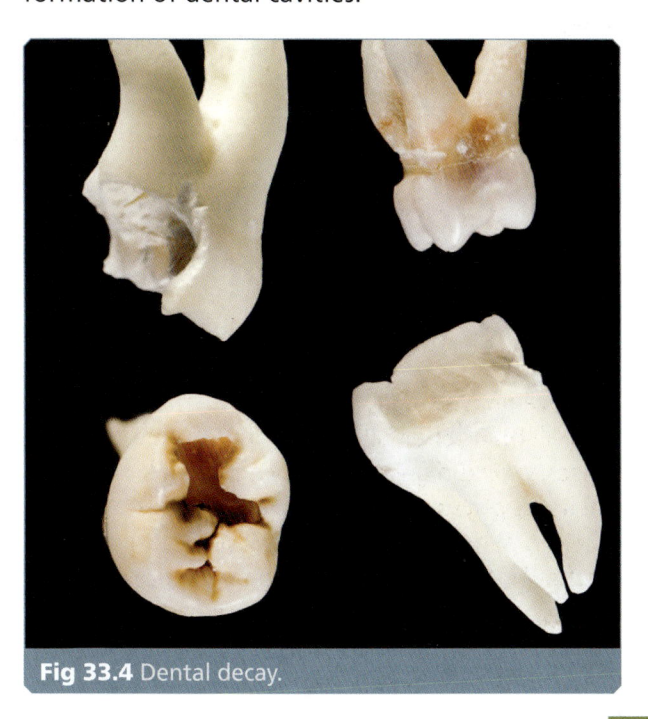

Fig 33.4 Dental decay.

Unit 3 The Organism

Pharynx
The pharynx functions in swallowing and ensuring the food travels down the **oesophagus.**

Oesophagus
The oesophagus is a muscular tube, approximately 30 cm long, through which food passes on its way to the stomach.

Food is actively pushed along by the muscles in the wall of the oesophagus. However, this muscular contraction is involuntary, meaning the body has no conscious control over it.

The muscle throughout the entire digestive system is smooth muscle. The contraction of this muscle occurs in waves that always push food along in one direction – downwards. This process is known as **peristalsis** (Fig 33.5).

> ! **Peristalsis** is rhythmical waves of contractions pushing food along the alimentary canal in one direction only.

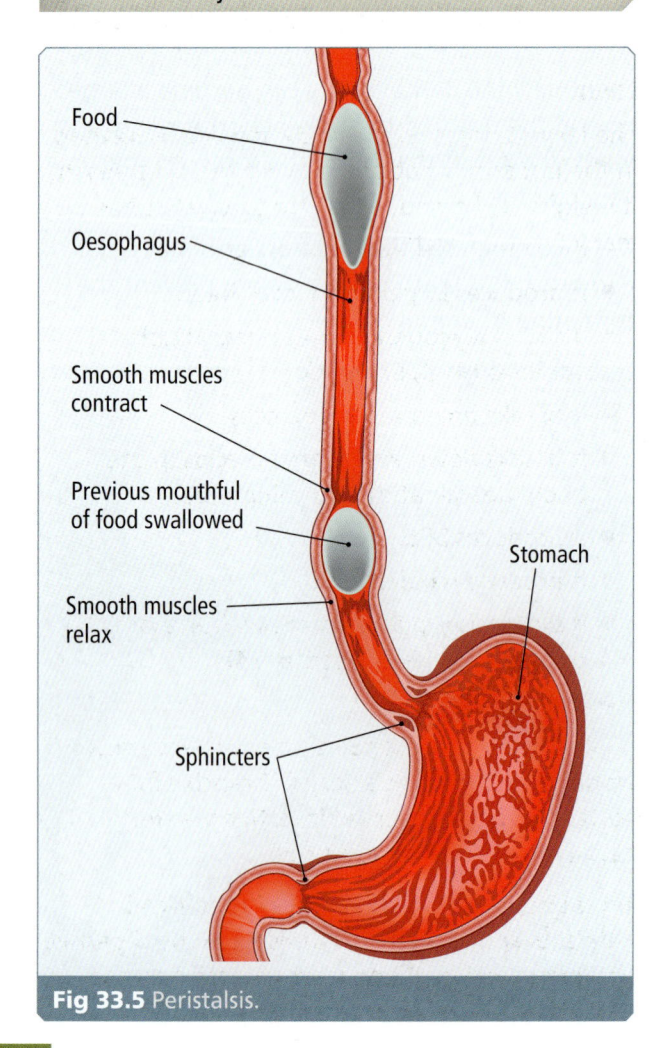

Peristalsis is a very important process in human nutrition. When peristalsis is slow or ineffective, the food can build up causing parts of the digestive system to distend (widen) and fill with food. This is called **constipation.**

Fibre reduces the risk of constipation. It is also thought to reduce the risk of colon cancer later in life by reducing the build-up of toxins.

Stomach
The stomach is a muscular bag sitting on the upper left-hand side of the abdomen (Fig 33.6). It holds approximately 1 L when full but can distend up to 2 L if enough food and drink are consumed.

It has a highly folded internal wall (Fig 33.7) that gives greater surface area for gastric glands.

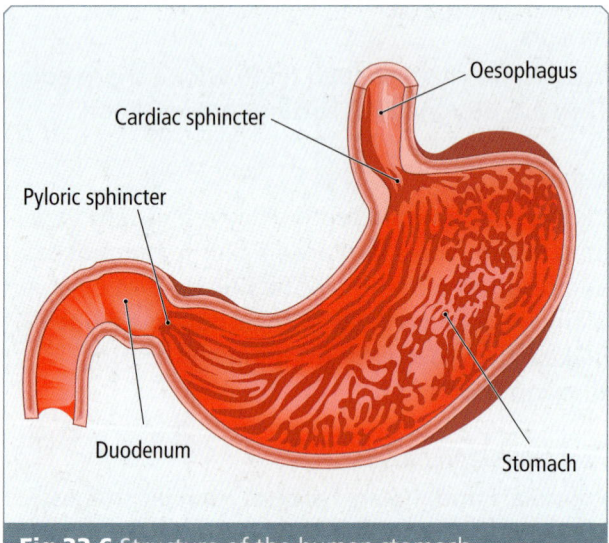

Fig 33.6 Structure of the human stomach.

Food enters the stomach through the **cardiac sphincter,** which is a muscle that controls the entry of food from the oesophagus. It also helps to prevent reflux **(heartburn).**

Food remains in the stomach for approximately one to two hours. During this time, it is mixed with gastric juice. Gastric juice is produced by thousands of gastric glands located in the wall **(mucosa)** of the stomach.

Gastric juice contains four main components:

- Water: This functions as the solvent in which food dissolves and enzymes act.
- Hydrochloric acid: This functions in killing pathogens and denaturing proteins, making them easier to digest. The pH of the stomach can be as low as 1.

Fig 33.5 Peristalsis.

- Mucous: This coats the internal wall of the stomach and protects it from the very acidic conditions of the stomach (as low as pH 1). The mucous is slightly alkaline which helps in protection.
- Pepsin: This protein-digesting enzyme digests proteins into smaller peptides. However, pepsin is first released as an inactive enzyme, called **pepsinogen**. Once in the lumen of the stomach, pepsinogen is converted to pepsin by the acidic conditions. The reason for this is so that it does not start digesting the cell contents before release. The optimum pH for the action of pepsin is 1–2.

The food is partially digested through action of the acid and proteases. This partially digested food is called chyme and is passed on to the duodenum through the **pyloric sphincter.**

As mentioned above, the stomach is also involved in mechanical digestion. It contracts forcibly every few seconds. This churns the food, mixing it with acid.

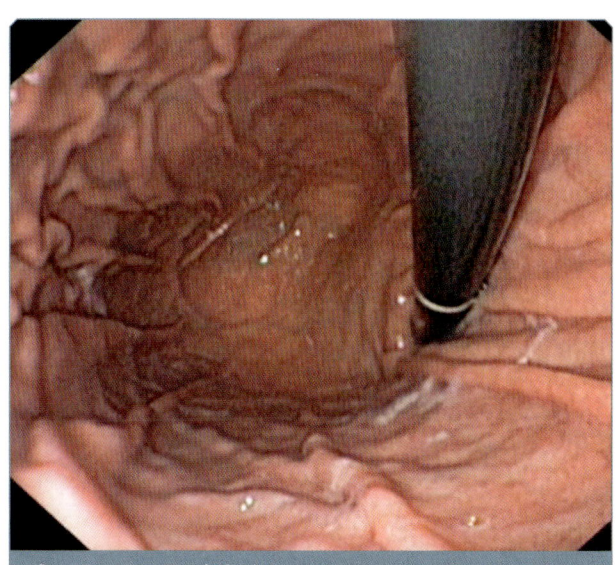

Fig 33.7 Stomach lining.

Stomach ulcers

Stomach (or gastric) ulcers (Fig 33.8) are a common disorder of the digestive system. Duodenal ulcers can also occur. They form in a number of ways, ranging from too much acid production or too much alcohol consumption to infections with a pathogenic bacterium.

Stomach ulcers can produce a constant dull pain in the upper abdomen. Left untreated, ulcers have the potential to become **perforated,** when the acid burns through the stomach wall. At this point, the contents of the stomach can start to leak out into the body cavity. This is a medical emergency and requires immediate surgery.

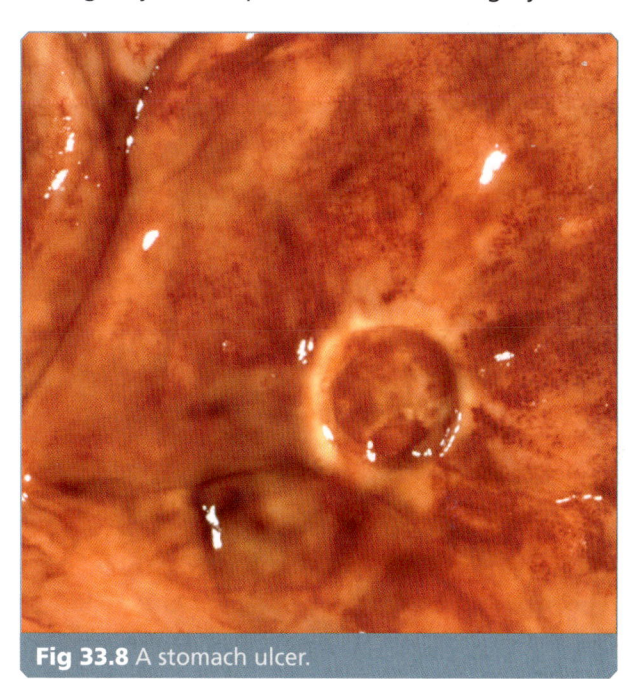

Fig 33.8 A stomach ulcer.

Liver

The largest organ in the body, the liver is located in the upper right abdomen next to the stomach. It weighs 1.5 kg and is vital for survival. It has many diverse functions:

- It produces large amounts of heat.
- It stores **glycogen, iron** and **fat-soluble vitamins (A, D, E and K).**
- It breaks down red blood cells.
- It breaks down excess amino acids in the body (deamination), forming urea.
- It produces **bile.**
- It produces **cholesterol.**
- It synthesises plasma proteins (for example, complement – see Chapter 34).
- It detoxifies alcohol.

We learned in Chapter 31 that the liver receives blood via the **hepatic artery** (a branch of the aorta) and from the small intestine via the **hepatic portal vein** (see below).

The hepatic portal vein carries blood rich in nutrients and white blood cells from the digestive system to the liver. Blood leaves the liver via the **hepatic vein** and is returned to the heart.

Fig 33.9 The structure of the liver.

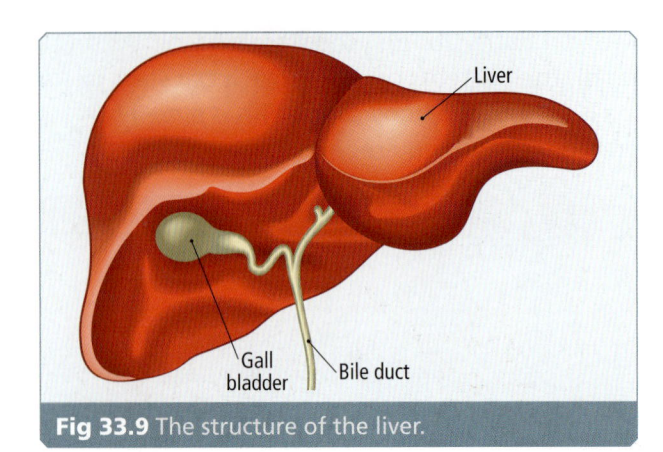

Bile and gall bladder

The liver produces bile, a dark green fluid. It is stored in the **gall bladder.** The gall bladder is a small bag-like organ that sits just underneath the liver.

Bile is released slowly when food passes through the duodenum. Bile contains **water, mucous, salts, cholesterol,** and **pigments** called **bilirubin** and **biliverdin.** These pigments are the breakdown products of **haemoglobin** from red blood cells. They give faeces its characteristic brown colour.

The water in bile provides the medium in which the active substances in bile travel and act.

The bile salts neutralise the acid from the stomach and function in emulsifying lipids.

> **Emulsification of lipids** is the breaking up of large fat droplets into smaller droplets.

Emulsification of lipids gives a larger surface area upon which enzymes can act. This speeds up the chemical digestive process.

Occasionally, gallstones form in the gall bladder and block the bile duct. They can be extremely painful and can prevent the release of bile into the duodenum. The bile pigments then enter the bloodstream and start to be deposited in the tissues of the body, such as the skin. The skin and white of the eyes then turn a characteristic yellow colour. In severe cases, gallstones may need to be removed surgically.

Pancreas

The pancreas is the other organ associated with the duodenum. It produces pancreatic juice that is released into the pancreatic duct along with bile.

The bile duct joins with the pancreatic duct to deposit both juices into the duodenum together and at the same time (Fig 33.10).

Pancreatic juice contains:

- **Sodium hydrogen carbonate,** which neutralises chyme from the stomach.
- **Lipase,** an enzyme that digests lipids into fatty acids and glycerol. It acts in the duodenum, where the pH is approximately 7 (neutral). This is due to the sodium hydrogen carbonate neutralising the acid.
- **Amylase,** which digests starch into maltose. It also acts in the duodenum.

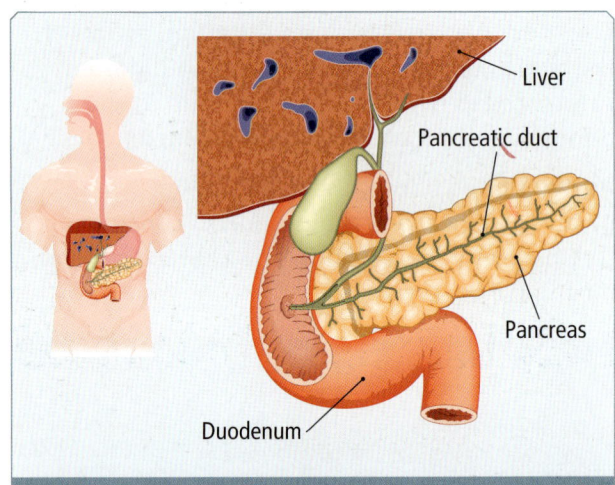

Fig 33.10 The structure of the bile duct, pancreatic duct and pancreas.

Small intestine

The small intestine is approximately 7 m long and is made up of the **duodenum** and **ileum.** It is called 'small' because its diameter is narrower than that of the large intestine. Food is moved along by strong rhythmical muscular contractions of the smooth muscle in the wall of the intestine. This is called **peristalsis.**

Duodenum

The duodenum is the first section of the small intestine. It is approximately 30 cm long and is involved in **chemical digestion.**

Pancreatic juice and bile are released into the duodenum to take part in chemical digestion.

Ileum

The ileum is much longer (approximately 6 m) and **convoluted,** meaning it is folded over on itself. It is responsible for **absorption of nutrients.**

The human digestive system Chapter 33

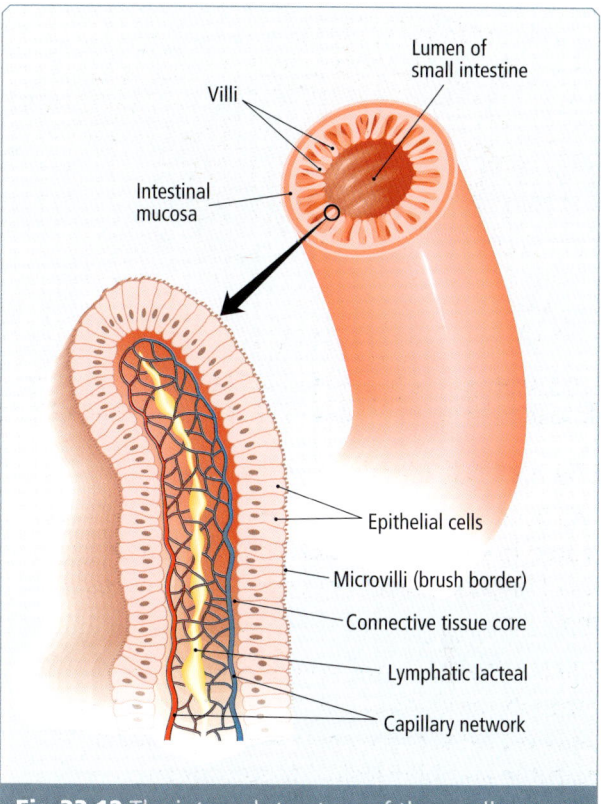

Fig 33.11 The folded surface of the ileum (villi).

Fig 33.12 The internal structure of the small intestine (ileum), showing villi and microvilli.

The internal wall (**mucosa**) of the ileum is highly specialised to carry out the role of absorption. The wall is highly folded, with each fold having many smaller folds or projections called villi (singular: villus) (Fig 33.11).

Villus
A villus is a small outfolding of the wall of the small intestine. Villi have adaptations that enable them to carry out their function of absorption very efficiently:

- They are very numerous.
- They have thin walls that are one cell thick.
- They have a good blood supply.
- They each have a lymph supply (lacteal).
- The cells have small cytoplasmic projections called microvilli to further increase the surface area.

The surface of the villi is composed of epithelial cells. Each epithelial cell has many microscopic cytoplasmic projections called microvilli (Fig 33.12). The folded nature of the ileum wall, along with villi and microvilli give the ileum an enormous surface area for absorption.

The surface where the microvilli are present is called the brush border. This is the location of absorption.

Hepatic portal system

Just underneath the epithelial cells of the small intestine is a huge network of blood capillaries responsible for transporting nutrients away. The capillaries all join together and carry blood from the digestive system to the liver via the hepatic portal vein. The collection of blood vessels connecting the small intestine to the liver (including the hepatic portal vein) is called the hepatic portal system.

The small intestine also has a network of lymph vessels. A lymph vessel enters each villus. Each lymph vessel in a villus is called a **lacteal**.

Lacteals absorb products of fat digestion (fatty acids and glycerol) and transport them back to the bloodstream. The lymph system carries lymph back to the bloodstream via the subclavian veins (*see* Chapter 32).

Fig 33.13 The process of absorption in the ileum. Individual biomolecules (such as glucose) are absorbed and transported by the bloodstream to body cells where they are metabolised.

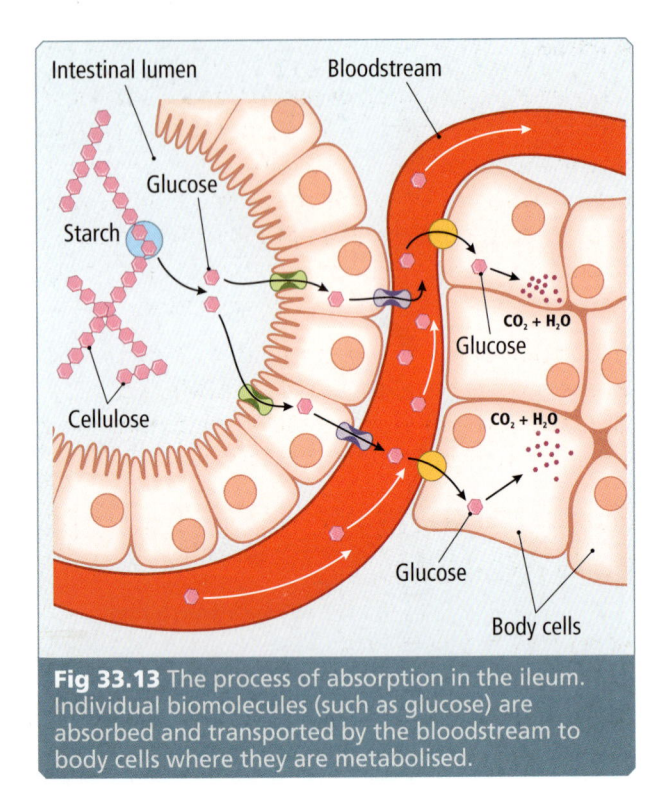

Large intestine

The large intestine is composed of the **caecum**, **appendix** and **colon** (Fig 33.14). Even though the large intestine is only approximately 1.5 m long, it has a large internal diameter, which gives it its name.

The large intestine receives food from the small intestine. The food, which is moved along by peristalsis, takes approximately 15 hours to travel the length of the large intestine.

Caecum

The first part of the large intestine is the caecum. The caecum's exact functions are not fully known. It is thought to be involved in the partial digestion of cellulose by bacteria. The caecum and the associated appendix are much larger in plant eaters and contain colonies of bacteria that have the ability to break down cellulose. The plant eater then uses these nutrients as a source of energy.

Appendix

The human appendix is a very small, blind-ended tube attached to the caecum. It is thought to be involved in protection against pathogens, but its exact functions are unknown.

As with the caecum, the appendix is much larger in herbivores. Sometimes it becomes infected (**appendicitis**) and swells, causing pain in the lower right abdomen. The pain can be chronic (dull pain that comes and goes) or acute (severe pain that comes on suddenly). If the pain is acute and severe, the appendix may need to be surgically removed.

Colon

The colon receives food from the caecum. There are four parts to the colon: the **ascending, transverse, descending** and **sigmoid** (meaning *S-shaped*) sections (Fig 33.14). The main function of the colon is to absorb water from the remaining food. This creates a semi-solid material called **faeces.**

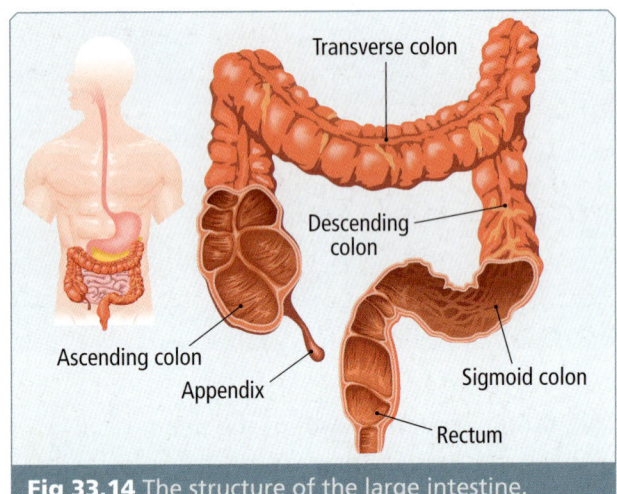

Fig 33.14 The structure of the large intestine.

Another function of the large intestine is to produce vitamins. It is estimated that there are nearly 1000 different species of 'good' bacteria living in the colon. These are called the **gut flora.** They are **symbiotic bacteria.** They receive a place to live and nutrients present in the gut. In return, they produce vitamins that are absorbed by the lining of the large intestine.

We often hear of 'good' bacteria present in various dairy products. In fact, nearly all types of dairy products contain these beneficial bacteria. Some species of bacteria living in the gut can digest cellulose, turning it into fatty acids that are then absorbed.

The bacteria help to maintain the health of the gut by preventing the growth of pathogenic bacteria. They also produce the vitamins K, B_1, B_2 and B_{12} (see Chapter 3). These are then absorbed into the bloodstream. If you have to go on a course of antibiotics, these 'good' bacteria are eliminated and it takes some time for the gut to be recolonised with beneficial bacteria. Beneficial bacteria are also often flushed out of the gut during episodes of diarrhoea.

Diarrhoea is caused by pathogenic infections in the gut and is a response to the bacteria or toxins produced by the harmful bacteria.

Role of fibre in the colon

Fibre is an essential component of the diet (Fig 33.15). Fibre is mostly composed of long chains of monosaccharides all joined together to form polysaccharides. The main polysaccharide found in fibre is **cellulose**.

Fibre has many different beneficial functions in the human alimentary canal. It helps to prevent constipation by stimulating **peristalsis**. It has also been shown to reduce the risk of developing colon cancer and to lower blood cholesterol levels and control glucose absorption. It may also have a role in preventing obesity as it gives a feeling of fullness.

Fibre is found in foods such as wholemeal bread, fruit and vegetables.

Fig 33.15 Foods rich in fibre help to prevent constipation.

Rectum

The rectum is a storage organ for faeces. Waves of peristalsis in the colon move undigested material into the rectum. The walls of the rectum expand as it fills. This stimulates stretch receptors that cause a spinal cord reflex (see Chapter 39). The reflex causes the walls of the rectum to start contracting, creating an urge for defecation **(egestion)**.

Defecation occurs through the anus. It is controlled by the anal sphincter muscle (anus). This is the only sphincter muscle of the digestive system that is under conscious control.

> **Egestion** is the elimination of undigested material (faeces) from the body.

Balanced diet

> A **balanced diet** is one that contains all seven major nutrients in the correct proportions.

The seven major nutrients are **carbohydrates, lipids, protein, fibre, vitamins, minerals** and **water**.

An imbalance in any one or a number of nutrients leads to malnutrition. Obesity is a type of malnutrition whereby too much carbohydrate and lipids are consumed.

The **food pyramid** is a useful guide to what amounts of each type of food should be consumed on a daily basis. There are four levels to the food pyramid (Fig 33.16).

- At the bottom level are carbohydrate-rich foods such as bread, potatoes and pasta. It is recommended that we consume six portions of carbohydrate per day.
- The second level contains fruit and vegetables. It is recommended we consume at least five portions of fruit and/or vegetables per day. **Remember your 'five-a-day'**.
- The third level contains dairy products and protein-rich foods such as meats and eggs. It is recommended that we consume three portions per day of dairy products and three portions of protein-rich foods per day.
- Finally, the very top of the pyramid contains sweet foods such as biscuits, cakes and chocolate (also known as **confectionery**). These foods should be taken very rarely. Ideally, they should not be eaten at all!

It is important to have variety in the diet. This means that a person should not eat two portions of chicken every day to satisfy the requirements of the food pyramid, but should eat fish, red meat and other proteins as well. This is to ensure that the correct levels of micronutrients (such as vitamins and minerals) are being taken.

The specific levels for each food group vary from person to person. A child will not require the same amount of nutrients as an adult. Similarly, an elderly person will require only a fraction of the nutrients that a highly active professional athlete would require.

Therefore, the food pyramid is only a guideline of the average amounts required by an average adult human.

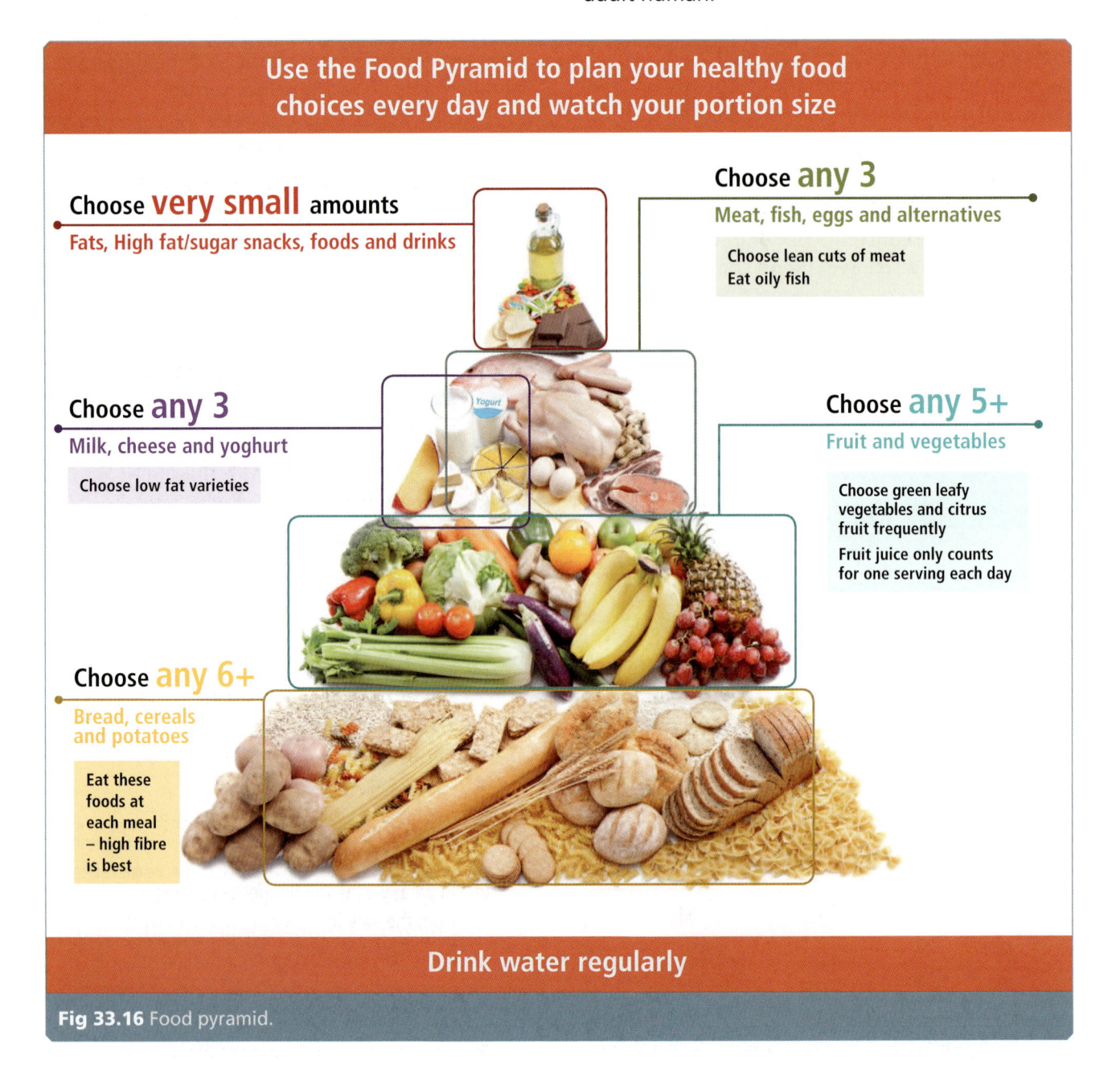

Use the Food Pyramid to plan your healthy food choices every day and watch your portion size

Choose very small amounts
Fats, High fat/sugar snacks, foods and drinks

Choose any 3
Meat, fish, eggs and alternatives
Choose lean cuts of meat
Eat oily fish

Choose any 3
Milk, cheese and yoghurt
Choose low fat varieties

Choose any 5+
Fruit and vegetables
Choose green leafy vegetables and citrus fruit frequently
Fruit juice only counts for one serving each day

Choose any 6+
Bread, cereals and potatoes
Eat these foods at each meal – high fibre is best

Drink water regularly

Fig 33.16 Food pyramid.

Chapter 33 Questions

1. (a) What is *nutrition*?
   (b) Distinguish between *autotrophic* and *heterotrophic* nutrition.
   (c) Distinguish between a *herbivore* and a *carnivore*.
   (d) What is an *omnivore*? Give **one** example.

2. (a) Describe the **four** stages of nutrition.
   (b) Explain why *egestion* is **not** a form of *excretion*. (Hint: *see* Chapter 37).

3. The diagram shows the human digestive system. Name the structures labelled A–S and give one function for **each** part.

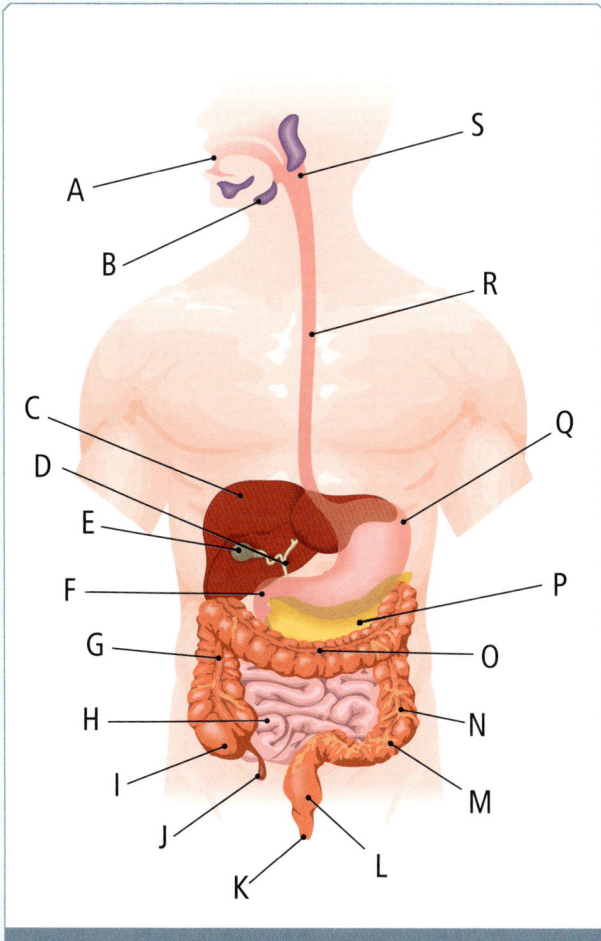

Fig 33.17 The human digestive system.

4. (a) What is the mouth also known as?
   (b) The mouth functions in both mechanical and chemical digestion. Explain how it carries out both types of digestion.

5. (a) What is the function of saliva, and where is it secreted from?
   (b) Name **two** components of saliva and give each of their functions.

6. (a) How many teeth are in a normal, healthy, mature human mouth?
   (b) What is the human dental formula?
   (c) Name the **four** types of human teeth and give **one** function for each type.
   (d) What type of tooth is a wisdom tooth?
   (e) Why are wisdom teeth often removed?

7. What is *smooth muscle*?

8. What is *peristalsis*?

9. (a) What is the function of the oesophagus?
   (b) Food is pushed down the oesophagus by peristalsis. What is the 'lump' of food that is swallowed called?

10. (a) What organ secretes gastric juice?
    (b) Name the **four** components of gastric juice.
    (c) Give the function of each component named above.
    (d) What is the mixture of food and gastric juice called?
    (e) What is the pH of the food mixture in the stomach? How does this pH help in the process of digestion?
    (f) What is a gastric ulcer? Give one way in which it might occur.

11. (a) What is the approximate length of the duodenum?
    (b) In what way is the duodenum protected from the very low pH material it receives from the stomach?

12. (a) Why are the liver and pancreas considered to be associated organs of the duodenum?
    (b) Give **three** general functions of the liver.
    (c) Give **two** functions of the liver that are specifically related to the digestive system.

13. (a) What is the *gall bladder*?
    (b) Where is the gall bladder located?

Unit 3   The Organism

(c) What condition, associated with the gall bladder, can cause skin colour to turn yellow?

(d) Name the **two** substances that cause the skin to turn yellow in this condition.

14 (a) Give **two** functions of the pancreas that are specifically related to the digestive system.

(b) Give **one** function of the pancreas that is not directly related to the digestive system. (Hint: see Chapter 38).

(c) Name **two** organ systems to which the pancreas belongs.

15 (a) The ileum follows the duodenum. What is the overall function of the ileum?

(b) What is the approximate length of the ileum?

16 (a) What is a *villus*?

(b) Draw a labelled diagram of a villus.

(c) Give **three** structural adaptations of a villus that enable it to carry out its function.

17 (a) What **two** organs are connected by the hepatic portal vein?

(b) What is the function of the hepatic portal vein?

18 (a) Name **three** parts of the large intestine.

(b) Why is it called the large intestine?

(c) Give the main function of the large intestine.

19 (a) Give **one** dietary way of reducing the risk of colon cancer?

(b) There is a large colony of bacteria in the colon. Give **two** functions of these bacteria.

(c) What name is given to the type of relationship between bacteria in the colon and humans?

(d) What effect might antibiotics have on these intestinal bacteria?

20 What is *appendicitis*?

21 What is the function of the rectum?

22 (a) What is meant by a *balanced diet*?

(b) Name the **seven** constituents that make up a balanced diet.

23 Draw a food pyramid, stating the foods at each level and the recommended daily intake of each.

Chapter 33 Sample examination questions

1 (a) (i) What is meant by a 'balanced' diet?

(ii) Distinguish between *autotrophic nutrition* and *heterotrophic nutrition*.

(b) (i) Explain the word *digestion*.

(ii) Give **one** role for **each** of the following types of teeth:
1. Incisors
2. Molars

(iii) Peristalsis begins when food enters the oesophagus. What is meant by *peristalsis*?

(iv) Describe the following changes that happen to food in the stomach:
1. Mechanical changes
2. Chemical changes

(v) What is the pH of the stomach contents?

(vi) Where does the partially digested food go when it leaves the stomach?

(c) The liver, the gall bladder and the pancreas all play a part in digestion. Digested food is carried to the liver where it is processed. Undigested food enters the large intestine.

(i) State:
1. **One** role of the pancreas in digestion.
2. **One** role of the gall bladder in digestion.

(ii) From what part of the digestive system does the digested food enter the blood?

(iii) Name the blood vessel that carries the digested food to the liver.

(iv) State **two** functions of the liver – other than the processing of digested food.

(v) The colon contains many symbiotic bacteria – mostly 'good' bacteria. State **two** benefits we get from these bacteria.

Section C, Question 13 Ordinary Level 2010

HL 2 (a) (i) Distinguish between *mechanical* and *chemical digestion*.

  (ii) Name a structure in the human digestive system, other than teeth, which is involved in mechanical digestion.

(b) The diagram shows the human digestive system.

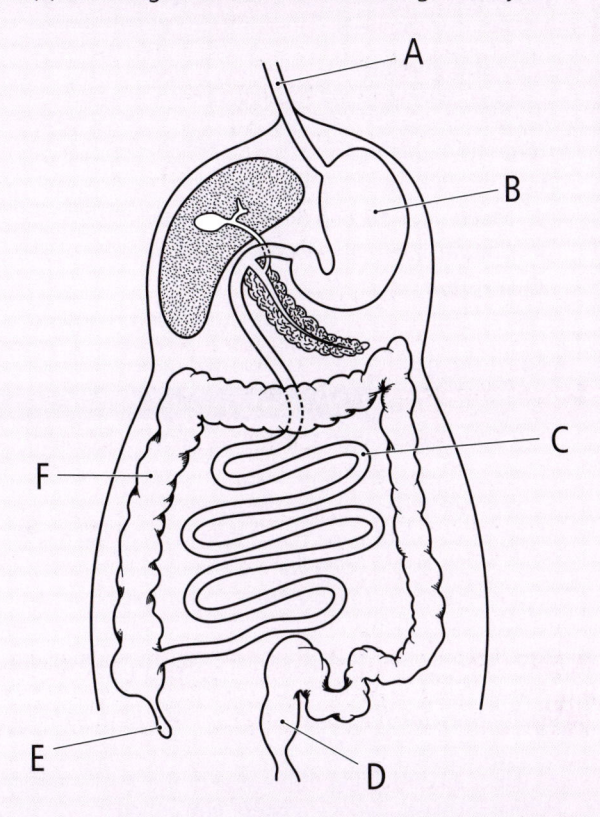

  (i) Name the parts A, B, C, D, E and F.

  (ii) Describe **two** functions of bile in relation to digestion.

  (iii) Answer the following in relation to a lipase:
   1. Where is it secreted?
   2. Where does it act?
   3. What is the approximate pH at its site of action?

(c) (i) What are symbiotic bacteria?

  (ii) Give **two** activities of symbiotic bacteria in the human digestive system.

  (iii) Name the part(s) of the digestive system in which the following are absorbed into the blood.
   1. The products of digestion
   2. Water

  (iv) Name a process involved in the passage of the products of digestion into the blood.

  (v) Explain how the structure that you have named in (iii) 1. is adapted for the absorption of the products of digestion.

Section C, Question 12 Higher Level 2008

Unit 3　The Organism

Chapter 33　Mind map

The digestive system

- **Herbivore:** an animal that eats only plant material.
- **Carnivore:** an animal that eats only animal material.
- **Omnivore:** an animal that eats both plant and animal material.

A **balanced diet** is one that contains all seven major nutrients in the correct proportions.

Food pyramid

- Carbohydrates: 6 portions per day.
- Fruit and vegetables: 5 portions per day.
- Dairy products: 3 portions per day.
- Protein: 3 portions per day.
- Confectionery: eat sparingly.

Digestion is the breaking down of food into its constituent molecules that can be absorbed into the bloodstream.

Stages of digestion

1. **Ingestion:** the taking in of food.
2. **Digestion:** the breaking down of food biomolecules into their constituent molecules.
   - **Mechanical:** action of teeth and peristalsis.
   - **Chemical:** enzyme action.
3. **Absorption:** small molecules pass directly into cells lining the gut. Either passive or active (requiring energy).
4. **Egestion:** getting rid of undigested material.

Structure of the human digestive system

- **Oral cavity:** where ingestion occurs, mechanical digestion (by teeth) and chemical digestion (by saliva) occurs. The food is formed into a round bolus before swallowing.
  - Tongue: functions in swallowing.
  - Teeth: function in mechanical digestion of food.
  - Incisors: cut through food.
  - Canines: tear and rip food.
  - Pre-molars and molars: chew and grind food.
  - Dental formula: 2(I ²⁄₂; C ¹⁄₁; PM ²⁄₂; M ³⁄₃)
- **Pharynx:** throat where food is pushed down into the oesophagus (swallowing).
- **Oesophagus:** long tube that pushes food by peristalsis down into the stomach.
- **Stomach:** muscular bag-like organ where food is mixed with gastric juice to form chyme.
  - Gastric juice contains water, mucous, hydrochloric acid and pepsinogen.
  - The mucous protects the delicate lining of the stomach from self-digestion.
  - The hydrochloric acid functions in denaturing enzymes, softening the food and killing pathogenic bacteria.
  - Pepsinogen is converted to active pepsin by the acidic conditions within the stomach. It then carries out its function of breaking down proteins into peptides.
- **Duodenum:** chyme from the stomach enters the duodenum and is mixed with pancreatic juice and bile.
- **Pancreatic juice:** secreted by the pancreas and consists of water, sodium bicarbonate and the enzymes, lipase and amylase.
  - Sodium bicarbonate acts to neutralise the acidic chyme.
  - Lipase digests fats into fatty acids and glycerol.
  - Amylase digests starch into maltose.
  - Bile consists of water, bile salts, and the pigments bilirubin and biliverdin.
  - Bile salts act as emulsifiers, which break large fat droplets into much smaller fat droplets.
  - The pigments are the breakdown products of haemoglobin. They give faeces its colour.
- **Liver:** produces bile, which is then stored in the gall bladder; stores glycogen and fat-soluble vitamins and iron; produces plasma proteins; breaks down excess amino acids (deamination).
- **Duodenum:** short section of the small intestine where most chemical digestion occurs.
- **Small intestine:** where most absorption of the products of digestion occurs.
  - Villus: an outfolding of the wall of the small intestine that increases surface area for absorption.
  - Each villus has a good blood supply, a lacteal and microvilli, further increasing the surface area for absorption.
  - Glucose and amino acids are carried away by the blood capillaries and fats are carried away by the lacteal, which is part of the lymphatic system.
  - The blood capillaries carry blood to the liver via the hepatic portal vein.
  - The lymphatic system carries fats to the subclavian vein where they enter the bloodstream.
- **Large intestine:** composed of the caecum and colon.
  - The caecum receives food from the small intestine. It is a small pouch-like organ where bacteria live and produce vitamins and break down cellulose.
  - The appendix is a small, blind-ended tube connected to the caecum. It is thought to function in defending against infection, although its exact function(s) are unknown.
  - Colon: where absorption of water occurs. There are bacteria present in the colon that break down cellulose and also produce vitamins.
- **Rectum:** storage organ. Faeces are stored in the rectum until release (defecation).
- **Anus:** located at the end of the human alimentary canal and controls the release of faeces.

The human defence system — Chapter 34

Learning objectives After studying this chapter, you should be able to:
- Describe the general defence system and its component parts.
- Describe the specific defence system and the antigen-antibody response.
- Define and describe *induced immunity*.
- Distinguish between *vaccination* and *immunisation*.
- HL ▶ Describe the role of B cells in the human immune system.
- ▶ Describe the roles and different types of T cells in the human immune system.

Introduction

The defence system protects us against disease. When a foreign particle/cell (pathogen) invades an organism, the defence system recognises it as foreign and gets rid of it by various mechanisms. In this way the human defence system is a response system.

> A **pathogen** is any organism that causes disease.

There are two parts to the defence system: **general** and **specific defence systems**.

General defence system

The general defence system is the first line of defence in the body. It is non-specific, meaning it does not specifically recognise individual pathogens. It is responsible for preventing the pathogen causing disease in the body.

The general defence system is itself divided into two parts: **the barrier system** and **non-specific cellular response**.

1 Barrier system

The barrier system includes any mechanism that prevents entry of pathogens. Examples include:

- The **skin** acts as a physical barrier to prevent entry of pathogens.
- **Sebaceous glands** in the skin produce sebum, which is an oily substance. Sebum maintains the integrity of the skin – without it the skin would become dry and crack, allowing pathogens to gain entry.
- **Mucous:** Mucous-producing membranes of the mouth, nose, throat, digestive system, respiratory system and reproductive tracts act by trapping pathogens and any small foreign particles.
- **Cilia** of the respiratory system beat rhythmically and push mucous out of the respiratory system. Coughing helps to move the mucous along more quickly. Eventually, the mucous reaches the top of the trachea where it is then swallowed.
- **Ear wax** traps pathogens and small foreign particles.
- **Tears** help to wash away pathogens and small particles that may reach the sensitive surface of the eye.
- **Stomach acid** kills most bacteria that enter the stomach.
- **Blood clotting** prevents the entry of bacteria. Any bacteria that entered before the clot is formed are destroyed by the second part of the general defence response or by the specific defence system (immune system).

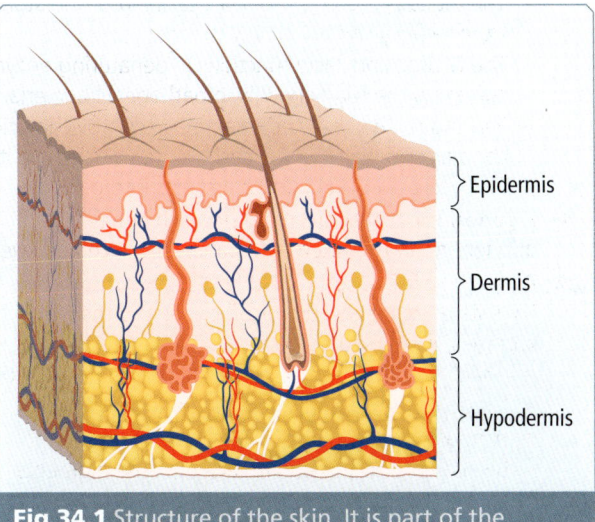

Fig 34.1 Structure of the skin. It is part of the general defence system.

2 Non-specific cellular response

The general defence system also has non-specific defence cells at its disposal. These responses are used if a pathogen manages to get past the barrier system. The non-specific cell responses are listed below:

- **Phagocytes** and **macrophages** are white blood cells capable of engulfing **any** foreign particles. They engulf them in a process known as **phagocytosis** (Fig 34.2).

- Chemicals are released that cause **inflammation** and attract white blood cells.
  - **Histamine** is an example of a chemical released by infected cells and tissues that causes inflammation. Hay fever is an example of a common condition where histamine is released.
  - **Complement** is a group of 30 proteins that circulate in the blood and lymph. Along with the specific defence system, they help to kill pathogens – they 'complement' the effect of the specific defence system. Complement proteins are part of the general defence system because the proteins do not change or adapt in response to pathogens and are produced in response to **all** pathogens. The complement proteins are made by the liver (see Chapter 33).
  - **Interferons** are signalling molecules that attract white blood cells to the site of an infection. They are also very effective against viruses as they **interfere** with viral replication, hence their name. They are also used as a **cancer treatment**. They are part of the general defence system as they are also chemicals that do not change or adapt. They are released in response to all infections.

- **Fever** raises internal body temperature, which denatures the enzymes and proteins in bacteria and viruses.

- **Lysozyme** is an enzyme present in tears and saliva that kills bacteria. It acts by breaking open the bacterial cell wall. It is non-specific as it acts on most bacteria and is therefore part of the general defence system.

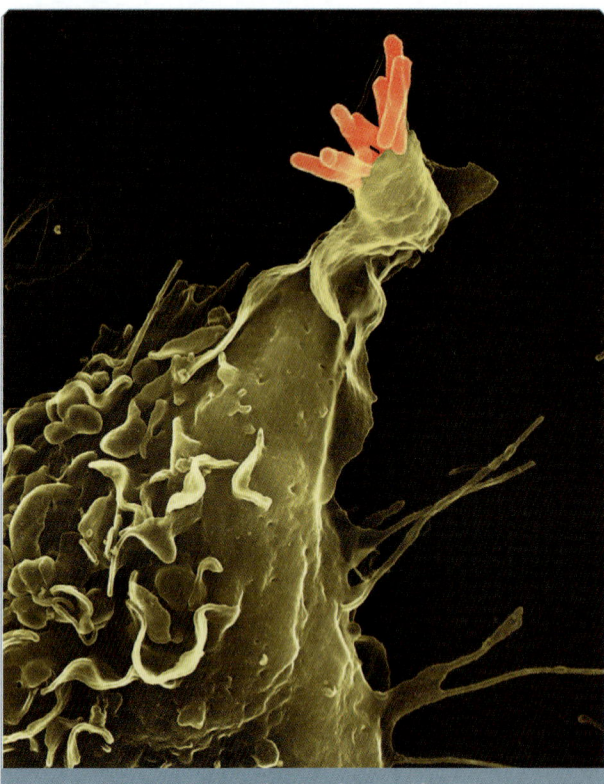

Fig 34.2 A phagocyte (yellow) engulfing bacteria (orange).

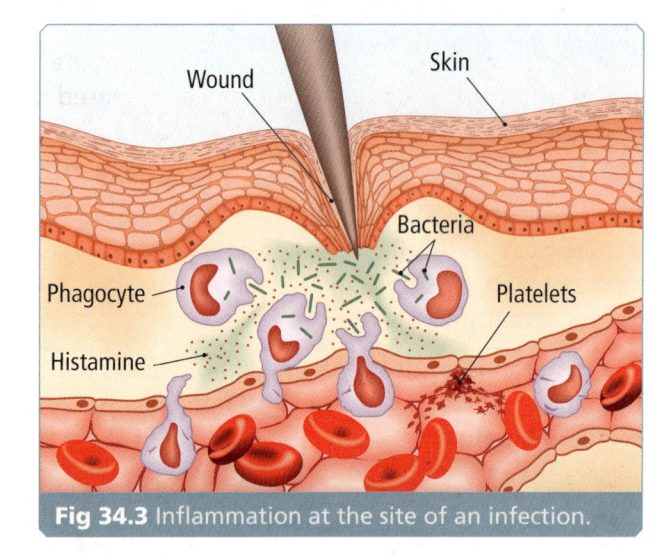

Fig 34.3 Inflammation at the site of an infection.

The human immune system

The immune system is the more common way of describing the specific defence system. It is responsible for fighting specific pathogens that cause disease and keeping the body 'immune' once the pathogen has been eliminated. In this way it is a response system. The immune system responds to specific pathogens. It consists of a range of white blood cells (immune cells) located mainly in the lymph nodes, thymus and spleen. It recognises individual organisms such as viruses, bacteria and other parasites as foreign invaders. The immune system consists of two main groups of white blood cells: **monocytes** and **lymphocytes**.

Monocytes

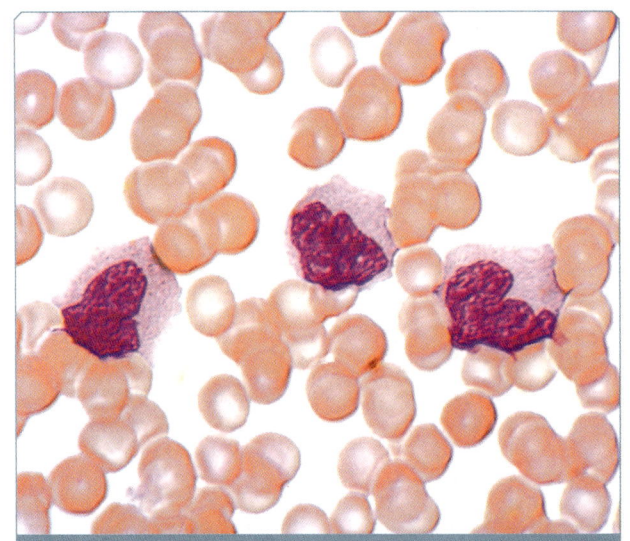

Fig 34.4 A monocyte (white blood cell) and red blood cells (RBC).

Monocytes are a type of white blood cell that are produced in the bone marrow and then released into the bloodstream and lymphatic system. Some types of monocyte develop into specialised **macrophage** cells.

The macrophage cells engulf bacteria and viruses and digest them (Fig 34.5).

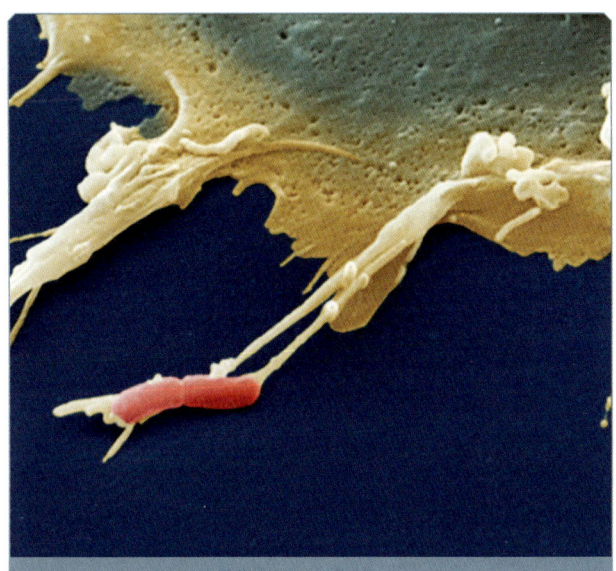

Fig 34.5 A macrophage extending its cell membrane to engulf bacteria.

Antigen-antibody response

Macrophages take some of the proteins from the pathogen and display them on the surface of their cells. These proteins are called antigens.

> **Antigens** are surface proteins that cause the production of antibodies.

Antigens are found on the cell wall of bacteria, the protein coat of viruses and the cell membrane of foreign cells such as protistan infections (for example, malaria) or organ transplants. They can also be found on cancer cells.

Immune cells respond to antigens by producing antibodies and engulfing or killing the invaders or cells infected with the invaders.

> **Antibodies** are proteins produced by lymphocytes in response to the presence of antigens.

Lymphocytes

Lymphocytes are white blood cells produced in the bone marrow that travel to areas of the lymphatic system to carry out their functions in keeping the body disease free.

Lymphocytes fight infections in two main ways:

1 Infected cells are killed by lymphocytes.
2 Lymphocytes recognise the pathogen and produce antibodies against it.

Immunity usually lasts a long time. A small number of the antibody-producing lymphocytes survive in the lymph nodes, thymus and spleen for many years.

If the body is exposed to the same type of pathogen again, the lymphocytes can multiply rapidly, producing antibodies very quickly to fight the infection.

Induced immunity

> **Induced immunity** is the stimulation of monocytes and lymphocytes to get rid of a specific antigen present in the body.

There are two ways in which the monocytes and lymphocytes are stimulated: **actively** and **passively**.

1 Active immunity

When lymphocytes produce antibodies against a specific pathogen, it is called **active immunity**.

> **Active immunity** is the production of antibodies by lymphocytes in response to a specific antigen.

Active immunity can occur in two ways: **natural active immunity** and **artificial active immunity**.

(i) Natural active immunity

> **Natural active immunity** occurs when lymphocytes produce antibodies in response to the body becoming infected with a pathogen from the environment.

When we get a cold, flu or sore throat or even chicken pox as children, natural active immunity is stimulated in the body.

Active immunity usually lasts a long time as some of the antibody-producing lymphocytes remain present in the body for many years. They live in the spleen, thymus and lymph nodes waiting for the same antigen to come along. If and when it does, the lymphocytes can multiply rapidly and are ready to produce the required antibody in very large amounts. Therefore, the body does not develop the symptoms of the illness.

(ii) Artificial active immunity

> **Artificial active immunity** occurs when lymphocytes produce antibodies in response to the pathogen being administered through vaccination.

As children, we are all vaccinated against various diseases, such as **polio, whooping cough, measles, mumps, rubella, meningitis** and **tuberculosis**.

These are all serious diseases that can kill. Therefore, it is very important that our immune system can deal with a serious pathogen if we become infected. When we are vaccinated against each of these diseases and come into contact with them, our immune system fights them off without us ever knowing we were infected.

> **Vaccination** is the administration, usually by injection, of a non-disease-causing dose of a pathogen or part of a pathogen (such as the antigen or toxin) which causes active immunity.

It is important to note that the vaccination is not a small dose, just a weakened one. The pathogens that cause disease are injected into our bodies in a weakened state (so they cannot actually cause the disease), to stimulate the body's lymphocytes to produce antibodies.

Fig 34.6 A vaccination dose being prepared.

Once antibodies are produced, they bind to the pathogen. Macrophages recognise the pathogen easily when antibodies are bound to it. The pathogen is therefore eliminated very quickly once antibodies are produced.

The antibody-producing lymphocytes live for a long time (as long as 20 years) in our bodies so that if the same infection occurs, the specific defence system can act quickly.

It is highly likely that the body will encounter the pathogen within the 20 years. Therefore, in general, vaccination is said to give life-long immunity. However, in the rare situation that the body does not encounter the pathogen, then immunity can be lost.

For example, immunity to the bacterium that causes **tetanus** can be lost and **'booster'** vaccinations are recommended every 10 years, as a precaution.

Other vaccinations include **measles, mumps** and **rubella (MMR)**, which it is recommended all babies receive; the **BCG** – a vaccine that gives immunity to **tuberculosis; polio,** a vaccine given by mouth; and **meningitis**.

The human defence system — Chapter 34

2 Passive immunity

When white blood cells are stimulated by administering external antibodies, it is called **passive immunity.**

> **Passive immunity** is the transfer of antibodies from one organism to another.

There are two types of passive immunity: **natural passive immunity** and **artificial passive immunity**.

(i) Natural passive immunity

> **Natural passive immunity** is when a baby receives antibodies directly from its mother either through the placenta before birth or via breast milk.

Antibodies received from the mother can stay in a baby's system and continue to offer a certain level of immunity for the first year of life.

Antibodies received from breast milk offer a higher level of immunity to the baby as the baby is receiving antibodies all the time. The protection continues for as long as the baby breast-feeds.

Fig 34.7 Breast-feeding gives the baby natural passive immunity for as long as the baby breast-feeds.

(ii) Artificial passive immunity

> **Artificial passive immunity** is when a person receives an injection of antibodies made in another organism.

Antibodies are administered when the person has contracted a serious disease that has the potential to cause serious harm or even death. The person usually contracts the disease due to having no immunity to the disease.

Rabies and tetanus are two diseases that can cause death if not treated with antibodies, as they do not give the body enough time to produce its own antibodies before causing death.

Antibodies must be administered by injection as they are protein. The protein antibodies would be digested if given by mouth.

Injected antibodies are very effective at disabling the bacterium and making it 'visible' to macrophages that then engulf the bacteria.

A disadvantage, however, is that passive immunity is very short-lived. The antibodies are not made by the body's own lymphocytes and therefore, no long-lived, antibody-producing lymphocytes are produced.

Immunisation

Immunisation is a general term that encompasses all types of artificial induced immunity such as **vaccination** and the **injection of antibodies**.

> **Immunisation** is the protection against pathogens, or the toxins of those pathogens, by vaccination or by injection of antibodies.

HL The human immune system – detailed study

Induced immunity requires specific immune cells called **monocytes** and **lymphocytes**.

Monocytes

Monocytes are a type of white blood cell, produced in the bone marrow that can develop into many different types of immune cell – the most common being macrophages.

Macrophages engulf bacteria and viruses, digest them within the cell and then place the digested pieces of bacteria and viruses (antigens) on their cell membrane (Fig 34.8). Macrophages also release chemicals called **cytokines** that stimulate other immune cells into action.

Other white blood cells called **lymphocytes** interact with the macrophages and are stimulated to act against the specific antigen.

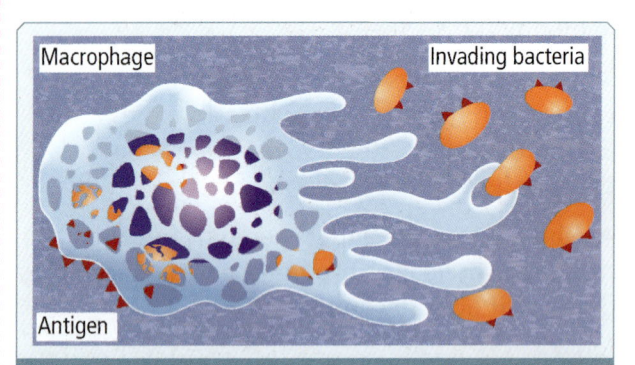

Fig 34.8 A macrophage with digested pieces of pathogens (antigens) on its surface.

Lymphocytes

Lymphocytes are a type of white blood cell, produced in the bone marrow. They are also sometimes called **leucocytes**. They are the main components of the specific defence system.

Lymphocytes interact with macrophages and the foreign antigens displayed on their surface. The lymphocytes then carry out a range of responses that eventually result in the elimination of the pathogen.

There are two main types of lymphocyte: **B cells** and **T cells**.

1 B cells

B cells were first discovered in birds. It was found that they developed in a small organ called a *bursa*. This is why they are called 'B' cells. It took another few years before researchers discovered that mammalian B cells develop in the **bone marrow** and mature in the **spleen**.

The fact that *'bone marrow'* and *'bursa'* both start with a 'B' is a fortunate coincidence!

B cells produce **antibodies** in response to a foreign antigen. They interact with the antigens present on the surface of macrophages that have digested a particular pathogen. This stimulates the B cell to make antibodies specifically against the antigen.

Each B cell produces only **one** type of antibody. There are two types of B cells: **plasma B cells** and **memory B cells**.

(i) Plasma B cells

B cells mature into plasma B cells in the spleen and lymph nodes.

As mentioned above, B cells interact with antigens present on the surface of macrophages as a result of macrophages engulfing pathogens (Fig 34.9).

B cells then multiply, becoming plasma B cells. Plasma B cells produce a large amount of a specific type of antibody against the antigen. This is called the **primary response**. The primary response can take up to two weeks to occur. Antibodies are produced in extremely large numbers and are released into lymph and blood.

Plasma B cells keep increasing in numbers during an immune response and continue to produce antibodies until the antigen is eliminated.

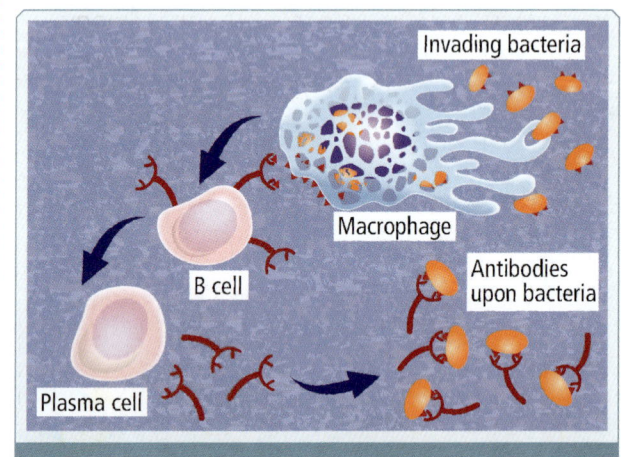

Fig 34.9 The specific nature of antigen-antibody interactions.

(ii) Memory B cells

Once the pathogen has been eliminated by the immune response, most of the plasma B cells die off. However, a small number survive. These are called memory B cells and they retain the ability to produce large numbers of a specific antibody. If the body is infected with the same pathogen, memory B cells can produce large numbers of antibodies in a very short space of time. This is called the **secondary response** and has the following important characteristics:

- Memory B cells respond to very small amounts of antigen.
- Memory B cells turn into plasma B cells very quickly and reproduce much more quickly than during the primary response.
- Antibodies are produced within a much shorter time period.
- Antibodies are produced in larger numbers than in the primary response.

Importantly, the characteristics of the secondary response enable us to avoid suffering the symptoms of the disease despite the pathogen being present in the body.

Antibody-antigen binding – specificity of antibodies

The shape of an antibody is complementary to the shape of its antigen (Fig 34.10).

We learned in Chapter 9 that enzymes bind to their substrates by having a complementary shape. Antibody-antigen binding occurs in much the same way. Any one type of antibody will bind to only one particular type of antigen. When the antibody binds to antigens on the surface of a pathogen, it is highlighted for destruction by macrophages. Once antibody production is in full swing, rapid elimination of the pathogen occurs.

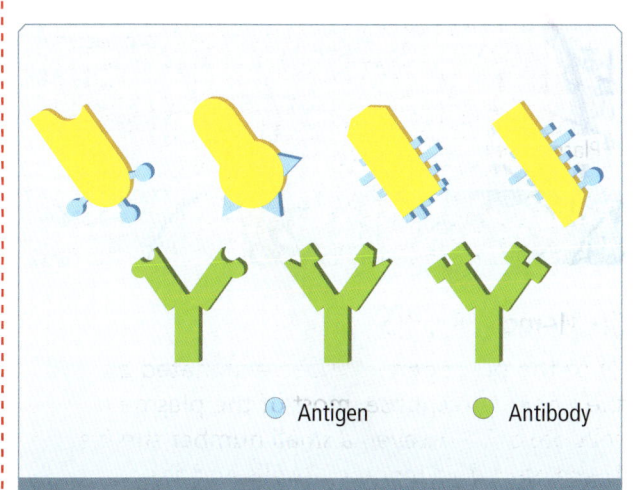

Fig 34.10 The specific nature of antigen-antibody interactions.

2 T cells

T cells are so-called because they move from the bone marrow, where they are produced, to the **thymus gland**, where they mature.

The thymus gland is especially important during childhood, as this is when it is most active. During adolescence the thymus begins to degenerate and is very small for the rest of our lives. There are **four** types of T cells: **helper T cells, killer T cells, suppressor T cells** and **memory T cells.**

(i) Helper T cells

Helper T cells are signalling cells that orchestrate the entire immune response against a pathogen. They do not directly kill or eliminate the pathogen. They work by activating other lymphocytes and monocytes to eliminate a pathogen or pathogen-infected cells. They do this by releasing cytokines.

Helper T cells interact with a macrophage presenting antigens on its surface. This stimulates the helper T cell to release cytokines. These cytokines cause the helper T cells to proliferate, but also stimulate other T cells and B cells to act against a pathogen.

As a result, helper T cells are extremely important to the overall immune response. If something goes wrong with helper T cells, the whole immune system is affected.

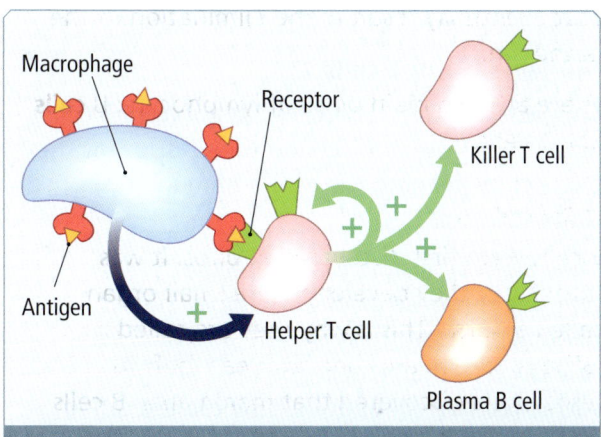

Fig 34.11 Stimulation of B cells and killer T cells by helper T cells.

HIV (human immunodeficiency virus) specifically targets and infects helper T cells, which affects the entire immune response in HIV-positive people. Infection with the

HIV virus results in a disease called AIDS (acquired immunodeficiency syndrome). Eventually, helper T cell numbers fall to very low levels, leaving HIV-positive patients vulnerable to secondary infections such as pneumonia, tuberculosis and flu. It is these secondary infections that eventually kill someone who is HIV-positive. This is due to their immune system being very weak.

(ii) Killer T cells

Killer T cells (also known as **cytotoxic T cells**) are capable of killing body cells that are damaged, abnormal, cancerous or infected with a virus.

They do this by first being activated by a helper T cell and then interacting with the target cell. They release chemicals called **perforins** (Fig 34.12), which form pores or holes in the cell membrane of the target cell. As a result, the target cell bursts.

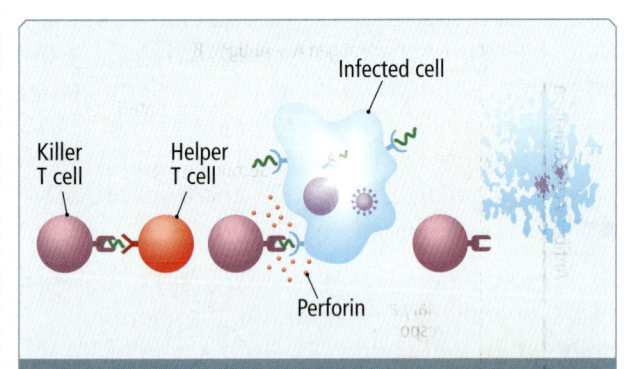

Fig 34.12 A killer T cell causing an infected cell to burst.

(iii) Suppressor T cells

Suppressor T cells (also called **regulatory T cells**) act as suppressors of the immune response. They also act by keeping the entire immune response under control.

They are responsible for stopping an immune response after a pathogen has been eliminated. They also help to maintain tolerance to the proteins present on the surface of normal body cells. These are called self-antigens. Tolerance to self-antigens ensures that the specific defence system does not start attacking the body's own tissues.

However, despite this in-built safety mechanism, the specific defence system occasionally produces antibodies against its own cells. This results in an autoimmune disease, which can vary in severity.

Examples of autoimmune diseases include **rheumatoid arthritis** (*see* Chapter 40) and **type I diabetes** (*see* Chapter 38).

As a consequence, there is great interest in this T cell subpopulation as they have the potential to treat autoimmune diseases. They could also possibly allow organ transplants to be accepted by the specific defence system, without the need for debilitating immune-system-suppressing drugs.

(iv) Memory T cells

Some T cells survive after an immune response is over. These T cells are called memory T cells. They survive for a long time as part of the specific defence system, usually in the spleen.

They 'remember' the antigen from the first encounter (primary response) and if the same antigen enters for a second time, the memory T cells proliferate very quickly and orchestrate an effective and fast secondary response to the pathogen (Fig 34.13).

Memory T cells and memory B cells give long-lived immunity (and often life-long immunity) against a particular pathogen.

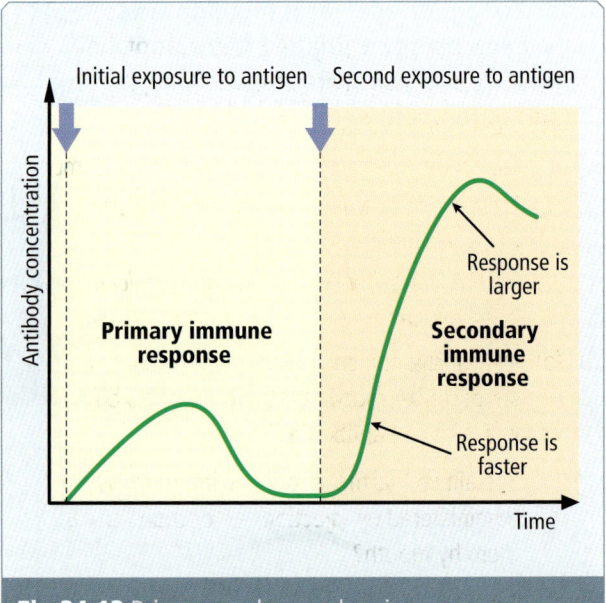

Fig 34.13 Primary and secondary immune responses.

Chapter 34 Questions

1. What is a *pathogen*?
2. Using your knowledge from previous chapters, give an example of each of the following:
   (a) **Bacterial** pathogen.
   (b) **Viral** pathogen.
   (c) **Fungal** pathogen.
3. Distinguish between the following pairs of terms:
   (a) *General defence system* and the *specific defence system*.
   (b) *Histamine* and *complement*.
   (c) *Monocyte* and *lymphocyte*.
   (d) *Antigen* and *antibody*.
   (e) *Vaccination* and *immunisation*.
4. Give **three** ways in which the general defence system acts.
5. Name **three** organs involved in the specific defence system.
6. Where are white blood cells produced?
7. Name the **two** general types of white blood cells.
8. Describe the way in which macrophages contribute to both the general and the specific defence systems.
9. Name **two** ways in which lymphocytes act during an immune response.
10. What type of biomolecules do antigens and antibodies belong to?
11. What is meant by saying that the shape of the antibody and antigen are *complementary*?
12. (a) Define *induced immunity*.
    (b) Distinguish between *active* and *passive* immunity.
    (c) Distinguish between *natural* and *artificial* active immunity.
    (d) Distinguish between *natural* and *artificial* passive immunity.
13. (a) Why must somebody who has developed a serious illness such as tetanus or rabies be injected with antibodies?
    (b) Explain why artificial passive immunity is administered by injection rather than taking them by mouth?
14. What is *immunisation*?
15. (a) What is a *vaccine*?
    (b) Give **two** examples of vaccines.
16. Explain why it is possible for immunity to be lost.

HL 17. (a) In what animals were B cells first discovered?
    (b) What does the 'B' in B cells refer to?
    (c) Where in the human body do B cells mature?
    (d) Name the **two** types of B cell and explain the function of each type.
18. (a) Where in the human body are T cells produced?
    (b) What does the 'T' in T cell refer to?
    (c) Where in the human body do T cells mature?
    (d) Name the **four** types of T cell.
    (e) Give **one** function for each type of T cell in the human body.
19. The graph shows the response by the body's immune system to two antigens: A and B. Anti-A and anti-B refer to antibodies produced in response to antigens A and B, respectively.

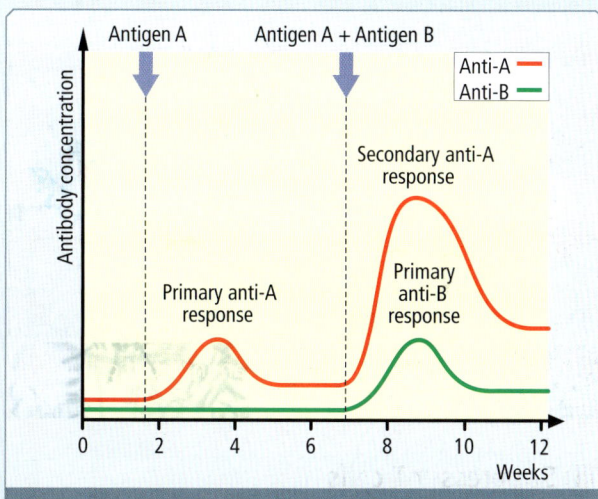

Fig 34.14 Primary and secondary immune responses.

   (a) Explain what is happening between approximately 3.5 and 4 weeks.
   (b) Name two cells that might be involved in this and state their specific effect.
   (c) Explain why anti-A levels decrease after week 4.
   (d) What cell/cells are contributing to the decrease in anti-A at week 4?
   (e) Why is there more anti-A after the second exposure of the immune system to antigen A?
   (f) Explain why there is less anti-B compared to anti-A between weeks 8 and 10.
   (g) Copy the graph and draw onto the graph a line representing exposure to antigen C at the same time as exposure to antigen A. The person had already been exposed to antigen C.

Unit 3 The Organism

Chapter 34 Sample examination questions

1. (i) What is meant by the term *immunity*?
   (ii) The skin is an important part of our immune system. Outline **two** ways in which the skin provides immunity.
   (iii) To help the immune system, many people receive vaccinations during their lifetime. What is meant by the term *vaccination*?

   Section C, Question 15 (c) (iii)–(v) Ordinary Level 2011

HL 2. (i) What is meant by the term *immunity*?
   (ii) Outline briefly the role of B lymphocytes in the human immune system.
   (iii) Distinguish between *active* and *passive* immunity.
   (iv) 'Vaccination gives rise to active immunity.' Explain this statement.
   (v) In certain situations a person is given a specific antibody rather than being vaccinated.
   1. Is this an example of active or passive immunity?
   2. Under what circumstances might an antibody, rather than a vaccination, be given?
   3. Comment on the duration of immunity that follows the administration of an antibody.

   Section C, Question 14 (c) Higher Level 2007

Chapter 34 Mind map

The defence system protects against disease.

A **pathogen** is a disease-causing organism.

Two parts to the defence system:
1. General defence system
2. Specific defence system

- The general defence system acts as a barrier. Examples of this barrier system are:
  - Skin.
  - Sebaceous glands in the skin.
  - Mucous-producing membranes of mouth, nose, throat, digestive system, respiratory system and reproductive tracts.
  - Cilia of the respiratory system.
  - Ear wax.
  - Tears.
  - Stomach acid.
  - Saliva.
  - Blood clotting.

- The general defence system can also act at the cellular level:
  - Macrophages engulf foreign particles.
  - Infected cells/tissues release histamines.
  - Complement and interferon are produced by the liver and viral-infected cells, respectively.
  - Lysozyme is released in the tears and saliva to kill bacteria.

- The human immune system consists of lymph nodes, thymus, spleen and white blood cells.
- There are two main types of white blood cell: monocytes and lymphocytes.
- Monocytes and lymphocytes are produced in the bone marrow.
- Monocytes develop into macrophages that engulf bacteria and viruses.
- Lymphocytes fight infections in two main ways:
  1. Infected cells are killed by lymphocytes.
  2. Lymphocytes recognise the antigens on the pathogen and produce antibodies against it.
  - Antigens are surface proteins that cause the production of antibodies.
  - Antibodies are proteins produced by lymphocytes in response to the presence of antigens.

- **Vaccination** is the administration, usually by injection, of a non-disease-causing dose of a pathogen or part of a pathogen (e.g. the antigen or toxin) which causes active immunity.
- **Immunisation** is the protection against pathogens, or the toxins of those pathogens, by vaccination or by injection of antibodies.

Types of immunity

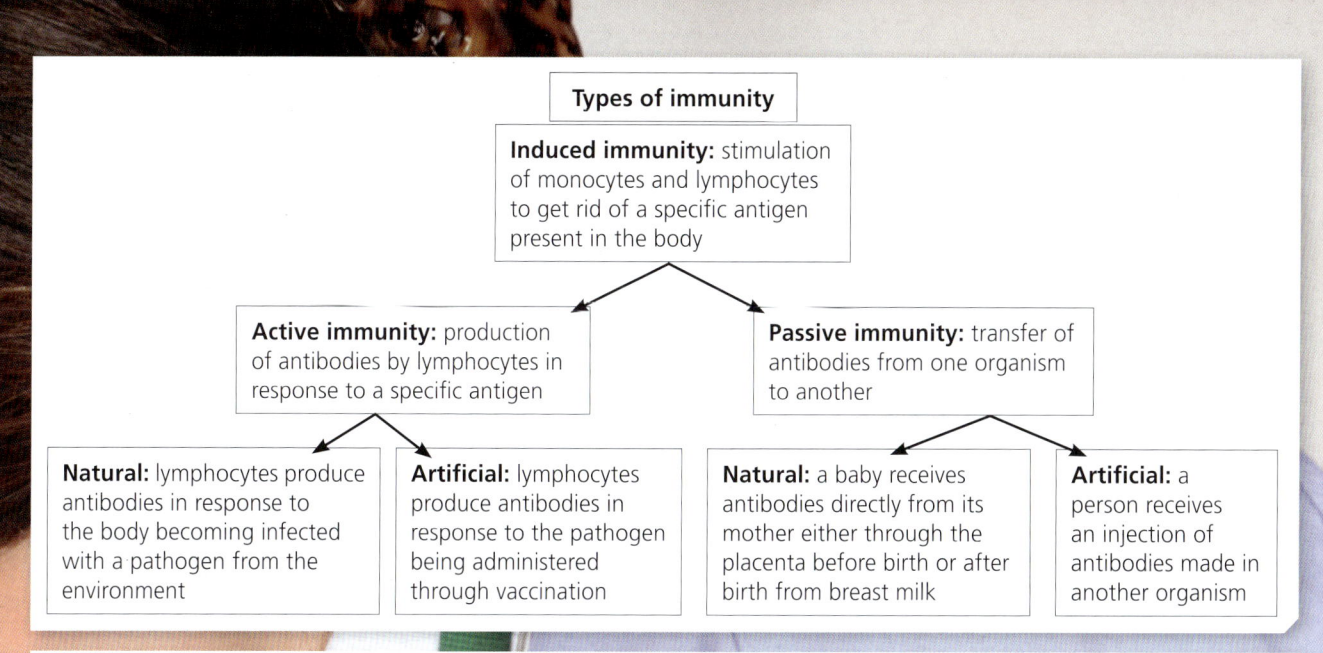

Induced immunity: stimulation of monocytes and lymphocytes to get rid of a specific antigen present in the body

Active immunity: production of antibodies by lymphocytes in response to a specific antigen

- **Natural:** lymphocytes produce antibodies in response to the body becoming infected with a pathogen from the environment
- **Artificial:** lymphocytes produce antibodies in response to the pathogen being administered through vaccination

Passive immunity: transfer of antibodies from one organism to another

- **Natural:** a baby receives antibodies directly from its mother either through the placenta before birth or after birth from breast milk
- **Artificial:** a person receives an injection of antibodies made in another organism

The human immune system – detailed study *(HL)*

There are two types of lymphocytes:

1. **B cells:** produced in the bone marrow, mature in the spleen and are responsible for the production of antibodies. There are two types:
   - **Plasma cells:** Produced very quickly in response to the presence of an antigen and extremely quickly if it is the second time the body has had the infection.
   - **Memory B cells:** 'Remember' the pathogen and reproduce rapidly to become antibody-producing plasma cells should the same pathogen re-enter the body.

2. **T cells:** produced in the bone marrow, mature in the thymus and have multiple functions in the control of pathogens. There are four types of T cell:
   - **Helper T cell:** Stimulate other lymphocytes and monocytes.
   - **Killer T cell:** Kill viral-infected cells, damaged cells and cancer cells by producing perforins that cause the cells to burst.
   - **Suppressor T cell:** Help to keep the immune response under control and stop an immune reaction once the pathogen has been eliminated.
   - **Memory T cell:** Remain behind after the immune reaction and 'remember' the antigen encountered. They produce a more rapid immune reaction should the same antigen re-enter the body.

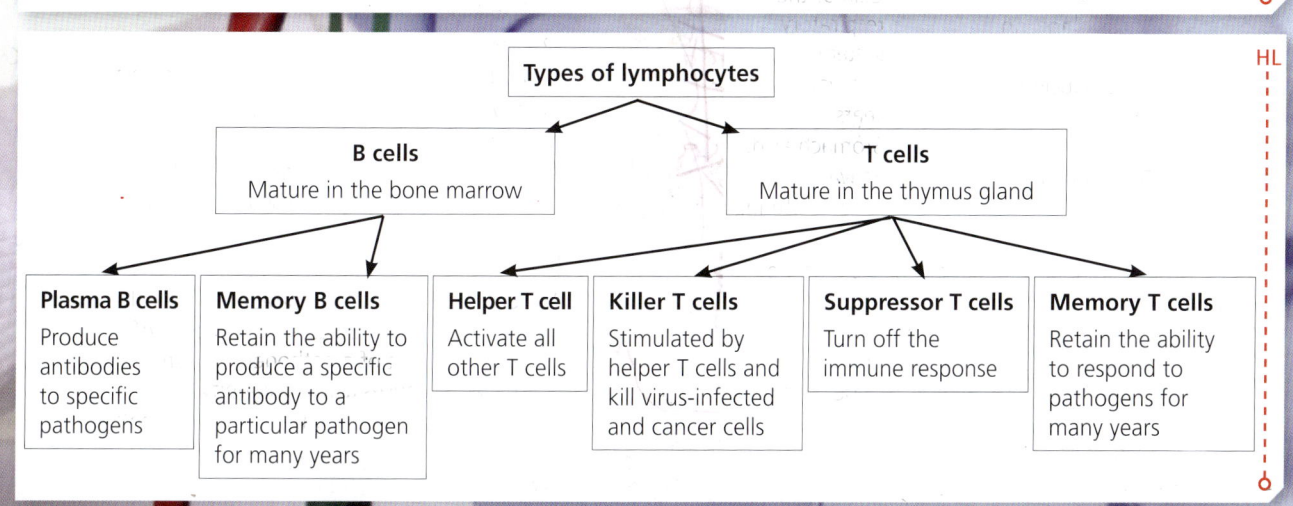

Types of lymphocytes *(HL)*

B cells — Mature in the bone marrow

- **Plasma B cells:** Produce antibodies to specific pathogens
- **Memory B cells:** Retain the ability to produce a specific antibody to a particular pathogen for many years

T cells — Mature in the thymus gland

- **Helper T cell:** Activate all other T cells
- **Killer T cells:** Stimulated by helper T cells and kill virus-infected and cancer cells
- **Suppressor T cells:** Turn off the immune response
- **Memory T cells:** Retain the ability to respond to pathogens for many years

Chapter 35 The human breathing system

Learning objectives After studying this chapter, you should be able to:
- Describe the structure and function of the human breathing system.
- Describe the essential features of alveoli in their function of gas exchange.
- Describe the mechanism of breathing and gas exchange in the alveoli.
- Describe either bronchitis or asthma under the headings of cause, prevention and treatment.
- **HL** Describe the role of carbon dioxide as the controlling factor in the human breathing system.

Introduction

The breathing, or respiratory, system is located in the chest, or thoracic, cavity. It is a type of excretory system composed of many individual organs.

The respiratory system functions in gas exchange, taking in oxygen and excreting water vapour and carbon dioxide.

The average human lung capacity is 5 L (men have an average of 6 L and women have an average of 4 L). However, lung capacity can be increased through exercise. The fittest athletes in the world are known to have lung capacities as high as 7 L!

Structure of the human breathing system

The breathing system consists of the **nasal cavity; buccal cavity (mouth); pharynx; epiglottis; larynx; trachea; rings of cartilage; bronchi; bronchioles; alveoli; diaphragm; pleural membranes; intercostal muscles;** and **rib cage.**

Nasal cavity

When you breathe in through your nose, the air passes through your nasal cavity. The nasal cavity produces a lot of mucous and has tiny hairs to filter the incoming air. The passages of the nasal cavity are moist to humidify (moisten and warm) the air flowing past. This allows for more efficient gas exchange in the lungs. The nasal passages can become blocked when we get a cold or flu. The sinuses are very close to the nasal cavity and become swollen during a viral infection, giving the feeling of a blocked nose. It takes a few days before the sinuses return to their normal size.

Buccal cavity

When you breathe in through your mouth, the air passes through your buccal cavity. We generally breathe through our mouths when we are exercising as we can take in a lot more air through our mouths than through our noses. Air flowing through your buccal cavity is not filtered, warmed or moistened.

Pharynx

The pharynx is the throat. Air will pass through the pharynx regardless of whether it came through the nose or mouth. The pharynx is affected whenever you get a sore throat. Sore throats are mostly caused by viruses, but can occasionally be caused by bacteria. The tonsils and adenoids (both part of the lymphatic system) can become swollen and infected during throat infections. A swollen and sore tonsil is called tonsillitis.

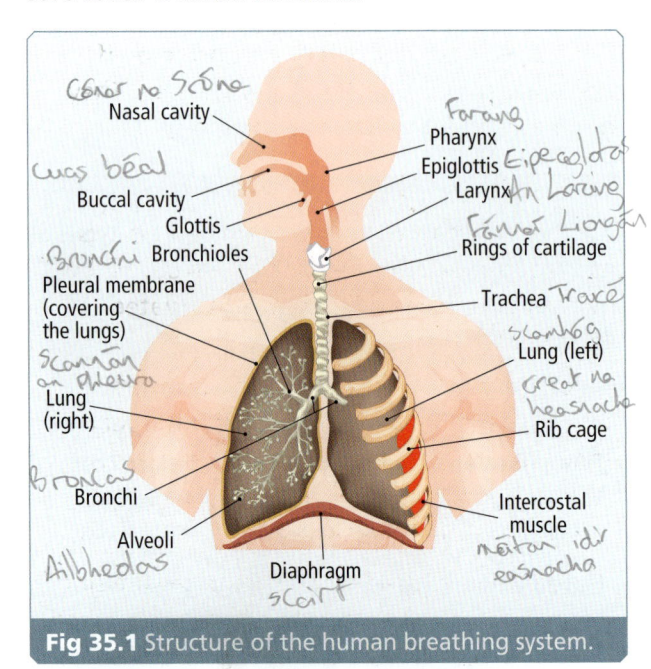

Fig 35.1 Structure of the human breathing system.

Epiglottis

The epiglottis is a flap of tissue located at the bottom of the pharynx that closes over the glottis during swallowing. This allows food to travel down the oesophagus. The glottis is the opening to the windpipe. Sometimes the epiglottis does not close over the glottis properly and 'food goes down the wrong way'. This stimulates the 'gag' reflex that prevents choking.

Larynx

The larynx is the voice box. It contains vocal cords and is responsible for producing sound. The vocal cords produce the sounds by modulating (changing the direction and/or speed) the flow of air leaving the lungs.

Trachea

The trachea (also known as the windpipe) directs the flow of air into and out of the lungs. Fast-moving air is at a lower pressure, which could leave the trachea at risk of collapsing. This is prevented by **rings of cartilage.**

Bronchi and bronchioles

There are two bronchi (singular: bronchus) in the human breathing system, one going to each lung. They direct air into the lungs. They are also supported by rings of cartilage to prevent them collapsing.

Bronchioles are small branches of the bronchi. They have a diameter of 1 mm or less. Bronchioles branch into more bronchioles of even smaller diameter (less than 0.5 mm). They terminate (end) at the air sacs (alveoli).

Alveoli

The alveoli (singular: alveolus) are tiny air sacs that are the site of gas exchange. Fig 35.2 shows the structure of alveoli and their associated blood supply.

Alveoli show adaptations that enable them to carry out their function of **gas exchange** very efficiently. Some of these characteristics are:

- They have very thin walls, allowing gases to diffuse more quickly.
- They have a good blood supply, maximising the amount of oxygen that can be absorbed and carbon dioxide excreted.
- They have elastic walls that enable exhalation to be a passive process through recoiling.
- They are very numerous – the average pair of human lungs contains 500 million alveoli, giving a gas exchange surface area of the size of a tennis court!
- They are moist. Moisture enables gases to dissolve and diffuse more quickly into the bloodstream and vice versa.

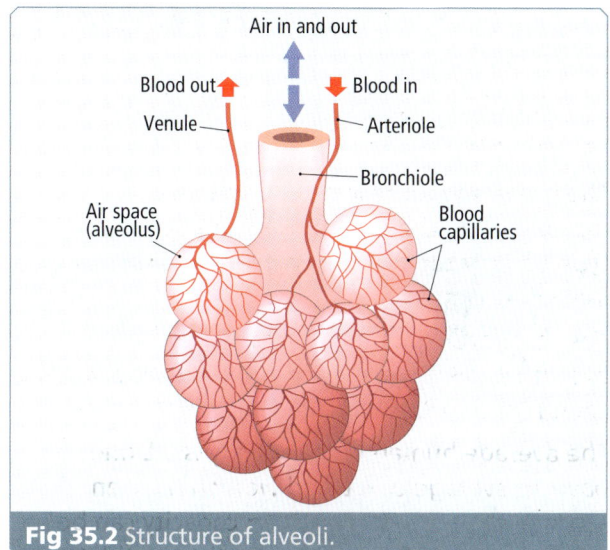

Fig 35.2 Structure of alveoli.

Lungs

The lungs are very large, elastic, spongy organs specialised for gas exchange. They are attached to the inside of, and protected by, the rib cage.

Diaphragm

The diaphragm is a sheet of muscle that seals off the bottom of the rib cage and separates it from the abdomen. It functions in inhalation, contracting and moving downwards into the abdomen. It does not take part in exhalation.

Pleural membranes

The pleural membranes are a two-membrane structure that cover the lungs and are attached to the inside of the rib cage. The very thin space in between is called the **pleural cavity.** This is filled with a fluid that allows friction-free movement between the two membranes during breathing.

Intercostal muscles

The intercostal muscles are muscles in between each rib. When they contract, they cause the rib cage to move upwards and outwards increasing the volume of the chest cavity. This causes air to rush into the lungs. They can be consciously and unconsciously controlled.

Rib cage

The rib cage is a series of 12 pairs of ribs that provides the support for breathing. Seven of these pairs are called 'true' ribs as they are directly attached to the sternum; three pairs are called 'false' ribs as they are attached to the sternum by cartilage only and two pairs are called 'floating' ribs as they are not attached to the sternum.

> **NOTE** The left lung is slightly smaller than the right lung. This is due to the position of the heart in the chest cavity. It is located slightly to the left of the sternum, meaning it impedes on the left lung slightly.

Gas exchange

Gas exchange involves the diffusion of gases into and out of the bloodstream. Remember the definition of diffusion.

> **Diffusion** is the movement of molecules from a region of high concentration to a region of low concentration.

Gases move in and out of the lungs by ventilation – the processes of inhalation and exhalation. The main gases involved in gas exchange are oxygen, carbon dioxide and water vapour.

The cells of the body need a constant supply of oxygen in order to carry out vital processes such as respiration. Therefore, the body takes in oxygen through the lungs. Oxygen is inhaled into the alveolus where there is a film of moisture. The oxygen gas dissolves into the moisture and then through the endothelial wall of the alveolus and into the bloodstream (capillary). The oxygen moves into red blood cells.

Most oxygen is carried by haemoglobin within the red blood cell (see Chapter 30), although a small amount is carried dissolved in the plasma.

Respiration produces the waste gas carbon dioxide, which needs to be excreted as it is an acidic gas. Carbon dioxide is carried dissolved in the plasma. In the lungs, carbon dioxide diffuses from the plasma through the endothelial wall of the alveolus into the film of moisture on the internal surface of the alveolus. The carbon dioxide then evaporates into the air space and is excreted out of the lungs.

Inhaled and exhaled air

- Inhaled air contains 21 per cent oxygen and 0.04 per cent carbon dioxide.
- Exhaled air contains 15 per cent oxygen and 5 per cent carbon dioxide.
- Oxygen diffuses into the bloodstream and carbon dioxide diffuses out of the bloodstream.
- Water vapour is also excreted by the lungs. Exhaled air is saturated with water vapour. The water vapour content of inhaled air varies and depends on weather conditions.

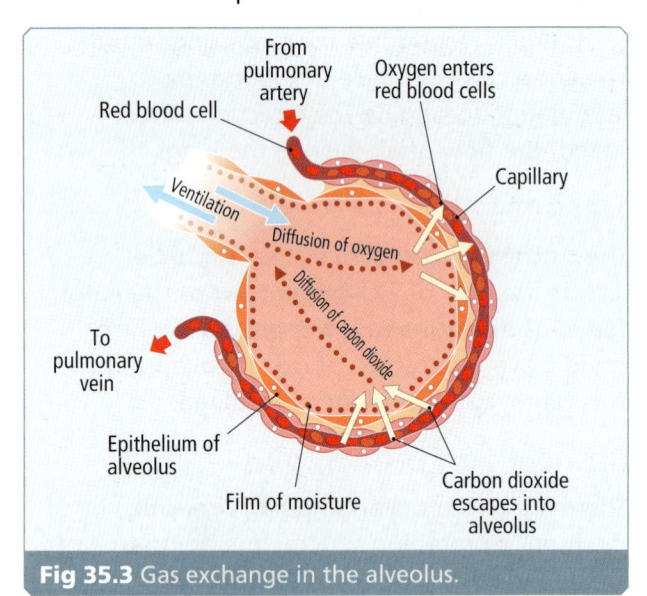

Fig 35.3 Gas exchange in the alveolus.

Mechanism of breathing

Breathing (also known as external respiration) is the process of taking in air from the atmosphere, exchange of gases at the alveoli and exhalation of air from the lungs.

The following describes the processes involved in inhalation and exhalation.

Inhalation

Inhalation is also called inspiration. Inhalation is an active process involving the brain and inspiratory muscles.

- The brain sends a signal to the inspiratory muscles, which are the **intercostal muscles** and the **diaphragm.**
- The intercostals and diaphragm contract.
- The diaphragm moves down and the intercostals cause the rib cage to move upwards and outwards.

- The volume of the thorax (chest cavity) increases.
- The thoracic air pressure decreases and air rushes in.

Exhalation

Exhalation is also called expiration. Exhalation is usually a passive process, meaning that it happens by itself due to the recoiling of the elastic lung tissue. However, it can also be active especially during heavy exercise when the body is trying to excrete as much carbon dioxide as possible. In that case, the stomach muscles and other muscles in the chest are recruited to forcibly expel air from the lungs. The process of passive exhalation is described below:

- The inspiratory muscles relax.
- This causes the elastic tissue of the lungs to return to its original position.
- The rib cage moves down and inwards.
- The diaphragm moves upwards.
- The volume of the chest decreases.
- Thoracic air pressure in the lungs increases and air rushes out.

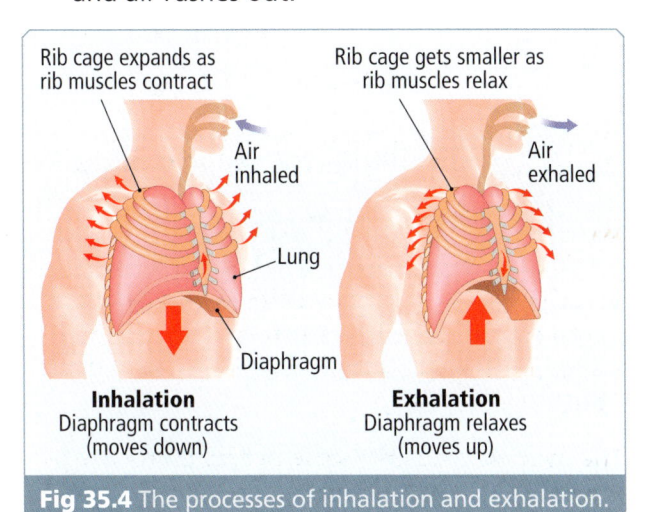

Fig 35.4 The processes of inhalation and exhalation.

HL Control of human breathing

Human breathing rate is determined by the level of carbon dioxide in the bloodstream. Carbon dioxide dissolves in the plasma to become carbonic acid (a weak acid). If there is too much carbon dioxide in the blood as a result of exercising, the pH of the blood will go down slightly.

Chemoreceptors throughout the body are extremely sensitive to very small changes in blood pH. When the pH decreases (becomes more acidic), the chemoreceptors send an electrical impulse to the brain telling it to increase the breathing rate. This causes more carbon dioxide to be excreted. The pH of the blood will then go back to normal.

Breathing disorders

> **NOTE** For the Leaving Certificate Biology exam, you are required to learn about one breathing disorder. Bronchitis and asthma are both listed here. You must learn one cause, one preventative measure and one treatment.

Bronchitis

Bronchitis is the inflammation of the mucous membranes of the breathing system, specifically the bronchi (hence the name).

Symptoms

There are two types of bronchitis: *acute* and *chronic*.

- Acute bronchitis involves a cough that lasts for only a few days.
- Chronic bronchitis also involves a cough but it can last for months.

Phlegm production can be characteristic of both types of bronchitis.

Cause

Bronchitis is a common condition, caused mainly by breathing system infections, such as colds and flu. It can also be caused by smoking or exposure to high levels of pollution.

Prevention

Avoid people with colds and flu. If you have a cold or flu, cover your mouth with a tissue when coughing and sneezing. Washing your hands regularly also reduces your risk of contracting a cold or flu. Avoid smoking and pollution.

Treatment

Treatment depends on whether the bronchitis is acute or chronic. If it is acute, it is most likely caused by a virus. Viruses are not affected by antibiotics; therefore, they are generally not an option. Treatment involves rest. If the bronchitis is chronic, then avoiding the factor causing the inflammation and irritation is the treatment. For example, stop smoking and avoid pollution.

Asthma

Asthma is a chronic inflammation of the bronchioles.

Symptoms

Wheezy breathing, tightness of the chest and shortness of breath are the main symptoms of asthma.

Cause

Asthma is caused by inflammation of the bronchioles. When they become inflamed, they narrow and can close completely causing an asthma attack. Inflammation of the bronchioles can be brought about by a number of external factors such as pollen, dust or air pollution. It can also be caused by exercise, which is a very common form. It has been found that up to 10 per cent of top athletes have exercise-induced asthma. Asthma can also be caused by breathing in cold air.

Prevention

Avoid allergens such as pollen, dust or air pollution. In the case of exercise-induced asthma, use an inhaler that keeps the bronchioles open.

Treatment

An inhaler is used to treat an asthma attack (Fig 35.5). Inhalers use drugs called bronchodilators such as salbutamol. These cause the constricted bronchioles to widen.

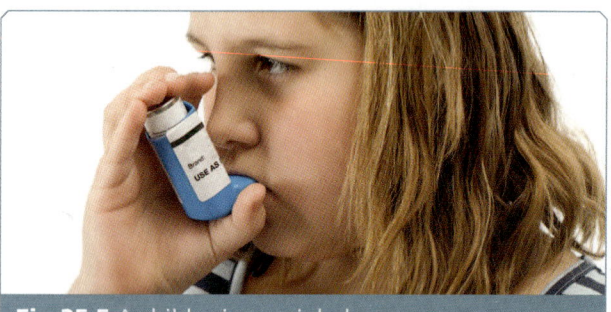

Fig 35.5 A child using an inhaler.

Practical activity: to investigate the effect of exercise on breathing rate

Breathing rate is the number of breaths per minute (bpm). One breath is counted as one inhalation **together with** one exhalation.

When measuring breathing rate after exercise, it is more accurate to count the number of breaths in 15 seconds and then multiply by four. This is because breathing rate will decrease over the course of one minute following exercise. When measuring breathing rate at rest, it is more accurate to count the number of breaths over one full minute.

NOTE: This practical activity is linked to the practical activity to investigate the effect of exercise on pulse rate on page 328. For the Leaving Certificate Biology syllabus, you must carry out one or the other.

Method

1. Measure your breathing rate three times while at rest. Average the result. This is your resting breathing rate.
2. Walk slowly for 3 minutes and recount your breathing rate.
3. Walk briskly for 3 minutes and recount your breathing rate.
4. Finally, run for 3 minutes and count your new breathing rate.
5. If you wish you can exercise vigorously by running as fast as you can for 3 minutes and then measure your breathing rate.
6. Record your results in a table.

Results

	Breathing rate (bpm)
Resting	
Walking slowly	
Walking briskly	
Running	

Conclusion

What have we learned from this practical activity?

- Exercise increases breathing rate.

Practical activity question

In carrying out this practical activity, you had to measure your breathing rate at rest. Explain how you did this and the reason for measuring it at least three times.

Chapter 35 Questions

1. What is another name for the chest cavity?
2. Fig 35.6 shows a diagram of the human breathing system. Label structures A–O and give each of their functions.

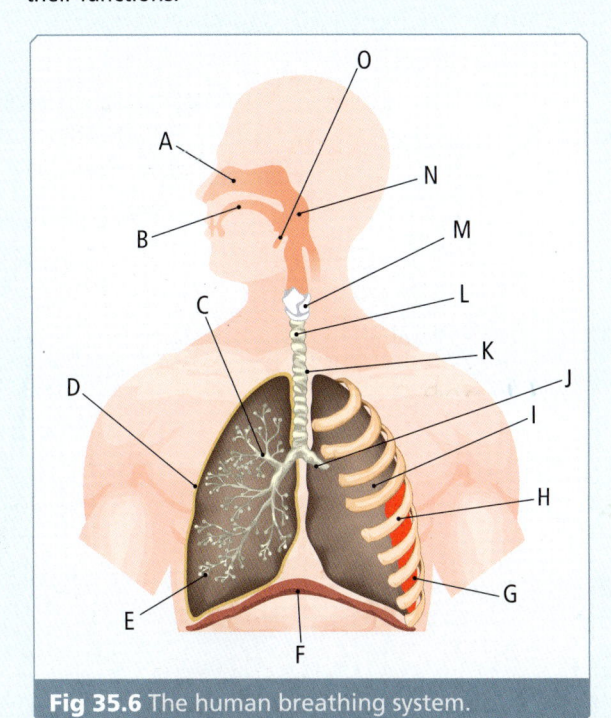

Fig 35.6 The human breathing system.

3. Distinguish between the following:
   (a) *Nasal cavity* and *buccal cavity*.
   (b) *Larynx* and *pharynx*.
   (c) *Oesophagus* and *trachea*.
   (d) *Glottis* and *epiglottis*.
   (e) *Bronchi* and *bronchioles*.
   (f) *Pleural membranes* and *pleural cavity*.
   (g) *Thorax* and *abdomen*.
4. (a) What major blood vessel supplies blood to the lungs?
   (b) What blood vessel carries blood away from the lungs?
5. To which major organ does blood travel on leaving the lungs?
6. Draw an alveolus and its associated blood supply.
   (a) On your diagram, show the direction of diffusion of the gases oxygen and carbon dioxide.
   (b) In what way is oxygen mostly transported in the bloodstream?
   (c) In what way is carbon dioxide mostly transported in the bloodstream?
   (d) State **three** ways in which the alveolus is adapted to carry out its function in gas exchange.
   (e) How many alveoli are in an average pair of human lungs?
7. What is *diffusion*?
8. Give the percentage differences of oxygen and carbon dioxide in inhaled air and exhaled air.
9. (a) Describe in detail the processes of inhalation and exhalation.
   (b) Explain why exhalation is normally a passive process.
   (c) Name a situation when exhalation is an active process.
   (d) What muscles are used during active exhalation?
10. Name **one** disorder of the human breathing system and state **one** symptom, **one** cause, **one** preventative measure and **one** treatment.
11. Breathing rate, like heart rate, increases during exercise. Give **two** reasons for this increase.
12. (HL) (a) What small gaseous compound is responsible for increasing breathing rate in the human?
    (b) Describe, in detail, how the compound you named in part (a) increases breathing rate in the human.

Chapter 35 Sample examination questions

1. (i) Draw a large labelled diagram of the human breathing tract and label the following parts: *larynx, trachea, bronchus, bronchiole*.
   (ii) What is the role of alveoli in the lungs?
   (iii) Name a breathing disorder.
   (iv) Suggest a possible cause of the breathing disorder that you have named in (iii) and state how it may be treated.

Section C, Question 14 (c) Ordinary Level 2008

Unit 3   The Organism

HL 2 The diagram shows microscopic detail from a human lung.

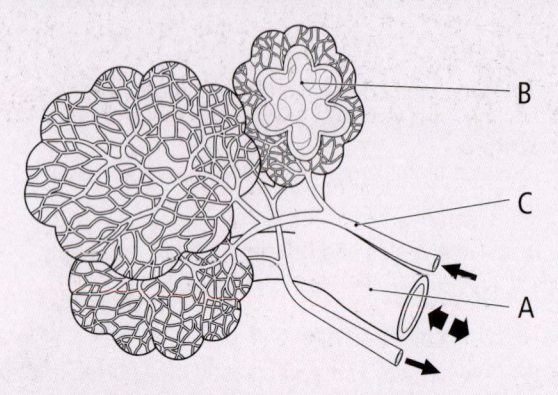

(i) Name the parts labelled A, B and C.

(ii) Give **two** features of the structures in the diagram that allow for efficient gas exchange.

(iii) Name a disorder of the breathing system and say how it may be:
  1. Caused.   2. Prevented.   3. Treated.

(iv) Which gas, dissolved in the blood, can trigger deeper or faster breathing?

Section C, Question 13 (c) Higher Level 2009

3 (a) (i) Draw a large diagram of the human breathing system. Label the *trachea, bronchus* and *lung*.

  (ii) State the function of the following: epiglottis, larynx.

  (iii) Describe briefly the role of the diaphragm and intercostal muscles in inhalation. In your answer refer to volume and thoracic air pressure.

(b) (i) Give **three** ways in which an alveolus is adapted for efficient gas exchange.

  (ii) Name the process involved in the passage of gas between the alveolus and the blood.

  (iii) Name a breathing disorder.

  (iv) In the case of the breathing disorder that you have named in (iii) state:
   1. A cause.
   2. A means of prevention.
   3. A treatment.

Section C, Question 13 (b) and (c) Higher Level 2007

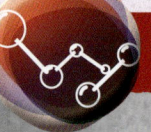

Chapter 35 Mind map

The **breathing system** is involved in gas exchange. Oxygen is absorbed and carbon dioxide and water vapour are excreted.

The breathing system is an excretory system located in the chest cavity or thorax.

Structure

- **Nasal cavity:** as air passes through the nasal cavity it is warmed, moistened and filtered.
- **Buccal cavity:** breathing through the mouth does not filter the air. It is used for breathing when exercising heavily.
- **Pharynx** is the throat.
- **Epiglottis:** a flap of tissue located at the bottom of the pharynx that closes over the glottis during swallowing. It prevents choking.
- **Larynx** is the voice box. It contains vocal cords and is responsible for producing sound.
- **Trachea:** (also known as the windpipe) directs the flow of air into and out of the lungs. It has rings of cartilage to prevent the trachea collapsing.
- **Bronchi and bronchioles:** Two bronchi direct air into the lungs. They are supported by rings of cartilage. Bronchioles are small branches of the bronchi.
- **Alveoli:** tiny air sacs. They are the site of gas exchange. Alveoli have adaptations:
  - Thin walls.
  - Good blood supply.
  - Elastic walls.
  - Numerous (500 million).
  - Moist.
- **Lungs:** large, elastic, spongy organs of gas exchange.
- **Diaphragm:** a sheet of muscle that seals off the bottom of the rib cage and separates it from the abdomen. Functions in inhalation, contracting and moving downwards into the abdomen. Does not take part in exhalation.
- **Pleural membranes:** consist of two membranes with a thin space called the pleural cavity between them. It is filled with a fluid that allows friction-free movement during breathing.
- **Intercostal muscles:** located between each rib. When they contract, they cause the rib cage to move upwards and outwards. They can be consciously and unconsciously controlled.
- **Rib cage:** consists of 12 pairs of ribs that provide the support for breathing.

The human breathing system   Chapter 35

- **Gas exchange:** the process of oxygen diffusing into the bloodstream and water and carbon dioxide diffusing out.
- **Diffusion:** the movement of molecules from a region of high concentration to a region of low concentration.
- Water vapour is also excreted by the lungs.

Inhaled and exhaled air

	Inhaled air	Exhaled air
Oxygen	21 per cent	15 per cent
Carbon dioxide	0.04 per cent	5 per cent
Water vapour	variable	saturated

Mechanism of breathing

1. **Inhalation:** an active process involving the brain and inspiratory muscles.
   - The brain sends a signal to the inspiratory muscles, which are the intercostal muscles and the diaphragm.
   - The intercostals and diaphragm contract.
   - The diaphragm moves down and the intercostals cause the rib cage to move upwards and outwards.
   - The volume of the thorax increases.
   - The thoracic air pressure decreases and air rushes in.
2. **Exhalation:** a passive process involving the recoil of the elastic lung tissue.
   - The inspiratory muscles relax.
   - This causes the elastic tissue of the lungs to return to its original volume.
   - The rib cage moves down and inwards.
   - The diaphragm moves upwards.
   - The volume of the chest decreases.
   - Thoracic air pressure in the lungs increases and air rushes out.

Bronchitis

- An inflammation of the mucous membranes of the breathing system, specifically the bronchi.
- Symptoms: cough that lasts from a few days to a few months with or without production of phlegm.
- Cause: breathing system infections such as colds and flu and also caused by heavy smoking and air pollution.
- Prevention: avoid people with colds and flu; regularly wash hands; avoid smoking and pollution.
- Treatment: rest and avoiding the factor causing the inflammation and irritation such as cigarette smoke and air pollution.

Asthma

- A chronic inflammation of the bronchioles.
- Symptoms: wheezy breathing, tightness of the chest and shortness of breath.
- Cause: inflammation and narrowing of the bronchioles caused by pollen, dust or air pollution. It can also be caused by exercise and cold air.
- Prevention: avoid allergens such as pollen, dust or air pollution. Use an inhaler.
- Treatment: use an inhaler during an episode of asthma.

Control of human breathing   HL

- Carbon dioxide dissolves in the plasma to become carbonic acid that reduces blood pH.
- Chemoreceptors send a signal to the brain which increases breathing rate.

Practical activity to investigate the effect of exercise on breathing rate

- One breath is counted as one inhalation together with one exhalation.
- Measure your breathing rate at rest.
- Walk slowly for 3 minutes and recount.
- Recount after a brisk walk and a run.
- Record your results in a table.

Chapter 36 Human skin (the integumentary system)

Learning objectives After studying this chapter, you should be able to:
- Draw a cross-section through the human skin.
- Describe the general structure of the skin.
- Describe the general functions of the skin and the excretory products of the skin.

Introduction

The skin is a system made up of many small organs (see below). The skin is the outer covering of an animal. It is also known as the **integumentary system** – a system that functions mainly in **protection**. Its main function is to act as a physical barrier to prevent entry of pathogens. In this role, the skin acts as part of the general defence system. It covers virtually the entire surface of the body.

Structure and function of the skin

The skin is composed of two main layers: the **epidermis** and **dermis**. There is also a **hypodermis** or **subcutaneous layer**.

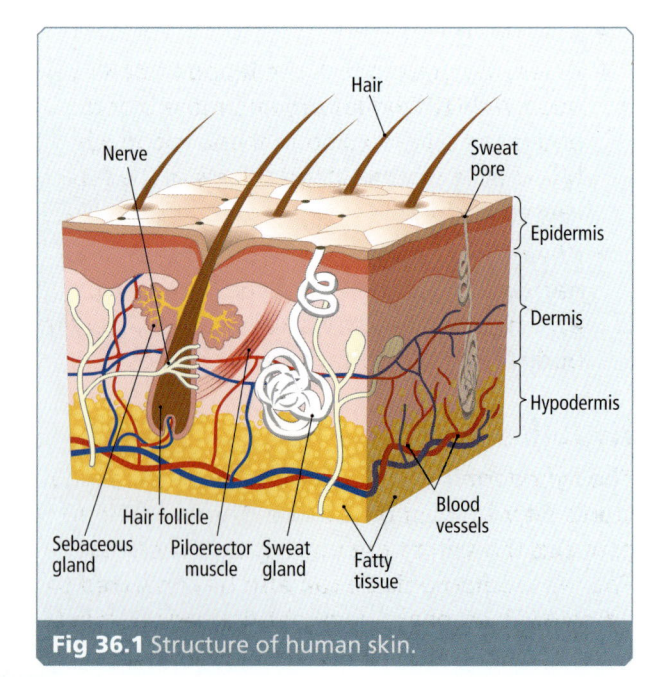

Fig 36.1 Structure of human skin.

The skin has a number of different functions:
- Protection.
- Sensing stimuli such as pain, temperature and touch.
- Storage of fat.
- Temperature regulation.
- Production of vitamin D.

Epidermis

The epidermis is the outermost layer of skin. It consists of **three** sub-layers: the **cornified layer; granular layer;** and **Malpighian layer.**

- The cornified layer is the outermost layer of the epidermis. It acts as the impermeable barrier to pathogens. It consists of dead cells that get brushed off continuously – which is where dandruff comes from. It is estimated that approximately 1 million dead cells are shed from the skin every day!

- The granular layer consists of cells filled with the protein keratin. As they move outwards towards the surface of the skin, they lose their nucleus and cell organelles and die. This layer gives skin its strength.

- The Malpighian layer is named after an Italian doctor, Marcello Malpighi, who was the first to identify it using a microscope. It is the deepest layer of the epidermis and contains cells called melanocytes that are responsible for producing melanin – the skin pigment that protects against ultraviolet (UV) radiation from the Sun. The Malpighian layer is also where all the cells in the epidermis originate before dying and being brushed off the cornified layer.

Dermis

The dermis lies below the epidermis and consists of the proteins **collagen** and **elastin**. These proteins give skin its strength and elasticity. The dermis contains many organs that have diverse functions.

Sweat glands

Sweat glands secrete **sweat** as part of the homeostatic mechanism of temperature regulation. When we are too hot, our sweat glands actively secrete sweat onto the surface of the skin through the sweat pore. Sweat consists mostly of water. However, there are trace amounts of urea and salt. Therefore, the skin, **to a very limited extent,** is also an excretory organ system. The water on the surface of the skin absorbs heat from the body and evaporates. This has a cooling effect on the body.

Sebaceous glands

Sebaceous glands are associated closely with hair follicles and are responsible for secreting **sebum,** a type of oil. Sebum maintains the integrity of the skin. However, too much sebum production can cause skin problems such as acne. Sebum blocks the hair follicle pores, giving bacteria the chance to multiply. This causes an immune reaction as there are a large number of macrophages present in the dermis. Acne is most common in adolescents, as sebum production increases dramatically in this age group. However, acne can occur at any age.

Sense organs

The skin has sense organs that respond to changes in temperature, pain and touch. These receptors function as a protective mechanism for the body. If a very hot object touches the skin, the temperature receptors send a signal to the central nervous system which responds by telling the muscles to contract and pull the affected area away from the heat source (see Chapter 39).

Hair follicles

Hair follicle distribution varies over the surface of the skin. The follicle is attached to a **piloerector** muscle (Fig 36.1). When we are cold, the piloerector muscle contracts, causing the hair to stand up away from the skin. These hairs help to hold a layer of warmer air close to the skin.

The piloerector muscles contracting also cause the formation of 'goose bumps' (Fig 36.2).

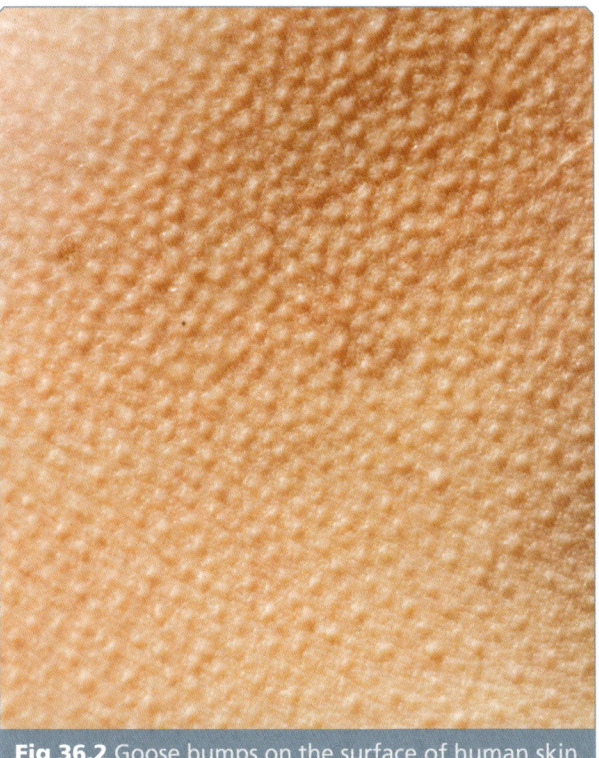

Fig 36.2 Goose bumps on the surface of human skin.

Blood vessels

The dermis has a good blood supply, bringing nutrients to the skin and waste products away. The blood vessels also function in temperature regulation.

- When you get too hot, the blood vessels open wide **(vasodilation)** and more blood enters the skin, causing redness. Too much blood entering the blood vessels in the face causes blushing.
- When we are too cold, the blood vessels narrow **(vasoconstriction)** and blood flows away from the skin. It is kept deep within the body to keep the vital organs functioning.

Hypodermis

The hypodermis is the deepest layer of the skin. It stores fat within adipose tissue. The hypodermis connects the skin to the underlying structures. The fat in adipose tissue can also be converted to vitamin D by sunlight. Sunlight-derived vitamin D is the main source of this vitamin to humans.

Unit 3 The Organism

Chapter 36 Questions

1. The skin is an *organ system* **not** an *organ*. Explain.
2. The skin has an upper layer and a lower layer. Name these **two** layers.
3. The upper layer is made of **three** sub-layers. Name each of these layers and give **one** function for each layer. Which of the layers is dead?
4. Name **three** proteins that are found in the skin.
5. Give **one** function of each of the following organs of the skin:
   (a) Temperature receptor.
   (b) Pain receptor.
   (c) Touch receptor.
   (d) Sebaceous gland.
   (e) Sweat gland.
   (f) Blood vessels.
6. Explain why the skin is part of the general defence system.
7. Explain how acne results. Why is it most common in adolescents?
8. Distinguish between *vasodilation* and *vasoconstriction*.
9. Explain how blushing occurs.
10. What is the function of the subcutaneous layer?
11. Where is adipose tissue located and what is its function?
12. Explain how the skin can produce vitamin D. What is vitamin D important for in the human body (*see* Chapter 3)?

Chapter 36 Sample examination questions

1. The diagram shows a section through human skin.

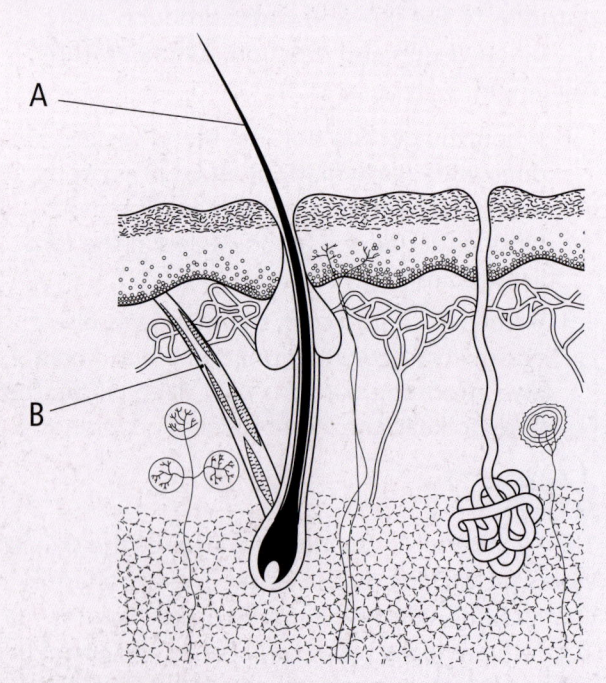

   (a) Name parts **A** and **B**.
   (b) Place **X** on the diagram to show where sweat reaches the skin surface.
   (c) Apart from water, name **one** other substance which is found in sweat.
   (d) Describe briefly **one** way by which the skin helps to retain heat in cold conditions.

   Section A, Question 6 Ordinary Level 2008

HL 2. (i) Draw a diagram of a section through human skin to show **two** structures involved in temperature regulation. Label each of these structures.

   (ii) For **one** of the structures that you have labelled in your diagram briefly describe its role in temperature regulation.

   Section C, Question 15 (c) (ii) and (iii) Higher Level 2007

3. Suggest a biological explanation for the following observation: A person's fingers may turn white when exposed to low temperature for a period of time.

   Section C, Question 15 (c) (v) Higher Level 2010

Chapter 36 Mind map

The skin is an organ system, also known as the integumentary system.

The skin is the outer covering of an animal. It has a number of different functions:
- Protection.
- Sensing stimuli such as pain, temperature, touch.
- Storage of fat.
- Temperature regulation.
- Production of vitamin D.

The skin consists of two main layers: epidermis and dermis.
- The epidermis consists of three layers: the cornified layer of dead skin cells; the granular layer of keratin-producing cells; and the Malpighian layer of melanocytes that produce melanin.
- The dermis consists of a thick layer of collagen and elastin-producing cells. It has many functions due to the many organs present in it, such as sense organs: temperature, pressure, and pain receptors; hair follicles; sweat glands; blood vessels and sebaceous glands.

Organs of the skin
- Sweat glands secrete sweat, consisting of mostly water and trace amounts of urea and salts.
- Sebaceous glands secrete sebum.
- Sense organs respond to changes in temperature, pain and touch.
- Hair follicles produce hairs that help keep warm air close to the skin.
- Blood vessels supply nutrients to the skin. They also dilate when too hot (vasodilation) and constrict when too cold (vasoconstriction).

The hypodermis (subcutaneous layer) contains mostly adipose tissue that stores fat. Certain types of cholesterol present in the adipose tissue can be converted to vitamin D by sunlight."

Chapter 37 The human urinary system

Learning objectives After studying this chapter, you should be able to:
- Describe the role of the urinary system in homeostasis.
- Describe the structure, functions and locations of all parts of the urinary system.
- Describe the excretory products of the urinary system.
- Describe how the kidneys regulate body fluids.
- Describe the basic process of urine production.
- HL ▶ Describe and draw the structure of the nephron and its blood supply.
- ▶ Describe the detailed process of urine production.

Introduction

The urinary system is crucial to **homeostasis**. It helps to maintain homeostasis through **excretion**.

> **Excretion** is the removal of waste products of metabolism.
>
> **Homeostasis** is the maintenance of a constant internal environment.

The kidneys are the main organ of the urinary system. The kidneys act as filters, continuously cleaning the blood and keeping it free of dangerous levels of waste products and toxins. Without the urinary system (for example, in the event of kidney failure), toxins would quickly build up in the bloodstream.

The kidneys filter out the unwanted chemicals and send them, in the form of urine, to the urinary bladder for storage until they are passed from the body. Urine consists of water, urea and salts. Urea is the breakdown product of protein. Any excess protein the body does not need is sent to the liver. The liver converts the protein to urea in a process called **deamination** (see Chapter 33). The urea is a nitrogen-containing compound that is released by the liver into the bloodstream and excreted by the kidney as part of urine.

The kidneys are just one of three types of excretory organ. The other two are the lungs and the skin.

- The lungs excrete water vapour and carbon dioxide.
- The skin excretes sweat.
- The kidneys excrete urine.

Structure of the urinary system

The urinary system consists of a number of organs:

- Kidneys
- Ureters
- Urinary bladder
- Urethra

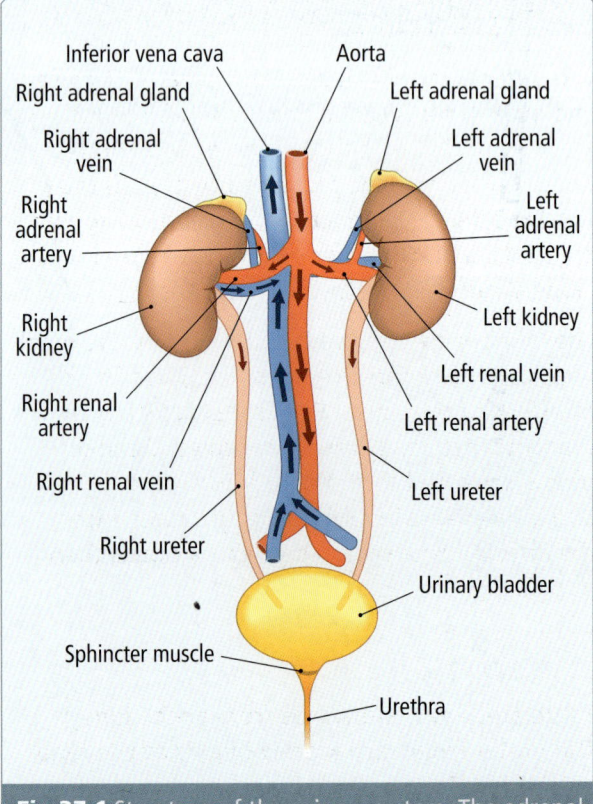

Fig 37.1 Structure of the urinary system. The adrenal glands are also shown, along with their blood supply.

1 Kidneys

The kidneys are bean-shaped organs located in the upper abdomen. The left kidney is slightly higher than the right one because of the position of the liver. Most people have two kidneys, but some people have only one while others have three!

The adrenal glands sit on top of each kidney. They secrete the hormone **adrenaline** (*see* Chapter 38).

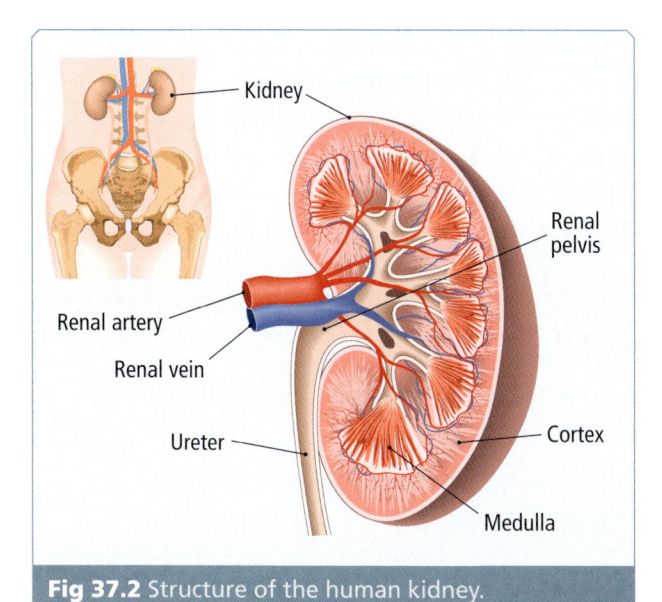

Fig 37.2 Structure of the human kidney.

The outer layer of the kidney is called the **cortex** and inner layer is called the **medulla**. The kidneys are surrounded by a thick layer of fat. This is because they are not protected by the rib cage. The fat offers a good level of protection against physical trauma. However, physical trauma to the kidneys can still result in a kidney tear.

The kidneys are supplied with blood by the **renal arteries** (one going to each kidney), which are branches of the aorta. Each renal artery then branches into many renal arterioles. Cleaned blood is drained from the kidney by the right and left **renal veins,** which in turn drain into the inferior vena cava. The clean blood is then returned to the heart.

2 Ureters

There are two ureters, one from each kidney. The ureter from each kidney begins at the renal pelvis (Fig 37.2).

The ureters carry urine to the **urinary bladder.**

3 Urinary bladder

The urinary bladder is a muscular, elastic organ that receives and stores urine from the kidneys via the two ureters.

Its maximum capacity varies greatly from person to person, but can be as much as 1 L. The urge to urinate is caused by the urinary bladder stretching as it fills. Stretch receptors in the muscular wall trigger a spinal cord reflex (*see* Chapter 39) that causes urination, also called **micturition.** This reflex can be overridden consciously up to a point. This is done by contracting the sphincter muscle and preventing the release of urine.

4 Urethra

The urethra is a tubule (narrow tube) leaving the urinary bladder that carries urine during urination. There is a small muscle at the top of the urethra that is called a sphincter. It remains contracted until urination, at which point it relaxes and allows urine to flow from the urinary bladder. The urethra in males (average length of 20 cm) is longer than in females (average length 4 cm).

Functions of the kidneys

Excretion

The primary role of the kidneys is in **excretion.** They filter the blood by extracting waste products and converting them to urine, which is released and passed onto the urinary bladder. Excretion helps to maintain homeostasis (*see* Chapter 29).

Osmoregulation

Osmoregulation is the control of the amount of water in the body. The kidneys can control the amount of water in the bloodstream by regulating the amount of water excreted. In this way, they can control the blood volume and therefore blood pressure.

For example, if blood pressure is low due to a lack of water in the bloodstream, then water is conserved by the kidneys producing a low volume of urine. This helps to maintain blood volume and therefore blood pressure. If blood pressure is too high due to the blood having too much water, then water will be excreted in the urine.

pH control

The kidneys can also control the pH of the blood, keeping it at the normal level of 7.4. They do this by producing acidic or alkaline urine. The kidneys produce slightly acidic urine when the blood pH is lower than 7.4 and slightly alkaline urine when the pH of the blood is higher than 7.4.

Diet also affects the pH of the urine. A diet high in protein will produce acidic urine and a diet high in fruits and vegetables keeps the urine alkaline.

Hormone production

The urinary system has other functions. The kidney produces the hormone erythropoietin, which stimulates the production of red blood cells in the bone marrow.

Urine production

Urine is the excretory product of the kidneys. It consists of **water, urea** and **salts**. It is formed by three processes that occur within the kidneys. These are **filtration, reabsorption** and **secretion**.

1 Filtration

Filtration occurs in the cortex of the kidney. The blood flows through tiny blood vessels within the kidney and many components of plasma are filtered out of the bloodstream. Water, salts, urea, glucose and amino acids (all components of plasma) get filtered through. Red blood cells, white blood cells, platelets and large plasma proteins such as antibodies are too large to be filtered through.

The liquid that results after filtration is called the filtrate. It contains wastes and useful substances that need to be reabsorbed.

2 Reabsorption

Reabsorption occurs in the cortex and medulla of the kidney. It is called 'reabsorption' because these substances have already been absorbed in the intestines (absorption of nutrients). Substances that the body needs, such as glucose and amino acids, are reabsorbed into the bloodstream.

3 Secretion

Secretion is the active transport of substances out of the blood into the tubules of the kidneys for excretion. Many drugs are excreted this way. The acidity or alkalinity of the urine is also caused by secretion.

Urination (micturition)

> **Urination** (micturition) is the passing of urine from the body.

Urine is formed in the kidney. It passes out of the kidney via the renal pelvis. It is transported to the urinary bladder via the ureters. The urinary bladder stores the urine until urination. Urination involves the passing of urine from the urinary bladder out of the body via the urethra.

HL The nephron – the functional unit of the kidney

The nephron is the functional unit of the kidney. It is where the three processes of urine formation occur.

There are approximately 1 million nephrons in each kidney. They are composed of four main parts: the **Bowman's capsule; proximal convoluted tubule; loop of Henle;** and **distal convoluted tubule.** The Bowman's capsules, proximal convoluted tubules and distal convoluted tubules of kidney nephrons are found entirely within the cortex. The loop of Henle straddles both the cortex and medulla (Fig 37.3).

The nephron filters the blood, producing urine. The urine drains from the nephron into a collecting duct. A number of nephrons are attached to each collecting duct. All collecting ducts drain into the renal pelvis.

The Bowman's capsule (sometimes called the glomerular capsule) is named after the English surgeon, Sir William Bowman, who was first to identify the capsule using a light microscope. It is a cup-like structure located in the cortex of the kidney and is the first structure of the nephron.

A ball of blood vessels called the **glomerulus** sits inside each Bowman's capsule. Blood flows through the vessels of the glomerulus from the **afferent arteriole** (which is a branch of the renal artery). It flows away from the glomerulus via the **efferent arteriole**.

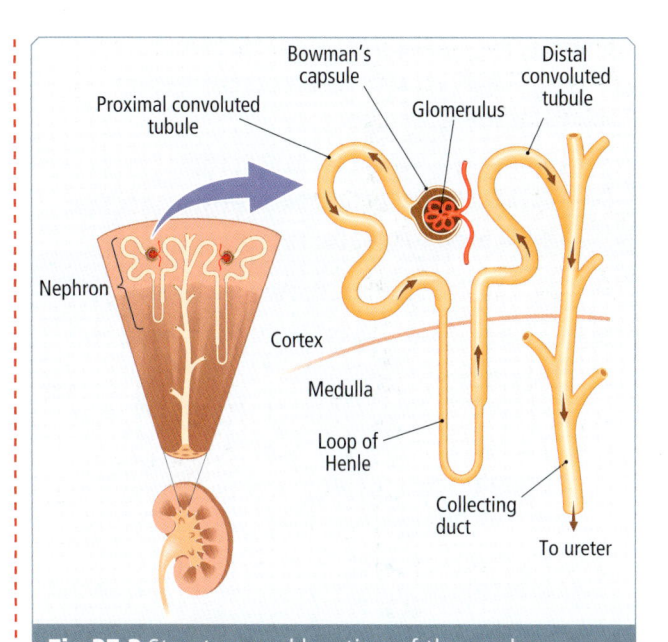

Fig 37.3 Structure and location of the nephron.

The efferent then carries blood all around the nephron for reabsorption of the useful components of the filtrate.

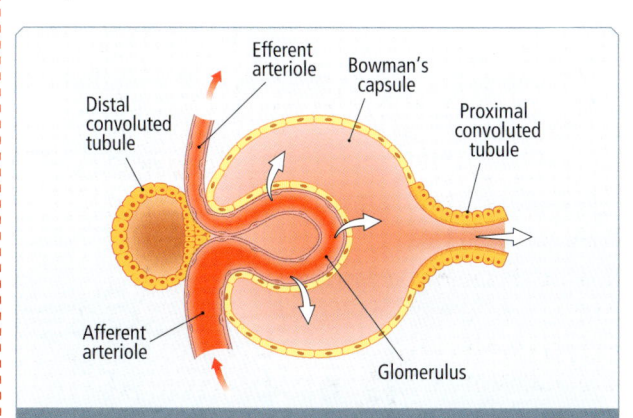

Fig 37.4 Structure of the Bowman's capsule.

The afferent arteriole is wider than the efferent arteriole. This is important to the function of the kidney in filtration. The narrower efferent arteriole creates high blood pressure within the glomerulus. This helps to make filtration in the Bowman's capsule more efficient. Blood pressure within the glomerulus is approximately three times normal blood pressure.

The Bowman's capsule is connected to the proximal convoluted tubule, which twists and turns before becoming the loop of Henle. The loop of Henle is named after Friedrich Henle, a German doctor who first identified it using a light microscope. The loop of Henle crosses both regions of the kidney (cortex and medulla) and carries the filtrate to the distal convoluted tubule, which is located in the cortex. The word 'distal' refers to the fact that the distal convoluted tubule is further away from the start of the nephron than the proximal (meaning 'close to') convoluted tubule.

The distal convoluted tubule twists and turns in much the same way as the proximal convoluted tubule before it attaches to the collecting duct.

Urine production – detailed process

Urine is the excretory product of the kidneys. It consists of water, urea and some salts. It is formed by three processes that occur within the nephron of the kidney. These are **filtration, reabsorption** and **secretion.**

1 Filtration

Filtration occurs in the Bowman's capsule and glomerulus of the nephron. Water, excess salts, urea, glucose and amino acids enter the lumen of the Bowman's capsule from the glomerulus. This fluid is called glomerular filtrate and contains wastes and useful substances. Cells and large proteins do not enter the glomerular filtrate as they are too big to diffuse through the porous capillary walls.

Both the Bowman's capsule and the glomerulus are adapted for the function of filtration by having the following characteristics:

- The Bowman's capsule is cup-shaped to hold the glomerulus and provide maximum surface area for filtration.
- The wall (endothelium) of the Bowman's capsule is one cell thick.
- The endothelium of the Bowman's capsule produce thin projections that wrap around the blood capillaries of the glomerulus. There are small gaps between the thin projections that allow for efficient filtration.
- The glomerulus has a high blood pressure that forces substances out of the capillary into the Bowman's capsule. The blood pressure within the glomerulus is three times normal blood pressure.
- The capillaries of the glomerulus are also one cell thick.

- The cell membranes of the capillaries of the Bowman's capsule are more porous than normal blood capillaries.

The rate at which filtration occurs is called the glomerular filtration rate and is approximately 125 ml per minute. This equates to 7.5 L per hour and 180 L per day! This means that all 6 L of blood in the body is filtered at least 30 times a day. Obviously, most of the glomerular filtrate has to be reabsorbed.

2 Reabsorption

The glomerular filtrate immediately enters the proximal convoluted tubule. The tubule is called 'proximal' because it is close to the start of the nephron. It is called 'convoluted' because it is a twisted and coiled tubule. More than 99 per cent of the glomerular filtrate is reabsorbed in the proximal convoluted tubule leaving a urine volume of approximately 1.5 L per day.

The proximal convoluted tubule is adapted to its function by having the following characteristics:

- It is a long and convoluted tubule, increasing surface area for reabsorption.
- Its walls are one cell thick, allowing diffusion to occur more easily.
- It has a good blood supply so that reabsorption into the blood can occur efficiently.
- Its internal wall has microvilli (tiny cytoplasmic projections) to further increase surface area for reabsorption.

The proximal convoluted tubule reabsorbs:

- All the glucose and amino acids. These substances are transported by active transport. Active transport requires energy in the form of ATP (see Chapter 10). All of the glucose and amino acids as well as other nutrients are pumped back into the bloodstream against their concentration gradients (meaning the concentration of the nutrients is higher in the bloodstream than in the proximal convoluted tubule).
- Most of the water by osmosis.
- Most salts (65 per cent).

The descending limb of the loop of Henle reabsorbs:

- Some water due to the cells of the medulla being more concentrated than the filtrate present within the tubule of the loop of Henle.
- Calcium and magnesium.

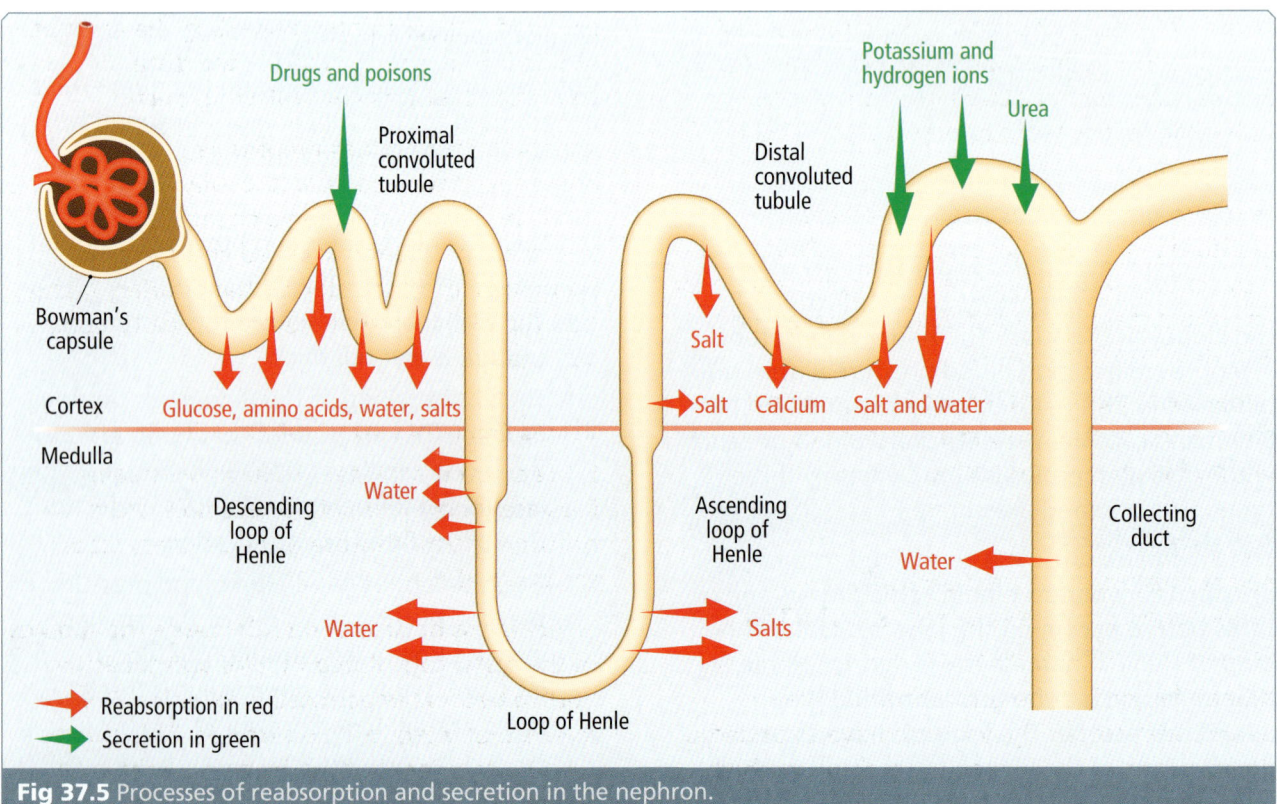

Fig 37.5 Processes of reabsorption and secretion in the nephron.

The ascending limb of the loop of Henle reabsorbs:
- The salts (that were not reabsorbed in the proximal convoluted tubule) by active transport (requiring ATP).

> **NOTE** Water cannot be reabsorbed in the ascending loop of Henle as it is impermeable to water.

The distal convoluted tubule reabsorbs:
- Water, depending on the concentration of a hormone (see below) in the bloodstream.
- Salts by passive transport.
- Urea, although it is undesirable. This is due to urea being highly concentrated within the tubule and relatively dilute in the cells of the cortex. The amount of urea that is excreted is far more than is reabsorbed and therefore does not have any negative effect on the kidneys.

The collecting duct reabsorbs:
- Water in response to changes in a hormone (see below) present in the bloodstream.

3 Secretion

Most secretion is by **active transport** and occurs in the convoluted tubules.

Potassium ions, hydrogen ions and urea are all actively secreted into the distal convoluted tubule against their concentration gradients. Secretion of hydrogen ions helps to regulate the acidity of the blood.

Even though small amounts of urea are reabsorbed in the distal convoluted tubules, it is also actively secreted out of the bloodstream back into the distal convoluted tubule. This requires energy in the form of ATP.

Other substances secreted into the proximal convoluted tubule include drugs such as antibiotics and painkillers.

Kidney failure

Sometimes the three processes of urine production do not work as they should. This can lead to kidney failure.

Kidney failure is quite common and those people with total kidney failure have to undergo dialysis. Dialysis is a process whereby a machine takes blood from the body and removes wastes and excess water from the blood before returning the blood to the body. Dialysis patients have to complete this process between five and seven times per week for 6 to 8 hours at a time (Fig 37.6). In the long term, kidney failure patients usually receive a kidney transplant.

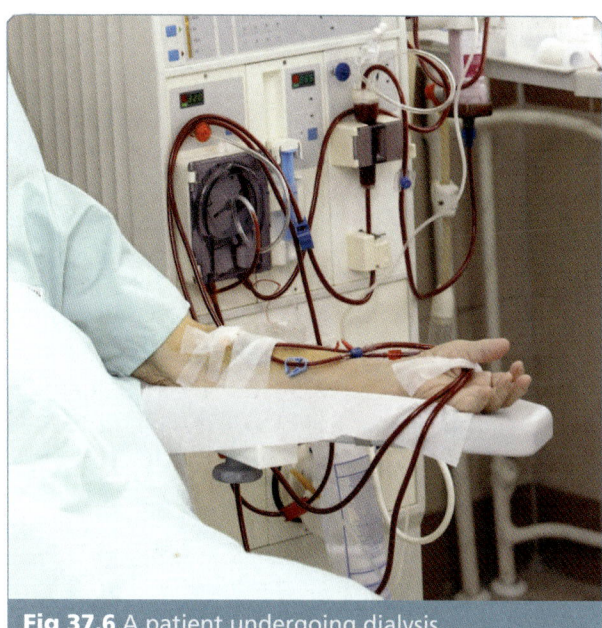

Fig 37.6 A patient undergoing dialysis.

HL Osmoregulation – detailed process

The kidney can control how much water is excreted. It does this by controlling the amount of water that is reabsorbed in the distal convoluted tubules and collecting ducts.

The brain contains **osmoreceptors** – cells that are sensitive to changes in the amount of water in the bloodstream. When a change is detected, the levels of a hormone called **anti-diuretic hormone (ADH)**, secreted by the pituitary gland (located at the base of the brain – *see* Chapter 38), change.

Blood becomes too dilute

If the amount of water in the bloodstream increases above normal (for example, from drinking too much water), the pituitary stops secreting ADH.

Lower levels of circulating ADH cause the tubules of the distal convoluted tubules and collecting duct to become impermeable to water. This means that water will be excreted. This creates very dilute urine that will be a very light yellow colour or even colourless.

Unit 3 The Organism

Blood becomes too concentrated

If the blood becomes too concentrated (the level of water in the blood decreases) through excessive sweating or lack of water intake, the pituitary begins to secrete ADH.

Increased circulating ADH levels cause the kidneys to reabsorb more water. This happens due to the ADH causing the distal convoluted tubules and collecting ducts to become more permeable to water. Water is reabsorbed into the bloodstream. In this way, the kidneys conserve water. As a result the urine produced is concentrated and will be a dark yellow colour.

The thirst centre in the brain is also stimulated giving the sensation of thirst.

Fig 37.7 It is recommended that males drink 3.7 L and females drink 2.7 L of water per day. However, it is important to note that this water can, and is, also obtained from food.

Chapter 37 Questions

1. Define the following terms:
   - (a) *Excretion*
   - (b) *Metabolism*
   - (c) *Homeostasis*
   - (d) *Deamination*
   - (e) *Micturition*
   - (f) *Osmoregulation*

2. (a) Along with the kidneys, what are the other **two** excretory organs in the human body?
   (b) List the excretory products of each excretory organ.
   (c) Which of the three excretory organs is the main excretory organ? Give a reason for your answer.

3. Briefly describe the formation of urine under the following headings:
   (a) Filtration (b) Reabsorption (c) Secretion

4. Distinguish between the following:
   - (a) *Cortex* and *medulla*
   - (b) *Ureter* and *urethra*
   - (c) *Urinary bladder* and *gall bladder* (see Chapter 33)
   - (d) *Plasma* and *urine*
   - **HL** (e) *Blood* and *glomerular filtrate*
   - (f) *Concentrated urine* and *dilute urine*
   - (g) *Proximal convoluted tubule* and *distal convoluted tubule*
   - (h) *Afferent arteriole* and *efferent arteriole*
   - (i) *Reabsorption* and *secretion*

5. Label A–S on the following diagram of the human urinary system and give the function of **each** part.

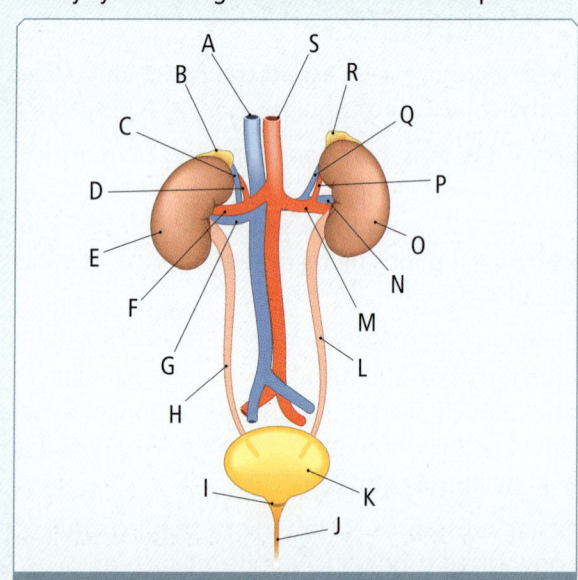

Fig 37.8 Structure of the human urinary system.

HL 6. Draw a sketch of a nephron and label the following parts: *afferent arteriole; efferent arteriole; glomerulus; Bowman's capsule; proximal convoluted tubule; loop of Henle; distal convoluted tubule; collecting duct.*

7. (a) Give **three** ways in which the nephron is adapted to its function of filtration.
   (b) Name **two** substances present in the blood that are not present in glomerular filtrate.

HL (c) Name **two** substances that are reabsorbed in the proximal convoluted tubule.
  (d) Name **two** substances reabsorbed in the loop of Henle.
  (e) Name **two** substances that are reabsorbed in the distal convoluted tubule.
  (f) Name **two** substances secreted into the nephron from the bloodstream.

(g) In secretion within the nephron, substances are usually moved against their concentration gradients. What type of transport is this called and what molecule is required for this movement?

8 What is meant by *osmoregulation*?

9 (a) Explain the hormonal response and renal (kidney) response to an episode of heavy exercise where the person sweated a lot.
  (b) Explain the hormonal response and renal response to a person drinking 2 L of water.

Chapter 37 Sample examination questions

1 (i) Explain the term *excretion*.
  (ii) Name **two** substances excreted by the kidney.
  (iii) The diagram shows the human urinary system. Name the parts labelled A, B and C.
  (iv) Name the parts of the kidney in which each of the following takes place:
    1. Filtration.   2. Reabsorption.
  (v) Name **one** other excretory organ in the body.

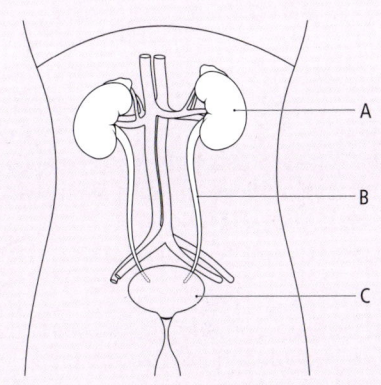

  (iv) In which cavity of the body are the kidneys located?
  (v) Name **one** substance, other than water, excreted in the urine.

NOTE: Question (b) (vi) has not been included here as you must study Chapter 38 before answering it.

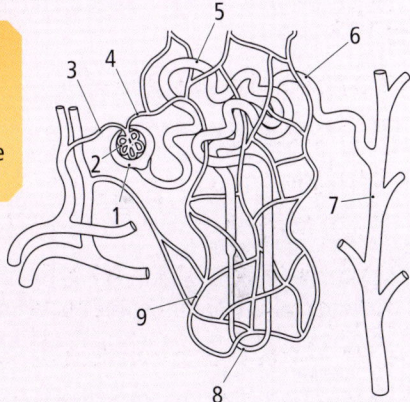

Section C, Question 14 (c) Ordinary Level 2011

HL 2 (a) (i) What is meant by the term *excretion*?
  (ii) Mention **one** method of excretion in flowering plants.
  (b) (i) Draw a large labelled diagram of a vertical section through a human kidney. Label the following parts of your diagram: *cortex, medulla, pelvis*.
  (ii) Indicate clearly on your diagram where reabsorption takes place.
  (iii) 1. Name the blood vessel that supplies blood to a kidney.
    2. From which blood vessel does the blood vessel referred to in (iii) arise?

  (c) (i) The diagram above shows the structure of a nephron and its associated blood supply.
    1. Name the parts numbered 1–6.
    2. Indicate clearly by number where filtration takes place.
    3. Name the hormone associated with changing the permeability of the structure at 7.
  (ii) A sample of urine was found to contain protein.
    1. Would you consider this to be normal?
    2. Explain your answer.
  (iii) A sample of urine was found to contain glucose.
    1. Would you consider this to be normal?
    2. Explain your answer.

Section C, Question 12 Higher Level 2011

Unit 3   The Organism

Chapter 37   Mind map

The urinary system is an excretory system crucial for homeostasis.

The urinary system consists of a number of organs:
- Kidneys
- Ureters
- Urinary bladder
- Urethra

- The kidneys are located in the abdomen. The left kidney is slightly higher than the right one.
- They are supplied with blood by the renal arteries and send clean blood back to the heart via the renal veins.
- The kidneys are surrounded by a thick layer of fat for protection.
- The kidneys function in excretion. They filter the blood and excrete waste products of metabolism.
- The kidneys also function in osmoregulation, controlling the amount of water released in the urine.
- The kidney has two layers: an outer cortex and an inner medulla.
- Filtration occurs and the urine produced flows into the renal pelvis where the ureters originate.
- The ureters carry urine from the kidney to the urinary bladder.
- The urinary bladder stores urine until ready to be released from the body (urination).
- The urethra carries the urine out of the body during urination, which is controlled by the sphincter muscle at the top of the urethra.
- The kidneys also produce the hormone erythropoietin, which increases red blood cell production.

Urine production
- Filtration occurs in the cortex of the kidney. Blood is filtered and water, urea, salts, amino acids and glucose are all taken out of the blood.
- Reabsorption is the process of taking useful substances back into the bloodstream. These include glucose, amino acids, and some salts. Most reabsorption occurs in the cortex but some also occurs in the medulla.
- Secretion is necessary to get rid of many drugs, excess salts and to control the pH of the blood. All secretion occurs in the cortex.

Urination is the passing of urine from the body.

HL
- The nephron is the functional unit of the kidney and consists of Bowman's capsule, proximal convoluted tubule, loop of Henle, and distal convoluted tubule.
- The Bowman's capsule, proximal convoluted tubule and distal convoluted tubule are entirely within the cortex. The loop of Henle straddles both the cortex and the medulla.

Urine production – detailed process   HL

1. **Filtration**
   - The blood is filtered through the glomerulus and Bowman's capsule.
   - The glomerulus and Bowman's capsule are adapted by having thin and porous walls and high blood pressure.

2. **Reabsorption**
   - Glomerular filtrate is formed in the Bowman's capsule and most is reabsorbed in the proximal convoluted tubule. All glucose, amino acids are reabsorbed here.
   - The proximal convoluted tubule has adaptations such as being long and has internal microvilli that increase the surface area for reabsorption. It also has a good blood supply.
   - Water is reabsorbed in the descending limb of the loop of Henle and salts are reabsorbed actively in the ascending limb.
   - The distal convoluted tubule reabsorbs water.

3. **Secretion**
   - Secretion occurs in both the proximal and distal convoluted tubules. Drugs, urea, hydrogen and potassium ions are actively transported into the nephron from the blood.

HL
- Osmoregulation is the maintenance of an organism's water content.
- The brain senses changes in the water content of the blood.
  - When the blood is concentrated, the pituitary secretes ADH which travels in the bloodstream and causes the distal convoluted tubule and collecting duct to become more permeable to water – water is reabsorbed.
  - When the blood is too dilute the pituitary stops secreting ADH and the tubules become impermeable to water – water is excreted.

The human endocrine system — Chapter 38

Learning objectives After studying this chapter, you should be able to:
- Define *hormone*.
- Locate the major endocrine glands in the human body.
- Name and describe the functions of one hormone for each of the major human endocrine glands.
- Describe, for any one named human hormone, its deficiency symptoms, excess symptoms and corrective measures.
- Describe two uses of hormone supplements in humans.
- **HL** Describe the negative feedback mechanism for any one named human hormone.

Introduction

The endocrine system is a hormonal or chemical system. It is a system of response. Hormones (chemicals) are released in response to other chemical signals. There are a number of organs (endocrine glands) involved but they are not directly linked to one another. Instead they are linked by the circulatory system. They communicate via hormones.

> A **hormone** is a chemical messenger produced by an endocrine gland, secreted directly into the bloodstream where it travels to a target tissue where it exerts a specific effect.

Many hormones, such as growth hormone and insulin, are proteins. Other hormones, such as testosterone and oestrogen, are steroids.

> An **endocrine** gland is a gland that secretes hormones directly into the bloodstream.

Examples of endocrine glands include the **pituitary gland,** the **pancreas, adrenal glands** and **testes.**

> An **exocrine** gland is a gland that secretes its product into a duct.

Examples of exocrine glands include the **pancreas, liver** and **testes.**

Notice that the pancreas and testes appear in both lists. This is because they show both endocrine function and exocrine function.

- The pancreas secretes pancreatic juice (*see* Chapter 33) into the pancreatic duct (exocrine secretion) and from there it travels into the duodenum. Different specialised cells within the pancreas secrete insulin into the bloodstream (endocrine secretion).
- The testes secrete sperm into the sperm ducts (exocrine secretion) and different specialised cells within the testes secrete testosterone into the bloodstream (endocrine secretion).

The endocrine system is a type of signalling system. In this respect, it is related to the nervous system (*see* Chapter 39). However there are some major differences between the two systems.

- The endocrine system is a chemical messaging system, whereas the nervous system is an electrical messaging system.
- Because of the above, the responses associated with the endocrine system are generally very slow, whereas those associated with the nervous system are very fast.
- The endocrine system affects wide areas of the body in general (there are exceptions), whereas the nervous system affects specific areas.
- The endocrine system usually has very long-lasting effects, whereas the nervous system usually has very short-lived effects.

Endocrine glands

There are ten main endocrine glands: **hypothalamus, pineal, pituitary, thyroid, parathyroids, thymus, pancreas, adrenals, testes** and **ovaries**.

However, there are many more endocrine glands that are less well known but secrete some very important hormones. For example, the heart, stomach, liver and kidneys all release very important hormones involved in homeostasis. Fig 38.1 shows the locations of six of the main endocrine glands. The other endocrine glands are shown in Fig 38.2 (pineal and hypothalamus), Fig 38.6 (parathyroids) and Fig 38.7 (thymus).

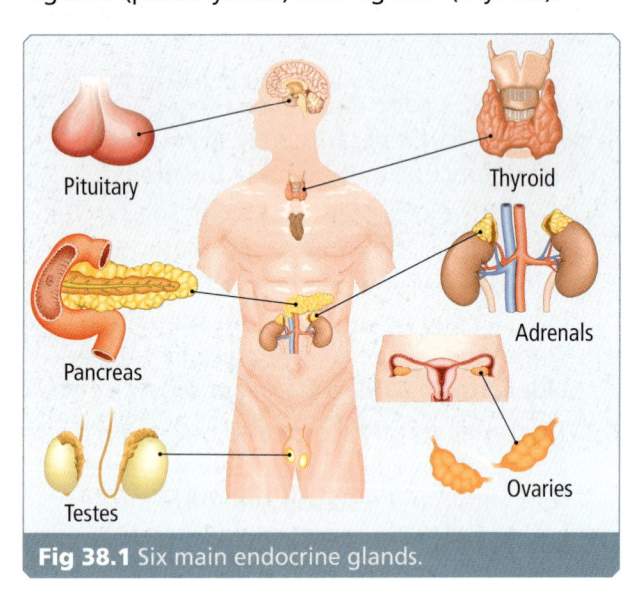

Fig 38.1 Six main endocrine glands.

Hypothalamus

The hypothalamus is part of the brain. It releases hormones that control the pituitary gland. In this way, it provides the link between the nervous system and the endocrine system.

As we will learn in Chapter 39, the hypothalamus controls basic functions such as hunger, thirst and body temperature.

Growth-hormone-releasing hormone (GHRH) is an example of a hormone secreted by the hypothalamus. This travels in the bloodstream to the pituitary where it stimulates the pituitary to secrete growth hormone.

Pineal gland

The pineal gland is also located within the centre of the brain. It is connected to the retina and therefore is sensitive to changes in day length. It secretes the hormone **melatonin,** which is responsible for controlling **circadian rhythms,** such as sleep patterns.

Pituitary gland

The pituitary gland is also known as the 'master' endocrine gland. This is because it controls many other endocrine glands in the body. It is about the size of a pea and is located at the base of the brain just below the hypothalamus (Fig 38.2).

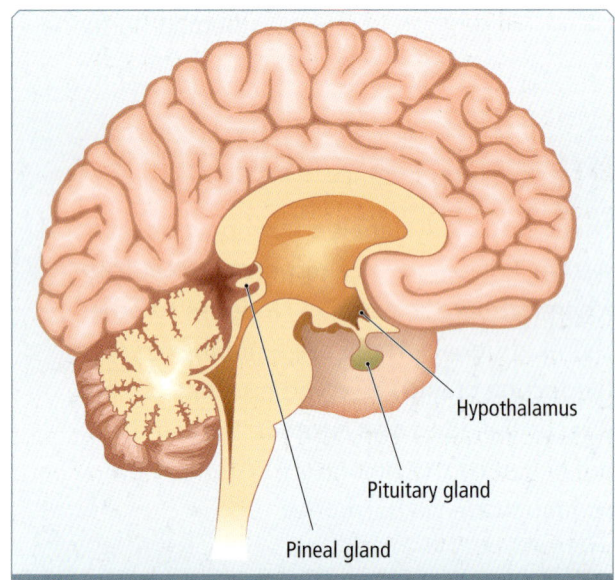

Fig 38.2 The locations of the three main endocrine glands in the brain: the hypothalamus, pineal and pituitary glands.

It is closely linked to the hypothalamus by a **portal system** (see Chapter 31) called the **hypophyseal portal system.**

The pituitary gland releases a range of hormones, such as:

- **Thyroid-stimulating hormone (TSH)**, which controls the release of thyroxine from the thyroid gland.
- **Luteinising hormone (LH)**, which controls ovulation in females and production of testosterone in males.
- **Follicle-stimulating hormone (FSH)**, which controls the formation of eggs in the ovaries and the formation of sperm in the testes.
- **Growth hormone (GH)**, which stimulates growth by causing every tissue in the body to increase in size.
- **Anti-diuretic hormone (ADH)**, which controls osmoregulation in the kidneys (see Chapter 37).

- **Prolactin**, which stimulates the formation of milk in the mammary glands (see Chapter 41).
- **Oxytocin**, which stimulates contractions of the uterus during childbirth (see Chapter 41).

Growth hormone

Deficiency symptoms

Occasionally the pituitary gland fails to produce enough GH or produces none at all. This causes a condition called **dwarfism,** where the person's bones fail to grow to the normal length. All newborns are routinely tested for GH levels.

Corrective measure

If it is found that GH levels are low, the child may need to be given GH throughout childhood to prevent dwarfism.

Excess symptoms

Occasionally the pituitary may produce too much GH. This is nearly always caused by a pituitary tumour. In these cases, the person may grow very tall (Fig 38.3). This condition is called **gigantism**.

Corrective measure

Surgery can remove the tumour and prevent excess GH being produced.

Thyroid

The thyroid gland is a butterfly-shaped endocrine gland located in the neck in front of the larynx (Fig 38.4). It produces the hormone **thyroxine,** which controls the rate of metabolism in the body.

The amount of thyroxine produced by the thyroid is controlled by the pituitary, which secretes **thyroid-stimulating hormone (TSH)**. TSH levels are in turn controlled by the **hypothalamus,** which produces **thyrotropin-releasing hormone (TRH)**.

Deficiency symptoms

Hypothyroidism is a condition where the thyroid gland does not produce enough thyroxine. It gives symptoms such as **weight gain, fatigue, hair loss** and a **very slow heart rate**. Severe symptoms include **goitre,** which is an enlargement of the thyroid gland.

Fig 38.3 Robert Pershing Wadlow (1918–1940) was the tallest man in medical history. By the time of his death at the age of 22, he had grown to 2.72 m (8 feet 11 inches) tall!

Hypothyroidism in babies and young children is called **cretinism**. However, as with growth hormone, thyroxine levels are routinely tested in newborn babies, so that treatment can be started early if required.

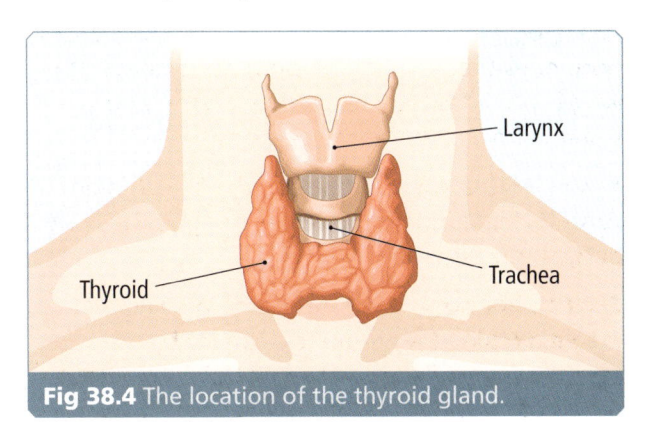

Fig 38.4 The location of the thyroid gland.

Corrective measure

Treatment of hypothyroidism depends on the cause. The most common cause is a **lack of iodine** in the diet. In this case, iodine tablets can be taken.

If it is not due to a lack of iodine, then thyroxine tablets are taken to treat the condition.

Excess symptoms

Hyperthyroidism is a condition where the thyroid produces too much thyroxine. The most common form of hyperthyroidism is **Graves' disease,** named after the Irish doctor Robert Graves who first described the condition.

Symptoms of hyperthyroidism include **exophthalmia** (protrusion of the eyeballs, Fig 38.5), **irritability, insomnia, fast heart rate** and **weight loss.**

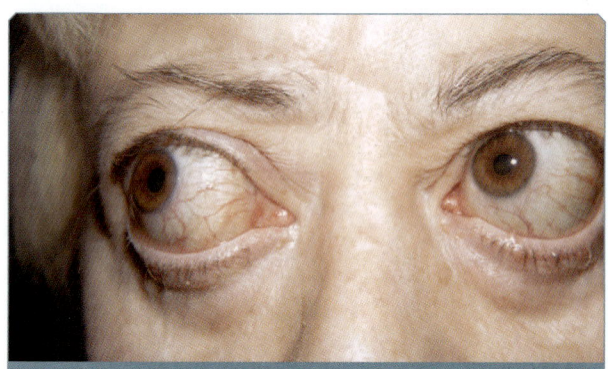

Fig 38.5 Exophthalmia (protrusion of the eyeballs in Graves' disease).

Corrective measure

Treatment for hyperthyroidism is usually anti-thyroid drugs or treatment with radioactive iodine to kill off some of the thyroid tissue.

If the hyperthyroidism is severe, surgery may be carried out to remove part of the thyroid gland.

Parathyroid glands

There are **four** parathyroid glands, which are located in the four corners of the thyroid gland. They produce **parathormone,** a hormone responsible for increasing calcium levels in the blood.

Parathormone increases the calcium levels of the blood by increasing absorption of calcium in the gut. It also stimulates the release of calcium from bone by stimulating the activity of the osteoclast cells in bone (see Chapter 40).

Thymus gland

As we learned in Chapter 34, the thymus is part of the immune system. However, it is also part of the endocrine system as it secretes a hormone called **thymosin.** The thymus is located just in front of the heart and behind the sternum.

Thymosin stimulates T cells to mature (see Chapter 34). Towards the end of adolescence, the thymus gland begins to degenerate and is very small in adults.

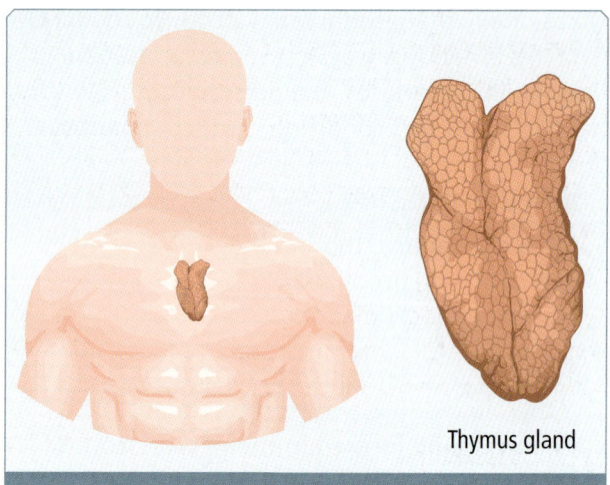

Fig 38.7 The location of the thymus gland.

Pancreas

The pancreas is an endocrine gland and an exocrine gland located deep within the abdomen. There are specialised groups of cells in the pancreas that produce insulin and other hormones. These are called **islets of Langerhans,** after German biologist Paul Langerhans, who in 1869, at the age of just 22, discovered these groups of cells using a microscope.

The islets of Langerhans produce **insulin.** Insulin stimulates all body cells to take in **glucose.** Therefore, insulin has the effect of removing glucose from the bloodstream.

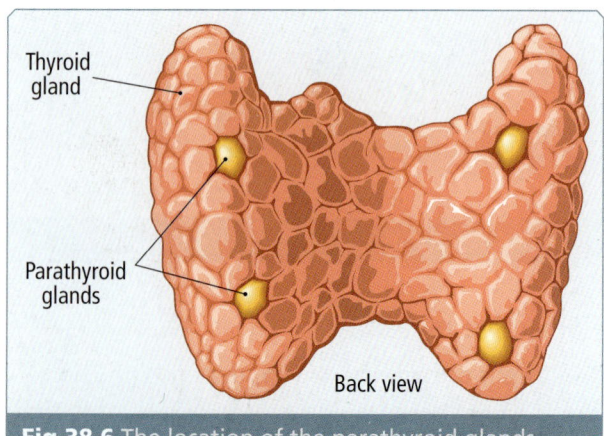

Fig 38.6 The location of the parathyroid glands.

Fig 38.8 The location of the pancreas.

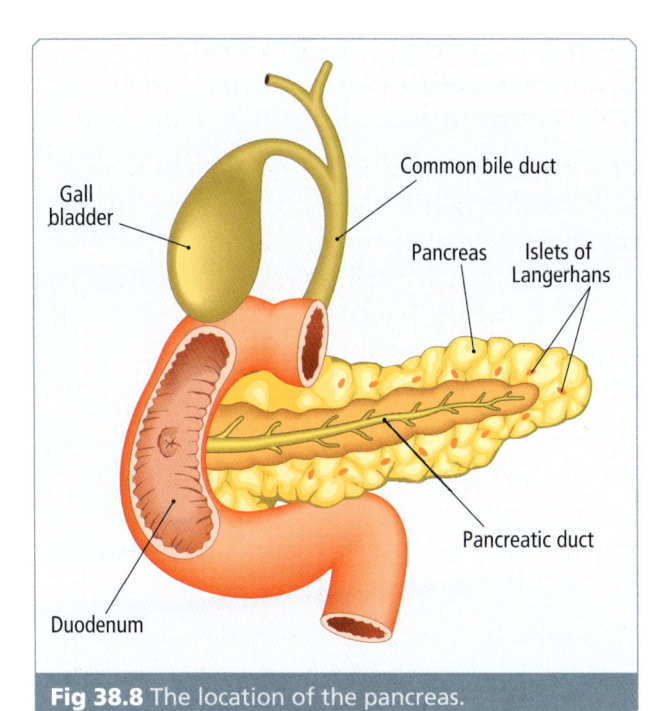

Deficiency symptoms

A deficiency of insulin results in glucose building up in the bloodstream. Too much glucose in the bloodstream is dangerous as it causes damage to delicate tissues such as nerves and capillary networks. Symptoms of high glucose levels are collectively known as **diabetes.**

There are two types of diabetes: **type I** and **type II**. The symptoms of diabetes are the same regardless of the type involved. These include **fatigue, frequent urination, thirst** and **hunger.**

Type I diabetes

Type I is also known as **early-onset diabetes** as it most often occurs in young children. It is usually caused by an inherited mutation where the child does not have the ability to produce insulin.

Treatment
The child must take insulin by injection for the rest of their lives.

Type II diabetes

Type II is also known as **late-onset diabetes** because it usually strikes in middle age or in the elderly. Type II diabetics can still produce insulin. However, the problem arises when not enough insulin is produced or cells have lost the ability to respond to the insulin.

Type II diabetes is usually caused by a poor diet throughout life, but can also be hereditary.

A high intake of sugary foods over many years and being overweight are risk factors for developing type II diabetes.

Treatment
The patient must follow a strict diet and take medication. The medication is usually taken as tablets. Some drugs work by stimulating the pancreas to produce more insulin and some work by stimulating body cells to be more sensitive to insulin.

Excess symptoms

Hyperinsulinism is a rare condition. It is usually caused by type I diabetics injecting too much insulin. This causes cells of the body to absorb too much insulin. When blood glucose levels drop, the patient is said to **'have a low'**.

Hyperinsulinism can also occur naturally; but this is extremely rare. This type of hyperinsulinism usually affects a person from birth and is called **congenital hyperinsulinism.**

Corrective measure

Treatment of hyperinsulinism involves getting the patient to consume an easily absorbed carbohydrate such as a chocolate bar or energy drink as soon as possible.

Adrenals

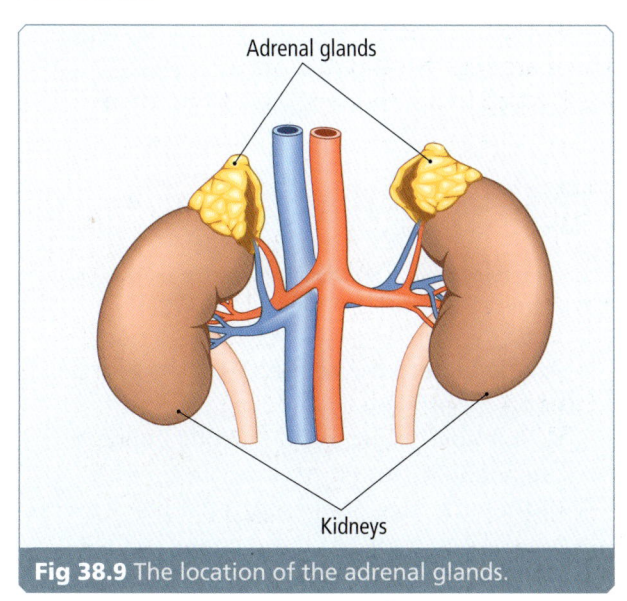

Fig 38.9 The location of the adrenal glands.

The adrenals are located on the top of each kidney. They are responsible for secreting **adrenaline**. This usually occurs following a dangerous, frightening or life-threatening event. For this reason it is often called the **'fight-or-flight'** hormone.

The fight-or-flight response is more applicable to the animal world. Either the organism stays to fight for their life or escapes from the dangerous situation (taking 'flight'). In both cases, the body of the organism requires maximum blood flow to organs needed in the fight-or-flight response.

Therefore, adrenaline functions by increasing blood flow to the brain, lungs, heart and skeletal muscles. Adrenaline reduces blood flow to less-necessary organs such as the intestines.

Testes

The testes are the male sex organs responsible for producing sperm and the male sex hormone **testosterone**. Testosterone is produced in response to a hormone from the pituitary called luteinising hormone (LH, see Chapter 41).

Testosterone affects most tissues in the male body. It is responsible for producing and maintaining male sexual characteristics such as wide shoulders, deep voice, facial and pubic hair and large musculature.

Ovaries

The ovaries are the female sex organs responsible for producing eggs and the female sex hormones **oestrogen** and **progesterone**. Both sex hormones are responsible for producing and maintaining female sexual characteristics such as breasts, pubic hair and wide hips (see Chapter 41).

Hormone supplements

> **NOTE** For Leaving Certificate Biology, you need to know of the use of two hormone supplements.

- **Anabolic steroids** are used by some sports people, both legally and illegally. Sports people such as professional body builders use anabolic steroids to increase the size of their muscles. Some sports people use anabolic steroids to both increase muscle size but also to aid recovery from extreme training sessions. This gives them an adaptive advantage over the competition as they can train harder and have a shorter recovery time.
- **Insulin** is used by type I diabetics. It must be injected directly into the bloodstream as it is a protein hormone.

Fig 38.10 A teenage boy self-injecting with insulin.

Control of hormone levels in the blood

Most hormone levels in the bloodstream are controlled by a **negative feedback mechanism**.

Thyroxine is an example of a hormone whose levels are controlled by negative feedback (inhibition).

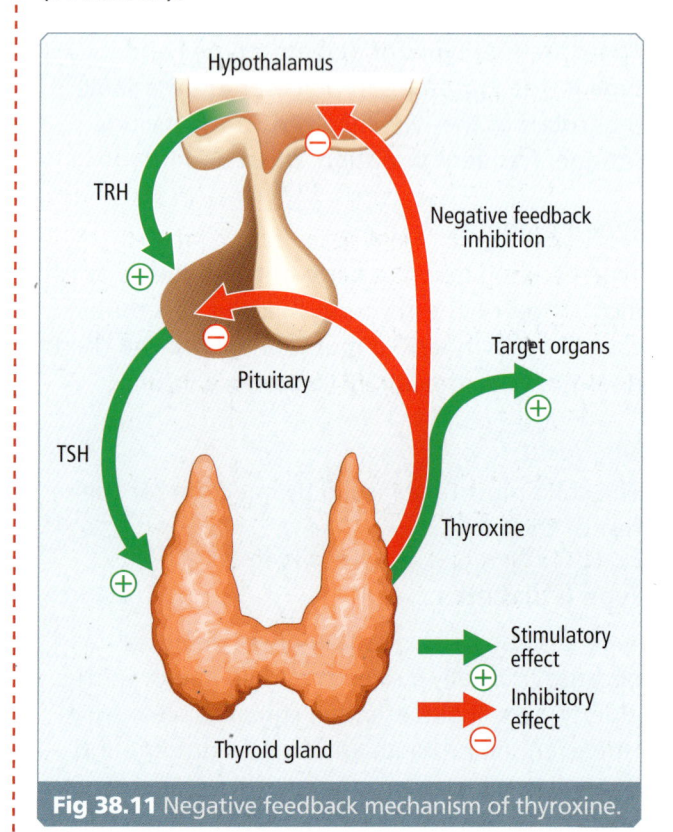

Fig 38.11 Negative feedback mechanism of thyroxine.

Thyrotropin-releasing hormone (TRH) is released by the **hypothalamus,** which stimulates the **pituitary** to release **thyroid-stimulating hormone (TSH)**.

TSH stimulates the thyroid gland to produce and release **thyroxine** (green arrows in Fig 38.11). As thyroxine levels increase, they negatively feedback on the pituitary and hypothalamus (red lines in Fig 38.11).

As a result the pituitary reduces the amount of TSH it produces, which in turn results in a reduction in the amount of thyroxine produced.

The lowered levels of thyroxine means that the inhibition of the pituitary decreases and the levels of TSH can once again increase.

Chapter 38 Questions

1. What is a *hormone*?

2. (a) Distinguish between an *endocrine* and an *exocrine* gland.
   (b) Give **one** example of an endocrine gland and **one** example of an exocrine gland.
   (c) Distinguish between a hormonal response and a nervous response in terms of:
      (i) Speed of response.
      (ii) Nature of response.
      (iii) Length of response.
      (iv) Area affected.

3. Give the location and **one** endocrine function of the hypothalamus.

4. Give the location and **one** endocrine function of the pituitary gland.

5. What is the function of melatonin and from which endocrine gland is it secreted?

6. What effect does parathormone have on the bones?

7. What hormone is responsible for the maturation of T cells?

8. (a) Explain how the pancreas is both an endocrine and an exocrine gland.
   (b) What are the products of each part of the pancreas?

9. Answer the following questions based on the adrenal glands:
   (a) Where are the adrenal glands located in the body?
   (b) What hormone is secreted from the adrenal glands?
   (c) Why is this hormone called the *'fight-or-flight'* hormone?
   (d) What effect does this hormone have on the body?

10. Name **one** human hormone and for the named hormone give **one** disease associated with:
    (a) An excess of the named hormone.
    (b) A deficiency of the named hormone.

11. Name **two** hormone supplements used by people in everyday life.

HL 12. Explain how the *negative feedback mechanism* works for a **named** hormone.

Unit 3 The Organism

Chapter 38 Sample examination questions

1. (i) What is a *hormone*?
   (ii) Draw an outline diagram of the human body and indicate on it the location of the following hormone-producing glands by using the following letters:

   W   Pituitary
   X   Thyroid
   Y   Pancreas (Islets of Langerhans)
   Z   Adrenals

   (iii) In the case of **one** of the hormone-producing glands that you have located in your diagram, state:

   1. The gland and a hormone that it produces.
   2. A function of this hormone.
   3. A deficiency symptom of this hormone.

   (iv) State **one** way in which hormone action differs from nerve action.

   Section C, Question 15 (b) Ordinary Level 2004

HL 2. (i) What is a *hormone*?
   (ii) State **two** ways in which hormones are similar to plant growth regulators.
   (iii) 1. What is meant by *feedback* in relation to hormone action?
   2. Give a brief account of the feedback mechanism for a **named** hormone.
   (iv) Describe **one** deficiency symptom of a **named** hormone.

   Section C, Question 11 (c) Higher Level 2011

Chapter 38 Mind map

The endocrine system is a hormonal system.

Differences between endocrine and nervous system responses:

Endocrine system	Nervous system
Chemical messaging system	Electrical messaging system
Slow response	Fast response
Affects wide areas of the body	Affects specific areas of the body
Long-lasting effects	Short-lived effects

- A **hormone** is a chemical messenger produced by an endocrine gland, secreted directly into the bloodstream. It travels to a target tissue where it exerts a specific effect.
- An **endocrine gland** is a gland that secretes hormones directly into the bloodstream, e.g. pituitary gland.
- An **exocrine gland** is a gland that secretes its product into a duct, e.g. salivary gland.

The human endocrine system — Chapter 38

Endocrine glands

- **Hypothalamus** is located in the centre of the brain just above the pituitary gland. It secretes growth-hormone-releasing hormone (GHRH) that stimulates the pituitary to release growth hormone.
- **Pituitary** gland is located at the base of the brain and secretes growth hormone that stimulates growth.
- **Pineal** gland is located in the centre of the brain and secretes melatonin that helps to control body rhythms such as sleep cycles.
- **Thyroid** gland is a butterfly-shaped gland in the neck that secretes thyroxine. Thyroxine controls the level of metabolism in the body.
- **Parathyroid** glands are four endocrine glands embedded in the thyroid gland that secrete parathormone. Parathormone is responsible for increasing calcium absorption from the gut and the removal of calcium from bone.
- **Thymus** gland is located just underneath the sternum. It secretes thymosin which is responsible for the maturation of T cells.
- **Pancreas** is located in the abdomen and secretes insulin, which is a protein hormone responsible for lowering blood sugar levels.
- **Adrenals** are located on top of each kidney. They secrete adrenaline, which increases blood flow to the brain, heart, lungs and skeletal muscles.
- **Testes** are located in the groin area of the male and secrete the hormone testosterone, which is responsible for producing and maintaining sexual characteristics in males such as deep voice, pubic and facial hair, large musculature and wide shoulders.
- **Ovaries** are located in the lower abdomen of the female and secrete the female hormones oestrogen and progesterone, which are responsible for producing and maintaining sexual characteristics in the female such as breasts, wide hips and pubic hair.

Insulin deficiency (diabetes)

- Diabetes is a disease with symptoms of thirst, hunger and frequent urination.
- There are two types of diabetes: type I and type II.
  - **Type I diabetes** is a condition where the person does not have the ability to produce insulin. They must take insulin injections for the rest of their lives.
  - **Type II diabetes** is more common than type I. The patient can produce insulin, but either they are not producing enough or it is not having an effect on the cells of the body. Treatment involves taking medication.

Negative feedback mechanism of hormone control HL

- Thyroxine controls its own secretion by negative feedback (inhibition) on the pituitary.
- When thyroxine levels decrease, the inhibition is removed and thyroid-stimulating hormone (from the pituitary) is secreted.
- This causes thyroxine levels to increase once again.

Hormone supplements

- **Anabolic steroids** are taken by body builders to increase and maintain a large muscle mass.
- **Insulin** is taken by type I diabetics to keep blood sugar levels under control.

Chapter 39 The human nervous system

Learning objectives After studying this chapter, you should be able to:
- Describe the structure of the nervous system under the headings: central nervous system and peripheral nervous system.
- Describe the structure and function of the neuron.
- Describe the basic movement of a nerve impulse and the structure and function of a synapse.
- Describe the roles and locations of the three types of neuron: sensory neuron, motor neuron and interneuron.
- Name the five senses and their respective organs and describe their respective functions.
- Describe the structure and function of the eye and ear and corrective measures for both long-sightedness and short-sightedness or one disorder of the ear.
- Describe the location and functions of cerebrum, hypothalamus, pituitary gland, cerebellum and medulla oblongata.
- Draw and label a cross-section of the spinal cord and describe the structure and functions of the reflex arc.

Introduction

The nervous system consists of a complex system of specialised organs, tissues and cells. It is a type of response system. It allows animals to **sense** and **respond** very quickly to changes in their environment (both internal and external).

The nervous system carries out its functions of sensing and responding to the environment by carrying messages around the body in the form of **electrochemical signals**. These signals are carried along by specialised cells called **neurons**, which can be up to 1 m in length!

In humans, and most animals, the nervous system consists of two main parts: the **central nervous system (CNS)** and the **peripheral nervous system (PNS)**.

- The central nervous system is composed of the **brain** and **spinal cord**.
- The peripheral nervous system is composed of all the nerves that carry messages to and from the central nervous system, as well as clusters of neurons called **ganglia** that are mostly located very near to the central nervous system. Ganglia contain the cell bodies of sensory neurons (*see* below).

Structure of the human nervous system

Fig 39.1 Structure of the human nervous system.

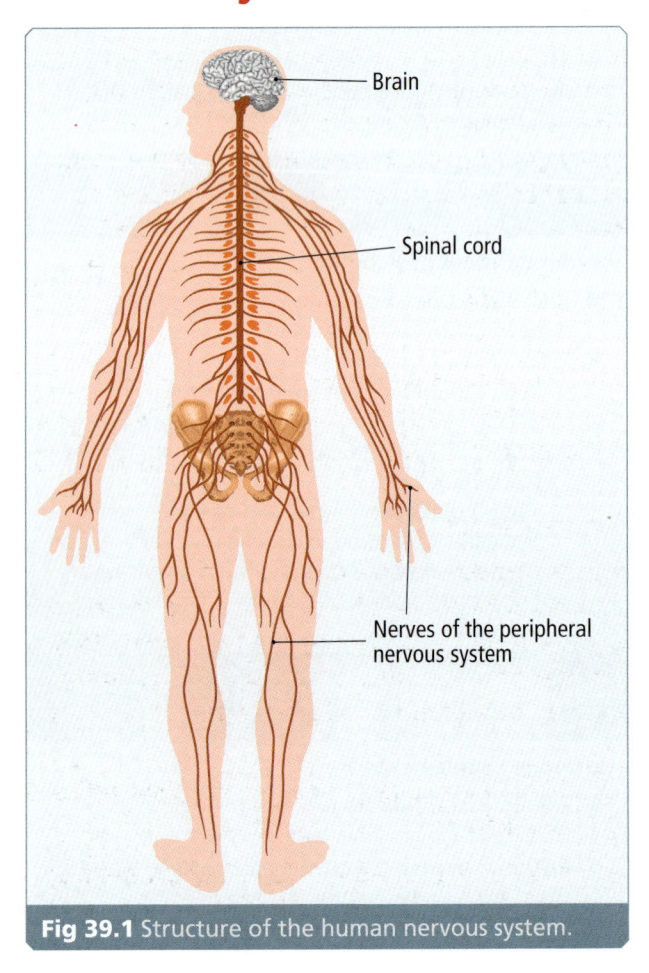

Neuron

> A **neuron** is a nerve cell specialised to carry electrochemical impulses.

The neuron is the basic functional unit of the nervous system. It carries electrochemical impulses from one region of the nervous system to another.

There are three main types of neuron in the body: **sensory neurons**; **interneurons** (or **association neurons**); and **motor neurons**.

Sensory neuron

As their name suggests, sensory neurons are responsible for carrying impulses from sense organs towards the central nervous system for processing.

Part of the sensory neuron is outside the central nervous system and part is inside.

> **Sensory neurons** carry impulses towards the central nervous system.

Interneuron

Interneurons are located entirely within the central nervous system (brain and spinal cord). They are responsible for 'integrating' incoming messages from sensory neurons. They then send messages on to other interneurons within the central nervous system and sometimes send messages on to motor neurons to carry out a physical response.

> **Interneurons** carry impulses from one neuron to another completely within the central nervous system.

Motor neuron

Motor neurons receive impulses from interneurons and send an impulse to a muscle or gland within the body. Any organ or tissue that carries out an action in response to a signal from the nervous system is called an **effector**.

> **Motor neurons** carry impulses from an interneuron to an effector.
>
> An **effector** is an organ or tissue that carries out an action in response to a signal from the nervous system.

Structure of a neuron

All neurons have the same basic components: **dendrites**; **cell body**; **nucleus**; **axon**; **myelin sheath** (**Schwann cells**); and **axon terminals**.

What distinguish the various types of neurons from each other are the lengths of the dendrites and axons.

Sensory neurons have very long dendrites and axons, with a cell body at a specific location in between (Fig 39.2).

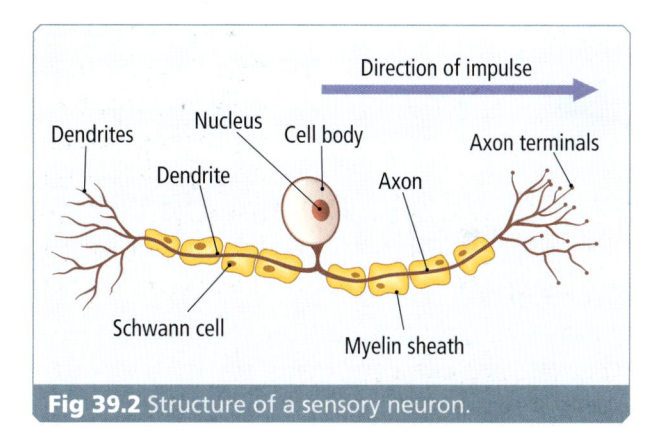

Fig 39.2 Structure of a sensory neuron.

Motor neurons have very short dendrites and very long axons (Fig 39.3).

In general, interneurons have very short dendrites and axons.

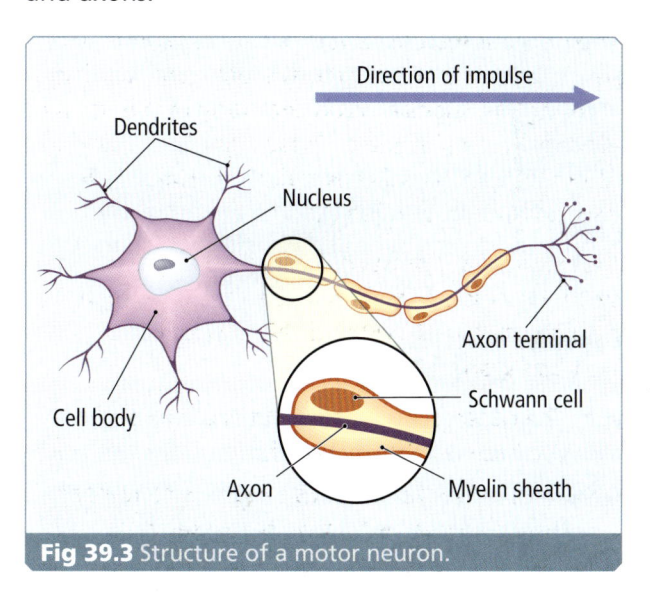

Fig 39.3 Structure of a motor neuron.

Neuron cell components

Dendrites

Dendrites are nerve endings that **receive** impulses from other neurons or from sensory cells. They transmit the impulse **towards** the cell body.

Cell body

The cell body is always located **between** the dendrites and the axon. It is responsible for the upkeep of the cell and for producing **neurotransmitters** – chemicals responsible for transmitting the impulse on to another neuron or effector.

> A neurotransmitter is a chemical substance released by a neuron to transmit a nerve impulse to another neuron or effector.

Axon

The axon is responsible for carrying an electrochemical impulse **away** from the cell body and onwards toward the axon terminals where the impulse will be transmitted on to another neuron or effector.

Myelin sheath

Myelin sheath is a substance made from lipid that wraps around axons and dendrites. It is made by a special type of cell called a Schwann cell. The Schwann cell wraps its cell membrane around the axon or dendrite a number of times to create the myelin sheath.

Myelin sheath protects the axon and dendrites and also has the effect of speeding up electrochemical impulses and maintaining their strength all the way to end of the axon or dendrite. Without it, impulses are not transmitted properly.

Axon terminals

Axon terminals are present at the end of the axon and contain **synaptic vesicles**, which in turn contain neurotransmitter chemicals.

Synaptic vesicles

Synaptic vesicles contain neurotransmitter chemicals. When an electrochemical impulse arrives at an axon terminal, it stimulates the tiny synaptic vesicles to fuse with the cell membrane. This releases the neurotransmitter substance into the small gap between neurons or between a neuron and an effector (*see* Fig 39.4 below).

Nerve impulse

Movement of the nerve impulse

The nerve impulse is a short-lasting electrochemical signal. This means that it is caused by the movement of chemical ions, specifically into the neuron.

As a nerve impulse begins to be generated, sodium ions begin rushing into the neuron. This sets up an electrical wave that travels along the length of the neuron. This is a nerve impulse. It travels the entire length of the neuron very quickly. The speed of a nerve impulse can reach 110 m/s in the human body!

Once the nerve impulse has passed along the neuron, the sodium ions are actively (requiring energy) pumped out of the neuron.

All of these events happen very quickly. Neurons are ready to conduct another nerve impulse after just one millisecond! This short rest period is called the **refractory period,** and is when the nerve readies itself to conduct another nerve impulse.

Transmission of the nerve impulse

Transmission of nerve impulses occurs at **synapses**.

> A synapse is a structure where two neurons come into close contact so that a nerve impulse can be transmitted between the two neurons.

A synapse consists of a pre-synaptic neuron (axon terminal) and a post-synaptic neuron (dendrite) that are very close to each other. However, they do not touch. The gap in between the two neurons is called the **synaptic cleft** (Fig 39.4).

On average, each neuron in the human body has 1000 synapses! Considering that there are approximately 100 billion neurons in the average human nervous system, there are therefore, approximately 100 trillion synapses in an entire human nervous system!

Function of the synapse

- Synapses transmit nerve impulses from one neuron to another.
- They transmit nerve impulses from a neuron to an effector, such as a muscle.
- They control the direction of the impulse – preventing it from travelling backwards. In this way synapses act as valves.
- They act as junctions allowing a nerve impulse to be split up and travel along many different neurons or join together from a number of neurons into one neuron.

Activation of neurotransmitter

When a nerve impulse arrives at an axon terminal (of the pre-synaptic neuron), synaptic vesicles are stimulated to fuse with the cell membrane. This releases a **neurotransmitter** into the synaptic cleft (gap between neurons).

Examples of neurotransmitter substances include **acetylcholine, noradrenaline** and **dopamine.**

As already mentioned, neurotransmitters are chemicals that transfer the nerve impulse from one neuron to another.

The neurotransmitter travels the small distance across the synaptic cleft to the post-synaptic neuron (dendrite). It is received by protein receptors present on the cell membrane of the post-synaptic neuron. This causes a new nerve impulse to be set up – sodium ions begin to rush into the cell.

Inactivation of neurotransmitter

Once the nerve impulse has been transferred, the neurotransmitter is broken down in the synaptic cleft by special enzymes or can also be reabsorbed by a re-uptake pump in the cell membrane of the pre-synaptic neuron.

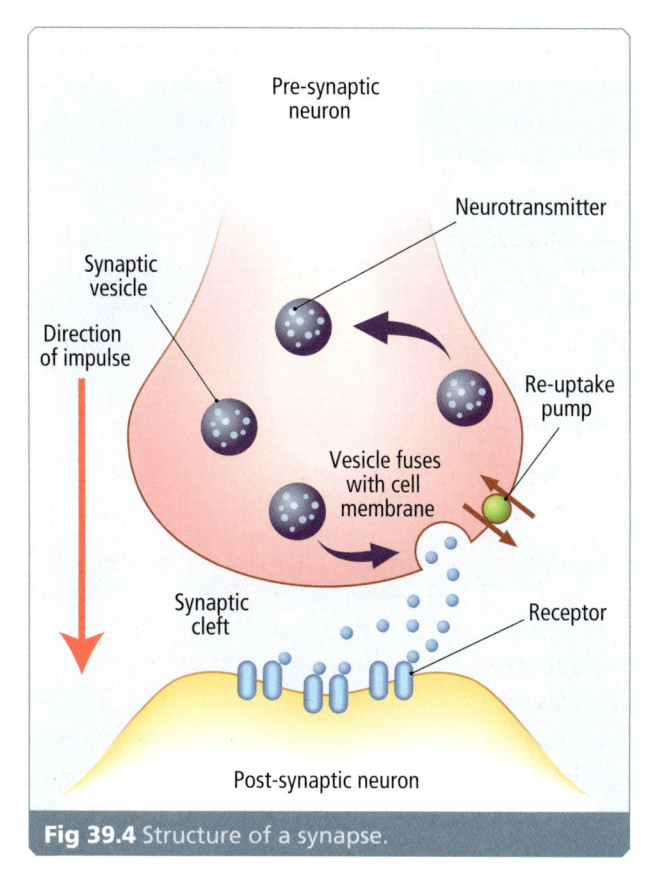

Fig 39.4 Structure of a synapse.

The senses

There are five senses: **sight; hearing; smell; taste** and **touch.** Each sense has its own specialised sense organ. The brain is the interpreting centre for all five senses.

1 Sight

The **eyes** are the sense organ of sight. Specifically, the **retina** is the sense organ that sends signals to the brain in response to light. Fig 39.5 shows the structure of the human eye.

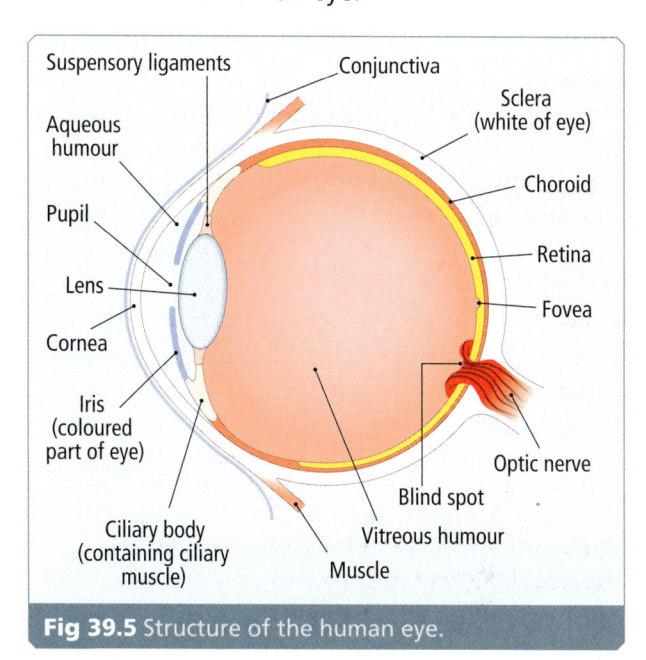

Fig 39.5 Structure of the human eye.

Functions of the parts of the eye

Conjunctiva

The conjunctiva covers the sclera and the cornea at the front of the eye. It produces a small amount of mucous, protecting the front of the eye by preventing entry of pathogens. Occasionally, the conjunctiva may become infected, a condition called conjunctivitis.

Cornea

The cornea is the transparent part of the sclera at the front of the eye. It protects the front of the eye; allows light into the eye; and refracts (bends) light slightly towards the lens.

Iris

The iris is the coloured part of the eye. It is a type of smooth muscle that can contract and relax, thereby controlling the amount of light entering the eye (Fig 39.6).

When the iris is contracted, the pupil is much smaller, letting less light into the eye. This happens in bright light.

When the iris is relaxed, the pupil is dilated (large), letting more light into the eye. This is the case in dark conditions.

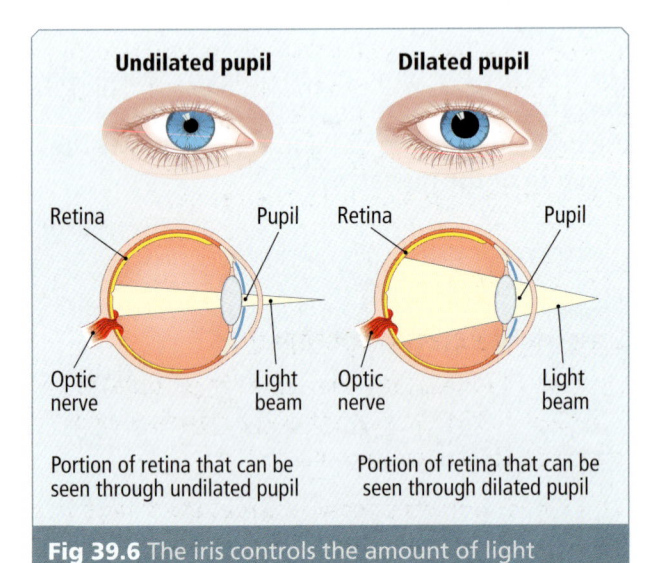

Fig 39.6 The iris controls the amount of light entering the eye.

Pupil

The pupil is a hole in the centre of the iris at the front of the eye. It lets light into the eye. Its size is controlled by the iris (Fig 39.6).

The pupil appears black in colour because light enters but does not leave the eye. The choroid layer inside the eye absorbs all the light entering.

Aqueous humour

The aqueous humour is a watery liquid present just inside the cornea that gives shape to the front of the eye. Sometimes the pressure of the aqueous humour can increase, causing damage to the eye, a condition known as glaucoma.

Vitreous humour

The vitreous humour is a viscous liquid that maintains the shape of the eyeball by maintaining an outward pressure on the sclera.

Ciliary body

The ciliary body (often referred to as the **ciliary muscle**) is a type of smooth muscle surrounding the lens. It contracts and relaxes, controlling the shape of the lens in a process known as **accommodation**.

- When the ciliary muscle is contracted, the lens becomes more convex (shorter and thicker). This has the effect of refracting (bending) incoming light rays more. When you are looking at close objects, the ciliary muscle is contracted (Fig 39.7).
- When the ciliary muscle is relaxed, the lens becomes less convex (thinner). This has the effect of refracting the incoming light rays less. When you are looking at distant objects, the ciliary muscle is relaxed (Fig 39.7).

The ciliary body is also responsible for producing the aqueous humour.

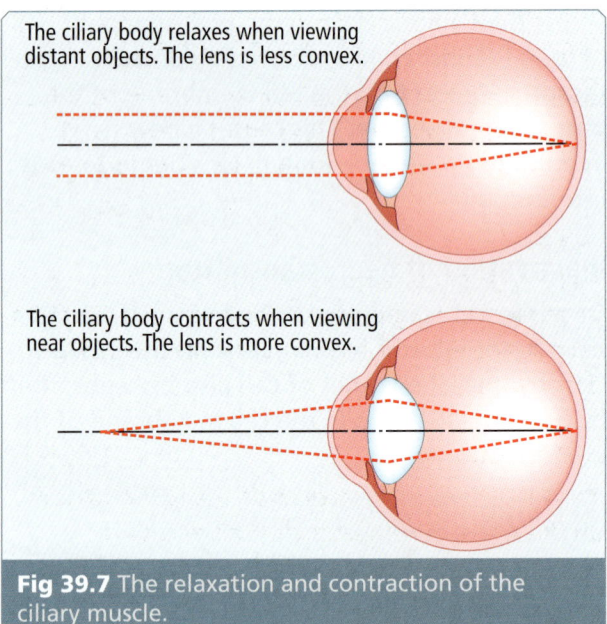

Fig 39.7 The relaxation and contraction of the ciliary muscle.

Suspensory ligament

The suspensory ligament attaches to and surrounds the ciliary body, providing a lever for the contraction of the ciliary muscle as well as holding the lens in place.

Lens

The lens is a transparent structure held in place by the ciliary muscle and suspensory ligament. It changes shape (called accommodation of the lens) in response to contraction and relaxation of the ciliary muscle (Fig 39.7).

Sclera

The sclera is the white of the eye. It covers the entire eye except for the transparent front part of the eye (cornea). It protects the eye and is the attachment surface for the external skeletal muscles that move the eye.

Choroid

The choroid is a heavily pigmented (with melanin) layer lying between the retina and sclera. It absorbs all light entering the eye. This helps to prevent internal reflection within the eye.

It also contains the blood vessels supplying the eye with nutrients and taking away wastes.

Retina

The retina is the light-sensitive structure of the eye. It contains light-sensitive cells called **rods** and **cones.**

Rods are sensitive to black and white light only. They are abundant all over the retina.

Cones are sensitive to colour (red, green and blue light) and are concentrated at the **fovea** of the retina – the position where light rays are focused.

Fovea

The fovea is the region of the retina where all the light rays converge. When you look directly at an object, the light rays from that object converge on your fovea.

Blind spot

The blind spot is the region of the retina where all the nerve fibres from the entire retina converge and exit the eyeball. There are no light-sensitive cells present on this region of the retina. All vertebrates have blind spots. However, marine invertebrate predators, such as the octopus, do not have a blind spot. There is no flaw on their retina.

The blind spot test helps to locate the blind spot (Fig 39.8).

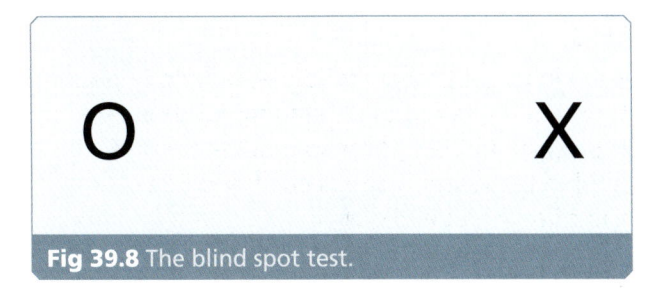

Fig 39.8 The blind spot test.

- To locate the blind spot in the left eye, cover the right eye and look at the 'X'. Move the head in or out until the 'O' disappears. At this point, the light from the 'O' is falling on the blind spot of the left eye.

- To find the blind spot in the right eye, cover the left eye and look at the 'O'. Move the head in or out until the 'X' disappears. At this point, the light from the 'X' is falling on the blind spot of the right eye.

Optic nerve

The optic nerve is a collection of sensory neurons that carry messages from the retina to the optic centre of the brain, called the **visual cortex.** This is the part of the brain responsible for interpreting messages from the retina.

Eye disorders

Long-sightedness (hyperopia)

Long-sightedness (also known as hyperopia) is an eye disorder where distant objects appear clear but near objects appear blurred.

When near objects appear blurred, the image is being focused behind the retina. It may be caused by the eyeball being too short or the focusing elements (ciliary body) being too weak.

Long-sightedness is corrected by placing convex lenses in front of the eyes (Fig 39.9).

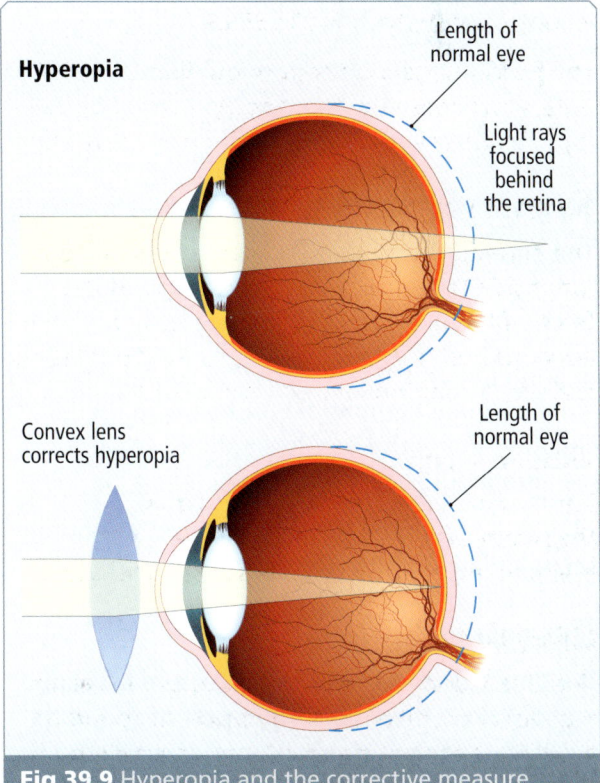

Fig 39.9 Hyperopia and the corrective measure (convex lens).

Short-sightedness (myopia)

Short-sightedness (also known as myopia) is an eye disorder where close objects appear clear but distant objects appear blurred.

When distant objects appear blurred, the image is being focused in front of the retina. It may be caused by the eyeball being too long or the focusing elements (ciliary body) being too strong.

Short-sightedness is corrected by placing concave lenses in front of the eyes (Fig 39.10).

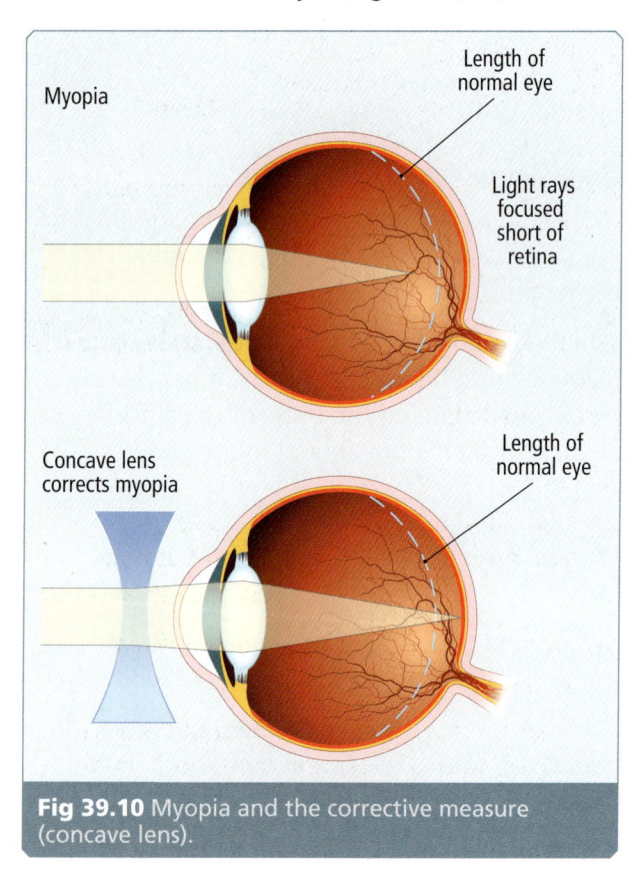

Fig 39.10 Myopia and the corrective measure (concave lens).

2 Hearing

Hearing involves the detection of sound. The **ears** are the organs responsible for **hearing.** The ear describes the entire auditory system, and not just the visible outer part of the ear.

The ear is composed of three sections: the **outer ear, middle ear** and **inner ear.**

Outer ear

The outer ear is exposed to the air and picks up sound waves. The visible outer part of the ear is called the **pinna.** It channels sound waves into the **auditory canal,** which in turn directs the sound waves towards the middle ear.

Middle ear

The blue section of Fig 39.11 is the middle ear. The middle ear is responsible for transferring sound waves on to the inner ear. The middle ear is filled with air and begins with the **eardrum** (also called the **tympanic membrane**). Sound waves enter the middle ear at the eardrum.

The eardrum vibrates in response to the sound waves it receives. It is connected to a series of **three** small bones called **ossicles.**

- The first bone is called the **hammer,** which is connected directly to the eardrum.
- The **anvil** and **stirrup** follow the hammer.

The ossicles are responsible for transferring vibrations on to the inner ear. They are capable of amplifying very soft sounds and dampening loud sounds.

The **Eustachian tube** is also part of the middle ear and is connected to the throat so that pressure differences between the outer and middle ear can be equalised through swallowing or yawning. This prevents stress and potential damage to the eardrum.

When we travel by air, the rapid increase in altitude creates a pressure difference between the outer ear and the middle ear. If you do not swallow, pressure builds up in the middle ear and can cause pain as the eardrum is being forced outwards. The pressure is equalised when the Eustachian tube (which is usually closed) opens with a small pop sound as we swallow.

Inner ear

The yellow section of Fig 39.11 is the inner ear. It functions in both hearing and balance.

The inner ear consists of the **cochlea** and the **vestibular apparatus.**

Cochlea

The cochlea (sensory organ of hearing) receives vibrations from the ossicles via the **oval window.** The oval window is an opening to the cochlea covered by a membrane. This membrane vibrates with the same frequency with which ossicles vibrate.

The cochlea is filled with lymph. Sound waves pass through the lymph and stimulate hair cells

Fig 39.11 The structure of the human ear.

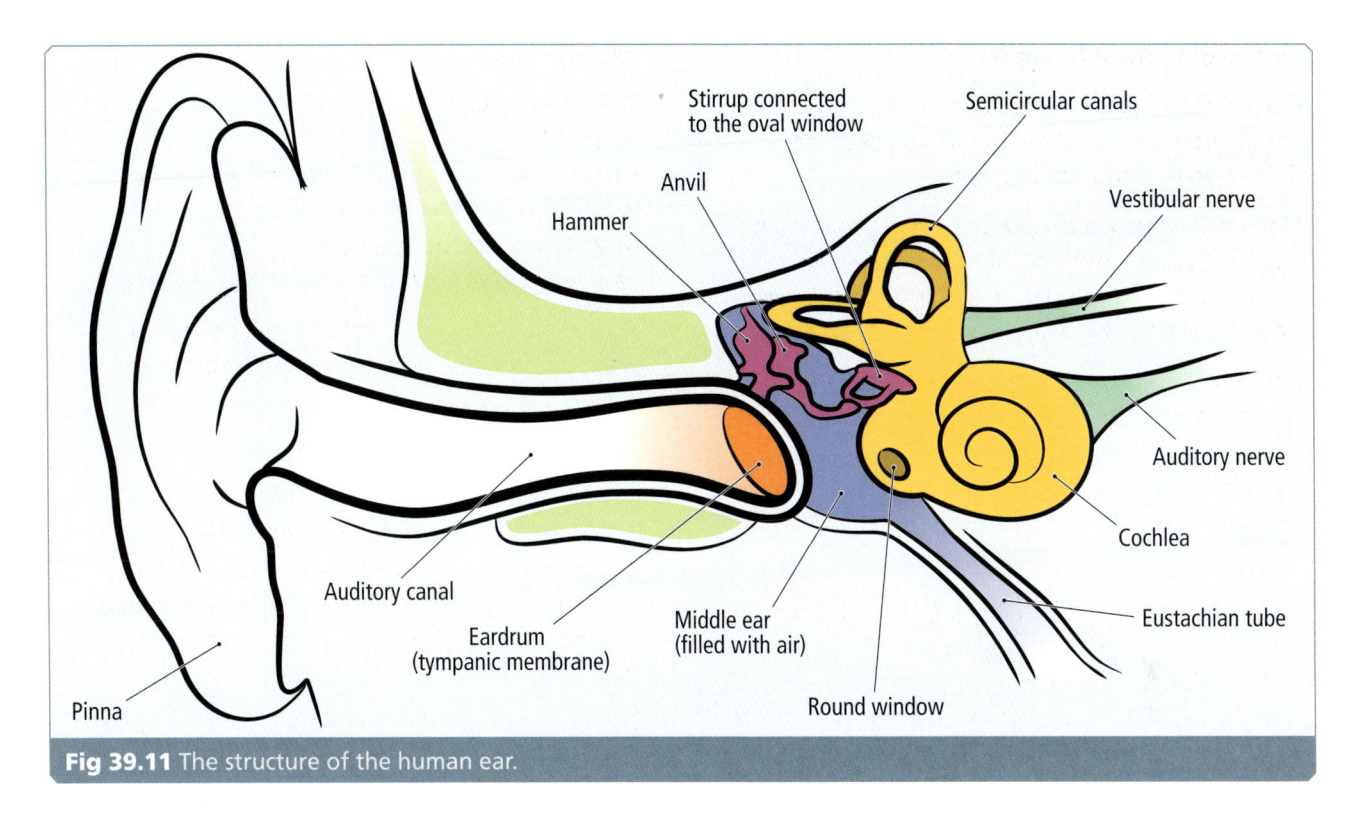

that line the inside of the cochlea. The hair cells sense vibrations within the lymph and produce electrochemical impulses.

The impulses are transferred on to the **auditory nerve,** which sends the messages to the brain for interpretation.

The **round window** is an opening in the cochlea into the middle ear. Lymph is kept within the cochlea by the round window membrane. The round window membrane vibrates with an opposite phase to the oval window. This means when the oval window vibrates in one direction, the round window vibrates in the opposite direction. This allows vibrations to be transferred throughout the lymph of the cochlea.

Vestibular apparatus

The **vestibular apparatus** is responsible for **balance,** another important function of the ear. The vestibular apparatus consists of **three semicircular canals** filled with lymph.

Each canal has hair cells lining its inner surface similar to the hair cells found in the cochlea. As the head moves, fluid moves through the semicircular canals stimulating the hair cells, which generate electrochemical impulses. These are sent to a part of the brain called the **cerebellum,** via the **vestibular nerve.**

Ear disorders

Glue ear

Glue ear (also known as *otitis media*) is inflammation of the middle ear and usually occurs with viral infections such as colds and flu.

Symptoms include pain in the ear, muffled hearing and pus formation.

Glue ear is most common in children because they have much shorter and more horizontal Eustachian tubes than adults.

Glue ear is usually treated using **ear drops** that contain decongestant drugs.

Occasionally, glue ear has to be treated by inserting a **grommet** in the eardrum to release the pressure within the middle ear. The grommet falls out as the eardrum heals itself.

> **NOTE** For Leaving Certificate Biology, you must learn **either** an ear disorder **or** long- and short-sightedness.

3 Smell

Smell is also known as the sense of **olfaction.** It is the ability of animals to sense odours. The nasal cavity is the organ involved in olfaction. It contains many cells responsible for sensing

Fig 39.12 Olfaction – the sense of smell.

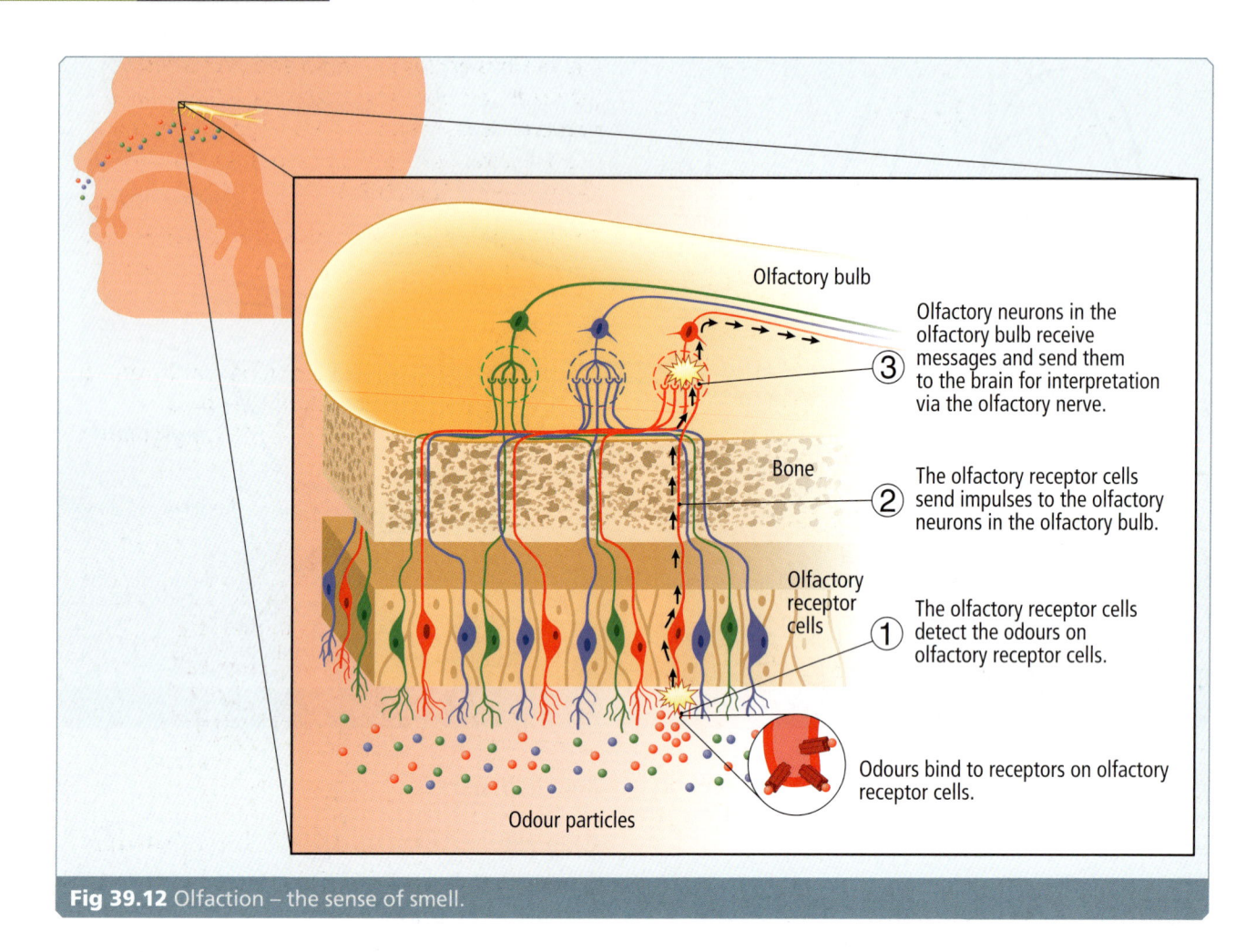

odours. Humans have approximately 40 million of these **olfactory receptor cells.** They are capable of detecting up to 10,000 different odours.

The olfactory receptor cells sense odours and transmit the messages in the form of electrochemical nerve impulses to the olfactory bulb at the top of the nasal cavity. The signals are then sent to the brain for interpretation via the **olfactory nerve.**

4 Taste

Taste is the sense associated with detecting flavours. We sense flavours via **taste buds** present on the upper surface of our tongues.

There are five basic tastes: **sweet, salt, bitter, sour** and **umami.**

Umami is a newly recognised savoury taste. Umami taste buds respond to a chemical called monosodium glutamate (MSG) – present in many foods (especially foods from southern Asia).

Recent research suggests that there is no definite tongue map of tastes – that taste buds for all five basic tastes are distributed relatively evenly over the upper surface of the tongue with no distinct patterns.

5 Touch

The **skin** (see Chapter 36) is the main organ system responsible for the sense of touch. There are touch receptors all over the skin, but their concentration varies. For example, the skin on the tips of the fingers has many touch receptors, whereas the skin of the back has relatively few.

The skin is also the organ system responsible for temperature and pain sensations. You do not need to know the names of these receptors for the Leaving Certificate Biology course.

The sense of touch is controlled by a part of the brain called the **somatosensory cortex.** All touch sensory information is sent from the skin to this area of the brain for interpretation.

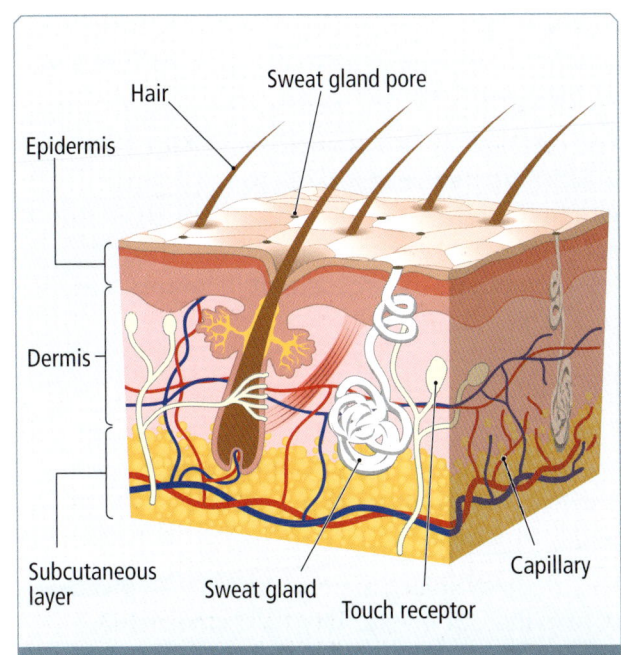

Fig 39.13 The structure of the human skin – the organ system responsible for touch, temperature and pain sensations.

The central nervous system

The brain

The human brain is the most complex organ in the body. It is the centre of the nervous system, where all nervous processes are interpreted and integrated.

The human brain is about 1.5 kg in mass and contains between 80 and 120 billion neurons.

All vertebrate, and most invertebrate, animals have a brain. However, the human brain is unique in its ability to reason, problem solve, imagine, generate language, memorise and be self-conscious.

Despite rapid advances in biology over the past few decades, we still know very little about our own brains.

- How do the 100 billion neurons interact in such a way as to enable humans to be self-conscious?
- Why do some people develop devastating brain diseases such as Alzheimer's and Parkinson's disease, whereas others are unaffected?

Scientists are tirelessly working to solve these problems.

The brain is enclosed within and protected by the skull. It is also surrounded by a triple layer of membranes called the **meninges**. Between the membranes of the meninges is a fluid, called **cerebrospinal fluid (CSF)**.

The function of the meninges and cerebrospinal fluid is protection of the brain and spinal cord.

Structure of the brain

The brain is composed of a number of different sections: **cerebrum, cerebellum; medulla oblongata; hypothalamus** and **pituitary gland** (Fig 39.14).

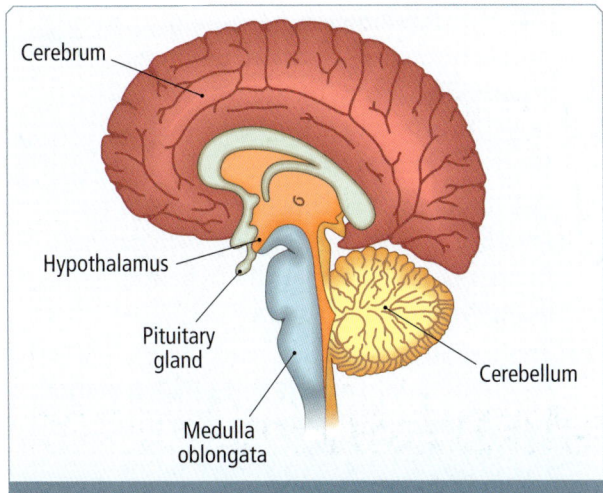

Fig 39.14 The structure of the human brain (transverse section).

Cerebrum

The cerebrum is the largest area of the brain. It is composed of two symmetrical hemispheres, called the left and right hemispheres.

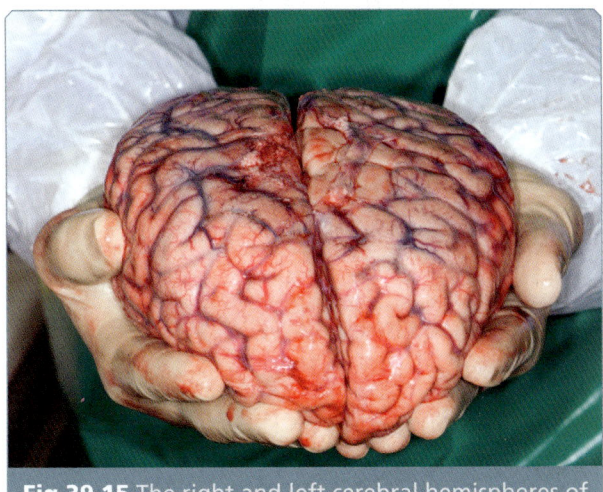

Fig 39.15 The right and left cerebral hemispheres of the human brain.

The left cerebral hemisphere controls the right side of the body and the right cerebral hemisphere controls the left side of the body.

The cerebrum has a highly folded surface. This enables a greater surface area for neurons.

The cerebrum can also be divided into four cerebral lobes: **frontal** lobe, **temporal** lobe, **parietal** lobe and **occipital** lobe. Each lobe has specific brain functions.

- The frontal lobe is much more highly developed in humans than in other animal species. It is involved in higher mental functions, such as **reasoning, short-term memory, intelligence, personality, planning, problem solving, emotion, language** and **social skills**. A part of the frontal lobe called the motor cortex (see Fig 39.16) functions in **movement**.
- The temporal lobe functions in **long-term memory, speech** and **hearing**. The part of the temporal lobe involved in hearing is called the auditory cortex.
- The somatosensory cortex of the parietal lobe functions in **movement** and **sensing stimuli**, such as **touch** and **body position**.
- The occipital lobe (also known as the occipital cortex) functions primarily in **vision**.

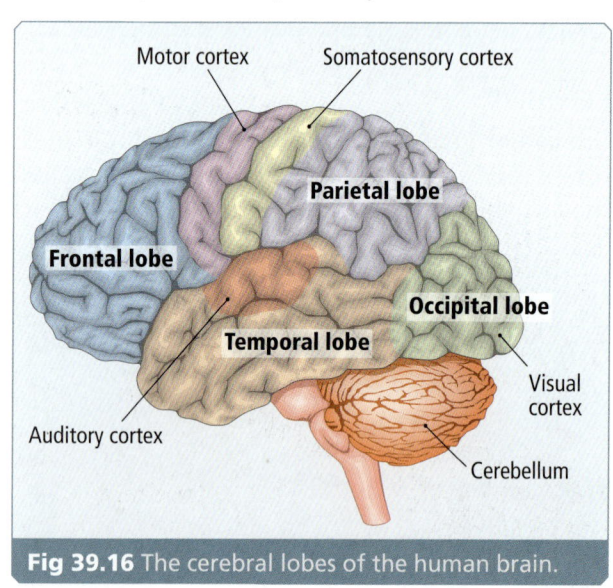

Fig 39.16 The cerebral lobes of the human brain.

Cerebellum

The cerebellum is located at the back of the head below the occipital lobe of the **cerebrum** (Fig 39.16). It is involved in the **control and coordination of movements**. The cerebellum is involved in the fine tuning of movement rather than initiating movement (which is the function of the cerebrum).

The cerebellum also plays an important role in **learning new motor tasks** to the point where the task is carried out without conscious control (involuntary motor control). This learning occurs to large extent in infants, but can also occur in adults.

Medulla oblongata

The medulla oblongata belongs to a part of the brain called the **brainstem**. The brainstem is a very important region involved in basic bodily functions.

The medulla oblongata is specifically involved in carrying out involuntary functions such as **breathing, heart rate, blood pressure, vomiting, coughing, sneezing** and **swallowing**.

Hypothalamus

The hypothalamus is a small region of the brain (roughly the size of an almond) located just below a structure called the thalamus and just above the brainstem.

The hypothalamus is responsible for linking the brain with the endocrine system, in conjunction with the pituitary gland (see below).

It secretes neurohormones, such as **growth hormone-releasing hormone** and **thyrotropin-releasing hormone** (see Chapter 38), which control the pituitary gland.

The hypothalamus is also responsible for controlling **body temperature, hunger** and **thirst**.

Pituitary gland

The pituitary gland is technically not part of the brain but is the link between the brain and the endocrine system.

The pituitary gland releases many hormones such as **growth hormone, thyroid-stimulating hormone** and many more (see Chapters 38 and 41).

Nervous system disorder

> **NOTE** For Leaving Certificate Biology, you must be able to state one possible cause, prevention and treatment for Parkinson's disease or paralysis. The following account is for Parkinson's disease.

Parkinson's disease

Cause and symptoms

Parkinson's disease is a degenerative nervous system disease. Symptoms include shaking and trembling of the hands and legs; a stiff and rigid body; difficulty walking; and a fixed stare. The disease occurs due to death of a specific group of neurons in an area of the brain called the *substantia nigra*.

These neurons are responsible for producing the neurotransmitter **dopamine**, which helps to control muscular movement and coordination. Patients with Parkinson's disease lack dopamine and develop the symptoms of Parkinson's.

The reason for the death of these neurons is unknown. It is thought that Parkinson's may be caused by exposure to pesticides.

Prevention

As it is thought that Parkinson's may be caused by exposure to pesticides, it is important to wear protective clothing, such as a mask, if using pesticides. We should also wash all fruit and vegetables thoroughly before eating.

Treatment

Parkinson's disease is treated with physiotherapy and exercises, as well as drugs, such as **levodopa**, that mimic the effect of dopamine in the brain.

Spinal cord

The spinal cord is a long (approximately 44 cm) bundle of nerve fibres that begins at the bottom of the brainstem and continues down through the centre of the back. It is covered by the meninges and bathed in cerebrospinal fluid for protection. It is almost fully enclosed within the vertebral column (*see* Chapter 40).

The spinal cord is responsible for carrying messages to and from the brain. There are 31 pairs (one on each side) of spinal nerves that leave the spinal cord. Each carries messages to and from a particular area of the body.

Just before entering the spinal cord, each spinal nerve divides into a **dorsal root** and **ventral root**. Dorsal refers to the back side and ventral refers to the front of the body. Each dorsal root has a **dorsal root ganglion,** which contains the cell bodies of sensory neurons.

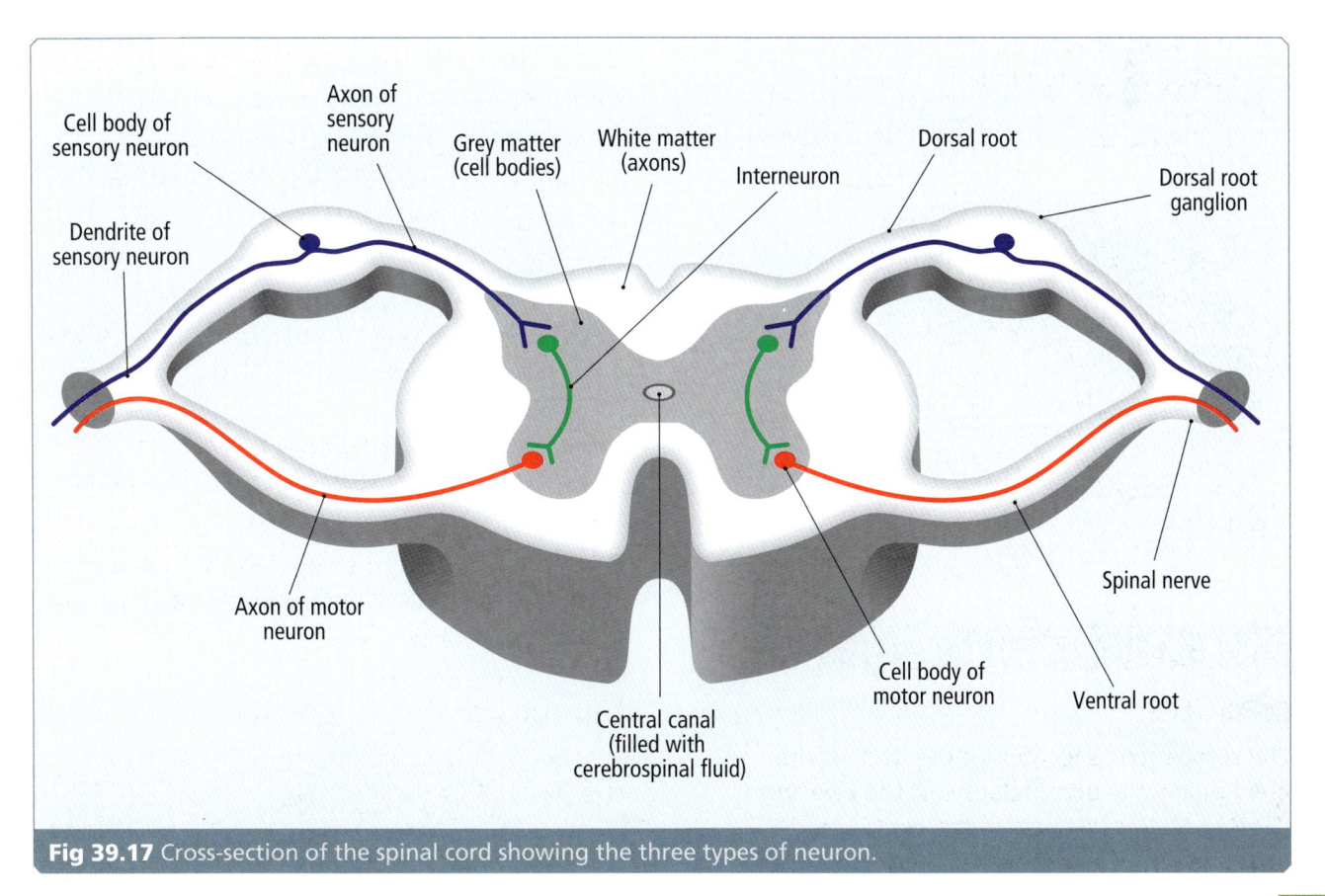

Fig 39.17 Cross-section of the spinal cord showing the three types of neuron.

Dorsal roots carry sensory neurons into the spinal cord, and ventral roots carry the axons of motor neurons away from the spinal cord.

The dorsal and ventral roots, along with the 31 pairs of spinal nerves emanating from the spinal cord, mark the beginning of the peripheral nervous system.

Fig 39.17 shows a cross-section through the spinal cord. The outer region of the cord is made up of **white matter.** White matter contains mostly axons that are covered in myelin sheath. This gives the matter its white appearance.

The inner region of the spinal cord is called **grey matter.** Grey matter contains mostly cell bodies and dendrites. This region appears a darker grey-brown colour because of the presence of capillaries.

Interneurons are present in the grey matter of the spinal cord. They are responsible for relaying messages from sensory neurons to motor neurons. In this capacity they function in reflex actions (see below). They also carry messages from sensory neurons to the brain.

The **central canal** is in the centre of the grey matter. It is filled with **cerebrospinal fluid** that is continuous throughout the spinal cord and is connected to the cerebrospinal fluid cavities of the brain.

Reflex action

> **Reflex actions** are involuntary responses to stimuli.

Reflex actions are evolutionary adaptations to protect the body against injury or harm. They are carried out by **reflex arcs.** Most reflex arcs consist of a **sensory neuron,** an **interneuron** and a **motor neuron.**

There are also very simple reflex arcs, called monosynaptic reflex arcs, which consist of only a sensory neuron and a motor neuron. The knee jerk reflex is an example of a monosynaptic reflex arc.

A very common reflex is the withdrawal reflex – the pulling of a hand away from a hot object (Fig 39.18). This reflex involves temperature receptors in the skin sensing heat, and sending a signal to the spinal cord. This signal is received by an interneuron that synapses with two neurons.

- The first is a motor neuron, which carries a message to the skeletal muscles of the arm, which contract and pull the arm away from the hot object.
- The second is another interneuron that carries the sensation of touching a hot object to the brain.
- The brain interprets the message after the arm has been pulled away. This is why the pain occurs after you have pulled your arm away.

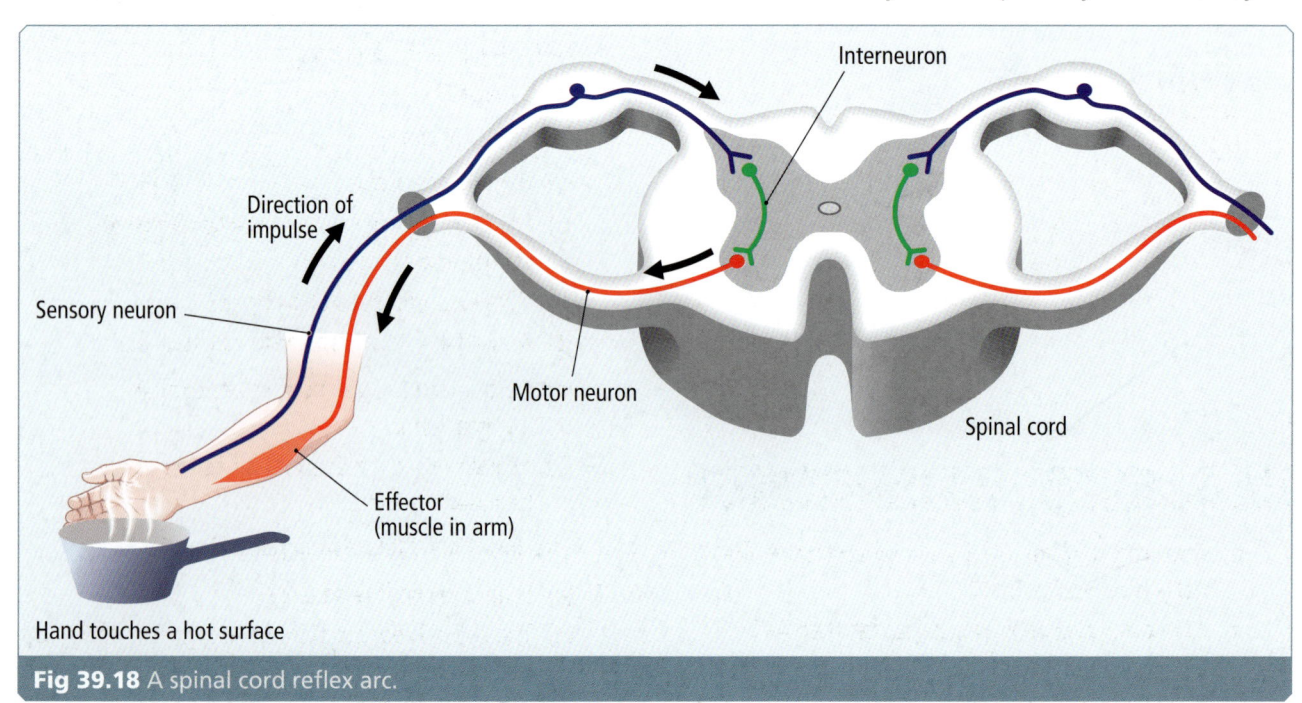

Fig 39.18 A spinal cord reflex arc.

Reflex actions occur very quickly – typically in just over one-tenth of a second.

Other less well-known reflex actions are: sneezing, shivering, blushing, accommodation of the lens to light hitting the retina, constriction of the iris in response to bright light, plantar reflex (curling of the toes when the bottom of the foot is touched), startle reflex, suckling reflex in babies and grasp reflex.

Comparison of the nervous system with the endocrine system

Both the nervous system and endocrine system involve the carrying of messages. It is useful to compare both systems in terms of their functions and how they carry out these functions.

	Endocrine system	Nervous system
Speed of response	Slow	Fast
Messages carried by	Chemical hormones	Electrochemical (ion movement)
Speed of transmission of message	Slow	Fast
Length of response	Long-lasting	Short-lived
Areas affected	Wide areas	Specific areas

Chapter 39 Questions

1. What are the **two** main parts of the nervous system?

2. (a) What is a *neuron*?
   (b) Name the **three** types of neuron and state the function of each type.
   (c) What type of neuron is shown in Fig 39.19 below?

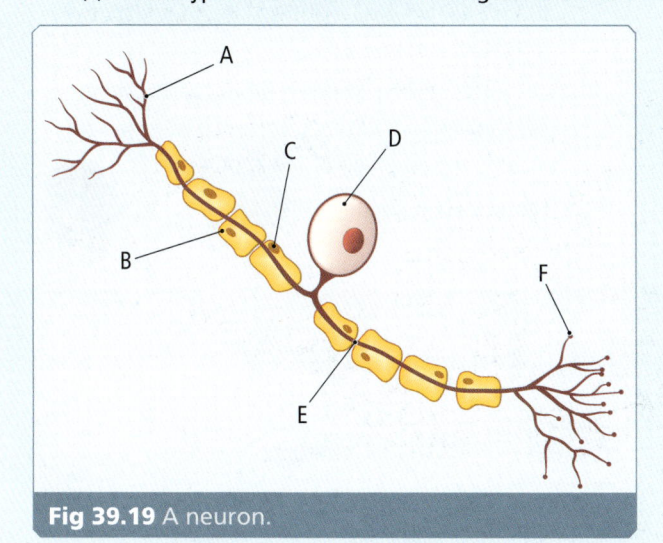

   Fig 39.19 A neuron.

   (d) Copy the diagram into your copy and name the parts labelled A – F.
   (e) Give **one** function for each part labelled A–F.
   (f) Indicate on your copy of the neuron the direction of the impulse.

3. Distinguish between:
   (a) *Dendrites* and *axon* terminals.
   (b) *Myelin sheath* and *Schwann cell*.
   (c) *Noradrenaline* and *adrenaline*. (Hint: see Chapter 38.)
   (d) *Pre-synaptic neuron* and *post-synaptic neuron*.

4. Define each of the following:
   (a) *Synapse*
   (b) *Synaptic cleft*
   (c) *Neurotransmitter*

5. (a) Using a diagram, describe the sequence of events at a synapse.
   (b) Give **two** functions of synapses.
   (c) Name **two** neurotransmitter substances.

6. (a) Explain how nerve impulses are carried along an axon.
   (b) Explain why there is a resting period between impulses.
   (c) How long is this resting period?

7. (a) What are the **five** senses?
   (b) The eye and ear are two sense organs associated with two of the five senses. Name the other **three** sense organs and their associated senses.

Unit 3   The Organism

8 (a) Draw the structure of the eye and label the following parts: *conjunctiva; cornea; iris; pupil; sclera; choroid; retina, lens; aqueous humour; vitreous humour;* and *ciliary body*.
   (b) Give **one** function of each part.
   (c) Distinguish between *myopia* and *hyperopia*.
   (d) Give the corrective measure for both myopia and hyperopia.

9 (a) Copy the following diagram of the human ear and label structures A–M.

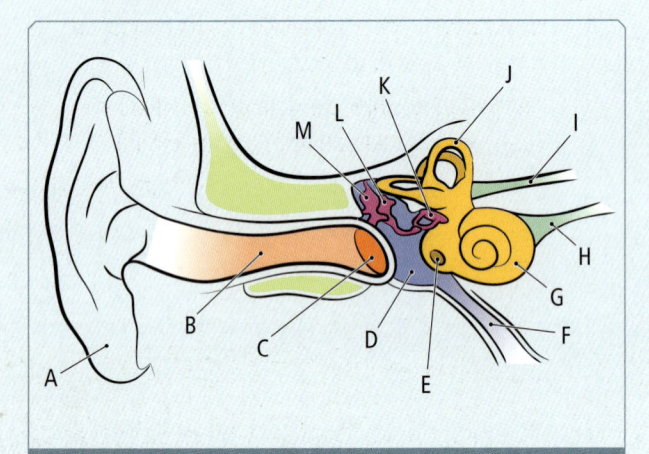

Fig 39.20 The structure of the human ear.

   (b) Give **one** function of each part.
   (c) Indicate, using the letter 'X', on the diagram the structures that contain lymph.
   (d) What is *glue ear* and how is it treated?

10 (a) Name **two** structures that function in protecting the brain.
   (b) The following diagram shows the main structures within the brain. Name structures labelled A–E and give **two** functions of **each** part.

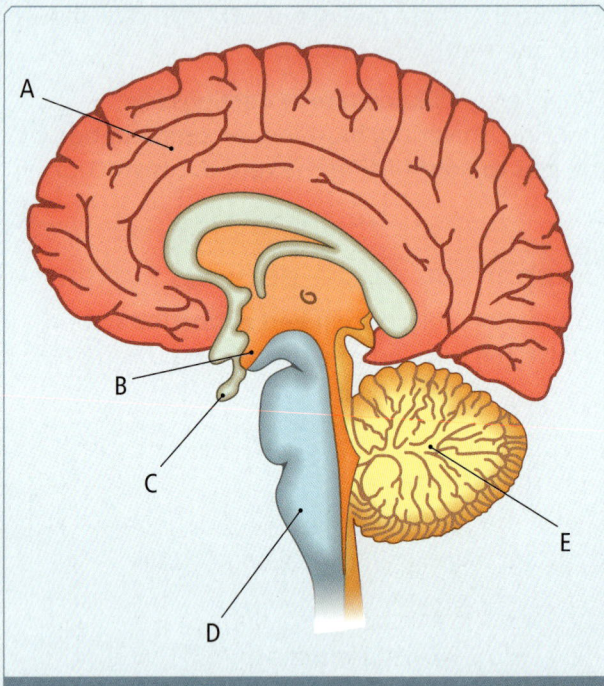

Fig 39.21 The structure of the human brain.

11 (a) Give **two** symptoms of Parkinson's disease.
   (b) What is the cause of Parkinson's disease?
   (c) Why is it difficult to prevent Parkinson's disease?
   (d) Give **one** precaution that might be taken to decrease the chances of developing Parkinson's disease.

12 (a) Draw a cross-section through the spinal cord and label the following parts: *white matter; grey matter; dorsal root; ventral root;* and *dorsal root ganglion*.
   (b) On your diagram, sketch a reflex arc including: *a sensory neuron, interneuron and motor neuron*. Include the direction of the impulse.
   (c) Name **two** common human reflexes.

Chapter 39 Sample examination questions

1 The diagram shows a vertical section through the human eye.
   (a) Name the parts labelled A, B, C.
   (b) Name the coloured part of the eye.
   (c) What is the function of the pupil in the eye?
   (d) In which labelled part would you find the rods and cones?
   (e) What is the function of the cones?

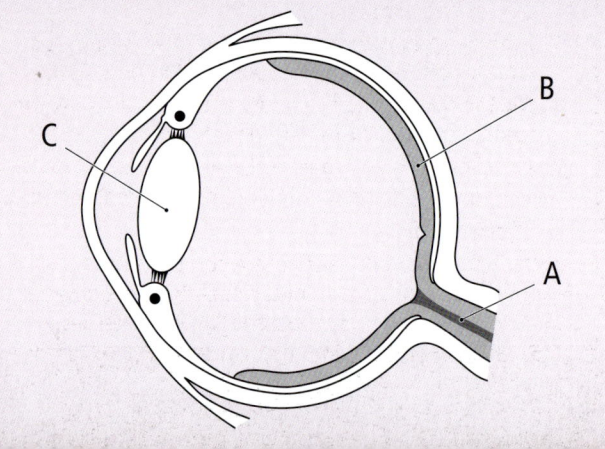

Section C, Question 6 Ordinary Level 2011

The human nervous system Chapter 39

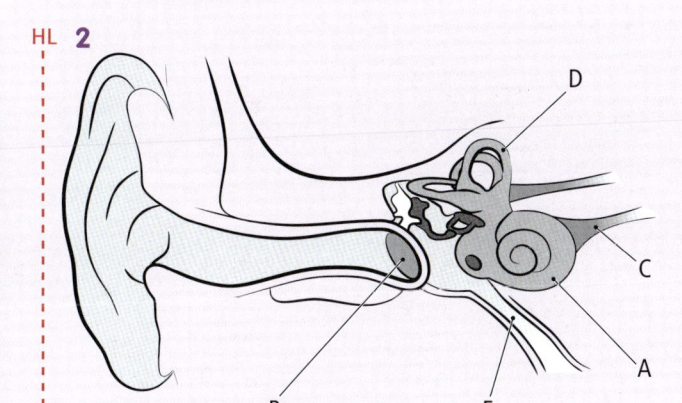

HL 2

(i) The diagram above shows the internal structure of the human ear.
1. Name the structures labelled A, B, C.
2. Give the functions of parts D and E.
3. Which letters denote the parts of the ear in which nerve impulses are generated?

(ii) In what part of *the eye* are nerve impulses generated?

(iii) Suggest **one** way by which the ear may be protected.

(iv) Explain how a corrective measure for a **named** defect of hearing **or** vision works.

Section C, Question 15 (a) Higher Level 2011

3 (i) Draw and label sufficient of two neurons to show a synaptic cleft.

(ii) Describe the sequence of events that allows an impulse to be transmitted across a synapse from one neuron to the next.

(iii) Suggest a possible role for a drug in relation to the events that you have outlined in (ii).

Section C, Question 15 (a) Higher Level 2004

Chapter 39 Mind map

The nervous system is responsible for sensing and responding to both the internal and external environment of an organism.

The **nervous system** is composed of the central nervous system (brain and spinal cord) and the peripheral nervous system (nerves and ganglia).

A **neuron** is a specialised nerve cell capable of transmitting electrochemical impulses from one nerve cell to another or to an effector.
- **Sensory neurons** carry impulses towards the central nervous system.
- **Interneurons** carry impulses from one neuron to another totally within the central nervous system.
- **Motor neurons** carry impulses from an interneuron (central nervous system) to an effector.
- An **effector** is an organ or tissue that carries out an action in response to a signal from the nervous system.

Structure of a neuron: neurons are composed of dendrites, cell body, axon, myelin sheath (formed by Schwann cells), axon terminals and synaptic vesicles.

Movement of a nerve impulse
- Nerve impulses are transmitted by movement of ions.
- Sodium ions rush into a neuron as a nerve impulse travels.
- The ions are actively pumped out again in preparation for conducting another nerve impulse.

Transmission of a nerve impulse
- A **synapse** is a structure where two neurons come into close contact so that a nerve impulse can be transmitted between the two neurons.
- A **neurotransmitter** is a chemical substance released by a neuron to transmit a nerve impulse to another neuron or effector. Examples of neurotransmitters are acetylcholine, noradrenaline and dopamine.
- Neurotransmitter is deactivated in the synaptic cleft by enzymes and/or reabsorbed into the pre-synaptic neuron.

Unit 3 — The Organism

The five senses

1. **Sight – the eye**
   - **Conjunctiva:** covers the sclera and the cornea at the front of the eye and functions in protection.
   - **Cornea:** the transparent part of the sclera at the front of the eye. It allows light into the eye.
   - **Iris:** the coloured part of the eye; contracts to control the amount of light entering the eye.
   - **Pupil:** a hole in the centre of the iris at the front of the eye; functions in letting light into the eye.
   - **Aqueous humour:** a watery liquid present just inside the cornea that gives shape to the front of the eye.
   - **Vitreous humour:** a viscous liquid that maintains the shape of the eyeball by maintaining an outward pressure on the sclera.
   - **Ciliary body:** a type of smooth muscle surrounding the lens; contracts and relaxes changing the shape of the lens in a process known as accommodation.
   - **Suspensory ligament:** attaches to and surrounds the ciliary body and holds the lens in place.
   - **Lens:** a transparent structure that focuses light onto the retina.
   - **Sclera:** the white of the eye. It covers the entire eye except for the cornea and functions in protection.
   - **Choroid:** a heavily pigmented (with melanin) layer lying between the retina and sclera; absorbs all light entering the eye helping to prevent internal reflection within the eye.
   - **Retina:** the light-sensitive structure of the eye containing light-sensitive cells called rods and cones. Rods are sensitive only to black and white light and cones are sensitive to colour (red, green and blue light).
   - **Fovea:** the region of the retina where all the light rays converge.
   - **Blind spot:** the region of the retina where all the nerve fibres from the retina converge and exit the eyeball. There are no light-sensitive cells on this part of the retina.
   - **Optic nerve:** a collection of sensory neurons that carry messages from the retina to the optic centre of the brain, called the visual cortex.
   - **Eye disorders**
     - **Long-sightedness (hyperopia):** near objects appear blurred. It is corrected by placing convex lenses in front of the eye.
     - **Short-sightedness (myopia):** distant objects appear blurred. It is corrected by placing concave lenses in front of the eye.

2. **Hearing – the ear** (the outer ear; middle ear; and inner ear)
   - **Outer ear:** picks up sound waves.
     - The visible outer part of the ear is the pinna. It channels sound waves into the auditory canal.
   - **Middle ear:** composed of the eardrum, three ossicles and the Eustachian tube. It is responsible for transferring sound waves to the inner ear. The middle ear is filled with air.
     - The eardrum vibrates in response to the sound waves it receives. The ossicles (hammer, anvil and stirrup) are attached to the eardrum and vibrate with the eardrum.
   - **Inner ear:** functions in both hearing and balance. The inner ear consists of the cochlea and the vestibular apparatus.
     - **Cochlea:** receives vibrations from the ossicles via the oval window. The cochlea is filled with lymph. Sound waves pass through the lymph and stimulate hair cells inside the cochlea and send a signal to the brain via the auditory nerve.
     - **Vestibular apparatus:** functions in balance. It consists of three semicircular canals filled with lymph. Each canal has hair cells lining its inner surface. As the head moves fluid moves through the semicircular canals stimulating the hair cells, which send signals to the brain via the vestibular nerve.
   - **Ear disorders – glue ear:** inflammation of the middle ear and occurs with viral infections such as colds and flu.
     - Symptoms include pain in the ear, muffled hearing and pus formation.
     - It is treated using ear drops that contain decongestant drugs.

3. **Smell – the nose**
   - The sense of smell is known as olfaction.
   - Olfactory receptor cells are responsible for sensing odours.
   - They then send a signal to the brain via the olfactory nerve.

4. **Taste – the tongue**
   - Taste buds sense the flavours in food.
   - There are five tastes: sweet, salt, bitter, sour and umami (savoury).

5. **Touch – the skin**
   - There are touch receptors all over the skin that function by sending a signal to the brain.

The human nervous system — Chapter 39

The central nervous system

1. The brain

- The brain is enclosed by the skull (protection). It is also surrounded by a triple layer of membranes called the meninges. Between the membranes of the meninges is a fluid, called cerebrospinal fluid (CSF).
- The brain is composed of a number of different sections: cerebrum; cerebellum; medulla oblongata; hypothalamus; and pituitary gland.
  - **Cerebrum:** divided into two cerebral hemispheres and functions in reasoning, memory, intelligence, personality, planning, problem solving, emotion, language and social skills.
  - **Cerebellum:** located at the back of the brain and functions in coordination of movements.
  - **Medulla oblongata:** located deep within the brain and functions in breathing, heart rate, blood pressure, vomiting, coughing, sneezing and swallowing.
  - **Hypothalamus:** located in the centre of the brain and functions in controlling body temperature, hunger and thirst and secreting some hormones that control the pituitary.
  - **Pituitary:** located just below the hypothalamus and functions in secreting growth hormone, thyroid-stimulating hormone and many others.
- **Parkinson's disease**
  - **Symptoms:** uncontrollable tremor of the arms and legs; a stiff and rigid body; difficulty walking; and fixed stare.
  - **Cause:** death of a specific group of neurons that produce dopamine.
  - **Prevention:** Parkinson's may be caused by exposure to pesticides. It is advisable to wear protective clothing if using pesticides and wash fruit and vegetables thoroughly.
  - **Treatment:** physiotherapy and exercises and drugs such as levodopa.

2. Spinal cord: responsible for carrying messages to and from the brain.

- Dorsal roots carry sensory neurons into the spinal cord; ventral roots carry the axons of motor neurons away from the spinal cord.
- Outer region of the cord is composed of white matter (axons).
- The inner region of the spinal cord is called grey matter (cell bodies and dendrites).

- **Reflex actions** are involuntary responses to stimuli.
- Withdrawal reflex: is the pulling away of a hand from a hot object.
- Temperature receptors in the skin send a signal to the spinal cord.
- This signal is received by an interneuron.
- A motor neuron is stimulated that sends a signal to a muscle that pulls the hand away.

Endocrine system versus nervous system

	Endocrine system	Nervous system
Speed of response	Slow	Fast
Messages carried by	Chemical hormones	Electrochemical (ion movement)
Speed of transmission of message	Slow	Fast
Length of response	Long-lasting	Short-lived
Areas affected	Wide effect	Local effect

Chapter 40 The human musculoskeletal system

Learning objectives After studying this chapter, you should be able to:
- Describe the structure and function of the skeleton.
- Describe the axial and appendicular skeletons.
- Describe the structure and functions of the parts of a long bone.
- Describe the types, locations and function of immovable, slightly movable and synovial joints.
- Describe the roles of cartilage and ligaments in joints.
- Describe the function of tendons in muscular system.
- Describe what an antagonistic muscle pair is and give an example.
- HL ▸ Describe the growth and development of bones.
- ▸ Describe the role of calcium, osteoblasts and osteoclasts in the structure of bone.

Introduction

The human musculoskeletal system consists of the skeleton and muscles (musculature) attached to the skeleton. The skeleton and muscles are structures of response. Muscles respond to electrical signals (nerve impulses) from the brain and spinal cord (see Chapter 39) and the skeleton responds to chemical signals from the endocrine system (see Chapter 38).

Most sources list the number of bones in the human skeleton as 206. However, some counting methods conclude that there are as many as 208 or even 213 bones. The differences arise when counting fused bones.

Functions of the human skeleton

The skeleton serves a number of important functions:

- **Shape:** The skeleton gives the body its functional shape.
- **Support:** The skeleton provides a rigid structure upon which many different tissues attach. This helps to keep various tissues and organs in their correct position within the body.

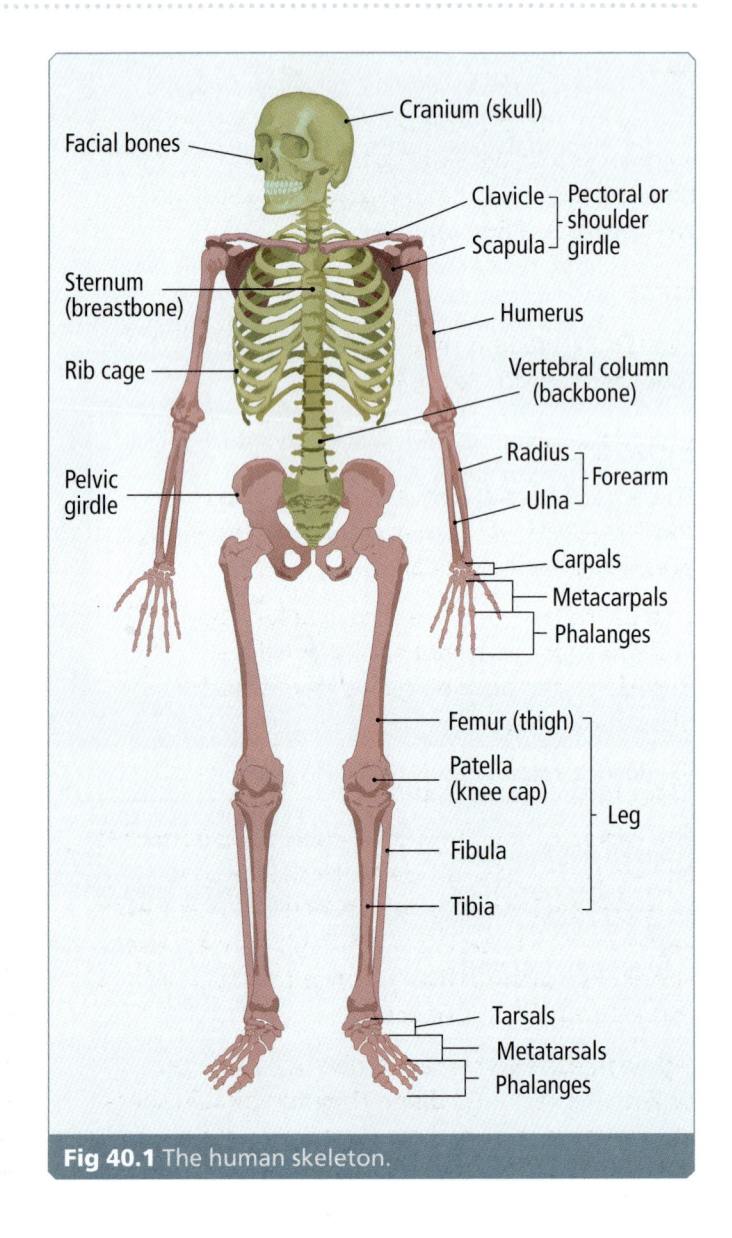

Fig 40.1 The human skeleton.

- **Movement:** The skeleton provides a rigid structure upon which muscles attach via tendons. The muscles use the bones of the skeleton as levers to create movement.
- **Protection:** The skeleton provides a very effective method of protecting the delicate internal organs of the body, such as the brain, spinal cord, heart and lungs.
- **Manufacture of blood cells:** The bone marrow of long bones such as the ribs, sternum and femur produce blood cells continuously.

Structure of the human skeleton

The human skeleton can be divided into the **axial skeleton** and the **appendicular skeleton**.

Axial skeleton

The axial skeleton (coloured green in Fig 40.1) is composed of the **skull (cranium), facial bones, vertebral column (spine), rib cage** and **sternum (breastbone).**

Skull

The skull is made from eight bones fused together. It **protects the brain.**

Facial bones

There are 14 facial bones (some fused and some freely movable joints) that protect the eyes, ears, nasal cavity and mouth.

One of the bones of the face is called the **mandible** (or **jaw bone**) and it functions in nutrition – the obtaining and mechanical digestion of food.

Vertebral column (spine)

The vertebral column is composed of 33 vertebrae (Fig 40.2). They are divided into five regions based on their shape and function: **cervical** (seven vertebrae); **thoracic** (12 vertebrae); **lumbar** (five vertebrae); **sacrum** (five fused vertebrae); and **coccyx** (four fused vertebrae).

Between each vertebra are discs of cartilage, called **intervertebral discs.** They function in shock absorption and also allow slight movement (**articulation**) between the vertebrae.

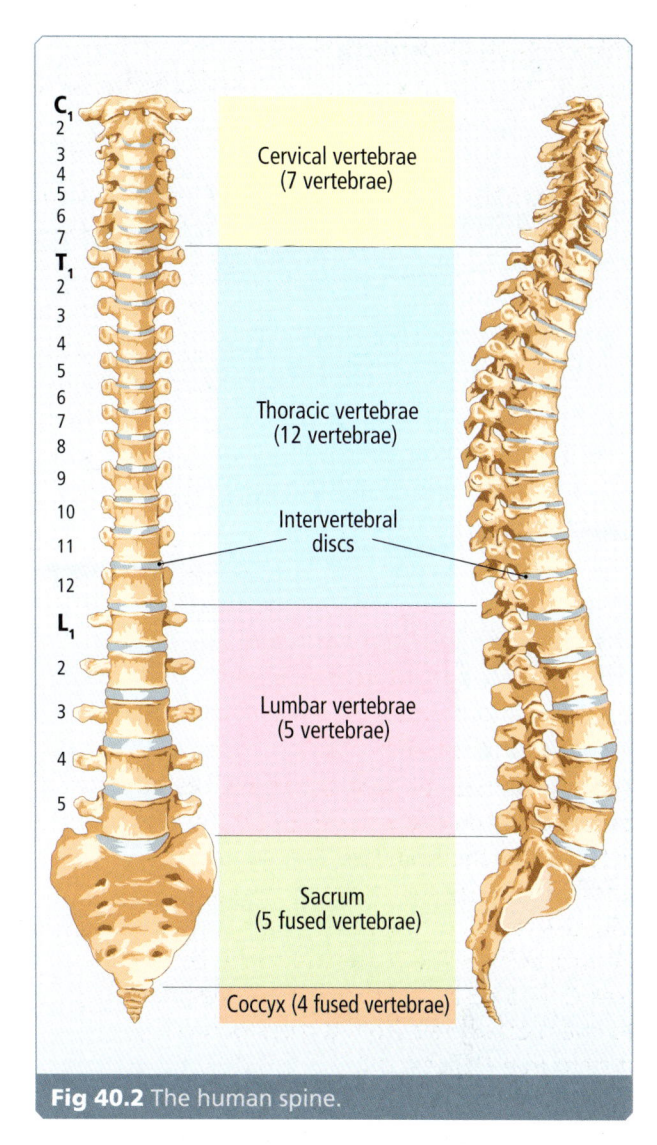

Fig 40.2 The human spine.

The lumbar vertebrae are the largest vertebrae as they have to withstand the most weight. Because of this, they are also the most commonly injured part of the spine. A disc between the lumbar vertebrae may bulge outwards pushing against a spinal nerve. This is called a **prolapsed disc,** or more often a 'slipped disc'. Spinal nerves leave the spinal cord very close to the vertebral discs. Pressure on a spinal nerve can result in pain, usually at the site of the disc. However, the pain can also appear to come from the leg as the spinal nerves from the lumbar vertebrae carry neurons to and from the legs.

The function of the vertebrae is to **support and give shape to the body; movement** (as muscles attach to the vertebrae); and **protection of the spinal cord** that runs through the centre of the vertebral column.

Unit 3 The Organism

Rib cage and sternum

The rib cage consists of 12 pairs of ribs (Fig 40.3). The ribs are all attached to the 12 thoracic vertebrae.

- The upper seven pairs of ribs are called **'true ribs'** because they directly attach to the sternum.
- The next three pairs are called **'false ribs'** because they are attached to the sternum via cartilage only.
- The final two pairs of ribs do not attach to the sternum at all and are called **'floating ribs'**.

The rib cage functions primarily in **breathing** (see Chapter 35). During inhalation (breathing in), the rib cage moves outwards and upwards. This occurs due to the **intercostal muscles** (between each rib) and the **diaphragm** contracting. This increases the volume of the chest cavity (thorax). During exhalation (breathing out), the intercostal muscles and diaphragm relax and the rib cage returns to its normal size.

The rib cage also has other important functions such as protection of the heart and lungs, and providing a framework for the attachment of the pectoral (shoulder) girdle.

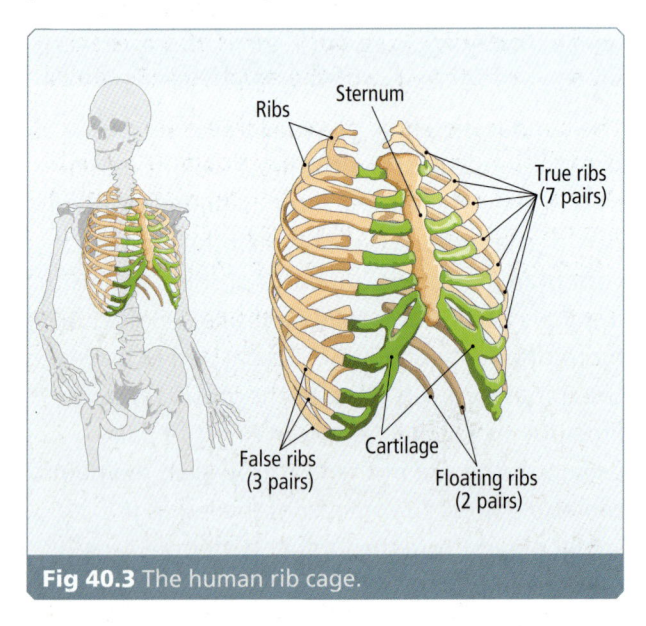

Fig 40.3 The human rib cage.

Appendicular skeleton

The appendicular skeleton (coloured purple in Fig 40.1) is composed of the **pectoral and pelvic girdles,** and **limbs**.

Pectoral (shoulder) girdle

The pectoral girdle consists of the **scapula (shoulder blade)** and **clavicle (collar bone)** and connects the upper arm to the axial skeleton (Fig 40.4). The pectoral girdles function in giving upper body mobility and strength.

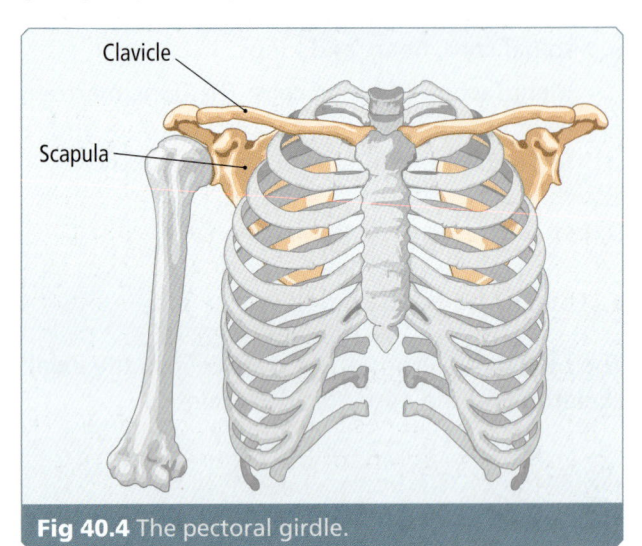

Fig 40.4 The pectoral girdle.

Pelvic (hip) girdle

The pelvic girdle consists of the **pelvis** (made up of three fused bones called **innominate** bones). The pelvis is connected to the sacrum (Fig 40.5).

The pelvic girdle gives strength and support to the body and also allows mobility of the lower limbs.

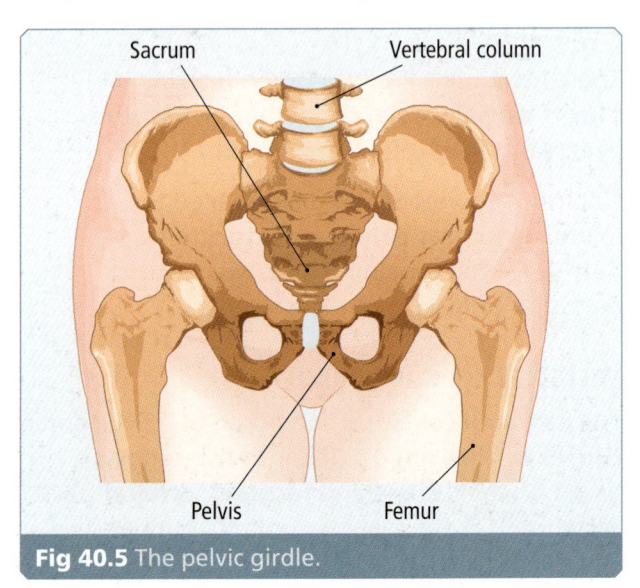

Fig 40.5 The pelvic girdle.

Limbs

The limbs (also known as **appendages**) consist of a total of 120 bones. There are 30 in each forelimb (arm, wrist and hand) and 30 in each leg.

The arm consists of the **humerus** in the upper arm and the **radius** and **ulna** in the forearm. The humerus is connected to the radius and ulna at a joint called the **elbow**. The radius is located on the thumb side and the ulna is on the 'little finger' side.

There are eight bones in the wrist, called **carpals**. They allow movement of the hand in relation to the forearm.

The five hand bones are called **metacarpals** and the 14 bones in the fingers are called **phalanges**.

The leg consists of the **femur** (thigh bone) in the upper leg and the **tibia** (shin bone) and **fibula** in the lower leg. The femur is the longest bone in the human body. The **patella (knee cap)** is located at the front of the knee in each leg. It functions in movement and protection.

There are seven bones in the ankle, called **tarsals**. They allow movement of the foot in relation to lower leg.

The five foot bones are called **metatarsals** and the 14 bones of the toes, similarly to the fingers, are called **phalanges**.

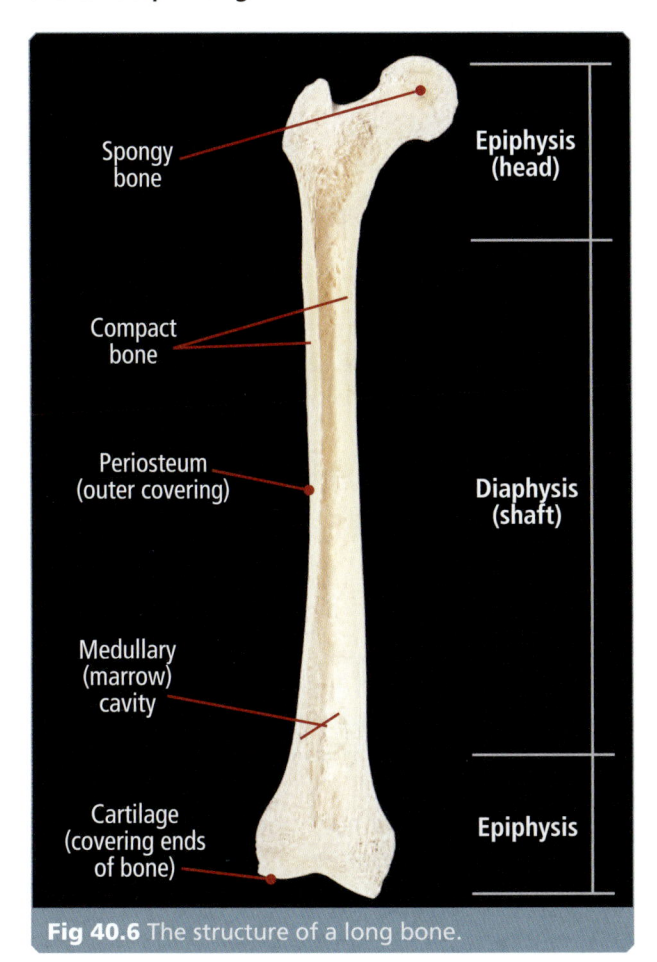

Fig 40.6 The structure of a long bone.

Structure of a long bone

A long bone is composed of a number of distinct regions: **periosteum, diaphysis, epiphysis, compact bone, spongy bone, medullary cavity (bone marrow)** and **cartilage**.

Periosteum

The periosteum is the outer covering of the bone. It contains nerve fibres and blood vessels. Ligaments and tendons attach to it.

Sometimes the periosteum can become inflamed (called periostitis) and can be very painful. Shin splints are a common example of periostitis.

Diaphysis

The diaphysis is the long, extended part of the bone (often called the shaft of the bone). It gives length and strength to the bone.

Epiphysis

The epiphysis is the head of the bone. In long bones there are two epiphyses. They enable movement (articulation) in a joint.

Compact bone

Compact bone is a type of dense connective tissue composed of calcium salts, magnesium salts and collagen fibres. Compact bone is located mostly in the diaphysis of the bone but is also present along the outer edge of the epiphyses (Fig 40.7).

The salts are secreted by bone cells present throughout the bone. They lay down new bone during growth and repair. Other types of bone cells are responsible for taking away the calcium salts when the body requires calcium in other areas.

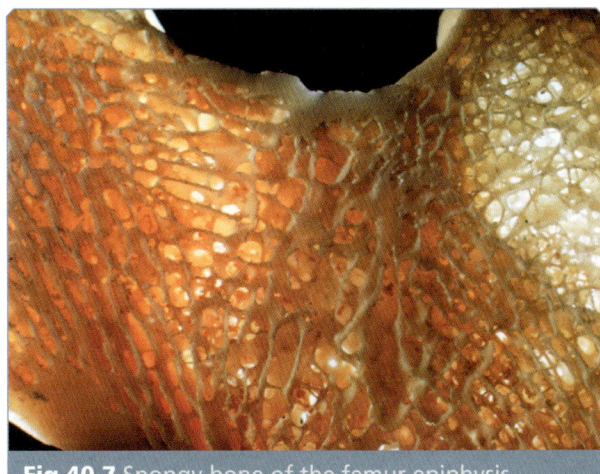

Fig 40.7 Spongy bone of the femur epiphysis.

Compact bone gives the bone its strength and rigidity. It is supplied by blood vessels and nerve fibres throughout its structure. This is why it is extremely painful to break a bone!

Spongy bone

Spongy bone looks much like a sponge when viewed under a microscope, hence its name. It is composed of bony bars and plates separated by irregular-shaped spaces (Fig 40.7).

Spongy bone is located mostly in the epiphyses of long bones. Bone marrow tissue (see below) can be found in the spaces of spongy bone.

Spongy bone provides support, strength and rigidity to the bone.

Medullary cavity (bone marrow)

The medullary cavity is more commonly known as the **bone marrow** (Fig 40.6). It is composed of two regions: **red marrow** and **yellow marrow.**

- Red marrow is where blood cells – such as red blood cells, white blood cells and platelets – are produced. It is found in the diaphysis and epiphyses. It is stimulated to produce red blood cells by erythropoietin (EPO), which is a hormone secreted by the kidneys.
- Yellow marrow is composed of adipose tissue for the storage of lipid. Yellow marrow can be converted to red marrow if needed.

Cartilage

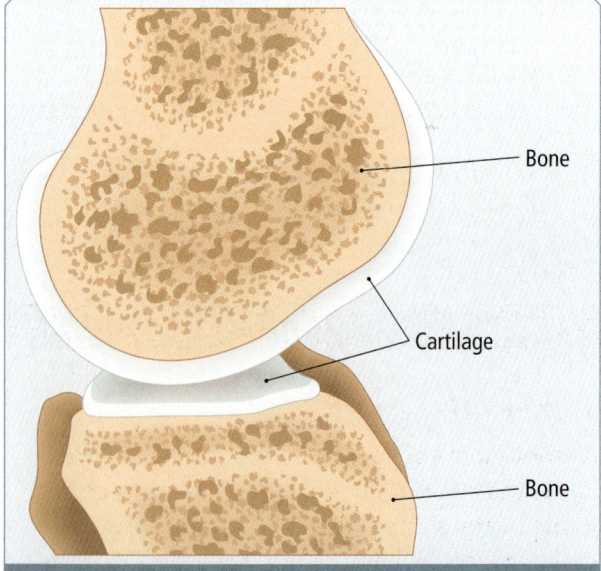

Fig 40.8 Cartilage is a flexible tissue present on the ends of bones.

Cartilage covers the ends of bones (Fig 40.8). It functions in shock absorption and provides a surface of contact with other bones, helping to provide friction-free movement. Cartilage is also found in other areas of the body such as the bronchi of the lungs (rings of cartilage), ears and nose.

Cartilage is a flexible tissue, made of collagen fibres. Cartilage is a unique tissue in that it does not have a blood supply. Therefore, if damaged, it heals extremely slowly if at all.

HL Development, growth and renewal of bone

Bone is a type of connective tissue that is living. As already mentioned, it is composed of collagen and has a blood and nerve supply. It also has living cells throughout its structure. As a result, if bone is damaged it can be repaired quite efficiently.

The cells present in bone are called **osteoblasts** and **osteoclasts.**

> **Osteoblasts** produce and lay down new bone.
> **Osteoclasts** digest and remove old bone.

Bone development

Bone development involves the conversion of cartilage to bone. In the foetus (unborn child), the skeleton is made of cartilage. As the foetus grows and develops, the cartilage is slowly converted to bone in a process called **ossification.**

> **Ossification** is the process of laying down new bone material by osteoblasts.

Bone growth

In children and adolescents, bone growth and development continue. A part of the bone of children remains in the form of cartilage to allow for increases in length. This region of cartilage, called the **growth plate** (Fig 40.9A and B), is present at the ends of each bone between the epiphyses and the diaphysis.

Towards the end of adolescence, the growth plates disappear through the process of ossification. Once the growth plates have disappeared, the bone cannot grow any longer and the individual has stopped increasing in height.

However, it is important to note that the diameter of the bone can still increase – and as a person ages their bones become thicker.

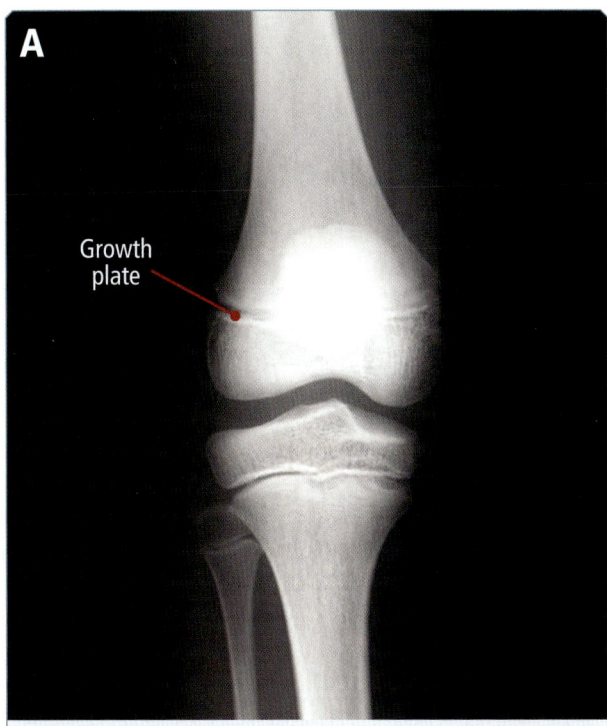

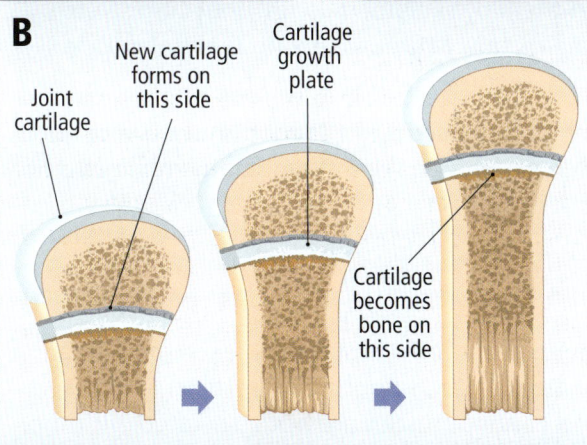

Fig 40.9 Growth plates in a child's bones. X-ray showing growth plates in the femur, tibia **(A)**; diagram showing the lengthening of a bone **(B)**.

Bone renewal

Throughout life, bone continues to be renewed. It is continually being broken down by osteoclasts and replaced by osteoblasts. However, this process is very slow due to the solid nature of bone.

Stress to the bones, through weight-bearing physical exercises or through injury, results in bone renewal. However, the bone will be laid down thicker than it was before the stress. This is called **bone remodelling.**

Bone renewal also depends on the diet and hormone levels within the body.

- Parathormone, a hormone released by the parathyroid glands, is responsible for removal of calcium from the bone. It does this by stimulating osteoclasts.
- Calcium-rich foods such as dairy products are very important for the maintenance of healthy bones. Without calcium in the diet, the bone will slowly become weaker due to calcium being removed from the bones by osteoclasts.

Joints

A **joint** is the location where two or more bones make contact.

Classification of joints

Joints can be classified based on structure and function: **immovable joints, slightly movable joints** and **freely-movable (synovial) joints.**

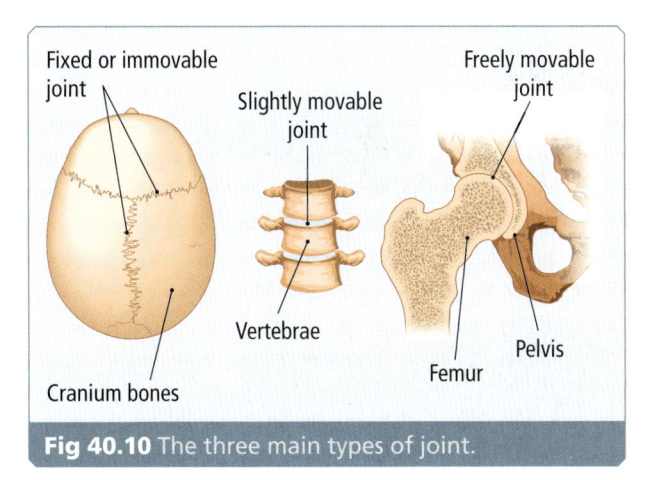

Fig 40.10 The three main types of joint.

1. Immovable joints

As their name suggests, immovable joints are joints that do not allow movement, such as the joints of the skull. There are eight bones that make up the skull (cranium). They fuse together in the first year of life forming a very strong bone that is responsible for protecting the brain.

2. Slightly movable joints

Slightly-movable joints permit a small amount of movement between the bones that make up the joint. Examples include the joints between each of the vertebrae of the spine; the joints between the ribs and the sternum; and the joints between the ribs and each of the 12 thoracic vertebrae.

The bones are held together strongly and rigidly by ligaments and also by the muscles surrounding the joints.

3. Freely movable joints

Freely movable joints are also known as synovial joints due to the presence of **synovial fluid** in the joint cavity. Synovial fluid allows greater friction-free movement. Synovial fluid is secreted by the **synovial membrane** that surrounds the joint. The entire joint is enclosed within a **fibrous capsule**.

The ends of the bones that make up synovial joints are covered in a thin layer of **cartilage**. This provides shock absorption and also contributes to the friction-free movement of the joint.

The bones are held together and the whole joint kept stable by ligaments and, to a lesser extent, the muscles surrounding the joint.

There are two main types of synovial joints: **hinge joints** and **ball-and-socket joints**.
- Examples of hinge joints include the elbow and knee.
- Examples of ball-and-socket joints include the hip and shoulder joints.

Synovial joints are the most common type of joint in the human skeleton. Fig 40.11 shows the structure of a typical synovial joint.

Ligaments and tendons

> **Ligaments** join bone to bone to form a joint.

Ligaments are a type of connective tissue composed of collagen fibres. They are very strong and are capable of withstanding huge stresses. Ligaments keep joints stable and prevent excessive movement in a joint.

Ligaments are slightly elastic. They can be stretched and will return to their original size and length. However, this is only the case up to a point. If a ligament is stretched too much it can tear or rupture.

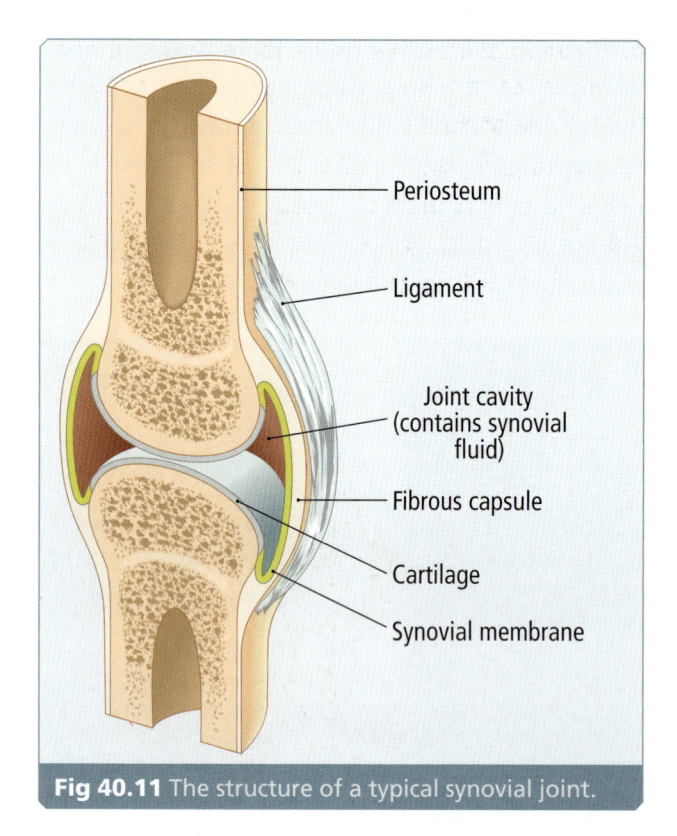

Fig 40.11 The structure of a typical synovial joint.

> **Tendons** join muscle to bone.

Tendons are also a type of connective tissue composed of collagen. They are also very strong, capable of withstanding the extreme forces put on them by skeletal muscles. They also stretch to a certain degree, allowing skeletal muscle contraction to be more forceful.

Neither ligaments nor tendons have a very good blood supply, making them relatively slow to heal if damaged.

Muscles

There are three types of muscles in the human body: **skeletal, smooth,** and **cardiac.** Smooth and cardiac muscles are not associated with the skeleton. This chapter describes skeletal muscle.

Skeletal muscle

Skeletal muscles are also known as **striated muscles.** This is because under the light microscope, narrow light and dark bands, called **striations,** can be seen along a muscle cell.

Skeletal muscle is composed of muscle fibre cells that are filled with contractile proteins called **actin** and **myosin**. Skeletal muscle is under voluntary control – meaning that we can control them consciously.

There are 640 skeletal muscles in the human body, each with their own distinct function! They are connected to bones via tendons. The bones act as levers during contraction.

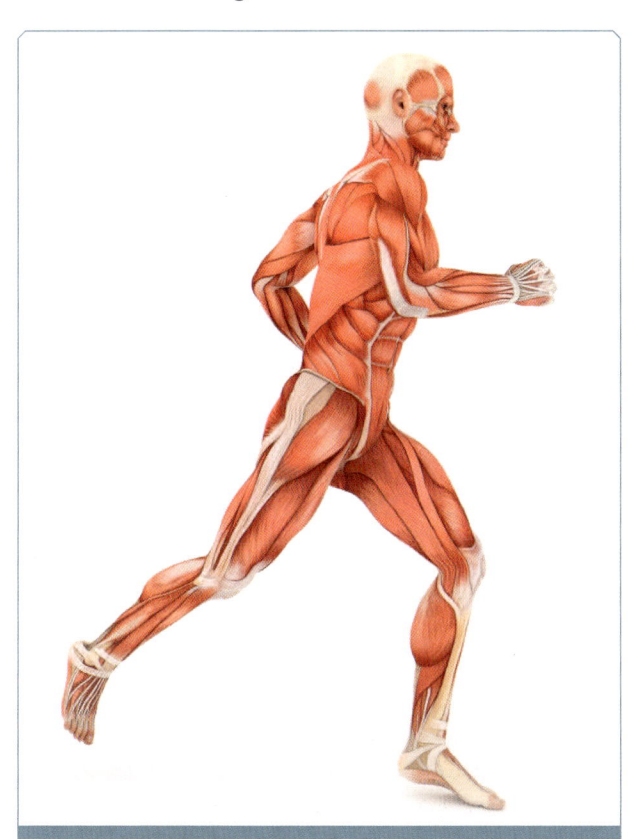

Fig 40.12 The skeletal muscle of the human body.

Skeletal muscles usually exist in pairs called **antagonistic muscle pairs**.

> **Antagonistic muscle** pairs are composed of two muscles that have opposite effects to each other.

The most commonly used example of an antagonistic muscle pair is the **biceps** and **triceps**.

- The biceps is located on the inside of the arm and is called the **flexor** – because it flexes the arm and closes the joint (elbow).
- The triceps is located on the outside or back of the arm and is called the **extensor** – because it extends the arm or opens the joint (elbow).

One important characteristic of antagonistic muscle pairs is that when one muscle of the pair is contracting the other is relaxing.

Disorders of the musculoskeletal system

> **NOTE** For Leaving Certificate Biology, you have to learn one disorder of the musculoskeletal system only.

Arthritis

Arthritis is inflammation of a joint of the skeletal system. There are two types of arthritis: **osteoarthritis** and **rheumatoid arthritis.**

Osteoarthritis

Osteoarthritis is a degenerative (gets steadily worse) disease that is more common in older people. It is caused by wear and tear of the joints over many years. The cartilage becomes worn down, and the bone eventually becomes exposed and damaged. This leads to a build-up of fluid in the joint (Fig 40.13).

Symptoms include pain and swelling in the joint. The ability to move the affected joint is also usually reduced.

Serious injury to the joint early in life can lead to early osteoarthritis. There may also be a genetic component to osteoarthritis.

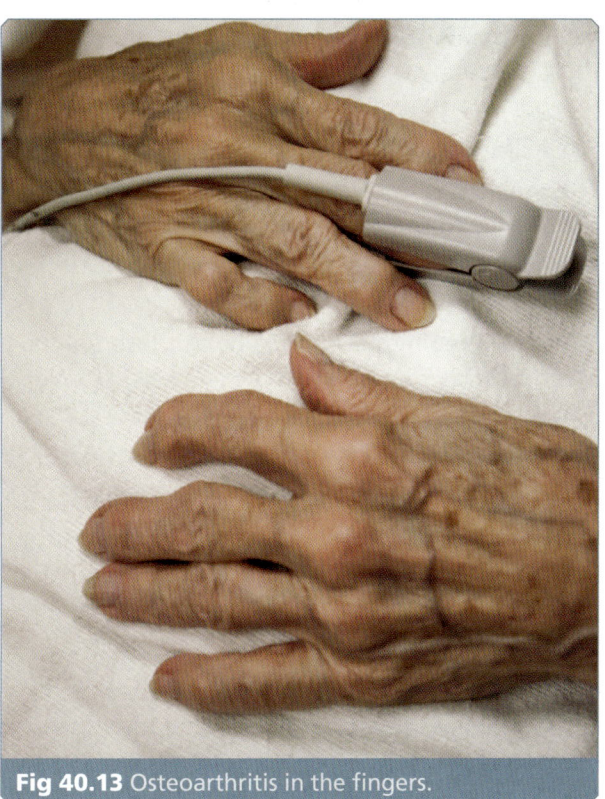

Fig 40.13 Osteoarthritis in the fingers.

The risk of getting osteoarthritis later in life can be reduced by taking care of the joints and limiting exercise or sports that involve considerable risk to the joints. It can also be reduced by limiting repetitive strain injuries and identifying them early.

Treatment of osteoarthritis involves **r**est, **i**ce, **c**ompression and **e**levation (RICE). Anti-inflammatory medication may also be prescribed by a doctor. In severe cases surgery to replace the joint is carried out. Hip replacements are a very common type of joint replacement surgery.

Rheumatoid arthritis

Rheumatoid arthritis is also an inflammatory degenerative disease. It mainly affects synovial joints of the skeletal system, but can affect other tissues.

The rheumatoid arthritis sufferer's immune system produces antibodies against its own cartilage. For this reason, rheumatoid arthritis is a type of autoimmune disease.

Symptoms of rheumatoid arthritis are the same as those for osteoarthritis, except that rheumatoid arthritis can lead to serious deformity of the joints affected (Fig 40.14).

Rheumatoid arthritis is much rarer than osteoarthritis. It affects women more often than men and can occur at any age, whereas osteoarthritis affects men and women equally and usually begins in old age.

There are no known measures to prevent the occurrence of rheumatoid arthritis. This is because scientists have not yet found the reasons behind the inflammatory response.

Treatment regimes are the same as those for osteoarthritis.

Osteoporosis

Osteoporosis is a disease in which the collagen within the bone is lost slowly over long periods of time. This leads to the bones becoming brittle and being at an increased risk of fracture. Osteoporosis usually affects elderly women.

There are no specific symptoms and often osteoporosis is not discovered in an elderly person until they have broken a bone. Common breaks that occur in osteoporosis are vertebral column, hip and wrist fractures.

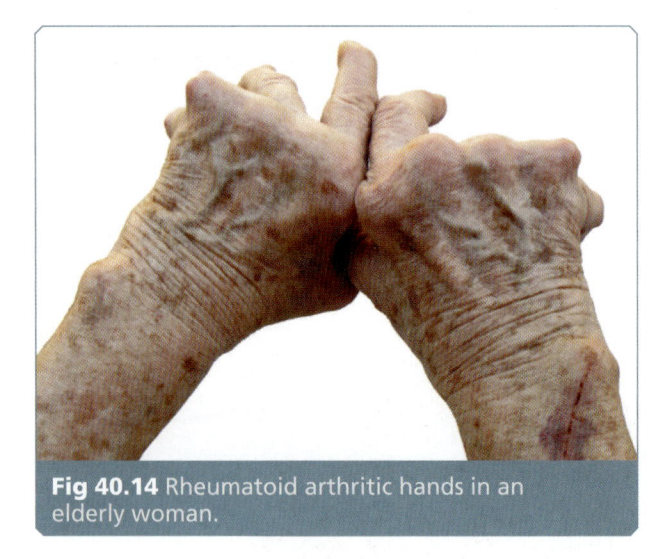

Fig 40.14 Rheumatoid arthritic hands in an elderly woman.

Preventative measures are to ensure a good dietary intake of calcium and vitamin D (*see* Chapter 3). Exercise also increases bone density and strength.

Bone anabolic drugs are used to treat osteoporosis. These drugs help to rebuild bone and the hormone calcitonin helps to inhibit the action of bone-digesting cells, thereby reducing the breakdown of bone by these cells.

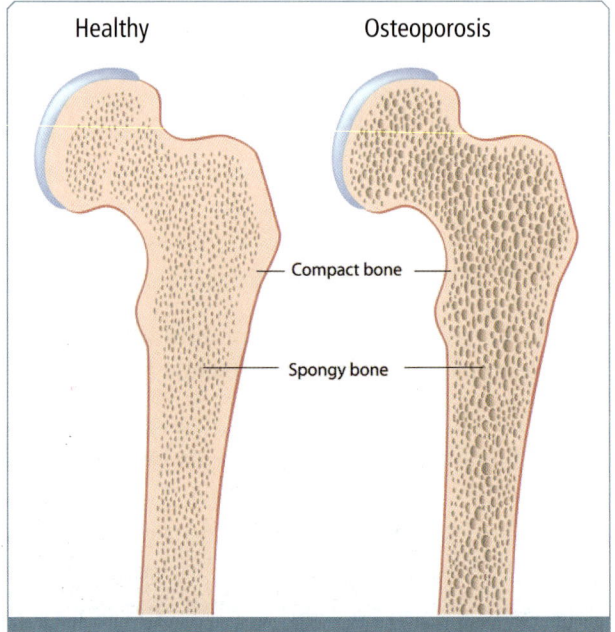

Fig 40.15 An artist's impression of a healthy bone and a bone affected by osteoporosis.

Chapter 40 Questions

1 Name the **three** types of muscle. Which is the only type under conscious control?

2 How many bones are there in the adult human skeleton?

3 Name parts labelled A–U on the following diagram of the human skeleton.

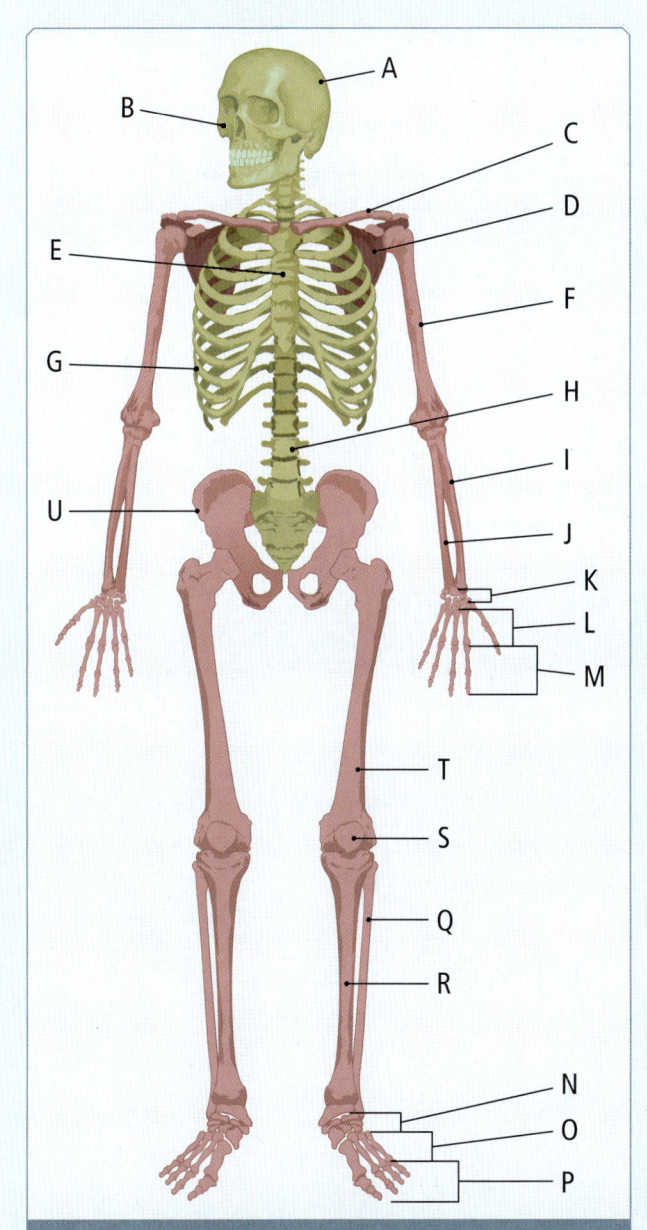

Fig 40.16 The structure of the human skeleton.

4 State **three** functions of the skeleton.

5 Name all the parts of the axial skeleton and give the main function of each part.

6 Distinguish between:
   (a) *Pelvic girdle* and *shoulder girdle*.
   (b) *Radius* and *ulna*.
   (c) *Carpals* and *metacarpals*.
   (d) *Tarsals* and *metatarsals*.

7 (a) How many vertebrae are there in the human spine?
   (b) Name the **five** regions of the spine and state how many vertebrae are present in each region.
   (c) Give **three** functions of the spine.
   (d) What is a *slipped disc*?
   (e) Explain why the pain of a slipped disc sometimes feels like it is coming from the leg.

8 What part of the skeleton are *innominate bones* associated with and how many are there?

9 (a) How many ribs and pairs of ribs are there in the human rib cage?
   (b) How many of these pairs are attached directly to the breastbone? What term is used to describe these ribs?
   (c) How many of these pairs are attached indirectly to the breastbone? What term is used to describe these ribs?
   (d) How many of these pairs are not attached at all to the breastbone? What term is used to describe these ribs?
   (e) What is another name for the breastbone?

10 (a) Make a sketch of a typical long bone and label the following: *periosteum*; *diaphysis*; *epiphysis*; *compact bone*; *spongy bone*; *medullary cavity*; and *cartilage*.
   (b) Give **one** function of each part.
   (c) Explain why cartilage is extremely slow to heal.
   (d) What **two** parts make up the medullary cavity?
   (e) Name the structure that enables growth of bones in children and adolescents.
   (f) Indicate on your diagram the location of the structure you have named in part (e).

Unit 3   The Organism

11 The diagram shows the structure of a typical synovial joint.

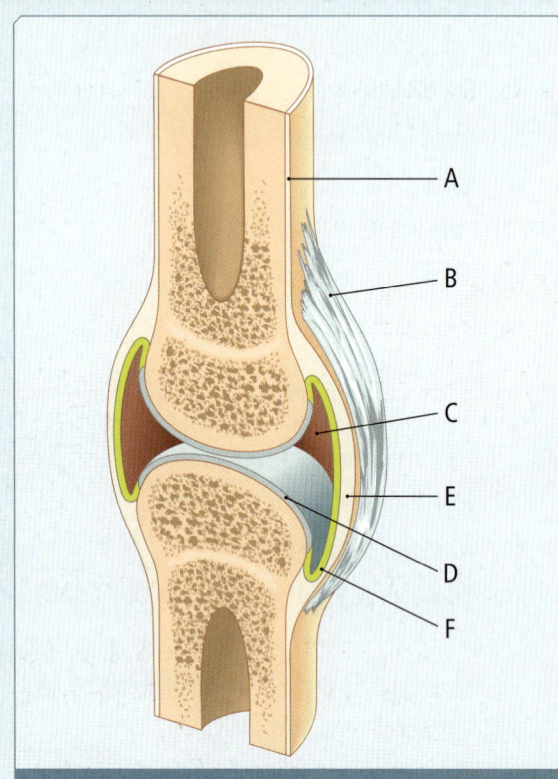

Fig 40.17 The structure of a typical synovial joint.

(a) Name the structures labelled A–F on the diagram and give the function of each part.
(b) Indicate on your diagram where a tendon might attach.
(c) Give **two** examples of joints that are synovial.
(d) What are the other **two** main types of joint? Give **one** example of each.

HL 12 (a) What is *ossification*?
(b) Distinguish between *osteoclasts* and *osteoblasts*.

13 Describe the effect of the following on the skeletal system:
(a) A diet low in calcium.
(b) Too much parathormone in the bloodstream.
(c) Regular, but not too much, sunlight exposure.

14 (a) What is an *antagonistic muscle pair*?
(b) Give **one** example and for this example state which is the flexor and which is the extensor.

15 For a named musculoskeletal disorder name one:
(a) Symptom
(b) Treatment
(c) Preventative measure

Answer the following multiple-choice questions:

16 The substances that make up compact bone are:
(a) Sodium and potassium salts and collagen
(b) Sodium and calcium salts and keratin
(c) Calcium and magnesium salts and collagen
(d) Potassium and sodium salts and myosin

17 The number of vertebrae in the spine is:
(a) 31   (c) 33
(b) 32   (d) 34

18 The number of cervical vertebrae is:
(a) 6   (c) 8
(b) 7   (d) 9

19 The number of ribs in the rib cage is:
(a) 6   (c) 24
(b) 12   (d) 36

20 Another name for the collar bone is the:
(a) Clavicle   (c) Scapula
(b) Humerus   (d) Stirrup

21 The innominate bones are the bones of the:
(a) Skull   (c) Wrist
(b) Hip   (d) Ankle

22 Osteoporosis is loss of:
(a) Calcium   (c) Cartilage
(b) Bone marrow   (d) Collagen

Chapter 40 Sample examination questions

1 The diagram shows the bones of the human arm.

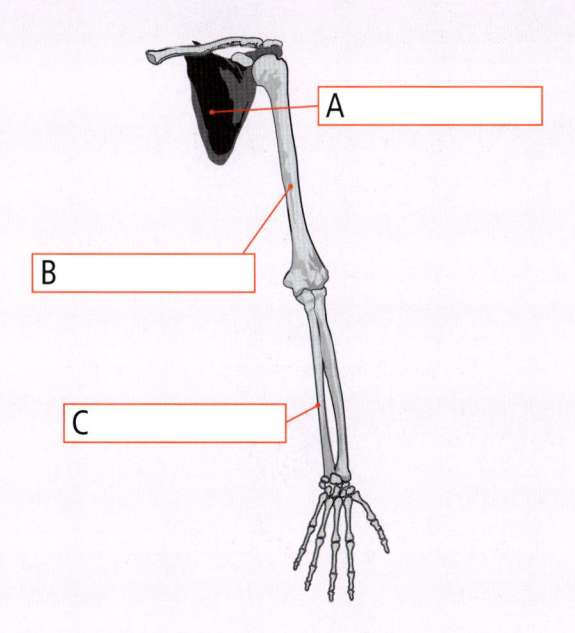

(i) Name the parts labelled A, B and C.
(ii) What structures attach a muscle to a bone?
(iii) Which upper arm muscle contracts to raise the lower arm?
(iv) What is meant by the term *antagonistic pair* in reference to muscles?
(v) Name the type of joint at the elbow.
(vi) Apart from movement, give **one** other function of the skeleton.
(vii) Suggest **one** reason why the bones of birds are almost hollow.

Section C, Question 15 (b) Ordinary Level 2010

HL 2 (a) The diagram shows a longitudinal section of a long bone.

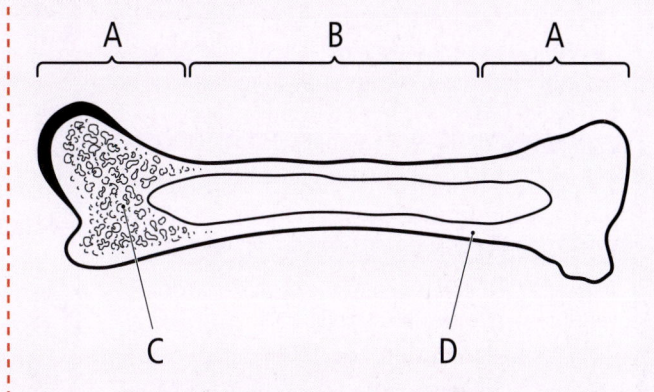

(i) Name the parts of the diagram labelled A, B, C, D.
(ii) Where are the discs in the human backbone?
(iii) What is the function of the discs in the human backbone?

(b) Give a role for **each** of the following in the human body:
(i) Yellow bone marrow.
(ii) Red bone marrow.

Section A, Question 4 Higher Level 2009

Chapter 40 Mind map

The musculoskeletal system is composed of the bones of the skeleton and the muscles.

- 206 bones in the mature adult human skeleton.
- Functions of the skeleton include: protection, support, shape, movement and manufacture of blood cells.

The skeleton is divided into the axial skeleton and the appendicular skeleton.

Axial skeleton composed of the skull, facial bones, vertebrae, rib cage and sternum.
- The skull (cranium) protects the brain.
- The facial bones protect the eyes, nasal cavity, ears and mouth.
- The vertebrae function in shape, support, movement, and protection of the spinal cord.
- The vertebral column is composed of 33 vertebrae divided into five regions:
  - Cervical (7 vertebrae)
  - Thoracic (12 vertebrae)
  - Lumbar (5 vertebrae)
  - Sacrum (5 fused vertebrae)
  - Coccyx (4 fused vertebrae)
- Between each vertebra are discs of cartilage, called intervertebral discs. They function in shock absorption and also allow slight movement (articulation) between the vertebrae.
- The rib cage protects the internal organs such as the heart and lungs, and functions in breathing.
- There are 12 pairs of ribs: 7 true pairs; 3 false pairs; and 2 pairs of floating ribs.
- The sternum functions in breathing (as the ribs attach to it) and protection.

A long bone is composed of: periosteum (outer covering), diaphysis (shaft of the bone), epiphysis (head of the bone), compact bone (strong and dense), spongy bone (bony bars and plates separated by small spaces), medullary cavity (bone marrow where blood cells are produced and where fat is stored) and cartilage (present on the ends of the bone for protection and shock absorption).

HL
- The cells present in bone are osteoblasts and osteoclasts.
- Ossification is the process of laying down new bone material by osteoblasts.
- Bone growth occurs during childhood and adolescence by ossification at the growth plates.
- Growth plates are present between the diaphysis and epiphyses.
- Osteoclasts function in removing minerals from bone.

- A **joint** is the location where two or more bones make contact.
- There are three types of joint: immovable joints (joints of the skull); slightly movable joints (joints between the vertebrae) and freely-movable (synovial) joints (e.g. knee).
- **Ligaments** join bone to bone to form a joint.
- **Tendons** join muscle to bone.

Antagonistic muscle pairs are composed of two muscles that have opposite effects to each other, e.g. biceps and triceps.

- **Arthritis** is painful inflammation of the joints caused by wear and tear or an immune reaction and is treated by anti-inflammatory drugs.
- **Osteoporosis** is a degenerative bone disease where the collagen is slowly lost and bones become brittle. It is treated with bone anabolic drugs.

Appendicular skeleton composed of the shoulder and hip girdles and the appendages (arms and legs).
- The pelvic girdle consists of the pelvis (consisting of 3 fused bones called innominate bones), which is connected to the sacrum. It gives strength and support to the body and also allows mobility of the lower limbs.
- The pectoral girdle consists of the scapula (shoulder blade) and clavicle (collar bone) and connects the upper arm to the axial skeleton.
  - The pectoral girdles function in giving upper body mobility and strength.
- The appendages include the arms, hands, legs and feet.
  - There are 30 bones in each appendage (total = 120).
  - Humerus (upper arm bone).
  - Radius and ulna (forearm bones) – the radius on the thumb side.
- The wrist bones are called carpals and there are 8 carpals.
- The bones of the hand are called metacarpals.
- The bones of the fingers are called phalanges.
- Femur (thigh bone) is the longest bone in the body.
- The patella (knee cap) is present at the front of the knee.
- The lower leg bones are the tibia (shin bone) and fibula.
- The bones of the ankle are called tarsals of which there are seven.
- The bones of the foot are called metatarsals.
- The bones of the toes are called phalanges.

The human reproductive system — Chapter 41

Learning objectives After studying this chapter, you should be able to:

- Describe the structure, function and main parts of the male and female reproductive systems.
- Describe the importance of meiosis in the formation of sperm and egg cells.
- Define *secondary sexual characteristics*.
- Describe the roles of oestrogen, progesterone and testosterone.
- Describe the main events of the menstrual cycle.
- **HL** Describe the detailed events of the menstrual cycle and its hormonal control.
- Describe one menstrual disorder: either endometriosis or fibroids.
- Describe copulation and the four methods of contraception.
- Describe the location of fertilisation.
- Describe male and female infertility, one possible cause for each and possible corrective measures.
- Describe implantation and placenta formation and function.
- Describe *in vitro* fertilisation.
- **HL** Describe the human embryo development from fertilised egg, morula, blastocyst, embryo, foetus and baby.
- Describe the three stages of childbirth.
- Describe lactation and breast-feeding and the benefits of breast-feeding.

Introduction

The human reproductive systems are divided into male and female systems. The structure and organs differ, as well as their products.

- The male reproductive system produces the male gamete, the sperm cell, and has organs specialised to deliver sperm into the female reproductive system.
- The female reproductive system produces the female gamete, the egg cell, and has organs specialised for the development of a new human.

Fig 41.1 Structure of the male reproductive system.

Male reproductive system

The male reproductive system consists of a number of different organs. The external part of the male reproductive system includes the **penis** and **testes**, which are held within a structure called the scrotum (Fig 41.1). The internal part of the reproductive system consists of a series of tubes and glands specialised to produce and carry semen, the fluid in which sperm swim.

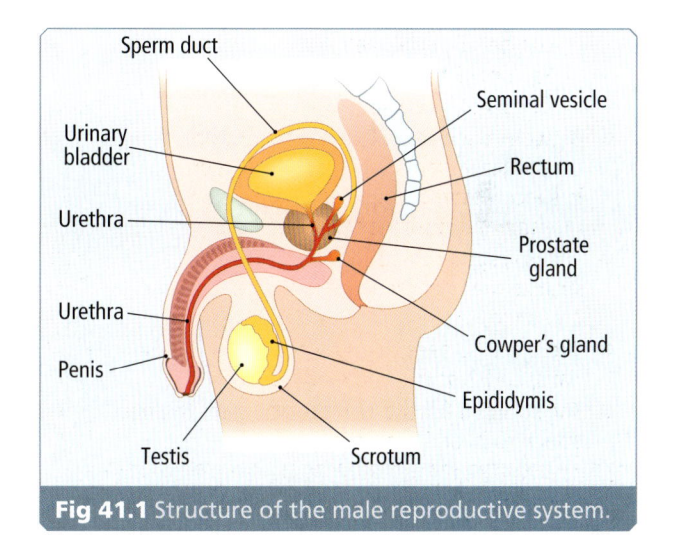

Parts of the male reproductive system

Penis

The penis is a muscular organ through which urine and semen travel. The tubule that carries these fluids is called the urethra and joins to the urinary bladder near the top of the penis.

The muscle of the penis can swell with blood, becoming erect. This occurs during sexual arousal and enables the penis to be inserted into the vagina.

Sperm ducts

The sperm ducts are also known as the vas deferens. There are two sperm ducts in the male reproductive system. They carry semen from the testes to the urethra. They join the urethra near the urinary bladder.

Prostate gland

The prostate gland is an exocrine gland located at the top of the penis just underneath the urinary bladder and is responsible for producing semen, the fluid in which sperm swim.

Prostate cancer is a common cancer in older men. The prostate gland swells and can obstruct the passing of urine.

Cowper's gland

Cowper's glands are a pair of exocrine glands located further back along the sperm ducts. They contribute to the production of semen.

Seminal vesicles

The seminal vesicles are a pair of exocrine glands also located along the sperm ducts. They also contribute to the production of semen.

Epididymis

The epididymis is a storage organ for sperm produced by the testes. The epididymis is located on top of each testis.

Sperm are stored and fully matured here before being released. If they are not released, they are broken down and absorbed by the cells of the epididymis.

Testes

The testes are a pair of glands located in the scrotum. The testes have an exocrine function (production of sperm) and an endocrine function (production of testosterone).

Sperm production

The testes produce sperm in response to **follicle-stimulating hormone** (FSH) – another hormone secreted by the pituitary. Sperm are produced through the process of **meiosis**.

Sperm are specialised cells containing three parts: the **head, midpiece** (or neck region) and **tail**.

- The head contains the haploid nucleus with 23 chromosomes. It also contains an **acrosome,** which enables the cell to gain entry to an egg cell.
- The midpiece contains many mitochondria. These are used for production of energy needed for movement.
- The tail propels the sperm along when inside the female reproductive tract.

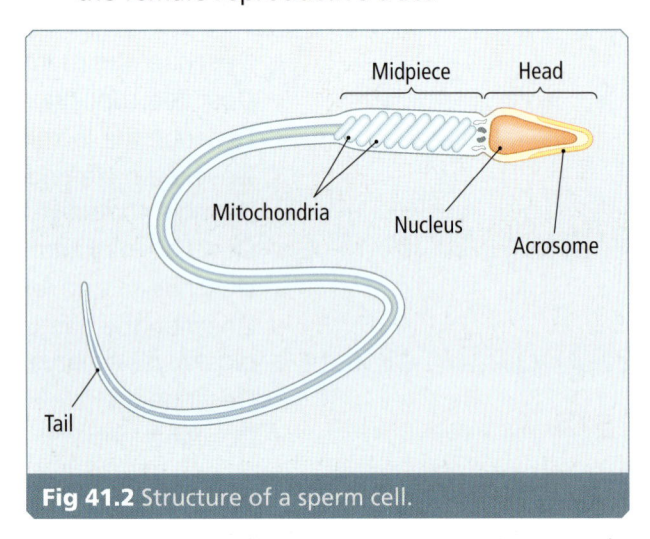

Fig 41.2 Structure of a sperm cell.

Endocrine function

The testes produce **testosterone** in response to a pituitary hormone called luteinising hormone (LH).

Scrotum

The scrotum is a pouch located underneath the penis that holds the testes outside of the body.

Sperm production requires a temperature (35°C) lower than body temperature. The exact reasons for this are unknown, but it is thought to be due to enzymes involved in sperm production requiring a lower optimum temperature. It is known that if the testes do not drop into the scrotum during development, the sperm will not be produced properly and the male may be sterile.

Female reproductive system

The female reproductive system consists of mostly internal organs. These organs include: the **vulva, vagina, cervix, uterus (womb), fallopian tubes (oviducts)** and **ovaries.**

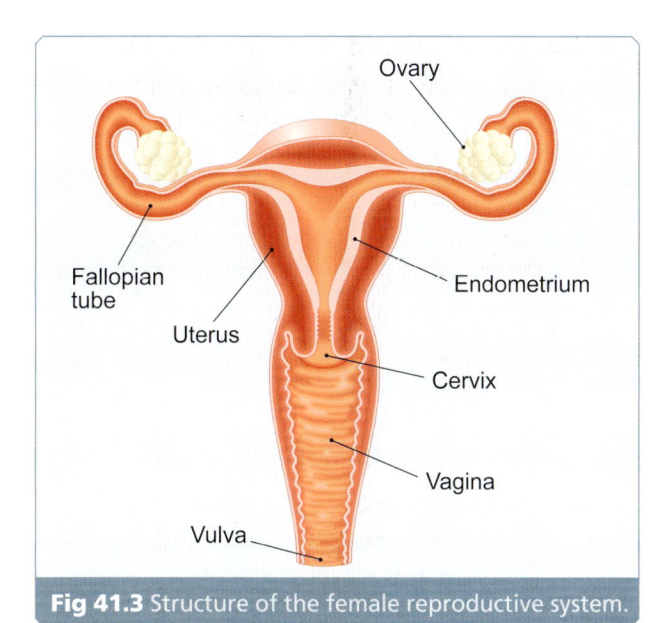

The human reproductive system Chapter 41

Fig 41.3 Structure of the female reproductive system.

Parts of the female reproductive system

Vulva
The vulva consists of a number of external genital organs (genitalia). They form the entrance to the vagina and function in sexual arousal.

Vagina
The vagina is a muscular organ approximately 7 cm long. It is also known as the **birth canal** and is the structure that receives the penis during sexual intercourse. The cells lining the vagina secrete an acidic mucous as a method of protection from infection.

Cervix
The cervix is located at the top of the vagina. It is the junction between the vagina and uterus.

Cervical cancer is a common cancer in women. It is thought to be caused by a viral infection of the cells of the cervix.

Uterus (womb)
The uterus is a muscular organ that is responsible for holding a developing baby during pregnancy. As a pregnancy continues, the uterus stretches. Towards the end of pregnancy, the muscular wall of the uterus starts to contract, helping to push the baby out during birth.

The uterus also goes through a repeating cycle of changes once every 28 days. This is called the **menstrual cycle** and occurs so that the uterus is ready for potential pregnancies once a month.

The lining of the uterus is called the **endometrium.** This layer undergoes the changes in the menstrual cycle once every 28 days.

Fallopian tubes
The fallopian tubes are also known as the **oviducts.** They connect the ovaries to the uterus.

The fallopian tubes capture the egg after it has been released by the ovary and transfer it to the uterus if it is fertilised by a sperm cell.

The cells lining the inside of the fallopian tubes contain cilia, which help to push the egg along to the uterus.

Ovaries
The ovaries are located at the ends of the fallopian tubes deep within the abdomen. The ovaries produce the egg cell, of which usually only one develops each month. Egg cells (also called **ova**) are produced through the process of **meiosis.**

Egg cell development
Egg cells are present in the female ovaries from birth. They remain in the ovaries, but their numbers decrease steadily throughout childhood until there are approximately 40,000 remaining at the beginning of puberty.

Approximately 20 egg cells develop further each month from puberty onwards. However, usually only one egg will become dominant each month and be released. The other egg cells degenerate.

Occasionally more than one egg is released, which if fertilised could lead to non-identical twins or even triplets!

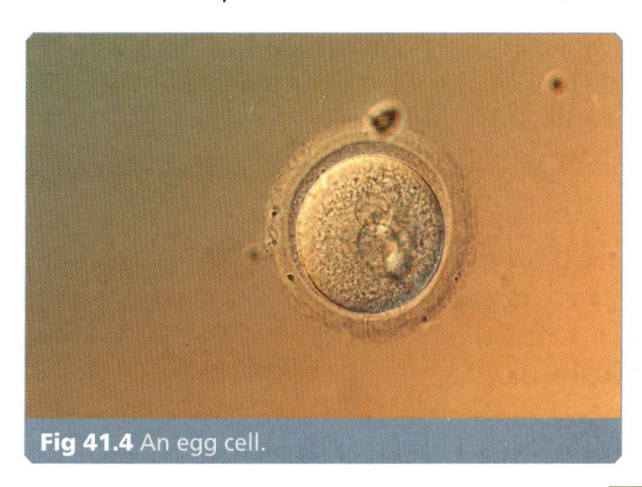

Fig 41.4 An egg cell.

Endocrine function

The ovaries are also an important endocrine gland, responsible for producing the sex hormones **oestrogen** and **progesterone**.

Role of meiosis in gamete formation

> **Meiosis** is a type of nuclear division that leads to four daughter cells being produced, each containing half the number of chromosomes as the parent cell.

Meiosis is extremely important in sexual reproduction in animals as it maintains the number of chromosomes in the resulting offspring. In humans, diploid cells have 46 chromosomes. In order to maintain this number in the offspring, gametes with 23 chromosomes need to be produced so that, at fertilisation, the diploid number of 46 chromosomes is re-attained.

Meiosis also enables variation in the offspring because of the random nature of chromosome arrangement at meiosis and also the swapping of genes (crossing over).

Secondary sexual characteristics

> **Secondary sexual characteristics** are features that distinguish males from females, but are not part of the reproductive system.

Secondary sexual characteristics in males include:
- Facial hair.
- Pubic hair.
- Enlargement of the larynx (Adam's apple) and deepening of the voice.
- Broadening of shoulders and chest.

Secondary sexual characteristics in females include:
- Pubic hair.
- Growth of breasts.
- Enlargement of hips.

Role of the sex hormones
The sex hormones in humans are: **testosterone**, **oestrogen**, and **progesterone**.

Testosterone
Testosterone is the male sex hormone. It is produced by the testes in response to another hormone called **luteinising hormone** (LH), which is secreted by the pituitary.

Testosterone is responsible for maintaining the male secondary sexual characteristics. It also plays a metabolic role: it increases muscle mass and bone density and reduces fat reserves.

Oestrogen and progesterone
Oestrogen and progesterone are the female sex hormones. Oestrogen is secreted by ovarian follicles within the ovary. Progesterone is also secreted by the ovaries.

- Oestrogen is responsible for formation and maintenance of the female secondary sexual characteristics and the repair and thickening of the endometrium during the menstrual cycle (*see below*). It also has metabolic roles. Oestrogen causes an increase in bone mass and fat storage in the female body.
- Progesterone is responsible for maintaining the endometrium during the menstrual cycle (*see below*).

Menstrual cycle

> The **menstrual cycle** is a series of cyclical changes that occur in the female reproductive system over a 28-day period.

The menstrual cycle is controlled by the endocrine system, principally the pituitary gland. The menstrual cycle begins at puberty at approximately 12–13 years of age. The first menstrual cycle is called **menarche**.

The menstrual cycle continues throughout a woman's life until the **menopause** – the time at which the menstrual cycle ceases. This occurs between the ages of 45 and 55.

The menstrual cycle is divided into three distinct phases: the **follicular phase**, **ovulation** and the **luteal phase**.

Fig 41.5 Egg development in the ovary.

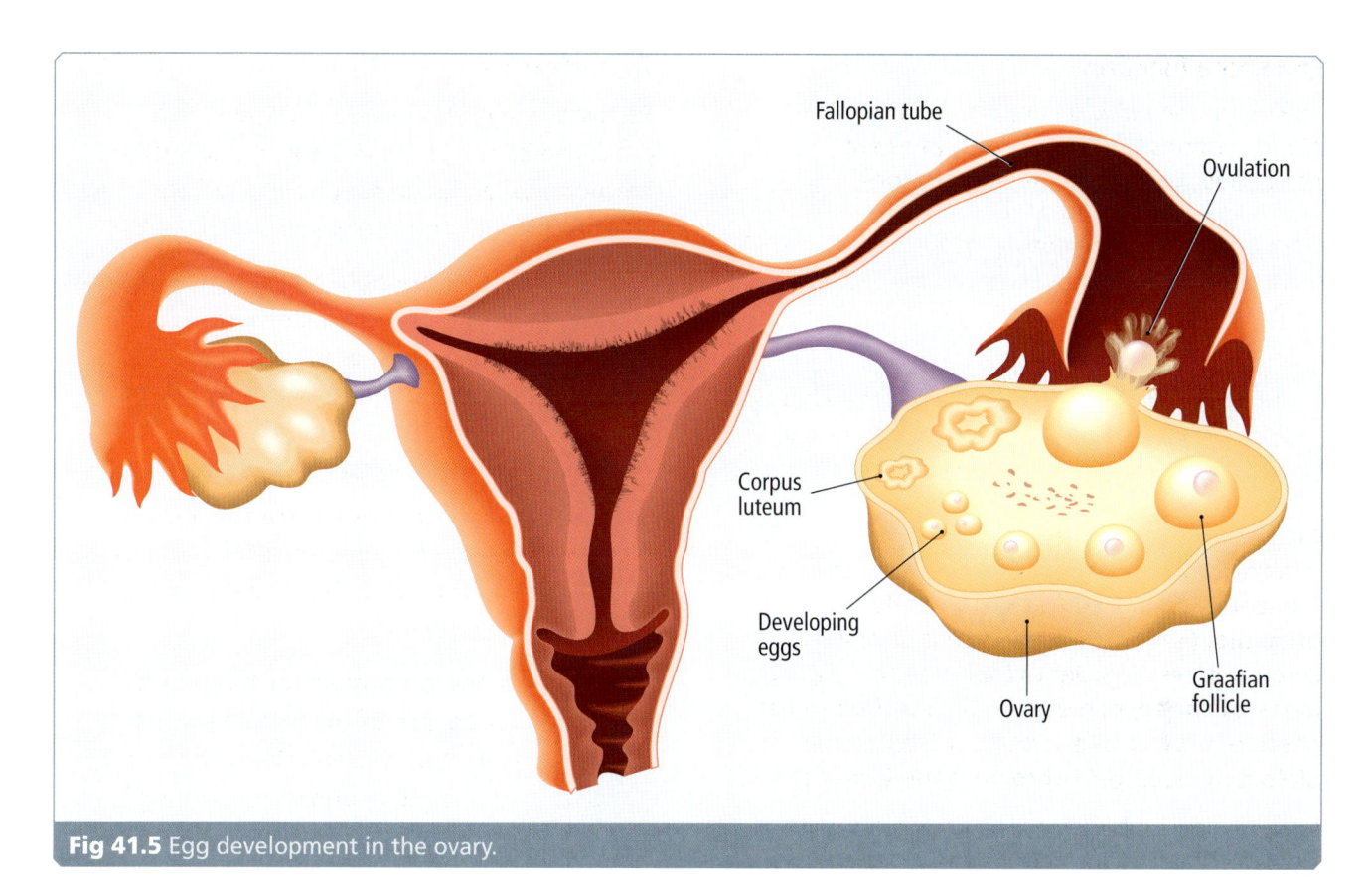

1 Follicular phase (days 1–13)

The follicular phase involves the formation of a mature egg cell. This process takes approximately two weeks.

During the first few days of the follicular phase, ovarian follicles, called **Graafian follicles,** are stimulated to grow in the ovary. Graafian follicles are collections of cells surrounding a central egg cell or ovum.

Usually only one follicle develops per cycle. This is due to the oestrogen from one dominant follicle inhibiting the other follicles from forming.

As the egg cell matures, the follicle increases in size and forms into a large fluid-filled sac. The Graafian follicle is also responsible for secreting oestrogen. As its size increases the amount of oestrogen secreted increases.

The follicular phase can be divided up into two stages: **menstruation** and the **proliferative stage.**

(i) Menstruation (days 1–5)

> **Menstruation** is the shedding of the endometrium (lining of the uterus).

During the first few days of the menstrual cycle, the female experiences bleeding from the vagina. This is the lining of the endometrium being shed when no pregnancy has occurred. This process is also known as **menses.**

Menstruation usually occurs over the course of five days. However, menstruation can be as short as two days and as long as seven days.

(ii) Proliferative stage (days 6–13)

The proliferative stage involves the repair of the endometrium. This occurs between days 6 and 13 of the menstrual cycle. The thickness of the endometrium also increases during this stage in readiness for a potential fertilised egg.

Oestrogen is the hormone responsible for the repair of the endometrium and progesterone is responsible for maintaining the endometrium for the rest of the cycle.

2 Ovulation (day 14)

> **Ovulation** is the release of an egg from the ovary.

Ovulation usually occurs on day 14 but can occur between days 13 and 15 of the menstrual cycle.

After the ovum has reached maturity, the follicle releases the egg from the ovary. Body temperature increases after ovulation. Following the release of the egg, the Graafian follicle becomes a yellow body, called the **corpus luteum.** Oestrogen levels decrease as a result. The menstrual cycle has now entered the luteal phase.

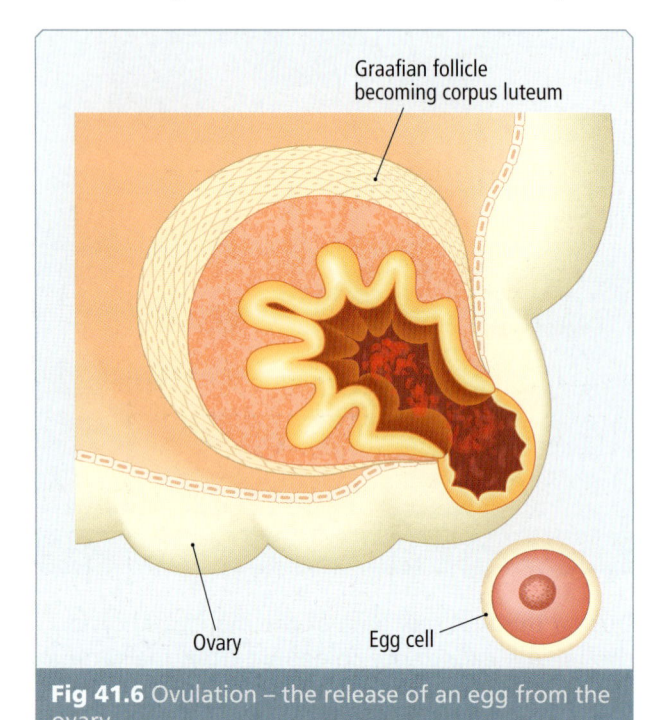

Fig 41.6 Ovulation – the release of an egg from the ovary.

3. Luteal phase (days 15–28)

The luteal phase lasts from days 15 to 28 of the menstrual cycle.

The corpus luteum, or yellow body, secretes progesterone and a small amount of oestrogen. Progesterone maintains the endometrium to the end of the cycle and also causes body temperature to increase slightly. This maintenance of the endometrium ensures the uterus is ready to receive a fertilised egg.

Towards the end of the luteal phase, the corpus luteum degenerates and a new cycle will begin.

Menstrual cycle – detailed study

As we have already learned, the menstrual cycle is divided into the follicular phase, ovulation and the luteal phase.

There are four main hormones involved in the control of the menstrual cycle: **follicle-stimulating hormone (FSH), luteinising hormone (LH), oestrogen** and **progesterone**.

The following describes the hormonal control of each phase.

1 Follicular phase (days 1–13)

The follicular phase is divided into two stages: **menstruation** and the **proliferative phase.**

Menstruation

Menstruation is the shedding of the lining of the uterus. It occurs due to low levels of progesterone and oestrogen caused by the degeneration of the corpus luteum from the previous cycle.

Proliferative stage

The proliferative stage involves the regeneration of the lining of the uterus and the development of the egg in the ovary.

Oestrogen and progesterone inhibit FSH secretion from the pituitary. During the early stages of the follicular phase, oestrogen and progesterone levels are low and therefore FSH is not inhibited. As a result, the pituitary gland begins to secrete **FSH**. This stimulates the formation of new Graafian follicles in the ovaries. As the follicles are developing, **oestrogen** levels begin to increase once again.

Usually only one Graafian follicle goes on to develop fully. This is due to the oestrogen from one dominant follicle inhibiting the secretion of FSH from the pituitary. This is an example of **negative feedback.** Lower levels of FSH, as a result of increasing oestrogen levels, prevent other follicles within the ovary developing.

The oestrogen levels continue to increase throughout the follicular phase.

Oestrogen is responsible for repairing the endometrium after menstruation and increasing its thickness. Towards the end of the follicular phase, the **oestrogen levels reach a critical level**, which is sensed by the pituitary gland. The pituitary gland responds by producing a surge of **LH** secretion.

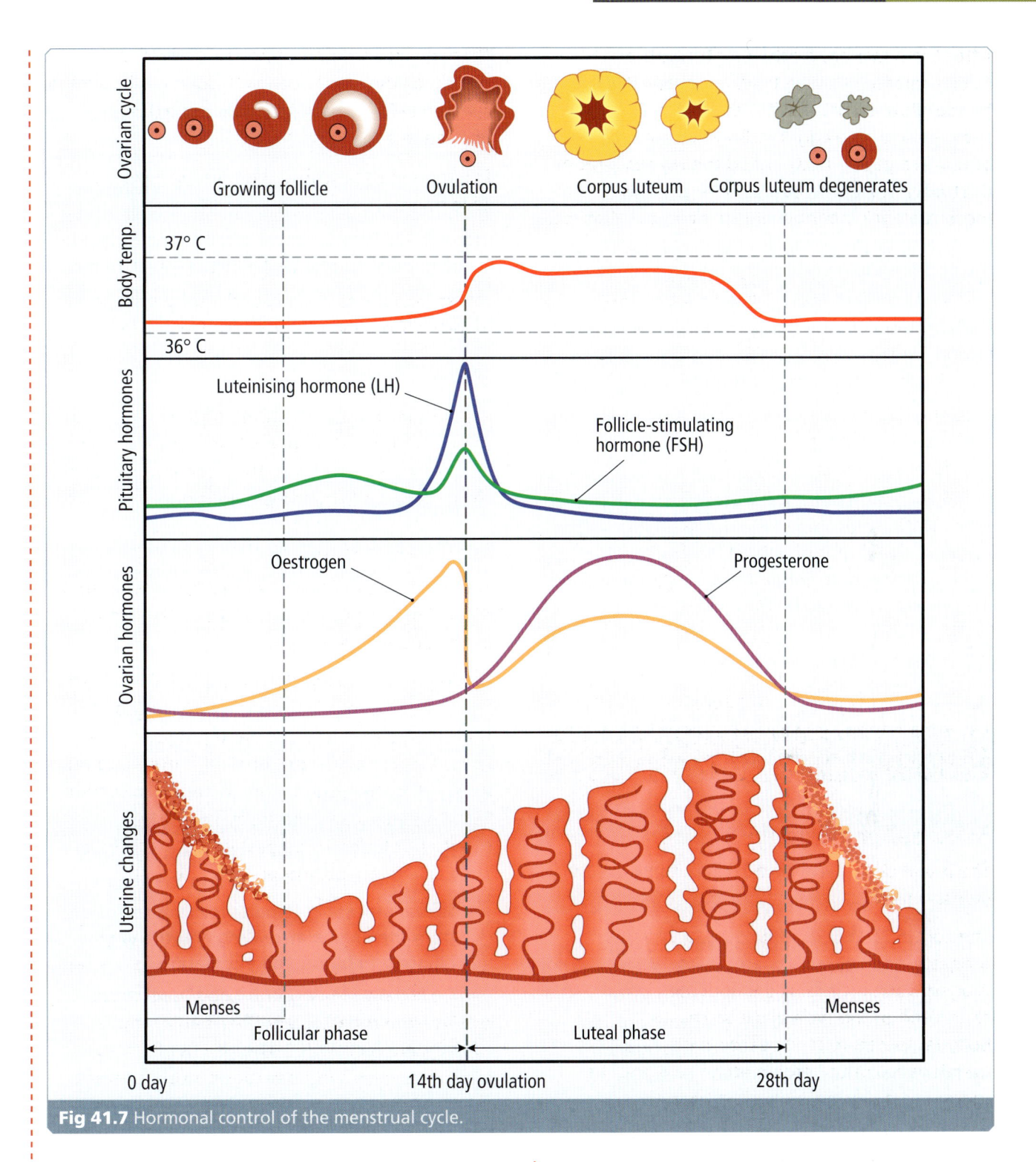

Fig 41.7 Hormonal control of the menstrual cycle.

2 Ovulation (day 14)

The **surge of LH** secretion causes **ovulation** – the release of the egg from the ovary, usually on day 14.

Following the release of the egg, the Graafian follicle becomes a yellow body, called the **corpus luteum**. Oestrogen levels decrease slightly as a result. The menstrual cycle has now entered the luteal phase.

3 Luteal phase (days 15–28)

The luteal phase lasts from days 15 to 28 of the menstrual cycle.

The corpus luteum, or yellow body, secretes **progesterone** and continues to secrete a lower amount of **oestrogen**. The progesterone causes the body temperature to increase in the days following ovulation. The oestrogen and the high levels of progesterone continue to exert a negative feedback effect on FSH. This prevents follicles developing within the ovaries.

Progesterone levels remain high during most of the luteal phase and only decrease towards the end of the phase. Progesterone is also responsible for maintaining the endometrium to the end of the cycle. This maintenance of the endometrium ensures the uterus is ready to receive a fertilised egg.

Towards the end of the luteal phase, the corpus luteum degenerates. As a result, progesterone and oestrogen levels drop off quite quickly.

The inhibition on secretion of FSH is removed and a new cycle will begin.

If fertilisation occurs, the fertilised egg produces a hormone that maintains the corpus luteum in the ovary. The maintenance of the corpus luteum for the first few weeks of pregnancy is critical as without it the endometrium would not be maintained and the pregnancy would be terminated.

Menstrual disorder

> **NOTE:** For Leaving Certificate Biology, you must be able to describe one disorder of the menstrual cycle from one of the following: endometriosis or fibroids.

Endometriosis

> **Endometriosis** is where the cells lining the uterus (endometrium) move and grow outside the uterus.

Endometriosis affects approximately 10 per cent of women and is more common in women who are of reproductive age and who suffer from infertility. Endometrial cells grow outside the uterus under the influence of the female sex hormones. The most common area for endometrial cells to grow is the ovaries.

Symptoms are pain around the pelvic area as cells grow within the body cavity around and on the ovaries. The pain can be severe in some cases. Infertility can be another symptom of endometriosis due to the formation of scar tissue around the ovary.

Treatments mostly involve pain medication and hormonal drugs that attempt to treat any hormonal imbalance. In severe cases, surgery may be required to remove scar tissue.

Fibroids

> **Fibroids** are benign tumours that grow in the muscular wall of the uterus.

Fibroids are the most common benign tumours in females and involve the smooth muscle of the uterus wall. They are most often found in women in the middle or later reproductive years. In most cases, fibroids are small and cause no symptoms. Occasionally fibroids can grow very large, in which case they can cause pain and heavy menstrual bleeding.

Treatments depend on the size and symptoms. Medication can reduce the size of the tumour and relieve pain. Ultrasound can be used to break up the tumour. In severe cases, the tumours are removed surgically.

In very rare circumstances, the whole uterus may need to be removed. This is called a **hysterectomy**.

Stages of sexual intercourse

Sexual intercourse is divided into three stages: **sexual arousal**, **copulation** and **orgasm**.

Sexual arousal

- Sexual arousal in males involves blood flowing into the penis. The penis becomes erect and can be inserted into the vagina.
- Sexual arousal in females involves secretions from the vagina increasing and the vagina filling with blood and elongating.
- An increase in heart rate and breathing rate and dilation of the pupils occur in both males and females during arousal.

Copulation

> **Copulation** is the insertion of an erect penis into the vagina.

The penis is moved within the vagina during copulation and sexual arousal reaches a maximum.

Orgasm

> **Orgasm** occurs when sexual arousal reaches a maximum (climax).

Orgasm in both males and females is caused by the contraction of pelvic muscles that surround the sex organs. Orgasm in males is accompanied by **ejaculation**.

> **Ejaculation** is the release of semen from the penis during sexual intercourse.

Ejaculation usually results in the release of approximately 10 ml of semen containing approximately 300 million sperm. Semen is composed of sperm cells and a liquid, containing water, mucous, fructose (as an energy supply for the sperm) and amino acids. It is slightly alkaline to neutralise the acidic nature of the vagina and cervix. This helps the sperm to survive and reach the uterus where they then swim up towards the egg present in the fallopian tube.

Fertilisation

> **Fertilisation** is the fusion of a sperm cell with an egg cell to form a diploid zygote.

Survival time of sperm and egg cells

- Sperm cells generally survive up to three days in the female reproductive tract.
- Egg cells, once released in ovulation, survive for up to two days. If no fertilisation has occurred, the egg is absorbed into the wall of the fallopian tube.

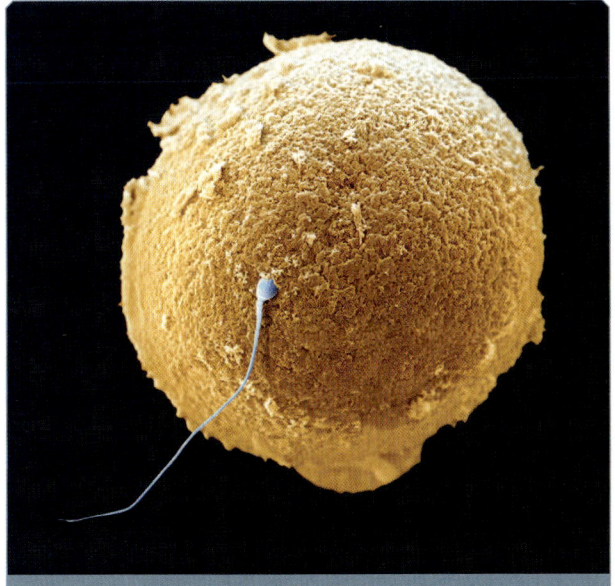

Fig 41.8 A scanning electron micrograph of a sperm cell fertilising an egg cell.

Location of fertilisation

Fertilisation in animals is also known as **conception**. Fertilisation always occurs in the fallopian tubes. Usually only one egg is released from one of the ovaries. The egg travels down the fallopian tube where sperm may be present. Sperm are attracted towards the egg by **chemotropism**.

Fertile period

> The **fertile period** of the menstrual cycle is the time at which the female is most likely to become pregnant.

The fertile period covers approximately five days before ovulation to two days after ovulation. If sexual intercourse occurs within this timeframe, the female is highly likely to become pregnant.

Implantation and placenta formation

> **Implantation** is the embedding of the embryo into the lining of the uterus.

By the time the fertilised egg reaches the uterus, it is a small ball of cells. Following successful implantation, the ball of cells continues to divide, eventually becoming an **embryo**.

The **placenta** begins to form at this stage. Outer layers of cells of the embryo form projections called villi, which push deeper into the endometrium. A mixture of embryonic and uterine tissue is formed, which develops into the placenta.

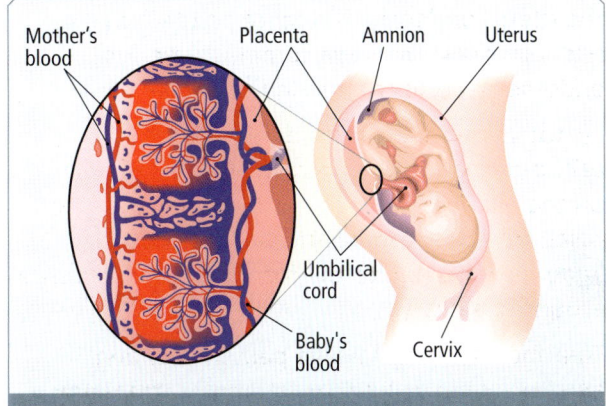

Fig 41.9 Structure of the placenta and organs surrounding the foetus.

The embryo continues to divide by mitosis and becomes a **foetus** after about eight weeks of pregnancy. The placenta continues to grow with the foetus and is fully functional after three months.

The placenta is attached to the foetus by the umbilical cord. The umbilical cord develops with no nerves. This is why it can be clamped and cut after birth without any pain to either mother or baby.

The placenta produces progesterone that maintains the pregnancy. Once the placenta is producing sufficient amounts of progesterone, the corpus luteum will degenerate.

The placenta is a unique organ in that it is made up of both the baby's tissue and the mother's tissue. It contains an intricate network of blood vessels from the baby and mother that are in very close contact. However, it is very important to note that the two bloods do not mix. This is because the mother could have a different blood type to the baby. If they were to mix, a **haemolytic reaction** (immune system reaction against red blood cells) may occur, which could be dangerous for the pregnancy.

Functions of the placenta

The placenta functions are:

- It allows nutrients, water, oxygen, antibodies, drugs and hormones to pass from the mother's bloodstream to the baby's bloodstream.
- It allows wastes produced by the baby, such as carbon dioxide and urea, to pass to the mother for excretion.
- It keeps the mother's blood separate from the baby's blood.

Development of the embryo

As soon as fertilisation has occurred, the diploid zygote begins to divide by mitosis to form two cells, four cells, eight cells and so on.

Eventually, enough divisions have occurred to produce a ball of undifferentiated (unspecialised) cells. This ball of cells is called the **morula**.

> A **morula** is a ball of undifferentiated cells that forms as a result of mitosis.

It is generally called a morula three days following fertilisation. The morula is pushed down the fallopian tube towards the uterus by the cilia of the fallopian tube.

The cells in the morula continue to divide by mitosis. Eventually, a fluid-filled sac appears within the morula. This has usually occurred after seven days. It is now called a **blastocyst** and is ready for implantation.

> A **blastocyst** is a fluid-filled sac containing an inner cell mass that gives rise to the embryo.

A ball of cells called the **inner cell mass** is present inside the blastocyst. At this stage, the cells are undifferentiated and are called **stem cells**. The inner cell mass gives rise to the embryo.

After about nine days, the blastocyst will reach the uterus and implant into the endometrium.

> **Implantation** is the embedding of the embryo in the lining of the uterus.

The outer layer of the blastocyst is called the **trophoblast**. This layer embeds deep into the endometrium by sending out long projections called **villi**. These villi, along with the mother's endometrial tissue, will ultimately give rise to the placenta.

The inner cell mass continues to divide by mitosis. The cells begin to differentiate into various tissues and the tissues begin to become organised into organs and organ systems. This occurs by the organisation of cells into three distinct germ layers: **ectoderm**, **mesoderm** and **endoderm**.

- The **ectoderm** gives rise to the skin and nervous system.
- The **mesoderm** gives rise to the musculoskeletal system, kidneys, lungs and heart.
- The **endoderm** gives rise to the liver, pancreas and the inner linings of the breathing, digestive and excretory systems.

A protective sac, called the **amnion**, begins to form around the embryo. It is filled with **amniotic fluid**. Its functions are protection and shock absorption.

By the end of the eighth week of pregnancy, all the major internal organs have formed. At this point everything is in miniature form and will increase in size as the pregnancy continues. Once the embryo reaches the eighth week it is called a **foetus.**

By the end of the 12th week of pregnancy, the placenta is fully functional and the foetus is increasing in size all the time.

- The eyes are low and widely spaced at this stage. Up until this point, the skeleton is made from cartilage. From the third month onwards, the cartilage becomes ossified, producing bone.
- Arms and legs begin to move as a result of the nerves and muscles maturing.
- The sex organs are now visible and easily distinguishable.
- The foetus begins to suck its thumb and the lungs start to inhale and exhale the surrounding amniotic fluid.
- The foetus's kidneys and digestive system also start to work. The foetus urinates and defecates into the amniotic fluid.

The foetus increases in size and strength for the remaining months of the pregnancy and the internal organs become mature in readiness for life outside the uterus.

Childbirth

Childbirth is the process of the baby moving out of the uterus and becoming an independent individual.

Human childbirth is divided into three stages: **labour, parturition** and **afterbirth.**

1 Labour

Labour involves physical changes in the reproductive system in readiness for the next stage, parturition. Labour can be a very short process (one hour) or a very long process (72 hours) depending on a number of factors.

Labour usually starts when the amniotic sac surrounding the baby bursts. This process releases the amniotic fluid and is often called 'the breaking of the waters'. It is caused by **contractions of the uterus,** which are brought about by the action of a hormone called **oxytocin.** Oxytocin is secreted by the pituitary.

The uterus contracts in waves that get more and more frequent as labour continues. The contractions cause the cervix to dilate. Once the cervix has dilated to 10 cm, the next stage of childbirth occurs.

2 Parturition

Parturition is the process of the baby being born. The cervix has dilated enough for the baby's head to pass through. Once the baby's head passes through the cervix, the rest of the baby's body usually follows very quickly and the baby passes through the vagina (birth canal).

The umbilical cord is then clamped and cut. No pain relief is required for this because it does not contain any nerves.

3 Afterbirth

The afterbirth involves the passing of the placenta from the uterus. This usually occurs a few minutes following the birth of the baby. It occurs due to continued contractions of the uterus.

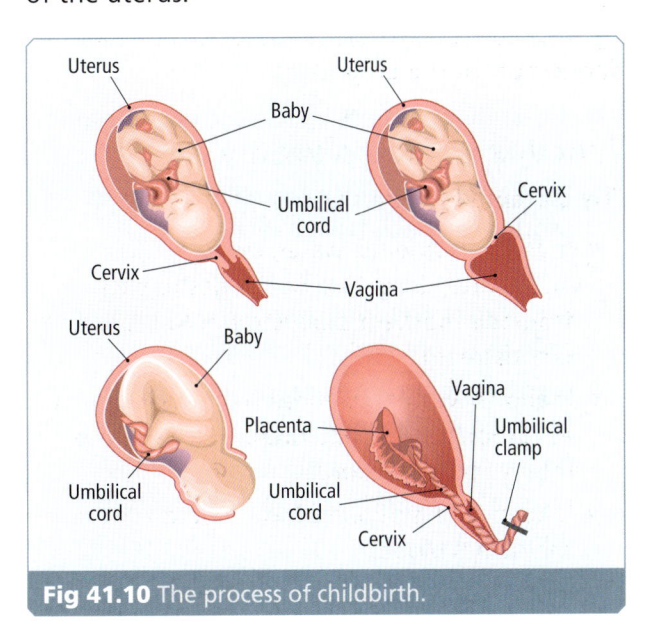

Fig 41.10 The process of childbirth.

Lactation

> **Lactation** is the production and secretion of milk by the breasts of the female.

Lactation begins to occur in the few days leading up to childbirth. It occurs in response to the pituitary hormone called **prolactin.**

During pregnancy prolactin is inhibited by the high levels of progesterone. Towards the end of pregnancy, progesterone levels decrease, which removes the inhibition on the pituitary. Prolactin is then secreted, stimulating lactation.

The breasts swell as they begin to produce milk. The breasts are a type of exocrine gland as they secrete their product (milk) into ducts.

After childbirth, the breasts secrete a thick yellow substance called **colostrum**. This is a very nutritious and concentrated form of milk and contains antibodies to protect the baby against disease in the first few days of life.

After the first few days, normal breast milk is produced.

Breast-feeding

> **Breast-feeding** is the feeding of a baby/infant directly from the breast.

Medical professionals recommend breast-feeding for babies up to at least six months of age. This is because breast-feeding has a number of advantages for both mother and baby:

- Breast milk contains all the correct nutrients in the correct proportions.
- Breast milk contains antibodies that help protect the baby from infections.
- Breast milk is the correct temperature.
- Breast milk does not pose any danger to the child as it contains no pathogens.
- Breast-feeding promotes a strong bond between mother and baby.
- Breast-feeding helps the mother's body recover more quickly from the effects of pregnancy.
- Breast-feeding is thought to reduce the chances of developing breast cancer later in life.

Birth control

> **Birth control** refers to procedures taken to control the number of offspring produced.

There are two main ways to control birth: **abortion** and **contraception**.

> **Abortion** is the physical removal of a foetus from the uterus.
>
> **Contraception** is the intentional prevention of pregnancy by stopping fertilisation or implantation from occurring.

There are four methods of contraception: **natural**, **mechanical**, **chemical** and **surgical**.

Natural contraception

Natural contraception is also known as the rhythm method. It involves avoiding sexual intercourse during the fertile period. It can be quite accurate if the couple keeps daily records of the female body temperature and other factors that change, such as vaginal mucous secretions.

Mechanical contraception

Mechanical contraception involves the use of barriers to the movement of sperm. These include male condoms, female condoms, diaphragms and domes.

Male condoms are placed over an erect penis; female condoms, diaphragms and domes are placed inside the female vagina before sexual intercourse. They prevent entry of sperm through the cervix.

Chemical contraception

Chemical contraceptives involve the use of spermicides and/or hormones. Spermicides are often used in conjunction with mechanical contraceptives. Most methods of mechanical contraceptives are coated in a layer of spermicide. The sperm are killed as soon as they come into contact with the spermicide.

Hormonal contraceptives are used by females in the form of the contraceptive pill, often simply called 'the pill'.

The contraceptive pill contains the hormones oestrogen and progesterone. The woman usually takes just one pill per day for three weeks out of four. This tricks the female reproductive system into thinking it is pregnant. The one week off the pill allows the renewal of the uterus via menstruation.

The contraceptive pill is the most effective method of contraception, and has an extremely low failure rate. Natural and mechanical methods have much higher failure rates, mainly due to not being used properly.

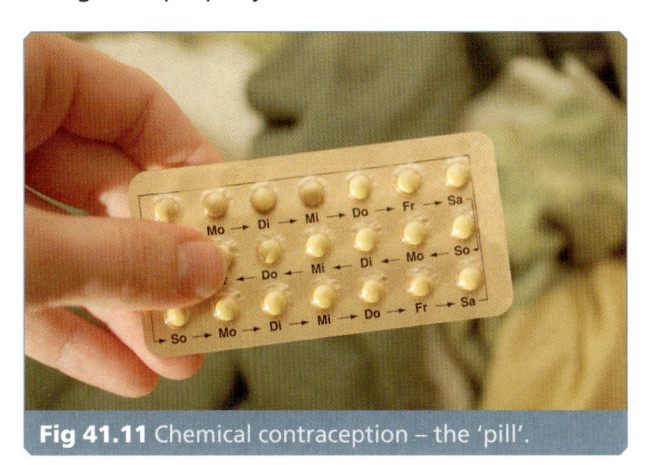

Fig 41.11 Chemical contraception – the 'pill'.

Surgical contraception

Surgical contraception is an extreme form of contraception because it can only rarely be reversed. Therefore, surgical contraception is considered only if the person does not want children at all. It involves ligation (tying and cutting) of the fallopian tubes in females (tubal ligation) and of the sperm ducts in males (vasectomy).

Infertility

> **Infertility** is the inability to contribute to conception.

There are many causes of infertility. As many as one in seven couples have difficulty in conceiving. Causes of infertility are generally divided evenly between the male and female.

Often, there appears to be no reason for an inability to conceive. A couple are described as infertile if, after 12 months of contraceptive-free sexual intercourse, they have failed to conceive.

> **NOTE** For Leaving Certificate Biology, you need to be able to describe one cause of male infertility and one cause of female infertility with a corrective measure for each.

Male infertility may be due to any of the following factors:

- Low sperm count.
- Low sperm mobility.
- Endocrine gland failure.

Female infertility may be due to the following factors:

- Fallopian tube blockage.
- Endocrine gland failure.

Corrective measures for infertile couples depend on the cause but may range from simple hormonal treatment to surgery. If these treatments do not work or in cases where there is no obvious cause of the infertility, *in vitro* **fertilisation (IVF)** may be used.

In vitro fertilisation (IVF)

> ***In vitro* fertilisation** is the process of fertilising an egg cell with a sperm cell outside the body, usually in a Petri dish, to produce a diploid zygote that is then implanted back into the uterus.

> **NOTE** *'In vitro'* is a Latin term specifically meaning 'within glass'. However, in terms of biology it refers to experiments on cells outside the body of an organism, or experiments on cells carried out in an artificial environment.

IVF is a medical technique of artificial fertilisation and implantation. It was developed in the 1970s. The first birth as a result of IVF was in 1979.

It is generally used for infertile couples who have failed to naturally conceive a child after 12 months of contraceptive-free sexual intercourse.

During the IVF process, the female is given fertility drugs during the early part of her menstrual cycle. This stimulates the formation of a number of eggs within the ovaries. These eggs are then surgically removed and each of them is fertilised with sperm. The resulting diploid zygotes are allowed to divide for a number of days to form a ball of cells (morulas) that are then implanted into the uterus of the female.

Usually a number of embryos are implanted to maximise the chances of pregnancy. As a result, IVF treatment carries a risk of multiple births, such as twins, triplets or even more!

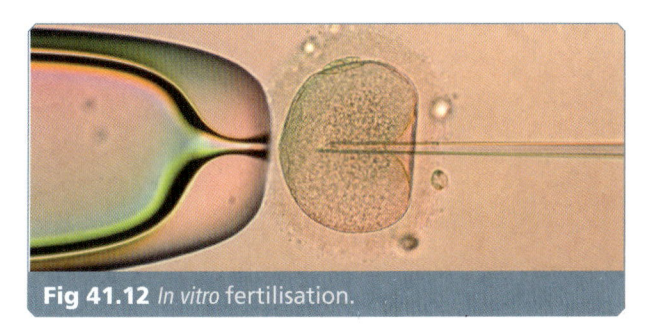

Fig 41.12 *In vitro* fertilisation.

Chapter 41 Questions

1. (a) Copy the following diagram of the male reproductive system. On your diagram write in the names of the parts labelled A–L.
   (b) Give **one** function of each part.
   (c) Indicate on your diagram the path taken by:
      (i) Sperm   (ii) Urine
   (d) Indicate, using the letter 'M', on your diagram the location of meiosis.

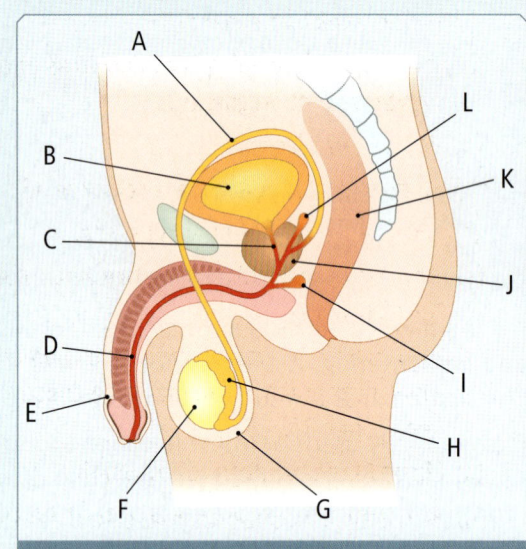

   Fig 41.13 The structure of the male reproductive system.

2. Draw a sperm cell and label the following parts: *head, acrosome, midpiece; mitochondria* and *tail*.

3. Explain why it is important for the testes to be outside of the body in a pouch.

4. (a) Draw a diagram of the female reproductive system and label the following parts: *vagina; cervix; uterus; endometrium; fallopian tube* and *ovary*.
   (b) What is another name for the:
      (i) Vagina?   (ii) Uterus?
   (c) Indicate, using the letter 'F', on your diagram the location of fertilisation.
   (d) Indicate, using the letter 'M', on your diagram the location of meiosis.

5. (a) What is *meiosis*?
   (b) Explain the importance of meiosis in human reproduction. (Hint: refer to the number of chromosomes.)

6. (a) What are *secondary sexual characteristics*?
   (b) Give **two** secondary sexual characteristics in:
      (i) Males.
      (ii) Females.

7. (a) What is meant by *sex hormones*?
   (b) Name the male sex hormone.
   (c) Name the **two** female sex hormones.
   (d) Give **two** roles for the male sex hormone.
   (e) Give **two** roles for **each** female sex hormone.

8. (a) What is meant by the *menstrual cycle*?
   (b) Name the **three** phases of the menstrual cycle.
   (c) Describe the main events of the first phase.
   (d) On what day of the cycle does the second phase usually occur?
   (e) What is the *corpus luteum*?
   (f) What is the function of the corpus luteum?

HL 9. The following diagram shows the hormonal control of the menstrual cycle:

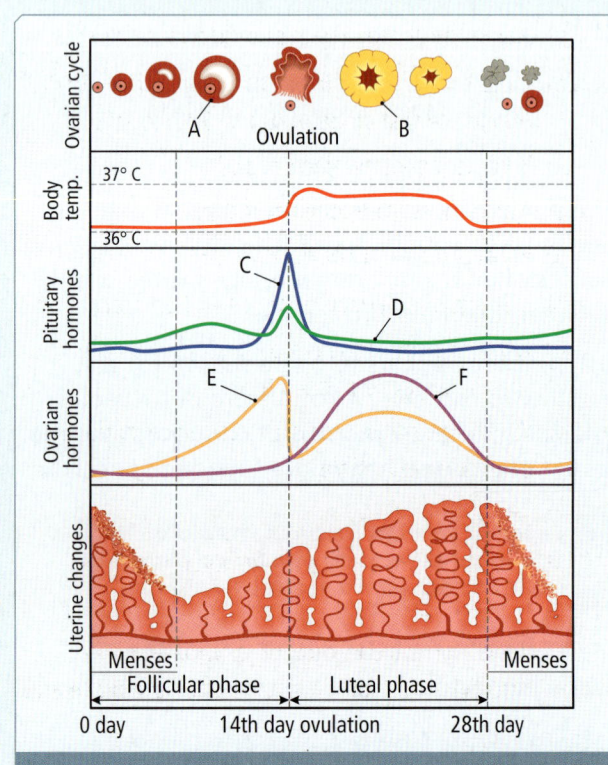

Fig 41.14 The hormonal control of the menstrual cycle.

(a) What hormone increases body temperature in the second half of the menstrual cycle?
(b) What is structure A?
(c) What is structure B?
(d) Explain the reasons for degeneration of structure B towards the end of the menstrual cycle.
(e) What is meant by *menses*?
(f) Name the hormones represented by lines C and D.
(g) What structures secrete the hormones represented by lines C and D?
(h) What is the significance of the spike in the level of hormone represented by line C?
(i) Name the hormones represented by lines E and F.
(j) What structure secretes the hormones represented by lines E and F?

10 Name and describe the cause, symptoms and treatment for a **named** menstrual disorder.

11 What is meant by the *fertile period*?

12 How long can the following survive in the female reproductive tract:
(a) Egg cell?
(b) Sperm cell?

13 What is *fertilisation*?

14 (a) Name the **three** stages of sexual intercourse.
(b) State **two** changes in the male and female bodies during the first stage of sexual intercourse.
(c) What is meant by *ejaculation*?
(d) Name **three** components of semen.

15 (a) What is meant by *birth control*?
(b) Distinguish between *abortion* and *contraception*.
(c) Name the **four** types of contraception and give a specific example of each type.
(d) Which one of the four types of contraception is generally irreversible?

16 (a) What is *infertility*?
(b) Give **two** possible causes for male infertility.
(c) Give **two** possible causes for female infertility.
(d) IVF is a possible treatment for infertility. What does IVF stand for? Briefly describe the process of IVF.

17 Distinguish between a *morula* and *blastocyst*.

HL
18 What is *implantation*?

19 Copy and complete the following table:

Embryonic germ layer	Organs/organ systems that develop
	1. 2.
	1. 2.
	1. 2.

20 (a) What is the *amnion*?
(b) What is the function of the amniotic fluid?

21 (a) What is the developing baby known as up to the eighth week of pregnancy?
(b) What is the developing baby known as after the eighth week of pregnancy?

22 (a) What is the *placenta*?
(b) From what tissues is the placenta formed?
(c) Give **two** functions of the placenta.
(d) How long does it take for the placenta to become fully functional?
(e) Explain why it is important that the mother's blood does not mix with the baby's blood? (Hint: *see* Chapter 30.)

23 (a) Name the **three** stages of childbirth.
(b) Name the hormone responsible for the first stage.
(c) Why can the umbilical cord be clamped and cut without the need for pain relief?

24 (a) What is *lactation*?
(b) What hormone is responsible for lactation? What endocrine gland secretes this hormone?
(c) What is *colostrum*?

Answer the following multiple-choice questions (note there may be two correct answers):

25 *Menstruation* is:
(a) The release of an egg from the ovary.
(b) The shedding of the endometrium.
(c) The repair of the endometrium.
(d) The widening of the cervix.

26 *Oestrogen* causes:
(a) Ovulation.
(b) Male secondary sexual characteristics.
(c) Female secondary sexual characteristics.
(d) Repair of the endometrium.

27 *Progesterone* causes:
  (a) Ovulation.
  (b) Repair of the endometrium.
  (c) Maintenance of endometrium.
  (d) Lactation.

HL 28 *Endometriosis* is:
  (a) The repair of the endometrium.
  (b) Growth of endometrial cells outside the uterus.
  (c) The shedding of the endometrium.
  (d) The growth of benign tumours in the uterus.

29 *Copulation* is:
  (a) The insertion of the erect penis into the vagina.
  (b) The production of sperm in the testes.
  (c) The development of the egg in the ovary.
  (d) One of the stages of childbirth.

30 *Testosterone* causes:
  (a) Female secondary sexual characteristics.
  (b) Sperm production.
  (c) Growth of body hair in males.
  (d) Increased muscle mass in the male.

Chapter 41 Sample examination questions

1 (i) Draw a large labelled diagram of the female reproductive system.
  (ii) Indicate clearly on your diagram where each of the following events takes place:
   1. Ovulation.
   2. Fertilisation.
  (iii) What does the term *infertility* mean?
  (iv) *In vitro* fertilisation is a method used to treat infertility.
   What is meant by the term *in vitro* in relation to fertilisation?
  (v) Give **one** cause of infertility in women.
  (vi) As a result of fertility treatment, an embryo develops successfully from an *in vitro* fertilisation. What is the next step for the embryo?

  Section C, Question 14 (a) Ordinary Level 2011

2 (a) The diagram shows the human male reproductive system.
  (i) Name the parts A, B, C and D.
  (ii) What is the function of part D?
  (iii) Name the principal male sex hormone.
  (iv) Name **two** male secondary sexual characteristics.

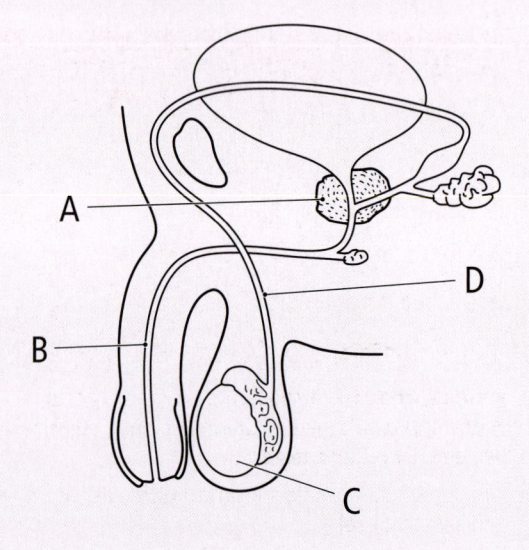

  (v) Draw a labelled diagram of a human sperm cell.

(b) The diagram shows a foetus in the uterus.
  (i) From what tissues is the placenta formed?
  (ii) Give **two** functions of the placenta.
  (iii) Describe the process of birth.
  (iv) Give any **one** biological benefit of breast-feeding.
  (v) List **two** methods of contraception.

Section C, Question 14 (a) and (b) Ordinary Level 2010

HL 3 (a) (i) Draw a diagram of the reproductive system of the human female.
  On your diagram indicate where the following occur:
    1. Meiosis.
    2. Fertilisation.
    3. Implantation.
  (ii) Give an account of the role of either oestrogen **or** progesterone in the menstrual cycle.
  (iii) Name a human female menstrual disorder. In the case of this disorder give:
    1. A possible cause.
    2. A method of treatment.

(b) (i) Give an account of the importance of the placenta during human development in the womb.
  (ii) From what tissues is the placenta formed?
  (iii) Outline how birth occurs.
  (iv) What is meant by *in vitro fertilisation*?
  (v) After implantation, the embryo first develops into a *morula* and then into a *blastocyst*. Explain the terms in italics.

Section C, Question 14 (a) and (b) Higher Level 2009

Chapter 41 Mind map

The human reproductive systems are divided into male and female systems.

The **male reproductive system** consists of: penis, sperm ducts, prostate gland, Cowper's gland, seminal vesicles, epididymis and testes.
- The penis is a muscular organ through which urine and semen travel.
- The sperm ducts (vas deferens) carry semen from the testes to the urethra.
- The prostate gland, Cowper's gland and seminal vesicles all contribute to the production of semen, the fluid in which sperm swim.
- The epididymis is a storage organ for sperm and is located on top of each testis.
- The testes are a pair of glands that produce sperm and testosterone.

The **female reproductive system** consists of: vulva, vagina, cervix, uterus (womb), fallopian tubes (oviducts) and ovaries.
- The vulva forms the external female genitalia.
- The vagina is a muscular tube that receives the penis during intercourse and is also known as the birth canal.
- The cervix is the junction between the vagina and uterus.
- The uterus is where a foetus develops.
- The fallopian tubes receive the egg from the ovaries and are the site of fertilisation.
- The ovaries are an endocrine gland that secretes the female sex hormones and are also the site of egg development.

Secondary sexual characteristics are features that distinguish males from females, but are not part of the reproductive system.

- **Role of testosterone:** causes and maintains secondary sexual characteristics such as pubic hair, facial hair, broad shoulders, and larger larynx. It also increases muscle mass and bone density and reduces fat reserves.
- **Role of oestrogen and progesterone:** oestrogen causes and maintains secondary sexual characteristics such as breasts, pubic hair and wide hips. It also causes an increase in body fat and bone mass as well as repair of the endometrium during the menstrual cycle. Progesterone is responsible for maintaining the endometrium during the menstrual cycle.

Meiosis produces haploid gametes so that at fertilisation, the diploid number is re-attained.

The menstrual cycle is a series of cyclical changes that occur in the female reproductive system over a 28-day period.

Events of the menstrual cycle:

- **Follicular phase**
  - **Menstruation:** the endometrium is shed during days 1–5.
  - **Proliferative stage (days 6–13):** Follicles begin to develop within the ovary. The endometrium is repaired.
- **Ovulation** occurs on day 14.
- **Luteal phase:** Endometrium is maintained from days 15–28 by high levels of progesterone.

Hormonal control of the menstrual cycle HL

- **Follicular phase (days 1–13):** is divided into two stages: menstruation and proliferative stages.
  - **Menstruation** is the shedding of the endometrium (lining of the uterus) due to low levels of oestrogen and progesterone.
  - The **proliferative stage** involves the regeneration of the lining of the uterus (by oestrogen) and the development of the egg in the ovary (by FSH secretion). Usually only one Graafian follicle develops fully. Towards the end of the follicular phase, the oestrogen levels reach a critical level causing the pituitary to secrete LH.
- **Ovulation:** LH stimulates ovulation. Ovulation is the release of an egg from the ovary.
- **Luteal phase:** The Graafian follicle changes into the corpus luteum that continues to secrete progesterone and oestrogen for the rest of the cycle.

Menstrual disorder: endometriosis HL

- Endometriosis is where the cells lining the uterus (endometrium) move and grow outside the uterus.
- Symptoms include abdominal pain.
- Treatment involves pain relief medication and possible surgery to remove scar tissue build-up.

Menstrual disorder: fibroids

- Fibroids are benign tumours of the uterus.
- They are thought to be caused by abnormal hormonal levels during the menstrual cycle.
- Most often they are small and they cause no problems. If they grow very large, they can cause pain and heavy menstrual bleeding.
- If they are small and cause no symptoms they are not treated. They are surgically removed if pain and bleeding occur.

Sexual intercourse is divided into three stages: sexual arousal, copulation and orgasm.

- **Sexual arousal** involves the erection of the penis in males and secretion of mucous in the vagina of females.
- **Copulation** is the insertion of an erect penis into the vagina.
- **Orgasm** is where sexual arousal reaches a maximum (climax).
- **Ejaculation** is the release of semen from the penis during sexual intercourse.

- **Fertilisation** is the fusion of a sperm cell with an egg cell to form a diploid zygote.
- The **fertile period** of the menstrual cycle is the time at which the female is most likely to become pregnant.
- Sperm can survive for 3 days inside the female reproductive tract and the egg can survive for 2 days after ovulation.

The human reproductive system — Chapter 41

Development of the embryo HL
- The diploid zygote divides by mitosis to form a morula after approximately 3–5 days.
- A morula is a ball of undifferentiated cells that forms as a result of mitosis.
- The morula continues to divide by mitosis and becomes a blastocyst, which moves into the uterus where it implants around day 9.
- Implantation is the embedding of the embryo into the lining of the uterus.
- A blastocyst is a fluid-filled sac containing an inner cell mass that gives rise to the embryo.
- The outer layer of the blastocyst is called the trophoblast.
- A group of cells inside the blastocyst is called the inner cell mass. This develops into the embryo.
- The inner cell mass organises itself into three distinct germ layers: ectoderm, mesoderm and endoderm.
  - Ectoderm: gives rise to the skin and nervous system.
  - Mesoderm: gives rise to the musculoskeletal system, kidneys, lungs and heart.
  - Endoderm: gives rise to the liver, pancreas and the inner linings of the breathing, digestive and excretory systems.

Development of the foetus HL
- A protective sac, called the amnion, begins to form around the embryo. It contains amniotic fluid and functions in protection and shock absorption.
- By the end of the eighth week of pregnancy, all the major internal organs have formed. The embryo is now called a foetus.
- The eyes are low and widely spaced at this stage and the skeleton is made from cartilage.
- From the third month onwards bone begins to form.
- Arms and legs begin to move.
- The sex organs are visible.
- The foetus begins to suck its thumb and inhales amniotic fluid.
- The foetus urinates and defecates into the amniotic fluid.
- The placenta is formed from the trophoblast layer of the embryo and tissue of the uterus.

- The placenta is fully functional 3 months into pregnancy.
- The placenta functions in transferring nutrients to the developing embryo/foetus and removing waste products of metabolism.

Childbirth involves three stages: labour, parturition and afterbirth.
- **Labour** begins with the breaking of the waters, contractions of the uterus and dilation of the cervix.
- **Parturition** is the process of the baby moving from the uterus through the birth canal to become an independent human.
- **Afterbirth** involves further contractions of the uterus to remove the placenta from the uterus.

- **Lactation** is the production and secretion of milk by the breasts of the female.
- Lactation is stimulated by prolactin – a pituitary hormone.

Birth control refers to procedures taken to control the number of offspring produced.
- **Abortion** is the physical removal of a foetus from the uterus.
- **Contraception** is the intentional prevention of pregnancy by stopping fertilisation or implantation from occurring.

Four methods of contraception: natural, mechanical, chemical and surgical.
- Natural involves using body rhythms to predict when the female is ovulating and avoiding intercourse around this time.
- Mechanical involves preventing the sperm reaching the egg by a physical barrier, such as a condom.
- Chemical involves preventing ovulation by the taking of the contraceptive pill. It also involves spermicides used together with mechanical contraception.
- Surgical involves the ligation (cutting and tying) of the fallopian tubes and the sperm ducts.

Infertility is the inability to contribute to conception.
- Male infertility can be due to:
  - Low sperm count.
  - Low sperm mobility.
  - Endocrine gland failure.
- Female infertility can be due to:
  - Fallopian tube blockage.
  - Endocrine gland failure.
- Corrective measures for infertility:
  - Hormonal treatment
  - **IVF:** *in vitro* **fertilisation** is the process of fertilising an egg cell with a sperm cell outside the body, usually in a Petri dish, to produce a diploid zygote that is then implanted back into the uterus.

Glossary

Entries in red are for Higher Level only.

A

Abiotic factor: anything that is non-living and has an effect on living organisms in an ecosystem.

Abortion: physical removal of a foetus from the uterus.

Absorption: the passage of single biomolecules from the gut into the cells lining the gut.

Acetyl coenzyme A: a two carbon compound that takes part in the Krebs cycle.

Acrosome: structure in the head of a sperm cell containing enzymes that enable the sperm cell to gain entry to the egg cell.

Active immunity: the production of antibodies by lymphocytes in response to a specific antigen.

Active site: area of an enzyme where the substrate enters and is changed into product(s).

Adenoids: lymphatic tissue located at the back of the nose.

ADH: anti-diuretic hormone – a hormone released by the pituitary.

Adhesion: sticking of water molecules to the sides of the xylem vessels.

Adipose tissue: groups of cells that store large amounts of triglycerides, usually under the skin.

ADP + P + energy → ATP + water

ADP: adenosine diphosphate.

Adrenaline: a hormone released by the adrenal glands that causes an increase in blood flow to the heart, lungs, brain and skeletal muscles.

Adrenals: endocrine glands located on top of each kidney that produce and release adrenaline.

Adventitious bud: present anywhere on the plant and can grow in unusual places.

Aerobic respiration: enzyme-controlled release of energy from food *using oxygen*.

Alimentary canal: length of the digestive system.

Allele: form of gene where a number of different types of the same gene exist.

Allergen: particle that causes an immune reaction.

Alveolus: air sac – the site of gas exchange.

Amoeba: aquatic single-celled protist.

Amylase: enzyme that breaks down starch to maltose.

Anabolic steroids: hormones that cause an increase in muscle mass.

Anabolism: building up of large molecules from smaller molecules using energy.

Anaerobic respiration: enzyme-controlled release of energy from food *without using oxygen*.

Anaphase: third stage of mitosis.

Animalia: a kingdom of similar organisms that includes all animals.

Antagonistic muscle pair: composed of two muscles that have opposite effects to each other.

Antibiotics: chemicals produced by microorganisms that prevent the growth of, or kill, other microorganisms.

Antibodies: proteins produced by lymphocytes in response to the presence of antigens.

Anti-codon: sequence of three bases present on transfer RNA that will be complementary to a codon present on messenger RNA.

Antigens: surface proteins that cause the production of antibodies.

Anther: male structure of the flower in which pollen develops.

Anus: sphincter muscle through which faeces is released.

Apical bud: present at the growth tips of a plant.

Apophysis: structure that supports the sporangium in fungi.

Appendix: small extension of the caecum thought to be involved in immune responses in the digestive system.

Aqueous humour: fluid in the front part of the eye that maintains the shape of the eye.

Artery: blood vessel that carries blood away from the heart in powerful pulses; has a thick wall, small lumen and no valves.

Arthritis: painful inflammation of a joint.

Artificial active immunity: pathogen is administered through vaccination.

Artificial passive immunity: injection of antibodies that were made in another organism.

Aseptic technique: procedure where contact with, or contamination by, microorganisms is avoided.

Asexual reproduction: the production of a new individual from one parent. The new individual is genetically identical to the parent.

Asthma: chronic inflammation of the bronchioles.

Athlete's foot: fungal infection of the skin of the foot.

ATP + water → ADP + P + energy

ATP: adenosine triphosphate.

Atrioventricular (AV) node: pacemaker located between the right atrium and right ventricle that causes ventricular contraction.

Autosome: chromosome that carries genes not associated with determining gender.

Autotrophic nutrition in bacteria is where the bacteria produce their own food.

Auxin: type of growth regulator in plants.

Axillary bud: present at the junction between the stem and petiole.

Axon: part of a neuron that transfers the impulse from the cell body to the terminals.

B

Balanced diet: a diet that contains all seven major nutrients in the correct proportions.

B cell: type of lymphocyte that produces antibodies.

Benedict's solution: blue reagent used to test for the presence of a reducing sugar.

Bile: greenish liquid produced by the liver and released by the gall bladder into the duodenum.

Bilirubin: bile pigment produced in the liver and released in bile.

Biliverdin: bile pigment produced in the liver and release in bile.

Binary fission: asexual reproduction in bacteria.

Biological organisation: different levels of complexity in an organism.

Biology: study of life.

Biomolecules: organic chemicals produced and found only within living organisms.

Bioprocessing: use of living cells or their components, such as enzymes, to make useful products or to carry out useful procedures.

Bioreactor: vessel in which a product is formed by a cell or cell component such as an enzyme.

Biosphere: region of the Earth where life can exist.

Biotic factor: anything that is living and has an effect on other living organisms in an ecosystem.

Birth control: procedures taken to control the number of offspring produced.

Blastocyst: fluid-filled sac containing an inner cell mass that gives rise to the embryo.

Blind spot: the region of each eye where the optic nerve leaves the eyeball.

Blood pressure: force blood exerts on the walls of blood vessels.

Bolus: swallowed ball of food.

Bowman's capsule: holds the glomerulus and is the site of filtration in the nephron.

Bronchioles: tiny air tubes that carry air to the alveoli.

Bronchitis: inflammation of the mucous membranes of the breathing system.

Bronchus: branch of the trachea that carries air to the lungs.

Bud: undeveloped shoot.

Buffer: solution used in experiments to maintain pH at a fixed value.

C

Caecum: first part of the large intestine.

Glossary

Cancer: a group of disorders in which cells lose control over the rate of mitosis and cell division.

Carpel: female part of the flower.

Cartilage: flexible solid connective tissue found at the ends of bones.

Capillary: blood vessel with a wall one cell thick; carries blood from arterioles to venules through tissues releasing nutrients and taking away wastes.

Canine: pointed tooth used for tearing food.

Carbon cycle: the process through which elemental carbon (in the form of biomolecules) is exchanged between living organisms and their environment.

Carnivore: animal that eats only animal material.

Carpals: bones of the wrists.

Catabolism: the breaking down of large molecules into smaller molecules with the release of energy.

Catalase: enzyme that breaks down hydrogen peroxide into oxygen gas and water.

Cell continuity: living cells arising from living cells of the same type.

Cell membrane: outer boundary of a cell made from phospholipids.

Cell plate: line of intracellular vesicles in a plant cell that forms into a new cell wall during cytokinesis.

Cellulose: type of carbohydrate that is the main component of plant cell walls.

Cell wall: structure found in bacteria, fungi and plants that maintains the shape of cells and functions in protection.

Cerebellum: part of the brain at the back of the head that is involved in fine movements and coordination of movement.

Cerebrum: largest area of the brain composed of two hemispheres.

Cervix: the junction between the vagina and the uterus in the female reproductive tract.

Chemosynthesis: process of making food from the chemicals present in the environment.

Chemotropism: growth of a plant in response to chemicals.

Chloroplast: cell organelle that carries out photosynthesis.

Choroid: dark pigmented layer in the eye.

Chromosome mutations: changes in the structure or number of chromosomes.

Chromosomes: tightly coiled and highly organised structures of DNA and protein.

Cilia: very long thin cytoplasmic protections (flagella-like) from cells lining various systems of the body that function in movement of substances.

Ciliary body: muscle that surrounds the lens and controls the shape of the lens.

Clavicle: collar bone.

Cleavage furrow: indentation of the cell membrane and cytoplasm of an animal cell during cytokinesis.

Climatic factors: weather conditions that have an effect on living organisms in an ecosystem.

Cloning: process of producing identical copies of a cell.

Cochlea: structure in the inner ear that converts sound vibrations into electrical impulses.

Codon: a sequence of three bases present on messenger RNA that codes for one amino acid.

Cohesion: sticking together of water molecules due to hydrogen-bonding.

Colon: large intestine.

Colour-blindness: condition where the individual cannot distinguish between different colours.

Columella: structure in fungi that supports the sporangium.

Community: a group of organisms living in a habitat that belong to many different species.

Compact bone: dense connective tissue.

Companion cell: part of phloem tissue.

Comparative anatomy: study of similarities and differences in the anatomy of living organisms.

Comparative biochemistry: study of similarities and differences in the chemistry of living organisms.

Comparative embryology: study of similarities and differences in the anatomy of the embryo from different species.

Competition: struggle between organisms for a resource that is in limited supply.

Complement: group of proteins produced by the liver that function as part of the general defence system.

Conclusion: an explanation of the results.

Conjunctiva: outer layer of the cornea that protects the front of the eye.

Conservation: wise management of our existing natural resources.

Contest competition: direct fight between two organisms for a resource that is in short supply.

Continuity of life: describes how cells arise from cells of the same type and organisms arise from other organisms of the same type.

Contraception: intentional prevention of pregnancy by stopping fertilisation or implantation from occurring.

Control: a factor in an experiment that provides a standard upon which the results of the experiment may be compared.

Copulation: insertion of an erect penis into the vagina.

Cornea: transparent part of the sclera that allows light to enter the eye.

Corpus luteum: remains of the Graafian follicle after ovulation.

Cotyledon: an embryonic seed leaf.

Cowper's gland: gland of the male reproductive system that contributes to the production of semen.

Cranium: skull.

Crenation: the process of an animal cell shrivelling up due to movement of water out of the cell.

Cross-pollination: the transfer of pollen from the anther to the stigma of a different plant but of the same species.

Cutting (1): process of removing a small piece of a parent plant and encouraging it to grow into an independent plant.

Cutting (2): removal of a gene from a piece of DNA using restriction enzymes.

Cytokinesis: the third stage of the cell cycle in which cell division occurs.

Cytoplasm: consists of the cytosol and cell organelles.

Cytosol: liquid portion of the cell composed mostly of water.

D

Data: results of measurements or observations.

Decline phase: stage of the bacterial growth curve where bacterial death is greater than bacterial reproduction.

Denatured enzyme: an enzyme that has lost its function due to a change in its shape.

Dendrites: part of a neuron that receives impulses.

Diabetes: a condition where the pancreas does not produce insulin or the tissues do not respond to insulin.

Diaphragm: domed-shaped sheet of muscle that takes part in inhalation.

Diaphysis: shaft of long bones.

Diastole: relaxation of the cardiac muscle.

2,4-dichlorophenoxyacetic acid (2,4-D): a type of synthetic weed-killer.

Dicotyledonous plants: plants that have two cotyledons in their seeds.

Diffusion: the movement of molecules from a region of high concentration to a region of low concentration.

Digestion: breaking down of food into its constituent molecules that can be absorbed into the bloodstream.

Dihybrid cross: genetic mating between two organisms where two genes are studied.

Diploid: two sets of chromosomes.

Dispersal: transfer of seeds and fruit away from the parent plant.

Diversity of life: large variety of living organisms present on Earth.

DNA (deoxyribonucleic acid): found in the nucleus of cells or nucleoid of bacteria.

DNA polymerase: enzyme that catalyses the formation of DNA from nucleotides.

Unit 2 Glossary

DNA profiling: a method of producing a unique pattern of bands from the DNA of a person so that it can be used for identification purposes.

Dominance: where one allele (the dominant one) masks the effect of another allele.

Dormancy: resting period for the seed when it undergoes no growth.

Double-blind testing: an experiment where neither the tester nor the patient know what treatment is being given.

Dry weight of a seed: mass of the seed minus the water.

Duodenum: first part of the small intestine where most digestion occurs.

E

Eardrum: thin membrane that receives sound waves and converts them into vibrations.

Ecological pyramid of numbers: the numbers of organisms at each trophic level in a food chain.

Ecology: branch of biology concerned with the study of the interactions of living organisms with each other and with their environment.

Ecosystem: community of organisms that interact with their environment.

Ectotherms: animals that cannot maintain a constant internal temperature. Their temperature fluctuates with the environmental temperature.

Edaphic factors: anything relating to the soil or geology of the land that have an effect on living organisms in an ecosystem.

Effector: organ or tissue that carries out an action in response to a signal from the nervous system.

Egestion: the getting rid of undigested material.

Ejaculation: release of semen from the penis during sexual intercourse.

Emulsification of lipids: breaking up of large fat droplets into smaller droplets.

Electron transport chain: part of the second stage of respiration that produces large amounts of ATP.

Endocrine gland: a gland that secretes hormones directly into the bloodstream.

Endometriosis: where the cells lining the uterus (endometrium) move and grow outside the uterus.

Endometrium: inner lining of the uterus.

Endosperm: triploid tissue that supplies the energy and nutrients for growth of the embryo during germination.

Endospore: thick and tough-walled, dormant and dehydrated bacterial cell formed during unsuitable conditions.

Endotherm: animal that maintains a constant internal temperature despite fluctuations in external temperature.

Enzymes: folded, globular-shaped protein catalysts that speed up reactions without being used up.

Epidermal tissue: a type of plant tissue that functions mainly in protection (shoot) and absorption (roots).

Epididymis: stores and matures sperm.

Epigeal germination: regrowth of the plant embryo where the cotyledon(s) move above ground.

Epiglottis: flap of tissue that closes over the glottis during swallowing.

Epiphysis: head of long bones.

Ethanol: a two-carbon compound formed as a result of anaerobic respiration in plants, fungi and some bacteria.

Ethene: a growth regulator in plants that ripens fruit.

Eukaryotic cell: cell that has a membrane-bound nucleus and membrane-bound organelles.

Eustachian tube: tube linking the throat with the middle ear.

Eutrophication: a process where water receives too many nutrients that stimulate excessive algal growth.

Evolution: genetic changes in species, over a long period of time, to produce new species in response to environmental stresses.

Excretion: getting rid of the waste products of metabolism.

Exine: tough outer layer of pollen grain.

Exocrine gland: gland that secretes its product into a duct.

Experiment: a test to determine the validity of hypotheses.

Expression: stimulation of a cell to produce the product of a particular gene.

Extracellular fluid: fluid surrounding cells of the body.

Faeces: undigested food released from the body.

Fallopian tubes: structures that carry the egg cell and sperm and where fertilisation occurs.

False ribs: three pairs indirectly attached to the sternum (by cartilage).

Fermentation: a type of anaerobic respiration.

Fermentation lock: used to hold limewater in the production of alcohol by yeast.

Fertile period: time of the menstrual cycle at which the female is most likely to become pregnant.

Fertilisation: fusion of two haploid gametes to produce a diploid zygote.

Fibroids: benign tumours that grow in the muscular wall of the uterus.

Filament: part of the stamen of the flower that holds the anther in a position most likely to involve transfer of pollen away from the flower.

Filtration: the removal of waste products and some useful substances from the blood by the kidneys.

Flagella: a type of bacterial tail that allows bacteria to move.

Floating ribs: two pairs not attached to the sternum.

Food processing: process of taking raw ingredients and converting them to food fit for consumption.

Food pyramid: guide as to the quantities of various foods to eat on a daily basis.

Food web: two or more interconnected food chains.

Fossil: the preserved remains of an organism, part of an organism or an imprint left by that organism.

Fovea: region of the retina where light rays are focused.

FSH: follicle-stimulating hormone – a hormone released by the pituitary that stimulates egg production in females and sperm production in males.

Fungi: a kingdom of similar organisms that includes yeast and bread mould.

G

Gall bladder: organ that stores bile before release.

Gametangia: structures in fungi between hyphae that contain many diploid cells as a result of sexual reproduction.

Gametes: haploid sex cells.

Gas exchange: diffusion of gases between the alveolus and bloodstream.

Gel electrophoresis: a procedure for separating DNA fragments as part of the DNA profiling method.

Gene expression: process by which the code in DNA is used to make a protein.

Gene: short region of a chromosome that contains a code for the production of a protein.

Gene mutations: changes in the structure of a single gene.

Generative nucleus: the nucleus that gives rise to sperm nuclei at fertilisation.

Genetic cross: diagram or table showing how characteristics are inherited.

Genetic engineering: artificial manipulation and alteration of genes.

Genetic screening: test of a person's DNA to see if an altered/mutated gene is present.

Genetics: study of inheritance.

Genotype: the genetic make-up of an individual.

Geotropism: growth of a plant in response to gravity.

Germination: regrowth of a plant embryo after a period of dormancy when environmental conditions are suitable.

GHRH: growth hormone-releasing hormone – a hormone released by the hypothalamus that

Glossary

stimulates the pituitary to produce growth hormone.

Gibberellins: growth regulators in plants used to increase the size of fruit.

Glomerulus: ball of blood vessels of a nephron where filtration occurs.

Glottis: opening to the trachea.

Glycolysis: first stage of respiration.

Graafian follicle: structure within which the egg cell develops prior to ovulation and the structure that produces oestrogen.

Grafting: process in which the foliage (scion) of one plant is joined to the root system (stock) of another.

Granum: stacks of thylakoid membranes in a chloroplast.

Grazing food chain: shows the sequence of organisms with one species at each trophic (feeding) level.

Grey matter: part of the spinal cord that contains cell bodies.

Ground tissue: a type of plant tissue that makes up the bulk of a plant, functions in support, storage and photosynthesis (in the leaf).

Growth hormone: released by the pituitary and causes increase in size of all tissues in the body.

Growth plate: area of bone growth that allows the bone to increase in length.

Growth regulator: chemical that controls growth in a plant.

Guard cell: controls the opening and closing of stomata.

H

Habitat: place where an organism lives.

Haemoglobin: red pigment present in red blood cells that carries oxygen in the blood.

Haemophilia: genetic condition where the individual does not have the ability to clot blood.

Haploid: one set of chromosomes.

Helper T cell: type of T cell that is involved in controlling the entire immune reaction to an infection.

Herbivore: animal that eats only plant material.

Heredity: passing on of characteristics from one generation to the next.

Heterotrophic nutrition: where bacteria obtain their food and nutrients from other living organisms.

Heterozygous: two alleles are different.

Histamine: chemical released as part of the inflammatory response.

Histones: proteins present in chromosomes.

Homeostasis: maintenance of a constant internal environment.

Homozygous: two alleles are the same.

Homologous pair: pair of chromosomes that carry genes controlling the same characteristics.

Hormone: chemical messenger produced by an endocrine gland, secreted directly into the bloodstream where it travels to a target tissue where it exerts a specific effect.

Human dental formula: $2(I^2/_2;\ C^1/_1;\ PM^2/_2;\ M^3/_3)$.

Hydrotropism: growth of a plant in response to water.

Hyperopia: long-sightedness.

Hyperthyroidism: a condition where the thyroid gland produces too much thyroxine.

Hyphae: tubular, thread-like structures present in fungi.

Hypogeal germination: the regrowth of the plant embryo where the cotyledons stay below the soil.

Hypothalamus: endocrine gland that is part of the brain and releases hormones that control the pituitary.

Hypothesis: educated guess or idea based on an observation.

Hypothyroidism: a condition where the thyroid gland does not produce enough thyroxine.

I

Immobilised enzymes: enzymes that are attached to or trapped in an inert insoluble material.

IAA: indoleacetic acid, a type of growth regulator in plants.

Ileum: small intestine.

Immunisation: protection against pathogens, or the toxins of those pathogens, by vaccination or by injection of antibodies or antidotes.

Implantation: embedding of a fertilised egg in the lining of the uterus.

Incisor: chisel-shaped tooth used for cutting food.

Intercostal: muscle between the ribs that functions in inhalation.

Interferon: chemicals released by viral-infected cells.

Interstitial fluid: fluid surrounding cells of the body.

***In vitro* fertilisation:** process of fertilising an egg cell with a sperm cell outside the body, usually in a Petri dish, to produce a diploid zygote that is then implanted back into the uterus.

Incomplete dominance: occurs when a cross between organisms of two different phenotypes (neither allele of an allelic pair is dominant or recessive with respect to each other) produces offspring with a third phenotype that is a mixture of the parental phenotypes.

Indolebutyric acid (IBA): a type of rooting powder.

Induced immunity: stimulation of monocytes and lymphocytes to get rid of a specific antigen present in the body.

Infertility: inability to contribute to conception.

Ingestion: process of taking in food.

Inheritance: the passing on of traits from one generation to the next.

Integuments: layers of tissue surrounding the embryo sac that give rise to the seed coat during seed development.

Interneurons: carry impulses from one neuron to another totally within the central nervous system.

Interphase: long period of the cell cycle during which the cell spends most of its life and carries out its everyday activities.

Intine: inner layer of pollen grain.

Iodine: red-yellow stain used to stain plant cells and test for starch.

Iodoform test: a chemical test involving potassium iodide and sodium hypochlorite that is used to test for the presence of alcohol.

Iris: coloured part of the eye that controls the amount of light entering the eye.

Islets of Langerhans: small collection of endocrine tissue located in the pancreas that produce the hormone insulin.

Isolation: process of removing DNA from a cell.

J

Joint: location where two or more bones make contact.

K

Karyotype: an image of the number and arrangement of chromosomes from a cell.

Killer T cell: type of lymphocyte that functions in killing viral-infected cells and abnormal cells using a chemical called perforin.

Krebs cycle: part of the second stage of respiration.

L

Lactation: production and secretion of milk by the breasts of the female.

Lacteal: small lymph vessel present in each villus of the small intestine.

Lactic acid: three-carbon compound formed as a result of anaerobic respiration in animals and some bacteria.

Lag phase: stage of the bacterial growth curve where bacteria are adjusting to a new environment.

Larynx: voice box.

Law/Principle: definite, factual explanation of an important aspect of nature.

Layering: process in which a stem of a parent plant is bent down into the soil and encouraged to grow into an independent plant.

Lens: transparent, flexible structure in the eye that focuses light on the retina.

Lenticels: small pores on a stem that function in gas exchange.

Life: describes an organic-based object that possesses the characteristics of metabolism and continuity of life.

Unit 2   Glossary

Ligaments: join bone to bone to form a joint.

Ligation: joining of a gene to a vector using DNA ligase.

Lignin: substance found in the xylem vessels and tracheids that give them their strength.

LH: luteinising hormone – a hormone released by the pituitary that stimulates ovulation in the female and testosterone production in the male.

Limewater: a base used to test for the presence of carbon dioxide.

Linked genes: genes present on the same chromosome.

Liver: largest internal organ in the body that has many metabolic functions.

Locus: the position of an allele or gene on a chromosome.

Log phase: stage of the bacterial growth curve where bacteria are reproducing rapidly.

Lymph: clear liquid that is collected among capillaries and is transported by the lymphatic system back to the bloodstream.

Lymph nodes: small ball-shaped organs of the lymphatic system that contain many white blood cells.

Lymphocyte: type of white blood cell.

Lymph vessel: narrow, dead-ending tube that transports lymph and are present in every tissue and organ throughout the body.

Lysosome: cell organelle responsible for making enzymes that digest structures within the cell.

M

Malpighian layer: layer of cells from which the outer layers of the skin originate. It also produces melanin.

Mandible: jaw bone.

Measles: a serious respiratory infection caused by a virus.

Medulla oblongata: part of the brainstem, deep within the brain.

Megaspore: cell that undergoes meiosis to form a haploid egg cell.

Meiosis: a type of nuclear division that leads to four daughter cells being produced, each containing half the number of chromosomes as the parent cell.

Melanin: brown skin pigment that protects against the harmful UV light rays from the Sun.

Memory B cell: type of lymphocyte that is capable of remembering an antigen and reproducing very quickly into plasma B cells in response to an antigen.

Memory T cell: type of lymphocyte that is capable of remembering an antigen and causing an immune reaction very quickly in response to an antigen.

Mendel's First Law of Segregation: each cell contains two factors for each trait. These factors separate at gamete formation so that each gamete contains only one factor from each pair of factors. At fertilisation the new organism will have two factors for each trait, one from each parent.

Mendel's Second Law of Independent Assortment: members of one pair of factors separate independently of another pair of factors during gamete formation.

Menstrual cycle: series of cyclical changes that occur in the female reproductive system over a 28-day period.

Menstruation: shedding of the endometrium (lining of the uterus).

Meristem: unspecialised cells in a plant continuously dividing by mitosis.

Meristematic tissue: composed of unspecialised cells that are dividing by mitosis all the time.

Metabolism: sum of all the chemical reactions occurring in an organism.

Metacarpals: bones of the hands.

Metaphase: second stage of mitosis.

Metatarsals: bones of the feet.

Methylene blue: a dark blue stain used for viewing animal cells under a microscope.

Microscope: instrument that magnifies small objects.

Microspore: cells that undergo meiosis to form pollen grains.

Microorganisms: living things that can be seen only with the aid of a microscope.

Microvilli: small extensions of the cytoplasm of epithelial cells lining the small intestine.

Middle lamella: cement that holds cell walls together in plants.

Mitochondrion: cell organelle responsible for producing energy.

Mitosis: nuclear division in which the number of chromosomes in the daughter nuclei is the same as the parent nucleus.

Molar: large tooth with cusps that chews and grinds food.

Monera: a kingdom of similar organisms that includes all bacteria.

Monocotyledonous plant: plant that has one cotyledon in its seeds.

Monocyte: type of white blood cell.

Monohybrid cross: a genetic mating between two organisms where one gene is studied.

Morula: ball of undifferentiated cells that forms as a result of mitosis.

Motor neurons: carry impulses from an interneuron to an effector.

MRSA: multi-resistant *Staphylococcus aureus*.

Mucosa: internal lining of the alimentary canal.

Mucous: thick fluid release by various glands in the body.

Mumps: painful infection of the salivary glands caused by a virus.

Mutagens: agents that increase the rate of mutations.

Mutation: change in the structure or amount of DNA in a cell.

Mycelium: collection of hyphae in fungi.

Myelin sheath: substance produced by a Schwann cell that insulates axons and dendrites.

Myopia: short-sightedness.

N

$NAD^+ + e^- \rightarrow NAD + e^- \rightarrow NAD^- + H^+ \rightarrow NADH$

NAD^+: nicotinamide adenine dinucleotide.

$NADP^+ + e^- \rightarrow NADP + e^- \rightarrow NADP^- + H^+ \rightarrow NADPH$

$NADP^+$: nicotinamide adenine dinucleotide phosphate.

Naphthalene acetic acid (NAA): a type of rooting powder.

Nasal cavity: series of spaces within the nose where air passes through.

Natural active immunity: when the body becomes infected with a pathogen from their environment.

Natural passive immunity: when a baby receives antibodies directly from its mother either through the placenta before birth or after birth from breast milk.

Natural selection: process by which particular traits become more common in a population due to that trait being advantageous to the species.

Nephron: functional unit of the kidney.

Neuron: a nerve cell specialised to carry electrochemical impulses.

Neurotransmitter: a chemical substance released by a neuron to transmit a nerve impulse to another neuron or effector.

Niche: functional role an organism plays in its habitat.

Nitrogen cycle: the process through which elemental nitrogen (in the form of biomolecules) is exchanged between living organisms and their environment.

Non-nuclear inheritance: the passing on of features from one generation to the next without the use of the nucleus.

Nucellus: nutritive layer in the embryo sac that supplies the energy and nutrients for egg cell development.

Nucleoid: region of a bacterial cell where DNA is to be found.

Nucleolus: structure within the nucleus responsible for making ribosomes.

Nucleotide: made up of a phosphate, sugar and a nitrogenous base.

Nucleus: membrane-bound organelle containing DNA and controls all chemical processes within the cell.

Glossary

Number of animals in a habitat: (Caught 1st x Caught 2nd) / (Marked 2nd)

Nutrient recycling: the process of exchanging important elements between living organisms and the environment.

Nutrition: the way in which living organisms obtain and use food.

O

Observation: the taking in of information received about the natural world.

Oestrogen: female sex hormone.

Olfaction: sense of smell.

Olfactory nerve: nerve that carries messages from the nasal cavity to the brain.

Omnivore: animal that eats both plant and animal material.

Optic nerve: nerve that carries messages from the eye to the brain.

Optimum activity of an enzyme: the condition(s) under which the enzyme works best.

Oral cavity: mouth.

Organ: group of tissues joined together to carry out a specialised function.

Organ system: group of organs that work together to carry out a number of linked functions.

Organelle: specialised membrane-bound compartment within a cell that has a specific function.

Orgasm: when sexual arousal reaches a maximum (climax).

Osmoregulation: control of the amount of water in an organism.

Osmosis: movement of water molecules from a region of high water concentration to a region of low water concentration across a semi-permeable membrane.

Ossicles: three tiny bones present in the ear for transfer of sound vibrations.

Ossification: process of laying down new bone material by osteoblasts.

Osteoblasts: bone cells that lay down new bone.

Osteoclasts: bone-digesting cells.

Osteoporosis: disease in which collagen is lost from the bone, making the bone brittle.

Ovary (1): endocrine organ in the female in which egg cells are produced.

Ovary (2): part of the carpel of the flower in which egg cells develop.

Ovulation: the release of an egg from the ovary.

Ovum: egg cell.

Oxidation **I**s **L**oss of electrons.

Oxytocin: a hormone released by the pituitary that causes the uterus wall to contract forcibly during childbirth.

P

Palaeontology: the study of fossils.

Pancreas: exocrine and endocrine gland located just below the stomach.

Parathormone: a hormone released by the parathyroid glands that increase the level of calcium in the blood.

Parathyroid glands: endocrine glands located in the thyroid gland of the neck that produce the hormone parathormone.

Parasitism: one organism, called the parasite, lives in or on another organism, called the host, and the host is harmed.

Parkinson's disease: degenerative disease where a small number of dopamine-producing neurons deep within the brain die.

Passive immunity: transfer of antibodies from one organism to another.

Pathogen: organism that causes disease.

Penis: muscular organ of the male reproductive system.

Pepsin: enzyme that breaks down proteins into peptides.

Pepsinogen: inactive form of pepsin.

Percentage gradient: (Rise / Run) x 100

Percentage cover: the area of ground occupied by aerial parts of plants.

Percentage frequency: the chances of finding a given species in a habitat.

Periosteum: outer covering of bone.

Peristalsis: rhythmical waves (in one direction) of contractions pushing food along the alimentary canal.

Petal: part of the flower usually involved in attracting insects.

Petri dish: shallow circular dish used for culturing or growing bacteria and other microorganisms.

Phalanges: bones of the fingers and toes.

Pharynx: throat.

Phenotype: the physical make-up of an individual.

Phloem: vascular tissue in plants that transports food.

Phospholipids: fats that are composed of one glycerol molecule, two fatty acids and one phosphate molecule.

Photolysis: the breaking up of water into oxygen gas, hydrogen ions and electrons using the energy in sunlight.

Photosynthesis: the process of producing sugars from carbon dioxide and water using sunlight as a source of energy.

Carbon dioxide + Water + Chlorophyll + Light → Glucose + Oxygen

$6CO_2 + 6H_2O$ + Chlorophyll + Light → $C_6H_{12}O_6 + 6O_2$

Photosystem: collection of approximately 300 chlorophyll pigments within the thylakoid membrane of a chloroplast.

Phototropism: growth of a plant in response to light.

Pineal: endocrine gland located in the brain that produces melatonin.

Pit: pore found in xylem tissue that allows movement of water.

Pituitary: 'master' endocrine gland located in the head just below the brain.

Placebo: a substance with no active medication used as a control in an experiment.

Plantae: kingdom of similar organisms that includes all plants.

Plasma: straw-yellow, liquid part of the blood.

Plasma B cell: type of lymphocyte that produces antibodies.

Plasmid: circular piece of DNA in bacteria that gives the bacteria special traits.

Plasmolysis: the process whereby a plant cell loses water and the cell membrane comes away from the cell wall.

Platelets: fragments of cells that take part in blood clotting.

Pleural membrane: thin membrane covering the lungs and allows friction-free movement during breathing.

Plumule: embryonic shoot.

Polar nuclei: two nuclei in the centre of an embryo sac that give rise to endosperm after fertilisation.

Pollination: the transfer of pollen from the anther to the stigma of a flower of the same species.

Pollution: any harmful addition to the environment.

Pooter: device used to trap small insects and arthropods.

Pondweed: aquatic plant used to measure the rate of photosynthesis.

Population: a group of organisms living in a habitat that belong to the same species.

Portal system: network of capillaries in one organ or tissue joined to another network of capillaries in another organ or tissue via a vein or veins.

Potato phosphorylase: enzyme that catalyses the formation of starch from glucose.

Predation: the catching, killing and eating of another organism.

Premolar: large tooth with cusps for chewing and grinding food.

Progametangia: swellings that grow on hyphae in fungi during sexual reproduction.

Progesterone: female sex hormone.

Prokaryotic cell: a tiny cell that has neither a membrane-bound nucleus nor membrane-bound organelles.

Unit 2 — Glossary

Prolactin: a hormone released by the pituitary in females that causes the breasts to produce milk.

Prophase: first stage of mitosis.

Prostate: gland of the male reproductive system that contributes to semen production.

Protein folding: the process a newly formed protein undergoes to take up its functional shape.

Protein synthesis: the making of protein using amino acids and the code in messenger RNA.

Protista: a kingdom of similar organisms that includes *Amoeba*.

Pseudopod: extension of cytoplasm in *Amoeba*.

Pulse: the alternate contraction and relaxation of an artery as blood passes through.

Pupil: hole in the iris that lets light through.

Purines: adenine and guanine.

Pyrimidines: thymine, cytosine and uracil.

Pyruvic acid: three-carbon end-product of the first stage of respiration.

Q

Quadrat: square made from wood, plastic or metal used to quantify plants or slow-moving animals in a habitat.

R

Rabies: a fatal nervous system disease caused by a virus.

Radicle: the embryonic root.

Reabsorption: process of taking back into the bloodstream useful substances that were filtered out of the bloodstream by the kidneys.

Receptacle: part of the plant that supports the flower.

Recessive: where an allele's effect is only expressed when in the homozygous condition.

Recombinant DNA: piece of genetically modified DNA that contains DNA from two or more different species.

Rectum: storage organ for undigested material.

Red blood cell: cell containing the pigment haemoglobin that is responsible for carrying oxygen around the body.

Red marrow: type of bone marrow that produces red blood cells.

Reducing sugar: a sugar that turns Benedict's solution brick-red in the presence of heat. Sucrose is not a reducing sugar.

Reduction **I**s **G**ain of electrons.

Reflex actions: involuntary responses to stimuli.

Reproduction: the way in which new offspring are produced from their parent(s).

Replicate: a repeat of an experiment.

Respiration: enzyme-controlled process of releasing energy from food.

Glucose + Oxygen → Energy + Water + Carbon dioxide

$C_6H_{12}O_6 + 6O_2 \rightarrow$ Energy $+ 6H_2O + 6CO_2$

Response: activity of an organism or part of an organism as a result of a stimulus.

Restriction enzyme: enzyme that cuts DNA at specific places.

Retina: light-sensitive surface of the eye.

Rhizoids: hyphae that grow down into a substrate.

Rhizopus: a type of bread mould.

Ribosome: found in the cytoplasm and take part in protein synthesis.

Rings of cartilage: structures of support that keep the trachea and bronchi open during breathing.

Ringworm: fungal infection of the skin.

RNA polymerase: enzyme that catalyses the formation of RNA from nucleotides.

Root pressure: build up of water in the xylem vessels of the roots causing water to move upwards.

Rubella: mild respiratory infection caused by a virus (often called German measles) – but can be serious if contracted during pregnancy as it can seriously harm the unborn child.

Runner: horizontal stem in plants used in asexual reproduction.

S

Saprophytic nutrition: process of obtaining food from dead organic matter.

Scapula: shoulder blade.

Schwann cell: a type of cell that produces myelin sheath.

Scientific method: a process of investigation carried out in order to explain observations made in the natural world.

Sclera: white of the eye that functions in protection.

Scramble competition: the struggle amongst a number of organisms for a resource in short supply and each organism gets a small share of the resource.

Scrotum: sac in which the testes are held.

Sebaceous gland: glands in the skin that produce sebum.

Secondary sexual characteristics: features that distinguish males from females, but are not part of the reproductive system.

Secretion: the process of transporting substances out of the blood by the kidneys.

Selection: process of killing any cells that did not take up the recombinant DNA.

Selective permeability: the property of cell membranes controlling what enters and leaves the cell.

Self-pollination: is the transfer of pollen from the anther to the stigma of the same plant.

Seminal vesicle: gland of the male reproductive system that contributes to semen.

Sensory neurons: carry impulses towards the central nervous system.

Sepal: protects the flower when it is in the bud.

Sex linkage: gene that is located on a sex chromosome.

Sexual reproduction: the production of a new individual from two parents. The new individual is genetically different to both parents.

Sickle-cell anaemia: genetic condition where the individual's red blood cells have faulty haemoglobin that causes the red blood cell to take up a sickle shape.

Sieve plate: porous end wall of a sieve tube cell that allows movement of food.

Sieve tube cell: part of phloem tissue.

Sino-atrial (SA) node: pacemaker located in the upper right atrium that causes atrial contraction.

Skin: outer protective covering present on all mammals.

Sodium alginate: substance obtained from seaweed that is used to immobilise enzymes.

Speciation: the formation of a new species following many changes in the structure of an organism until the new species cannot interbreed to produce fertile offspring with the original species.

Species: group of similar organisms that are capable of interbreeding to produce fertile offspring.

Specificity: refers to an enzyme ability to react with only one substrate.

Sperm cell: haploid gamete in male animals.

Sperm duct: carries sperm during ejaculation.

Sperm nuclei: nuclei in plants that take part in fertilisation during sexual reproduction.

Sphygmomanometer: instrument that measures blood pressure.

Spleen: lymphatic organ located just to the left of the stomach.

Spongy bone: contains bony bars and plates separated by irregular-shaped spaces.

Sporangiophore: hypha that grows vertically upwards.

Sporangium: structure in fungi that holds spores.

Stamen: male part of the flower.

Stationary phase: stage of the bacterial growth curve where bacterial reproduction equals bacterial death.

Sterile: state of being free from microorganisms.

Sternum: breastbone.

Stigma: part of the carpel of a flower upon which the pollen is trapped.

Stimulus: anything that causes a response in an organism.

Stolon: horizontally growing hyphae in fungi.

Stoma (stomata): pores located mostly on the underside of a leaf that function in gas exchange.

Glossary

Stomach: bag-like organ that mixes swallowed food with gastric juice.

Stroma: liquid part of the chloroplast.

Style: part of the carpel of a flower which holds the stigma in a position most likely to capture pollen.

Sucker: a root sprout in certain plants used as a type of sexual reproduction.

Suppressor T cell: type of lymphocyte involved in stopping the immune reaction to an infection once the pathogen has been eliminated.

Survival phase: stage of the bacterial growth curve where bacteria form endospores due to harsh conditions.

Suspensory ligament: ligament in the eye that holds the lens in place.

Symbiosis: a biological relationship in which two species live in close proximity to each other and interact regularly in such a way as to benefit one or both of the organisms.

Synapse: structure where two neurons come in to close contact so that a nerve impulse can be transmitted between the two neurons.

Synaptic cleft: gap between two neurons in close contact.

Synaptic vesicle: tiny cytoplasmic organelle that contains neurotransmitter.

Synovial fluid: fluid that lubricates freely movable joints.

Systole: contraction of cardiac muscle.

T

Tapetum: nutritive layer in the anther that supplies energy and nutrients for developing pollen.

Tarsals: bones of the ankles.

Taxonomy: study of classification of living organisms.

T cell: type of lymphocyte involved in the specific defence system.

Telophase: fourth stage of mitosis.

Tendons: join muscle to bone.

Testes: endocrine and exocrine gland present only in males that produces testosterone and sperm.

Tetanus: a fatal muscular system disease caused by a virus.

Tetrad: group of four cells in the early stages of pollen grain development.

Theory: comprehensive explanation of an important aspect of nature supported by results gathered over a long period of time.

Thigmotropism: growth of a plant in response to touch.

Thylakoid membrane: structure within a chloroplast that contain chlorophyll pigments.

Thymosin: a hormone released by the thymus gland that stimulates white blood cells to become mature and fully functional.

Thymus: endocrine gland located in the chest that produces thymosin.

Thyroid: endocrine gland located in the neck that produces thyroxine.

Tissue: group of similar cells with a shared function.

Tissue culture: growth of tissue and/or cells outside of the organism.

Tissue culturing (also called micropropagation): growth of a large number of plantlets in a nutrient medium from small tissue samples.

Tonsils: lymphatic tissue located on either side of the back of the throat.

Trachea: windpipe.

Traits: physical and chemical characteristics that a living organism possesses.

Transcription: the synthesis of mRNA *using* a DNA template.

Transformation: uptake of recombinant DNA into a bacterial cell.

Translation: making of protein *using* the code in mRNA.

Transmission electron microscope: a type of specialised microscope that magnifies extremely small objects up to 1,000,000 times.

Transpiration: loss of water vapour from the surface of a plant.

Transpiration stream: movement of water through a plant.

TRH: thyrotropin-releasing hormone – a hormone released by the hypothalamus that stimulates the pituitary to release thyroid-stimulating hormone.

Triglycerides: lipids composed of one glycerol molecule and three fatty acids.

Triplet (or codon): a sequence of three bases present on messenger RNA that codes for one amino acid.

Tropism: growth response of a plant to a stimulus.

True ribs: seven pairs directly attached to the sternum.

TSH: thyroid-stimulating hormone – a hormone released by the pituitary that causes the thyroid gland to produce thyroxine.

Tube nucleus: nucleus responsible for producing the pollen tube after pollination.

Turgor: the pressure of the contents of a cell against its cell wall.

U

Urinary bladder: bag-like organ that stores urine until release from the body.

Urination (micturition): the passing of urine from the body.

Urine: mixture of urea, salts and water produced by the kidneys.

Urethra: tube that carries urine from the bladder and semen from the testes.

Uterus: womb where the baby develops.

V

Vaccination: the administration, usually by injection, of a non-disease-causing dose of a pathogen or part of a pathogen (e.g. the antigen or toxin) which causes active immunity.

Vacuole: fluid-filled sac present in mainly plant cells.

Vagina: muscular organ of the female reproductive tract that receives the penis during sexual intercourse.

Variable: factor that is changed in the course of an experiment.

Variation: difference amongst members of the same species.

Vascular tissue: a type of plant tissue that functions in transport of substances around a plant.

Vector: a piece of DNA (such as a bacterial plasmid) that will carry the gene of interest into a host cell.

Vegetative propagation: asexual reproduction in plants.

Vein: a blood vessel that carries blood towards the heart in an even flow; has a thin wall, large lumen and valves.

Vertebrae: spinal bones.

Vestibular apparatus: series of tubes that gives the brain information on the position of the head.

Vestibular nerve: nerve that carries messages from the semicircular canals to the brain.

Villus: small out-folding of the wall of the small intestine.

Visking tubing: semi-permeable membrane used to demonstrate osmosis.

Vitreous humour: viscous fluid in the main part of the eye that maintains the shape of the eye.

Vulva: external female genitalia.

W

White blood cells: cells responsible for fighting infection.

White matter: part of the spinal cord that contains mostly axons and dendrites.

Xylem: vascular tissue in plants that transports water and minerals.

Yellow marrow: type of bone marrow that stores fat.

Z

Zygospore: tough-walled spore produced by fungi during sexual reproduction that can survive harsh conditions.

Zygote: is a diploid cell that results from fertilisation.

Index

2,4-dichlorophenoxyacetic acid (2,4-D) 272

A

abdomen 375
abiotic factors 32–33, 73–74
abortion 434
ABO system 310
abscisic acid 269, 292
abscission 292
absorption 337
 of nutrients 342
accidental discovery 7
accommodation 396
 of the lens 405
acetate grid 274
acetylcholine 395
acetyl coenzyme A 135
acidic urine 376
acidophiles 221
acne 371
acrosome 424
actin 22–23, 417
activation of neurotransmitter 395
active immunity 354
active site 104
active site theory 104
active transport 261–262, 378–379
adaptations 34, 74–75
 competitive 74
 structural 74
 behavioural 74
adenine 157, 162
adeno-associated virus (AAV) 246
adenoids 332–334, 362
adenosine triphosphate 118
adhesion 262
adipose tissue 371, 414
ADP 118
adrenal artery 374
adrenal glands 374–375, 383, 387-388
adrenaline 375, 388
adrenal vein 374
adventitious bud 253
adventitious root 254
aerobic bacteria 220
aerobic respiration 132–143
aerotolerant anaerobic bacteria 220
afferent arteriole 377
afferent lymph vessels 333
afterbirth 433
agar plates 234
agitation system 112
AIDS (acquired immunodeficiency syndrome) 244, 358
air space 252, 263–264
air temperature 73
air thermometer 65
alcohol 110, 136, 139–140, 225, 298, 341
 testing for (iodoform test) 140
alcohol fermentation 133–134
algae 239

alimentary canal 337
alkaline urine 376
alkaliphiles 221
alkaloid 273
allele 172
allergens 286
allergic rhinitis 286
alveoli 362–367
amino acid 22, 168, 378
ammonia 43–44
amnion 432
amniotic fluid 432
Amoeba 213, 239–240
amphibians 304
amylase 104, 297, 338, 342
amylose (starch) 18
anabolic steroids 388
anabolism 27, 104
anaemia 25
anaerobic jar 296
anaerobic respiration 133–134
analysis 78
anaphase 149
anatomical adaptations (plants) 273
anchorage 253
anemometer 65, 68
angiogram 320
angiosperms 248
animal cells 84, 88–89
animal dispersal 292
animalia 214
animal pollination 287
animal tissues 94
antagonistic muscle pairs 417
anther 284–285
antibiotics 224, 231
 overuse of 224
antibodies 310, 353, 356, 434
anti-diuretic hormone (ADH) 379, 384
antigen-antibody response 353, 357
antigens 353
anti-thyroid drugs 386
anus 337–338
anvil 398
aorta 319–322, 326
apical bud 253
apical dominance 272
apical meristems 272
apophysis 232
appendages 412
appendicitis 344
appendicular skeleton 412–413
appendix 338, 344
apples 290
apricots 290
aqueous humour 395–396
arteriole 317, 319
artery 317
arthritis 417
articulation 411, 413
artificial active immunity 354
artificial genetic manipulation 290

artificial passive immunity 355
artificial vegetative propagation 281
asbestos fibres 151
ascending colon 338, 344
asepsis 234
aseptic technique 234
asexual reproduction 150, 232, 266, 279
asparagus 266
aspect 73
assessment 78
association neurons 393
asthma 366
atherosclerosis 324
athlete's foot 231, 236
ATP 118, 134, 378
atria 321
atrial diastole 322
atrial systole 322
atrioventricular node (AV node) 322
auditory canal 398–399
auditory cortex 402
auditory nerve 399
auricles 326
autoclave 234
autoimmune disease 358
autosomes 144, 172
autotrophic nutrition 219
autotrophic organisms 248
auxin 269, 271–272
auxin treatment 290–291
axial skeleton 411–412
axil 253
axillary buds 253, 280
axon 393–394
axon terminals 393–394
azidothymidine (AZT) 246

B

bacillus 217
backbone 410
backed blade 256
bacteria 43, 212, 216, 352
 beneficial 222
 denitrifying 44
 E. coli 223
 economic importance of 222
 good 344
 harmful 222
 lactic acid 222
 meningitis 223
 of decay 44, 220
 pathogenic 222
 strep throat 222
 symbiotic 344
 tuberculosis 222
bacteriophage 243
balance 399
balanced 132–143
ball-and-socket joints 416
bananas 291
bark 273
barnacles 60, 63
barrier system 351
batch cultures 112, 137
batch food processing 224
B cells 356
BCG 354
beach erosion 78

beaker 114
beans 290
beating tray 65–66
beer 110
beetles 317
begonia 256
behavioural adaptation 74
belt transect 65, 71–72
Benedict's reagent 17, 114
beneficial bacteria 222
benign cancer 151
beriberi 25
biceps 417
biconcave 308
bicuspid valve 321, 322
bile 341
bile duct 338, 342
bile salts 342
bilirubin 309, 342
biliverdin 309, 342
binary fission 217–218
biological organisation 11
biomolecules 15–26
bioprocessing 110–112
 with immobilised cells 138
bioreactor 112, 137, 224
biosphere 32, 216, 230
biotic factors 33
birds 304
birth canal 425, 433
birth control 434–435
birth defects 273
bitter 400
Biuret reagent 24
bladder wrack 60
blastocyst 432
blind spot 395, 397
blood 308–313, 317
blood clotting 313, 351
blood groups 310–313
blood pressure 323–324, 375, 402
blood vessels 316–317, 371
blushing 405
bolus 338
bone anabolic drugs 418
bone development 414
bone-digesting cells 418
bone growth 414–415
bone marrow 356
bone remodelling 415
bone renewal 415
booster 354
botanist 4
Bowman's capsule 377
brain (human) 392, 401–405
 brainstem 402
 brain (structure of) 401–402
breaking dormancy 292
breastbone 410
breast-feeding 355, 434
breast milk 355
breathing 402
 breathing disorders 365
 breathing rate 366
 breathing system (human) 362–366
broad bean seeds 297
broad-bladed leaf 251
bronchi 362–363
bronchioles 362–363
bronchitis 365

bronchodilators 366
brush border 343
buccal cavity 337, 362
buds 249, 252, 280
budding 231
buffer 106, 109
bug pot 65
Bunsen 298
burdock fruits 292
bursa 356
busy Lizzy 256
butter 222
button mushrooms 236

C

caecum 338, 344
caffeine 273
calcitonin 418
calcium 15, 26, 306, 378, 386, 418
calcium alginate beads 111, 138
calcium chloride 113
calcium salts 413
Calvin cycle 124
camouflage 39
cancer 151, 194
 benign 151
 carcinogens 151
 chemotherapy 151
 common causes
  asbestos fibres 151
  cigarette smoke 151
  human papillomavirus 151
  radon gas 151
  ultraviolet (UV) light 151
 malignant 151
 metastasis 151
 mutations 151
 oncogenes 151
 research 246
 treatment 352
canines 339
canopy layer 62
capillaries 318–319
capsid 243
capsule 216
capsule (lymph nodes) 333
capture-recapture method 72
carbohydrates 15–16, 123, 126, 265
carbon 15, 42
carbon cycle 42
carbon dioxide 43, 123, 306
 uptake 263
carcinogens 151
cardiac (heart) cycle 322–325
cardiac muscle 321, 416
cardiac sphincter 340
carnivores 336
carotid arteries 319–320
carpals 410, 413
carpel 284
carrier 186
carrier-binding method 111
carrots 265–266
cartilage 413–414, 416
Casablanca lily 273
catabolism 27, 103
catalase 104, 106, 108–109

Index

catechin 273
celery 106, 109, 266
cell body 393–394
cell continuity 144
cell elongation 272
cells
 animal 84, 88
 cheek 88
 cheek companion 255
 components 84
 continuity 144
 cycle 147–150
 division 147
 division (cytokinesis) 148, 150
 egg 171–172, 288
 elongation 272
 equator (middle) 149
 eukaryotic 89
 growth 150
 guard 251, 252, 263, 264
 haploid daughter 285
 membrane 84
 microspore mother 285
 onion 90
 plant 84, 90
 plate 150
 prokaryotic 89
 red blood 308
 repair 150
 sieve tube 255
 somatic 145
 triploid 146
 wall 85
 white blood 308, 312, 352
cellular energy 103
cellulose 18, 345
central canal 403–404
central nervous system (CNS) 392, 401–405
centriole 149
centromere 149
cerebellum 399, 401–402, 402
cerebrospinal fluid (CSF) 401, 403–404
cerebrum 401
cervical cancer 425
cervix 411, 425
characteristics of life 10
cheese-making 110, 222
chemical adaptations (plants) 273
chemical contraceptives 434
chemical digestion 337, 342
chemical elements present in food 15
chemoreceptors 365
chemosynthesis (nitrifying bacteria) 219
chemotherapy 151
chemotropism 271, 289, 306, 431
Chernobyl nuclear disaster 194
chicken pox 245
childbirth 433
chimpanzee 214
chitin 230
chlorine 15
chlorophyll 121, 123, 250, 260
chloroplast 121–122
chloroplasts 85
choking 363
cholesterol 341–342

chordae tendineae 321
choroid 395, 397
chromatin (uncoiled DNA) 147–148, 156
chromium 15
chromosome diagram 183
chromosome mutations 194
chromosomes 144–145, 147, 156
 dedicated 149
 diagram 183
 duplicated homologous 158
 duplicated 156
 homologous 158
 mutations 194
 sex 144, 156
 X 145
 Y 145
chyme 342
cigarette smoke 151, 194
cilia 351, 425
ciliary body 395–396
ciliary muscle 396
classification of joints 415–416
clavicle (collar bone) 410, 412
cleavage furrow 150
clematis 281
climatic factors 33
Clinistix glucose test strips 114
clock glass 256
cloning 205–206
closed circulatory system 316–317
clownfish 61
coarse focus wheel 86–87
cobalt 15
cocaine 273
coccus 216
coccyx 411
cochlea 398–399
cockles 60
coding DNA 155
co-dominance 177
codon
 amino acid 168
 start 168
 stop 168
cohesion 262
cohesion-tension model 262
cold-blooded 304
collagen 22–23, 318, 371, 413, 416, 418
collar bone 412
colon 344
colony 231
colostrum 434
colour-blindness 185
columella 232
commercial rooting powders 272
common blenny 60
common prawns 60
community 36
compact bone 413
companion cells 255
comparative anatomy 199
comparative biochemistry 200
comparative embryology 200
compass 65
competition 36

competitive adaptation 74
complement 341, 352
complementary base pairing 158
complex viruses 243
concave lenses 398
conception 431
conclusions 3
 analysing 3–4
condensation reaction 16
condoms 434
cones 397
confectionery 345
congenital hyperinsulinism 387
conifer trees 273, 287
connective tissue 94, 413, 416
constipation 340
constriction of the iris 405
consumers
 primary 34–35
 secondary 34
 tertiary 34
 top 35
contest competition 36
continuity of life 10–11, 14
continuous-flow cultures 112, 137–138
continuous-flow food processing 224–225
contraception 41, 434
contraceptive pill 434–435
contractile proteins 416
contractile vacuoles 240
control (experimental) 5
control of human breathing 365
convex lenses 397
convoluted 342
copper 15, 26
copper sulfate 24
copulation 430
corn 290
cornea 395–396
cornified layer 370
corn lily 273
coronary artery 320, 326
coronary vein 320
corpus luteum 428
corrosive 4
cortex 250, 375–377
cosmic rays 194
cotton wool 274, 296
cotyledons 248, 289, 294–295
coughing 402
covalent binding 111
cover slip 88, 90
Cowper's gland 423–424
crabs 60, 63
cranium (skull) 410
crenation 99
cress seeds 296
cretinism 385
crossing over 184
cross-pollination 287
cryptosporidium 213, 239
cryptozoic trap 65–66
cucumbers 291
cultures
 batch 137
 continuous-flow 137–138
current 73
cusps 339
cuticle 252

cutting 203, 281
cyclopamine 273
cyclopia 273
cystic fibrosis 160, 187
cytokines 356
cytokinesis (cell division) 150
cytoplasm 84
cytosine 157
cytosol 84, 134
cytotoxic T cells 358

D

dandelion 287, 291
dark stage 124, 126–127
Darwin, Charles 198
 On the Origin of Species 198
data (collecting and interpreting) 3
daughter nuclei 147
deadwood 62
deamination 341, 374
death and decay 43
death cap fungus 236
decline phase 221
dedicated chromosomes 149
deep vein thrombosis (DVT) 313, 318
degree of exposure 73
denaturation 220
denatured enzyme 106
dendrites 393
denitrifying bacteria 43–44
dental cavities 339
deoxygenated blood 317
deoxyhaemoglobin 309
deoxyribose 157, 166
dermal (or epidermal) tissue 248
dermatitis 25
dermis 351, 370–371
descending colon 338, 344
destroying angel (fungus) 236
detritus 62
developed countries 41
developing countries 41
development of the embryo 432–433
Devil's backbone 280
diabetes 387
diaphragm 86, 362, 363, 364, 365, 412, 434
diaphysis 413
diastolic pressure 323
dicot 248
dicotyledonous 248
diet 325
dietary minerals 26
diffusion 12, 99, 332, 364
digestion 337
digestive system (human) 336–346
dihybrid crosses 181
diploid 145–146, 172, 232, 285
diploid zygote 289
dip net 65
disaccharides (sugars) 16
discovery, accidental 7
discs of cartilage 411
disease 41
disinfectant 235, 298

disorders of the musculoskeletal system 417
dissection board 326
distal convoluted tubule 377
distilled water 274
diuretics 325
diversity of life 10–11
Dixon, Henry 262
DNA (deoxyribonucleic acid) 85, 155–161, 200
 bases
  adenine 157
  cytosine 157
  guanine 157
  thymine 157
 coding 155
 common genetic diseases
  cystic fibrosis 160
  haemochromatosis 160
 complementary base pairing 158
 cutting 159
 double helix 156
 double-stranded 156
 fragments 160
 gel electrophoresis 159
 genetic screening 160
 isolation 159
 junk 155
 nitrogenous bases 157
 non-coding 155
 pattern analysis 160
 polymerase 104, 158
 profiling 159–160
 recombinant 204
 replication 158
 separation 159
 technology 157
dog whelk 60, 63
dolphin 214
domain 103
domes 434
dominance 173
dopamine 395, 403
dormancy 292–293
dorsal root 403
dorsal root ganglion 403
double-blind testing 5–6
double circulation 319
double helix 156
double-stranded 156
Down's syndrome 194–195
dried brewer's yeast 113
dry fruits 290
dry weight 294
duck down 286
duodenal ulcers 341
duodenum 338, 340, 342
duplicated chromosomes 185
dwarfism 385

E

ear disorders 399
ear drops 399
eardrum 398
eardrum (tympanic membrane) 399
early-onset diabetes 387
ears 398
ear wax 351
E. coli bacteria (*Escherichia coli*) 110, 203, 217, 220, 223
ecology 32–55

451

Unit 2 Index

local issues 78
pyramid of numbers 34
relationships 35–39
economic importance of bacteria 222
economic importance of fungi 236
economic and medical importance of viruses 244
ecosystems 32, 56–81
 human impact on 44–49
 study of 56–81
ectoderm 432
ectoplasm 239
ectotherms 304
edaphic factors 33
effector 393
efferent lymph vessels 333
effluent 112
egestion 337, 345
egg cell 171, 172, 288
 development 425
ejaculation 431
elastic tissue 318, 365
elastin 371
elbow 413, 416
electrofishing 65, 67
 equipment 65
electron acceptor 125
electron microscope 242
electrons 118, 134–135
electron transport chain 135–136
Elodea 122, 127
embryo 289, 431
 development of 432
embryonic seed leaf 289
embryo sac 284, 288
 development 285
emotion 402
emulsification 342
enamel 339
endocrine glands 383–384, 388
 failure 435
endocrine secretion 383
endocrine system (human) 383–389
endoderm 432
endometriosis 430
endometrium 425
endoplasm 239
endosperm 289, 294
endospermic seed 289
endospore 218–219
endothelial wall 364
endothelium 317–319, 332
endotherms 304
energy carriers 118–119
energy flow 33–35
entrapment 138
enzymes 103–117, 220, 337–338
enzyme-substrate complex 104
epicotyl 293, 295
epidermal tissue 94
epidermis 250, 252, 254, 264, 273, 286, 351, 370
epididymis 423–424
epigeal 294
epiglottis 362–363
epiphysis 413
epithelial tissue 94
equator (middle) of cell 149
erosion

beach 78
erythrocytes 308
erythropoietin 376, 414
ethanol 161, 274
ethanol fermentation 136
ethene 269, 272, 291
eukaryotic cells 89
Eustachian tube 398–399
evolution 193–200
 evidence for 199
excretion 12, 374–375
exercise 325, 328, 366, 403, 418
exhalation 364–365
exine 286
exocrine secretion 383
exophthalmia 386
experimentation 3
expiration 365
exposure (degree of) 73
expression 206
extensor 417
external solute concentrations 221
extracellular fluid 332
eye disorders 397
eyepiece 86–87

F

facial bones 410–411
factors 180
 abiotic 32–33, 73–74
 biotic 33
 climatic 33
 edaphic 33
facultative anaerobic bacteria 220
faeces 344
fallopian tubes 425
 blockage 435
false fruits 290
'false' ribs 364
famine 41
fats 20–21
 storage of 370
fat droplets 240
fat-soluble vitamins (A, D, E and K) 341
fatty acids 342
fauna 57
feeding pump 112
female condoms 434
female reproductive system 424–426
femur (thigh bone) 410, 412–413
fermentation 133
 alcohol 134–135
 ethanol 136
 industrial 137–138
 lactic acid 133, 136
fermentation lock 139
fertile period 431
fertilisation 172, 288–289, 431
fever 352
fibre 345
fibroids 430
fibrous capsule 416
fibrous proteins 22
fibrous root 253
fibula 410, 413
'fight-or-flight' hormone 388
filament 284–285
filter paper 274

filtration 376–377
fine focus wheel 86–87
first filial generation 174
'five-a-day' 345
flagellum 216
flammable 4
Fleming, Alexander 7, 224, 231
flexor 417
flight socks 313, 318
'floating' ribs 412, 364
flora 57
flower 249
flowering plants 248, 279
flu 243–244
foetus 432–433
follicle-stimulating hormone (FSH) 384, 428
follicular phase 427–428
food
 availability 40
 webs 34
food chain 34, 75–77
 grazing 33
food, chemical elements present in 15
food processing 224–225
food pyramid 345
food vacuoles 240
food web 75–77
foot and mouth virus 245
forearm 410
fossil fuels 42
fossils 199
fovea 395, 397
freely-movable joints 416
frontal lobe 402
fructose 16
fruit 345
fruit formation 290–291
fume cupboard 5
fungal spores 286
fungi 43, 213–214, 230–236
 economic importance of 236
 harmful effects of 236
 of decay 231
funnel 114

G

'gag' reflex 363
galactose 16
gall bladder 338, 342
gallstones 342
gametangium 232
gamete formation 285–286, 426
gametes 171–172
gamma radiation 194
ganglia 392
gas exchange 264, 363–364
gastric glands 340
gel electrophoresis 159
gene expression 155
gene mutations 194
general defence system 351–352, 370
generative nucleus 286, 288
genes 145–146, 155–156
genetic crosses 174–179
genetic engineering 203–207, 222, 246

applications of (animals) 206–207
applications of (plants) 206
genetic manipulation 290
genetics 171–192
genetic screening 160
genetic variation 295
genome 145
 human 145, 155
genotype 173–174
geotropism 270
geranium 256
germinating seed 294
germination 293–294, 296–298
giant sequoias 262
gibberellins 272, 293
gigantism 385
global warming 42
globular proteins 22, 309
glomerulus 377
glottis 338, 362–363
glucagon 306
glucose 16, 114, 121, 126, 265, 306, 378, 386
glucose isomerase 110–111
glue ear 399
glutaraldehyde 111
glycerol 304, 342
glycoalkaloids 266
glycogen 18, 341
glycolysis 134
goitre 385
good bacteria 344
goose bumps 305, 371
goose grass 292
Graafian follicles 427
grafting 281
grains 290
granular layer 370
granum 122
grasp reflex 405
Graves' disease 386
grazing food chain 33
green fluorescent protein (GFP) 207
green iguana 304
grey heron 60
grey matter 403–404
grommet 399
ground level 62
ground stakes 65
ground tissue 95, 248, 252, 254, 264
 cortex and pith 250
growth (cells) 150
growth curve 221
growth hormone (GH) 384–385, 402
growth-hormone-releasing hormone (GHRH) 384, 402
growth plate 414
growth regulators 269, 293
guanine 157
guard cells 251–252, 263–264
gums 339
gut 337
gut flora 344

H

habitat 32
 seashore 60–61

woodland 57–59
haemochromatosis 160
haemoglobin 23, 194, 197, 309, 342, 364
haemolytic reaction 432
haemophilia 186
hair cells 398–399
hair follicles 371
hammer 398
haploid 145–146, 171, 230, 289
haploid daughter cells 285
haploid nuclei 285
harmful bacteria 222
harmful effects of fungi 236
hay fever 286
hazel 287
head (sperm) 424
hearing 398, 402
heart 317
heart attack 324
heartburn 340
heart rate 328, 402
heat denaturation 106
heating 293
helper T cells 357
hepatic artery 319–320, 341
hepatic portal system 321, 343
hepatic portal vein 319, 321, 341
hepatic vein 319–320, 341
hepatitis 245
hepatovirus 245
herbivores 336
heredity 155
herring gulls 60
heterotrophic nutrition 220, 336
heterotrophs 337
heterozygous 172–173
High Pressure Processing (HPP) 221
hinge joints 416
hip joints 416
hip replacements 418
histamine 352
histones 156, 203
HIV (human immunodeficiency virus) 244, 357
homeostasis 304–306, 374
homologous chromosomes 158
homologous pair 145, 172
homozygous 172–173
hormone production 376
hormones 383
hormone supplements 388–389
horticulturists 123
host 220
house dust 286
human brain 401–405
human breathing (control of) 365
human breathing system 362–366
human circulatory system 316–325
human endocrine system 383–389
human genome 155

452

Index

Human Genome Project 157
human immune system 355–358
human impact on ecosystems 44–49
human musculoskeletal system 410–418
human nervous system 392–405
human papillomavirus 151
human population 40–41
human reproductive system 423–435
human skeleton
  functions of 410–411
human skin (integumentary system) 370–373
human urinary system 374–380
humerus 410, 413
humus 43, 73
hydrochloric acid 340
hydrogen 15
hydrogen bonding 158, 262
hydrogen peroxide 106, 109
hydrolysis 26, 338
hydrotropism 271, 306
hyperopia 397
hyperthermophiles 220
hyperthyroidism 386
hyphae 231
hypocotyl 293–294
hypodermis 351, 370–371
hypogeal 295
hypophyseal portal system 384
hypothalamus 384, 389, 401–402
hypothesis 2
hypothyroidism 385
hysterectomy 430

I

IBA 281
identification keys 57–58
  seashore animal and plant 65
  woodland animal and plant 65
ileum 338, 342
iliac arteries 319–320
iliac veins 319–320
immobilised cells
  advantages of 138
  bioprocessing with 138
  uses of 138
immobilised enzymes 111
immovable joints 415
immunisation 355
implantation 431–432
inactivation of neurotransmitter 395
incisors 339
incomplete dominance 177
incubator 275, 298
indoleacetic acid (IAA) 271–272, 274–275
indolebutyric acid (IBA) 272
induced fit model 104
induced immunity 353
industrial fermentation 137–138

inferior vena cava 321, 326, 374
infertility 435
inflammation 352
ingestion 337
inhalation 364
inhaler 366
inheritance 155, 171–192
  blood groups 311
inner cell mass 432
inner ear 398–399
inner membrane 122
innominate bones 412
inoculating loop 234
insects 304, 317
insomnia 386
inspiration 364
insulin 222, 306, 383, 386, 388
integumentary system (human skin) 370–371
integuments 288
intelligence 402
intercostal muscles 362, 364, 412
interdependence 56
interferons 246, 352
interior vena cava 319
interneurons 393, 403
internodes 249–250, 256
interphase 147
interstitial fluid 332
intertidal zone 63
intervertebral discs 411
intestinal mucosa 343
intine 286
invertase 113
invertebrates 317
inverted pyramids of numbers 35
in vitro fertilisation (IVF) 435
involuntary motor control 402
iodine 15, 19, 90, 298, 385
iodoform test 140
ionic binding 111
iris 395
iron 15, 26, 113
irritant 4, 106, 113
islets of Langerhans 386
isolation 203
ivy 270

J

jaw bone 411
joint cavity 416
joint replacement 418
joints (classification of) 415–416
Joly, John 262
jugular veins 319, 320
junk DNA 155

K

karyotype 144, 146
  egg cell 146
  sperm cell 146
keratin 22, 370
keys
  identification 57–58
kidneys 374–375
  functions of 375–376
killer T cells 358
kingdoms 212

knee caps 410
knee jerk 404
knee joint 416
Krebs cycle 135

L

labour 433
lactase 111
lactation 433–434
lacteals 332, 334, 343
lactic acid bacteria 222
lactic acid fermentation 133, 136
Lactobacillus casei 222
lactose 16
lag phase 221
lamina 251
language 402
large central vacuole 85
large intestine 344
larynx 362–363
late-onset diabetes 387
lattice 111
law 4
layering 281
leaf 249, 280
leaf blade 251
leaf litter 62
leaf storage organ 266
leaf yeast 234
left atrium 321
left coronary artery 320
left ventricle 321
lens 395–396
lenticels 249
lettuce mosaic virus 245
leucocytes 312, 356
levodopa 403
lichens 60, 213
life 10
life, characteristics 10
life, continuity of 14
life-long immunity 358
ligaments 416
ligase 204
ligation 203–204
liger 196
light-dependent stage 124
light-independent stage 124
light intensity 127–128
light meter 65, 68
light microscope 85, 87–88
lightning 44
light source 86
light stage 124
light year 6
lignin 255, 262
lily 287
limbs 412–413
limewater 139
limpets 60–61, 63
line transect 65, 71–72
linkage 183
lipase 342
lipids 20
lipoprotein envelope 243
littoral zone 63
liver 338, 341, 374, 383
lock and key model 104
locus 172–173
log phase 221
long-sightedness (hyperopia) 397
long-term memory 402

loop of Henle 377, 378
low sperm count 435
low sperm mobility 435
lumbar 411
lumen 317
lung capacity 362
lungs 362–363
luteal phase 428, 429
luteinising hormone (LH) 384, 426, 428
lymph 332, 398–399
lymphatic system (human) 332–334
lymph nodes 332–333
lymphocytes 312, 353, 356
lymph vessels 332
lysosomes 85, 240
lysozyme 338, 352

M

macrophages 312, 352–353, 371
magnesium 15, 26, 123, 378
  salts 413
malaria 353
male condoms 434
male reproductive system 423
malignant cancer 151
Malpighian layer 370
maltose 16, 297
mammals 304
mammal traps 65–66
mandible (jaw bone) 411
manganese 15
manufacture of blood cells 411
marine worms 60, 63
measles 245, 354
mechanical contraception 434
mechanical digestion 337
mechanism of phototropism 272
medical importance of viruses 244
medulla 375–377
medulla oblongata 401–402
medullary cavity (bone marrow) 413–414
megaspore mother cells 285
meiosis 151–152, 171, 193, 232, 285, 426
melanin 370, 397
melanocytes 370
membrane (nuclear) 148
memory B cells 356
memory T cells 358
menarche 426
Mendel, Gregor 179–181
Mendel's First Law of Segregation 180–181
Mendel's Laws of Genetics 180
Mendel's Second Law of Independent Assortment 180
meninges 401, 403
meningitis 354
meningitis bacteria (*neisseria meningitidis*) 223

menopause 426
menses 427
menstrual cycle 426–427, 428–430
menstrual disorder 430
menstruation 427–428
meristem 249, 252
meristematic zone 254
mesenteric arteries 319–320
mesoderm 432
messenger RNA (mRNA) 166–167
  codon base 168
  triplet base 168
metabolism 10–11, 14, 103, 304
metacarpals 410, 413
metaphase 149
metastasis 151
metatarsals 410, 413
methylated spirits 161
methylene blue 88
metre stick 65
microencapsulation 111
microorganisms 2, 207, 221
  decline phase 221
  lag phase 221
  log phase 221
  stationary phase 221
  survival phase 221
micropyle 288–289
microscope 85–86
  coarse focus wheel 86–87
  diaphragm 86
  eyepiece 86–87
  fine focus wheel 86–87
  light source 86
  nosepiece/turret 86
  objective lenses 86–87
  stage 86–87
  stage clips 86
microspore mother cells 285
microvilli (brush border) 343
microvillus 343
middle ear 398–399
middle lamella 85
midpiece (sperm) 424
midrib 251
minerals
  dietary 26
minus (–) strain 232
mites 286
mitochondria 85, 240, 424
mitochondrion 132
mitosis 147, 149–150, 285, 289
MMR 354
molars 339
molybdenum 15
Monera (Prokaryotae) 212
monocot 248
monocotyledonous 248
monocytes 312, 353, 355
monohybrid crosses 174
monosaccharides 16, 134
monosodium glutamate (MSG) 400
monosynaptic reflex arcs 404
monoterpenes 273
morphine 273
motor cortex 402
motor neurons 393
mouth 337–338

453

Unit 2 Index

movement 402
speed of 39–40
movement (skeleton) 411
MRSA (multi-resistant *Staphylococcus aureus*) 197, 224
mucosa 340, 343
mucous 338, 341–342, 351
mumps virus 245, 354
muscle (eye) 395–396
muscles 416–417
muscular tissue 94
musculoskeletal system (disorders of) 417–418
mushrooms 213, 230
mussels 60
mustard 296
mutagens 194
mutations 151, 160, 194–195
mycelium 232
mycologists 230
mycology 230
myelin sheath 393–394
myopia 398
myosin 22–23, 417

N

NAD+ 134
NADH 118
NADPH 118
naphthalene acetic acid (NAA) 272
nasal cavity 362, 400
natural active immunity 354
natural contraception 434
natural genetic manipulation 290
natural passive immunity 355
natural vegetative propagation 280
nectar 287
needles 273
negative feedback 428
mechanism 388
nephron 376
nerve impulse 394–395
movement of 394
nervous system disorder 402–403
nervous system (human) 392–405
nervous tissue 94, 322
neuron 393–394
neuron (structure) 393
neurotransmitters 394–395
niche 35
nicotinamide adenine dinucleotide phosphate 118
nicotine 273
night-blindness 25
nitrates 43–44
nitrifying bacteria 43
nitrites 43
nitrogen 15, 42
cycle 42
fixation 42
nitrogen-fixing bacteria 42
nitrogen gas 44
nitrogenous bases 157
nodes 249–250
non-endospermic seed 289

non-nuclear inheritance 187
non-parental types 183
non-specific cellular response 351, 352
noradrenaline 395
northern gannet 60
nosepiece/turret 86
nucellus 288, 289
nuclear division 147
nuclear membrane 148
nuclear pores 166
nucleoid 216
nucleolus 85
nucleotide 157–158
nucleus 84–85, 240
nutrient agar 234, 297
nutrient recycling 41–44
nutrients (absorption) 342
nutrition 11–12, 14–31, 231
stages 336–338
nuts 290

O

objective lens 86–87
objective method 70–71
obligate anaerobic bacteria 220
obligate parasites 242, 244
observation 2
occipital lobe 402
odours 400
oesophagus 338, 340
oestrogen 388, 426, 428
oils 20
olfactory bulb 400
olfactory nerve 400
olfactory receptor cells 400
omnivores 336
oncogenes 151
onion bulbs 280
onion cells 90
onions 266
On the Origin of Species 198
open circulatory systems 316–317
optic nerve 395, 397
optimum activity 105–106
oral cavity (mouth) 338–339
oranges 290
organelle 84
organisation 316
biological 11
organism (size of) 40
organs 96–97
organ systems 97
orgasm 430–431
osmoreceptors 379
osmoregulation 240, 306, 375
osmosis 99–100, 261, 378
ossicles 398
ossification 414
osteoarthritis 417–418
osteoblasts 414–415
osteoclasts 386, 414–415
osteomalacia 25
osteoporosis 418
ostia 316–317
otitis media 399
outer ear 398
outer membrane 122
oval window 398–399

ovarian follicles 427
ovary (human) 388, 425
ovary (plants) 284, 288, 290
overbreeding 198
oviducts 425
ovulation 427–429
ovule 289
ovum 428
oxidation 118, 136
oxidising 4
oxygen 15, 121, 265, 293
oxygenated blood 317
oxygenators 127
oxygen-independent 134
oxyhaemoglobin 309
oxytocin 385, 433

P

pacemaker 321–322
palaeontology 199
pancreas 338, 342, 383, 386–387
pancreatic juice 383
papillary muscle 321
parallel venation (in plants) 251
paramyxovirus 245
parasite 220
parasitic fungi 231
parasitic nutrition 220
parasitism 39
parathormone 306, 386, 415
parathyroid glands 306, 386
parental types 183
parietal lobe 402
Parkinson's disease 403
parsnips 265
partially upright pyramids of numbers 35
parturition 433
passive immunity 355
passive transport 99, 261
patella (knee cap) 410, 413
pathogen 351
pathogenic 33, 222
pathway 1 (cyclic pathway) 125
pathway 2 (non-cyclic pathway) 125
pattern analysis 160
peaches 290
pea plants 179
pea pods 292
pears 290
pectoral (shoulder) girdle 410, 412
pedigree studies 187
pellagra 25
pelvic (hip) girdle 410, 412
pelvis 412
penicillin 7, 224, 231
penicillium 7
penis 423
pentadactyl limb 199
pepsin 104, 341
pepsinogen 341
percentage
cover 70–71
frequency 69–70
gradient 68
perforins 358
pericarp 290
periosteum 413, 416

periostitis 413
peripheral nervous system (PNS) 392
peristalsis 340, 342, 345
periwinkles 60–61, 63
personality 402
perspiration 305
pesticides 403
petal 284
petiole 249, 251
petiole storage organ 266
Petri dishes 3, 234, 274, 296–297
petroleum jelly 235
pH 105, 220–221
phagocytes 352
phagocytosis 312, 352
phalanges 410, 413
pharynx 338, 340, 362
pH control 376
phenotype 173–174
phlegm 365
phloem 248, 250, 252, 254–255
phosphates 118, 157
phospholipids 20–22
phosphorus 15
photolysis 123, 125
photosynthesis 121–126, 265
photosynthesis (purple-sulfur bacteria) 219
photosystems 122, 124, 125
phototropism 270
mechanism of 272
pH regulation 306
physical adsorption 111
physical barrier 370
physiotherapy 403
phytoplankton 61, 121
piloerector muscle 371
pineal gland 384
pink clematis 270–271, 287
pinna 398, 399
pipefish 60
pitfall trap 65–66
pith 250
pits 255
pituitary gland 379, 383–385, 389, 401–402
placebos 5–6
placenta 431
functions of 432
placenta formation 431
plankton 60
net 65, 67
planning 402
planning and design, careful 4
plant adaptations 273
plantae 214
plantar reflex 405
plant cells 84, 90
plant embryo 289
plant growth regulators (uses of) 272
plant organs 97
plants 206, 248–255
plant tissues 94–96
plan view map 62, 64
plasma 308, 332
plasma B cells 356
plasma proteins 341
plasmids 203–204, 216
plasmolysis 101

platelets 308, 313, 352
pleural membranes 362–363
plums 290
plumule 289, 293, 295
plus (+) strain 232
point mutations 194
poison ivy 273
polar division 218
polar nuclei 284, 285, 288
polio 354
poliomyelitis 245
polio virus 245
pollen grain 172, 286, 288
development 285
pollen tube 288–289
pollination 287–288
pollinators (insects) 273
pollution (seashore) 78
polyacrylamide gel 111
polysaccharides 18
pondweed 127
pooter 65
population 36
dynamics 39–41
human 40–41
porous glass beads 111
portal system 321, 384
post-synaptic neuron 395
potassium 15
potassium iodide 140
potato 266
potato phosphorylase 104
powdery mildews 213
pre-chilling 293
predation 37–38
predator-prey relationships 39–40
premolars 339
pressure 221
pre-synaptic neuron 395
primary consumers 34–35
primary immune response 358
primary response 356
primary root 249
principle 4
principles of experimentation 4–6
problem solving 402
producer 34–35
product 104
progametangia 232
progesterone 388, 426, 428
prokaryotes 216
prokaryotic cells 89
prolactin 385
prolapsed disc 411
proliferative stage 427–428
prophase 149
prostate cancer 424
prostate gland 423–424
protease 110, 161
protected species 57
protection 370
protection (skeleton) 411
protein folding 167
proteins 22–24
fibrous 22
globular 22
protein synthesis
process 167–168
transcription 166–167
translation 168
Protista (Protoctista) 213, 239–240

Index

protistan infections 353
Protista (Protoctista) 213, 239–240
Protoctista (Protista) 213, 239–240
protons 118, 134–135
proximal convoluted tubule 377–378
pseudopods 240
pulmonary artery 319, 321–322, 326
pulmonary circuit 319
pulmonary embolism 313
pulmonary vein 321, 326
pulse 322–323
pulse rate 328
Punnett square 175
pupil 395–396
pure-breeding (homozygous) 172, 181
purines 158
pyloric sphincter 340–341
pyramid of numbers 75–77
   ecological 34
   inverted 35
   partially upright 35
   upright 35
pyrimidines 158
pyruvic acid 134

Q

quadrat 65, 69
   graduated 70–71
   qualitative method 69
   quantitative 57
      method 69
   quantitative study
      animals 72–73
      plants and animals 69–73

R

rabies virus 242, 245, 355
radicle 289, 293–294
radioactive iodine 386
radish 296
   seeds 274
radius 410, 413
radon gas 151, 194
random selection 5
reabsorption 376, 378
reaction centre chlorophyll 124
reasoning 402
receptacle 284, 290
receptor 395
recessive 173
recombinant DNA 204
recombinants 183
rectum 338, 344–345, 423
recycling
   nutrient 41–44
red blood cells 308
red marrow 414
reducing sugar 17
reduction 118, 134
reflex action 404
reflex arcs 404
refractory period 394
refrigerator 296
regulatory T cells 358
relationships, ecological 35–39
renal arteries 319–320, 374–375
renal pelvis 375

renal veins 319–320, 374, 375
rennin 110–111
repair (cells) 150
replication 5
reporting and publishing results 4
reproduction 12
   asexual 150
reproductive system (human) 423–435
reptiles 304
resource 36
respiration 132–143
   aerobic 132–143
respiratory system 362
response 12
   flowering plant 269–272
restriction enzymes 159, 203
results, reporting and publishing 4
reticulate (net) venation (in plants) 251
retina 395, 397
re-uptake pump 395
Rhesus factor 311–312
Rhesus incompatibility 311
Rhesus monkey 311
rheumatoid arthritis 358, 418
rhizoids 232
Rhizopus (common bread mould) 231–233, 236
rhubarb 266
rhythm method 434
rib cage 362–365, 410–412
ribose 118, 162
ribosomal RNA (rRNA) 168
ribosomes 85, 162, 166
RICE 418
rickets 25
right atrium 321
right coronary artery 320
right ventricle 321
rings of cartilage 362, 363
ringworm 236
ripening of fruit 291
RNA (ribonucleic acid) 162
   bases
      adenine 162
      cytosine 162
      guanine 162
      uracil 162
   complementary to DNA code 162
   messenger (mRNA) 166–167
   polymerase 162, 167–168
   ribosomal (rRNA) 168
   ribosomes 162
   single-stranded 162
   transfer (tRNA) 168
   translation 166
roan 178
rock louse 60
rock pool 63
rocky seashore 63–64
rods 397
rod-shaped bacteria 217
rod-shaped virus 243
root 280
root hairs 254
rooting powders (commercial) 272
root pressure 260–262
root sprout 280

root storage organ 265–266
root system 249, 253–254
rope 65
rose 287
roseate tern 60
round viruses 243
round window 399
rubella 354
runners 280

S

saccharides 16
Saccharomyces 110
sacrum 411, 412
safety procedures 4–5
salbutamol 366
salinity (salt content) 73
saliva 338
salivary amylase 103
salivary gland 338
salt 400
salt content (salinity) 73
salts 338, 342, 374, 376, 378
sample size, large 5
sand sieve 65
SA node 322
saprophytic fungi 231
saprophytic nutrition 220
saturation point 127
scalpel 326
scapula (shoulder blade) 410, 412
scarification 293
Schwann cells 393
scientific method 2–9
   limitations 6–7
scion 281
sclera 395–396
scramble competition 36
scrotum 423–424
scurvy 25
sea anemones 60, 63
sea cucumber 60–61, 63
seagrass 60
seagulls 60
sea scorpion 60
seashore
   habitat 60–61
   pollution 78
   rocky 63–64
sea slugs 60
sea urchins 60–61, 63
seaweed 61, 63, 239
sebaceous glands 351, 371
sebum 371
secondary consumers 34
secondary immune response 358
secondary response 357
secondary root 249
secondary sexual characteristics 426
secretion 376, 379
seed bank 295
seed dispersal 291
seed leaf 289
seedling growth
   stages of 294–295
seed reproduction 295
seed structure 289
selection 205–206
selective permeability 99
selenium 15

self dispersal 292
selfed 182
self-pollination 287
semen 424, 431
semicircular canals 399
semilunar valve 321
seminal vesicles 423–424
semi-permeable membrane 99–100
senses 392
   organs 371
sensor probes 112
sensory neurons 393
sepal 284
septum 320, 321–322
serial dilution 274
serrated wrack 60
sex chromosomes 144, 172
sex hormones
   role of 426
sex linkage 183, 185
sexual arousal 430
sexual intercourse
   stages of 430–431
sexual reproduction (human) 423–441
sexual reproduction (flowering plant) 284–295
shape (skeleton) 410
sheep's heart 326
shingles 245
shin splints 413
shivering 305, 405
shoot system 249–253
short-sightedness (myopia) 398
short-term memory 402
shoulder blade 412
shoulder girdle 410
shoulder joints 416
shrub layer 62
sickle-cell anaemia 194, 197
sieve plates 255
sieve tube cells 255, 265
sight 395–398
sigmoid colon 338, 344
single-cell protein 225
sinoatrial node (SA node) 322
sinuses 362
size of organism 40
skeletal muscles 416–417
skimmed milk plates 297–298
skin 351–352, 400
skull (cranium) 410–411, 415
slightly movable joints 416
slipped disc 411
slope 73
small intestine 342
small lumen 318
smallpox 242
smell 399–400
smoking 324
smooth muscles 317–318, 416
snakelocks anemone 61
snapdragon 177
sneezing 402, 405
social skills 402
sodium 15
sodium alginate 111, 113
sodium hydrogen carbonate 338, 342

sodium hydroxide 24
sodium hypochlorite 140
soil 62
   pH meter 65
   sieve 65, 67
   soil pH 73
   temperature 73
   thermometer 65
   type 73
solar energy 103
somatic cell 145
somatosensory cortex 400, 402
sour 400
speciation 195
specific heat capacity 26
specificity 104
speech 402
speed of movement 39–40
sperm 171, 383
sperm ducts 423–424
spermicide 434
sperm nuclei 288, 289
sperm production 424
spherical bacteria 217
sphincter 375
   muscle 374
sphygmomanometer 324
spiders 304, 317
spina bifida 25
spinal cord 392, 403–404
spinal nerve 403
spindle fibres 149
spines (anatomical adaption) 273
spine (vertebral column) 411
spiral-shaped bacteria 217
spiral wrack 60
spirillum 217
spirit level 65, 68
splash zone 63
spleen 332–333, 356
sponges 60
spongy bone 413–414
sporangiophores 232
sporangium 232
spores 232
spotted knapweed 273
stage (microscope) 86
stage 1 133
stage 2 133
stage clips 86
stages of nutrition 336–338
stamen 284–285
Staphylococcus aureus 216
starch 19, 124, 265, 297
starch agar 297–298
starch (amylose) 18
starfish 60, 63
start codon 168
startle reflex 405
stationary phase 221
stem 249–250, 280
stem cells 432
stem storage organ 266
sterile 234
sternum (breastbone) 364, 410–412
stigma 284, 288
stimulus 269
stinging hairs 273
stirrup 398–399
stock 281
stolons 232, 280
stoma 251–252, 264

455

Unit 2 Index

stomach 338, 340
stomach acid 351
stomach ulcers 341
stomata 123, 251, 261, 263
stomatal closing 263–264
stomatal opening 263–264
stop codon 168
storage of fat 370
storm petrels 60
strawberries 290
stream flow meter 65
strep throat bacteria (*Streptococcus pyogenes*) 222
striated muscles 416
string 65
stroke 324
stroma 122
structural adaptation 74
structure of a neuron 393
structure of the human skeleton 411–414
struggle for existence 198
style 284, 288
subclavian arteries 319–320
subclavian veins 319–320, 332
subcutaneous layer 370
subjective method 70
submerged aerator 112
substantia nigra 403
substrate 104
succulent fruits 290
sucker 280
suckling reflex 405
sucrose 16, 265
sugars 157
suitable temperature 294
sulfur 15
sunlight 121–122
supercoiling 156
superior vena cava 320–321, 332
support (skeleton) 410
suppressor T cells 358
surgical contraception 435
survival of the fittest 196
survival phase 221
suspensors 232
suspensory ligaments 395
SV40 virus 246
swallowing 363, 402
sweat 305, 371
  glands 371
sweep net 65, 67
sweet 400
sweet chestnut 287
swine flu 245
sycamore trees 291
symbiosis 38–39
symbiotic bacteria 344
synapse 394
  function of 394
synaptic cleft 394
synaptic vesicles 394–395
synovial fluid 416
synovial membrane 416
systemic circuit 319
systolic pressure 323

T

tail (sperm) 424
tap 114
tape measure 65
tapetum 286
tap roots 253, 265
tarsals 410, 413
taste 400
  bitter 400
  salt 400
  sour 400
  sweet 400
  umami 400
taste buds 400
taxonomy 212
T cells 357, 386
tears 351
teeth 338–339
telophase 149
temperature 105
  air 73
  receptors 371
  regulation 304, 370, 371
  soil 73
  suitable 294
  water 73
temporal lobe 402
tendons 416
tension 262
tertiary consumers 34
testa (seed coat) 289, 293
testes 383, 388, 423–424
testosterone 383, 388, 426
tetanus 354, 355
thalidomide 7
theory 4
  of natural selection 196, 198–199
thermophiles 220
thigmotropism 270
thirst 306
thoracic 411
  air pressure 365
  cavity 362, 365
thorns 273
threonine deaminase 2 (TD2) 273
throat 362
thrombocytes 313
thylakoid membrane 122
thymine 157, 166
thymosin 386
thymus gland 332–334, 357, 386
thyroid-stimulating hormone (TSH) 384–385, 389, 402
thyrotropin-releasing hormone 402
thyrotropin-releasing hormone (TRH) 385, 389
thyroxine 305, 385–386, 388–389
tibia (shin bone) 410, 413
tissue 94–96
  culture 96
tobacco mosaic virus (TMV) 243, 245
tomatoes 291
tomato mosaic virus 245
tongue 338
tonsillitis 334, 362
tonsils 332–334, 362
top consumer 35
touch 400
  receptors 400
toxic 4
toxins 374
trace elements 15
trachea 362–363
tracheids (xylem) 255
traits 171
transduction 204–205
transfection 204–205
transfer RNA (tRNA) 168
transformation 204–205
translation 166–167
transmission (nerve impulse) 394
transpiration 250, 260–262, 304
transpiration stream 261
transverse colon 338, 344
triceps 417
tricuspid valve 321–322
triglycerides 20, 22
triploid 146
trisomy 21 194
trophic level 34
trophoblast 432
tropism 269–271
trowel 65
true fruits 290
'true' ribs 364, 412
truffles 231, 236
tubal ligation 435
tube nucleus 286, 288
tuber 266
tuberculosis 354
tuberculosis bacteria (*Mycobacterium tuberculosis*) 222
tulip 287
tullgren funnel 65, 68
turbidity 114
turgidity 101, 264
turgor 101
tympanic membrane 398
Type I diabetes 358, 387
Type II diabetes 387

U

ulna 410, 413
ultrastructure of animal cells 84
ultrastructure of plant cells 84–90
ultraviolet (UV) light 151, 160, 194, 370
umami 400
umbilical cord 433
universal donors 310
universal recipients 310
upright pyramids of numbers 35
uracil 162
urea 374, 376
ureters 374–375, 377
urethra 374–375, 423
urinary bladder 374–375, 423
urinary system (human) 374–380
urinary system structure 374–375
urination (micturition) 376
urine production 376–378
uterus (womb) 425

V

vaccination 354
vagina 425
valve 317
variable 4
variation 193–200
varicella zoster virus 245
varicose veins 318, 323
vascular bundles 250, 252
vascular tissue 95, 248, 255, 269
vasectomy 435
vasoconstriction 305, 371
vasodilation 305, 371
vectors 203, 204, 246
vegetable oil 296
vegetables 345
vegetarians 336
vegetative propagation 279–282, 295
vein problems 318
veins 251, 317–318
vena cava 320, 321
ventilation 364
ventral root 403
ventricle 321
ventricular diastole 322
ventricular systole 322
venule 319
vertebral column 410, 412
  cervical 411
  coccyx 411
  lumbar 411
  sacrum 411
  thoracic 411
vessels (xylem) 255
vestibular apparatus 398, 399
vestibular nerve 399
villi 343, 432
viral replication 244
virology 242
viruses 242–246
  adeno-associated (AAV) 246
  assembly 244
  attachment 244
  complex 243
  economic importance of 244
  entry 244
  foot and mouth 245
  genetic engineering 246
  hepatovirus 245
  influenza 244
  lettuce mosaic 245
  mumps 245
  paramyxovirus 245
  polio 245
  rabies 245
  release 244
  replication 244
  rod-shaped 243
  round 243
  SV40 246
  swine flu 245
  tobacco mosaic (TMV) 245
  tomato mosaic 245
  varicella zoster 245
vision 402
visking tubing 100
visual cortex 397, 402
vitamins 24–25
  fat-soluble (A, D, E and K) 341
  vitamin A 25
  vitamin B_1 25
  vitamin B_2 25
  vitamin B_3 25
  vitamin B_5 25
  vitamin B_6 25
  vitamin B_7 25
  vitamin B_9 25
  vitamin B_{12} 25
  vitamin C 25
  vitamin D 25, 231, 371, 418
  vitamin E 25
  vitamin K 25, 222
vitreous humour 395–396
vocal cords 363
voice box 363
vomiting 402
vulva 425

W

Wallace, Alfred Russel 198
war 41
warm-blooded 304
washing-up liquid 106, 108, 109
waste products 374
water 26, 123, 293, 338, 340, 342, 374, 376, 378
water temperature 73
water bath 106, 108–109
water dispersal 291
water melon 290
water moulds 239
water transport 262
wave action 73
waxy cuticle 261
weed-killer 273
wheezy breathing 366
white blood cells 308, 312, 352
white matter 403–404
wholemeal bread 345
whooping cough 354
wind dispersal 291
windpipe 363
wind pollination 287
wind speed 73
wisdom teeth 339
withdrawal reflex 404
womb (uterus) 425
woodland habitat 57–59
worms 317
wound 352

X

X rays 194
xylem 248, 250, 252, 254–255, 262

Y

yeast 110, 138–140, 213, 230–231
  dried brewer's 139
  leaf 234
yellow marrow 414
yoghurt 222, 225

Z

zinc 15
zone of differentiation 254
zone of elongation 254
zone of protection 254
zygospore 232
zygote 172